东莞统计年鉴

DONGGUAN STATISTICAL YEARBOOK

2012

（总第 22 期　NO.22）

东　莞　市　统　计　局
国家统计局东莞调查队　编

Compiled by

Dongguan Municipal Bureau of Statistics

Survey Office of the National Bureau of Statistics in Dongguan

中国统计出版社

China Statistics Press

（京）新登字 041 号

图书在版编目（CIP）数据
东莞统计年鉴. 2012 / 东莞市统计局，国家统计局东莞调查队编.
—北京：中国统计出版社，2012. 8
ISBN 978 - 7 - 5037 - 6631 - 2

Ⅰ. ①东…
Ⅱ. ①东… ②国…
Ⅲ. ①统计资料 - 东莞市 - 2012 - 年鉴
Ⅳ. ①C832. 653 - 54

中国版本图书馆 CIP 数据核字（2012）第 182760 号

东莞统计年鉴 - 2012

作　　者/ 东莞市统计局　国家统计局东莞调查队
责任编辑/ 陈越月
封面设计/ 冯　坚　钟锦漩
出版发行/ 中国统计出版社
通信地址/ 北京市西城区月坛南街 57 号
办公地址/ 北京市丰台区西三环南路甲 6 号
邮　　编/ 100826
电　　话/（010）63376907
网　　址/ http://csp. stats. gov. cn
印　　刷/ 东莞市本色印刷有限公司
经　　销/ 新华书店
开　　本/ 890 × 1240 毫米　1/16
字　　数/ 1300 千字
印　　张/ 36. 38 印张
印　　数/ 1 - 1350 册
版　　别/ 2012 年 9 月第 1 版
版　　次/ 2012 年 9 月第 1 次印刷
书　　号/ ISBN 978 - 7 - 5037 - 6631 - 2/C. 2704
定　　价/ 350. 00 元

编　者　说　明

一、《东莞统计年鉴—2012》（以下简称年鉴）是一部反映东莞国民经济和社会发展情况的资料性年刊，本书收录了东莞 2011 年大量的统计数据和历史主要年份的一些主要统计数据，旨在全面系统地反映东莞在经济和社会方面的发展变化，为社会各界和海内外人士了解和研究东莞提供翔实的资料。

二、全书分三部分。第一部分，概述；第二部分，统计资料，具体分为综合、人口与劳动力、农业、工业、固定资产投资与建筑业、运输邮电、国内贸易、价格指数、对外经济贸易与旅游、财政、金融与保险、人民生活、社会事业、能源、镇街主要指标、村（居）委会主要指标、历年国民经济和社会发展主要指标、东莞与全国、全省、三角洲主要指标比较等 17 部分；第三部分，基本单位情况。

三、本年鉴资料大部分来自政府统计部门和调查队的各种定期统计报表、抽样调查资料，部分来自中央省属单位和市属各主管部门的统计资料。

四、使用本年鉴时，请注意指标的统计口径，计量单位及计算价格。本年鉴指标计算所采用的价格除注明外均为当年价格。

五、年鉴统计表中的符号说明：“#”表示其中主要项；“空格”表示该项统计指标数据不详或无该项数据。

六、本年鉴在编辑出版过程中，得到省统计局、有关部门和镇街的大力支持，在此表示衷心感谢。限于编辑水平，本书难免有疏漏之处，敬请批评指正。

《东莞统计年鉴－2012》
编委会和编辑出版人员

目　　录
CONTENTS

第一部分　概　述
Part One　Outline

第二部分　统计资料
Part Two　Statistics

一、综　合
General Survey

二、人口与劳动力
Population and Labor Force

三、农业
Agriculture

四、工业
Industry

五、固定资产投资与建筑业
Investment in Fixed Assets and Construction

六、运输邮电

Transport, Postal and Telecommunication Services

七、国内贸易
Domestic Trade

八、价格指数
Price Indices

九、对外经济贸易与旅游
Foreign Trade and Tourism

十、财政、金融与保险
Finance, Banking and Insurance

十一、人民生活
People's Living Conditions

十二、社会事业
Social Undertakings

十三、能源

Energy

十四、镇街主要指标
Main Indicators of Towns

十五、村（居）委会主要指标
Main Indicators of Villagers'（Neighborhood）Committees

十六、历年国民经济和社会发展主要指标
Main Indicators of National Economy and Social Development over Years

十七、东莞与全国、全省、三角洲城市主要指标比较
Comparison of Main Indicators between Dongguan and China, Guangdong Province, the Cities of the Pearl River Delta

第三部分　基本单位情况
Part Three　Basic Units

东莞市生产总值(亿元)

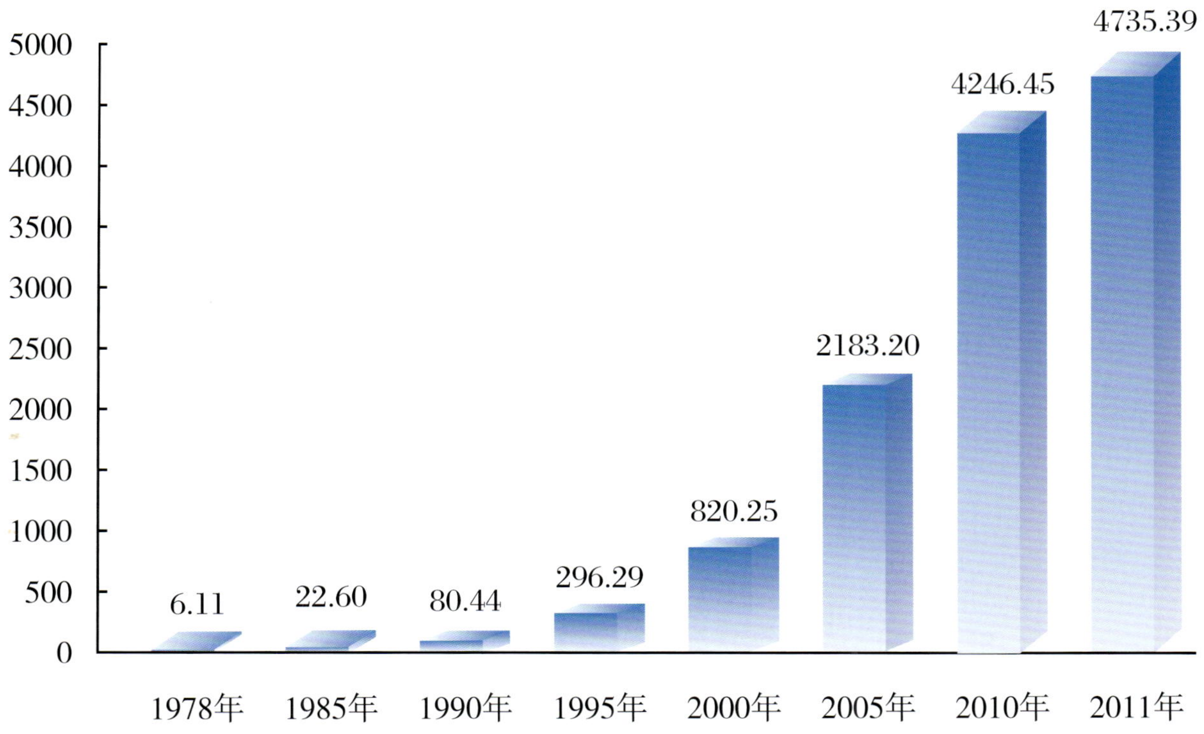

东莞市生产总值构成(%)

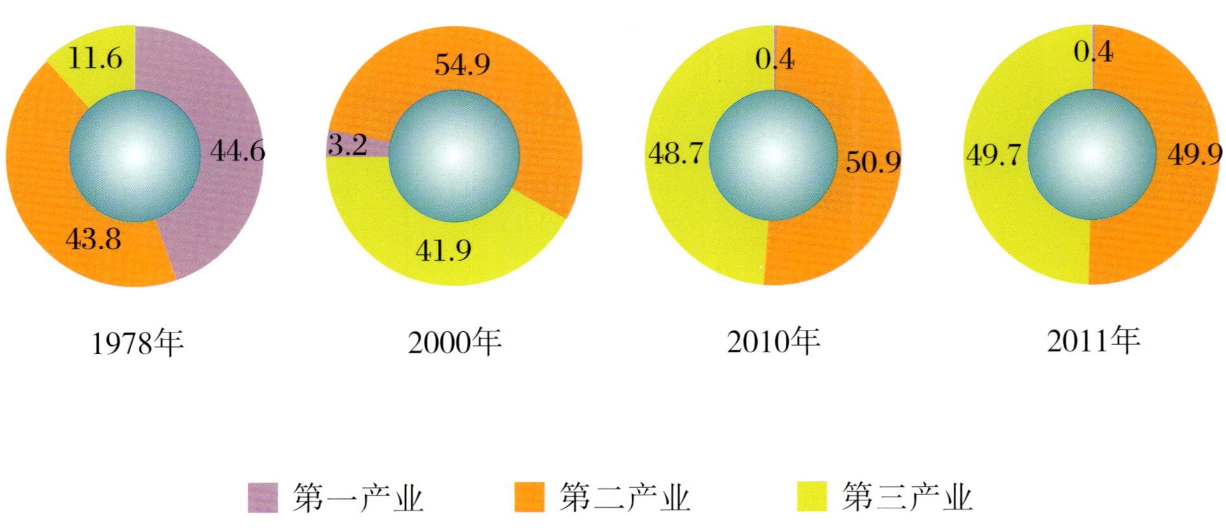

工业增加值（亿元）

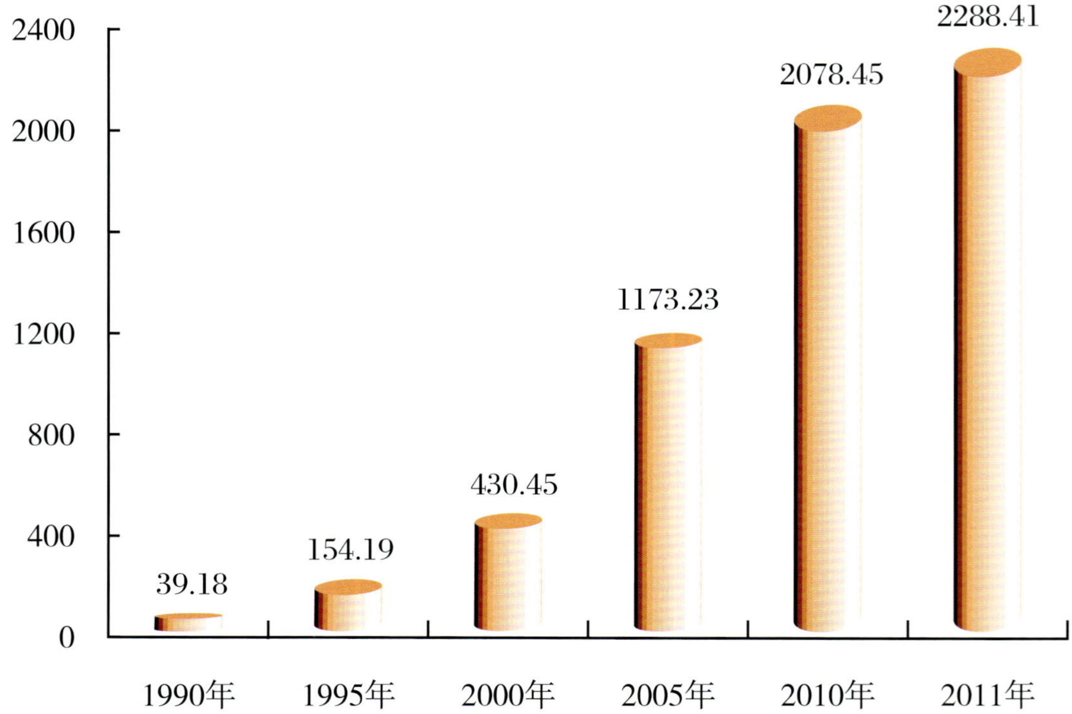

规模以上制造业增加值行业结构(%)

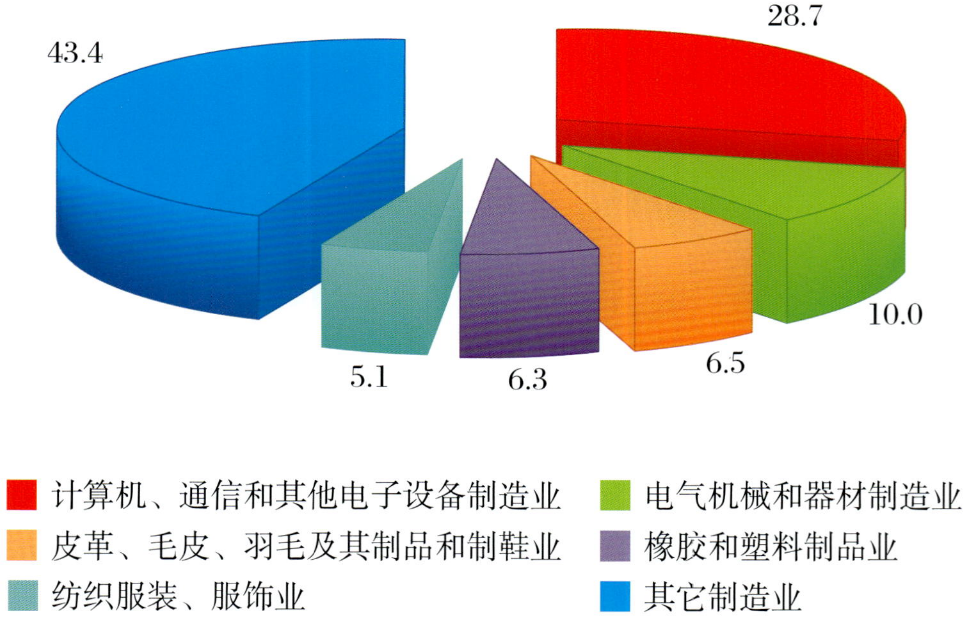

进口总额、出口总额（亿美元）

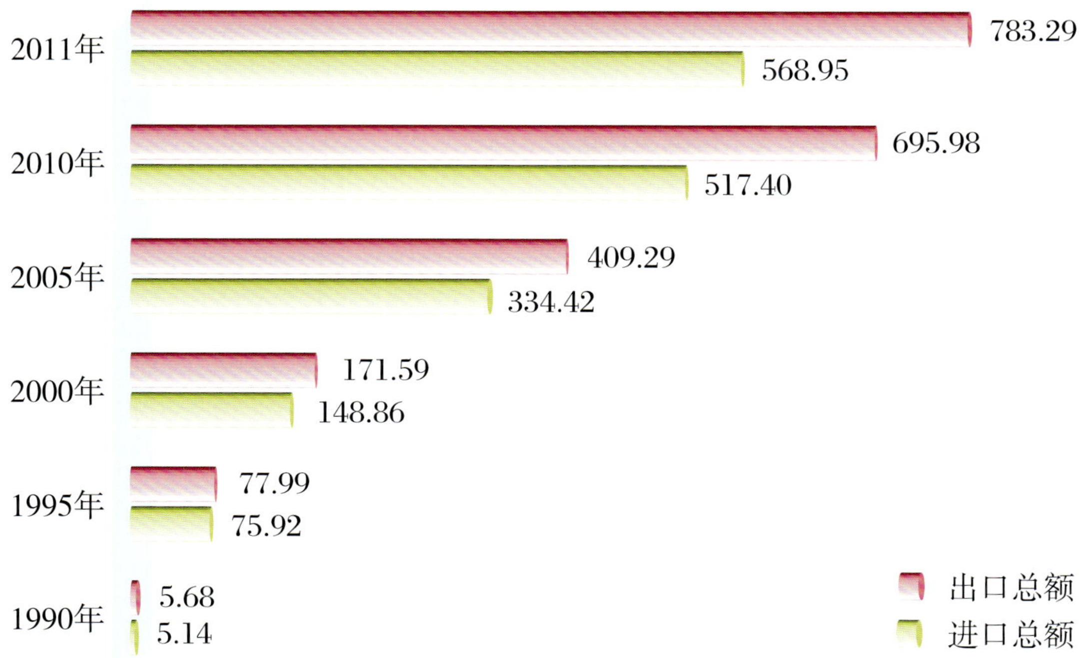

当年实际利用外资（新口径）（亿美元）

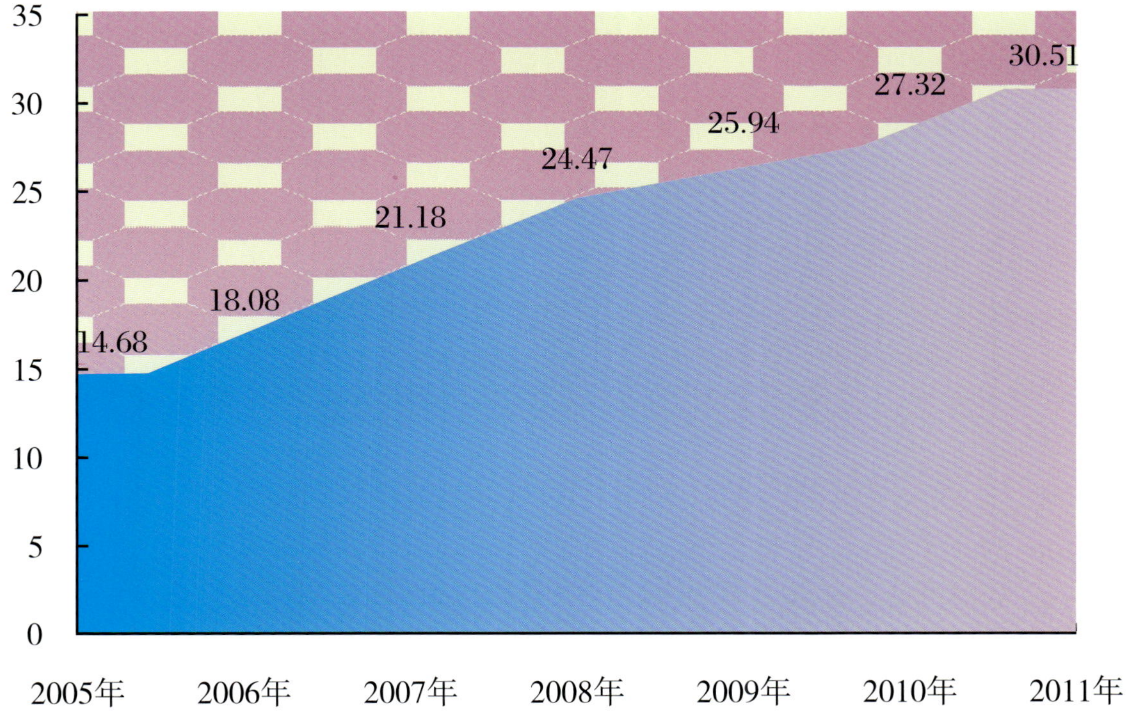

来源于东莞的财政收入（亿元）

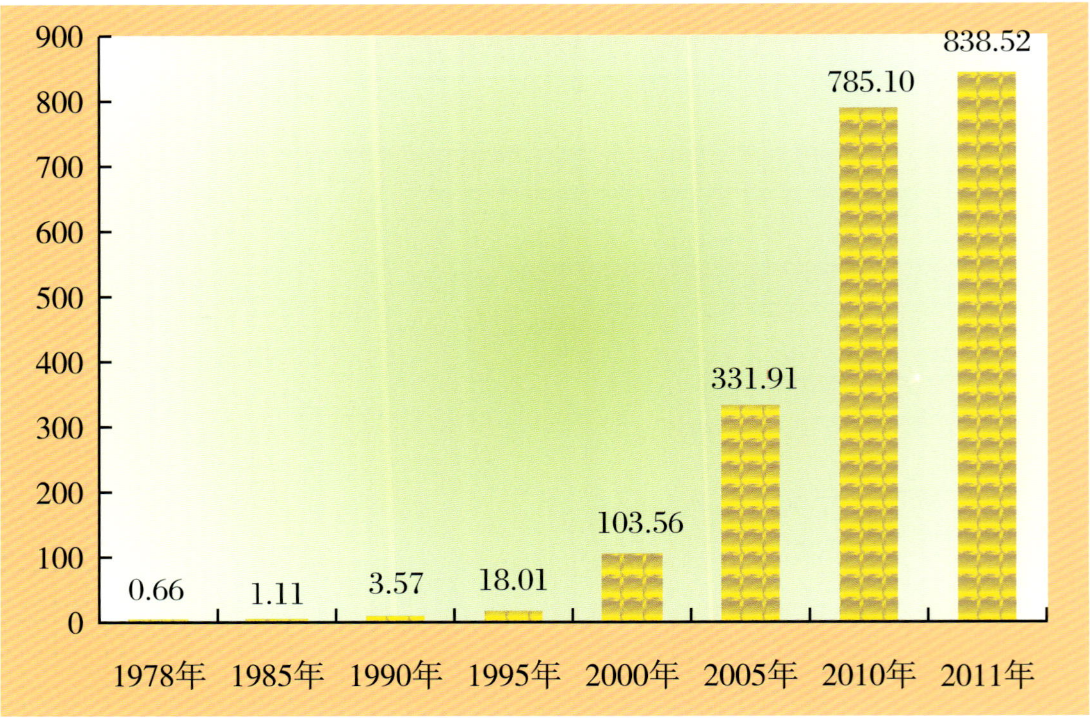

注：1995年及以前年份，来源于东莞的财政收入不含关税。

各项人民币存贷款余额(亿元)

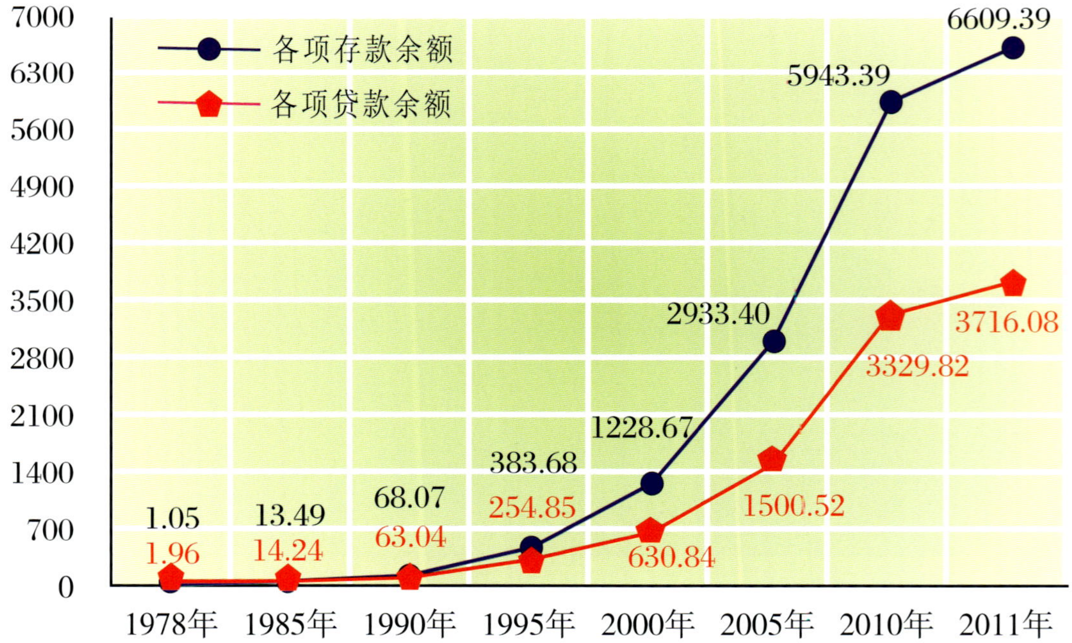

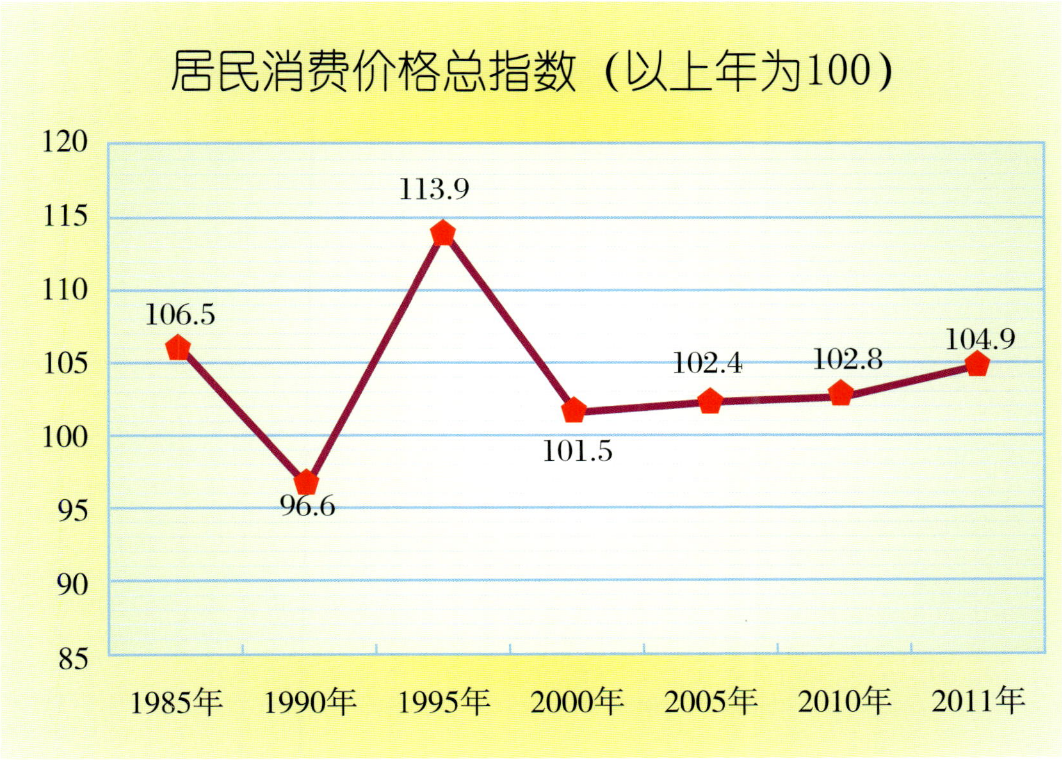
居民消费价格总指数（以上年为100）
120
115
110
105
100
95
90
85
106.5
96.6
113.9
101.5
102.4
102.8
104.9
1985年
1990年
1995年
2000年
2005年
2010年
2011年

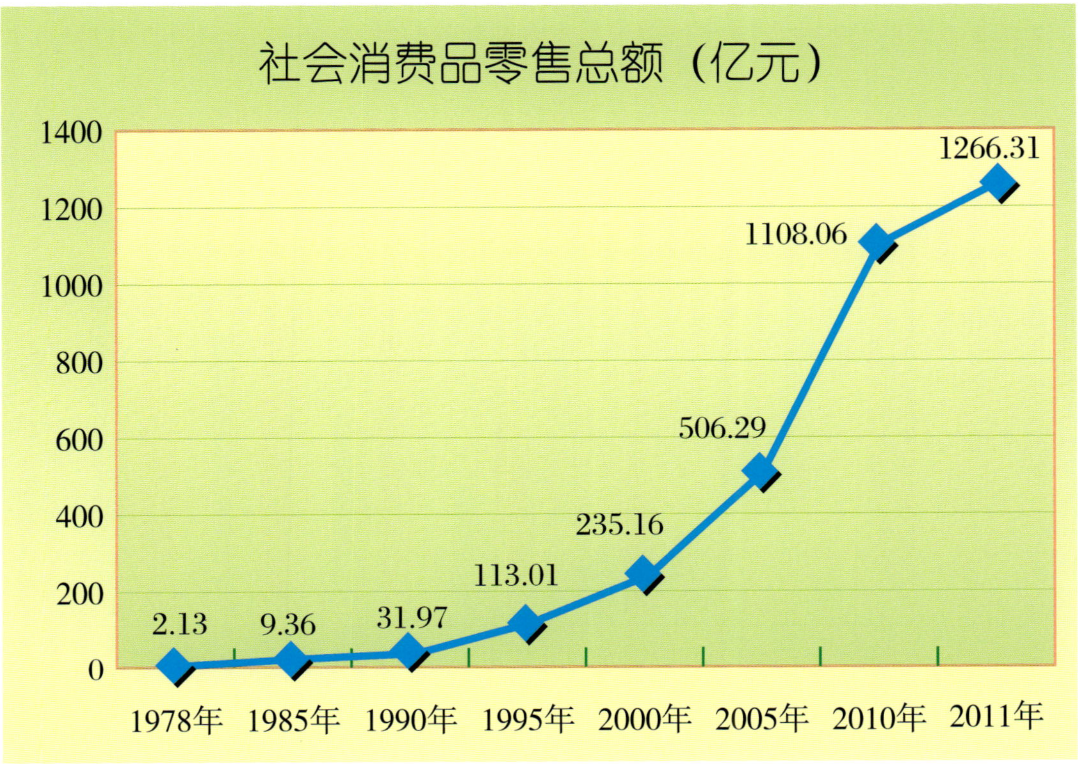
社会消费品零售总额（亿元）
1400
1200
1000
800
600
400
200
0
2.13
9.36
31.97
113.01
235.16
506.29
1108.06
1266.31
1978年
1985年
1990年
1995年
2000年
2005年
2010年
2011年

城乡居民人民币储蓄存款余额(亿元)

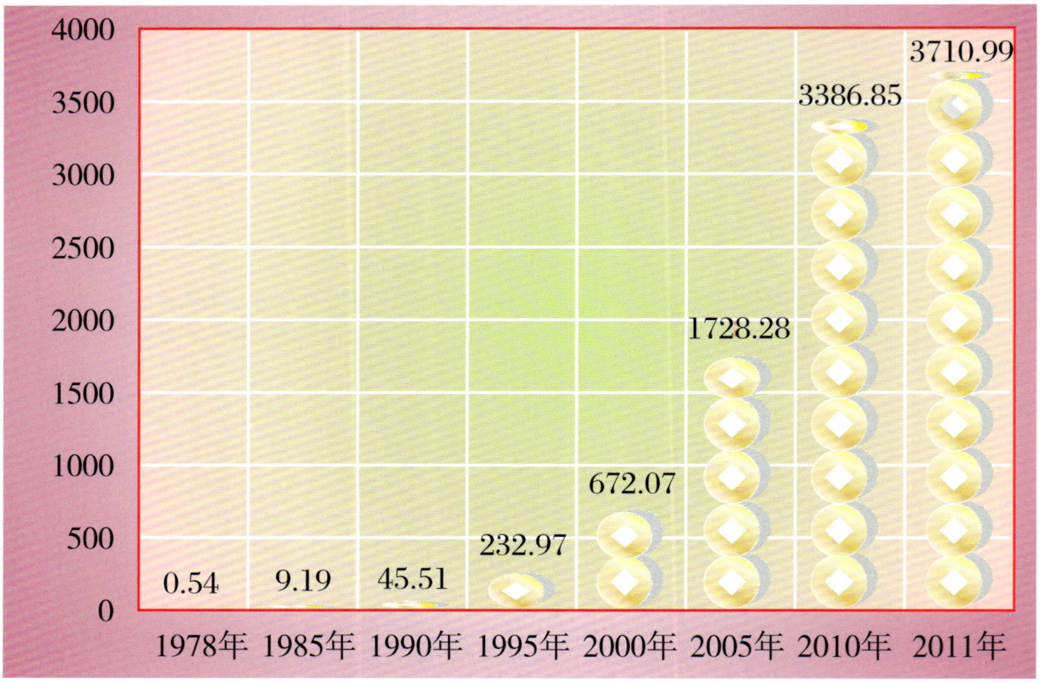

城乡居民收入(元)

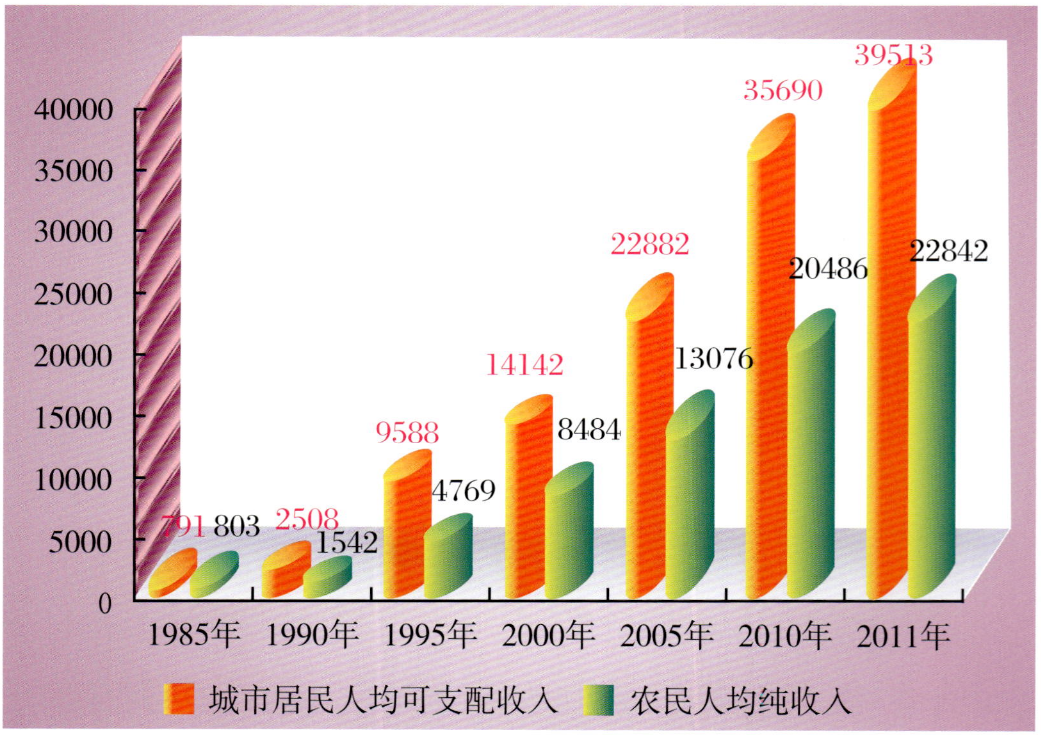

注：农民人均纯收入采用农村住户抽样调查口径，相应调整了往年数。

固定资产投资总额(亿元)

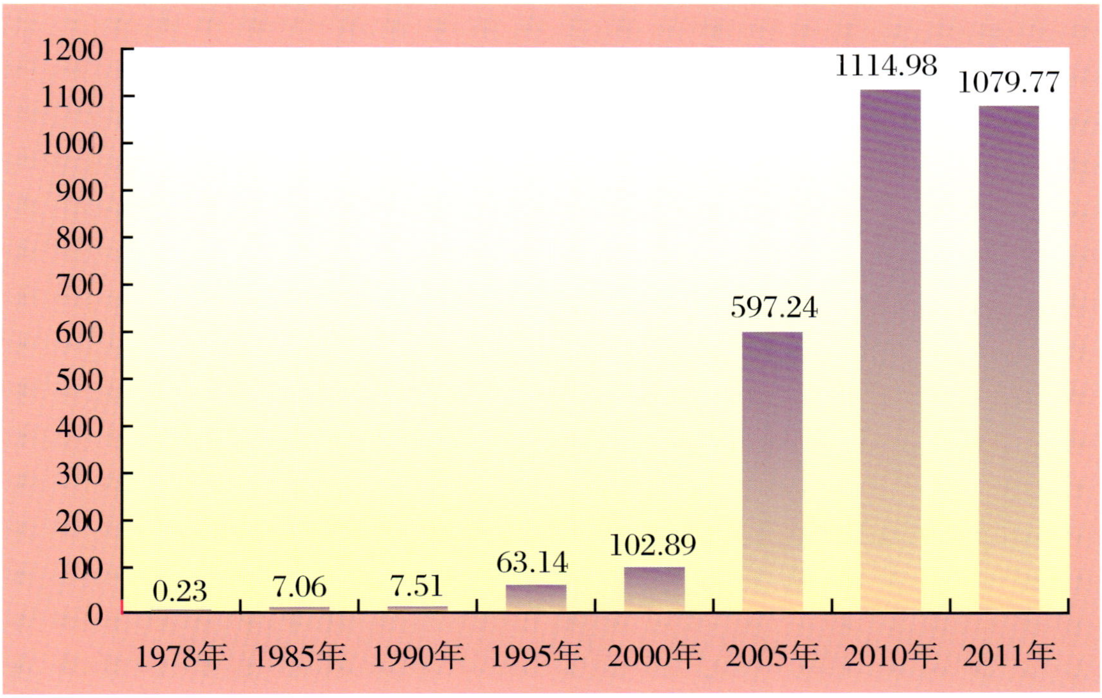

总供电量和总售电量(亿千瓦时)

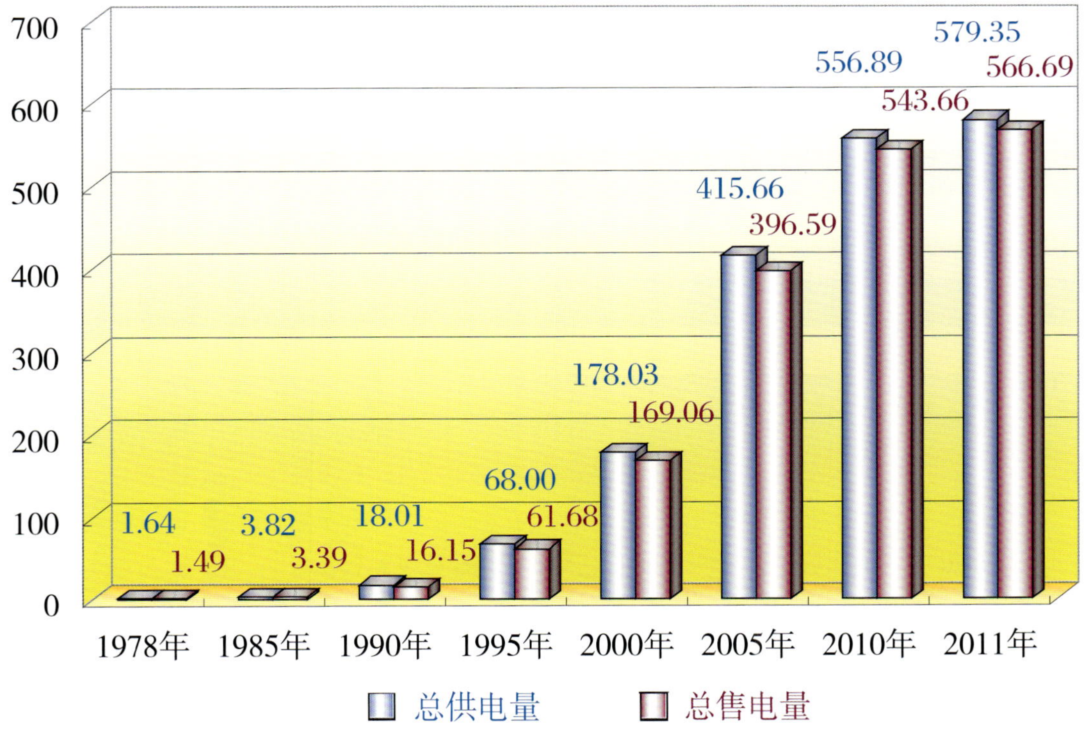

公路密度（公里/百平方公里）

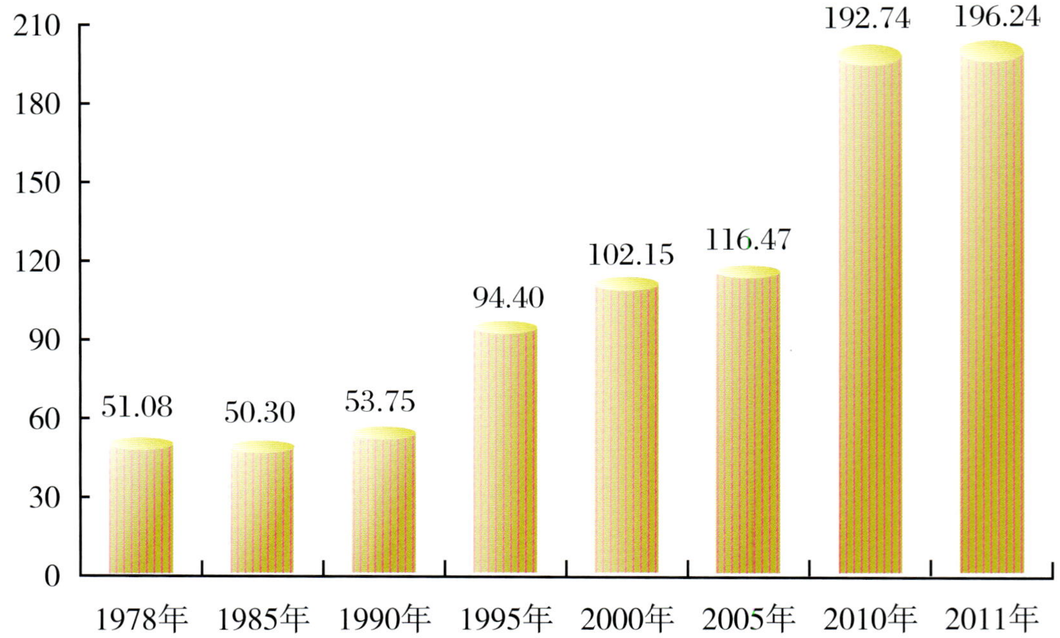

注：公路密度2000年起含高速公路，2006年起含专用公路和村道。

本地电话用户、移动电话用户（万户）

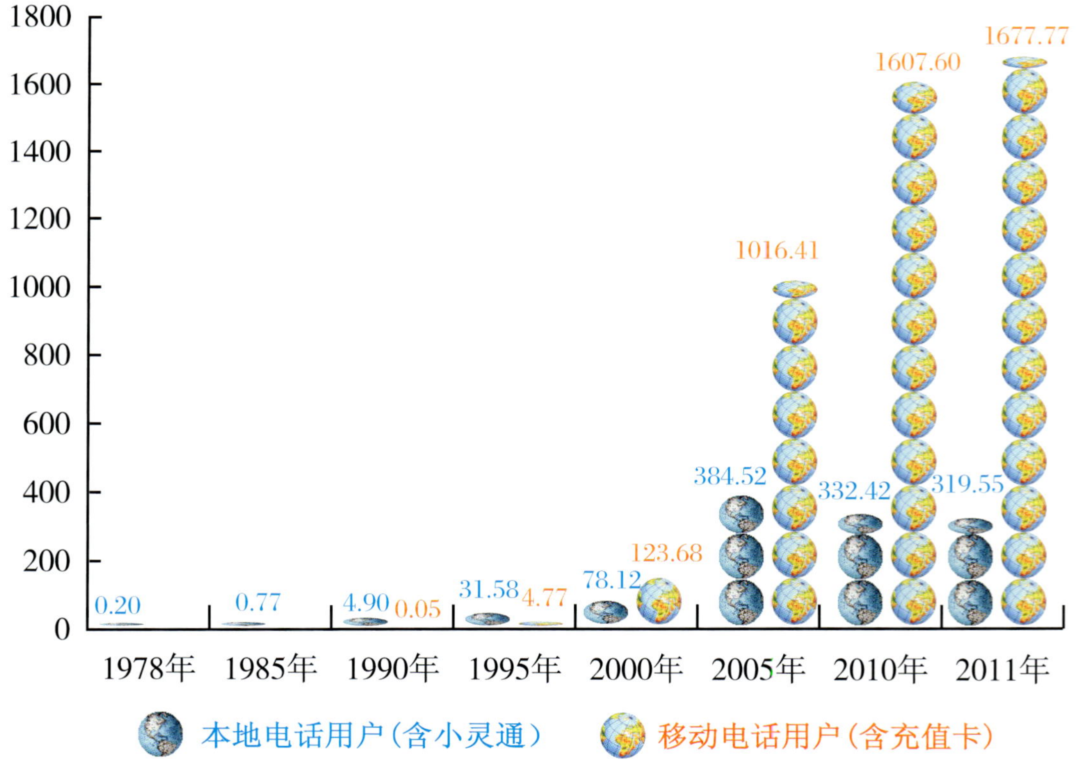

第一部分　概　述

Part One　Outline

2011 年东莞市国民经济和社会发展统计公报

2011 年，在市委、市政府的坚强领导下，全市上下深入贯彻落实科学发展观，全面实施《珠江三角洲地区改革发展规划纲要》，深入推进经济社会双转型，切实抓好结构调整等工作，确保了东莞经济平稳增长，呈现出城市综合实力稳步增强、产业结构持续优化、人民生活不断改善、社会事业全面进步的良好局面。

一、经济发展

经济总量

初步核算，2011 年东莞生产总值（GDP）4735.39 亿元，比上年增长 8.0%。分产业看，第一产业增加值 17.71 亿元，下降 0.4%；第二产业增加值 2377.40 亿元，增长 6.8%；第三产业增加值 2340.28 亿元，增长 9.3%。三大产业比例为 0.4∶50.2∶49.4。从经济类型看，公有制经济增加值 1171.94 亿元，增长 4.1%，占全市生产总值的 24.7%；民营经济增加值 1773.48 亿元，增长 10.8%，占 37.5%；外资经济增加值 1789.98 亿元，增长 7.9%，占 37.8%。在第三产业中，交通运输、仓储和邮政业增长 14.5%，批发和零售业增长 8.0%，住宿和餐饮业增长 6.1%，金融业下降 0.8%，房地产业增长 6.6%，其他服务业增长 12.8%。人均地区生产总值 57470 元，增长 5.4%。

图一 2005-2011年地区生产总值及增长速度

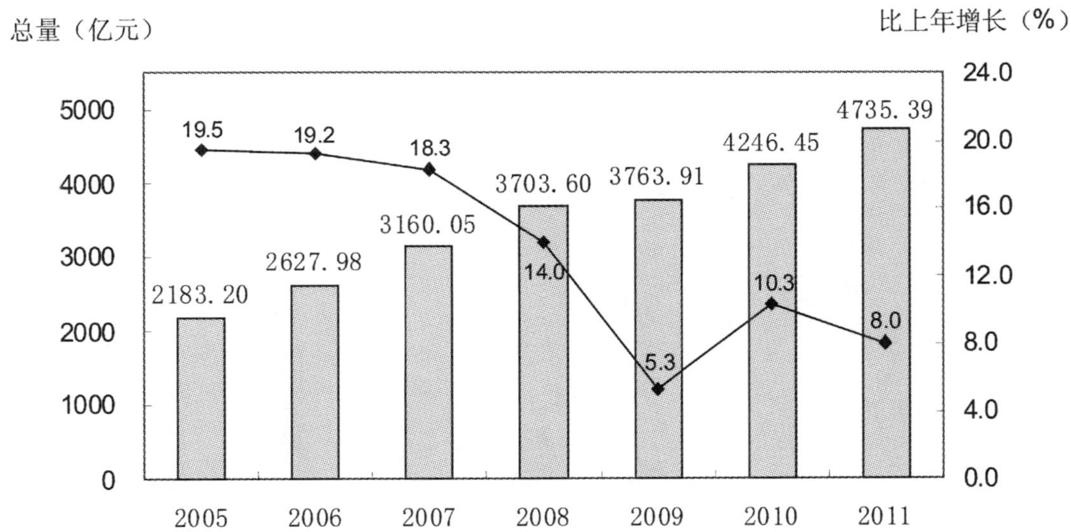

全年来源于东莞的财政收入 838.52 亿元，增长 16.2%。市财政一般预算收入 313.06 亿元，增长 18.3%。其中增值税 71.93 亿元，增长 14.8%；营业税 45.33 亿元，增长 18.6%；企业所得税 26.59 亿元，增长 18.2%；个人所得税 11.20 亿元，增长 21.3%；城市维护建设税 22.14 亿元，增长 94.5%；房产税 10.63 亿元，增长 14.6%；契税 23.06 亿元，增长 23.3%。市财政一般预算支出 351.92 亿元，增长 21.4%。其中，一般公共服务支出 32.62 亿元，公共安全支出 47.83 亿元，教育支出 83.23 亿元，科学技术支出 18.14 亿元，文化体育与传媒支出 14.31 亿元，社会保障和就业支出

24.38 亿元，医疗卫生支出 13.79 亿元，节能环保支出 22.81 亿元，城乡社区事务支出 29.74 亿元，农林水事务支出 18.04 亿元，交通运输支出 25.28 亿元。全年全市税收总额 843.57 亿元，增长 17.9%。其中国税 523.41 亿元，增长 19.1%；地税（含耕地占用税和契税）320.16 亿元，增长 16.0%。

转型升级

加快加工贸易转型升级，出台了“全国加工贸易转型升级试点城市”建设工作方案，支持企业引进先进技术、优化生产模式、拓展内销市场；出台了《外经贸转变增长方式“十个 100”计划实施方案》和《关于进一步加强对外招商引资工作的指导意见》；召开“全市推进外经贸稳增长调结构促平衡工作会议”，并出台 28 条措施，明确了以市镇两级企业收费减负、融资支持以及五年转型升级扶持资金为重点的财政支持，连续三年每年增设 2 亿元促进口资金等。全年有 1122 家来料加工企业转为法人企业，累计转型企业超过 3500 家，上规模来料加工企业基本实现转型。全市新增外资企业研发机构 202 家，增加 52 家；其中，外资企业研发中心 14 个，增加 5 个。全年新签、增资及实际到资超千万美元项目 156 宗，增加 29 宗。启动实施“686”民营企业上市梯度培育工程，建立市一级民营企业上市后备企业资源库。认定首批资源库企业 68 家，推荐其中 10 家成为第四、五批上市后备企业，推动 3 家企业成功上市。加强内资引进，全年引进内资项目 643 宗，协议投资金额 427.53 亿元，实际投资金额 285.96 亿元。区域自主创新能力进一步提升。在高端电子信息、半导体照明和太阳能光伏 3 个领域开展 2011 年粤港招标东莞专项工作，立项 5 个，资助 5000 万元。

固定资产投资

全年固定资产投资 1079.77 亿元，增长 8.1%。按登记注册类型分，国有经济投资 124.35 亿元，下降 23.3%，占固定资产投资总额的 11.5%；集体经济投资 122.37 亿元，下降 1.4%，占 11.3%；民营经济投资 460.07 亿元，增长 17.7%，占 42.6%；外商及港澳台商投资 220.29 亿元，增长 12.9%，占 20.4%。

在固定资产投资总额中，房地产开发投资 373.76 亿元，增长 25.0%。从产业投向看，投资集中在第二、三产业。第二产业投资 351.30 亿元，其中制造业投资 302.31 亿元；第三产业投资 727.87 亿元。全年完成投资 5000 万元以上项目 302 个，共完成投资 475.85 亿元。其中，工业类项目 151 个，完成投资 201.34 亿元。完成投资 1 亿元以上的项目有 97 个，共完成投资 332.39 亿元。其中，工业类项目 44 个，完成投资 125.57 亿元。

图二　2005－2011年固定资产投资总额及其增长速度

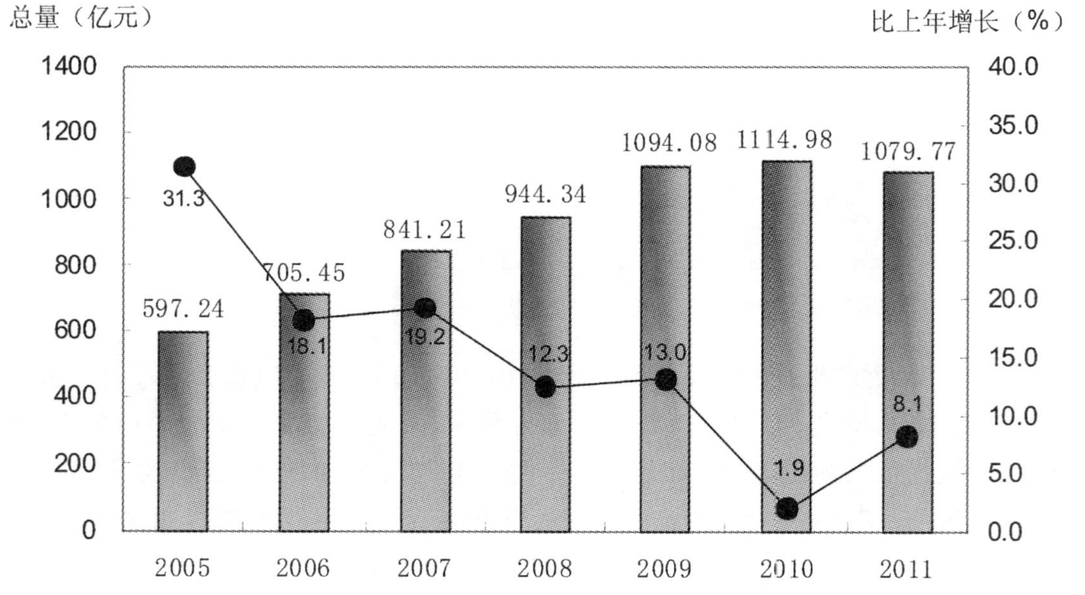

注：从 2011 年起，固定资产投资统计起点由 50 万元提高到 500 万元，2011 年的增速按同口径计算。

表一：2011 年分行业固定资产投资额情况

行　　业	投资额（万元）	增长（%）
总　计	10797662	8.1
农、林、牧、渔业	5994	387.7
制造业	3023124	9.3
电力、燃气及水的生产和供应业	487845	-28.3
建筑业	1468	-25.6
交通运输、仓储和邮政业	1111422	-8.6
信息传输、计算机服务和软件业	199193	0.9
批发和零售业	264068	79.2
住宿和餐饮业	46117	-50.7
金融业	19395	-18.3
房地产业	4040535	18.2
租赁和商务服务业	74593	66.0
科学研究、技术服务和地质勘查业	77528	-16.0
水利、环境和公共设施管理业	1007314	48.5
居民服务和其他服务业	17109	-24.9
教育	235049	12.9
卫生、社会保障和社会福利业	73711	-46.5
文化、体育和娱乐业	70148	-36.4
公共管理和社会组织	42529	-70.9

价格

全年居民消费价格总水平上涨 4.9%。其中居住类上涨 4.3%，娱乐教育文化用品及服务类上涨 0.3%，衣着类上涨 1.4%，食品类上涨 11.1%，医疗保健和个人用品类上涨 2.4%，烟酒及用品类上涨 1.5%，交通和通信类上涨 0.1%，家庭设备用品及维修服务类上涨 5.5%。此外，全年商品零售价格上涨 4.7%。工业生产者出厂价格上涨 2.9%。

图三 2005-2011年居民消费价格总指数（上年=100）

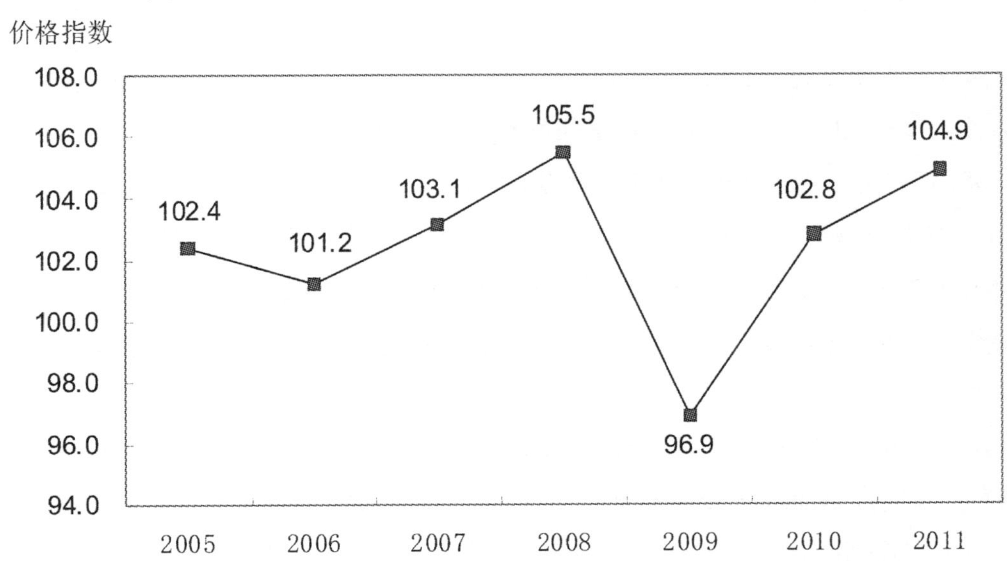

表二：2011 年价格变动情况

类　　别	价格指数（上年 = 100）	比上年升降幅度（%）
居民消费价格指数	104.9	4.9
食 品	111.1	11.1
其中：粮食	114.6	14.6
肉禽及其制品	114.5	14.5
油脂	110.3	10.3
蛋	118.0	18.0
鲜菜	95.3	-4.7
水产品	122.0	22.0
烟酒及用品	101.5	1.5
衣 着	101.4	1.4
家庭设备用品及维修服务	105.5	5.5
医疗保健和个人用品	102.4	2.4
交通和通信	100.1	0.1
娱乐教育文化用品及服务	100.3	0.3
居 住	104.3	4.3
商品零售价格指数	104.7	4.7
工业生产者出厂价格指数	102.9	2.9

农业

全年全市完成农业总产值 30.66 亿元，下降 0.1%。其中种植业产值 16.02 亿元，增长 3.3%，占农业总产值的 52.2%；林业产值 0.21 亿元，下降 29.6%，占 0.7%；牧业产值 6.38 亿元，下降 8.4%，占 20.8%；渔业产值 7.14 亿元，增长 0.1%，占 23.3%。全年粮食种植面积 4.15 万亩，粮食产量 1.29 万吨；水产品产量 7.82 万吨，增长 2.6%；蔬菜产量 38.90 万吨，下降 1.0%；生猪出栏 27.91 万头，下降 17.1%；家禽出栏 732.33 万只，下降 1.9%。

全年新增农民专业合作社 9 家、省级农业龙头企业 1 家，新增省名牌产品（农业类）5 个，有 20 个产品通过无公害农产品、绿色食品和有机产品认证。

工业

全年全市规模以上工业实现增加值 1797.3 亿元，增长 7.5%。在规模以上工业中，重工业增加值 959.98 亿元，增长 8.0%，占 53.4%；轻工业增加值 837.32 亿元，增长 3.1%，占 46.6%。大中型企业完成增加值 1388.07 亿元，占规模以上工业增加值的 77.2%。按登记注册类型分，国有控股工业增加值 132.75 亿元，增长 4.8%；集体工业增加值 35.87 亿元，增长 16.7%；外商投资工业增加值 603.29 亿元，增长 6.3%；港澳台商投资工业增加值 759.90 亿元，增长 2.5%；私营经济工业增加值 171.30 亿元，增长 6.8%。规模以上工业实现利润总额 260.65 亿元，综合经济效益指数为 131.52，资产负债率为 60.1%。

全年全市规模以上五大支柱产业完成增加值 1249.87 亿元，增长 8.0%，略高于规模以上工业平均增速；四个特色产业完成增加值 187.21 亿元，下降 2.6%。规模以上电子信息制造业增加值 692.48 亿元，增长 10.7%；实现利润总额 93.98 亿元，增长 5.9%。

表三：2011 年规模以上工业主要产品产量

产品名称	计量单位	产 量	增长（%）
电子元件	万只	101254508	-1.8
机制纸及纸板（外购原纸加工除外）	吨	10213204	1.6
瓷质砖	平方米	22333672	7.0
发电量	万千瓦时	3762253	4.9
家具	件	64181360	-7.4
服装	万件	107297	-1.6
玩具	千元	10459959	1.7
钢化玻璃	平方米	5433287	-10.5
模具	套	428255	2.1
不锈钢日用制品	吨	36510	22.9
皮革鞋靴	万双	31905	-15.1
电话单机	部	44433728	-4.0
组合音响	台	28274323	-7.0
印制电路板	平方米	16109240	-4.0
彩色电视机	台	5414621	1.1
金属切削工具	万件	11296	-16.6
电力电缆	千米	367142	-1.9
布	万米	9958	-23.8
表	只	16697231	7.5
化学纤维	吨	4324	-22.4
光电子器件	万只	1272661	37.8
印刷专用设备	吨	9392	-0.6
移动通信手持机（手机）	台	43362412	113.4
电工仪器仪表	台	5825445	19.8
塑料加工专用设备	台	33962	-7.7
家用电风扇	台	18108071	-7.7
显示器	台	7202	-70.6

建筑业

全年全市建筑业实现增加值 77.79 亿元，下降 12.2%。建筑企业完成总产值 133.50 亿元，增长 10.8%；施工面积 759.11 万平方米，增长 3.5%；竣工面积 396.15 万平方米，增长 27.0%。建筑企业按施工产值计算的全员劳动生产率为人均 22.99 万元，增长 1.5%。

交通运输、仓储和邮政业

全年全市交通运输、仓储和邮政业实现增加值 93.69 亿元，增长 14.5%。

年末全市境内公路通车里程（含乡村道路）4827.53 公里，公路密度 196.24 公里/百平方公里。其中等级公路 4715.73 公里，密度为 191.70 公里/百平方公里；高速公路 251.38 公里，密度为 10.22 公里/百平方公里。年末全市机动车保有量 141.71 万辆，增长 5.2%。其中汽车保有量 106.14 万辆，增长 15.3%。公路货物运输量 8210 万吨，货物周转量 53.13 亿吨公里；水路货物运输量 1955 万吨，货物周转量 134.35 亿吨公里。全年公路运输完成客运量 8.03 亿人次，旅客周转量 145.68 亿人公里；

水路运输完成客运量31万人次，旅客周转量2029万人公里。全年港口旅客吞吐量31.27万人次，货物吞吐量6848.12万吨。

全年完成邮电业务收入164.86亿元，增长6.1%。其中电信业务收入157.49亿元，增长5.7%；邮政业务收入7.37亿元，增长16.6%。全年邮政发送信函5148万件，特快专递167万件，邮政汇款汇出金额206.15亿元。

国内贸易

全年全市批发和零售业实现增加值458.74亿元，增长8.0%；住宿和餐饮业实现增加值168.62亿元，增长6.1%。

全年全市社会消费品零售总额1266.31亿元，增长15.0%，扣除物价因素影响，实际增长9.6%。分行业看，批发零售贸易业零售额1150.61亿元，增长15.2%；住宿餐饮业零售额115.70亿元，增长13.5%。

在限额以上批发和零售业、住宿和餐饮业零售额中，按登记注册类型分，内资企业实现零售额552.08亿元，增长18.5%，占限额以上零售额的87.3%。其中，国有企业占2.6%，集体企业占3.7%，有限责任公司占33.4%，私营企业占33.5%，外资企业占11.7%。

在限额以上批发和零售业中，食品、饮料、烟酒类零售额增长17.8%；服装鞋帽、针、纺织品类增长26.7%；日用品类增长12.3%；汽车类增长20.3%。

图四　2005—2011年社会消费品零售总额及其增长速度

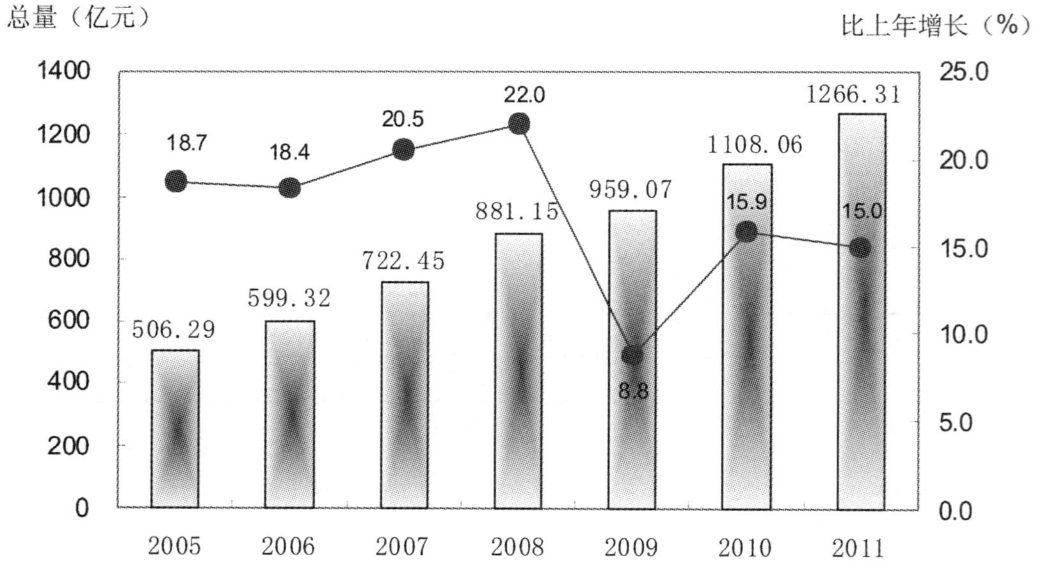

注：社会消费品零售总额2010年和2011年统计口径均有调整，增长速度按同口径计算。

金融业

全年全市金融业实现增加值182.59亿元，下降0.8%。

全年新增各类金融机构4家。年末全市有各类金融机构87家，其中银行类机构27家（含2家代表处），保险类机构38家，证券期货类机构22家。年末全市金融机构各项人民币存款余额6609.39亿元，比年初增长11.2%。其中城乡居民储蓄存款余额3710.99亿元，增长9.3%；单位存款余额2733.83亿元，增长10.9%；财政性存款余额31.39亿元，下降8.3%。各项人民币贷款余额3716.08亿元，增长11.6%。在个人消费贷款余额中，个人住房贷款余额741.77亿元，增长5.4%；个人汽车消费贷款余额15.20亿元，下降30.2%。全市金融机构不良贷款率比年初下降0.42个百分点。

年末全市各类证券公司共开户89.48万户，比上年增加7.41万户。全年股票总成交额8209.25亿元，下降25.3%。年末保证金余额69.80亿元，下降48.8%。

年末全市有各类保险公司38家，保险中介机构43家。保险从业人员2.8万人。全年保费收入163.65亿元，增长2.5%。其中财产险保费收入55.10亿元，增长17.9%；人寿险保费收入108.55亿元，下降3.9%。全年保险赔款与给付金额36亿元，其中财产险赔款27亿元，综合赔付率为49.04%。人身险赔款与给付9亿元。

图五　2005－2011年城乡居民储蓄存款余额及其增长速度

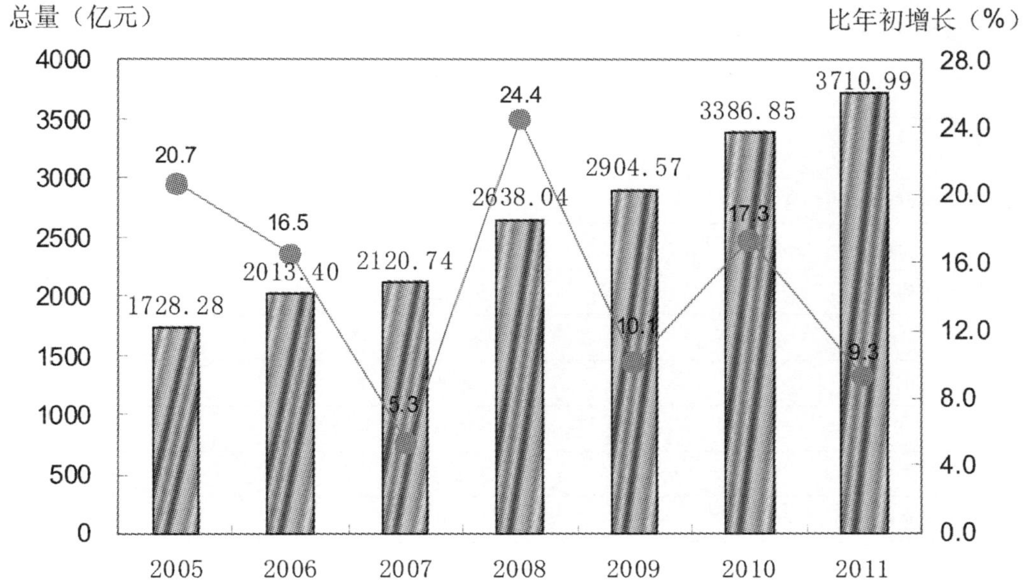

房地产业

全年全市房地产业实现增加值358.55亿元，增长6.6%。全年完成房地产开发投资373.76亿元，增长25.0%。商品房施工面积2396.55万平方米，增长16.3%；竣工面积242.28万平方米，下降18.3%；销售面积595.61万平方米，增长16.5%，其中商品住宅销售面积540.68万平方米，增长15.1%。全年商品房销售额459.61亿元，增长23.0%，其中商品住宅销售额413.33亿元，增长23.7%。

民营经济

年末全市民营登记注册户数48.01万户，下降2.6%。其中私营企业增长较快，达到10.47万户，增长18.1%；个体工商户37.33万户，下降7.2%。全年规模以上民营工业完成增加值257.71亿元，增长12.0%；民营经济完成固定资产投资460.07亿元，增长17.7%；民营经济消费品零售额1006.63亿元，增长14.3%；民营经济缴税总额314.41亿元，增长20.4%。

二、对外开放

对外贸易

全年全市进出口总额1352.24亿美元，增长11.2%。其中进口568.95亿美元，增长9.4%；出口

783.29 亿美元，增长 12.5%。

按贸易方式分，一般贸易出口 134.11 亿美元，增长 40.6%；加工贸易出口 634.78 亿美元，增长 7.6%；其他出口 14.40 亿美元，增长 38.3%。

按登记注册类型分，国有企业出口 70.30 亿美元，下降 36.3%；三资企业出口 542.81 亿美元，增长 22.6%；集体企业出口 14.23 亿美元，增长 0.6%。

按出口的地区分，对亚洲出口 408.65 亿美元，增长 15.3%；对北美洲出口 199.75 亿美元，增长 5.2%；对欧洲出口 135.86 亿美元，增长 12.0%；对拉丁美洲出口 24.38 亿美元，增长 39.3%；对大洋洲出口 9.66 亿美元，增长 12.2%。

全年机电产品出口 556.16 亿美元，增长 12.4%，占出口总额的 71.0%；高新技术产品出口 273.42 亿美元，增长 13.0%，占 34.9%。

表四：2011 年主要商品出口情况

商品名称	金额（万美元）	增长（%）
自动数据处理设备及其部件	612054	15.9
服装及衣着附件	461285	18.4
自动数据处理设备的零件	347125	4.2
鞋类	307241	-0.9
家具及其零件	339959	5.9
静止式变流器	376054	4.5
游戏机	122646	45.1
有线电话机（包括无绳电话机）	192614	17.2
纺织纱线、织物及制品	164309	8.1
数字式相机	128944	-19.8
电视、收音机及无线电讯设备的零附件	144218	-10.5
玩具	172040	5.4
旅行用品及箱包	181550	16.1
电线和电缆	173136	13.8
电视机（包括整套散件）	96155	-0.4
通断保护电路装置及零件	161770	20.6
塑料制品	127124	11.8
录、放像机	161883	22.3
手持或车载无线电话机	138393	42.8

吸收外资

按新口径统计，全年全市新签外商直接投资项目 1324 宗，合同外资金额 35.08 亿美元，增长 35.1%。实际利用外资 30.51 亿美元，增长 11.7%。其中电子及通信设备制造业实际利用外资 6.57 亿美元，增长 8.0%；专用设备制造业实际利用外资 1.99 亿美元，增长 27.8%。全市新签投资总额超 1000 万美元项目 68 宗，增加 22 宗；新增世界 500 强企业投资项目 5 宗，世界 500 强企业增资 4 宗；新签第三产业项目合同外资 5.25 亿美元，占全市的 15.0%，比上年提高 1.1 个百分点。外商进入商贸领域加快。全市新签批发和零售业项目 102 宗，合同吸收外资 2.82 亿美元，增长 36.7%，占第三产业吸收外资的 53.8%。

全市外资企业共设立研发机构202家，增加52家。全市新增外商投资的服务外包企业13家，占我市历年吸收服务外包项目的29.9%。

表五：2011年分行业利用外资情况

行业名称	合同外资金额（万美元）	增长（%）	实际利用外资（万美元）	增长（%）
总计	350836	35.1	305052	11.7
农、林、牧、渔业	1580	56.4	559	801.6
制造业	293826	31.9	259793	7.5
纺织业	12846	-0.5	16659	130.6
纺织服装、鞋、帽制造业	11480	-12.5	11424	25.0
家具制造业	2417	32.4	3977	-35.4
通用设备制造业	5808	-11.1	8814	16.9
专用设备制造业	13806	-28.3	19921	27.8
电气机械及器材制造业	37409	79.3	27742	9.8
通信设备、计算机及其他电子设备制造业	83647	25.7	65660	8.0
金属制品业	17182	65.4	11056	6.6
塑料制品业	29467	65.9	18327	30.8
文教体育用品制造业	12113	148.6	7559	-12.7
造纸及纸制品业	17140	112.7	15643	-26.2
其他制造业	50511	24.4	53011	-4.8
信息传输、计算机服务和软件业	200	-74.4	1045	858.7
批发和零售业	28232	36.7	23568	77.6

旅游

年末全市有星级酒店91家，比上年减少6家。其中五星级酒店21家，四星级酒店25家，三星级酒店31家，二星级酒店13家，一星级酒店1家。全市有旅行社57家，其中国际旅行社9家，国内旅行社45家，其他3家。全年接待国际及港澳台游客357.42万人次，增长9.2%。其中接待外国游客121.45万人次，增长11.7%；接待港澳台游客235.97万人次，增长7.9%。国际旅游外汇收入9.10亿美元，增长34.6%。全年接待国内游客2258.05万人次，增长17.4%。国内旅游总收入249.37亿元，增长30.3%。全年东莞组团外出旅游183.23万人次，增长19.1%。其中，国内旅游167.42万人次，增长20.4%；出境旅游15.81万人次，增长7.5%。

三、城市建设

城市绿化

年末全市建成区土地面积854.3平方公里，公共设施用地面积71.01平方公里。林业用地面积90.54万亩，森林覆盖率为36.9%，林地绿化率为97.8%；城市建成区绿地率为42.3%，绿化覆盖率为44.5%，人均公园绿地面积16.46平方米；全市已建成公园广场1039个，面积1.05万公顷。

公用事业

年末全市有公交线路 99 条，公交运营车辆 1417 辆，运营出租小汽车 7671 辆。全年市内公共汽车客运量为 2. 13 亿人次。

全市自来水日供水能力达到 700 万立方米，全年自来水供水总量 17. 34 亿立方米。年末供水管道总长度 2. 26 万公里。全年总售电量 566. 69 亿千瓦时，增长 4. 2%，其中工业用电 445. 76 亿千瓦时，增长 2. 3%；照明用电 119. 69 亿千瓦时，增长 11. 8%。年末液化石油气家庭用户 117. 61 万户，天然气家庭用户 17. 88 万户。全年液化石油气供应量 33. 81 万吨，天然气供气量 3. 65 亿立方米。

信息化

2011 年末全市固定电话用户（含小灵通）319. 55 万户，比上年减少 12. 87 万户；移动电话用户 1677. 77 万户，增加 70. 17 万户，其中充值卡用户 1432. 99 万户，减少 5715 户。全年长途电话通话时长 213. 63 亿分钟，其中对国际及港澳台电话通话时长 2. 89 亿分钟。年末互联网用户 190. 72 万户，比上年增加 36. 8 万户；宽带接入用户 184. 43 万户，增加 34. 35 万户。

图六　2005-2011年年末电话用户数

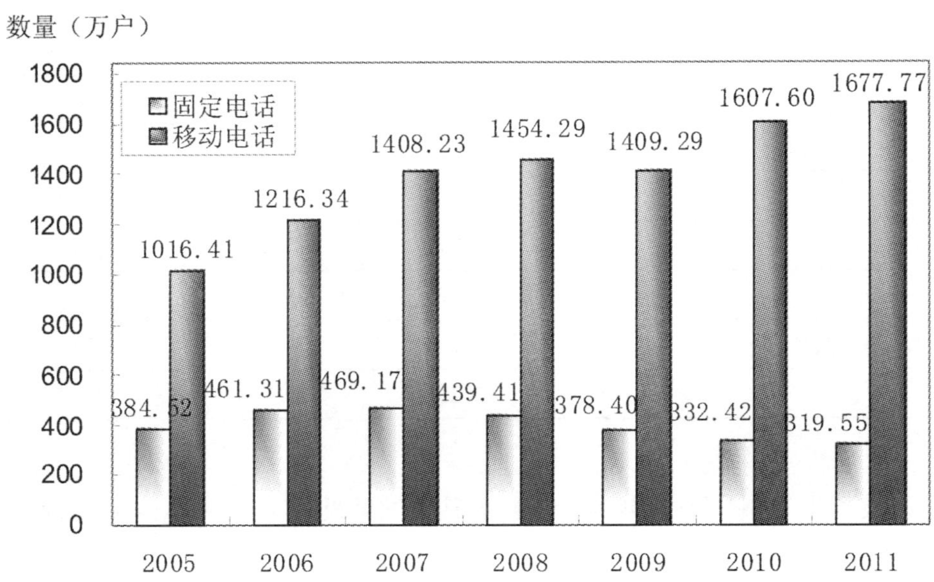

注：固定电话含小灵通，移动电话用户含充值卡用户。

四、社会事业

科技

2011 年，全市累计技术合同项目 163 项，技术合同金额 3. 20 亿元；获得省级科技进步奖 13 项，市级科技进步奖 77 项；科技合作有新进展，产学研项目立项数 85 项，国际合作项目立项 5 项，其中国家立项 2 项，省级立项 3 项；专业镇 18 个；国家级工程中心 2 个，省级工程中心 42 个；国家高新技术企业 413 家、省民营科技企业 852 家；全年专利申请量 2. 45 万件，专利授权量 1. 94 万件，其中发明专利申请量和授权量分别为 4214 件和 758 件，增幅分别为 34. 1% 和 71. 5%。

教育

全市有幼儿园 749 所，比上年增加 22 所，其中公立集体办园 175 所，民办园 574 所。共有省、市一级幼儿园96所。3－6周岁在园（班）幼儿22.77万人，入园（班）率为95.2%。

全市有小学324所，比上年减少6所；在校学生57.83万人；适龄儿童入学率达100%，本市毕业生升学率达100%。全市有初中161所，在校学生18.94万人，初中入学率为100%，辍学率为0.15%，毕业生5.47万人，毕业生升学率为98%。

全市高中阶段学校有64所（含民办学校20所），在校学生12.18万人，其中普通高中（含完中）38所，在校学生7.36万人，中职学校26所（含技工学校1所），在校学生4.82万人。高中阶段教育毛入学率为93.6%，比上年提高0.1个百分点。

全市有5所成人高等教育机构，32所乡镇成人文化技术学校，277所民办培训机构，年培训量近50万人次，各类成人高等学历教育规模达3.16万人（不含本市高校内的成人学历教育在校生数）。全市共有2.13万人报名参加成人高考，5.24万人报名参加全国高等教育自学考试。

全市有普通高等院校6所。其中本科院校3所，专科院校3所。在校学生4.51万人。全年普通高等院校共招收本科、专科学生1.68万人，毕业生9463人。2011年全市参加高考总人数2.23万人，高考升学人数2.14万人；高职类升学人数3357人。

文化

年末全市有群众艺术馆1个，文化站33个，公共图书馆622个，博物馆31个，文化广场769个，艺术表演场所63个，电影放映单位52个，网吧1048间，公共文化设施建筑面积700.76万平方米。全市有公共广播节目56套，公共电视节目37套。全年共出版报纸5220.62万份，各类杂志108.96万册，图书6.96万册，《东莞日报》发行3131.7万份，电影放映18.54万场次，观众407.49万人次。

卫生

年末全市有医疗机构2249个，其中门诊、诊所、医务室、卫生站、社区卫生服务机构等基层医疗机构2170个。全市卫生技术人员3.96万人，医院病床2.28万张。全市建成并投入使用的社区卫生服务中心（站）390个，覆盖了全市594个村（社区）。全年诊疗总人数上升3.5%。

体育

全年全市运动员共获得151枚金牌、118枚银牌、102枚铜牌。其中夺得国际赛金牌8枚；全国赛金牌27枚；广东省赛金牌116枚、银牌101枚、铜牌95枚。

全年举办市级综合和单项比赛62次，参加人数14.33万人次；举办镇街级单项比赛420次，参加人数46.58万人次。全市有体育彩票发行网点196个，销售总额9.57亿元，体彩公益金6934.71万元。

社会福利与救助

年末全市有收养类福利事业单位45个，其中社会福利院1个，儿童福利院1个，敬老院31个，敬老院供养老人873人。社会福利事业单位34个，收养2689人，安排“四残”人员就业296人，全年社会救济3.26万人。全市居民最低生活保障支出6300万元，社会救济福利事业费用2.16亿元，自然灾害生活救助支出268.9万元，慈善基金结余2.23亿元。全市纳入“五保户”对象有1210人，“五保户”费用支出1723.5万元。32个镇街全部建立了社会保障网络，纳入城市居民最低生活保障范围的有3796户9415人，纳入农村居民最低生活保障范围的有8744户21959人。

社会稳定和安全生产

全年刑事案件破案宗数增长9.4%，群众信访总量上升6.6%。年末累计建成平安社区（村）574

个，其中当年创建21个。全年共发生各类伤亡事故4525宗，下降7.9%；死亡540人，受伤5015人，分别下降5.9%和6.5%；直接经济损失662.31万元，下降26.1%。其中，道路交通事故4490宗，下降7.8%；造成死亡495人，受伤4999人，分别下降5.9%和6.6%。亿元地区生产总值生产安全事故死亡率为0.114，道路交通事故万车死亡率为3.49。

资源和环境保护

全年雨日天数161天，日照时数2120.1小时，平均气温22.1摄氏度，相对湿度71%，降水量1298.6毫米。

年末全市有森林公园18个，林业用地面积90.54万亩，生态公益林37.63万亩，林木积蓄量272.98万立方米，林木总生长量15.99万立方米。

五、人民生活

人口

年末全市户籍人口184.77万人。全年出生人口1.99万人，出生率为10.92‰；死亡人口8728人，死亡率为4.79‰；人口自然增长率为6.13‰。年末全市常住人口825.48万人，其中城镇常住人口731.38万人。人口城镇化率为88.6%。

就业

全年接收大中专毕业生1.64万人。人才市场求职登记人数112.58万人次；成功应聘人数42.16万人次，增长5.2%。年末城镇实有登记失业人数1.11万人，全年失业人员安置就业人数1.13万人，城镇登记失业率为2.1%。

居民收入

初步统计，2011年全市职工年平均工资21739元，其中，城镇在岗职工年平均工资50398元。城市居民人均可支配收入39513元，农村居民人均纯收入22842元，分别增长10.7%和11.5%。

图七　2005-2011年城市居民人均可支配收入及其增长速度

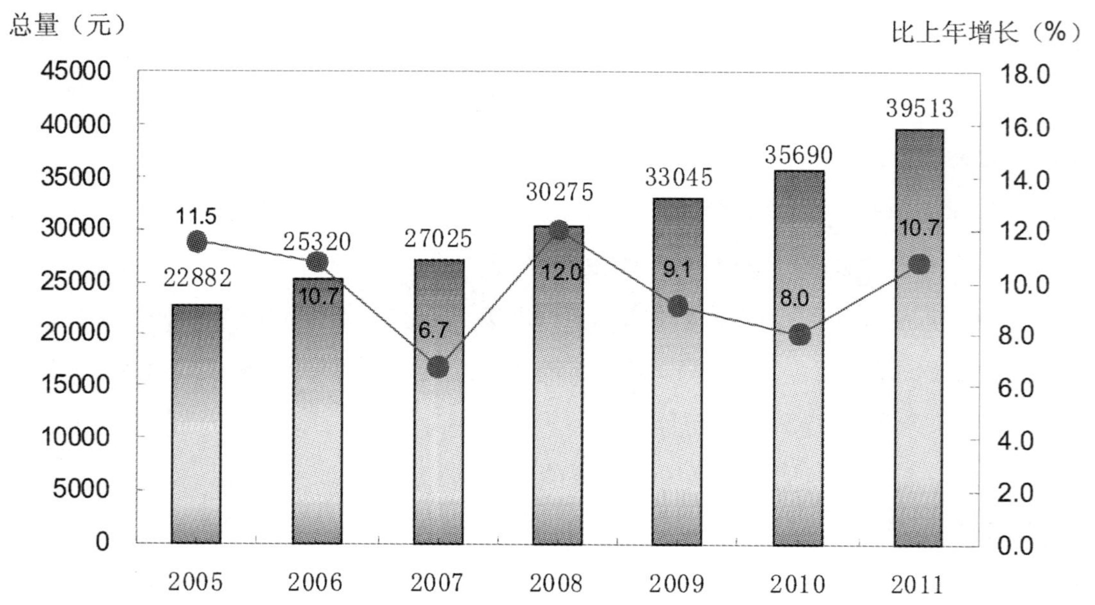

图八　2005-2011年农民人均纯收入及其增长速度

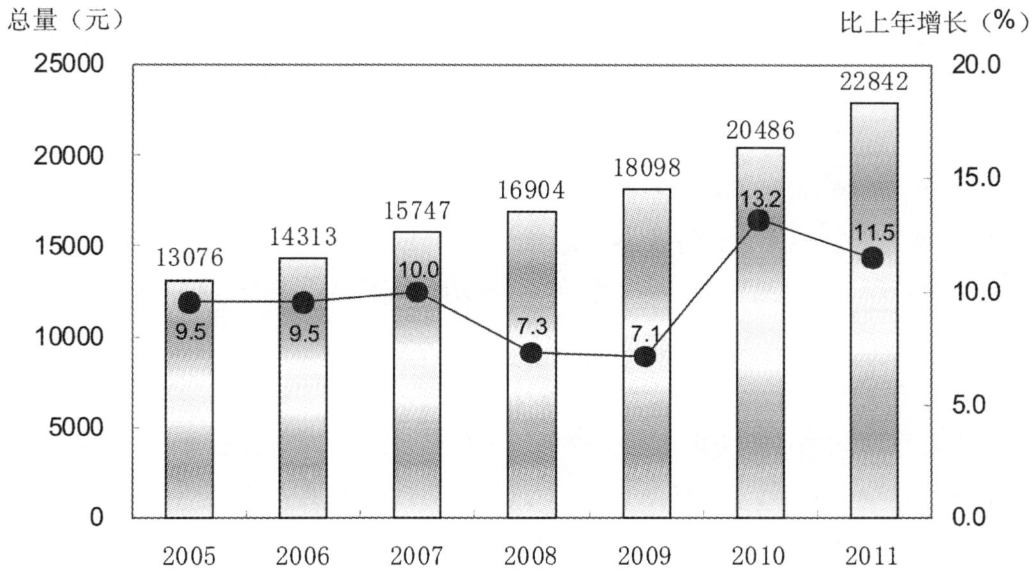

居民消费

全年城市居民人均消费性支出 27495 元，增长 6.8%。其中食品消费支出 9513 元，增长 8.9%；衣着消费支出 1806 元，增长 5.9%；居住消费支出 2128 元，增长 1.9%；家庭设备用品及服务支出 1902 元，增长 7.4%；医疗保健支出 1251 元，下降 3.3%；交通和通信支出 6035 元，增长 1.9%；教育文化娱乐服务支出 3886 元，增长 12.9%；其他商品和服务支出 974 元，增长 26.0%。城市居民家庭恩格尔系数为 34.6%。全年农民生活消费现金支出 13342 元，其中食品消费支出占 37.8%，衣着消费支出占 4.7%，居住消费支出占 16.7%，家庭设备用品及服务支出占 4.1%，医疗保健支出占 4.7%，交通通讯支出占 19.2%，教育文化娱乐服务支出占 8.7%，其他商品和服务支出占 4.1%。

表六：2011 年城市居民收支情况

指　　标	金额（元）	增长（%）
城市居民人均可支配收入	39513	10.7
#工资性收入	27272	1.8
财产性收入	7481	56.8
转移性收入	4374	35.8
城市居民人均消费性支出	27495	6.8
食品	9513	8.9
衣着	1806	5.9
居住	2128	1.9
家庭设备用品及服务	1902	7.4
医疗保健	1251	-3.3
交通和通信	6035	1.9
教育文化娱乐服务	3886	12.9
其他商品和服务	974	26.0

年末平均每百户城市居民家庭耐用消费品拥有量：家用空调272台，组合音响72套，移动电话280部，家用电脑136台，淋浴热水器138台，家用汽车80辆。城市居民人均住房建筑面积65.75平方米。平均每百户农村居民家庭耐用消费品拥有量：彩电167台，洗衣机107台，淋浴热水器133台，移动电话276部，影碟机69台，家用空调223台，家用电脑108台，家用汽车61辆。

社会保障

年末全市参加职工基本养老保险481.05万人，基本医疗保险602.41万人，失业保险299.38万人，工伤保险479.44万人。全年社会保险基金总收入179.40亿元，保险基金总支出83.87亿元，年末保险基金累计余额470.38亿元。全年累计征缴各项保险（不含机关养老保险）基金157.24亿元，增长25.6%。

国民经济和社会发展中存在的主要困难和问题是：产业结构调整仍需继续推进，企业的自主创新能力有待提高，资源环境问题日益突出，社会管理压力依然较大，均衡发展水平尚待提升，城市管理模式仍较粗放。要立足优化发展，围绕好中求进，以建设“三区四城”为目标，明确以加快转变经济发展方式、推进产业结构调整为主线，重点发展大项目、大园区、大产业，全面推进“三重”建设，吸引承接高端产业、优质项目，向“三重”要增量、要创新、要动力、要发展。

注：1. 本公报数为初步统计数，最后统计数据以《东莞统计年鉴－2012》为准。

2. 地区生产总值、各行业增加值、农业总产值绝对数按当年价格计算，增长速度按可比价格计算。

3. 五大支柱产业：电子信息制造业（即通信设备、计算机及其他电子设备制造业）、电气机械及设备制造业（包括电气机械及器材制造业，仪器仪表及文化、办公用机械制造业，通用设备制造业，专用设备制造业以及交通运输设备制造业）、纺织服装鞋帽制造业（包括纺织业，纺织服装、鞋、帽制造业以及皮革、毛皮、羽绒及其制品业）、食品饮料加工制造业（包括食品制造业，饮料制造业，农副产品加工业）、造纸及纸制品业。

四个特色产业：玩具及文体用品制造业（即文教体育用品制造业）、家具制造业、化工制品制造业（包括化学原料及化学制品制造业，橡胶制品业，石油加工、炼焦业及核燃业）、包装印刷业（即印刷业、记录媒介的复制）。

4. 全市职工年平均工资的调查范围为东莞市辖区内除农户以外各类经济实体，具体包括：①辖区内中央、省、市属各类企业、事业、机关单位；②各镇街办企业；③村及村以下办企业；④私营企业和个体工商户。

城镇在岗职工年平均工资的调查范围包括：①东莞市辖区内中央、省、市属全部独立核算的企业、事业、机关单位；②莞城、石龙、虎门3个镇街范围内镇街属单位（不包括莞城、石龙、虎门3个镇以下及其它镇街的单位、全市的私营单位和个体工商户）。

以上两个指标的调查范围不同，调查结果不同，请勿误用。

5. 农村居民人均纯收入采用农村住户抽样调查口径。

6. 阅读本公报时，请注意统计指标的时间、口径和计算方法等。

Dongguan Statistical Communique on National Economic and Social Development 2011

In 2011, under the strong leadership of the municipal government, with the guidance of scientific concept of development, in full operation of the 〈regional reform and development planning programs of the pearl river delta (2008 –2020)〉,giving prominence to changing the way of development, ensuring the growth of economy development steadily, presenting the situation of the enhanced the comprehensive strength of the city, effortful modulate the industry structure, improving people's livelihood continuously, social undertakings got continued progress.

Economical development

Ⅰ Economic aggregate

According to preliminary accounting, Dongguan realized a GDP of RMB 473.54 billion in 2011, up by 8.0% over the previous year calculating at comparable price. In specific terms, primary industry contributed RMB 1.771 billion to the overall growth, down by 0.4%; secondary industry contributed RMB 237.74 billion, up by 6.8%; and tertiary industry contributed RMB 234.03 billion, showing an increase of 9.3%. The added value of primary, secondary and tertiary industries respectively accounted for 0.4%, 50.2% and 49.4% of the GDP of Dongguan for the year 2011. The added value of the public economy realized RMB 117.19 billion, up by 4.1%, of the private economy realized RMB 177.35 billion, up by 10.8%, of the foreign economy realized RMB 179.00 billion, up by 7.9%, account for 24.7%, 37.5% and 37.8% of the GDP of Dongguan for the year 2011 respectively. In the tertiary industry, the growth of the transportation, storage and postal services 14.5%, of the wholesales and retail trade 8.0%, of the housing and catering services 6.1%, of the finance down by 0.8%, of the real estate 6.6%, of the others 12.8%. The per capita GDP was RMB 57, 470, up by 5.4%.

Figure 1:Gross Domestic Product and Its Growth, 2005-2011

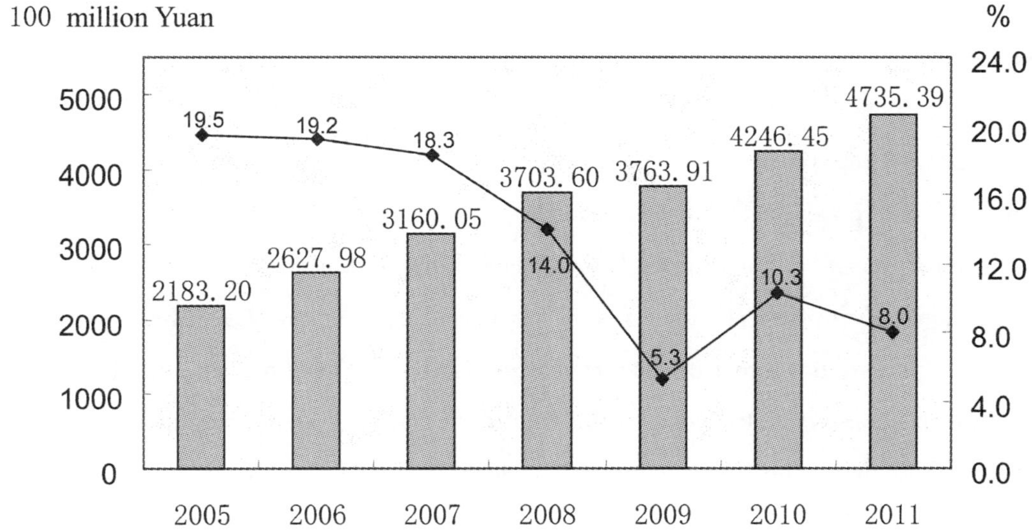

Fiscal revenue rooted in Dongguan was RMB 83. 85 billion for the year, up by 16. 2% , in which, the General budgeted revenue was RMB 31. 31 billion, up by 18. 3%. Among the General budgeted revenue, for the value-added tax revenue was RMB 7. 19 billion, up by 14. 8% ; for the business tax revenue was RMB 4. 53 billion, up by 18. 6% ; for the enterprise income tax revenue was RMB 2. 66 billion, up by 18. 2% ; for the individual income tax revenue was RMB 1. 12 billion, up by 21. 3% ; for the city maintenance and construction tax revenue was RMB 2. 21 billion, up by 94. 5% ; for the house property tax revenue was RMB 1. 06 billion, up by 14. 6% ; for the deed tax revenue was RMB 2. 31 billion, up by 23. 3%. General budget expenditures amounted to RMB 35. 19 billion, increasing by 21. 4% , in which, the general public services expenditures totaled RMB 3. 26 billion; the expenditure for public security amounted to RMB 4. 78 billion; for education was RMB 8. 32 billion; for science and technology was RMB 1. 81 billion; for culture, sports and media expenditures totaled RMB 1. 43 billion; for safety net and employment effort was RMB 2. 44 billion; for medical and health care services was RMB 1. 38 billion; for environmental protection was RMB 2. 28 billion; for urban and rural community affairs was RMB 2. 97 billion; for agriculture, forestry and water conservancy was RMB 1. 80 billion; for transportation was RMB 2. 53 billion. Industrial and commercial tax revenue for the year was RMB 84. 36 billion, up by 17. 9% , in which, the national tax revenue was RMB 52. 34 billion, up by 19. 1% , and the local tax revenue was RMB 32. 02 billion, up by 16. 0%.

Ⅱ Economy structure transformation and upgrading

To speed up transformation and upgrading of improvement trade, Dongguan introduced the construction scheme of transformation and upgrading of improvement trade pilot cities to support the introduction of advanced technologies, to optimize the mode of production, expand the domestic market; introducing the 〈The Implementation plan of change the mode of foreign economy growth〉 and 〈Guiding Opinions on further strength of the foreign investment attraction〉; giving the 28 measures on fiscal support on reducing charges, financial support and support fund of ransformation and upgrading improvement trade by the added RMB 0. 2 billion for import fund For three consecutive years. There were 1122 processing enterprises turn into corporate enterprises, over 3500 enterprises complete the transformation cumulatively, the basic realization of the transformation on the scale processing enterprises, and there were 202 new foreign-funded R & D institutions in the city, an increase of 52 units, among them, 14 foreign-funded R & D center, an increase of 5 units. 156 projects of the new signing, capital increase and actual capital respectively of the year, an increase of 29 projects. To start implementation on the 686 projects of introducing the private enterprises listing, establishment the resource library of reserve private enterprises for listing on municipal. For that, 68 enterprises in the resource library were determined, 10 enterprises in the resource library were recommended for the forth and the fifth reserve enterprises for listing, promoting 3 enterprises listing successfully. Giving the emphasis on domestic investment introduction, 643 domestic investment projects were introduced all over the year, the contractual investment realized RMB 42. 75 billion, the actual investment realized RMB 28. 60 billion. The capability of Independent innovation was further enhanced. Introducing on bidding of the high-end electronic information, semiconductor lighting and solar PV fields by the Guangdong & Hong Kong the special work on 2011, and 5 projects were certificated, got RMB 50 million supported.

Ⅲ Investment in fixed assets

The total investment in fixed assets reached RMB 107. 98 billion in 2011, an increase of 8. 1% over previous year. Specifically, state owned economy investment RMB 12. 44 billion, down by 23. 3% , collective economic investment RMB 12. 24 billion, down by 1. 4% , private economic investment RMB 46. 01 billion, up by 17. 7% , foeign and Hong Kong、Macao and Taiwan investment RMB 22. 03 billion, up by 12. 9% , account for 11. 5% , 11. 3% , 42. 6% and 20. 4%.

The investment in real estate development increased 25. 0% to RMB 37. 38 billion. With regard to industry, the investment was concentrated toward the secondary and tertiary industries. Investment in secondary industry was RMB 35. 13 billion, including manufacturing industry investment of RMB 30. 23 billion; investment in tertiary industry was RMB 72. 79 billion. The total completed investment reached 47. 59 billion, 302 project units above 50 million investment completed around the year, specifically, 151 industry project units reached RMB 20. 13 billion. 97 project units above 100 million investment completed around the year reached RMB 33. 24 billion, specifically, 44 industry project units reached RMB 12. 56 billion.

Figure 2: Investment in Fixed Assets and Its Growth, 2005-2011

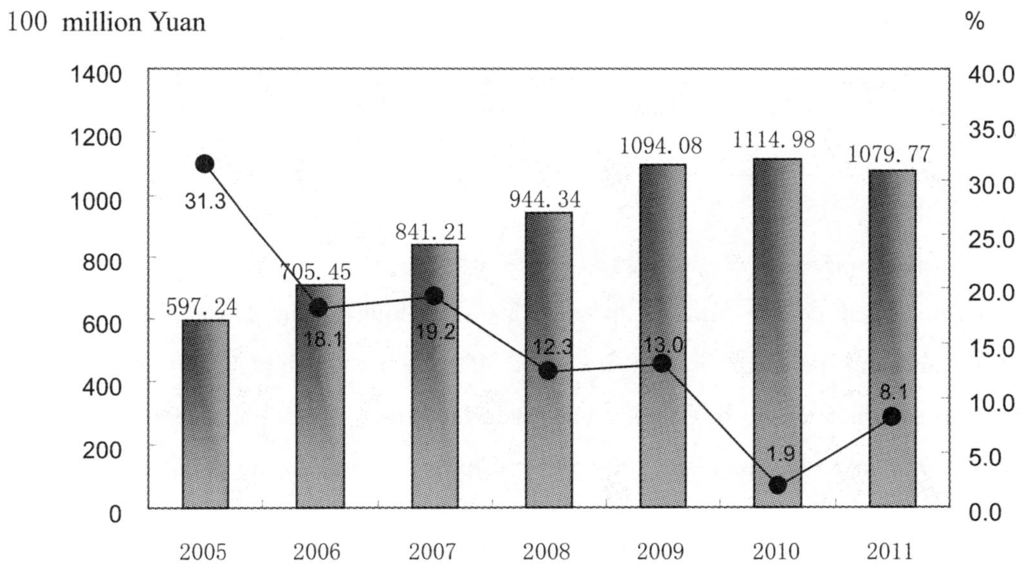

Notes: Investment in Fixed Assets include inter–regional projects from 2011.

Table 1: Investment in Fixed Assets by Sector in 2011

Sector	Investment	Increase over 2010 (%)
Total	10797662	8. 1
Farming, Forestry, Animal Husbandry and Fishery	5994	387. 7
Manufacture	3023124	9. 3
Production and Supply of Electric power, Gas and Water	487845	–28. 3
Construction	1468	–25. 6
Transport, Storage and Postal Services	1111422	–8. 6

Continue

Sector	Investment	Increase over 2010 (%)
Information Transmission, Computer Services and Software	199193	0.9
Wholesale and Retail Trade	264068	79.2
Hotel and Catering Services	46117	-50.7
Finance	19395	-18.3
Real Estate	4040535	18.2
Leasing and Business Services	74593	66.0
Scientific Research, Technical Services and Geologicl Prospecting	77528	-16.0
Water Conservancy, Environment and Public Facilities Management	1007314	48.5
Resident Services and Other Services	17109	-24.9
Education	235049	12.9
Health Care, Social Security and Social Welfare	73711	-46.5
Culture, Sports and Recreation	70148	-36.4
Public Administration and Social Organization	42529	-70.9

Ⅳ Prices

2011 CPI (consumer price index) was up by 4.9% in Dongguan, among which residence up by 4.3%, recreational, education and culture articles up by 0.3%, clothing up by 1.4%, food prices went up by 11.1%, healthy care and personal articles up by 2.4%, tobacco, liquor and articles up by 1.5%, transportation and communication up by 0.1%, household facilities, articles and services up by 5.5%. 2011 retail price up by 4.7% and PPI (producer price index) up by 2.9% over the pervious year.

Figure 3: Change in Consumer Prices, 2005-2011

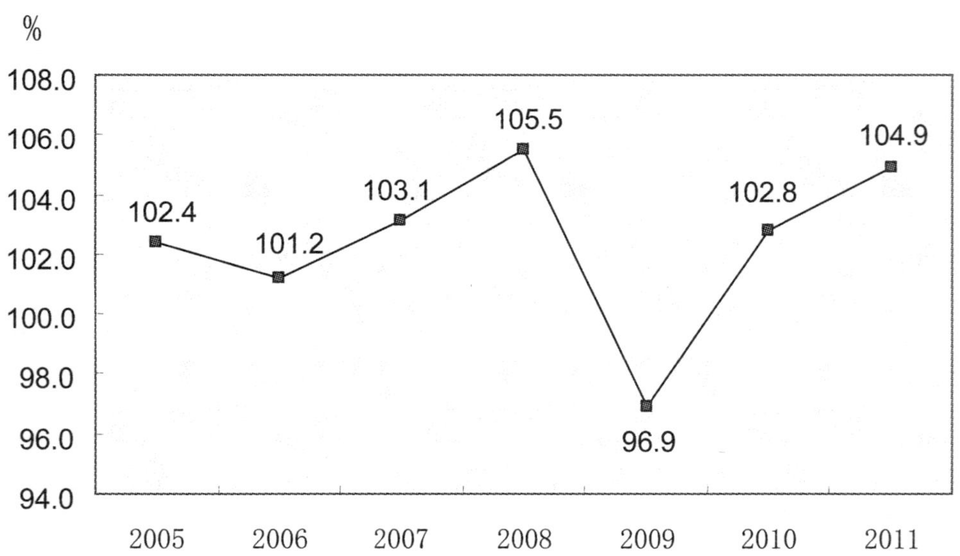

Table 2: Change of Prices in 2011

Item	Price Index (%)	Increase over 2010 (%)
Consumer Price Index	104. 9	4. 9
Food	111. 1	11. 1
Of Which: Grain	114. 6	14. 6
Meal, Poultry and Processed Products	114. 5	14. 5
Oil or Fat	110. 3	10. 3
Eggs	118. 0	18. 0
Fresh	95. 3	-4. 7
Aquatic Products	122. 0	22. 0
Tobacco, Liquor and Articles	101. 5	1. 5
Clothing	101. 4	1. 4
Household Facilities, Articles Services	105. 5	5. 5
Health Care and Personal Articles	102. 4	2. 4
Transportation and Communication	100. 1	0. 1
Recreation, Education and Culture Articles	100. 3	0. 3
Residence	140. 3	4. 3
Retail Price Index	104. 7	4. 7
Producer Price Index	102. 9	2. 9

Ⅴ Agriculture

In 2011, the gross output value of agriculture forestry animal husbandry and fishery was RMB 3. 07 billion, down by 0. 1% calculating at comparable price. Specifically, the output value of agriculture was RMB 1. 60 billion, up by 3. 3%, account for 52. 2%; the output value of forestry was RMB 21 million, down by 29. 6%, account for 0. 7%; the output value of animal husbandry was RMB 638 million, down by 8. 4%, account for 20. 8%; the output of fishery increased 0. 1% to RMB 714 million, account for 23. 3%. In 2011, the sown area of grain was 27. 66 million m^2. The total output of grain was 12. 9 thousand tons; the total output of aquatic products was 78. 2 thousand tons, up by 2. 6%; the total output of vegetables was 389. 0 thousand tons, down by 1. 0%. The number of slaughtered fattened hogs was 279. 1 thousand heads, down by 17. 1%; and that of poultry was 7. 32 million (heads), down by 1. 9%.

In 2011, there was a approved leading agricultural enterprises at the provincial level, 9 new farmer' s specialized cooperation units, 5new famous brand products. At the end of 2011, there was 20 eco-friendly foods obtain the certification.

Ⅵ Industry

In 2011, the total added value of the sector industry above the designated size was RMB 179. 73 billion, up by 7. 5%. Specifically, heavy industry realized an output value of RMB 96. 00 billion, up 8. 0%, accounting for 53. 4% of the output value of industry above the designated size; that of light industry was RMB 83. 73 billion, up by 3. 1%, accounting for 46. 6%. The added value of medium-sized enterprises RMB 138. 81 billion, accounting for 77. 2%. Specifically, the added value of the state owned industry was RMB 13. 28

billion, up by 4. 8, of the collective industry was RMB 3. 59 billion, up by 16. 7%, of the foreign industry was RMB 60. 33 billion, up by 6. 3%, of the Hong Kong, Macao and Taiwan investment industry was RMB 75. 99 billion, up by 2. 5%, of the private industry was RMB 17. 13 billion, up by 6. 8%. Which realized total profit RMB 26. 07 billion, the assets liability ratio was 60. 1%; and the comprehensive index of economic efficiency levels was 131. 52.

In 2011, the total added value of 5 pillar industry was RMB 124. 99 billion, up by 8. 0%, which is little high than the average growth rate of the industry above the designated size. The added value of Four Characteristic Industries was RMB 18. 72 billion, down by 2. 6%. The added value of electronic information and manufacturing enterprises above designated size was RMB 69. 25 billion, up by 10. 7%, showing a total profit of RMB 9. 40 billion, up by 5. 9% over the previous year.

Table 3: Output of Major Industrial Products of Industrial Enterprises above the Designated Size and the Growth Rates in 2011

Industry	Unit	Qty	Increase over 2010 (%)
Electronic Components	10000 Pcs	101254508	-1. 8
Machine-made Paper &Paperboard	Tons	10213204	1. 6
Porcelain	Sqm	22333672	7. 0
Electricity	10000 kilowatt-hours	3762253	4. 9
Furniture	Pcs	64181360	-7. 4
Garment	10000 Pcs	107297	-1. 6
Toy	1000 Yuan	10459959	1. 7
Tempered glass	Sqm	5433287	-10. 5
Mould	Sets	428255	2. 1
Daily stainless steel products	tons	36510	22. 9
Leather Shoes	10000 pairs	31905	-15. 1
Telephone sets	Sets	44433728	-4. 0
Hi-Fi stereo Components Players	Sets	28274323	-7. 0
Print circuit board	Sqm	16109240	-4. 0
Color TV	Sets	5414621	1. 1
Metal-cutting Tools	10000 units	11296	-16. 6
Power Cable	1000 meters	367142	-1. 9
Fabric	10000 meters	9958	-23. 8
Watch	Pcs	16697231	7. 5
Chemical Fibers	Tons	4324	-22. 4
Opto-electronic instruments	10000 Pcs	1272661	37. 8
Printing equipment	Tons	9392	-0. 6
Mobile Telephone	Sets	43362412	113. 4
Electricians Instruments and Meters	Sets	5825445	19. 8
Equipments for plastics processing	Sets	33962	-7. 7
Household electric fan	Sets	18108071	-7. 7
Monitor	Sets	7202	-70. 6

Ⅶ Construction

The added value of construction was RMB 7.78 billion, down by 12.2% over the previous year. The output value of buildings completed of construction enterprises in Dongguan was RMB 13.35 billion, up by 10.8% over the previous year; the floor space of buildings under construction was 7.59 million m^2, up by 3.5%; the floor space of buildings completed was 3.96 million m^2, up by 27.0%. Calculated at the output value of buildings completed, the overall labor productivity was RMB 229, 900 per person, up by 1.5% over the previous year.

Ⅷ Transportation, storage, post and telecommunications

The added value of the transportation, storage, post and telecommunications sector reached RMB 9.37 billion in 2011, up by 14.5% over the previous year.

At the end of 2011, the total length of highways in Dongguan (including the highway in the rural area) was 4827.53 kilometers; the highway density was 196.24 kilometers per 100 km^2. Among them, the length of expressway and class I to IV highways was 4715.73 km, the density was 191.70 km per 100 km^2; Among which, the length of expressways in the whole city reached 251.38 kilometers, and the density reached 10.22 km per 100 km^2. The possession of motor vehicles reached 1.42 million units, up by 5.2%. The possession of civil motor vehicles was 1.06 million units, up by 15.3%. The freight traffic of highways was 82.1 million tons, the freight ton-kilometers of highways was 5.31 billion ton-kilometers; the freight traffic of waterways was 19.55 million tons, the freight ton-kilometers of waterways was 13.44 billion ton-kilometers. The passenger traffic of highways was 0.80 billion by the end of 2011, the passenger-kilometers of highways was 14.57 billion passenger-km, the passenger traffic of waterways was 310 thousand persons by the end of 2011, the passenger-kilometers of waterways was 20.29 million passenger-km. The volume of freight handled in Dongguan' s coastal ports was 68.48 million tons and passenger traffic was 0.31 million persons.

The total business volume of postal and telecommunication services was RMB 16.49 billion in the year, up by 6.1% over the previous year. Specifically, the business volume of telecommunications was RMB 15.75 billion, up by 5.7%; the business volume of post was RMB 0.74 billion, up by 16.6%. In 2011, 51.48 million letters were posted, 1.67 million EMS were posted, the amount of postal remittance was RMB 20.62 billion.

Ⅸ Domestic trade

The total value-added of wholesale & retail sales was RMB 45.87 billion in 2011, up by 8.0% over the previous year; that of the lodging and catering industry was RMB 16.86 billion, up by 6.1%.

The total retail sales of consumer goods reached RMB 126.63 billion, up by 15.0% over the previous year (up by 9.6% in real terms). Specifically, the retail value of wholesale and retail trades reach RMB 115.06 billion, up by 15.2%, the lodging and catering industry reached RMB 11.57 billion, up by 13.5%.

With regard to enterprises above designated size of wholesale and retail trades, the asles value of domestic enterprises reached RMB 55.21 billion, up by 18.5%, account for 87.3%, in which, the sales value of the state owned enterprises, collective enterprises, Limited liability company, private enterprises and foreign enterprises account for 2.6%, 3.7%, 33.4%, 33.5% and 11.7% respectively.

the sales value of food, beverages, tobacco and liquor, clothing, shoes, hats and textiles, daily necessities, automobiles increased 17.8%, 26.7%, 12.3%, 20.3% over the previous year.

Figure 4: The Retail Sales of Consumer Goods and Its Growth,2005—2011

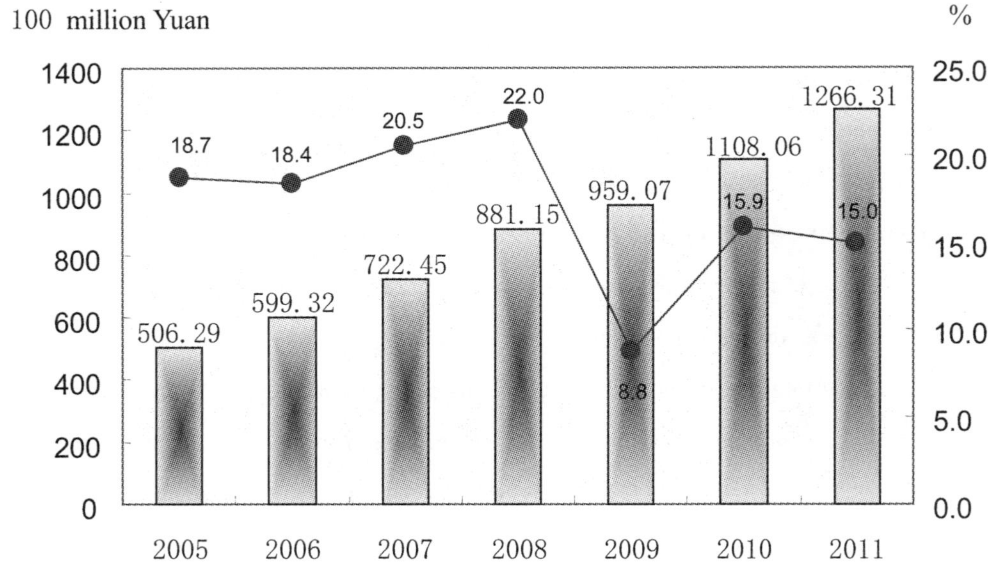

Ⅹ Finance

By the end of 2011, the added value of finance was RMB 18. 26 billion, down by 0. 8%.

In 2011, there were 87 financial institutions, including 4 newly added. Specifically, there were 27 banking institutions, 38 insurance companies, 22 security companies. The year-end balance of RMB savings in domestic financial institutions totaled 660. 94 billion, up by 11. 2% since the beginning of the year, in which, deposits by enterprises totaled RMB 273. 38 billion, an increase of 10. 9% over the previous year; residents' savings totaled RMB 371. 1 billion, up by 9. 3%, fiscal deposits amounted to RMB 3. 14 billion, down by 8. 3%. The year-end balance of RMB loans in domestic financial institutions totaled RMB 371. 61 billion, up by 11. 6% since the beginning of the year. With respect to the personal individual consumption loans, the balance of personal housing loans reached RMB 74. 18 billion, up by 5. 4% over the previous year; personal auto loans totaled RMB 1. 52 billion, down by 30. 2%. The NPLs of Dongguan financial institutions reduced 0. 42 index over the beginning of the year.

The total investors of all kinds of security companies was 894. 8 thousand by the end of 2011, increased about 74. 1 thousand accounts over the previous year. The total turnover of stock trading was down by 25. 3% to RMB 820. 93 billion. The guarantee fund balance totaled RMB 6. 98 billion, down by 48. 8% over the previous year.

The total number of insurance institutions reached 38 units, The insurance intermediary institutions amounts to 43. the employee of them amount to 28 thousand. Insurance institutions earned premiums of RMB 16. 37 billion, up by 2. 5% over the previous year, in which, property insurance premiums was RMB 5. 51 billion, up by 17. 9%, and life insurance premiums was RMB 10. 86 billion, down by 3. 9%. The claim and payment reached RMB 3. 6 billion, including property insurance indemnity of RMB 2. 7 billion, the loss ratio reached 49. 04%, and life insurance indemnity of RMB 0. 9 billion.

Figure 5: **Savings Deposits Of Urban And Rural Households and Its Growth, 2005-2011**

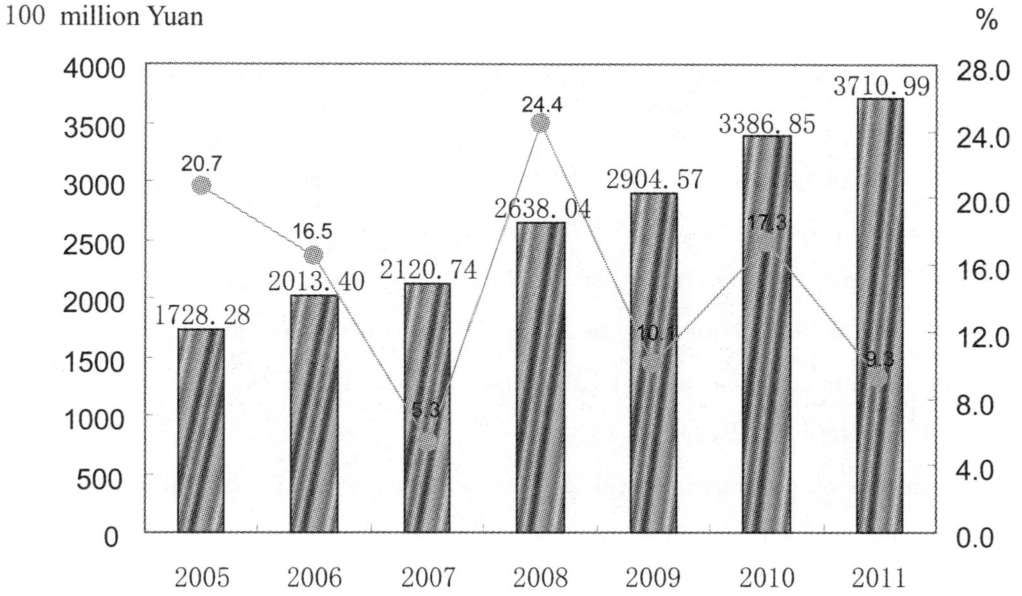

Ⅺ Real estate

The value-added of real estate was RMB 35.86 billion, up by 6.6% over the previous year. The total investment in real estate reached RMB 37.38 billion in 2011, an increase of 25.0% over the previous year. The total floor space under construction of commercialized buildings was 23.97 million m^2, up by 16.3% over the previous year; the total floor space completed reached 2.42 million m^2, down by 18.3%; the floor space of commercialized buildings sold amounted to 5.96 million m^2, up by 16.5%, in which, the floor space of residential buildings sold this year was 5.41 million m^2, up by 15.1% over the previous year. The total sales value of commercialized buildings was RMB 45.96 billion, up by 23.0% over the previous year, specifically the sales value of residential buildings was RMB 41.33 billion, up by 23.7%.

Ⅻ Private economy

The number of private units registered was 480.1 thousand, down by 2.6% over the previous year, in which, private enterprises was 104.7 thousand units, up by 18.1% over the pervious year and self-employed individuals was 373.3 thousand, down by 7.2% over the previous year. The added value of the private enterprises above designated size was RMB 25.77 billion, up by 12.0% over the previous year; the total investment in fixed asset of the private economy reached RMB 46.01 billion, up by 17.7%; the total retail sales of consumer goods of private economy was RMB 100.66 billion, up by 14.3% over the previous year; the total tax payable was RMB 31.44 billion, up by 20.4%.

Reform and opening up

Ⅰ Foreign trade

The total value of imports and exports in 2011 reached US $135.22 billion, up by 11.2% over the previous year, of which the total value of imports reached US $56.90 billion, up by 9.4%; the total value of exports reached US ＄78.33 billion, up by 12.5%.

Divided by mode of trade, the export value of general trade reached US ＄13.41 billion, representing an increase of 40.6%; The export value of processing trade reached US ＄63.48 billion, up by 7.6%; other trades for export reached US ＄1.44 billion, representing an increase of 38.3%.

Divided by registration type, the export value of state-owned enterprise reached US ＄7.03 billion, down by 36.3%; the export value of foreign funded enterprises reached US ＄54.28 billion, up by 22.6%; the export value of collective enterprise reached US ＄1.42 billion, up by 0.6%.

Divided by regions of export, the exports to Asia reached US ＄40.87 billion, up by 15.3%; the exports to North America reached US ＄19.98 billion, up by 5.2%; the exports to EU reached US ＄13.59 billion, up by 12.0%; the exports to Latin America reached US ＄2.44 billion, up by 39.3%; the exports to Oceania reached US ＄0.97 billion, up by 12.2%.

The total export volume of electromechanical products reached US ＄55.62 billion, up by 12.4%, accounting for 71.0% of the total exports. The export of hi-tech products reached US ＄27.34 billion, up by 13.0%, accounting for 34.9% of total export value of the entire city.

Table 4: Main Export Commodities in Value and the Growth Rates in 2011

Unit: 10000 US dollars

Commodities	Value	Increase over 2010 (%)
Automatic Data processing machines and components	612054	15.9
Clothes and clothing accessories	461285	18.4
Parts of automatic Data processing machines	347125	4.2
Shoes	307241	-0.9
Furniture and components	339959	5.9
Static converters	376054	4.5
Game machines	122646	45.1
Cable telephone (including cordless telephone)	192614	17.2
Spinning Yarn, Fabric and Products	164309	8.1
Digital cameras	128944	-19.8
Parts of Television, Radio and Wireless Telecommunication Equipment	144218	-10.5
Toys	172040	5.4
Traveling articles and cases (value)	181550	16.1
Insulated Wire or Cable	173136	13.8
TV sets (including a complete set of spare parts)	95155	-0.4
Electric Apparatus for Switching or Protecting Electrical Circuits	161770	20.6
Plastic Articles	127124	11.8
Video Recorder and Video Player	161883	22.3
Handle Mobiles and Car Telephones	138393	42.8

Ⅱ Foreign investment absorbance

According to new statistical information, the number of recently signed projects of foreign direct investment was 1324, the amount of contracted foreign capital reached US ＄3.51 billion, up by 35.1% over the previous year. The amount of foreign capital actually utilized reached US $3.05 billion, up by 11.7%, in which, the amount of foreign capital actually utilized by manufacture of electronic equipment and communication equipment reached US $0.66 billion, up by 8.0%; the amount of foreign capital actually utilized by manufacture of special purpose machinery reached US $0.20 billion, up by 27.8%. The number of recently signed projects which investments were over US $10 million was 68, representing an increase of 22 units over the previous year; the number of capital increasing projects of world's top 500 enterprises was 4, and the number of new investment of world' s top 500 enterprises was 5; the recently signed projects of tertiary industry reached US $0.53 billion, accounting for 15.0% of the entire city, raising 1.1 percentage points over the previous year. The step of foreign investment entering business domain was getting faster. The number of recently signed projects of wholesale and retail trade was 102 units, the amount of contracted foreign capital reached US $0.28 billion, up by 36.7%, accounting for 53.8% of total contracted foreign capital of tertiary industry.

Foreign-funded enterprises of whole city had established 202 research and development organizations, representing an increase of 52 units over the previous year. The number of service outsourcing enterprises of new foreign investment was 13, accounting for 29.9% of introducing service outsourcing projects in the city.

Table 5: Total Value of Foreign Capital Actually Utilized and the Growth Rates by Sector in 2011

Unit: 10000 US dollar

Sector	contracted foreign capital	Increase over 2010 (%)	Foreign Capital Actually Utilized Value	Increase over 2010 (%)
Total	350836	35.1	305052	11.7
Agriculture, Forestry, Animal Husbandry and Fishing	1580	56.4	559	801.6
Manufacturing	293826	31.9	259793	7.5
Textile Industry	12846	-0.5	16659	130.6
Manufacture of Textiles, garments, shoes and hats	11480	-12.5	11424	25.0
Manufacture of furniture	2417	32.4	3977	-35.4
Manufacture of General Machinery	5808	-11.1	8814	16.9
Manufacture of Special Purpose Machinery	13806	-28.3	19921	27.8
Manufacture of Electric Machinery and Equipment	37409	79.3	27742	9.8
Manufacture of Communication Equipment, Computers and other Electronic Equipment	83647	25.7	65660	8.0
Manufacture of Metal Products	17182	65.4	11056	6.6
Manufacture of Plastics Products	29467	65.9	18327	30.8
Manufacture of stationery and sporting Products	12113	148.6	7559	-12.7
Manufacture of papermaking and Paper Products	17140	112.7	15643	-26.2
Manufacture of others	50511	24.4	53011	-4.8
Information Transmission, Computer Services and Software	200	-74.4	1045	858.7
Wholesale and Retail Trade	28232	36.7	23568	77.6

Ⅲ Tourism

At the end of 2011, the number of star-rated hotels in whole city was 91, reducing 6 units over previous year, including 21 five-star hotels, 25 four-star hotels, 31 three-star hotels, 13 two-star hotels and 1 one-star hotel. There were 57 travel agencies, including 9 international travel agencies, 45 domestic travel agencies and 3 other travel agencies. The number of tourists from foreign economic zones, including Hong Kong, Macao and Taiwan was 3. 57 million, up by 9. 2% over the previous year, among them, the number of foreign tourists was 1. 21 million, up by 11. 7% over the previous year; the number of tourists from Hong Kong, Macao and Taiwan was 2. 36 million, up by 7. 9%. The foreign exchange income from international tourism increased 34. 6% to US $0. 91 billion. The number of domestic tourists was 22. 58 million, up by 17. 4% over the previous year, and the total income from domestic tourism increased 30. 3% to RMB 24. 94 billion.

The number of tourists of Dongguan out on tours was 1. 83 million in 2011, up by 19. 1%, of which, the tourists who were traveling domestic areas totaled 1. 67 million, up by 20. 4%; traveling aboard totaled 158. 1 thousand, up by 7. 5%.

Urban construction

Ⅰ Urban greening

At the end of 2011, the total developed areas reached 854. 3 sq km. in Dongguan. The land used for public facilities reached 71. 01 sq km. The area of afforested land was 90. 54 thousand hectares; forest cover rate reached 36. 9%, the green cover rate in afforested land reached 97. 8%. The green space rate of urban built-up area reached 42. 3% in the city, the green covered area was 44. 5%. Per capita park green area was 16. 46 sq. m. The number of park plaza was 1039 and the total area numbered 10500 hectares.

Ⅱ Public utilities

There were 99 bus lines, 1417 public transit vehicles and 7671 taxis in operation at year-end of 2011. Passenger' s traffic numbered 213 million by public transportation in 2011.

The daily water supply capacity was 7 million cubic meters and the annual volume of water supply totaled 1. 73 billion cubic meters in Dongguan. At the end of 2011, the total length of water supply pipelines reached 22. 6 thousand kilometers. The total sold electricity was 56. 7 billion Kwh, an increase of 4. 2%. In specific terms, industrial electricity was 44. 58 billion Kwh, up by 2. 3% and lighting electricity was 11. 97 billion Kwh, up by 11. 8%. At the end of 2011, the total of households using liquefied petroleum gas numbered 1. 18 million, and the households using natural gas numbered 178. 8 thousand. The total LPG supply was 338. 1 thousand tons, and the supply of natural gas was 365 million cubic meters.

Ⅲ Infomationization

The number of fixed telephone subscribers (including PHS) at year-end of 2011 was 3. 2 million, a decrease of 128. 7 thousand subscribers over 2010. The number of mobile phone subscribers reached 16. 78 million, an increase of 701. 7 thousand subscribers, of which by recharge card was 14. 33 million, decreasing by 5. 72 thousand. The length of long-distance calls totaled 21. 36 billion minutes in 2011, of which those connected to overseas nations and to Hong Kong, Macao and Taiwan were 289 million minutes. At the end of 2011, there were 1. 91 million internet subscribers, increasing by 368 thousand, and 1. 84 million broad band subscribers, increasing by 343.5 thousand.

Figure 6: Numbers of Telephone Subscribers at Year-end, 2005-2011

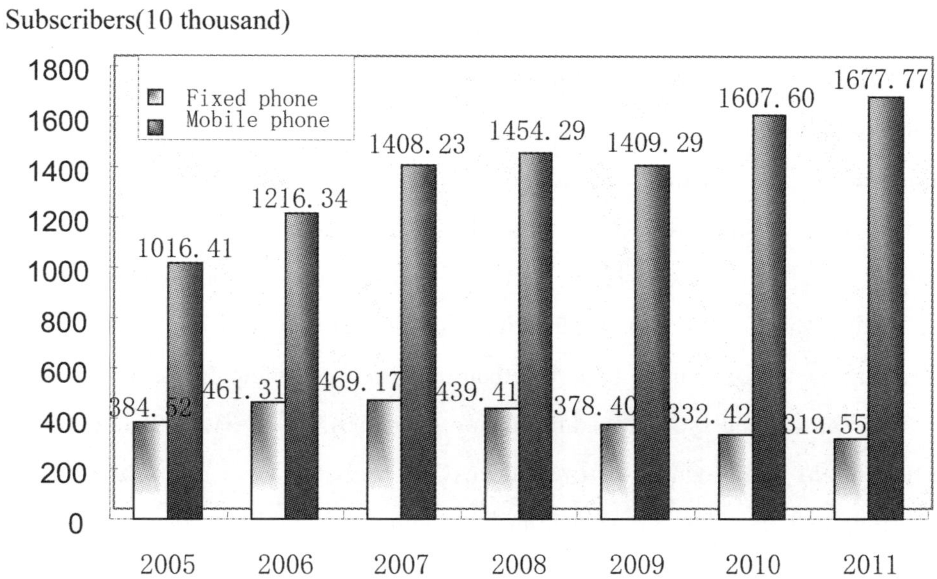

Note: Fixed phone subscribers include PHS (personal handy phone system), and mobile phone subscribers include recharge card subscribers

Social Undertaking

Ⅰ Science and technology

In 2011, 163 technology contract projects were signed, amount of RMB 320 million. 13 provincial and 77 municipal prizes for progress in science and technology were granted. Scientific and technological cooperation achieved new progress. 85 IUR (Industry-University-Research) projects were approvaled, international cooperation projects were approved, including 2 national-level and 3 provincial-level projects. There were totally 18 professional towns, 2 national engineering centers, 42 provincial engineering center,s 413 national high-tech enterprises and 852 private technology enterprises in Dongguan. The number of patents application accepted and granted reached 24.5 thousand units and 19.4 thousand units respectively. Of the total, 4214 patent applications of invention were accepted, and 758 of them were granted, up by 34.1% and 71.5% respectively over the previous year.

Ⅱ Education

There were 749 kindergartens in Dongguan, 22 more than the previous year, of which 175 were founded by education departments and collectives, 574 were founded by private institutions. 96 kindergartens were certified as Provincial or Municipal 1st Class kindergarten. There were 227.7 thousand aged 3-6 years old children enrolled, and the enrollment rate reached 95.2%.

There were 324 primary schools in Dongguan, decreased 6 units over the previous year; there were 578.3 thousand students enrolled in primary school; school-age children enrollment ratio had reached 100%, and the promotion rate from primary schools to junior secondary schools of Dongguan residents was 100%. There were 161 junior secondary schools, with 189. 4 thousand enrolled students and 54. 7 thousand graduated students. For Dongguan's registered residents, the net enrollment ratio of junior secondary schools, drop-out rate and graduation rate were 100%, 0. 15% and 98% respectively.

There were 64 senior secondary schools (including 20 private schools) with 121. 8 thousand students enrolled (including technical school) in Dongguan. Of the total, there were 38 senior secondary schools (including six-grade secondary schools) with 73. 6 thousand students and 26 secondary vocational schools (including 1 technical school) with 48. 2 thousand students. The promotion rate from junior secondary schools to senior secondary school of Dongguan residents was 93. 6%, 0. 1 points of percentage over the previous year.

There were 5 adult institutions of higher education, 32 township cultural and technical schools for adults, and 277 private training institutions, more than 500 thousand people participated in various types of training by adult education. Scale of various types of adult higher education up to 31. 6 thousand people (Excluding students who participate in adult education by colleges and universities in Dongguan). A total of 21. 3 thousand people participated in adult college entrance examination and 52. 5 thousand people participated in National higher education self-study exam.

There were 6 institutions of regular higher education. 3 of them were universities with full undergraduate courses and the other 3 were collages with specialized courses. There were 45. 1 thousand total enrollments. In 2011, there were totally 16. 8 thousand new-enrolled students and 9463 graduated students. In 2011, there were 22. 3 thousand students participated in the entrance examinations for colleges and universities, and 21. 4 thousand of those students passed and entered into colleges and universities. There were 3357 people passed the higher vocational exam.

Ⅲ Culture

At the end of 2011, there were 1 mass art center, 33 cultural stations, 622 public libraries, 31 museums, 769 cultural squares, 63 arts performance places, 52 movie screening units and 1048 internet cafes. Public cultural facilities construction area reached 7 million square meters. Dongguan had 56 public radio programs and 37 public television programs. In 2011, 52. 21 million copies of newspapers, 1. 09 million copies of magazines and 69. 6 thousand copies of books were published respectively. Dongguan Daily had 31. 32 million copies circulation. There were 185. 4 thousand film screenings and 4. 07 million viewers in 2011.

Ⅳ Health and medicine

At the end of 2011, Dongguan had 2249 heath care institutions, including 2170 grass-roots health care institutions such as outpatient departments, clinics, health stations, infirmaries and community health service centers, with 39. 6 thousand medical technical personals and 22. 8 thousand hospital beds. In Dongguan, 390 community health service institutions had been built and put into service, covering more than 594 villages (communities)throughout the city. The patients who received treatment throughout the year were increased by 3.5%.

Ⅴ Sports

Dongguan athletes won 151 gold (above provincial level), 118 silver and 102 bronze medals in 2011, including 8 gold medals in international tournaments, 27 gold medals in national tournaments. In provincial tournaments, athletes won 116 gold, 101 silver and 95 bronze medals.

Dongguan held 62 municipal integrated and individual competitions, in which over 143. 3 thousand people participated. There were 465. 8 thousand participants who took part in 420 township individual competitions. Dongguan had 196 sports lottery distributions outlets, which total sale was RMB 957 million and public welfare fund of sports lottery was RMB 69. 35 million.

Ⅵ Social welfare and relief

At the end of 2011, there were 45 adoptive welfare institutions, of the total, 1 social welfare institute, 1 children's welfare institute and 31 gerocomiums, with 873 old people who were maintained in geocomiums. There were 34 social welfare institutions with 2689 people adopted. There were 296 " four types of disability" people employments arranged and 32. 6 thousand persons received social assistance in 2011. The expenditure of urban minimum living allowance was RMB 63 million. Expenditure of social relief totaled RMB 216 million. Expenditure of social relief for natural disaster was RMB 2. 69 million, the balance of Charitable Fund was RMB 223 million. 1210 persons were brought into the "Five-Guaranteed households" project, and which cost RMB 17. 24 million. All the 32 towns in Dongguan had established social security network. 3796 households counting up to 9415 persons were brought into the urban minimum living allowance project and 8744 households counting up to 21959 persons were brought into township receiving minimum living allowance project.

Ⅶ Social stability and Safe production

The detected criminal cases increased by 9. 4% all over the year. An increase of 6. 6% was shown in total acceptance of mass petitions. At the end of 2011, 574 municipal safe communities have been built, 21 of them were built in 2011. In 2011, 4525 cases of industrial accident occurred in Dongguan, decreased by 7. 9% over the previous year; 540 persons died and 5015 people were injured, decreased by 5. 9% and 6. 5% respectively; direct economic losses was RMB 6. 62 million, decreased by 26. 1%. Of the total, the number of road traffic accidents was 4490, decreased by 7. 8%, which resulted in 495 deaths and 4999 injured, a decrease of 5. 9% and 6. 6% respectively. Production-related accident mortality rate per 100 million GDP was 0. 114 and road traffic mortality rate per 10 thousand vehicles was 3. 49.

Ⅷ Resource and environmental protection

Throughout the year, rainy days numbered 161 days; sunshine hours were 2120. 1 hours; average temperature was 22. 1 degrees Celsius; relative humidity was 71%. Precipitation of the year was 1298. 6 millimeters.

At the end of 2011, there were 18 forest parks, 600. 1 square kilometers of Forest area and 250. 9 square kilometers of ecological public forest, which contained 2. 73 million cubic meters of tree storage and 159. 9 thousand cubic meters of total tree growth in Dongguan.

People's living conditions

Ⅰ Population

At the end of 2011, Dongguan's registered population reached 1. 85 million. The year 2011 saw 19. 9 thousand births, a crude birth rate of 10. 92 per thousand, and 8, 728 deaths, a crude death rate of 4. 79 per thousand. The natural growth rate was 6. 13 per thousand. The permanent population reached 8. 25 million. Of this total, the permanent urban population was 7.31 million, the urbanization rate of 2011 reached 88.6%.

Ⅱ Employment

In 2011, 16400 college graduates were employed. Talent market registered numbered 1.13 million; 421.6 thousand person-time were applied, up by 5.2%. The number of urban registered unemployment was 11.1 thousand, and 11.3 thousand were settled down. The registered urban unemployment rate was 2.1%.

Ⅲ Income

In 2011, the average annual salary was RMB 21, 739. Of this total, the average annual salary of the urban full-employed staff and workers was RMB 50, 398. The per capital annual disposable income of urban households increased by 10.7% over the previous year to RMB 39, 513, and the per capita annual disposable income of rural households increased by 11.5% over the previous year to RMB 22, 842.

Figure 7: Per Capital Disposable Income of UrbanHouseholds and Its Growth, 2005-2011

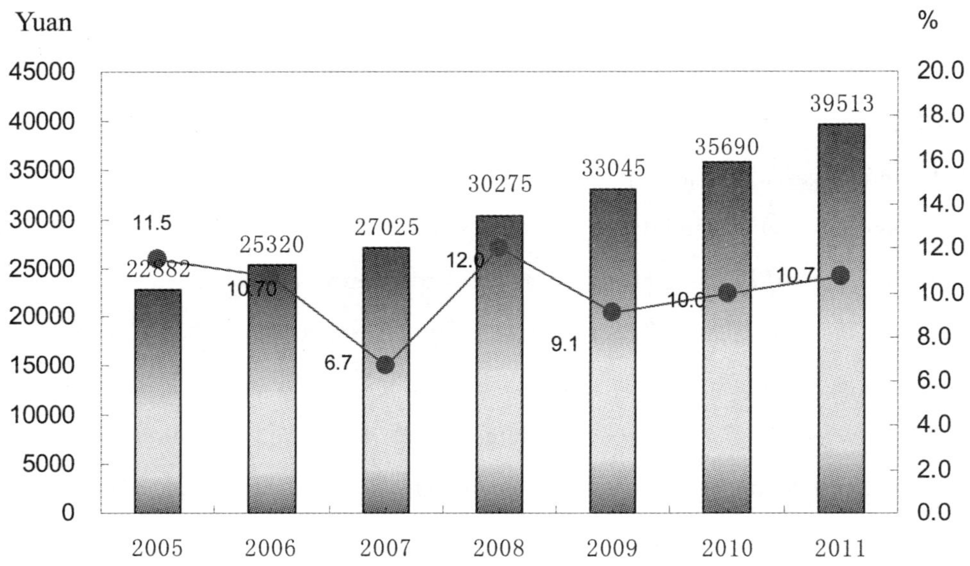

Figure 8: Per Capital Disposable Income Of Rural Households and Its Growth, 2005-2011

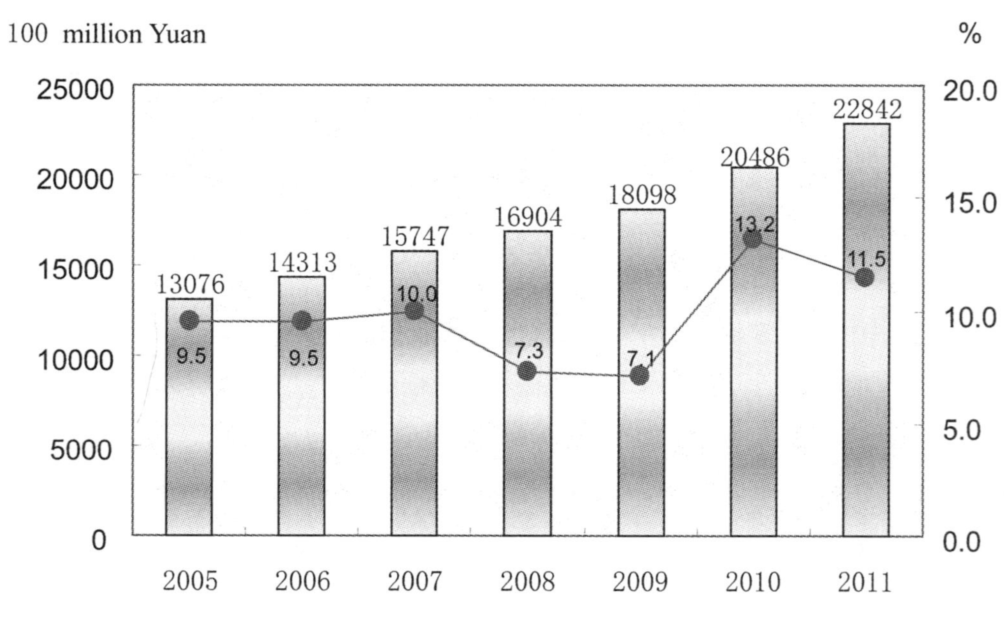

Ⅳ Consumer Expenditure

The annual per capital consumption expenditure of urban residents was RMB 27, 495, increased by 6. 8%. Of this total, the expenditure on food was RMB 9, 513, up by 8. 9%; the expenditure on clothing was RMB 1, 806, up by 5. 9%; the expenditure on residence was RMB 2, 128, up by 1. 9%; the expenditure on household facilities, articles and services was RMB 1, 902, up by 7. 4%; the expenditure on health care and medical services was RMB 1, 251, down by 3. 3%; the expenditure on transport and communications was RMB 6, 035, up by 1. 9%; the expenditure on education, cultural and recreation services was RMB 3, 886, up by 12. 9%; and the expenditure on miscellaneous goods and services was RMB 974, up by 26. 0%. The annual per capital cash expenditure of rural residents was RMB 13, 342. Of this total, 37. 8% was spent on food; 4. 7% on clothing; 16. 7% on living; 4. 1% on household facilities, articles and services; 4. 7% on health care and medical services; 19. 2% on transport and communications; 8. 7% on education, cultural and recreation services; 4. 1% on miscellaneous goods and services.

Table 6: Income and Expenditure Of Urban Households 2010

Item	Income or expenditure (yuan)	Increase over 2010 (%)
Per Capita Disposable Income of Urban Residents	39513	10. 7
Income from Wages and Salaries	27272	1. 8
Income from Properties	7481	56. 8
Income from Transfer	4374	35. 8
Per Capita Consumption Expenditure of Urban Residents	27495	6. 8
Food	9513	8. 9
Clothing	1806	5. 9
Residence	2128	1. 9
Household Facilities, Articles and Services	1902	7. 4
Health Care and Medical Services	1251	-3. 3
Transport and Telecommunication	6035	1. 9
Educational, Cultural Recreation Services	3886	12. 9
Miscellaneous Goods and Services	974	26. 0

The ownership of major durable consumer goods per 100 urban households at the year-end were: 272 air conditioners, 72 Hi-Fi stereo component system, 280 mobile phones, 136 computers, 138 water heaters, 80 cars. The per capital housing floor space of urban households was 65. 75 square meters. The ownership of major durable consumer goods per 100 rural households at the year-end were: 167 color TV, 107 washing machines, 133 water heaters, 276 mobile phones, 69 disc players, 223 air conditioner, 108 computers, 61cars.

Ⅴ Social Security

At year-end, the number of employee joining basic pension insurance was 4. 81 million, in special terms, the basic medical care system was 6. 02 million, the unemployment insurance was 2. 99 million persons; the injury insurance was 4. 79 million persons. The annual total revenue of social insurance fund was RMB 17. 94 billion, the total expense at year-end of the insurance fund was RMB 8. 39 billion, and the accumulated balance of the insurance fund was RMB 47. 04 billion. The cumulative collection fund throughout the year to various kinds of insurance (excluding the organs pension insurance) was RMB 15.72 billion, an increase of 25.6%.

The main difficulties and problems in national economy and social development include: industrial restructuring needs to be continuously pusing forward, independent innovation capacity of enterprises needs to be improved, resources and environmental problems have become increasingly critical, social management is still under high pressure, the level of balanced development has to be enhanced, urban management mode is still extensive. Our work should stick to the idea of optimal development and make progress based on previously well estabilished results. We should aim at the goal of building " three districts, four cities", clearly regard speeding up the transformation of economic development and promoting industrial restructuring as the main theme, focus on the development of large projects, industrial parks, large industries, and comprehensively promote the " triple" construction to attract high-end-undertaking industries, high-quality projects, and obatin increment, innovation, power, and development from the " triple" construction.

政 府 工 作 报 告

REPORT ON THE WORK OF THE GOVERNMENT

——2011 年 1 月 7 日在东莞市第十五届人民代表大会第一次会议上

东莞市人民政府代市长　袁宝成

各位代表：

现在，我代表市人民政府向大会报告过去五年的政府工作，并对今后五年和 2012 年工作提出建议，请予审议，并请政协各位委员和其他列席人员提出意见。

过去五年工作回顾

市第十四届人民代表大会第一次会议以来的五年，是东莞发展进程中不平凡的五年。五年来，在上级和市委的坚强领导下，全市上下深入落实科学发展观，全面实施《珠江三角洲地区改革发展规划纲要》，扎实推进经济社会双转型，较好地完成了市十四届人大一次会议确定的各项目标任务，东莞综合实力稳步增强，产业结构持续优化，人民生活不断改善，城市形象日益提升，获得全国文明城市、全国双拥模范城、国家园林城市、国家环保模范城市、中国制造业名城、中国十大最关爱民生城市等荣誉。

——积极应对挑战，经济实力迈上了新的台阶。2008 年以来，我市面临复杂多变的经济形势，经受了转型发展的考验和国际金融危机的冲击，在宏观环境较为困难的情况下，保持了经济的平稳健康发展。初步预计，全市生产总值从 2006 年的 2628 亿元增加到 2011 年的 4735 亿元，年均增长 11.1%。来源于东莞的财政总收入、市财政一般预算收入、进出口总额、金融机构各项存款余额分别达到 839 亿元、313 亿元、1347 亿美元和 6400 亿元，是五年前的 2.2 倍、2.1 倍、1.6 倍和 1.9 倍。**以落实规划纲要统领发展全局。**深化“五个一体化”合作，加快深莞惠融合步伐，推动省、市重大项目实施，“四年大发展”各项目标任务完成良好。**以一揽子举措应对金融危机。**开展“稳定企业扎根发展”系列活动，设立多个 10 亿元专项资金帮扶企业。实行领导挂钩督导、审批绿色通道、要素资源倾斜等制度，促进重点项目建设提速，年均固定资产投资超过 1000 亿元。实施八大商贸促进工程，开展“莞货全国行”活动，社会消费品零售总额年均增长 16.3%。**以园区开发打造新增长极。**松山湖升级为国家级高新区，工业总产值、税收年均分别增长 40% 和 65%，台湾高科技园开园并引进了一批大型项目。虎门港建成 3 万吨级以上深水泊位 12 个，港口年吞吐量超过 6000 万吨。生态园基础设施和环境建设基本完成，升级为省级生态工业园区和循环经济示范园区。长安新区规划报批进展良好。各镇街工业集聚区加快整合提升。园区经济成为全市发展的重要增长极。**以扶持镇村推动协调发展。**提高镇街财政分成比例，落实贷款贴息政策，开展市内“双到”扶贫，实施生态补偿、镇村基础建设补助和公共管理支出补助，有效增强了基层发展的活力。2011 年镇街平均可支配收入比 2006 年翻了 1 番，村组两级平均可支配收入达到 3239 万元。

——深入调整结构，转型升级取得了突出成效。制定“1 + 26”政策体系，试点先行，加强引导，推动产业结构调整，实现了三大产业结构、经营模式、技术品牌、企业结构、市场结构、资源配套的优化。**加工贸易转型步伐加快。**在全国首创不停产转型模式，推动 3500 家来料加工企业转为独立法人企业，442 家外资企业设立了研发机构，新增 632 家加工贸易企业开展品牌经营。全市外贸依存度从 254% 下降为 187%，外企内销比重从 26.4% 上升到 32.8%。东莞被确定为全国加工贸易转型升级试点城市。**自主创新能力有效增强。**市财政每年投入 10 亿元，2011 年提高到 20 亿元，深入实施“科技东莞”工程。全市研发经费增长 2.4 倍，新增各类创新平台 105 个，企业参与各类标准修订 223 项。拥有国家高新技术企业 415 家、省级以上名牌名标 528 个，省创新科研团队数量和专利授权量居全省第二，社会创新意识和企业创新能力不断增强。**招商引资和企业培育有新进步。**深化与港台地区的经贸合作，拓展对日韩欧美的重点招商，五年累计实际利用外资 128.4 亿美元，引进超千万美元项目 430 宗、世界 500 强项目 44 宗。2008 年以来实际引进内资 694 亿元、超亿元项目 278 宗。现代产业体系“四个 30 项目”、民营 50 强企业不断壮大，新增上市企业 8 家，年主营业务收入百亿元企业实现零的突破。**现代服务业和战略性新兴产业加快发展。**推动珠三角新兴物流城市建设，积极打造电博会、外博会、漫博会、台博会等品牌展会，推进“大麦客”等商业模式创新，金融、物流、会展、动漫等产业蓬勃发展，生产性服务业加快集聚，农业产业园建设扎实推进，三大产业比例从 0.5∶57.3∶42.2 调整为 0.3∶50.5∶49.2。设立战略性新兴产业培育资金，启动五年倍增计划，新增全省战略性新兴产业基地 3 个。**产业和劳动力“双转移”积极推进。**市财政投入 3 亿元建设莞韶、莞惠产业转移园。全市新接收粤东西北地区劳动力 23 万人。

——坚持环境取胜，城乡面貌得到了切实改善。五年引导全社会共投入城建资金 2500 多亿元，推动城市建设从中心城区向全市范围延伸，从基础设施向环境建设延伸，从拉开框架向完善功能延伸，强化了市区地位，优化了镇村形象，提升了城乡一体化水平，改善了水环境和空气质量，城市环境考核排名从全省第九升至第三。**基础设施日趋完善。**城际轨道和市内轻轨启动建设，莞深高速三期、莞惠高速、龙大高速、环城路、西部干道等高快速路建成通车，新建改造镇村联网路 373 公里，新建水利防灾减灾工程 370 项、110 千伏及以上输变电工程 76 项、天然气管网 790 公里，城市承载力稳步增强。**城市功能不断强化。**“四院一中心”、第六水厂等投入使用，市篮球中心基本建成，中央商务区、中央商圈和生态休闲区规划建设全面启动，市区首位度不断提高，辐射带动作用更加突出。加快打造各镇街标志性片区，推进成熟社区、宜居社区和名村建设，镇街配套更加成熟。**城乡环境持续优化。**划定 1104 平方公里生态控制线范围，建成森林公园 8 个、乡村公园 1031 个、绿道 638 公里，森林覆盖率、建成区绿化率分别达到 36.9% 和 45.4%。投入 200 多亿元建成 34 座污水处理厂及截污主干管网工程，污泥处理厂、医疗废物处理中心投入使用，运河综合整治取得实效，城镇生活污水处理率、生活垃圾无害化处理率分别达到 77.3% 和 56.6%。圆满完成“十一五”节能减排任务。深入开展农村环境“五整治”，全面铺开“三旧”改造，促进了城市更新与城乡一体。**城市管理水平提升。**实行城管综合执法，推广“市场化 + 监理制”的市政管理模式，建立健全各项管理制度，推进生活垃圾分类试点，城市管理的制度化、专业化、社会化水平不断提高。

——**强化社会管理，有力维护了和谐稳定**。落实维稳第一责任，着力提升社会管理水平，保障了社会稳定，增进了社会和谐。**公共安全管理不断加强**。每年将治安列为十件实事之首，加强治安防控，严打恶性和多发性犯罪，群众安全感增强，东莞获评全国社会治安综合治理优秀市。紧盯消防、交通、建筑、公共卫生、食品药品安全和产品质量等重点领域，深入推进大排查、大整治、大培训、大建设，全面提升安全生产管理水平。各类安全事故宗数、死亡人数、直接经济损失，比五年前分别下降33.9%、35.5%和41.3%。**矛盾纠纷有效化解**。完善信访调解网络，健全维稳综治体系，加强矛盾隐患排查，提升应急管理能力，强化劳动监察执法和劳资关系调解，群众信访总量下降19.8%，纠纷调处成功率达97.4%。**新莞人服务管理逐步优化**。成立新莞人服务管理机构，全面实施以居住证为载体的服务管理“一证通”制度，实行新莞人积分入户、子女积分入学政策，接受1.8万名新莞人积分入户、13.3万名新莞人子女入读义务教育阶段公办学校。新莞人参加各类社保超过2020万人次。

——**践行为民宗旨，民生事业实现了全面发展**。把改善民生作为政府工作的出发点和落脚点，坚持每年办好十件实事，带动民生工作全面开展。五年来，市财政共投入688亿元用于民生发展，城市居民可支配收入和农村居民纯收入均增长56%。**就业创业扶持有力**。市财政每年安排10亿元实施“创业东莞”工程，累计培训劳动力20万人次，援助就业困难人员7万多人，城乡登记失业率控制在3.5%以内。向4400多人次提供小额创业贷款3.2亿元。最低工资标准提高到1100元。**社保体系日益健全**。农（居）民与职工基本养老实现统筹发展，退休金分别增长104%和55%。城乡基本医疗实现同等保障，医保最高支付限额提高到20万，医疗门诊报销70%。建立低保自然增长、临时物价补贴和高龄津贴制度，低保标准提高到440元，户籍困难家庭住房保障基本实现应保尽保。**教育水平稳步提升**。办学管理实现市镇统筹，省教育强镇实现全覆盖，义务教育实现全免费，高中阶段学校布局调整基本完成，职业教育、民办教育、高等教育加快发展，每万户籍人口大学入学人数全省第一。**文化事业繁荣发展**。推进图书馆、博物馆、文化广场建设，实现了村（社区）文化设施“五个有”全覆盖，完善了公共文化服务网络，创作了一批文艺精品，形成了一系列文化惠民活动品牌。设立5年共50亿元的专项资金，推动文化新城向文化名城跨越提升。**卫生、体育等各项事业持续进步**。推进以公益性为方向的新一轮医改，启动公立医院改革试点，建立基本药物制度，建成社区卫生服务机构390个。成功防控甲型H1N1流感、基孔肯雅热等疫情。年均人口自然增长率6.12‰。成功承办亚运会举重赛事，群众体育广泛开展，篮球运动屡获殊荣。积极做好残疾人康复、教育、就业服务。提前完成援建汶川映秀任务，大力援建新疆生产建设兵团农三师，对口援助西藏林芝、广西河池等地区，扎实推进韶关、云浮“双到”扶贫。国防双拥、外事侨务、海洋渔业、民族宗教、统计审计、气象防灾、档案方志、科普、打私、工青妇幼等工作取得新的进展。

——**不断改进作风，政府执行力进一步提高**。深入转变政府职能，着力建设阳光、高效、为民的政府。**改革创新力度不断加大**。市政府工作部门从37个精简为32个，市直临时议事协调机构精简53%，行政审批事项精简33%。铺开简政强镇改革，向中心镇和市属园区下放经济社会管理权限500多项。开展村级体制改革试点，推进村民自治、经济发展、公共服务等职能分离。稳妥实施事业单位分类改革和人事制度改革。**依法行政水平有效提高**。加强法治政府建设，制定重大行政决策程序规定和行政处罚裁量标准，健全政府法律顾问、专家咨询论证、征求公众意见等制度。市长办公会向媒体开放，推行公共企事业单位办事公开，以网络、微博等方式强化了政群互动。自觉接受市人大、市政协及社会各界监督，五年来共办结人大代表、政协委员意见建议2576件，回复率和满意率均达

100%。**廉政和效能建设持续推进。**严格落实廉政责任制，严控由财政出资举办的晚会、展览、庆典、论坛活动，严控楼堂馆所建设。建立市镇领导挂钩督导制度，将重要工作纳入行政问责范围，加强督促检查，狠抓工作落实。推进并联审批与网上审批，强化效能监察和电子政务建设，精简会议和文件。深入实施改进机关作风六项制度，组织明查暗访，每年开展“市民评机关”活动，优化了机关作风，提升了政府形象。

各位代表！过去五年，全市上下风雨兼程，励精图治，经受了严峻考验，战胜了重重困难，迈出了科学发展、转型发展的坚实步伐。这些成绩的取得，离不开中央、省委省政府和市委的正确领导，以及历届班子打下的坚实基础；离不开市人大、市政协与各民主党派的监督支持；离不开全市人民、驻莞部队、武警官兵的实干奋进，以及港澳台同胞、海外侨胞和国际友人的共同努力。在此，我代表市政府，向所有参与、支持和关心东莞经济社会发展的各界人士，表示衷心的感谢和崇高的敬意！

成绩令人振奋，经验弥足珍贵。实践充分证明：**唯有**坚持深入转型、加快升级，才能破解发展难题，转变发展方式。**唯有**坚持政府主导、市场主体，才能强化转型发展的科学导向，激发全社会的创造活力。**唯有**坚持产业强市、特色发展，才能发挥比较优势，巩固城市地位。唯有坚持关注基层、民生为本，才能促进协调发展，让改革成果更多更好地惠及老百姓。**唯有**坚持求真务实、强化执行，才能将上级和市委的决策部署，转化为推动东莞发展的有效举措。**唯有**坚持着眼大局、团结奋进，才能凝聚干事创业力量，推动东莞不断实现新的发展。

与此同时，我们也要清醒地看到经济社会发展面临的问题和存在的隐忧：**一是产业结构调整任重道远。**对传统发展模式的路径依赖仍然较强，产业核心竞争能力、自主创新能力和抗御风险能力仍待提升，新产业带动、大项目支撑力度不足。**二是资源环境问题日益突出。**土地、能源等要素供给越来越紧张，节能减排、生态建设和环境治理任务艰巨。**三是社会管理压力依然较大。**社会治安形势虽然有所好转，但与人民群众的期望仍有差距，安全事故还时有发生，矛盾排查调处与化解还不彻底，社会管理的体制机制和方法手段仍需优化。**四是均衡发展水平尚待提升。**个别镇村负债较重，集体经济稳健增长和持续增收面临考验，市内扶贫任务比较艰巨。**五是城市管理模式仍较粗放。**交通秩序、环境卫生、设施管养、内涝防治、违法建筑等方面的问题不可忽视，城市的精细化管理水平有待进一步提升。**六是政府自身建设仍需加强。**政府的创新意识、行政效能、服务水平等还有待改善，一些政府工作人员存在小富即安、小进则满、不求有功、但求无过的浮躁思想与懒散作风。对此，我们将以高度的使命感与紧迫感，认真有效加以解决。

今后五年奋斗目标和主要任务

未来五年，是面临重大挑战的发展转型期。从国际环境看，金融危机仍在延续，世界经济复苏的不稳定性、不确定性上升，东莞外向依存度较高，吸引外商投资、扩大外贸出口、稳定企业经营面临严峻考验。**从国内环境看，**全面开发开放步伐加快，区域竞争日益激烈，新开发城市大力招商引资，吸引了我市部分产业外移，而长三角、环渤海地区不少兄弟城市后来居上，在发展新兴产业方面形成了先发优势，我市产业结构调整面临严峻考验。**从珠三角区域看，**广州、深圳的中心城市地位突出，对我市的高端产业、人才等具有强大的磁吸效应，而惠州等周边城市成本和要素优势明显，对我市扩张期产业也具有较强的承接能力。如何找准自身定位，实施差异化发展战略，增强比较优势，集聚优势产业资源，是摆在我市面前的重大课题。**从自身实际看，**目前我市的人均收入已达到世界中等水平，传统的产业体系、发展方式无法为经济增长与企业增收提供足够动力，经济减速下行与社会矛盾凸显的趋势令人警惕，如果不能及时转变发展方式，以科技和制度创新注入新的动力，就无法跨越“中等收入陷阱”，甚至陷入发展停滞与矛盾冲突。内外困难倒逼转型，克服困难有赖转型，根本出路在于转型。

未来五年，是实现高水平崛起的战略机遇期。当前形势，危中有机。世界经济格局的深刻变化，加速了全球产业布局的调整；复杂严峻的外部环境，倒逼基层和企业加快转型升级的步伐。内需市场长期向好，国内新兴产业发展和创新成果转化不断加快，提供了巨大的增长空间。作为加工贸易转型升级、民政改革发展、“三旧”改造等全国、全省试点城市，我市拥有先行先试的宝贵机遇。改革开放30多年形成的对外开放优势、产业配套优势、城市环境优势，为未来发展奠定了良好基础。与广州、深圳等城市相比，我市在要素成本、配套成本、物流成本、行政成本、生活成本等方面，具有一定的综合优势，如果发挥利用得好，有利于吸引高端项目和人才。过去五年，东莞在结构调整、自主创新、体制改革等方面已经破了题、开了局。因此，只要我们抓住机遇，主动调整产业结构，加快转变发展方式，就有充分的信心实现高水平崛起。

实现高水平崛起，我们既要继承历届班子的宝贵经验与务实传统，也要与时俱进，锐意创新，不断开创工作新局面。未来五年工作中，我们一定要认真处理好**五个方面的关系：**

一是发展速度与发展质量的关系。坚持质量优先，速度服从质量，宁可在提升发展质量的过程中暂时减速，也不能追求低效益、高消耗、不可持续的速度。与此同时，要加快转型升级，培育新一轮增长的动力，释放内涵式发展的潜力，拓展高质量发展的空间，有效应对经济下行的压力，全面实现新的加速发展，通过几年的结构调整和扎实工作，让东莞在全省、全国重新领跑。

二是新兴产业与传统产业的关系。坚持“做大增量、调整存量、以增量扩张稀释存量”的思路，集中资源发展创新型产业尤其是战略性新兴产业，培育一批产值过千亿元的产业和超百亿元的企业，构建新的经济支柱与发展支撑。同时，要以工业化与信息化的融合改造提升传统产业，推动技术、设计、商业模式与分工体系的创新，加快转移淘汰高消耗、高污染、低效益的产业环节，提升核心竞争力与综合效益，更好地融入创新型经济体系，改善整个经济结构。

三是对外开放与对内开放的关系。外源型经济是我市的特色，必须通过深化对外合作、拓展海外市场、承接新兴产业转移等手段，不断保持和扩大先发优势。与此同时，必须深挖对内开放的潜力，大力开拓内需市场，积极引进国内大型央企、龙头民企、科技型中小企业和相关创新机构，使东莞成为国内外产业资源、创新资源高度集聚的城市。

四是市场调节与政府引导的关系。在经济转型的过程中，要把政府引导与市场机制结合起来，寓引导调节于主动服务之中，充分利用成本收益等价值规律，善于结合产业规划、功能区划、要素配置、资源价格、资助奖励等调控手段，有针对性地抓好项目发展与产业提升，对优质的初创型企业“雪中送炭”，加速孵化培育，对扩张期成长型企业“锦上添花”，助推做大做强，使市场调节更具导向性与时效性。

五是城市发展与群众生活的关系。城市发展既要服务于产业发展，更要服从于群众生活。要完善城市的设施、功能和布局，也要完善城市的环境、管理和服务，努力提供低成本、高品质的城市生活；要突出东莞的生态优势与自然特色，也要延续东莞的人文脉络与组团格局，努力塑造有特色、受认同的城市形象；要高水平普及教育、医疗、文化等公共服务，也要高水平满足群众在依法行政、社会公平、政府廉洁等方面的要求，让城市发展给全市人民带来全面的福祉。

未来五年，政府工作的**总体要求**是：**全面贯彻市第十三次党代会精神，以科学发展为主题，以转变经济发展方式为主线，以加快转型升级、打造创新型经济为重点，以建设幸福东莞为宗旨，努力把东莞打造为全省科技和产业融合发展的示范区、结构调整和转型升级的样板区、创新社会管理的引领区，成为广东现代制造业名城、创新创业之城、生态文明之城、平安和谐之城，实现东莞的高水平崛起。**

未来五年，全市发展的**主要目标**是：**生产总值年均增长8%以上，人均生产总值年均增长7.5%以上，进出口总额年均增长8%以上，研究与开发经费支出占生产总值比例2.4%，城市居民人均可支配收入和农民人均纯收入年均增长8%以上，单位生产总值能耗降低19.5%，全市综合经济实力大幅提升，产业结构明显优化，城市竞争力和可持续发展能力显著增强；市民生活品质持续改善，做到人均收入更丰、就业机会更多、社会保障更强、文明程度更高、幸福感更强。**

未来五年，政府工作的**主要任务**是：

一、致力打造创新型经济强市

创新型经济，就是以科技与产业融合为目标、以知识和人才为依托、以创新为动力、以新技术和新产品为着力点、以创新产业为标志的经济。发展创新型经济，是东莞实现高水平崛起的必然要求，是我市未来五年经济建设的核心任务，也是发展方式转变的核心内容。只有建立起创新型经济，推动经济发展从要素驱动、投资驱动向创新驱动转变，才能破除传统发展模式的路径依赖，防止落入“中等收入陷阱”；才能与韩国、新加坡、台湾等国家和地区一样，成功实现经济转型，步入良性发展轨道；才能拓展新的发展空间，引入新的发展动力，迎来新的增长拐点，实现新的发展格局。这要求我们在今后五年，把打造创新型经济作为经济建设的主攻方向，作为实现高水平崛起的主抓手，更坚定、更明确地把政府工作的重点放到产业建设上来，深入推进产业结构调整，推动东莞从产业大市向产业强市迈进。

主攻产业高端，构建创新型经济体系。以传统产业优势突出、战略性新兴产业形成规模、现代服务业支撑有力、都市型农业高效集约为目标，积极构建创新型经济体系。推动传统支柱产业加快拓展产业链条，抢占研发、设计、先进制造与营销等高端环节，提升产业竞争力与综合效益。加快战略性新兴产业的引进和培育，着力发展新一代信息技术、新一代互联网、新能源、新材料、节能环保、生物等产业，努力打造一批超千亿元战略性新兴产业集群。推动现代服务业加快聚集和拓展，突出发展与制造业配套的金融服务外包、物流仓储、研发设计、电子商务、文化创意等生产性服务业，积极发展总部经济、会展经济，打造珠三角新兴物流城市和金融强市。结合环境建设与生态修复，着力发展生产、生态、休闲、观光一体化的都市型农业。

夯实承载平台，优化创新型经济布局。完善园区承接创新型产业的载体功能，科学开发建设松山湖、虎门港、生态园、长安新区及各镇街工业集聚区，实施各镇街（园区）差异化发展战略。把大市区打造为金融中心、总部经济集聚中心和产业服务中心，加快建设以松山湖为龙头的园区经济带、以虎门港为核心的物流经济带、以主城区为核心的商贸经济带，加快形成现代服务业、高新技术产业、先进制造业、临港产业、都市型农业等集聚区，构建起“一个核心区、三大经济带、五大产业集聚区”的创新型产业格局。

集聚龙头项目，引领创新型经济发展。主动接受广州、深圳及港台等地辐射，积极承接高端产业转移，强化市级统筹，加强招商选资，在引进世界500强企业、大型跨国公司、大型央企和龙头民企上实现新突破。定向扶持一批优质企业做大做强，发挥大项目、大企业辐射效应，打造龙头项目配套企业群，力争带动一批现有产业集群整合提升、促进一批新兴产业集群有效形成。鼓励外资企业增资扩产和设立区域总部，协助拓展新兴市场和内销市场，增强产业植根性，提升开放型经济水平。

推进自主创新，增强创新型经济动力。完善"科技东莞"政策体系和服务体系，推动企业自主创新的资源投入与绩效提升，不断提高科技创新对经济增长的贡献率。集中财政专项资金力量，突出重点扶持一批关系城市未来发展的战略性、创新型产业项目。优化创新资源配置，建设和完善一批国家级、省级创新平台，加快突破一批共性和关键技术。深入实施人才东莞战略，加大创新科研团队和领军人才的引进培育力度，引导企业善待人才、用好人才，为创新型经济发展提供智力保障。大力扶持民营经济尤其是民营制造业发展，增强自主发展和抗御风险能力。

壮大现代金融，助推创新型经济提速。建设东莞金融商务区和松山湖金融改革创新服务区，在试点基础上推动科技金融、物流金融发展，加强莞台金融合作。扶持地方金融机构完善管理、整合壮大、扩张上市。有针对性地引进外资金融机构和跨境金融服务。加大优质企业上市培育力度，积极发展创业投资、产业基金等新型金融组织，引导形成多层次的投融资平台，促进金融、科技与产业融合发展，建设和完善现代金融体系。

二、致力建设宜居生态城市

按照"强心、宜居、内畅、外联"的思路，统筹布局各种公共设施和资源，建设更加宜居的生态城市。

打造中心突出、组团清晰的城市格局。以提高城市首位度为目标，高标准规划建设中央商务区、中央商圈和生态休闲区，努力把主城区打造成城市形象展示区和高级人才集聚区。合理布局全市性和片区性重大基础设施，把松山湖、虎门港、生态园、长安新区打造成产业升级引领区，把各镇打造成配套完善、各具特色的城市节点。促进布局集中、产业集聚、土地集约，遏制土地低效利用与城市无序扩张。

完善覆盖城乡、联接内外的基础网络。积极构建内聚外联的轨道交通网、一环六横六纵三连的高快速路网、四通八达的主干支次路网和便捷顺畅的公交体系，形成市内"半小时生活圈"、周边城市"一小时通勤圈"，全面融入珠三角交通一体化网络。健全城市供水、排水、治水体系，推进电信网、广播电视网、互联网三网融合，建设智慧城市和无线城市，完善城乡全覆盖的水电气设施和通讯网络。

塑造富有特色、现代品位的城市风格。加强重点区域、重点建筑的规划设计，加快城市更新改造，打造城市亮点和建筑精品。结合轨道交通的发展，沿线高起点规划、高标准建设一批城市综合体。借鉴世界先进城市经验，塑造人性化、生态化、特色化的公共环境，构筑错落有致、宽敞大气的城市空间。充分发挥我市江河湖库密集的资源禀赋和环境特色，加快推进沿江沿河的综合开发，彰显滨水特色，塑造生态形象。

营造生态良好、环境优美的人居环境。坚持环境建设与资源开发并举，生态保护与污染治理并重，加快森林公园、市镇和社区公园、绿道、慢行道等建设，推进绿化覆盖与生态控制。深入治理水系和大气污染，大力推行清洁生产，发展循环经济，推进节能减排。完善公共配套与休闲设施建设，加强城市精细化管理，使东莞成为最适宜创业与居住的城市之一。

三、致力提高市民幸福水平

建立健全幸福东莞指标体系，加快推进以改善民生为重点的社会建设，加强和创新社会管理，提高市民生活品质，提高社会净福利水平。

力保社会安定有序。坚持集中整治与长效管理相结合，积极构筑公共安全管理新模式，进一步完善社会治安立体防控体系、安全生产与食品药品安全监管体系、防灾减灾与应急管理体系，进一步完善利益协调、诉求表达、矛盾调处和权益保障机制，确保人民生命财产安全，确保矛盾纠纷有效化解，确保社会大局和谐稳定。

力推区域均衡发展。完善城乡统筹发展机制，逐步扩大公共财政对村级公共服务投入，减轻基层负担，促进城乡协调。帮助欠发达镇村加快发展，通过财税激励、项目支撑、结对帮扶等手段，增强欠发达镇村发展能力，确保发展速度不低于全市平均水平。创新集体经济发展模式，探索建立现代企业制度，开展多元化经营，实现集体资产保值增值。

力促发展成果共享。加强就业创业服务，健全工资正常增长机制。完善基本养老、基本医疗和最低生活保障制度，实现户籍人口社保全覆盖、新莞人参保率稳步提升、各类保障待遇逐步提高。完善住房保障机制，健全社会救助体系，加快发展慈善事业，加强残疾人保障服务。推进医药卫生体制改革，在解决看病难、看病贵问题上取得根本突破。促进基本公共服务均等化和优质化，稳步向新莞人群体覆盖，努力让每个市民都学有所教、劳有所得、病有所医、老有所养、住有所居。

四、致力提升文化软实力

以提升全民素质为核心，深化文化体制改革，优先发展教育事业，积极培育城市文明，全面提升城市软实力。

高水平建设文化名城。以满足人民精神文化需求为出发点和落脚点，用好文化专项资金，推进文化体制改革，实施文化惠民工程，保护历史街区和建筑，鼓励文艺精品创作，扶持文化产业发展，努力建设全国公共文化服务名城、国家历史文化名城、全国现代文化产业名城、岭南文化精品名城。

全方位打造教育高地。着眼于人的全面发展，整合教育资源，推动教育创新，力争在发展学前教育、提升义务教育优质均衡水平、促进职业教育与产业发展紧密结合、强化高等教育服务功能、推进特殊教育发展等方面实现新突破，建成省推进教育现代化先进市，教育综合竞争力达到国内先进地区水平。

深层次彰显文明形象。大力弘扬“海纳百川、厚德务实”的城市精神，深入开展文明创建活动，提升市民文明素质，提高城市文明程度。深化“六五”普法，强化全社会的法治意识。关爱弱势群体，推广志愿者服务，树立文明有序、和谐融洽的城市形象。

五、致力加强政府自身建设

深入转变政府职能，崇尚实干，激励创新，优化服务，依法行政，进一步改进机关作风，提升政府形象。

着力打造实干型政府。以提高效能为导向，树立奋发有为的意识，强化真抓实干的作风，全面推行“问题管理”模式，有效提升政府执行力。厉行勤俭节约，减少文山会海，强化工作问责，集中精力抓发展、抓落实，确保工作定一件、干一件、成一件。

着力打造创新型政府。深化简政强镇改革，加快形成有利于统筹发展、提升效能的行政管理体制。深化行政审批制度改革，进一步精简审批事项，优化办事流程。深化财政制度改革，积极构建公共财政体系。整合相关国有资产，建设政府投资平台，以金融创新手段筹集资金，推动城市建设与产业建设。积极培育发展社会组织，鼓励社会力量参与社会管理、提供公共服务。

着力打造服务型政府。牢固树立服务意识，高度重视社情民意，不断改进工作方法，强化督促指导和现场办公，及时解决社会关注的热点难点问题。实行“一站式”服务，加强政府电子政务建设，大力推广网上审批，严格执行服务承诺制，进一步提高服务水平，提升群众满意度。

着力打造法治型政府。坚持科学民主决策，落实重大行政决策程序，健全行政听证、社会公示、决策评估等制度。主动接受人大政协及社会各界监督。推进依法行政，深化政务公开，畅通诉求渠道，全面保障人民群众的知情权、表达权、参与权和监督权。完善行政执法责任制，落实行政过错责任追究制。扎实推进廉政建设和反腐败斗争，健全明查暗访长效机制，坚决整治损害群众利益的不正之风。

2012年工作安排

千里之行，始于足下；五年宏图，重在开局。2012年是我市推动高水平崛起的起步之年，是打造创新型经济的破题之年。政府工作的总体要求是：**深入贯彻党的十七届六中全会、中央经济工作会议、省委十届十一次全会和市第十三次党代会精神，以科学发展观为指导，进一步增强忧患意识和使命意识，立足优化发展，围绕好中求进，以建设“三区四城”为目标，以创新型经济为主抓手，突出抓产业、上项目，提升城市品质，高度关注民生，为实现高水平崛起开好局、起好步。**

——**立足优化发展，**就是要坚定不移地推进产业结构调整，加快构建以现代产业体系为核心的创新型经济，加快提升自主创新能力，在产业建设上迈出坚实步伐。

——**围绕好中求进，**就是要积极应对严峻复杂的发展形势，保持经济平稳健康可持续增长；加强和创新经济社会管理，最大限度减少不和谐因素，保持社会大局稳定。

——**提升城市品质，**就是要围绕承接优质产业、吸引优秀人才、提高生活质量，进一步完善城市功能，优化空间布局，改善人居环境，使东莞成为创业热土、宜居城市。

——**高度关注民生，**就是要强化执政为民宗旨，加快发展以民生为重点的各项社会事业，着力提升公共服务水平，办好十件民生实事。

综合考虑各方面因素，今年全市发展的**预期目标是：全面完成珠三角规划纲要“四年大发展”各项目标任务，生产总值同比增长8%，人均生产总值增长7.5%，市财政一般预算收入增长10%，固定资产投资总额增长9%，社会消费品零售总额增长12%，外贸出口总额增长8%；现代服务业增加值占服务业增加值比重61.5%，先进制造业、高技术制造业增加值占规模以上工业增加值比重分别达到42.7%和29.5%，发明专利申请量和授权量分别增长12%和28%；城市居民人均可支配收入和农民人均纯收入增长8%，单位生产总值能耗下降4.25%，城镇登记失业率、居民消费价格涨幅分别控制在3%以内和4%左右。**

围绕以上目标要求，重点抓好八个方面工作：

一、深入调整结构，切实推动产业建设

经济发展的根本动力在于产业。必须紧紧抓住产业建设这个关键，扎扎实实发展创新型经济。

加快培育壮大战略性新兴产业。着力引进大、高、精、尖项目，培育骨干企业，扩张产业规模，力争在新兴产业的重点领域、关键环节率先突破。加快省级薄膜太阳能光伏、物联网、半导体照明等产业基地建设，抓好宏威、中镓、华为等项目建设。实施“智慧东莞”工程，推进物联网和云计算运用，争取建立省战略性新兴产业云计算基地。探索政府引导、社会参与等方式，建立战略性新兴产业投资引导基金。

加快加工贸易和传统产业转型。深入推进全国加工贸易转型升级试点工作，落实“稳增长、调结构、促平衡”方针，继续实施外经贸“十个100”计划。落实促进优势传统产业发展和转型升级的指导意见，分行业制定具体实施方案。深入推进品牌带动战略，积极发展工业设计和动漫设计，推动企业技术、产品和管理升级。

加快打造现代服务业集聚板块。推进生产性服务业功能区建设，加快引进培育物流采购、客户服务、产品展示、资金结算等中心。推进中央商圈的整合提升，启动南城国际商务区建设，加快各镇中心区的服务产业集聚。研究出台发展楼宇经济优惠政策，积极引进地区总部和区域总部。继续办好电博会、漫博会、台博会等展会，力争将外博会升级为国家级博览会。探索制定鼓励电子商务、移动支付等新兴业态发展的政策，加快发展物流、金融、软件、新一代互联网、旅游休闲等产业。

二、强化创新驱动，集聚高端资源要素

进一步完善创新体系、集聚创新资源、优化创新环境，使科技创新成为转型升级的核心推动力。

促进科技、产业、金融有机结合。围绕培育新兴产业和提升优势产业，组织关键技术攻关，加快培育壮大一批创新型骨干企业。探索建立产业风险投资引导资金，大力引进风投、创投机构及种子基金，充分利用社会资本，加速孵化一批成长性创新企业。加快金融商务区和金融改革创新服务区建设步伐。积极推动松山湖高新区进入“新三板”扩容试点。在有条件的地区开展土地资本、金融资本、产业资本“三资融合”试点。建立企业专利动态数据库，支持企业开展专利权质押融资。鼓励发展中小企业担保机构、小额贷款公司等新型经济金融组织。

加强创新载体建设。加快组建国家半导体光源产品质量监督检验中心、华南设计创新园、北京大学光电研究院等公共创新平台。创新投入和管理机制，强化产权激励和绩效管理，充分发挥公共平台服务功能。加快散裂中子源项目建设。积极推动松山湖科技平台与各镇街企业对接合作。做大做强专业镇技术创新平台。引导有条件的企业设立技术中心等机构，创建一批国家级、省级企业研发平台。

优化科技创新环境。完善科技政策体系，加强科技专项资金管理，整合金融与社会资本，提高资金使用效率与引导功能。发挥政府牵线搭桥作用，促进产学研更紧密合作。积极发展技术评估、技术转移、科技信息等中介服务机构和行业协会组织，加快组建技术产权交易中心，促进科研成果应用转化。

实施人才强市战略。创新人才政策体系，有效发挥“人才东莞”专项资金作用。大力实施“十百千万”行动计划，积极引进培育创新科研团队、领军人才、紧缺人才和高技能人才。认真解决人才入户、配偶就业、子女入学等问题。重奖有突出贡献的杰出人才。推进留学人员创业园、博士后流动站等建设。采取校企合作、订单培训等方式，加快培养与产业发展相适应的技能型、实用型人才。

三、优化园区平台，引进培育龙头项目

发挥园区的产业集聚作用，着力实施大企业、大项目引领战略，进一步优化企业结构，提升产业集中度。

科学推进园区建设。进一步明确松山湖产业定位，吸引大项目和科研平台进驻。办好台湾高科技园，承接以色列产业园落户。加强虎门港的货源聚集，做好增值服务。科学定位生态园，完善基础设施和功能配套，争取引进一批高端企业。抓紧长安新区用海规划报批，加快土地资源整合。提升各镇街工业集聚区建设水平，增强大项目承载能力。严格筛选入园企业和项目，确保产出效益最大化。

瞄准优质项目重点招商。建立市级招商统筹协调机制，促进招商信息共享。落实重大项目快速反应机制，加强与知名投资中介的合作，集中力量引进大型央企、民企，引进日韩台等国家和地区的高科技项目。主动承接广州、深圳等城市的高端优质产业转移项目。加大土地统筹与闲置地盘活力度，科学安排用地指标。办好首届世界莞商代表大会。

加强龙头企业和上市公司培育。抓好总部企业认定，建立大企业储备库，筛选一批年产值10亿元以上的企业进行重点培育。加强政府服务，推动品牌企业、大型企业增资扩产。切实帮助企业解决土地产权等历史遗留问题，争取新增上市企业2—3家、年主营业务收入百亿元企业2家。

四、深化开放协作，确保经济平稳发展

积极应对外部环境挑战，高度重视帮扶企业和镇村发展，进一步加强区域合作，保障经济平稳发展。

不遗余力帮扶企业解困。坚持市镇领导走访重点企业制度，帮助解决实际困难，增强企业经营信心。规范镇村收费项目，积极争取省级收费减免。实施10亿元融资支持计划，帮助企业获得贷款和直接融资。积极争取用电指标，科学安排错峰用电，保障企业能源供给。加强劳务对接，缓解用工难题。优化中小企业服务，帮助搭建营销平台。

有效改善强化经济管理。落实对镇村的超收分成、贷款贴息、生态补偿等措施，减轻欠发达镇重大基建资金负担。逐步加大对农村的转移支付力度。安排1.39亿元推进市内“双到”扶贫，确保两个“80%”目标任务顺利完成。加强镇街政府性债务管理。完善农村集体资产管理实施办法，严控一般性支出和超前分配，减轻债务负担，防范经济风险。

多策并举促进内外均衡。认真落实省政府促进进口的二十七条意见。设立每年2亿元、连续3年的进口扶持资金，资助先进生产设备进口。开展“莞货全国行”活动。大力支持企业扩大内销市场，巩固欧美等传统市场，拓展东盟等新兴市场。落实促进民营经济发展上水平的实施意见，支持民营资本进入先进制造业、战略性新兴产业，实施“686”民营企业上市梯度培育工程、“323”高成长型中小工业企业培育计划，鼓励民营企业开展进出口业务和对外合作。

抢抓机遇深化区域协作。主动对接穗深港，从观念、交通、产业、市场和人才等方面，积极融入世界级城市群的发展。落实珠江口东岸地区紧密合作框架协议，加强深莞惠三市重大规划衔接，强化产业发展、交通运输、环境生态、社会公共事务等领域的合作。落实“双转移”战略，加快莞韶、莞惠产业转移园建设。全面完成韶关、云浮“双到”扶贫工作。做好对口支援新疆生产建设兵团农三师、西藏林芝、广西河池、重庆巫山等工作。

五、统筹城乡建设，提升城市承载能力

以重点项目建设为抓手，进一步完善基础设施，改善城乡环境，提升城市功能，持续增强城市承载力和辐射力。

突出城市功能提升。加快市民艺术中心、工人文化宫、篮球中心、网球中心、雅园新村二期等功能配套项目建设，积极配合穗莞深、莞惠城际轨道建设，推进市域轨道R2线、东莞新火车站建设和东莞东站升级改造。加快中央生态休闲区建设。加强地下空间综合开发。

突出设施水平提升。建成沿江高速、虎岗高速虎门港支线一期、东莞大道延长线、S120石排至桥头段。加快建设博深高速、从莞高速、虎岗高速延长线、虎门港支线二期和沿海公路。推进石大公路、东部快速企石至桥头段、S256南城至虎门段、S358长安至虎门段、S357樟木头至谢岗段的升级改造。加快梨川大桥、东平大桥建设。抓紧整治市主干公路堵塞点。建成110千伏及以上输变电工程10项。加快东江与水库联网供水二期工程，有效整合基层水厂，推进供水管网改造，建设水质质监网络，组建市水务投资集团。编制全市排水规划，加强城市内涝整治，启动127宗防灾减灾工程。

突出环境质量提升。落实用水总量控制、用水效率控制、水功能区限制纳污“三条红线”，实行最严格的水资源管理制度。加快截污次支管网建设，推进运河综合整治与内河涌治理。完善“三旧”改造政策及流程，健全土地出让金返拨机制，完善2万亩用地手续。加快垃圾处理厂的新建改造，推广生活垃圾分类处理，争取城镇生活垃圾无害化处理率达85%。加快7个环保专业基地建设。改造提升旗峰公园，基本建成黄牛埔和碧湖森林公园。推进生态景观林建设，实施退果还林工程。建成29个名村、300公里市级绿道。严格落实节能减排任务，深入开展清洁空气行动，加强空气质量PM值的监测。

六、推进社会建设，提高民生保障水平

全面发展社会事业，积极解决群众关注的难点热点问题，让全市人民更好地分享发展成果。

深化医疗体制改革。强化医疗卫生事业公益性质，明确政府补偿机制，抓好公立医院改革试点。落实社区卫生服务机构基本药物零差率销售，推动公立医院优先使用基本药物。健全基层医疗卫生服务体系，落实基本公共卫生和重大公共卫生服务项目。剥离镇街公立医院的疾病预防控制和卫生监督功能。组建市传染病后备医院。制定扶持中医药发展的具体措施。进一步完善医患纠纷调解机制。

提高社会保障水平。扩大社保覆盖面，推行全国统一的社保卡。出台临时救助办法。扩建市社会福利中心。将高龄津贴发放范围扩大至70岁以上户籍老人。加快残疾人服务设施建设。做好社会工作，设立扶持社会组织发展专项资金，创建20个社区综合服务中心示范点，规范购买社工服务制度。开展公益创投活动，办好第三届“东莞慈善日”。

激发就业创业活力。推广“村民车间”就业形式，帮助户籍劳动力特别是家庭困难人员就业。实施青年就业见习和培训计划，帮助高校毕业生就业。开展农民工专场招聘，做好新莞人就业服务。加快人力资源市场信息网络建设，建立就业信息收集发布制度。发挥小额贷款、创业奖励等的作用，激发社会创业活力。

全面发展民生事业。完善体育设施，推动群众体育发展。维护物价稳定，抓好“菜篮子”工程，兴建平价商店。加强房地产调控，防止过度发展房地产项目。拓宽商业贷款转公积金贷款业务，制定公租房管理办法，扩大保障房申请范围，有序推进农民公寓建设。优先发展公共交通，逐步推广新能源汽车，提高公交服务水平。稳定低生育水平，统筹人口发展，提高人口素质。继续做好国防人防、双拥共建、外事侨务、普法教育、民族宗教、统计审计、气象防灾、档案方志、科普、打私、工青妇幼等工作。

七、加强社会管理，有效维护安定和谐

坚持服务与管理并举，加大治理力度，理顺管理体制，不断提高社会管理水平，营造稳定和谐的社会环境。

强化社会治安综合治理。紧盯群众反映最强烈的治安问题，深入开展专项整治行动，严打多发性和恶性违法犯罪行为。坚持科技强警，完善公安指挥中心平台，加强联网报警和视频监控。逐步整合村（社区）治安联防队伍。加强商业区、车站码头、公园等重点场所的巡逻防控，提高街面见警率和出警效率，切实增强群众安全感。

加强公共安全管理。落实安全生产“一岗双责”，建立重大事故隐患监控信息系统。深化“三小”场所、人员密集场所等重点部位整治，打好“清剿火患”战役，筑牢消防安全“防火墙”。发挥综治信访维稳中心作用。加强矛盾纠纷调处化解和欠薪逃匿预警监控。深入开展“三打两建”行动和食品药品安全专项整治。强化应急管理与处置。

深化镇村体制改革。深入推进简政强镇改革，统一机构设置，规范权责关系。稳妥推进村级体制改革，探索推广社区政务服务中心。改革集体经济体制，探索推动从建设物业、分散收租向成立物业公司集中管理运营转变。

提升新莞人服务管理水平。加强新型社区建设，完善新莞人享受基本公共服务政策体系，提高就业培训、子女入学、医疗卫生等公共服务水平。落实居住证制度，强化出租屋管理。实施新莞人社会融入工程，开展商旅优惠、专列返乡等特色服务，增强城市认同感和归属感。

八、加快文化建设，着力提升城市文明

深化文化体制改革，强化社会主义核心价值体系建设，进一步提高市民素质，提升城市文明程度。

推动文化名城建设。完善文化专项资金使用管理办法。创建国家公共文化服务体系示范区，实施创建示范达标工程和文化惠民提升工程。编制历史文化名城保护规划，推动虎门销烟遗址等历史文化项目建设。出台文化产业扶持政策，积极发展创意设计等产业，培育文化龙头企业，支持本土传媒做大做强。扶持文化创作基地，打造特色文艺精品。统筹发展公益性文化事业，鼓励社会资本进入经营性文化服务领域。实施文化人才“三个 100”工程。

推动教育体系完善。提高财政对教育拨款比例。加快学前教育改革发展，理顺幼儿园管理体制，每年投入 1 亿元补助各类幼儿园，年内新增公办幼儿园 15 所。推进公办中小学等级学校创建。加快职教城建设，建成高技能公共实训中心、东莞理工学校新校区、市技师学院，创建 2—3 所省级以上示范性中职学校。筹建酒店管理职业技术学院和光明职业技术学院，推进与香港理工大学合作办学，扶持本土高校发展。

推动城市文明提升。巩固全国文明城市地位，开展文明创建活动，加强爱国主义和理想信念教育，引导市民践行道德规范，弘扬尊老爱幼传统。加强未成年人思想道德建设，健全心理健康教育网络。广泛开展志愿服务活动。不断加强政府自身建设，坚持依法行政，提升政府服务，以良好政风带动社会风气转变、带动城市文明升华、带动发展步伐提速。

各位代表！团结凝聚力量，实干铸就伟业。我们在攻艰克难中成就了一个又一个东莞奇迹，也将在奋进拼搏中迎来一个又一个新的辉煌。未来的蓝图已经绘就，前进的号角再次吹响。让我们以邓小平理论和“三个代表”重要思想为指导，以科学发展观为统领，深入贯彻落实中央和省的决策部署，在中共东莞市委的领导下，团结和依靠全市人民，锐意创新，扎实进取，为加快转型升级、建设幸福东莞、实现高水平崛起而努力奋斗！

名词注解：

五个一体化：指珠三角基础设施、产业布局、基本公共服务、城乡规划和环境保护五个一体化。

四年大发展：珠三角规划纲要的目标为“一年开好局，四年大发展，十年大跨越。”其中“四年大发展”是指从2009年到2012年要实现第一阶段目标，珠三角地区率先建成全面小康社会。

“1+26”政策文件：“1”是指《关于推进产业结构调整促进产业转型升级的意见》，“26”是指《东莞市推进加工贸易转型升级工作方案》、《东莞市转型升级实施“三旧改造”土地管理暂行办法》等26项具体配套政策文件。

现代产业体系“四个30项目”：即30个战略性新兴产业项目、30个先进制造业项目、30个优势传统产业项目、30个现代服务业项目。

“大麦客”商业模式：指我市部分台商企业以“大麦客”统一品牌，打造集内销仓储批发为一体的大卖场经营模式。

村（社区）文化设施“五个有”：即有一个总面积不少于200平方米的综合文化活动室、有一个村（社区）图书室或农家书屋、有一个建筑面积在1000平方米以上的文体广场、有一个面积不少于40平方米的文化信息共享工程服务网点、有一批文化活动和体育健身器材。

中等收入陷阱：是指当一个国家或地区的人均收入达到中等水平后，由于不能顺利实现经济发展方式的转变，导致经济增长动力不足，最终出现经济停滞的一种状态。

“问题管理”模式：参照企业管理理念，针对政府部门及其工作人员在履行职责中存在的问题，以电子政务系统为依托，通过建立落实问题报告、处理反馈、分析评估、奖惩激励等制度而采取的一种问题前置处理机制。

薄膜太阳能光伏：指用硅、硫化镉、砷化镓等薄膜为基体材料，利用半导体光伏效应的太阳能电池技术。

物联网：通过信息传感设备，把物体与互联网相连接，进行信息交换和通信，以实现对物体的智能化识别、定位、跟踪、监控和管理的一种网络。

半导体照明：又称LED照明，指利用固体半导体芯片作为发光材料，制造照明器具的技术。

云计算：指一种基于互联网的计算方式，可以将大量用网络连接的计算资源统一管理和调度，构成一个计算资源池，将共享的软硬件资源和信息，按需提供给终端计算机和其他设备。

外经贸“十个100”计划：即培育百家总部形态企业、壮大百家内销龙头企业、扶持百家自主品牌企业、发展百家高新技术企业、打造百家“升转”示范企业、锻造百名外经贸“专才”、拜访百家目标企业总部、落实百家千万美元项目、引进百家新兴产业项目、帮扶百家民企“走出去”。

种子基金：指专门投资于创业企业研究与发展阶段的投资基金。

新三板：即“代办股份转让系统”，是专门为国家级科技园区非上市的高科技公司股份转让提供的交易平台，主要解决初创期高新技术企业股份转让及融资问题。

“三资融合”：指以民营企业为主体，通过推动土地资本、金融资本、产业资本“三资融合”，创新土地开发、盈利和“园区一体化”合作模式，为民营科技企业解决融资、土地、创新服务等问题，促进高端产业集聚，吸引创新资源，推动产业转型升级。

“十百千万”行动计划：即引进培育10个创新科研团队、100名领军人才、1000名紧缺人才、10000名高技能技术管理人才。

市内“双到”扶贫两个“80%”目标：即帮扶89个欠发达村和4000户贫困户减负增收，到2012年实现80%的欠发达村村组两级集体经营性年纯收入达到150万元或增长10%以上，80%以上已结对帮扶的有劳动能力低保户脱贫。

“686”民营企业上市梯度培育工程：即保持市一级上市民营企业后备资源库有60家以上的储备，每年推动其中8家企业进入上市辅导程序，6家企业进入发行申报程序或实现上市（含境外上市）。

“323”高成长型中小工业企业培育计划：即发掘培育300家成长性好、自主创新能力强、发展潜力大的中小工业企业，择优扶持20家以上优质企业，使其充分享受各级扶持政策，推动实现其中3家以上企业纳入上市后备资源库。

空气质量PM值：指单位大气中固体或液体颗粒状物质的含量，是测量空气质量的重要指标之一。

公益创投：指政府、企业或基金会出于解决社会问题等公益目的，进行非营利性投资，帮助有需要的企业和个人创业。

“三打两建”行动：今年全省统一部署的专项工作，主要内容是打击欺行霸市、打击制假售假、打击商业贿赂，建设社会信用体系、建设市场监管体系。

文化人才“三个100”工程：即从全市相关企事业单位、社会团体中选拔100名优秀人才充实文化人才队伍，从文化系统中选拔100名优秀干部到先进地区挂职锻炼，在全国范围内公开招聘100名各艺术门类专业优秀人才。

2012年市政府十件实事

一、改善社会治安。深入推进“大巡警”机制建设，确保20%的警力用于巡逻，切实提高路面见警率；设立专线电话，实行有奖举报，确保举报核查率100%、处理率100%，坚决取缔“老虎机”赌博活动；严厉打击路面违法犯罪，全年警情减少1100起以上，同比下降5%以上。

二、强化食品安全监管。投入6000万元，提高食品抽检频次，全年抽检蔬菜样本65万份、生猪及肉品样本38万份，水产品820批次、生产环节3000批次、流通环节6000批次、餐饮服务环节2000批次，定期发布不合格食品抽检信息；实行有奖举报，定期开展专项行动，坚决取缔黑作坊、黑工厂、黑窝点、黑市场；全市创建50个示范食堂，推动100个C级以下集体食堂升级为B级；建设动物卫生远程视频监控系统，对生猪屠宰实行全过程监管。

三、加快教育发展。投入9亿元，全年新增公办（集体办）幼儿园15所，增加6000个公办幼儿园学位；对全市各类幼儿园进行财政补助；提供新莞人子女积分入学公办学位17900个，比上年增长10%；基本建成东莞职教城二期房建工程，东莞理工学校新校区和市技师学院投入使用。

四、实施扶贫帮困。投入8.2亿元，帮扶89个欠发达村和4000户贫困户减负增收，年内实现80%的欠发达村村组两级集体经营性年纯收入达到150万元或增长10%以上、80%以上已结对帮扶的有劳动能力低保户脱贫；推动6700名登记失业人员就业，帮扶2700名家庭困难人员实现再就业，实现东莞生源家庭困难大中专毕业生全部就业；建成10个镇街康复就业服务中心，为残疾人提供康复、就业和日间照料等服务。

五、完善社区服务。投入3.1亿元，打造7个市级名村、22个镇级名村；再创建20个社区综合服务中心示范点；为1000名孤寡老人家庭安装“平安铃”，为2500名符合条件的老人提供居家养老服务。

六、加强社会保障。投入9000万元，完成15万户籍妇女“两癌”筛查；将高龄津贴发放对象扩大到70岁以上老人；不断扩大包括新莞人及其子女在内的医疗保险覆盖面，做到应保尽保。

七、实施防灾减灾。投入3.8亿元，完成10宗防灾减灾工程；基本完成市区内涝整治应急三期北侧分流工程。

八、提升公共文化服务水平。投入1.3亿元，建立专兼结合的村（社区）公共文化管理服务队伍；全市实现公共电子阅览室全覆盖；完善数字公共文化服务载体；推进人均藏书增长计划，新增公共图书馆藏书56万册，全市人均藏书达到1册以上；开展“百场培训、千场演出、万场电影”到村（社区）、到企业活动。

九、整治环境污染。投入3.4亿元，完成桥头小海河整治和生态修复工程，基本完成同沙水库截污管网工程和尾水排放工程；年内淘汰或改造小功率工业燃煤锅炉200台。

十、提升宜居环境。投入4.7亿元，建成300公里城市和社区绿道，全市达到900公里；基本建成黄江镇黄牛埔森林公园和凤岗镇碧湖森林公园；完成市区10个交通拥堵点整治。

第二部分　统计资料

Part Two　Statistics

一、综　合

General Survey

1-1 东莞行政区划（2011年）

Divisions of Administrative Areas in Dongguan (2011)

镇街	村（居）委会		
	个数		名称
合计	村委会	350	
	社区居委会	244	
莞城	社区居委会	8	东正 市桥 北隅 西隅 罗沙 博厦 兴塘 创业
石龙	村委会	7	西湖 忠维 林屋 蒲溪 新维 王屋洲 黄家山
	社区居委会	3	中山东 中山西 兴龙
虎门	社区居委会	30	虎门寨 东方 则徐 大宁 树田 白沙 沙角 怀德 博涌 镇口 村头 新联 九门寨 居岐 金洲 南面 北栅 小捷滘 北面 陈村 东风 武山沙 黄村 南栅 龙眼 宴岗 赤岗 路东 新湾 民泰
东城	社区居委会	23	岗贝 花园新村 东泰 温塘 桑园 周屋 余屋 鳌峙塘 峡口 柏洲边 上桥 下桥 樟村 梨川 堑头 主山 石井 同沙 光明 牛山 立新 火炼树 星城
万江	社区居委会	28	万江墟 万江 石美 莫屋 拔蛟窝 黄粘洲 蚬涌 谷涌 小享 滘联 上甲 新村 新谷涌 共联 水蛇涌 大莲塘 牌楼基 严屋 大汾 流涌尾 金泰 曲海 坝头 胜利 官桥滘 简沙洲 新和 新城
南城	社区居委会	17	宏远 胜和 元美 亨美 三元里 篁村 新基 周溪 袁屋边 白马 石鼓 蛤地 西平 雅园 水濂 新城 鸿福
中堂	村委会	15	潢涌 三涌 湛翠 凤冲 袁家涌 吴家涌 鹤田 中堂 一村 东向 蕉利 槎滘 下芦 马沥 四乡
	社区居委会	5	中心 斗朗 红锋 东泊 江南
望牛墩	村委会	21	李屋 望东 扶涌 赤滘 五涌 下漕 上合 聚龙江 望联 洲湾 洲涡 杜屋 寮厦 芙蓉沙 官桥涌 横沥 福安 石排 官洲 朱平沙 锦涡
	社区居委会	1	望牛墩
麻涌	村委会	13	麻一 麻三 麻四 大步 东太 新基 川槎 鸥涌 华阳 南洲 大盛 漳澎 黎滘
	社区居委会	2	麻涌 麻二
石碣	村委会	14	石碣 唐洪 黄泗围 西南 单屋 梁家村 沙腰 刘屋 水南 四甲 鹤田厦 涌口 横滘 桔洲
	社区居委会	1	城中
高埗	村委会	18	冼沙 卢溪 宝莲 塘厦 草墩 护安围 保安围 三联 横滘头 低涌 朱磡 新联 欧邓 芦村 高埗 凌屋 上江城 下江城
	社区居委会	1	新创
道滘	村委会	13	南城 南丫 闸口 大鱼沙 小河 永庆 北永 昌平 厚德 九曲 大罗沙 大岭丫 蔡白
	社区居委会	1	兴隆
洪梅	村委会	9	洪屋涡 新庄 梅沙 氹涌 黎洲角 夏汇 尧均 乌沙 金鳌沙
	社区居委会	1	洪梅
沙田	村委会	16	中围 和安 大流 泥洲 杨公洲 福禄沙 阇西 民田 先锋 西大坦 穗丰年 大泥 齐沙 稔洲 义沙 西太隆
	社区居委会	2	横流 滨港
厚街	社区居委会	24	竹溪 厚街 珊美 宝屯 三屯 陈屋 赤岭 河田 寮厦 汀山 环冈 大迳 新围 桥头 南五 新塘 涌口 双岗 溪头 沙塘 宝塘 下汴 白濠 湖景
长安	社区居委会	13	涌头 沙头 霄边 上沙 咸西 厦岗 锦厦 厦边 上角 乌沙 新民 长盛 新安

1-1　续表

(2011年)

镇街	村（居）委会		
	个数		名称
寮步	村委会	20	西溪　凫山　石龙坑　石步　良边　富竹山　塘唇　向西　霞边　上屯　下岭贝　竹园　上底　药勒　刘屋巷　浮竹山　陈家埔　井巷　小坑　长坑
	社区居委会	10	寮步　塘边　横坑　岭厦　新旧围　缪边　牛杨　泉塘　坑口　良平
大岭山	村委会	21	太公岭　大塘朗　下高田　连平　鸡翅岭　马蹄岗　金桔　大沙　百花洞　大塘水朗　杨屋　矮岭冚　颜屋　大片美　梅林　元岭　大岭　新塘　旧飞鹅　大环
	社区居委会	3	大岭山　农场　领居
大朗	村委会	16	高英　洋乌　洋坑塘　松柏朗　黎贝岭　松木山　犀牛陂　水平　宝陂　石厦　杨涌　沙步　新马莲　佛子凹　蔡边　水口
	社区居委会	12	大朗　佛新　巷头　巷尾　大井头　屏山　竹山　求富路　长塘　黄草朗　圣堂　长富
黄江	社区居委会	7	新市　田美　三新　梅塘　宝山　北岸　长龙
樟木头	社区居委会	10	圩镇　樟罗　百果洞　樟洋　石新　柏地　官仓　裕丰　金河　樟新
清溪	村委会	20	浮岗　上元　清厦　铁松　铁场　谢坑　青皇　大埔　长山头　三中　九乡　三星　渔樑围　厦坭　大利　土桥　重河　松岗　罗马　荔横
	社区居委会	1	清溪
塘厦	社区居委会	22	塘厦　三局　林村　石潭埔　四村　振兴围　大坪　莆心湖　平山　诸佛岭　桥陇　龙背岭　石鼓　田心　横塘　蛟乙塘　凤凰岗　莲湖　沙湖　石马　清湖头　塘新
凤岗	村委会	11	雁田　官井头　油甘埔　凤德岭　塘沥　黄洞　竹塘　竹尾田　三联　五联　天堂围
	社区居委会	1	凤岗
谢岗	村委会	11	黎村　窑山　南面　大龙　大厚　赵林　稔子园　五星　曹乐　谢岗　谢山
	社区居委会	1	泰园
常平	村委会	31	岗梓　塘角　苏坑　袁山贝　金美　还珠沥　朗贝　桥沥　卢屋　九江水　朗洲　陈屋贝　司马　霞坑　漱旧　漱新　黄泥塘　元江元　横江厦　沙湖口　白石岗　松柏塘　上坑　木棆　下墟　板石　田尾　白花沥　桥梓　麦元　土塘
	社区居委会	2	常平　新民
桥头	村委会	11	田头角　李屋　朗厦　岗头　屋厦　禾坑　邓屋　邵岗头　东江　山和　石水口
	社区居委会	6	桥头　田新　莲城　大洲　迳联　岭头
横沥	村委会	16	石涌　隔坑　半仙山　田头　田坑　横沥　村头　长巷　田饶步　六甲　村尾　水边　新四　山厦　月塘　张坑
	社区居委会	1	恒泉
东坑	村委会	14	东坑　坑美　角社　塔岗　黄麻岭　初坑　凤大　黄屋　寮边头　长安塘　新门楼　井美　彭屋　丁屋
	社区居委会	2	草塘　骏达
企石	村委会	19	铁岗　深巷　湖美　博夏　上洞　江边　旧围　清湖　东平　上截　下截　东山　莫屋　杨屋　新南　南坑　铁炉坑　企石　霞朗
	社区居委会	1	宝石
石排	村委会	18	石排　下沙　福隆　庙边王　沙角　黄家壆　赤坎　向西　水贝　田寮　横山　埔心　谷吓　塘尾　李家坊　田边　中坑　燕窝
	社区居委会	1	太和
茶山	村委会	16	上元　茶山　下朗　横江　增埗　卢边　寒溪水　南社　塘角　博头　冲美　粟边　孙屋　超朗　京山　刘黄
	社区居委会	2	茶山圩　茶溪
松山湖	社区居委会	1	松山湖
虎门港	社区居委会	1	虎门港

1-2 历年东莞行政区划

Divisions of Administrative Areas in Dongguan over Years

单位：个

年 份	镇 街	村(居)委会		
			村委会	社区居委会
1978	33	526	496	30
1979	33	531	501	30
1980	33	545	515	30
1981	34	554	524	30
1982	34	561	531	30
1983	34	561	531	30
1984	34	542	512	30
1985	33	546	516	30
1986	33	560	530	30
1987	34	580	537	43
1988	33	582	542	40
1989	33	583	544	39
1990	33	583	543	40
1991	33	586	546	40
1992	33	590	549	41
1993	33	590	549	41
1994	33	592	551	41
1995	33	592	551	41
1996	33	593	552	41
1997	33	594	551	43
1998	32	594	551	43
1999	32	593	546	47
2000	32	675	546	129
2001	32	678	546	132
2002	32	678	546	132
2003	32	616	487	129
2004	32	596	440	156
2005	32	596	404	192
2006	32	596	394	202
2007	32	591	386	205
2008	32	591	383	208
2009	32	598	383	215
2010	32	599	383	216
2011	32	594	350	244

注：2010年起社区居委会数含松山湖园区及虎门港。

1-3 主要年份户数、人口与自然资源

Number of Households, Population and Natural Resources in Main Years

项　　目	单 位	1978年	1985年	1990年	1995年	2000年	2005年	2010年	2011年
一、户　数									
年末户籍总户数	万户	24.82	28.95	32.73	36.43	41.40	46.50	53.05	53.90
#非农业户	万户	4.37	6.97	8.91	10.06	11.44	18.90	27.08	27.69
二、人口与劳动力									
年末常住人口	万人			175.62	336.45	644.84	656.07	822.48	825.48
年末户籍人口	万人	111.23	120.85	131.85	143.65	152.61	165.65	181.77	184.77
#非农业人口	万人	18.49	25.49	30.87	35.38	39.61	65.84	92.09	94.46
人口密度(常住人口)	人/平方公里			712	1365	2616	2662	3343	3356
人口密度(户籍人口)	人/平方公里	451	490	535	583	619	672	739	751
三、土　地									
土地面积	平方公里	2465	2465	2465	2465	2465	2465	2460	2460
年末耕地面积	万亩	118.39	96.67	88.26	70.86	66.33	50.29	57.69	
人均耕地面积	亩	1.06	0.80	0.67	0.49	0.43	0.30	0.32	
建成区面积	平方公里				82.48	147.68	620.31	798.48	854.30
#城区建成区面积	平方公里					28.13	108.10	91.65	100.80
四、气　候									
年降水量	毫米	1748.3	1678.0	1602.9	1664.8	2019.3	1837.6	2165.9	1298.6
年平均气温	摄氏度	21.9	21.8	22.8	22.4	23.2	22.7	22.4	22.1
极端最高气温	摄氏度	35.7	35.8	37.8	36.2	37.0	37.4	36.1	36.2
极端最低气温	摄氏度	2.7	4.2	4.3	6.7	5.6	1.8	1.9	3.2
年日照时数	小时	1958.8	1671.7	1910.2	1935.7	2059.5	1736.3	1699.7	2120.1
五、森　林									
有林地面积	万亩		78.34	83.48	91.48	92.16	89.23	87.30	87.38
林木蓄积量	万立方米		155.97	167.18	123.02	136.11	175.38	255.82	272.98
森林覆盖率	%		28.6	31.4	29.7	30.6	33.1	36.7	36.9
六、水资源									
大陆海岸线总长度	公里	61.4	61.4	61.4	61.4	115.9	92.1	97.2	97.2
海水养殖可养面积	万亩	5.0	5.0	5.0	5.5	2.6	16.9	2.0	1.1
淡水养殖可养面积	万亩	30.0	30.0	30.0	28.0	14.3	30.7	10.0	10.0

注：1. 人均耕地面积按户籍人口计算。
2. 大陆海岸线从2000年起以咸水为界定。
3. 常住人口2006-2010年数据，根据东莞市第六次全国人口普查数据结果重新修订，下同。

1-4 历年土地与自然资源

Land and Natural Resources over Years

年　份	土地面积 (平方公里)	气　候				
		年　降 水　量 (毫米)	年平均 气　温 (摄氏度)	极端最高 气　温 (摄氏度)	极端最低 气　温 (摄氏度)	年日照 时　数 (小时)
1978	2465	1748.3	21.9	35.7	2.7	1958.8
1979	2465	2007.1	21.9	36.5	2.9	1991.4
1980	2465	1434.7	22.3	37.7	3.3	2157.1
1981	2465	2394.9	22.1	35.6	3.2	1792.2
1982	2465	1454.1	22.1	37.5	3.8	1754.1
1983	2465	1947.1	21.8	35.8	3.3	1909.7
1984	2465	1444.5	21.5	35.9	3.1	1749.2
1985	2465	1678.0	21.8	35.8	4.2	1671.7
1986	2465	1665.2	22.2	35.9	3.0	2098.1
1987	2465	1908.8	22.9	37.0	4.3	1816.6
1988	2465	1735.0	22.0	37.0	7.0	1836.5
1989	2465	1567.2	22.5	37.6	5.2	1926.0
1990	2465	1602.9	22.8	37.8	4.3	1910.2
1991	2465	1219.6	23.0	36.6	1.2	1968.8
1992	2465	1827.1	22.3	37.0	4.5	1854.5
1993	2465	2393.6	22.5	35.6	3.0	1965.7
1994	2465	1809.1	23.0	38.2	5.4	1828.6
1995	2465	1664.8	22.4	36.2	6.7	1935.7
1996	2465	1547.4	22.7	37.1	3.4	2036.0
1997	2465	2074.0	22.8	36.3	6.1	1558.1
1998	2465	1844.5	23.6	36.5	5.6	1699.0
1999	2465	1614.5	23.3	37.8	3.1	2015.8
2000	2465	2019.3	23.2	37.0	5.6	2059.5
2001	2465	2042.6	23.3	36.6	6.6	1978.2
2002	2465	1557.4	23.6	36.7	4.5	2046.9
2003	2465	1416.7	23.0	36.1	3.8	2268.7
2004	2465	1705.8	22.8	38.0	3.5	2192.9
2005	2465	1837.6	22.7	37.4	1.8	1736.3
2006	2465	2412.0	22.7	36.8	4.7	1616.4
2007	2465	1806.9	22.9	35.9	6.7	1876.7
2008	2465	2710.9	22.2	36.8	4.8	1879.3
2009	2465	1881.6	22.8	36.3	5.3	1967.8
2010	2460	2165.9	22.4	36.1	1.9	1699.7
2011	2460	1298.6	22.1	36.2	3.2	2120.1

注：土地面积数据由市国土资源局提供，下同。

1-4 续表

年份	森林			水资源		
	森林面积(万亩)	林木蓄积量(万立方米)	森林覆盖率(%)	大陆海岸线总长度(公里)	海水养殖可养面积(万亩)	淡水养殖可养面积(万亩)
1978				61.4	5.0	30.0
1979	44.4	110.3	14.7	61.4	5.0	30.0
1980				61.4	5.0	30.0
1981				61.4	5.0	30.0
1982				61.4	5.0	30.0
1983				61.4	5.0	30.0
1984	76.6	160.5	21.9	61.4	5.0	30.0
1985	78.3	156.0	28.6	61.4	5.0	30.0
1986	82.4	157.8	30.0	61.4	5.0	30.0
1987	83.9	183.9	34.5	61.4	5.0	30.0
1988	84.3	169.1	34.7	61.4	5.0	30.0
1989	80.9	164.8	31.1	61.4	5.0	30.0
1990	83.5	167.2	31.4	61.4	5.0	30.0
1991	85.0	169.2	31.6	61.4	5.0	29.0
1992	86.3	169.8	31.3	61.4	5.5	29.0
1993	87.3	168.9	31.9	61.4	5.5	28.0
1994	86.1	116.8	28.3	61.4	5.5	28.0
1995	91.5	123.0	29.7	61.4	5.5	28.0
1996	91.9	115.7	29.9	61.4	5.5	28.5
1997	93.5	121.1	29.9	61.4	5.7	28.7
1998	93.4	126.0	30.1	61.4	5.7	28.7
1999	92.2	120.4	30.1	115.9	4.8	28.7
2000	92.2	136.1	30.6	115.9	2.6	14.3
2001	93.3	146.0	31.2	116.0	2.8	12.9
2002	93.8	155.0	31.7	115.9	4.1	11.7
2003	93.3	165.1	32.2	92.1	4.2	10.4
2004	93.3	165.1	32.2	92.1	4.0	10.0
2005	89.2	175.4	33.1	92.1	16.9	30.7
2006	88.9	194.4	35.1	92.1	16.6	30.5
2007	89.1	215.1	35.5	92.1	16.9	30.7
2008	88.6	227.9	36.2	97.2	2.5	15.0
2009	90.1	241.4	36.5	97.2	2.0	10.0
2010	87.3	255.8	36.7	97.2	2.0	10.0
2011	87.4	273.0	36.9	97.2	1.1	10.0

1-5 主要年份国民经济主要指标

Main Indicators on National Economy in Main Years

项　　目	单位	1978年	1985年	1990年	1995年	2000年	2005年	2010年	2011年
一、国民经济核算									
地区生产总值	亿元	6.11	22.60	80.44	296.29	820.25	2183.20	4246.45	4735.39
第一产业	亿元	2.72	6.15	13.28	21.43	25.91	20.55	16.57	17.88
第二产业	亿元	2.68	11.66	40.53	166.97	450.71	1227.86	2160.82	2366.20
#工业	亿元			39.18	154.19	430.45	1173.23	2078.45	2288.41
第三产业	亿元	0.71	4.80	26.63	107.89	343.64	934.78	2069.07	2351.32
二、农村经济									
农业总产值	亿元	4.24	9.12	23.64	42.69	54.64	42.05	28.31	30.66
农村集体经营总收入	亿元			7.18	41.23	77.50	120.57	143.38	148.48
年末耕地面积	万亩			88.26	70.86	66.33	50.29	57.69	
三、工　业									
规模以上工业企业指标									
工业增加值	亿元			23.76	111.02	360.11	979.34	1708.31	1642.45
主营业务收入	亿元	2.69	9.23	47.27	275.84	988.91	3912.15	7708.17	8454.92
年末固定资产原值	亿元	0.78	1.68	14.29	60.14	728.85	1856.09	3216.25	3304.96
年末固定资产净值	亿元	0.51	1.20	11.95	46.26	470.19	1105.26	1783.69	1823.77
流动资产合计	亿元	0.26	0.58	1.74	21.28	529.82	1873.28	3788.83	4173.21
资产总额	亿元		1.73	13.51	52.98	1122.60	3345.33	6001.71	6612.71
负债总额	亿元					563.04	1858.09	3525.30	3877.06
资产负债率	%					50.2	55.5	58.7	58.6
利税总额	亿元					84.10	183.10	469.59	483.30
综合效益指数	%					114.0	119.9	130.3	128.3
四、能源消费									
地区能源消费总量(等价值)	万吨标准煤						1885.78	2812.65	2896.05
地区能源消费总量(当量值)	万吨标准煤						1800.14	2438.84	2512.46
电力消耗	亿千瓦时						419.83	562.00	586.07
单位GDP能耗(等价值)	吨标准煤/万元						0.864	0.619	0.632
单位GDP能耗(当量值)	吨标准煤/万元						0.825	0.599	0.548
规模以上工业综合能源消费量(当量值)	万吨标准煤						1203.77	1496.06	1482.56

注：1.2005年以前地区生产总值采用全国第一次经济普查资料修订的数据；2005-2008年采用第二次经济普查资料修订的数据；2004年以前使用旧行业分类，2004年起使用新行业分类，下同。
2.规模以上工业企业1997年及以前为独立核算企业口径，1998-2005年为全部国有及年销售收入500万元以上非国有企业口径，2006-2010年为年主营业务收入500万元及以上口径，2011年起为年主营业务收入2000万元及以上口径，下同。
3.2005年以前工业相关数据采用第一次经济普查资料修订的数据，2008年采用第二次经济普查资料修订的数据，下同。
4.单位GDP能耗(等价值)和单位GDP能耗(当量值)2006-2010年按2005年可比价计算；2011年开始按2010年可比价计算。

1-5 续表 1

项目	单位	1978年	1985年	1990年	1995年	2000年	2005年	2010年	2011年
五、运输邮电									
公路通车里程	公里	1259	1240	1325	2327	2518	2871	4751	4828
#高速公路	公里					89	154	217	251
旅客周转量	亿人公里	0.94	9.52	32.22	44.62	100.19	118.53	129.07	145.88
水　运	亿人公里	0.43	0.43	0.15	0.19	0.14	0.33	0.20	0.20
公　路	亿人公里	0.51	9.10	32.07	44.43	100.05	118.20	128.87	145.68
货物周转量	亿吨公里	1.51	17.16	18.47	26.46	40.47	42.48	109.03	187.48
水　运	亿吨公里	1.42	5.86	11.25	13.66	15.86	15.23	57.95	134.35
公　路	亿吨公里	0.09	11.30	7.22	12.80	24.60	27.25	51.08	53.13
港口货物吞吐量	万吨	293	276	233	201	746	2280	5657	6848
邮政业务收入	亿元							6.32	7.37
电信业务收入	亿元							149.02	157.49
局用交换机容量	万门		1.14	6.98	52.29	103.13	286.25	365.02	357.00
年末移动电话交换机总容量	万户				4.80	154.20	1059.10	1657.00	2066.00
本地电话用户	万户	0.20	0.77	4.90	31.58	78.12	384.52	332.42	319.55
移动电话用户(含充值卡)	万户			0.05	4.77	123.68	1016.41	1607.60	1677.77
#充值卡	万户					42.71	839.58	1433.56	143.30
互联网用户	万户				0.05	13.78	52.90	153.92	190.72
六、供用电									
总供电量	亿千瓦时	1.64	3.82	18.01	68.00	178.03	415.66	556.89	579.35
#网供	亿千瓦时	1.64	3.39	11.18	38.48	134.91	342.26	547.33	569.93
总售电量	亿千瓦时	1.49	3.39	16.15	61.68	169.06	396.59	543.66	566.69
#工业用电	亿千瓦时	1.08	2.21	11.93	48.79	134.58	330.31	435.57	445.76
七、固定资产投资									
固定资产投资总额	亿元	0.23	7.06	7.51	63.14	102.89	597.24	1114.98	1079.77
#房地产开发	亿元				8.52	11.25	144.43	298.99	373.76
房地产开发当年房屋施工面积	万平方米						1160.20	2060.54	2396.55
房地产开发当年房屋竣工面积	万平方米						132.90	296.59	242.28
商品房销售面积	万平方米						321.90	511.25	595.61
商品房销售额	亿元						119.40	373.77	459.61
新增固定资产	亿元						173.30	577.86	578.89
固定资产交付使用率	%						29.0	51.8	53.6
八、国内贸易									
批发和零售业商品销售总额	亿元	7.49	23.16	43.41	155.69	279.19	824.82	1957.18	2346.18
社会消费品零售总额	亿元	2.13	9.36	31.97	113.01	235.16	506.29	1108.06	1266.31

注：1. 2006年起公路通车里程含专用公路和村道，与往年数据不可比，下同。
2. 1995年全社会固定资产投资总额含沙角C厂投资126374万元。
3. 2009年起，客货运输量中，公路和水路运输量统计改用新调查方法，与往年不可比，下同。
4. 2005年以前国内商业相关数据采用第一次经济普查资料修订的数据，2005-2008年采用第二次经济普查资料修订的数据，下同。

1-5 续表 2

项　　目	单 位	1978年	1985年	1990年	1995年	2000年	2005年	2010年	2011年
九、物价指数(以上年价格为100)									
商品零售物价总指数	%	100.4	106.9	94.9	109.7	100.1	103.0	103.2	104.7
居民消费价格总指数	%		106.5	96.6	113.9	101.5	102.4	102.8	104.9
消费品价格指数	%		106.9	94.9	109.7	100.1	103.0	102.8	105.7
服务项目价格指数	%		103.3	111.0	128.9	112.8	100.4	102.6	103.0
十、对外经济贸易、旅游									
进出口总额(海关口径)	亿美元			10.82	153.91	320.45	743.72	1213.38	1352.24
进口总额	亿美元			5.14	75.92	148.86	334.42	517.40	568.95
出口总额	亿美元			5.68	77.99	171.59	409.29	695.98	783.29
#一般贸易	亿美元				2.32	2.09	17.55	95.41	134.11
来料加工装配	亿美元				43.46	83.43	161.17	195.54	169.35
进料加工	亿美元				32.02	85.84	230.43	394.62	465.43
其他	亿美元				0.19	0.22	0.14	10.40	14.39
新签利用外资协议(合同)数	宗						773	869	1324
合同外资金额(新口径)	亿美元						29.80	25.97	35.08
实际利用外资(新口径)	亿美元						14.68	27.32	30.51
全年接待旅游人数	万人次			125	89	291	1156	2251	2615
#国际及港澳台旅游者	万人次			27	27	106	169	327	357
旅游外汇收入	万美元					7617	28189	67592	90975
十一、财政、金融									
来源于东莞的财政收入	亿元	0.66	1.11	3.57	18.01	103.56	331.91	785.10	838.52
市财政一般预算收入	亿元				11.56	30.47	103.97	277.84	313.06
市财政一般预算支出	亿元	0.18	0.50	2.28	12.42	33.61	117.04	289.83	351.92
金融机构各项人民币存款余额	亿元	1.05	13.49	68.07	383.68	1228.67	2933.40	5943.39	6609.39
金融机构各项人民币贷款余额	亿元	1.96	14.24	63.04	254.85	630.84	1500.52	3329.82	3716.08
十二、人民生活									
全市职工平均工资	元							16108	21739
城镇在岗职工平均工资	元	474	1456	3552	9682	14051	28253	46576	50398
城市居民人均可支配收入	元		791	2508	9588	14142	22882	35690	39513
城市居民人均消费性支出	元		689	2038	9220	12529	21768	25733	27495
农民人均纯收入	元	149	803	1542	4769	8484	13076	20486	22842
城乡居民人民币储蓄存款余额	亿元	0.54	9.19	45.51	232.97	672.07	1728.28	3386.85	3710.99

注：1. 城镇在岗职工工资总额和人均工资2000年前是城镇职工工资，2000年起是城镇在岗职工工资，不含乡镇及以下办企业职工，下同。
2. 全年接待旅游人数和旅游外汇收入2002年起是旅游局口径，与往年数不可比。
3. 农民人均纯收入采用农村住户抽样调查口径，相应调整了往年数，下同。
4. 1995年及以前年份，来源于东莞的财政总收入不含关税，下同。

1-6 主要年份国民经济和社会发展主要比例与效益指标

Main Indicators on National Economy and Social Development in Main Years

项　　目	单 位	1990年	1995年	2000年	2005年	2010年	2011年
一、户籍人口							
出生率	‰	17.07	17.59	12.11	10.62	10.90	10.92
死亡率	‰	4.76	4.84	4.59	4.60	4.68	4.79
自然增长率	‰	12.31	12.75	7.52	6.02	6.23	6.13
人口性别比(男/女)	%	97.1	100.4	102.4	103.1	103.1	103.0
二、地区生产总值中三次产业比重							
第一产业	%	16.5	7.2	3.2	0.9	0.4	0.4
第二产业	%	50.4	56.4	54.9	56.2	50.9	49.9
工　业	%	48.7	52.0	52.5	53.7	48.9	48.3
建筑业	%	1.7	4.3	2.5	2.5	1.9	1.6
第三产业	%	33.1	36.4	41.9	42.8	48.7	49.7
三、全社会劳动生产率	元/人				59743	70910	75477
(按全社会从业人员、增加值计算)							
第一产业	元/人				14238	24017	29980
第二产业	元/人				50634	51150	49512
第三产业	元/人				86154	122064	163827
四、农　业							
农业总产值中“五业”比例							
种植业	%	54.9	45.7	39.6	27.0	55.4	55.2
林　业	%	1.8	2.1	0.7	0.4	1.0	0.7
牧　业	%	19.2	30.0	41.4	57.7	19.6	20.8
副　业	%	11.1	6.2	3.5			
渔　业	%	13.3	16.1	14.9	14.9	24.0	23.3
五、工　业							
规模以上工业企业效益							
固定资产利税率	%	8.5	10.7	11.5	9.9	26.3	26.5
资金利税率	%	6.3	7.7	7.5	5.5	7.8	7.3
产值利税率	%	5.4	10.0	9.2	4.6	6.1	5.7

注：2002年起农业中副业并入种植业。

1-6 续表 1

项 目	单 位	1990年	1995年	2000年	2005年	2010年	2011年
六、建筑业							
技术装备率	万元/人		0.37	0.43	0.68	1.02	0.98
产值利税率	%		3.9	5.4	7.5	8.1	7.4
劳动生产率(按总产值计算)	元/人	18636	42766	60849	108136	218076	207555
七、固定资产投资							
固定资产投资相当于地区生产总值比例(投资率)	%	9.3	17.0	12.5	27.4	26.3	22.8
全社会房屋建筑面积竣工率	%	45.2	34.1	60.7	22.5	20.7	12.8
八、财 政							
来源于东莞的财政收入相当于地区生产总值比例	%	4.4	6.1	12.6	15.2	18.5	17.7
市财政一般预算支出相当于地区生产总值比例	%	2.8	4.2	4.1	5.4	6.5	7.4
九、外经外贸							
利用外资结构							
外商直接投资	%	41.2	63.6	66.0	75.2	86.4	94.8
外商其他投资	%	58.8	36.4	34.0	24.8	13.6	5.2
实际利用外资额相当于协议规定外商投资额比例(旧口径)	%	80.6	31.9	89.7	78.9	103.0	86.9
进出口总额比例							
进口总额	%	47.5	49.3	46.5	45.0	42.6	42.1
出口总额	%	52.5	50.7	53.6	55.0	57.4	57.9
#一般贸易	%		3.0	1.2	4.3	13.7	17.1
来料加工装配	%		55.7	48.6	39.4	28.1	21.6
进料加工	%		41.1	50.0	56.3	56.7	59.4
其他	%		0.2	0.2		1.5	1.9
十、交通、邮电通信业							
货运量中各种运输方式比例							
公 路	%	58.2	55.7	63.3	71.7	82.0	80.8
水 运	%	41.8	44.3	36.7	28.3	18.0	19.2

1-6 续表 2

项 目	单 位	1990年	1995年	2000年	2005年	2010年	2011年
十一、金 融							
各项人民币存款相当于生产总值比例	%	84.6	129.5	149.8	134.5	140.0	139.6
各项人民币贷款相当于生产总值比例	%	78.4	86.0	76.9	68.8	78.4	78.5
各项人民币存款余额中主要存款比例							
#企业存款	%	17.1	23.3	35.7	29.2	25.6	
财政性存款	%	1.2	2.2	0.3	0.9	0.8	0.5
储蓄存款	%	66.9	60.7	54.7	58.9	57.0	56.1
农业存款	%	7.4	6.2	5.9	4.1	5.8	
各项人民币贷款余额中主要贷款比例							
#短期贷款	%	90.5	64.6	84.2	48.9	37.1	39.8
中长期贷款	%	2.1	10.8	7.4	46.7	59.1	55.7
十二、科技、教育、文化、卫生							
科教文卫事业费占财政支出比例	%	28.7	24.5	25.8	17.8	28.6	36.8
学龄儿童入学率	%	99.9	100.0	100.0	100.0	100.0	100.0
小学毕业生升学率	%	95.4	99.2	99.8	99.9	100.0	100.0
初中毕业生升学率	%	44.1	85.4	90.3	94.1	97.9	98.0
普通高中毕业生升学率	%	31.2	64.9	70.5	96.5	95.1	94.5
每一教师负担学生数							
普通高等学校	人		13.7	20.1	15.4	17.6	18.5
中等职业技术学校	人	20.6	21.8	19.0	18.2	20.3	20.0
普通中学	人	20.7	21.1	22.4	19.8	17.7	17.2
小学	人	24.0	24.2	34.3	27.5	23.3	23.3
十三、人民生活							
城市居民消费结构							
食品类	%	63.5	39.5	32.3	27.7	33.9	34.6
衣着类	%	4.7	6.6	3.9	5.9	6.6	6.6
其 他	%	31.8	53.9	63.8	66.4	59.5	58.8

1-7 国民经济主要指标分月变化情况（2011年，累计绝对数）

Main Indicators on National Economy by Month
(2011, Accumulative Figures in Value Terms)

项　　目	单位	1 月	1-2 月	1-3 月	1-4 月	1-5 月	1-6 月
规模以上工业增加值	亿元		293.11	443.17	604.47	702.05	848.56
#国有经济	亿元		1.08	14.99	21.09	32.11	39.61
外资型经济	亿元		229.03	336.57	462.15	535.47	646.19
#民营企业	亿元		47.93	72.91	96.18	101.52	122.90
#八大支柱产业	亿元		193.27	283.90	385.93	431.44	520.44
规模以上工业销售产值	亿元		1224.49	1873.06	2554.44	3218.96	3889.87
规模以上工业出口产品产值	亿元		639.40	936.10	1292.26	1631.03	1978.02
规模以上工业产品产销率	%		99.7	99.7	99.5	99.6	99.6
规模以上工业企业主营业务收入	亿元		1419.83	1865.79	2540.18	3201.10	3866.21
规模以上工业企业利税总额	亿元		79.16	89.59	119.32	150.56	175.92
固定资产投资总额	亿元		72.72	157.40	240.11	331.04	426.79
#房地产开发	亿元		25.19	63.12	93.15	120.57	154.52
来源于东莞的财政收入	亿元	98.97	146.52	205.56	290.92	364.08	426.65
市财政一般预算收入	亿元	32.26	58.78	81.10	106.67	129.66	156.82
市财政一般预算支出	亿元	41.72	62.68	89.48	118.00	143.21	174.81
金融机构各项人民币存款余额	亿元	5748.72	5803.27	6220.51	5989.59	6100.28	6364.30
#城乡居民储蓄存款余额	亿元	3306.38	3298.45	3507.34	3376.75	3417.96	3564.79
金融机构各项人民币贷款余额	亿元	3392.57	3415.83	3463.97	3494.69	3527.82	3553.84
进出口总额(海关口径)	亿美元	110.36	178.92	291.17	400.99	511.86	624.71
#出口总额	亿美元	63.26	101.47	164.56	226.84	290.03	357.00
新签项目宗数	宗	83	149	269	418	628	846
合同规定外商投资额	亿美元	4.08	6.06	8.73	11.64	15.69	19.88
实际利用外资(不含对外借款)	亿美元	2.56	4.37	7.30	9.42	12.23	15.00
社会消费品零售总额	亿元	111.45	220.69	310.26	411.68	511.15	617.29
居民消费价格总指数	%	104.7	103.9	104.4	104.6	104.4	104.4
#服务项目价格指数	%	105.7	103.9	104.2	104.0	103.5	103.1
总供电量	亿千瓦时	41.00	70.30	116.30	162.44	212.69	266.60
总售电量	亿千瓦时	47.06	83.24	115.55	160.15	206.25	254.32
邮电业务收入	亿元	13.84	26.23	39.68	53.38	67.18	81.03
城市居民人均可支配收入	元			13501			21903
城市居民人均消费性支出	元			6463			12707

注：1. 物价指数以上年同期为100；各项指标1-12月累计不等于年报数。
　　2. 城市居民收支为季报数据。

1-7 续表

(2011年，累计绝对数)

项　　目	单位	1-7 月	1-8 月	1-9 月	1-10 月	1-11 月	1-12 月
规模以上工业增加值	亿元	1002.06	1175.60	1325.12	1488.19	1639.83	1797.30
#国有经济	亿元	47.91	56.52	65.58	73.49	81.12	88.21
外资型经济	亿元	761.93	891.59	1003.83	1128.71	1243.22	1363.19
#民营企业	亿元	145.38	169.65	190.26	213.04	235.01	257.71
#八大支柱产业	亿元	614.61	723.27	816.05	918.46	1014.42	1113.42
规模以上工业销售产值	亿元	4598.15	5386.43	6070.92	6830.17	7526.44	8253.61
规模以上工业出口产品产值	亿元	2341.13	2762.06	3114.85	3512.29	3877.13	4255.50
规模以上工业产品产销率	%	99.7	99.5	99.5	99.7	99.6	99.6
规模以上工业企业主营业务收入	亿元	4569.39	5281.52	6034.46	6792.15	7485.95	8790.80
规模以上工业企业利税总额	亿元	206.69	241.66	278.60	314.35	348.68	382.71
固定资产投资总额	亿元	507.87	610.91	755.52	834.11	921.82	1079.77
#房地产开发	亿元	183.68	220.66	264.68	296.26	322.62	373.76
来源于东莞的财政收入	亿元	521.23	581.17	647.49	734.53	787.97	838.52
市财政一般预算收入	亿元	181.38	202.90	227.31	252.71	281.55	313.07
市财政一般预算支出	亿元	195.04	240.96	258.72	285.31	312.63	356.41
金融机构各项人民币存款余额	亿元	6210.83	6214.49	6360.84	6239.00	6281.63	6609.39
#城乡居民储蓄存款余额	亿元	3470.58	3445.69	3586.44	3482.98	3508.73	3710.99
金融机构各项人民币贷款余额	亿元	3578.43	3612.41	3632.02	3656.07	3667.42	3716.08
进出口总额(海关口径)	亿美元	743.41	871.46	996.28	1110.18	1232.95	1352.24
#出口总额	亿美元	425.42	500.04	573.15	638.77	711.93	783.29
新签项目宗数	宗	966	1090	1191	1242	1292	1324
合同规定外商投资额	亿美元	22.78	27.20	30.06	31.49	33.73	35.08
实际利用外资(不含对外借款)	亿美元	18.04	21.65	25.17	27.05	28.13	30.51
社会消费品零售总额	亿元	724.08	832.24	939.67	1049.62	1160.12	1266.31
居民消费价格总指数	%	104.5	104.6	104.8	104.8	104.9	104.9
#服务项目价格指数	%	103.0	102.8	102.8	102.8	103.0	103.0
总供电量	亿千瓦时	325.13	385.82	439.62	486.94	533.62	579.35
总售电量	亿千瓦时	306.45	362.50	421.84	472.72	521.48	566.69
邮电业务收入	亿元	94.92	109.03	123.12	136.86	150.76	164.86
城市居民人均可支配收入	元			30798			39513
城市居民人均消费性支出	元			20107			27495

1-8 国民经济主要指标分月变化情况（2011年，比上年同期增长）

Main Indicators on National Economy by Month

(2011, Compare with Same Period of Preceding Year %)

项　　目	单位	1 月	1-2 月	1-3 月	1-4 月	1-5 月	1-6 月
规模以上工业增加值	%		18.2	22.7	16.2	14.5	11.5
#国有经济	%		-21.2	6.2	3.4	7.3	4.4
外资型经济	%		17.3	21.6	15.0	13.1	9.7
#民营企业	%		25.4	36.2	26.3	24.1	21.6
#八大支柱产业	%		21.4	25.3	17.8	15.5	12.2
规模以上工业销售产值	%		26.2	31.7	23.2	21.6	18.1
规模以上工业出口产品产值	%		25.1	31.0	21.2	17.7	13.4
规模以上工业产品产销率	%		-0.2	0.6	0.2	0.1	0.5
规模以上工业企业主营业务收入	%		22.6	20.8	19.1	18.3	16.7
规模以上工业企业利税总额	%		10.2	9.2	7.2	8.4	6.2
固定资产投资总额	%		15.3	11.9	8.2	7.1	6.6
#房地产开发	%		67.2	54.8	42.6	48.3	45.2
来源于东莞的财政收入	%	17.0	12.9	13.2	16.6	23.1	24.4
市财政一般预算收入	%	34.4	38.6	17.5	18.4	21.9	25.0
市财政一般预算支出	%	115.3	41.0	23.8	25.8	25.4	19.5
金融机构各项人民币存款余额	%	-3.3	-2.4	4.6	0.7	2.6	7.0
#城乡居民储蓄存款余额	%	-2.6	-2.8	3.3	-0.5	0.7	5.0
金融机构各项人民币贷款余额	%	1.9	2.6	4.0	5.0	5.9	6.7
进出口总额(海关口径)	%	27.4	18.9	19.1	17.7	15.9	14.1
#出口总额	%	27.7	17.7	19.8	19.5	17.3	15.9
新签项目宗数	%	22.1	43.3	70.3	101.0	117.7	139.7
合同规定外商投资额	%	174.1	69.4	72.1	73.4	77.7	78.7
实际利用外资(不含对外借款)	%	8.5	5.6	6.0	6.2	6.4	7.5
社会消费品零售总额	%	18.0	18.8	16.1	16.0	15.7	15.8
居民消费价格总指数	%	4.7	3.9	4.4	4.6	4.4	4.4
#服务项目价格指数	%	5.7	3.9	4.2	4.0	3.5	3.1
总供电量	%	-1.3	4.2	5.0	5.6	4.9	5.4
总售电量	%	6.9	-4.2	0.1	2.1	4.5	3.3
邮电业务收入	%	7.6	5.4	3.1	3.8	5.4	5.8
城市居民人均可支配收入	%			12.0			11.6
城市居民人均消费性支出	%			-10.2			-4.7

1-8 续表

(2011年，比上年同期增长)

项　　目	单位	1-7 月	1-8 月	1-9 月	1-10 月	1-11 月	1-12 月
规模以上工业增加值	%	10.3	10.5	9.0	8.5	7.6	7.5
#国有经济	%	4.6	3.9	3.8	3.3	2.9	3.4
外资型经济	%	8.7	8.5	6.1	5.3	4.1	4.1
#民营企业	%	20.3	20.7	16.9	15.6	12.6	12.0
#八大支柱产业	%	11.1	12.0	9.7	8.7	7.6	7.4
规模以上工业销售产值	%	17.1	17.2	14.5	13.5	11.9	11.5
规模以上工业出口产品产值	%	12.0	12.8	10.4	9.5	8.2	8.0
规模以上工业产品产销率	%	0.5	0.4	0.4	0.5	0.5	0.5
规模以上工业企业主营业务收入	%	15.8	14.6	13.8	12.9	12.2	11.4.
规模以上工业企业利税总额	%	6.2	7.7	7.3	3.5	2.2	0.2
固定资产投资总额	%	6.9	7.6	8.0	8.2	8.2	8.1
#房地产开发	%	39.2	36.1	26.8	31.5	31.0	25.0
来源于东莞的财政收入	%	23.7	25.0	24.7	23.7	21.0	16.2
市财政一般预算收入	%	26.0	23.3	24.0	23.4	26.6	18.3
市财政一般预算支出	%	15.4	27.7	18.5	18.3	18.2	15.5
金融机构各项人民币存款余额	%	4.5	4.5	7.0	4.9	5.7	11.2
#城乡居民储蓄存款余额	%	2.3	1.5	5.7	2.6	3.4	9.3
金融机构各项人民币贷款余额	%	7.5	8.5	9.1	9.8	10.1	11.6
进出口总额(海关口径)	%	12.9	13.0	12.5	12.0	11.7	11.2
#出口总额	%	14.3	14.0	13.4	12.6	12.6	12.5
新签项目宗数	%	130.0	107.2	91.8	79.7	66.3	52.4
合同规定外商投资额	%	62.6	55.5	47.5	41.7	38.5	35.1
实际利用外资(不含对外借款)	%	7.8	7.6	8.1	8.5	8.2	11.7
社会消费品零售总额	%	16.0	16.0	15.5	15.4	15.3	15.0
居民消费价格总指数	%	4.5	4.6	4.8	4.8	4.9	4.9
#服务项目价格指数	%	3.0	2.8	2.8	2.8	3.0	3.0
总供电量	%	4.4	4.5	4.1	3.8	4.0	4.0
总售电量	%	3.8	3.5	3.7	3.3	3.4	4.2
邮电业务收入	%	5.5	5.2	5.1	4.7	5.0	6.1
城市居民人均可支配收入	%			11.6			10.7
城市居民人均消费性支出	%			4.9			6.8

1-9 历年地区生产总值

Gross Domestic Product over Years

年 份	地区生产总值 (万元)	第一产业	第二产业	第三产业	人均地区生产总值 (元)
1978	61122	27235	26781	7106	553
1979	66233	26460	29244	10528	593
1980	72199	26323	33290	12586	643
1981	91131	32772	42980	15379	802
1982	114322	37257	58137	18927	991
1983	130340	39847	68962	21531	1115
1984	159632	45671	78091	35869	1350
1985	226033	61475	116584	47973	1885
1986	300167	81416	135735	83016	2462
1987	392859	98236	177249	117373	3170
1988	554583	118888	282771	152924	4408
1989	609202	126568	279724	202910	4768
1990	804401	132787	405290	266325	6173
1991	959073	134523	503220	321330	5095
1992	1108922	144115	592701	372106	5038
1993	1570491	143953	873114	553424	5850
1994	2170341	174796	1194928	800616	6357
1995	2962892	214306	1669723	1078863	7421
1996	3617502	248645	1994826	1374031	8444
1997	4485981	256388	2432816	1796777	9747
1998	5579964	259437	3056779	2263749	11265
1999	6672386	257863	3670519	2744004	12494
2000	8202530	259087	4507072	3436372	13679
2001	9918905	260968	5405092	4252845	15268
2002	11869374	248791	6488109	5132474	18131
2003	14525186	228165	7981954	6315068	22174
2004	18060258	227087	10160382	7672789	27554
2005	21831961	205546	12278624	9347791	33287
2006	26279791	120089	15065985	11093717	39173
2007	31600489	118991	17546573	13934924	45057
2008	37036004	148251	19016068	17871685	50471
2009	37639142	147877	18230836	19260428	48988
2010	42464527	165719	21608153	20690656	52798
2011	47353949	178776	23662018	23513155	57470

注：1. 地区生产总值绝对值按当年价计算，指数按可比价计算,下同。
2. 人均地区生产总值1990年及以前按户籍人口计算，1991年起按常住人口计算，与以前年份不可比。
3. 人均地区生产总值2006-2010年数据，根据东莞市第六次全国人口普查数据结果重新修订，下同。

1-10 历年地区生产总值指数

Indices of Gross Domestic Product over Years

年份	地区生产总值指数(上年=100)	第一产业	第二产业	第三产业	人均地区生产总值指数(上年=100)	人均地区生产总值指数与地区生产总值指数之比
1979	99.5	86.5	107.0	146.4	98.6	0.991
1980	102.7	90.3	117.3	113.9	102.0	0.993
1981	116.6	115.0	122.1	110.8	115.4	0.989
1982	116.9	105.3	131.0	117.6	115.1	0.985
1983	110.4	104.8	115.7	111.3	108.9	0.987
1984	114.2	109.0	107.0	140.9	112.9	0.988
1985	132.3	118.9	144.5	132.7	130.5	0.986
1986	126.1	111.9	110.3	174.7	124.0	0.983
1987	122.5	111.6	127.7	126.0	120.5	0.984
1988	115.7	90.6	143.7	103.0	114.0	0.985
1989	107.1	99.8	106.2	113.7	105.5	0.985
1990	123.2	104.4	127.6	128.0	120.8	0.980
1991	117.5	103.1	121.5	118.6	108.8	0.926
1992	108.3	100.0	112.6	105.1	92.6	0.855
1993	127.9	79.4	139.2	129.0	104.8	0.820
1994	122.5	107.2	124.7	122.3	96.3	0.786
1995	127.4	110.5	135.1	116.8	108.9	0.855
1996	117.5	109.4	115.5	123.5	109.5	0.932
1997	119.6	104.5	119.8	121.8	111.3	0.931
1998	121.8	100.9	122.1	124.5	113.1	0.929
1999	119.7	102.3	120.6	120.3	111.0	0.928
2000	119.7	99.8	120.7	120.0	106.6	0.891
2001	119.9	103.0	121.6	118.9	110.7	0.923
2002	120.5	97.6	122.6	119.1	119.6	0.992
2003	120.5	90.2	122.3	119.7	120.4	0.999
2004	121.0	90.0	125.6	115.8	120.9	0.999
2005	119.5	102.3	120.0	119.3	119.4	0.999
2006	119.2	58.9	121.9	117.1	116.6	0.978
2007	118.3	89.9	114.8	123.3	113.1	0.957
2008	114.0	110.6	106.1	124.0	109.0	0.956
2009	105.3	102.3	99.7	111.4	100.5	0.955
2010	110.3	101.6	116.7	104.1	105.3	0.955
2011	108.0	100.5	107.0	109.0	105.4	0.976

1-11 历年地区生产总值产业构成

Composition of Gross Domestic Product over Years

单位：%

年　份	地区生产总值	第一产业	第二产业	第三产业
1978	100.0	44.6	43.8	11.6
1979	100.0	40.0	44.2	15.9
1980	100.0	36.5	46.1	17.4
1981	100.0	36.0	47.2	16.9
1982	100.0	32.6	50.9	16.6
1983	100.0	30.6	52.9	16.5
1984	100.0	28.6	48.9	22.5
1985	100.0	27.2	51.6	21.2
1986	100.0	27.1	45.2	27.7
1987	100.0	25.0	45.1	29.9
1988	100.0	21.4	51.0	27.6
1989	100.0	20.8	45.9	33.3
1990	100.0	16.5	50.4	33.1
1991	100.0	14.0	52.5	33.5
1992	100.0	13.0	53.5	33.6
1993	100.0	9.2	55.6	35.2
1994	100.0	8.1	55.1	36.9
1995	100.0	7.2	56.4	36.4
1996	100.0	6.9	55.1	38.0
1997	100.0	5.7	54.2	40.1
1998	100.0	4.7	54.8	40.6
1999	100.0	3.9	55.0	41.1
2000	100.0	3.2	55.0	41.9
2001	100.0	2.6	54.5	42.9
2002	100.0	2.1	54.7	43.2
2003	100.0	1.6	55.0	43.5
2004	100.0	1.3	56.3	42.5
2005	100.0	0.9	56.2	42.8
2006	100.0	0.5	57.3	42.2
2007	100.0	0.4	55.5	44.1
2008	100.0	0.4	51.3	48.3
2009	100.0	0.4	48.4	51.2
2010	100.0	0.4	50.9	48.7
2011	100.0	0.4	49.9	49.7

1-12 各行业增加值项目（2011年）

Composition of Value-added by Industry (2011)

单位:万元

项 目	增加值	劳动者报酬	生产税净额	固定资产折旧	营业盈余
地区生产总值	47353949	20524700	5281218	10967298	10580732
第一产业	178776	166111		12665	
第二产业	23662018	11047898	2279223	5765545	4569351
工业	22884117	10638809	2133463	5698738	4413106
建筑业	777901	409089	145761	66807	156245
第三产业	23513155	9310691	3001995	5189089	6011381
交通运输、仓储和邮政业	1109497	418665	78904	361959	249969
交通运输和仓储业	1062925	398321	76935	356226	231442
邮政业	46573	20343	1969	5733	18528
信息传输、计算机服务和软件业	1855216	304592	98872	318224	1133529
批发和零售业	4628747	2028878	1840333	186779	572758
住宿和餐饮业	1694750	1380673	87722	215274	11082
金融业	1830659	527860	231724	32076	1038999
#银行业	1543001	455669	136764	28302	922266
房地产业	4076705	168790	422619	2461433	1023863
房地产开发经营	1396387	73604	364928	20255	937601
物业管理	202918	70272	13546	100561	18539
房地产中介服务	23090	10626	3088	3151	6224
其他房地产活动	169070	14288	41057	52225	61500
居民自有住房服务	2285241			2285241	
租赁和商务服务业	4531670	1875184	148083	776108	1732294
科学研究、技术服务和地质勘查业	313083	86124	16812	128128	82019
水利、环境和公共设施管理业	101154	48125	3684	29607	19738
居民服务和其他服务业	930775	759171	29336	85816	56451
教育	791935	627695	4001	151166	9074
卫生、社会保障和社会福利业	497516	363307	8003	59325	66880
文化、体育和娱乐业	248093	122166	31258	79944	14724
#娱乐业	156221	73673	25159	64221	-6831
公共管理和社会组织	903354	599460	644	303250	

1-13 主要年份支出法地区生产总值

Gross Domestic Product by Expenditure Approach in Main Years

项　　目	1995年	2000年	2005年	2010年	2011年
支出法地区生产总值(万元)	2962892	8202530	21831961	42464527	47353949
最终消费	1502524	4342481	11201390	22984391	26194232
资本形成总额	1210079	2369818	7148513	12757774	12692672
货物和服务净出口	250290	1490232	3482058	6722362	8467045
资本形成率(投资率)(%)	40.8	28.9	32.7	30.0	26.8
最终消费率(消费率)(%)	50.7	52.9	51.3	54.1	55.3

1-14 主要年份资本形成总额及构成

Gross Capital Formation and Its Composition in Main Years

项　　目		1995年	2000年	2005年	2010年	2011年
资本形成总额(万元)		1210079	2369818	7148513	12757774	12692672
固定资产形成总额		884671	1775228	6115306	10513989	11221377
存货增加		325407	594590	1033207	2243785	1471295
比重(资本形成总额=100)	固定资产形成总额	73.1	74.9	85.5	82.4	88.4
	存货增加	26.9	25.1	14.5	17.6	11.6

1-15 主要年份最终消费支出及构成

Final Consumption Expenditure and Its Composition in Main Years

项　　目		1995年	2000年	2005年	2010年	2011年
最终消费(万元)		1502524	4342481	11201390	22984391	26194232
居民消费		1262972	3752814	9798031	19852461	22421136
政府消费		239552	589666	1403359	3131930	3773095
比重(最终消费=100)	居民消费	84.1	86.4	87.5	86.4	85.6
	政府消费	15.9	13.6	12.5	13.6	14.4

1-16 全市企业和个体工商户登记注册年末实有数量(2005-2011年)

Enterprises and Self-employed Individuals Registered at Year-end (2005-2011)

单位：户

项　　目	2005年	2006年	2007年	2008年	2009年	2010年	2011年
工商登记户数合计	353266	403403	476125	504978	505502	518513	506061
内资企业	13898	12953	13401	13074	12493	12439	12820
#国有	1977	1554	1404	1313	1141	1058	1014
集体	6478	4989	4487	3385	2899	2180	1968
有限责任公司	1606	1468	1493	7017	7886	7649	8271
外商投资企业	7675	7695	7973	9437	9748	10113	11240
#合资	1013	822	718	860	1206	1120	1197
合作	482	379	307	218	197	179	177
独资	6177	6492	6946	6956	7678	8280	9492
“三来一补”企业	9552	8206	7417	6552	5748	4906	4047
私营企业	29017	38282	48955	63241	74229	88650	104689
个体工商户	293124	336267	398379	412674	403284	402405	373265

注：本表数据来源于市工商局。

1-17 个体工商户情况（2011年）

Statistics on Self-employed Individuals (2011)

项　　目	户　数（户）	从业人员（人）	资金数额（万元）	其中城镇		
				户　数（户）	从业人员（人）	资金数额（万元）
合　　计	373265	853589	848186	202426	435083	433701
农、林、牧、渔业	218	783	5034	92	328	1880
工　业	61331	265614	298600	24334	102415	114819
建筑业	739	1925	3410	442	1092	1480
交通运输、仓储和邮政业	1566	4253	5525	916	2375	2858
信息传输、计算机服务和软件业	1786	2780	1479	1051	1517	846
批发和零售业	247681	423963	373767	141532	238296	216442
住宿和餐饮业	27654	76677	81439	15716	44558	49434
房地产业	47	91	111	40	77	91
租赁和商务服务业	2337	5502	6261	1536	3598	4048
居民服务和其他服务业	28995	69279	64584	16152	38995	36300
卫生、社会保障和社会福利业	29	63	110	24	51	88
文化、体育和娱乐业	401	1520	6668	269	1044	4630
其他行业	481	1139	1199	322	737	785

注：本表数据来源于市工商局。

1-18 私营工商企业基本情况（2011年）

Basic Statistics on Private Industrial & Commercial Enterprises (2011)

项目	户数(户)	投资者人数(人)	雇工人数(人)	注册资本(万元)	其中：1. 独资企业 户数(户)	投资者人数(人)	雇工人数(人)	注册资本(万元)
合计	104689	196017	635206	12908860	7867	7746	77191	281374
农、林、牧、渔业	598	944	9316	84628	310	302	6946	25565
工业	37307	72514	257658	3759879	4086	4079	46146	118096
建筑业	4768	8771	28120	874675	31	31	159	279
交通运输、仓储和邮政业	1962	3570	10411	278480	20	20	96	226
信息传输、计算机服务和软件业	2047	3767	13420	243135	512	507	4940	51101
批发和零售业	35528	63864	186380	2877665	1587	1557	5574	13720
住宿和餐饮业	1171	1819	14477	207290	365	344	4878	44786
房地产业	3109	6065	16127	945505	5	5	16	38
租赁和商务服务业	9234	18603	47594	1946670	235	222	874	2976
居民服务和其他服务业	4188	6547	23974	240275	553	514	5198	15258
卫生、社会保障和社会福利业	25	43	320	18296				
文化、体育和娱乐业	809	1490	5983	91351	131	131	2198	8667
其他行业	3943	8020	21426	1341012	32	34	166	662

1-18 续表

项目	2. 合伙企业 户数(户)	投资者人数(人)	雇工人数(人)	注册资本(万元)	3. 有限责任公司 户数(户)	投资者人数(人)	雇工人数(人)	注册资本(万元)
合计	936	2447	7432	145278	95617	185036	548709	12144991
农、林、牧、渔业	85	215	1234	5761	200	403	1029	38562
工业	345	834	3109	21022	32843	67360	207548	3479961
建筑业	1	3	5	25	4725	8737	27891	874372
交通运输、仓储和邮政业	3	8	12	95	1936	3540	10288	277659
信息传输、计算机服务和软件业	141	339	862	14080	1381	2919	7537	176554
批发和零售业	85	186	345	4240	33768	61729	180222	2813576
住宿和餐饮业	56	145	725	10280	747	1330	8850	152224
房地产业	4	11	12	30	3095	6042	16083	928510
租赁和商务服务业	118	440	493	83878	8862	17890	46136	1833594
居民服务和其他服务业	65	157	473	2710	3557	5873	18273	221307
卫生、社会保障和社会福利业					24	43	315	18296
文化、体育和娱乐业	22	48	121	1458	655	1311	3656	81226
其他行业	11	61	41	1699	3824	7859	20881	1249150

注：本表数据来源于市工商局。

1-19 历年总供用电

Gross Electricity Supply over Years

单位：万千瓦时

年　份	总供电量	#网供	总售电量	#工业用电	#农村工业用电	照明用电
1978	16375	16376	14909	10828		1741
1979	19271	19271	17325	12474		2338
1980	21659	21569	19663	13407		3372
1981	22247	22247	19902	14194		4650
1982	26871	26351	23502	14618		6272
1983	31527	31527	27461	17496		8052
1984	32617	28566	28403	18019		9484
1985	38183	33907	33907	22139		9934
1986	39305	35100	35099	25567		10204
1987	64258	45129	57083	38076		16657
1988	94842	66295	84738	60226		22347
1989	120861	76762	108387	80050	60116	26139
1990	180142	111800	161479	119322	70459	39677
1991	240471	139841	216657	157062	99767	56504
1992	320003	180902	288688	210373	144391	25578
1993	436231	242205	393962	287400	205687	103583
1994	585763	393312	530232	416128	297479	110357
1995	680030	384764	616788	487873	386413	125135
1996	800300	506062	727093	569317	423898	153093
1997	949296	612907	866456	702811	519325	180583
1998	1094816	724758	1009086	781811	597601	221750
1999	1327788	973427	1234183	965945	756713	261629
2000	1780290	1349134	1690557	1345766	1104301	337044
2001	2077248	1649458	1965858	1567083	1400915	584700
2002	2585474	2219054	2471342	2070709	1877278	392879
2003	3216468	2846679	2835389	2401970	2071712	424869
2004	3728441	3196454	3502821	2966131	2539962	527332
2005	4156629	3422603	3965892	3303140	2873734	652514
2006	4644506	3676492	4455157	3686266	3234929	759384
2007	5078933	4167125	4825614	3956118	3483474	859851
2008	5073489	4423085	4873204	3928108	3424868	935510
2009	4888467	4318868	4781895	3761046	3292716	1011494
2010	5568902	5473261	5436637	4355690	3841990	1070692
2011	5793482	5699321	5666889	4457615	3919883	1196914

1-20 企业景气指数（2011年）

Business Climate Index (2011)

项　　目	一季度	二季度	三季度	四季度
企业景气指数	136.40	136.96	143.72	130.91
按行业门类分				
工业	138.89	134.35	143.98	129.96
建筑业	120.00	133.33	126.67	126.67
交通运输、仓储和邮政业	140.00	140.00	113.33	106.67
批发和零售业	141.72	151.31	152.55	144.18
房地产业	129.88	125.37	119.20	119.37
社会服务业	125.00	140.00	150.00	130.00
信息传输、计算机服务和软件业	135.55	157.14	167.32	153.04
住宿和餐饮业	147.70	125.02	145.02	125.02
按企业登记注册类型分				
国有企业	155.56	177.78	177.78	177.78
集体企业	109.09	145.45	136.36	118.18
股份合作企业	200.00	100.00	100.00	200.00
有限责任公司	124.15	132.06	136.71	123.44
股份有限公司	131.16	170.63	138.28	129.18
私营企业	134.67	136.66	149.16	124.16
港、澳、台投资企业	133.96	128.18	141.19	135.77
外商投资企业	145.19	129.00	137.05	119.33
按企业规模分				
大型	148.91	150.01	156.25	150.58
中型	130.00	131.43	132.86	108.57
小型	123.33	128.81	135.59	125.42
按观察指标分				
生产总量	73.69	128.48	133.96	90.76
盈利(亏损)变化	78.55	118.21	122.69	90.34
流动资金	125.89	120.75	120.75	124.72
货款拖欠	112.13	108.45	107.69	94.47
劳动力需求	120.86	114.04	124.29	111.64
固定资产投资	92.69	120.56	113.08	109.61
产品订货	100.19	119.84	131.24	105.85
企业融资	105.55	98.20	109.18	98.65

1-21 企业家信心指数（2011年）

Entrepreneurs' Confidence Index (2011)

项　　目	一季度	二季度	三季度	四季度
企业家信心指数	143.16	136.17	137.88	124.61
按行业门类分				
工业	143.40	133.77	137.24	124.76
建筑业	126.67	126.67	133.33	120.00
交通运输、仓储和邮政业	140.00	126.67	100.00	80.00
批发和零售业	140.85	139.22	148.97	129.67
房地产业	120.61	103.23	82.15	76.69
社会服务业	155.00	155.00	165.00	140.00
信息传输、计算机服务和软件业	180.00	171.43	167.32	167.32
住宿和餐饮业	126.89	136.62	131.62	135.02
按企业登记注册类型分				
国有企业	166.67	177.78	155.56	177.41
集体企业	127.27	118.18	118.18	118.18
股份合作企业	200.00	100.00	100.00	100.00
有限责任公司	136.73	136.38	137.91	120.33
股份有限公司	160.54	138.77	136.17	127.08
私营企业	140.51	149.16	149.16	136.66
港、澳、台投资企业	139.53	126.90	132.51	126.60
外商投资企业	141.25	128.22	125.32	107.64
按企业规模分				
大型	160.65	151.04	150.23	143.24
中型	134.29	125.71	134.29	115.71
小型	128.33	132.20	123.73	111.86

1-22 各行业企业景气指数（2011年）

Business Climate Index by Sector (2011)

指　　标	一季度	二季度	三季度	四季度
总指数				
工业				
企业综合生产经营	138.89	134.35	143.98	129.96
生产成本	66.23	48.97	37.27	80.18
生产总量	57.71	138.01	144.80	85.65
产品订货	108.01	124.22	143.41	119.79
#国外订货	104.99	117.07	109.34	96.27
产品销售量	61.24	139.83	150.28	86.45
产品销售价格	107.67	99.72	113.85	100.04
产成品库存	129.26	130.59	132.76	119.30
盈利(亏损)变化	74.77	118.89	127.87	90.14
流动资金	132.91	127.50	130.07	140.52
企业融资	110.96	100.79	121.01	105.65
货款拖欠	115.71	102.71	103.48	85.17
劳动力需求	125.20	117.50	131.34	107.72
固定资产投资	83.16	131.01	129.58	121.33
科技创新	121.05	108.40	111.74	106.14
原材料及能源购进价格	42.86	43.79	63.81	73.74
原材料及能源供应	137.42	127.95	140.00	134.14
建筑业				
企业综合生产经营	120.00	133.33	126.67	126.67
工程合同	73.33	100.00	100.00	120.00
#国(境)外合同	100.00	100.00	80.00	93.33
建筑工程量	60.00	100.00	86.67	106.67
新开工工程量	66.67	100.00	106.67	126.67
技术设备能力	180.00	173.33	180.00	173.33
工程进度	93.33	126.67	113.33	133.33
工程结算收入	93.33	93.33	86.67	93.33
建筑材料购进价格	20.00	40.00	20.00	66.67
工程结算成本	53.33	66.67	53.33	73.33
盈利(亏损)变化	100.00	106.67	86.67	86.67
流动资金	146.67	133.33	120.00	146.67
企业融资	133.33	120.00	100.00	106.67
工程款拖欠	140.00	120.00	120.00	113.33
劳动力需求	120.00	120.00	100.00	106.67
固定资产投资	106.67	106.67	106.67	106.67
交通运输、仓储和邮政业				
企业综合生产经营	140.00	140.00	113.33	106.67
业务预订	120.00	100.00	120.00	73.33
业务量	113.33	113.33	133.33	73.33
业务收费价格	113.33	106.67	106.67	100.00

1-22 续表 1

指　　标	一季度	二季度	三季度	四季度
业务成本	53.33	53.33	33.33	53.33
盈利(亏损)变化	100.00	73.33	140.00	93.33
流动资金	113.33	120.00	86.67	100.00
企业融资	100.00	100.00	93.33	73.33
货款拖欠	126.67	100.00	100.00	120.00
劳动力需求	133.33	86.67	80.00	100.00
固定资产投资	113.33	113.33	106.67	100.00
批发和零售业				
企业综合生产经营	141.72	151.31	152.55	144.18
购货合同	109.50	122.83	125.66	114.07
商品购进价格	65.43	70.96	59.47	79.47
商品销售	69.45	102.04	132.78	116.23
#出口	83.33	100.00	113.33	101.70
商品销售价格	118.25	114.72	114.37	110.53
商品库存	133.56	120.75	115.08	116.64
经营费用	75.68	84.79	70.96	52.98
竞争能力	131.97	137.65	133.81	136.55
盈利(亏损)变化	95.51	132.58	117.12	119.10
流动资金	101.01	115.20	106.89	99.77
企业融资	91.29	94.83	98.16	96.32
货款拖欠	100.00	111.10	105.93	108.16
劳动力需求	113.72	107.06	111.10	113.42
固定资产投资	103.33	108.16	96.52	106.46
房地产业				
企业综合生产经营	129.88	125.37	119.20	119.37
土地开发	89.40	100.89	87.30	87.26
完成投资	90.58	125.90	73.26	76.12
新开工面积	105.60	105.75	85.15	86.74
房屋竣工面积	91.25	94.08	64.18	82.04
商品房预售面积	48.94	95.73	56.27	47.37
商品房销售面积	79.09	100.02	87.84	41.21
商品房销售价格	103.84	99.33	93.23	87.85
空置商品房面积	163.18	140.76	133.29	163.18
盈利(亏损)变化	72.43	99.10	108.28	54.36
流动资金	113.73	86.24	87.02	74.33
企业融资	102.72	56.31	62.00	62.75
货款拖欠	121.39	128.10	122.58	102.37
劳动力需求	100.22	110.43	95.26	97.85
固定资产投资	116.89	92.42	78.38	97.62
社会服务业				
企业综合生产经营	125.00	140.00	150.00	130.00
服务预订	90.00	120.00	140.00	75.00

1-22　续表 2

指　　标	一 季 度	二 季 度	三 季 度	四 季 度
竞争能力	145.00	155.00	155.00	155.00
旅游客源	83.33	100.00	166.67	50.00
收费服务价格	105.00	80.00	125.00	70.00
业务量	105.00	120.00	135.00	75.00
营业成本	60.00	60.00	40.00	85.00
盈利(亏损)变化	70.00	120.00	120.00	80.00
流动资金	125.00	115.00	110.00	105.00
企业融资	95.00	105.00	95.00	90.00
货款拖欠	95.00	125.00	115.00	105.00
劳动力需求	115.00	95.00	125.00	115.00
固定资产投资	95.00	110.00	90.00	80.00
信息传输、计算机服务和软件业				
企业综合生产经营	135.55	157.14	167.32	153.04
产品销售	103.23	128.57	131.61	123.14
产品订货	117.16	123.27	130.41	100.51
竞争能力	185.57	171.43	166.15	173.29
销售(收费)价格	88.38	87.55	80.41	95.36
营业收入	66.07	138.75	138.75	101.71
营业成本	93.93	50.00	39.82	46.96
盈利(亏损)变化	87.14	144.70	116.13	101.71
流动资金	121.60	131.61	138.09	138.09
企业融资	100.50	115.49	144.72	122.63
货款拖欠	106.05	88.09	119.16	103.55
劳动力需求	119.38	149.34	142.86	148.80
固定资产投资	101.60	114.29	90.35	83.21
住宿和餐饮业				
企业综合生产经营	147.70	125.02	145.02	125.02
业务预订	99.33	118.75	130.31	133.63
业务量	112.71	125.55	140.31	140.00
竞争能力	142.70	145.02	131.10	131.10
客房出租	60.00	100.00	100.00	100.00
收费服务价格	104.73	114.73	110.00	113.12
营业收入	95.95	98.75	130.31	140.00
营业成本	52.80	50.00	54.97	43.40
盈利(亏损)变化	90.95	103.51	123.51	113.20
流动资金	121.60	115.00	135.00	131.60
企业融资	98.92	103.90	93.90	93.92
货款拖欠	107.57	105.82	98.93	99.74
劳动力需求	136.89	126.88	136.91	145.02
固定资产投资	102.97	122.97	113.38	117.97

1-23 企业宏观经济景气状况

Macro Economic Climate Situations of Enterprises

指　　标	2003年	2004年	2005年	2006年	2007年	2008年	2010年	2011年
一季度								
企业家信心指数	140.35	140.73	133.95	137.41	144.75	85.12	137.75	143.16
企业家对本行业景气状况判断(%)								
乐观	49.22	49.12	39.84	45.56	53.43	21.32	42.95	48.11
一般	41.90	42.49	54.26	46.28	37.89	42.48	51.84	46.94
不乐观	8.88	8.39	5.90	8.16	8.68	36.20	5.21	4.95
二季度								
企业家信心指数	130.04	139.03	132.04	134.53	142.57	96.52	135.42	136.17
企业家对本行业景气状况判断(%)								
乐观	44.42	49.19	40.67	45.15	53.04	24.00	43.01	41.61
一般	41.20	40.65	50.71	44.22	36.51	48.52	49.40	52.94
不乐观	14.38	10.16	8.62	10.63	10.45	27.48	7.59	5.45
三季度								
企业家信心指数	140.85	139.05	131.86	140.03	143.21	122.30	138.73	137.88
企业家对本行业景气状况判断(%)								
乐观	46.18	49.10	41.32	46.79	52.47	32.43	45.56	46.37
一般	48.49	40.85	49.22	46.46	38.28	57.44	47.61	45.14
不乐观	5.33	10.05	9.46	6.75	9.25	10.13	6.83	8.49
四季度								
企业家信心指数	140.20	133.60	133.05	141.76	148.18	128.02	142.00	124.61
企业家对本行业景气状况判断(%)								
乐观	47.03	45.05	43.59	49.91	54.11	36.40	49.37	37.04
一般	46.13	43.51	45.86	41.94	39.96	55.22	43.25	50.53
不乐观	6.83	11.44	10.55	8.15	5.93	8.38	7.38	12.43

1-24 企业综合生产经营状况

Comprehensive Production and Management Situations of Enterprises

指　　标	2003年	2004年	2005年	2006年	2007年	2008年	2010年	2011年
一季度								
企业景气指数	138.81	135.69	132.79	133.80	138.02	98.83	136.08	136.40
企业家对生产经营景气状况判断(%)								
良好	46.13	41.55	42.26	42.90	49.06	23.01	44.87	46.21
一般	46.55	52.59	48.27	48.00	39.90	52.81	46.33	43.98
不佳	7.32	5.86	9.47	9.10	11.04	24.18	8.80	9.81
二季度								
企业景气指数	119.33	138.85	134.75	135.51	141.44	114.33	135.80	136.96
企业家对生产经营景气状况判断(%)								
良好	38.17	45.61	43.39	43.95	48.04	27.65	42.61	44.40
一般	43.00	47.64	47.96	47.61	45.36	59.03	50.57	48.15
不佳	18.83	6.75	8.65	8.44	6.60	13.32	6.82	7.45
三季度								
企业景气指数	139.73	138.48	131.49	141.85	147.21	131.17	143.78	143.72
企业家对生产经营景气状况判断(%)								
良好	43.67	46.38	38.46	47.09	52.18	39.20	50.79	50.04
一般	52.40	45.74	54.57	47.67	42.84	52.78	42.20	43.63
不佳	3.93	7.88	6.97	5.24	4.98	8.02	7.01	6.33
四季度								
企业景气指数	142.20	135.06	131.09	141.19	142.76	133.40	143.47	130.91
企业家对生产经营景气状况判断(%)								
良好	46.34	44.44	39.85	45.90	51.67	41.72	49.68	41.02
一般	49.52	46.18	51.39	49.38	39.42	49.96	44.11	48.86
不佳	4.14	9.38	8.76	4.72	8.91	8.32	6.21	10.12

1-25 历年国民经济主要指标人均水平

The Per Capita Level of Main National Economic Indicators over Years

年　份	人均地区生产总值（元）	人均地方财政收入（元）	人均出口总　额（美元）	人均消费品零售额（元）	人均固定资产投资额（元）	人　均用电量（千瓦时）	年末人均储蓄存款余额（元）
1978	553	60	36	192	21	135	49
1979	593	59	48	224	15	155	64
1980	643	60	69	281	21	175	104
1981	802	60	81	354	33	175	178
1982	991	70	94	417	157	204	238
1983	1115	73	102	447	157	235	328
1984	1350	72	110	625	254	240	520
1985	1885	93	146	781	589	283	761
1986	2462	132	191	1004	945	288	1068
1987	3170	163	216	1214	1145	461	1519
1988	4408	215	253	1959	1315	674	1965
1989	4768	250	273	2116	392	848	2529
1990	6173	274	436	2454	576	1239	2592
1991	5095	236	879	1943	732	1154	3074
1992	5038	263	1217	2073	883	1350	3580
1993	5850	385	1318	2615	1345	1617	4131
1994	6357	277	1548	3070	5074	1911	5130
1995	7421	366	2468	3577	1998	1952	6924
1996	8444	268	2553	3489	1879	2021	8300
1997	9747	278	2774	3564	1608	2114	9758
1998	11265	324	2799	3753	1650	2162	10740
1999	12494	344	2851	3806	1662	2322	10890
2000	13679	503	2834	3884	1700	2792	10422
2001	15268	693	2923	4244	1932	3026	12212
2002	18131	845	3626	4907	2926	3775	15297
2003	22174	1030	4275	5645	4876	4329	18788
2004	27554	1261	5369	6506	6940	5344	21836
2005	33287	1585	6240	7719	9106	6047	26343
2006	39173	1922	7062	8934	10516	6641	29364
2007	45057	2658	8588	10301	11994	6881	29577
2008	50471	2851	8931	12008	12869	6641	35146
2009	48988	3009	7180	12482	14239	6224	36950
2010	52798	3455	8653	13777	13863	6760	41179
2011	57470	3799	9506	15368	13104	6877	45037

注：1. 人均指标1991年以前按户籍人口计算，1991年起按常住人口计算；时点数按年末人口计算，时期数按年平均人口计算。
2. 人均指标2006-2010年数据，根据东莞市第六次全国人口普查数据结果重新修订，下同。

主要统计指标解释

Explanatory Notes on Main Statistical Indicators

国内（地区）生产总值　指按市场价格计算的一个国家（或地区）所有常住单位在一定时期内生产活动的最终成果。国内（地区）生产总值有三种计算方法，即生产法、收入法和支出法。三种方法分别从不同的方面反映国内（地区）生产总值及其构成。

增加值　指常住单位生产过程创造的新增价值和固定资产的转移价值。它可以按生产法计算，也可以按收入法计算，按生产法计算，它等于总产出减去中间投入；按收入法计算，它等于劳动者报酬、生产税净额、固定资产折旧和营业盈余之和。

劳动者报酬　指劳动者因从事生产活动所获得的全部报酬，包括劳动者获得的各种形式的工资、奖金和津贴，既包括货币形式的，也包括实物形式的，还包括劳动者所享受的公费医疗和医药卫生费、上下班交通补贴和单位支付的社会保险费、住房公积金等。对于个体经济来说，其所有者所获得的劳动报酬和经营利润不易区分，这两部分统一作为劳动者报酬处理。

生产税净额　指生产税减生产补贴后的差额。生产税指政府对生产单位从事生产、销售和经营活动以及因从事生产活动使用某些生产要素（如固定资产、土地、劳动力）所征收的各种税、附加费和规费。生产补贴与生产税相反，指政府对生产单位的单方面转移支付，因此视为负生产税，包括政策性亏损补贴、价格补贴等。

固定资产折旧　指一定时期内为弥补固定资产损耗按照规定的固定资产折旧率提取的固定资产折旧，或按国民经济核算统一规定的折旧率虚拟计算的固定资产折旧。它反映了固定资产在当期生产中的转移价值。各类企业和企业化管理的事业单位的固定资产折旧是指实际计提的折旧费；不计提折旧的政府机关、非企业化管理的事业单位和居民住房的固定资产折旧是按照统一规定的折旧率和固定资产原值计算的虚拟折旧。

营业盈余　指常住单位创造的增加值扣除劳动者报酬、固定资产折旧和生产税净额后的余额。它相当于企业的营业利润加上生产补贴，但要扣除从利润中开支的工资和福利等。

三次产业　根据社会生产活动历史发展的顺序对产业结构的划分，产品直接取自自然界的部门称为第一产业，初级产品进行再加工的部门称为第二产业，为生产和消费提供各种服务的部门称为第三产业。它是世界上通用的产业结构分类，但各国的划分不尽一致。我国的三次产业划分是：

第一产业：农林牧渔业

第二产业：工业（包括采矿业，制造业，电力、燃气及水的生产和供应业）和建筑业。

第三产业：除第一、二产业以外的其他行业。第三产业包括：交通运输、仓储和邮政业，信息传输、计算机服务和软件业，批发和零售业，住宿和餐饮业，金融业，房地产业，租赁和商务服务业，科学研究、技术服务和地质勘查业，水利、环境和公共设施管理业，居民服务和其他服务业，教育，卫生、社会保障和社会福利业，文化、体育和娱乐业，公共管理和社会组织，国际组织。

景气指数　亦称景气度，是对企业景气调查中的定性指标通过定量方法加工汇总，综合反映某一特定调查群体或某一社会经济现象所处的状态或发展趋势的一种指标，景气指数介于 0－200 之间，100 为景气指数的临界值；当景气指数大于 100 时，表明经济状况趋于上升或改善，处于景气状态；当景气指数小于 100 时，表明经济状况趋于下降或恶化，处于不景气状态。

企业景气指数　亦称企业综合生产经营景气指数，是根据企业家对本企业综合生产经营情况的判断与预期（通常为对“良好”、“一般”、“不佳”的选择）而编制的指数，用以综合反映企业的生产经营状况。

企业家信心指数 亦称宏观经济景气指数，.是根据企业家对企业对外部市场经济环境与宏观政策的认识、看法、判断与预期（通常为对“乐观”、“一般”、“不乐观”的选择）而编制的指数，用以综合反映企业家对宏观经济环境的感受与信心。

发展速度 用以反映社会经济发展程度的相对指标，根据两个时期发展水平的对比而得。由于比较的标准时期不同，发展速度可分为定基发展速度和环比发展速度两种。

增长速度 发展速度 - 1（或 100%）就是增长速度。即增长速度=发展速度 - 1（或 100%）。

平均每年增长速度 我国计算平均增长速度有两种方法，一种是习惯上经常使用的“水平法”，又称几何平均法，是以间隔最后一年的水平同基期水平对比来计算平均每年增长（或下降）的速度；另一种是“累计法”又称代数平均法或方程法，是以间隔年内各年水平的总和同基期水平对比来计算平均每年增长（或下降）的速度。具体计算方法，可参照中国财经出版社出版的《平均增长速度查对表》。

在一般正常情况下，两种方法计算的平均每年增长速度比较接近，但在经济发展不平衡出现大起大落时，两种方法计算的结果差别较大。

本《年鉴》内所列的平均每年增长速度都是用水平法计算的。从某年到某年平均增长速度的年份，均不包基期年在内。如 1981-2011 年平均每年增长速度，是以 1980 年为基期，2011 年为报告期，年份从 1981 年算起，共 31 年。

二、人口与劳动力

Population and Labor Force

2-1 历年总人口数与人口密度

Total Population and Density over Years

单位：万人

年 份	户籍人口	按性别分		按农业、非农业分		外来暂住人口	常住人口	人口密度(人/平方公里)
		男	女	农业人口	非农业人口			
1949	68.24	32.87	35.37	56.29	11.95			
1952	71.68	34.53	37.15	58.69	12.99			
1957	77.48	37.50	39.98	62.52	14.96			
1962	79.64	38.07	41.57	64.42	15.22			
1965	86.46	41.83	44.63	70.28	16.18			
1970	98.56	47.91	50.65	81.26	17.30			
1975	107.94	52.70	55.24	90.37	17.57			
1978	111.23	54.34	56.89	92.74	18.29			451
1979	112.04	54.45	57.59	92.86	19.18			455
1980	112.70	54.43	58.27	92.87	19.83			457
1981	114.46	55.36	59.10	94.08	20.38			464
1982	116.19	56.28	59.91	95.32	20.87			471
1983	117.59	57.05	60.54	96.36	21.23			477
1984	118.95	57.80	61.15	96.47	22.48			483
1985	120.85	58.84	62.01	95.36	25.49			490
1986	123.01	59.95	63.06	96.53	26.48	15.62		499
1987	124.86	61.02	63.84	97.20	27.66	25.29		507
1988	126.76	62.09	64.67	97.96	28.80	36.89		514
1989	128.76	63.27	65.49	98.82	29.94	47.19		522
1990	131.85	64.96	66.89	100.99	30.86	65.59	175.62	712
1991	133.65	66.10	67.55	101.79	31.86	80.58	200.01	811
1992	136.06	67.55	68.51	103.35	32.71	114.48	227.78	924
1993	138.92	69.20	69.72	105.18	33.74	121.70	259.41	1052
1994	141.40	70.64	70.76	106.85	34.55	139.09	295.43	1198
1995	143.65	71.97	71.68	108.27	35.38	142.18	336.45	1365
1996	145.25	72.92	72.33	109.11	36.14	143.32	383.17	1554
1997	147.12	74.04	73.08	110.15	36.97	144.68	436.38	1770
1998	148.77	74.99	73.78	110.93	37.84	199.11	496.97	2016
1999	150.82	76.18	74.64	112.09	38.73	244.81	565.98	2296
2000	152.61	77.22	75.39	113.00	39.61	254.72	644.84	2616
2001	153.89	77.94	75.95	113.52	40.37	457.82	654.43	2655
2002	156.19	79.14	77.05	115.17	41.02	433.65	654.84	2657
2003	158.96	80.65	78.31	102.09	56.87	440.45	655.25	2658
2004	161.97	82.25	79.72	100.49	61.48	486.95	655.66	2660
2005	165.65	84.07	81.58	99.81	65.84	584.98	656.07	2662
2006	168.31	85.43	82.88	97.89	70.42	586.76	685.66	2782
2007	171.26	87.00	84.26	97.59	73.67	557.80	717.02	2909
2008	174.86	88.88	85.98	98.06	76.80	552.50	750.60	3045
2009	178.73	90.78	87.95	97.27	81.46	429.96	786.08	3189
2010	181.77	92.27	89.50	89.68	92.09	411.47	822.48	3343
2011	184.77	93.76	91.01	90.31	94.46	413.62	825.48	3356

注：1. 人口密度1990年以前户籍人口计算，1990年起按常住人口计算。
　　2. 常住人口2006-2010年数据，根据东莞市第六次全国人口普查数据结果重新修订，下同。

2-2 主要年份户籍人口与劳动力指标

Main Indicators of Household Population and Labor in Main Years

指　　标	单 位	1985年	1990年	1995年	2000年	2005年	2010年	2011年
年末户籍人口	人	1208515	1318526	1436525	1526090	1656541	1817709	1847691
#农业人口	人	953582	1009857	1082703	1130002	998159	896789	903139
人口性别比(女性人口=100)	%	94.9	97.1	100.4	102.4	103.1	103.1	103
人口密度	人/平方公里	490	535	583	619	672	739	751
人口出生率	‰	15.4	17.1	17.6	12.1	10.6	10.9	10.9
人口死亡率	‰	4.5	4.8	4.8	4.6	4.6	4.7	4.8
人口自然增长率	‰	10.8	12.3	12.8	7.5	6.0	6.2	6.1
人口净迁移率	‰	3.0	1.9	1.9	2.2	16.4	12.0	11.5
城镇新登记的失业人员人数	人			6536	6524	7080	3207	5545
城镇失业人员安置就业人数	人				5683	6088	3796	11345

2-3 历年户籍人口自然变动情况

Changes of Household Population over Years

年　份	出　生		死　亡		自然增长	
	人　数（人）	出生率（‰）	人　数（人）	死亡率（‰）	人　数（人）	自然增长率(‰)
1978	20728	18.73	5451	4.92	15277	13.81
1979	26931	24.13	5755	5.13	21176	19.00
1980	27428	24.41	5747	5.10	21681	19.31
1981	24828	21.86	6016	5.29	18812	16.57
1982	21991	19.07	5681	4.93	16310	14.14
1983	19573	16.74	6100	5.21	13473	11.53
1984	18380	15.54	5841	4.94	12539	10.60
1985	18432	15.37	5439	4.54	12993	10.83
1986	20049	16.44	5955	4.88	14094	11.56
1987	19962	16.11	5502	4.44	14459	11.67
1988	21077	16.75	5863	4.66	15214	12.09
1989	23457	17.06	5966	4.67	17491	12.39
1990	22238	17.07	6208	4.76	16030	12.31
1991	23771	17.91	6070	4.57	17701	13.34
1992	26040	19.31	6485	4.81	19555	14.50
1993	25270	18.38	6833	4.97	18437	13.41
1994	24152	17.88	6319	4.51	17833	13.37
1995	25312	17.59	6898	4.84	18414	12.75
1996	24635	17.05	7333	5.08	17302	11.97
1997	24106	16.50	6448	4.41	17658	12.09
1998	22563	15.31	6553	4.45	16010	10.86
1999	21673	14.55	6460	4.34	15213	10.22
2000	18260	12.11	6923	4.59	11337	7.52
2001	17083	11.16	6344	4.14	10739	7.01
2002	16029	10.35	6873	4.44	9156	5.91
2003	16204	10.34	7346	4.69	8858	5.65
2004	17312	10.86	7814	4.90	9498	5.96
2005	17301	10.62	7497	4.60	9804	6.02
2006	16819	10.14	7103	4.28	9716	5.86
2007	17482	10.39	7418	4.41	10064	5.98
2008	18382	10.77	7752	4.54	10630	6.23
2009	18584	10.67	7587	4.36	10997	6.31
2010	19509	10.90	8367	4.68	11142	6.23
2011	19884	10.92	8728	4.79	11156	6.13

2-4 历年户籍人口迁移变动情况

Changes of Household Migration over Years

年份	迁入		迁出		总迁移		净迁移	
	人数（人）	迁入率（‰）	人数（人）	迁出率（‰）	人数（人）	总迁移率（‰）	人数（人）	净迁移率（‰）
1978	10148	9.2	13179	11.9	23327	21.1	-3031	-2.7
1980	13345	11.9	28624	25.5	41969	37.4	-15279	-13.6
1985	19205	16.0	15636	13.0	34841	29.1	3569	3.0
1990	13485	10.4	11061	8.5	24546	18.8	2424	1.9
1991	12628	9.5	12531	9.4	25159	19.0	97	0.1
1992	14622	10.8	11168	8.3	25790	19.1	3454	2.5
1993	10801	7.9	4886	3.6	15687	11.4	5915	4.3
1994	10127	7.2	6406	4.6	16533	11.8	3721	2.7
1995	10312	7.2	7675	5.4	17987	12.6	2637	1.9
1996	9273	6.4	11508	8.0	20781	14.4	-2235	-1.6
1997	10284	7.0	9469	6.5	19753	13.5	815	0.6
1998	12400	8.4	11253	7.6	23653	16.0	1147	0.8
1999	15049	10.0	11497	7.6	26546	17.6	3552	2.4
2000	15618	10.2	12314	8.1	27932	18.3	3304	2.2
2001	15968	10.4	11099	7.2	27067	17.6	4869	3.2
2002	20214	12.9	8033	5.1	28247	18.1	12181	7.8
2003	27143	17.1	7173	4.5	34316	21.6	19970	12.6
2004	29621	18.3	7618	4.7	37239	23.0	22003	13.6
2005	43026	26.0	15798	9.5	58824	35.5	27228	16.4
2006	30710	18.2	11442	6.8	42152	25.0	19268	11.4
2007	26940	15.7	4847	2.8	31787	18.6	22093	12.9
2008	33595	19.2	5974	3.4	39569	22.6	27621	15.8
2009	36387	20.4	7381	4.1	43768	24.5	29006	16.2
2010	28534	15.7	6651	3.7	35185	19.4	21883	12.0
2011	28623	15.5	7425	4.0	36048	19.5	21198	11.5

2-5 主要年份外来暂住人口和外来劳动力

Temporary Residents and Labor in Main Years

单位：人

项　目	1995年	1997年	1998年	1999年	2000年	2001年	2002年	2003年
一、外来暂住人口总计	1421754	1446830	1991122	2448134	2547221	4578163	4336453	4404467
(一) 按性别分								
男	581304	554193	850266	1084492	1155277	2138218	1973316	2198324
女	840450	892637	1140856	1363642	1391944	2439945	2363137	2206143
(二) 按来自地区分								
省内	371816	298510	402267	504722	485889	731931	722894	665549
省外	1023510	1130981	1569963	1921206	2041959	3826830	3593034	3720408
#湖南省	253574	243384	330241	391491	377257	718295	685311	663487
四川省	223727	227077	294149	387730	319039	622166	555569	591145
广西自治区	149478	140483	183734	236936	240923	442904	394088	432738
湖北省	84727	89140	143662	173787	196697	359872	389735	443603
江西省	67562	83272	118685	149000	157323	294740	294086	339518
港澳台	23729	16048	17557	20664	17547	17975	18856	16986
国外	2699	1291	1335	1542	1826	1427	1669	1524
二、外来劳动力总计	1265368	1307279	1831939	2161487	2448415	4496771	4260142	4327312
按行业分								
工业	1084860	1114235	1577922	1609539	2043270	3681099	3573355	3753904
农业	54714	57214	68143	113324	88195	174936	127584	85109
商业	52965	67242	100041	282938	187015	283277	300642	278632
服务业	72829	68588	85833	155686	129935	357459	258561	209667

注：本表根据市公安局统计数据整理。

2-5 续表

单位：人

项　目	2004年	2005年	2006年	2007年	2008年	2009年	2010年	2011年
一、外来暂住人口总计	4869462	5849785	5867555	5577988	5525022	4299615	4114745	4136177
(一) 按性别分								
男	2347115	2746833	2775718	2666292	2657712	2093055	2010869	2054179
女	2522347	3102952	3091837	2911696	2867310	2206560	2103876	2081998
(二) 按来自地区分								
省内	747804	1036417	1012637	986062	1012341	889160	791665	900560
省外	4096599	4747692	4807064	4551507	4468505	3367565	3275768	3194930
#湖南省	812976	844053	875904	816688	828779	604891	587153	571601
四川省	581272	642170	617644	553907	533496	441758	411005	370717
广西自治区	483329	574634	556961	497438	488226	396425	405051	387198
湖北省	490063	514760	531987	521529	517519	391650	353414	350490
江西省	329715	376526	367094	355798	353738	269133	252936	264965
港澳台	21700	59798	44653	36321	37329	35630	37665	31731
国外	3359	5878	3201	4098	6847	7260	9647	8956
二、外来劳动力总计	4733903	5534248	5669798	5389490	5303008	4134581	3912274	3947135
按行业分								
工业	4078400	4676454	4820388	4480800	4227211	3361306	3191436	3277984
农业	98272	107933	124942	102519	97597	74982	92451	82025
商业	315021	420810	412180	460114	560345	430183	402786	358941
服务业	242210	329051	312288	346057	417855	268110	225601	228185

2-6 历年外来暂住人口与外来劳动力

Temporary Residents and Labor over Years

单位：人

年　份	外来暂住人口总计	按性别分		按省内省外分		外来劳动力	工　业	农　业	商　业	服务业
		男　性	女　性	本　省	外　省					
1986	156222					104091	87154	9849	2509	4579
1987	252895					180285	154842	13110	4181	8152
1988	368913					292499	260237	16911	5797	9554
1989	481850					405287	365840	19893	7763	11791
1990	655902			333180	322722	572044	518971	25576	10793	16704
1991	805790			360379	445411	701982	633400	25838	17945	24799
1992	1144753	440500	704253	494278	650475	1071048	874149	62324	88087	46488
1993	1217010	529096	687914	370770	846240	1126813	933147	40177	88524	64965
1994	1390884	547435	843449	380790	1010094	1241814	1069478	52146	39869	80321
1995	1421754	581304	840450	371816	1023510	1265368	1084860	54714	52965	72829
1996	1433157	606524	826633	305821	1106749	1276626	1084330	64732	61092	66472
1997	1446830	554193	892637	298510	1130981	1307279	1114235	57214	67242	68588
1998	1991122	850266	1140856	402267	1569963	1831939	1577922	68143	100041	85833
1999	2448134	1084492	1363642	504722	1921206	2161487	1609539	113324	282938	155686
2000	2547221	1155277	1391944	485889	2041959	2448415	2043270	88195	187015	129935
2001	4578163	2138218	2439945	731931	3826830	4496771	3681099	174936	283277	357459
2002	4336453	1973316	2363137	722894	3593034	4260142	3573355	127584	300642	258561
2003	4404467	2198324	2206143	665549	3720408	4327312	3753904	85109	278632	209667
2004	4869462	2347115	2522347	747804	4096599	4733903	4078400	98272	315021	242210
2005	5849785	2746833	3102952	1036417	4747692	5534248	4676454	107933	420810	329051
2006	5867555	2775718	3091837	1012637	4807064	5669798	4820388	124942	412180	312288
2007	5577988	2666292	2911696	986062	4551507	5389490	4480800	102519	460114	346057
2008	5525022	2657712	2867310	1012341	4468505	5303008	4227211	97597	560345	417855
2009	4299615	2093055	2206560	889160	3367565	4134581	3361306	74982	430183	268110
2010	4114745	2010869	2103876	791665	3275768	3912274	3191436	92451	402786	225601
2011	4136177	2054179	2081998	900560	3194930	3947135	3277984	82025	358941	228185

2-7 主要年份城镇职工年末人数

Number of Employed Persons in Urban Areas at Year-end in Main Years

单位：人

项　　目	1985年	1990年	1995年	2000年	2005年	2010年	2011年
合　　计	122951	131631	178724	164080	188579	226268	246083
第一产业	2432	2053	620	476	483	625	966
第二产业	64525	72993	110885	76153	80596	87136	82164
工　业	60571	68508	105782	68354	79359	84992	80648
采矿业			130	62	59	52	54
制造业			99194	62790	71569	77544	72885
电力、燃气及水的生产和供应业			6458	5502	7731	7396	7709
建筑业			5103	7799	1237	2144	1516
第三产业	55994	56585	67219	87451	107500	138507	162953
#金融业	2270	4291	9487	13945	16584	20706	28004
房地产业	1551	2529	73	387	427	488	490
公共管理和社会组织	5854	7887	9711	15733	28542	41676	43341

注：2000年起为城镇在岗职工人数。

2-8 历年分行业城镇职工人数

Numbers of Employers by Sector in Urban Areas over Years

单位：人

年 份	年末城镇职工人数合计	第一产业	第二产业	#工业	第三产业
1978	81971	2875	41179	38729	37917
1979	96807	3051	44905	42251	48851
1980	98587	2637	47374	44737	48576
1981	106626	2897	52638	50370	51091
1982	114119	2133	56391	52418	55595
1983	115926	1978	58139	53246	55809
1984	117627	1933	59129	54916	56565
1985	122951	2432	64525	60571	55994
1986	132744	2252	73922	65674	56570
1987	136666	2359	76393	69985	57914
1988	127098	2702	69385	64631	55011
1989	131039	2397	73042	68738	55600
1990	131631	2053	72993	68508	56585
1991	145873	2083	84992	79389	58793
1992	154712	2043	89713	82611	62955
1993	176578	1933	107296	92212	67349
1994	160872	621	95378	83322	64873
1995	178724	620	110885	105782	67219
1996	174964	497	98061	91228	76406
1997	164987	616	82513	76619	81858
1998	164047	779	80510	70499	82758
1999	163917	583	76905	68860	86429
2000	164080	476	76153	68354	87451
2001	164226	444	76181	69260	87601
2002	164209	431	75384	68348	88394
2003	165978	522	73357	72118	92099
2004	175415	565	78003	76786	96847
2005	188579	483	80596	79359	107500
2006	199878	483	84618	83328	114777
2007	205640	487	81448	79949	123705
2008	207234	459	77982	76563	128793
2009	225990	477	94365	92943	131148
2010	226268	625	87136	84992	138507
2011	246083	966	82164	80648	162953

注：2000年起城镇职工为城镇在岗职工口径。

2-9 主要年份国有单位分行业年末职工人数

Number of Employed Persons in State-owned Units at Year-end by Sector in Main Years

单位：人

指　　标	1985年	1990年	1995年	2000年	2005年	2010年	2011年
合　　计	56534	63469	71165	78216	94902	121690	137735
按企业、事业、机关单位分							
企业	40201	43538	38022	31988	20401	20348	27928
事业	11362	13072	23147	31506	46382	60310	67531
机关	4971	6859	9996	14722	28119	41032	42276
按国民经济行业分							
第一产业	2264	1956	712	476	483	625	966
第二产业	22373	22877	17363	11658	4442	4888	4985
工　业	20919	19390	14610	10119	3471	3638	3735
采矿业	423	72	130	62	59	52	54
制造业	19625	16912	12908	6611	1217	981	1007
电力、燃气及水的生产和供应业	871	2406	1572	3446	2195	2605	2674
建筑业	1454	3487	2753	1539	971	1250	1250
第三产业	31897	38571	53090	66082	89977	116177	131784
交通运输、仓储及邮政业					3381	2182	5129
信息传输、计算机服务和软件业					2243	2275	2274
批发和零售业					1582	1790	1641
住宿和餐饮业							
金融业	943	2215	5634	7343	9401	9319	13921
房地产业	138	149	44	98	244	329	336
租赁和商务服务业					676	1437	1441
科学研究、技术服务和地质勘查业					1496	1928	2075
水利、环境和公共设施管理业					484	542	596
居民服务和其他服务业					95	105	157
教育					23301	26138	26314
卫生、社会保障和社会福利业					17134	26795	32860
文化、体育和娱乐业					1398	1661	1699
公共管理和社会组织	4971	6859	9563	15372	28542	41676	43341
国际组织							

注：2000年起为城镇在岗职工人数，下同。

2-10 主要年份城镇集体单位分行业年末职工人数

Number of Employed Persons in Urban Collective-owned Units at Year-end by Sector in Main Years

单位：人

指 标	1985年	1990年	1995年	2000年	2005年	2010年	2011年
合 计	63383	58749	64923	50592	44251	35106	33956
按企业、事业、机关单位分							
企业	58258	54671	63194	49257	43200	34245	33095
事业	4062	3050	1581	974	1051	861	861
机关	1063	1028	148	361			
按国民经济行业分							
第一产业	168	97	33				
第二产业	39858	41795	52334	34958	32778	23765	21884
工 业	37358	40979	49984	28698	32527	22879	21626
采矿业		433					
制造业		40458	48600	27268	30772	21497	20540
电力、燃气及水的生产和供应业		88	1384	1430	1755	1382	1086
建筑业	2500	998	2350	6260	251	886	258
第三产业	23357	16857	12556	15634	11473	11341	12072
交通运输、仓储及邮政业					3446	3543	3156
信息传输、计算机服务和软件业					45	40	
批发和零售业					2078	1818	1859
住宿和餐饮业					307	289	291
金融业	1327	2076	3844	3437	4184	4533	5713
房地产业			29	289	183	159	154
租赁和商务服务业					843	677	645
科学研究、技术服务和地质勘查业					16	56	56
水利、环境和公共设施管理业					237	112	98
居民服务和其他服务业							
教育							
卫生、社会保障和社会福利业					92	64	34
文化、体育和娱乐业					42	50	66
公共管理和社会组织	1063	1028	148	361			
国际组织							

2-11 主要年份其他所有制单位分行业年末职工人数

Number of Employed Persons in Other Ownership Units at Year-end by Sector in Main Years

单位：人

指　　标	1985年	1990年	1995年	2000年	2005年	2010年	2011年
合　　计	3034	9413	42636	35272	49426	69472	74392
按企业、事业、机关单位分							
企业	2312	9413	42597	35272	49426	69472	74392
事业	722		39				
机关							
按国民经济行业分							
第一产业							
第二产业	2294	8321	41188	29537	43376	58483	55295
工　业	2294	8321	41188	29537	43361	58475	55287
采矿业		48					
制造业		8273	37686	28911	39580	55066	51338
电力、燃气及水的生产和供应业			3502	626	3781	3409	3949
建筑业					15	8	8
第三产业	740	1092	1448	5735	6050	10989	19097
#交通运输、仓储及邮政业					412	702	7112
信息传输、计算机服务和软件业					240	220	220
批发和零售业					1530	2607	2788
住宿和餐饮业					678	450	456
金融业			9	3165	2999	6854	8370
房地产业	722						
租赁和商务服务业					191	156	151
卫生、社会保障和社会福利业							

2-12 主要年份工业、建筑业企业年末城镇职工人数

Number of Urban Employed Persons in Industrial and Construction Enterprises at Year-end in Main Years

单位：人

指　　标	1985年	1990年	1995年	2000年	2005年	2010年	2011年
一、工业总计	105782	91228	82474	68354	79359	84992	80648
（一）按经济类型分							
国有经济单位	14610	15121	14477	10119	3471	3638	3735
城镇集体经济单位	49984	38822	32620	28698	32527	22879	21626
其他各种经济单位	41188	37285	35377	29537	43361	58475	55287
（二）按工业行业分(大类)							
非金属矿采选业	130	43	66	62	59	52	54
农副食品加工业	4664	4419	3978	2884	249	398	392
食品制造业	1842	542	583	368	159	137	202
饮料制造业	3944	2976	2814	584	570	1400	1428
烟草制品业							
纺织业	2722	1561	1547	1990	1928	1252	1313
纺织服装、鞋、帽制造业	11769	13199	6749	4162	5068	6628	6730
皮革、毛皮、羽毛(绒)及其制品业	3692	2756	1688	106	209	167	183
木材加工及木、竹、藤、棕、草制品业	1190	1056	910	362	45		
家具制造业	433	192	154	29	5246	6036	
造纸及纸制品业	1697	1540	938	1079	1241	976	1016
印刷业和记录媒介的复制	2065	1493	1734	773	1074	986	863
文教、体育用品制造业	7192	1463	1173	9	254	249	249
石油加工、炼焦及核燃料加工业							
化学原料及化学制品制造业	1921	1325	1284	869	662	1204	1263
医药制造业	1115	915	689	2719	1890	1927	1918
化学纤维制造业	25	25					
橡胶制品业		9	520	148			
塑料制品业	3783	3855	3235	1418	1739	2259	2537
非金属矿物制品业	4909	3882	3159	1939	3556	1126	1278
黑色金属冶炼及压延加工业							
有色金属冶炼及压延加工业	59	205	205	86	74	83	80
金属制品业	2862	1767	1664	2226	768	482	494
通用设备制造业	2097	2825	2666	1308	890	1093	1117
专用设备制造业	1819	942	1968	560	240	1533	1382
交通运输设备制造业	1729	972	827	375	329	1976	1619
电气机械及器材制造业	14755	10017	11197	16028	13638	12792	15769
通信设备、计算机及其他电子设备制造业	14129	12589	14310	14121	17812	21330	18191
仪器仪表及文化、办公用机械制造业	4884	6617	8107	7262	13759	12812	14150
工艺品及其他制造业				1385	130	673	676
电力、热力的生产和供应业	6068	4993	5199	4579	6487	5687	5783
水的生产和供应业	390	415	590	923	1244	1709	1926
二、建筑业总计	5103	6833		7799	1237	2144	1516
国有经济单位	2753	1462	1362	1539	971	1250	1250
城镇集体经济单位	2350	4771	4532	6260	251	886	258
其他各种经济单位		600			15	8	8

2-13 按经济类型分行业城镇职工人数及构成（2011年）

Employed Persons in Urban Areas by Registration Status and Sector (2011)

项　　目	合　计	国有经济单位	城镇集体经济单位	其他经济单位
合　　计(人)	246083	137735	33956	74392
第一产业	966	966		
第二产业	82164	4985	21884	55295
工　业	80648	3735	21626	55287
采掘业	54	54		
制造业	72885	1007	20540	51338
电力、燃气及水的生产和供应业	7709	2674	1086	3949
建筑业	1516	1250	258	8
第三产业	162953	131784	12072	19097
交通运输、仓储及邮政业	15397	5129	3156	7112
信息传输、计算机服务和软件业	2494	2274		220
批发和零售业	6288	1641	1859	2788
住宿和餐饮业	747		291	456
金融业	28004	13921	5713	8370
房地产业	490	336	154	
租赁和商务服务业	2237	1441	645	151
科学研究、技术服务和地质勘查业	2131	2075	56	
水利、环境和公共设施管理业	694	596	98	
居民服务和其他服务业	157	157		
教育	26314	26314		
卫生、社会保障和社会福利业	32894	32860	34	
文化、体育和娱乐业	1765	1699	66	
公共管理和社会组织	43341	43341		
国际组织				
占全部职工人数的比重(%)	100	55.97	13.80	30.23
第一产业	0.39	0.39		
第二产业	33.39	2.03	8.89	22.47
工　业	32.77	1.52	8.79	22.47
采矿业	0.02	0.02		
制造业	29.62	0.41	8.35	20.86
电力、燃气及水的生产和供应业	3.13	1.09	0.44	1.60
建筑业	0.62	0.51	0.10	0.00
第三产业	66.22	53.55	4.91	7.76
交通运输、仓储及邮政业	6.26	2.08	1.28	2.89
信息传输、计算机服务和软件业	1.01	0.92		0.09
批发和零售业	2.56	0.67	0.76	1.13
住宿和餐饮业	0.30		0.12	0.19
金融业	11.38	5.66	2.32	3.40
房地产业	0.20	0.14	0.06	
租赁和商务服务业	0.91	0.59	0.26	0.06
科学研究、技术服务和地质勘查业	0.87	0.84	0.02	
水利、环境和公共设施管理业	0.28	0.24	0.04	
居民服务和其他服务业	0.06	0.06		
教育	10.69	10.69		
卫生、社会保障和社会福利业	13.37	13.35	0.01	
文化、体育和娱乐业	0.72	0.69	0.03	
公共管理和社会组织	17.61	17.61		
国际组织				

主要统计指标解释

Explanatory Notes on Main Statistical Indicators

人口数 指一定时点、一定地区范围内的有生命的个人的总和。年度统计的年末人口数是指每年12月31日24时的人口数。

常住人口 包括居住在本乡镇街道、户口在本乡镇街道或户口待定的人；居住在本乡镇街道、离开户口所在的乡镇街道半年以上的人；户口在本乡镇街道、外出不满半年或在境外工作学习的人。

外来暂住人口 指户口登记地在外县、市而目前在本市暂住的人口。

性别比 反映两性人口之间比例的指标。指在总人口中或在各年龄人口中，男性人数与女性人数之比。通常用每100个女性人口相应有多少男性人口表示。

出生率（又称粗出生率） 指在一定时期内（通常为一年）平均每千人所出生的人数的比率，一般用千分率表示。

死亡率（又称粗死亡率） 指在一定时期内（通常为一年）一定地区的死亡人数与同期平均人数（或期中人数）之比，一般用千分率表示。

人口自然增长率 指在一定时期内（通常为一年）人口自然增加数（出生人数减死亡人数）与该时期内平均人口数（或期中人数）之比，一般用千分率表示。

总迁移率 是反映人口迁移变动总规模的相对指标，是某地区一定时期内（通常为一年）迁入人数及迁出人数之和与同时期平均人口数之比，一般用千分率表示。

净迁移率 是反映人口迁移变动的相对指标之一，是某地区一定时期内（通常为一年）迁入与迁出相抵销后的余额与同时期平均人口数之比，一般用千分率表示。

政策生育率 是指一定时期内（通常为一年）计划内出生人数与总出生人数之间的比率，一般用百分率表示。

节育率 指一定时期内（通常为一年）已落实节育措施的已婚育龄妇女人数与同期已婚育龄妇女人数之间的比率，一般用百分率表示。

从业人员 指在劳动年龄内，有劳动能力，参加社会劳动取得劳动报酬或经营收入的人口。

职工 在单位工作，以工资为生活费主要来源的从业人员。

城镇集体经济单位职工 指在城镇集体经济单位及其管理部门工作，并由其支付工资的各类人员。

其他经济单位职工 指在联营经济、股份制经济、外商投资经济、港、澳、台投资经济单位工作，并由其支付工资的各类人员。

三、农　业

Agriculture

3-1 主要年份农业指标

Main Indicators of Agriculture in Main Years

指　　标	单　位	1978年	1980年	1985年	1990年	1995年	2000年	2002年	2003年
镇(街)总劳动力	人	467757	478599	544734	598911	639985	727328	754294	851484
第一产业	人	390585	368322	283425	269460	202138	189349	151487	130930
第二产业	人	51422	94576	167116	228114	283050	362666	394770	486298
第三产业	人	25750	15701	94193	101337	154797	175313	208037	234256
年末耕地面积	亩	1183926	1177400	966725	882602	708595	663304	500694	492433
农业机械总动力	千瓦	248760	354250	667750	1003980	795120	586063	361552	308159
水利建设总投资	万元	413	927	886	5428	16900	35550	38921	40320
化肥施用量(实物量)	吨	113296	100776	150083	235836	124263	103570	76634	69896
农药施用量	吨	4276	3382	2951	3453	1924	1836	1485	1355
农村用电量	万千瓦时	5667	7355	14365	82545	406327	1312931	1927589	2239886
农业总产值(当年价)	万元	42394	41943	91244	236412	426901	546383	536729	490206
主要农产品产量									
粮　食	吨	532308	529381	488705	494259	227441	204136	53732	30500
糖　蔗	吨	508976	447318	526033	538712	233803	49359	15025	2564
花　生	吨	14157	29015	20963	13411	3724	1960	865	395
水　果	吨	26457	23688	189350	282410	243231	129367	189343	146414
水产品	吨	30900	25471	32641	68508	74778	95076	82361	75756
肉　类	吨	26920	27652	33298	62191	97572	179032	188774	154615
#猪 肉	吨	22790	23461	25759	40130	68649	149648	165344	135344
禽　蛋	吨	425	398	2424	6906	5431	4367	4052	3597
森林覆盖率	%			28.6	31.4	29.2	30.6	31.7	32.2

注：本表部分镇街农村劳动力含部分外来劳动力，下同。

3-1 续表

指　标	单　位	2004年	2005年	2006年	2007年	2008年	2009年	2010年	2011年
镇(街)总劳动力	人	798954	830705	847361	837283	842933	870156	878912	913251
第一产业	人	119347	110612	92819	85246	82059	77502	72856	58767
第二产业	人	434172	447207	460758	441523	436029	447662	448637	465239
第三产业	人	245435	272886	293784	310514	324845	344992	357419	389245
年末耕地面积	亩	489448	502937	491535	483740	479260	516623	576883	
农业机械总动力	千瓦	299152	229297	212312	192990	154344	159010	367988	379028
水利建设总投资	万元	66726	59437	53583	73032	96075	64935	78308	83436
化肥施用量(实物量)	吨	59126	52749	49716	47661	43699	43364	41445	42307
农药施用量	吨	1201	1090	1017	1000	1006	1060	819	858
农村用电量	万千瓦时	2880220	2970738	2979221	3489058	3373402	3567469	3950486	4319019
农业总产值(当年价)	万元	441912	420496	212632	199782	255307	253077	283092	306621
主要农产品产量									
粮　食	吨	30374	20004	10040	9864	11902	11912	12482	12890
糖　蔗	吨	1437	450	379	1953	2580	1249	800	845
花　生	吨	216	114	99	73	130	113	115	78
水　果	吨	175389	151255	139582	131571	101541	91544	75540	73866
水产品	吨	71526	67381	47059	47292	72282	73323	76268	78229
肉　类	吨	146184	171737	34891	20257	24052	25457	28830	26010
#猪　肉	吨	128286	159169	30199	14862	17946	19095	22339	19074
禽　蛋	吨	3435	1355	371	361	146	515	386	643
森林覆盖率	%	33.0	33.1	35.1	35.5	36.2	36.5	36.7	36.9

注：1. 2010年起，农业机械总动力数据采用农业局统计口径，下同。
　　2. 2011年起，农村用电量数据采用供电局统计口径，下同。

3-2 主要年份农村经济比例和效益指标

Main Indicators of Proportions and Efficiency in Rural Economy in Main Years

指　　标	单　位	1985年	1990年	1995年	2000年	2005年	2010年	2011年
一、农村各产业劳动力比例								
第一产业	%	52.0	45.0	31.6	26.0	13.3	8.3	6.4
第二产业	%	30.7	38.1	44.2	49.9	53.8	51.0	50.9
第三产业	%	17.3	16.9	24.2	24.1	32.9	40.7	42.6
二、劳动生产条件								
平均每一农业人口用电量	千瓦时	150	826	3778	11666	29762	44051	47822
每亩耕地农业机械总动力	瓦特	691	1138	1122	884	455	638	
平均每亩耕地化肥施用量	公斤	155	267	175	156	105	72	
平均每亩耕地农药施用量	公斤	3.05	3.91	2.72	2.77	2.17	1.42	
三、增加值率								
农业增加值率	%			57.8	56.9	51.9	58.5	58.3
四、劳动生产率(平均每个劳动力创造或生产的)								
农业总产值	元	1703	3977	6737	7828	5062	3221	3357
农业增加值	元			3892	4453	2627	1886	1958
粮食产量	吨	0.91	0.83	0.36	0.29	0.02	0.01	0.01
蔬菜产量	吨	0.59	0.75	0.88	0.94	0.55	0.45	0.43
糖蔗产量	吨	0.98	0.91	0.37	0.07			
水果产量	吨	0.35	0.48	0.38	0.19	0.18	0.09	0.08
畜牧总肉产量	吨	0.06	0.10	0.15	0.26	0.21	0.03	0.03
#猪　肉	吨	0.05	0.07	0.11	0.21	0.19	0.03	0.02
水产品产量	吨	0.06	0.12	0.12	0.14	0.08	0.09	0.09

注：劳动生产率中产值部分按当年价计算。

3-3 农村集体(经联社、经济社两级)资产负债及收益分配

Assets，Liabilities and Income Distribution of Rural Collective Economy

单位：亿元

指　　标	2005年	2007年	2008年	2010年	2011年
一、资产负债情况					
资产总额	929.60	1088.58	1135.14	1228.20	1234.95
负债总额	221.56	267.42	275.38	292.15	280.42
资产负债率(%)	23.83	24.57	24.25	23.79	22.71
净资产	708.04	821.16	859.70	936.05	954.53
二、收益分配情况					
经营总收入	120.57	140.19	141.02	143.38	148.48
#直接经营收入	12.83	14.31	12.73	14.39	13.38
物业出租收入	77.02	86.44	89.79	91.65	96.72
管理费收入	13.07	10.30	8.66	7.51	8.10
结汇收入		6.41	5.12	3.52	2.95
农业发包及上交收入	3.17	2.57	2.25	2.09	2.33
投资收益	5.07	6.87	7.43	7.07	7.36
其他收入	9.40	13.29	15.05	17.15	17.64
经营总费用	48.05	58.39	63.34	66.45	69.47
#直接经营费用	6.46	8.11	8.50	8.59	8.50
租赁费用	24.05	26.41	28.61	32.62	33.59
经营税金		1.37	1.51	1.90	2.11
管理费用	9.34	11.50	12.61	12.46	14.34
其他支出	7.92	10.99	12.11	10.89	10.93
经营纯收入	72.52	81.80	77.68	76.93	79.01
收益分配总额	64.57	77.32	82.90	92.79	98.54
可弥补分配的收益总额	3.29	7.92	8.71	15.79	17.43

3-4 历年农产品人均拥有量

Per Capita Possession of Agricultural Products over Years

单位：公斤

年 份	粮 食		# 稻 谷		蔬 菜	
	按总人口	按农业人口	按总人口	按农业人口	按总人口	按农业人口
1949	312	378	304	368		
1952	379	463	364	444		
1957	373	463	337	419		
1962	414	514	392	486		
1965	513	632	502	618		
1970	463	562	451	546		
1975	473	565	452	539		
1980	471	570	462	558	111	134
1985	408	510	397	497	260	330
1990	379	495	368	480	337	440
1995	160	211	148	196	388	515
1996	168	224	155	207	411	548
1997	169	225	155	207	436	582
1998	167	224	151	203	450	603
1999	165	222	149	200	443	597
2000	135	181	121	163	431	582
2001	83	113	71	97	459	623
2002	34	54	27	43	418	653
2003	19	30	13	20	352	549
2004	19	30	8	12	329	530
2005	12	20	7	12	278	461
2006	6	10	4	8	212	364
2007	6	10	4	7	200	351
2008	7	12	3	6	224	399
2009	7	12	4	7	224	412
2010	7	14	5	10	216	438
2011	7	14	5	10	211	431

注：本表按户籍人口计算。

3-4 续表

单位：公斤

年份	水果		猪肉		水产品	
	按总人口	按农业人口	按总人口	按农业人口	按总人口	按农业人口
1949					5	6
1952					5	6
1957					5	7
1962					8	10
1965	53	66			12	14
1970	71	87			17	20
1975	34	41			20	24
1980	21	26	21	25	23	27
1985	158	197	21	27	27	34
1990	218	283	31	40	53	69
1995	171	226	48	64	52	70
1996	143	190	58	77	56	76
1997	113	151	68	91	63	84
1998	77	103	84	112	65	88
1999	91	122	87	117	63	84
2000	85	115	97	131	61	82
2001	98	132	109	148	58	79
2002	121	190	106	165	53	82
2003	92	143	85	133	48	74
2004	108	175	79	128	44	71
2005	91	152	96	159	41	68
2006	83	143	18	31	28	48
2007	77	135	9	15	28	48
2008	58	104	10	18	41	74
2009	51	94	11	20	41	75
2010	42	84	12	25	42	85
2011	40	82	10	21	42	87

3-5 主要年份基层组织情况

Basic Statistics on Rural Grassroots Units in Main Years

指　　标	单位	1985年	1990年	1995年	2000年	2005年	2010年	2011年
一、农村基层组织								
镇街政府	个	33	33	33	32	32	32	32
社区居委会、村委会	个	528	583	594	593	596	599	594
二、镇街户籍总户数	户	289512	327344	364273	414007	465008	530497	539044
#农业户	户	219846	238221	263669	299576	275988	259691	262105
三、镇街户籍总人口	人	1208515	1318526	1436525	1526090	1656541	1817709	1847691
#农业人口	人	953582	1009857	1082703	1130002	998159	896789	903139
四、镇街劳动力	人	544734	598911	639985	727328	830705	878912	913251
按性别分								
男性	人	260439	289258	315892	364866	427840	475996	490951
女性	人	284295	309653	324093	362462	402865	402916	422300
按行业分								
农、林、牧、渔业	人	283425	269460	190061	174201	110612	72856	58767
工业	人	133685	194485	254999	335545	414017	416197	431269
建筑业	人	33431	33629	28051	27121	33190	32440	33970
交运仓储和邮政业	人	20142	29005	40032	31291	40619	40124	41074
信息传输、计算机服务和软件业	人					16889	31432	33524
批发与零售业	人					65051	82662	87052
住宿和餐饮业	人					32953	48728	51327
其他行业	人					117374	154473	176268

3-6 历年耕地面积

Area of Cultivated Land over Years

单位：亩

年 份	年末实有 耕地面积	当 年 新增面积	当 年 减少面积	粮食占用 耕地面积
1949	1398338			1260357
1952	1445016			1283151
1957	1435861			1199575
1962	1214417	15405	75905	1053985
1965	1199611	4142	11473	956905
1970	1203350	11359	8818	944903
1975	1193180	1246	6402	922916
1978	1183926	288	6515	874967
1979	1182292	120	1754	896347
1980	1177400	177	5069	856824
1981	1159963	279	17716	824166
1982	1146458	1086	14591	834028
1983	1121311	216	25363	837642
1984	1077659	664	44316	784763
1985	966725	1655	112589	691895
1986	889780	2350	79295	624471
1987	887369	1986	22271	618066
1988	877308	12374	22435	609332
1989	885694	13885	5499	626334
1990	882602	6991	10083	621564
1991	878980	962	4584	614994
1992	845159	100	33921	532296
1993	753746	6319	97732	391736
1994	718144	11169	46771	382238
1995	708595	12227	21776	394913
1996	674588	6270	40277	391610
1997	663013	6350	17925	382890
1998	663045	156	124	376133
1999	663122	1684	1607	381933
2000	663304	1632	1450	354980
2001	643648	4410	24066	255771
2002	500694		150	116989
2003	492433	1922	10183	81939
2004	489448	625	3610	85988
2005	502937	291	4302	76037
2006	491535		11403	34366
2007	483740		7795	32314
2008	479260	375	4855	40795
2009	516623	9	1212	41561
2010	576883	65649	5362	41922
2011				

3-7 历年耕地面积变动情况

Changes of Cultivated Land over Years

单位：亩

年 份	当年增加耕地面 积	#新开荒	围 海造 田	当年减少耕地面 积	#国家基建占用	种 果占 用	鱼 塘占 用
“六五”时期累计	3900	1152		214575	6687	148244	33462
1981	279	91		17716	1275	7577	4507
1982	1086	215		14591	505	3345	8073
1983	216	135		25363	788	19590	2152
1984	664	148		44316	1122	31072	7694
1985	1655	563		112589	2997	86660	11036
“七五”时期累计	33250	2507	600	38017	9587	9138	2698
1986							
1987							
1988	12374	1199		22435	6971	5379	1871
1989	13885	651	100	5499	1433	330	151
1990	6991	657	500	10083	1183	3429	676
“八五”时期累计	30777	569	150	204784	5339	101880	44542
1991	962	95	150	4584	1463	430	57
1992	100	5		33921	1090	17435	3154
1993	6319	270		97732	808	64790	19032
1994	11169	139		46771	645	16031	16162
1995	12227	60		21776	1333	3194	6137
“九五”时期累计	16092	443	175	61383	2824	26550	9637
1996	6270	194	19	40277	532	16382	5597
1997	6350			17925	797	10168	4027
1998	156		156	124	85		
1999	1684	148		1607	128		
2000	1632	101		1450	1282		13
“十五”时期累计	7248			42311	3114	14531	5704
2001	4410			24066	1406	14434	5704
2002				150			
2003	1922			10183	1587		
2004	625			3610	121		
2005	291			4302		97	
“十一五”时期累计	66033	23627		30627			
2006				11403			
2007				7795			
2008	375			4855			
2009	9			1212			
2010	65649	23627		5362			
“十二五”时期累计							
2011							

3-8 历年农村劳动力(按性别、产业分)

Rural Labor Force over Years (by Sex and Industry)

单位：人

年 份	合 计	按性别分		按产业分		
		男	女	第一产业	第二产业	第三产业
1949	329182			281700		
1952	280506			228550		
1957	329204			269365		
1962	328354			267466		
1965	359464			294760		
1970	445768			376585		
1975	451207			427304		
1978	467757			390585	51422	25750
1979	468059			373438		
1980	478599	227496	251103	368322	94576	15701
1981	484346	231033	253313	367225		
1982	502066	239398	262668	360387	106294	35385
1983	512240	262608	249632	305715	145787	60738
1984	526766	253922	272844	248406	178527	99833
1985	544734	260439	284295	283425	167116	94193
1986	557048	265132	291916	277085	187920	92043
1987	571077	272044	299033	269984	204802	96291
1988	582425	281299	301126	270357	216508	95560
1989	589920	281420	308500	273377	215634	100909
1990	598911	289258	309653	269460	228114	101337
1991	601467	286328	315139	261271	232797	107399
1992	612142	298997	313145	239845	253218	119079
1993	625571	311208	314363	219230	267438	138903
1994	627366	313942	313424	200833	245562	180971
1995	639985	315892	324093	202138	283050	154797
1996	639492	316928	322564	206543	286166	146783
1997	643671	320844	322827	208030	284919	150722
1998	661604	329713	331891	205300	297418	158886
1999	668473	333136	335337	207432	300506	160535
2000	727328	364866	362462	189349	362666	175313
2001	743662	377491	366171	174786	383363	185513
2002	754294	384417	369877	151487	394770	208037
2003	851484	439406	412078	130930	486298	234256
2004	798954	412687	386267	119347	434172	245435
2005	830705	427840	402865	110612	447207	272886
2006	847361	445915	401446	92819	460758	293784
2007	837283	446755	390528	85246	441523	310514
2008	842933	451325	390608	82059	436029	324845
2009	870156	468137	402019	77502	447662	344992
2010	878912	475996	402916	72856	448637	357419
2011	913251	490951	422300	58767	465239	389245

注：本表农村劳动力包含部分外来劳动力。

3-9 历年农村劳动力(按主要行业分)

Rural Labor Force over Years (by Main Sectors)

单位：人

年 份	合 计	农 业	工 业	建筑业	交通仓储邮电通讯业	商饮业
1949	329182	281700				
1952	280506	228550				
1957	329204	269365				
1962	328354	267466				
1965	359464	294760	2626			
1970	445768	376585	9178			
1975	451207	427304	10293			
1978	467757	390585	46651	4771	2515	2441
1979	468059	373438	85306			
1980	478599	368322	94576			
1981	484346	367225	87204			
1982	502066	360387	92860	13434	15580	3158
1983	512240	305715	124791	20996	8129	5916
1984	526766	248406	147324	31203	15804	12808
1985	544734	283425	133685	33431	20142	16970
1986	557048	277085	150136	37784	25049	18417
1987	571077	269984	167354	37448	25832	20919
1988	582425	270357	181234	35274	27280	21698
1989	589920	273377	183107	32527	28491	21582
1990	598911	269460	194485	33629	29005	22652
1991	601467	261271	201152	31645	29787	25813
1992	612142	239845	222722	30496	32777	29991
1993	625571	219230	236994	30444	39612	33629
1994	627366	200833	245562	28425	39479	35798
1995	639985	202138	254999	28051	40032	36974
1996	639492	206543	258227	27939	41092	40166
1997	643671	208030	258432	26487	37375	37702
1998	661604	205300	271099	26319	36939	38880
1999	668473	207432	273914	26592	37323	39284
2000	727328	189349	335545	27121	31291	48088
2001	743662	174786	357527	25836	32153	50512
2002	754294	151487	361418	33352	34919	57997
2003	851484	130930	451920	34378	35517	62978
2004	798954	119347	398596	35576	38406	83901
2005	830705	110612	414017	33190	40619	98004
2006	847361	92819	427500	33258	43295	102259
2007	837283	85246	406910	34613	41687	113141
2008	842933	82059	402895	33134	40827	117545
2009	870156	77502	413929	33733	40299	123631
2010	878912	72856	416197	32440	40124	131390
2011	913251	58767	431269	33970	41074	138379

注：本表农村劳动力包含部分外来劳动力。

3-10 历年农业总产值及指数

Gross Output Value and Indices of Agriculture over Years

年　　份	农业总产值	种植业	#粮食	水果	林业	牧业	副业	渔业
一、农业总产值(万元)								
1978	42394	29425	21006	1404	312	5665	3843	3149
1980	41943	28054	17178	1570	238	6313	4460	2878
1985	91244	57684	19986	1913	759	12652	13930	6219
1986	122988	79251	18869	34831	2425	18078	14294	8940
1987	148414	90502	21593	39295	2330	23324	20328	11930
1988	203685	109531	29776	33939	4732	36915	26007	26500
1989	221079	117464	35488	30276	4316	45313	25491	28495
1990	236412	129032	34543	44268	4324	45405	26202	31449
1991	242587	130986	30256	44250	4038	47839	27084	32640
1992	271293	148412	28551	56967	5307	57163	22384	38026
1993	284539	130666	18519	39505	5489	78919	22728	46737
1994	347451	158315	22426	44798	6735	101117	21020	60263
1995	426901	194921	29030	59567	8850	128089	26494	68547
1996	497161	213018	33620	55763	9149	155112	32890	86992
1997	514373	232721	35329	53483	4383	176254	19442	81573
1998	536047	220614	34338	29852	5472	193404	23467	93090
1999	537442	236429	35549	47159	5640	197474	22404	75495
2000	546383	216318	19893	46423	3649	226293	19006	81118
2001	559280	228740	12895	48496	5309	245444	7655	72132
2002	536729	224452	5680	49790	2346	242928		67003
2003	490206	218039	3377	54346	1414	203477		67276
2004	441912	172481	3489	46992	2247	199912		67272
2005	420496	113577	4194	35130	1746	242534		62639
2006	212632	126923	2232	29801	3101	50638		31968
2007	199782	124627	2446	27434	3238	38354		33562
2008	255307	138205	3326	22551	3585	53221		60296
2009	253077	140221	3170	22986	2232	49982		60642
2010	283092	156698	3389	22804	2937	55499		67958
2011	306621	169304	3562	28917	2109	63758		71450

注：绝对数按当年价格计算，指数按可比价格计算。从2002年起种植业包含副业产值。下同。

3-10 续表

年份	农业总产值	种植业	#粮食	水果	林业	牧业	副业	渔业
二、指数(1978=100)								
1978	100.0	100.0	100.0	100.0	100.0	100.0	100.0	100.0
1980	98.0	100.3	98.1	89.0	65.6	81.4	146.7	88.3
1985	138.9	131.3	84.6	719.8	154.2	130.7	411.3	127.5
1986	174.6	158.0	78.8	1159.9	677.2	183.5	470.3	166.7
1987	186.4	160.1	80.0	1354.9	416.9	194.9	637.0	241.0
1988	182.1	143.5	79.8	959.0	476.4	215.1	766.8	262.2
1989	181.9	138.0	84.5	784.5	372.4	225.4	812.9	288.4
1990	195.3	150.6	85.7	1005.4	320.6	238.5	827.4	316.2
1991	199.5	149.4	77.3	961.8	286.4	262.1	859.5	335.9
1992	211.3	163.7	60.0	1255.3	325.7	289.3	697.3	356.7
1993	175.5	115.7	32.9	720.2	281.8	320.1	670.2	332.3
1994	188.4	123.9	32.8	905.8	235.5	364.3	582.0	382.1
1995	207.8	132.8	36.8	1022.0	337.0	410.4	731.1	407.0
1996	216.3	122.6	39.3	791.4	312.7	465.1	900.2	467.4
1997	225.0	129.1	40.0	835.4	167.7	532.0	563.1	540.4
1998	227.3	103.6	39.9	407.7	225.3	612.8	612.0	659.7
1999	242.8	140.2	39.9	981.4	297.4	616.2	52.7	686.0
2000	243.3	111.5	32.9	593.1	214.9	697.5	269.1	769.6
2001	246.3	111.8	20.5	634.6	233.4	750.0	146.4	766.0
2002	263.2	150.9	8.5	1336.5	124.5	730.2		652.5
2003	209.7	105.7	4.6	654.3	62.1	600.5		666.2
2004	213.5	118.0	3.3	899.9	123.9	563.1		647.9
2005	222.2	107.7	2.2	861.4	171.4	662.2		653.8
2006	121.0	108.3	2.4	683.1	246.6	155.2		590.7
2007	105.6	102.7	2.3	667.9	261.7	93.6		584.9
2008	118.3	106.0	3.9	520.6	286.3	109.5		899.5
2009	122.2	109.4	4.3	507.1	178.9	116.9		929.2
2010	126.2	107.6	4.6	415.3	205.2	132.2		982.2
2011	126.1	111.2	4.7	425.7	144.5	121.1		983.2

3-11 历年农业增加值

Added Value of Agriculture over Years

单位：万元

年 份	农业增加值	种植业	林业	牧业	副业	渔业
1978	27235	18903	200	3639	2469	2023
1980	26323	17606	149	3962	2799	1806
1985	61475	38864	511	8524	9385	4190
1986	81416	52463	1605	11967	9462	5918
1987	98236	59904	1542	15438	13455	7897
1988	118888	63932	2762	21547	15180	15468
1989	126568	67248	2471	25942	14594	16313
1990	132787	72474	2429	25503	14717	17664
1991	134523	72636	2239	26528	15019	18100
1992	144115	78839	2819	30366	11891	20200
1993	143953	66106	2777	39926	11498	23645
1994	174796	79645	3388	50870	10575	30317
1995	214306	97851	4443	64301	13300	34411
1996	248645	106537	4576	77576	16449	43507
1997	256388	115999	2185	87853	9691	40660
1998	259437	106773	2648	93604	11358	45054
1999	257863	113438	2706	94747	10749	36222
2000	259087	102575	1730	107305	9012	38465
2001	260968	106733	2477	114528	3572	33658
2002	248791	104041	1087	112605		31058
2003	228165	101486	658	94708		31313
2004	227087	88633	1155	102730		34569
2005	218212	84774	1162	97864		34412
2006	123936	88073	1913	17938		16011
2007	118991	86597	1997	13586		16810
2008	148250	96984	2212	18851		30202
2009	147877	98420	1378	17703		30375
2010	165719	110209	1812	19658		34040
2011	178777	119104	1301	22583		35789

注：绝对数按当年价格计算，从2002年起种植业包含副业产值。

3-12 历年农作物播种面积

Total Sown Area of Farm Crops over Years

单位：亩

年 份	农作物总播种面积	粮食	#稻谷	薯类	大豆	甘蔗	#糖蔗	花生	蔬菜(瓜)
1949	2118931	1908828	1783035	100391	40369	32165		39038	30000
1952	2514170	2245205	2035558	170547	37000	60682		47305	32000
1957	2834694	2482883	2015230	303587	53598	87062		53009	41934
1962	2339543	2072742	1795654	222978	31356	70793		67854	36415
1965	2384567	1824562	1681802	105758	24329	102528		113797	48988
1970	2618966	1908766	1752465	102205	31519	116639		118469	56668
1975	3029981	2055514	1739862	82594	43076	129778		141213	68061
1978	2859494	2072184	1715230	66400	36764	131200	130676	155021	68743
1979	2585334	1937441	1676936	62537	37993	110580	110123	185434	63959
1980	2436118	1756854	1624873	49665	39261	92397	91908	232541	58550
1981	2267521	1606926	1525072	48999	32143	131453	131103	264903	63768
1982	2204381	1600137	1511345	57188	35450	125787	124431	217612	82982
1983	2193087	1635344	1530918	71430	32029	110684	109283	152335	119370
1984	2165276	1576777	1468801	77105	31718	98449	96224	173198	153636
1985	1950081	1395692	1293847	70997	28982	96627	91884	159918	139795
1986	1791221	1257126	1174464	54993	31469	67920	63729	152214	159100
1987	1795990	1250934	1165554	57850	28471	63655	59637	130292	184744
1988	1792952	1236359	1151493	55368	27929	69694	66505	113882	208930
1989	1834039	1284184	1199979	55964	26200	85238	82666	101077	211217
1990	1848814	1286028	1194153	61281	26444	85977	83246	97808	229532
1991	1791266	1226573	1138043	60107	22785	90137	87356	85537	238418
1992	1561497	963947	889074	51273	20688	76184	72845	67897	318193
1993	1068053	551155	499223	34449	12843	43720	40594	39062	361826
1994	1009468	536191	482051	32615	7542	36346	34621	25344	367122
1995	1078363	598547	527594	43346	7058	28521	26488	24779	379362
1996	1083418	628347	559499	37989	8276	32620	30880	20805	363331
1997	1082610	624091	560506	32629	8190	41427	40166	18490	369113
1998	1101826	624383	558668	34799	7028	48602	47772	16824	385151
1999	1088854	626481	558508	36329	5597	31641	30889	14305	388173
2000	986022	527689	465616	31754	5290	7566	6775	11969	407304
2001	854229	338467	283351	31214	3947	4610	3290	9405	465659
2002	634205	148184	112388	18265	1983	3193	2299	4746	445447
2003	509504	84782	54970	11154	1550	1879	626	2823	380252
2004	462244	81207	31108	24683	816	868	373	1544	350412
2005	410648	62084	34356	9390	1006	950	55	574	315537
2006	333854	34366	25159	4100	183	575	55	556	241070
2007	320500	32314	19534	5330	253	1676	281	340	236490
2008	352222	40352	18781	4381	443	2330	340	586	287618
2009	370740	41421	18629	5047	140	4144	209	838	306270
2010	369257	41922	26124	3192		2944	100	713	300622
2011	366840	41461	26412	4247	418	2395	116	456	297537

3-13 历年农作物产量

Total Output of Farm Crops over Years

单位：吨

年 份	粮食	#稻谷	薯类	大豆	甘蔗	#糖蔗	花生	蔬菜（瓜）
1949	210694	205180	4889		52229	49229	1464	
1952	269458	258860	9641		181901	177696	3545	
1957	288047	260432	22623		170880	160314	3280	
1962	331207	313352	15213		134012	133755	3813	
1965	437106	427809	8165		348519	293622	7232	
1970	450808	438293	9703		397251	395964	9629	
1975	507151	484425	7685		361756	359666	11108	
1978	532308	501074	6458	1948	511492	508976	14157	135603
1979	535342	516263	6568	1982	366424	364084	19100	127918
1980	529381	518591	5432	2245	449907	447318	29015	124859
1981	447540	439534	6318	1722	678160	676074	35506	132846
1982	543349	532998	8430	2162	707764	699174	29930	123117
1983	561246	548073	11345	1875	553174	553105	19662	168878
1984	558216	545548	10946	1980	569225	554919	23076	230454
1985	488705	476399	10304	1771	556983	526033	20963	314539
1986	455243	443760	9422	2050	382608	354759	20056	427138
1987	462830	451032	10058	1920	378094	349749	17019	414261
1988	460929	448923	9950	1965	420391	400045	15119	412436
1989	487648	474476	11052	2023	528463	511031	13746	410879
1990	494259	479350	12452	2184	557102	538712	13411	444377
1991	473663	458425	12998	1838	619884	601734	11510	446204
1992	368083	354298	11070	1763	543657	523271	9323	523806
1993	202097	192018	7366	1035	343133	326389	5594	572376
1994	202356	189688	7929	668	313851	302669	3678	537442
1995	227441	210876	10758	647	246707	233803	3724	557807
1996	243204	224469	11271	806	285732	274531	3120	597732
1997	246901	227163	11487	811	354420	346469	2879	641403
1998	247194	223938	13916	758	411555	406644	2588	668753
1999	247287	223403	14580	566	242773	238774	2204	668822
2000	204136	183485	9730	610	54095	49359	1960	658196
2001	128366	109881	9920	426	33387	24768	1556	706775
2002	53732	42508	5420	244	20224	15025	865	653272
2003	30500	20423	3415	215	8019	2564	395	560523
2004	30374	12230	9803	138	4763	1437	216	532116
2005	20004	11941	2733	147	4433	450	114	460204
2006	10040	7548	1314	31	3167	379	99	356347
2007	9864	6467	1732	48	10834	1953	73	342703
2008	11902	6007	1381	95	15286	2580	130	391192
2009	11912	6560	1437	19	23044	1249	113	400335
2010	12482	8768	668		15952	800	115	392904
2011	12890	9137	888	53	14239	845	78	389014

3-14 主要年份农作物播种面积、亩产及总产量

Sown Area, Yield Per Acreage and Total Output of Farm Crops in Main Years

单位：亩、公斤、吨

指 标	1978年			1985年			1990年		
	播种面积	亩产	总产量	播种面积	亩产	总产量	播种面积	亩产	总产量
一、粮食作物	2072184	257	532308	1395692	350	488705	1286028	384	494259
按品种分									
稻谷	1715230	292	501074	1293847	368	476399	1194153	401	479350
小麦									
旱粮	290554	85	24776	30848	65	2002	30594	80	2457
薯类	66400	97	6458	70997	145	10304	61281	203	12452
按季节分									
春收				30978	131	4042	33352	174	5790
夏收	1127790	248	279552	649856	377	244755	614059	399	244890
#早稻	814852	309	251907	620409	389	241413	587821	410	241018
秋收	944394	268	252757	714858	336	239907	638617	381	243579
#晚稻	900378	277	249167	673438	349	234985	606332	393	238332
二、大豆	36764	53	1948	28982	61	1771	26444	83	2184
三、经济作物				306406			209120		
#甘蔗	131200	3899	511492	96627	5765	556983	85977	6480	557102
糖蔗	130676	3895	508976	91884	5725	526033	83246	6471	538712
果蔗	524	4802	2516	4743	6525	30950	2731	6734	18390
油料作物				160186	131	20974	97808	137	13411
#花生	155021	91	14157	159918	131	20963	97808	137	13411
四、其他作物				219001			327222		
#蔬菜	68743	1973	135603	139795	2250	314539	229532	1936	444377

3-14 续表 1

单位：亩、公斤、吨

指　　标	1995年			2000年			2005年		
	播种面积	亩产	总产量	播种面积	亩产	总产量	播种面积	亩产	总产量
一、粮食作物	598547	380	227441	527689	387	204136	62084	322	20004
按品种分									
稻谷	527594	400	210876	465616	394	183485	34356	348	11941
小麦									
旱粮	27607	210	5807	30319	360	10921	18338	291	5330
薯类	43346	248	10758	31754	306	9730	9390	291	2733
按季节分									
春收	17880	224	4008	20787	287	5966	9665	312	3019
夏收	282978	388	109914	245110	392	96015	23286	306	7136
#早稻	255886	405	103592	225985	397	89729	14713	351	5164
秋收	297689	381	113519	261792	390	102155	29133	338	9850
#晚稻	271708	395	107284	239631	391	93756	19643	345	6777
二、大豆	7058	92	647	5290	115	610	1006	146	147
三、经济作物	62092			35221			18011		
#甘蔗	28521	8650	246707	7566	7150	54095	950	4666	4433
糖蔗	26488	8827	233803	6775	7285	49359	55	8182	450
果蔗	2033	6347	12904	791	5987	4736	895	4450	3983
油料作物	24779	150	3724	11969	164	1960	574	199	114
#花生	24779	150	3724	11969	164	1960	574	199	114
四、其他作物	410666			417822			329547		
#蔬菜	379362	1470	557807	407304	1616	658196	315537	1458	460204

3-14 续表 2

单位：亩、公斤、吨

指　　标	2009年			2010年			2011年		
	播种面积	亩产	总产量	播种面积	亩产	总产量	播种面积	亩产	总产量
一、粮食作物	41421	288	11912	41922	298	12482	41461	311	12890
按品种分									
稻谷	18629	352	6560	26124	336	8768	26412	346	9137
小麦									
旱粮	17745	221	3915	12606	242	3046	10384	271	2812
薯类	5047	285	1437	3192	209	668	4247	209	888
按季节分									
春收	6257	254	1588	5202	221	1150	4186	242	1015
夏收	17314	302	5221	17948	306	5501	18070	315	5701
#早稻	9117	332	3031	12017	330	3965	12878	339	4367
秋收	17850	286	5103	18772	311	5831	19205	321	6174
#晚稻	9512	371	3529	14107	340	4803	13534	352	4770
二、大豆	140	136	19				418	127	53
三、经济作物	16440			14084			16924		
#甘蔗	4144	5561	23044	2944	5418	15952	2395	5945	14239
糖蔗	209	5976	1249	100	8000	800	116	7284	845
果蔗	3935	5539	21795	2844	5328	15152	2279	5877	13394
油料作物	838	135	113	713	161	115	456	171	78
#花生	838	135	113	713	161	115	456	171	78
四、其他作物	312739			313251			308455		
#蔬菜	306270	1307	400335	300622	1307	392904	297537	1307	389014

3-15 主要年份农机总动力、水利、化肥、农药及农村用电量

Basic Statistics on Total Power of Agricultural Machinery, Water Conservancy, Consumption of Chemical Fertilizers and Pesticides, and Electricity Consumed in Rural Areas in Main Years

指　　标	单　位	1978年	1985年	1990年	1995年	2000年	2005年	2010年	2011年
一、农业机械总动力	千瓦	248760	667750	1003980	795120	586063	229297	367988	379028
耕作机械	千瓦	42550	116200	157910	83482	51848	16386	24079	25947
排灌机械	千瓦	104050	149900	178280	112392	91745	36251	99716	104926
收获机械	千瓦	6180	39130	84130	54722	51084	969	2280	2400
运输机械	千瓦	16930	273270	322950	397735	184949	41678	12463	14363
二、水利建设完成土石方	万立方米	957	295	737	891	927	682	442	742
土方	万立方米	932	266	693	835	864	611	386	569
石方	万立方米	25	29	44	56	63	71	56	173
水利建设总投资	万元	413	886	5428	16900	35550	59437	78308	83436
#各级自筹资金	万元	247	720	4956	14500	33026			
水利建设使用劳动工日	万工日	696	136	994	1019	1200	732		
三、化肥施用实物量	吨	113296	150083	235836	124263	103570	52749	41445	42307
#氮肥	吨	86371	66846	84642	43441	30214	14439	10214	10653
磷肥	吨	23164	37147	52483	28939	23939	10967	8055	8269
钾肥	吨	3761	13544	26131	16915	14606	6403	5030	5113
复合肥	吨		13117	39098	34968	34811	20940	18146	18272
四、农药施用量	吨	4276	2951	3453	1924	1836	1090	819	858
五、农村用电量	万千瓦时	5667	14365	82545	406327	1312931	2970738	3950486	4319019
#农村工业用电量	万千瓦时			70459	386413	1104301	2873735	3841990	3919883
平均每一农业人口用电量	千瓦时		150	826	3778	11666	29762	44051	47822

注：农业机械总动力数据从2010年起采用农业局统计口径，数据与往年不可比，下同。

3-16 历年水果面积及产量

Planted Area and Output of Fruits over Years

年份	年末实有水果面积(亩)	#香(大)蕉	荔枝	水果总产量(吨)	#香(大)蕉	荔枝
1949		15659	19300		15911	1391
1952		21827	20050		21633	1976
1957		21827	18242		19469	1976
1962		15547	22844		7766	255
1965		19343	27966	45421	28259	14259
1970		24831	37482	69480	47257	18775
1975		24232	41045	36821	32238	2727
1978	93245	18828	46678	26457	18867	4959
1979	91021	17977	46697	23346	12165	8667
1980	88444	15582	46743	23688	10894	7884
1981	97468	18042	48230	46909	25513	15599
1982	114730	28439	50669	58196	40872	7042
1983	159260	39749	63349	77225	42079	20724
1984	235311	66506	84183	105851	69186	14714
1985	407416	125998	115428	189350	133503	19304
1986	609347	171168	168820	307743	210439	18577
1987	609569	158874	175366	363085	222826	17439
1988	548482	99256	176979	263710	126655	7699
1989	476598	54867	164782	221418	69410	6165
1990	452729	54185	160355	282410	73555	16994
1991	440442	56481	154456	343155	85702	6201
1992	420661	81331	139584	344751	97986	22972
1993	360130	86299	117557	271346	80982	717
1994	325336	67595	121236	264875	92072	12703
1995	322876	62351	142370	243231	86466	23324
1996	326291	59822	159403	206276	77768	14804
1997	319556	57583	188220	165016	80355	22572
1998	310873	46377	208899	114106	78978	2885
1999	285514	48975	198144	136317	82169	35218
2000	297618	71454	189862	129367	108913	9107
2001	275428	86578	156019	150115	132292	7059
2002	209924	76764	109948	189343	135209	45339
2003	199634	82024	95812	146414	130688	9012
2004	183375	84812	80115	175389	150669	18312
2005	176845	75452	83357	151255	123986	21026
2006	173470	73493	81395	139582	124601	8615
2007	163448	66904	80313	131571	116833	10107
2008	178337	64141	94953	101541	86817	8498
2009	177281	52761	103364	91544	75341	10240
2010	170536	47420	100136	75540	60236	8266
2011	167667	42874	101458	73866	55291	11032

3-17 历年林业生产

Basic Statistics on Forestry Production over Years

年 份	林业用地面积(亩)	#杉	松	桉	当年育苗面积(亩)	当年幼林抚育面积(亩)	当年迹地更新面积(亩)	当年四旁植树(万株)
1952					15			3
1957					144			15
1962					333	3740		47
1965					2028			307
1970	711996	20266	596098	8100	531	6783	423	12
1975	711375	59992	572746	35216	693	29200	4343	40
1978	700570	63994	541492	49008	485	32900	5365	44
1979	705764	67104	543210	50439	880	14900	4745	30
1980	740052	70665	568729	56272	316	9500	3924	15
1981	743697	67236	584674	49994	133	12500	931	12
1982	698715	63730	535072	52925	500	11945	2531	19
1983	769893	67423	574171	56724	361	40464	3193	17
1984	739402	66107	552721	58092	501	106982	5120	15
1985	761460				801	120000	4479	150
1986	706823	61438	510042	60581	33231	210540	16908	22
1987	714664	57824	526254	75498	1728	53759	28007	35
1988	729896	59351	512451	90998	3667	70275	34467	37
1989	691944	53293	490370	103887	2101	64950	31241	58
1990	709240	47054	484397	133706	3464	56647	15782	54
1991	709306	44432	459015	148127	609	53827	22294	63
1992	662919	39326	422527	149944	762	60764	28184	49
1993	628612	36213	400816	144346	677	28511	13318	57
1994	1016138	43815	382482	129473	2492	28127	9689	34
1995	1015223	43661	360591	125133	4273	25130	11140	48
1996	1014972	9654	248288	115878	699	21000	23143	133
1997	1014954	8843	235410	113928	823	23745	22462	218
1998	1014876	8367	222147	112005	387	36000	22273	417
1999	1009965	10890	221585	133500	506	29863	29000	522
2000	1009037	29940	526797	280618	625	47145	13515	425
2001	1007298	9678	189930	133464	705	45000	38000	357
2002	900335	8265	187665	138525	516	46500	13700	98
2003	890877	6540	66206	105666	420	38910	10425	147
2004	980942				255	60000	8472	625
2005	934700	3086	2860	100145	195	61005	3383	253
2006	930162	3716	60890	162125	15	25320	3900	480
2007	926760	3870	62363	149440	255	43320	4701	600
2008	923097	3873	59864	145340	255	49571	4548	610
2009	921000	3719	58375	143690	610	56545	6184	60
2010	909900	3719	56987	142971	285	37278	5889	18
2011	905370	3719	56801	141945	345	41085		22

3-18 历年畜牧业生产及产品产量

Production of Animal Husbandry and Output of Livestock Products over Years

年 份	耕牛年末存栏量（头）	羊年末存栏量（头）	生猪饲养量（头）	生猪存栏量（头）	生猪出栏量（头）	三鸟饲养量（万只）	三鸟出栏量（万只）	畜牧总肉量（吨）	#猪肉	禽蛋总产量（吨）
1949	52475		147266	82266	65000	256	159			
1952	58530		243000	117082	125918	329	205			
1957	62444		300529	154756	145773	400	249			339
1962	47004		185961	103034	82927	339	248			394
1965	53105		640968	369391	271577	421	276			2989
1970	56665		900481	593310	307171	310	163			1614
1975	55292		920100	633527	286573	364	187			1141
1978	53004		1018060	672919	345141	428	219	26920	22790	425
1979	50595		995408	626435	368973	379	187	29209	25647	367
1980	53385		799568	501380	298188	420	209	27652	23461	444
1981	58619		703659	449638	254021	476	252	28011	23387	1284
1982	64067		791518	526106	265412	568	309	33037	27374	679
1983	69117		842198	489887	352311	630	370	35695	28872	1256
1984	70992		784473	458804	325669	652	369	33260	26301	1899
1985	62763		790505	471268	319237	832	414	33298	25759	2424
1986	62874		812102	428545	383557	940	655	43302	30920	5159
1987	58577		781957	396082	385875	1235	862	46120	32588	5478
1988	54723		811945	402035	409910	1400	1020	56125	35067	6734
1989	52713		846598	407317	439281	1565	1136	58563	38270	7109
1990	48760	1559	870782	410875	459907	1592	1188	62191	40130	6906
1991	44121	1396	930377	420919	509458	1806	1336	68844	44702	5924
1992	32259	1068	981698	448586	533112	1889	1419	67983	45492	5845
1993	18688	783	982084	404352	577732	2185	1647	76562	49470	4990
1994	14219	863	1089793	434904	654889	2334	1730	85448	57920	5521
1995	12207	1593	1250597	469355	781242	2501	1881	97572	68649	5431
1996	12945	1806	1407080	490161	916919	2418	1851	116058	83404	5862
1997	12675	2391	1772892	619114	1153778	2608	1863	128992	99300	6295
1998	10522	2159	2217247	776851	1440396	2291	1742	153513	123874	4738
1999	6811	1508	2573310	900285	1673025	2228	1667	159889	130494	4742
2000	5550	1675	2894126	967056	1927070	2362	1784	179032	149648	4367
2001	4618	1851	3255780	1079397	2176383	2226	1683	198423	168353	4441
2002	2919	1931	3075523	927477	2148046	1962	1557	188774	165344	4052
2003	1727	1789	2525252	742101	1783151	1652	1282	154615	135344	3597
2004	1024	1936	2444990	785289	1659701	1396	1048	146184	128286	3435
2005	827	998	2487962	214120	2273842	1314	1072	171737	159169	1355
2006	82	242	530959	110396	420563	485	312	34891	30199	371
2007	399	415	292234	88648	203586	525	341	20257	14862	361
2008	55		454117	195016	259101	758	574	24052	17946	106
2009	94		464727	183904	280823	767	576	25457	19095	515
2010	224	60	511356	174933	336423	761	591	28830	22339	386
2011	200	50	455875	176805	279070	706	547	26010	19074	643

3-19 历年水产品产量及养殖面积

Output and Cultured Area of Aquatic Products over Years

年 份	水产品产量(吨)	海水产量	海水捕捞	海水养殖	淡水产量	淡水捕捞	淡水养殖	养殖面积(亩)	海水养殖	淡水养殖
1949	3175	1475	1475		1700		1700	27390		27390
1952	3365	1565	1565		1800		1800	26167		26167
1957	4185	2410	2410		1775		1775	36016		36016
1962	6321	3521	3521		2800		2800	100822		100822
1965	9946	5693	5693		4253		4253	93502		93502
1970	16214	10878	10878		5336		5336	72176		72176
1975	21879	15026	15026		6853		6853	83398		83398
1978	30900	23307	23307		7593		7593	89040		89040
1979	22309	13878	13878		8431		8431	94916		94916
1980	25471	17069	17069		8402		8402	95549		95549
1981	24905	15669	15669		9236		9236	104069		104069
1982	27695	16120	16120		11575		11575	112586		112586
1983	30292	17330	17330		12962		12962	116943		116943
1984	32465	18025	18025		14440		14440	119456		119456
1985	32641	15422	15214	208	17219		17219	131350	5301	126049
1986	46534	28439	25918	2521	18095		18095	138651	16078	122573
1987	65679	45214	42793	2421	20465		20465	163225	15036	148189
1988	68087	44111	42926	1185	23976	182	23794	137966	9670	128296
1989	62306	37189	35372	1817	25117	1194	23923	123090	10350	112740
1990	68508	41002	38423	2579	27506	2177	25329	136174	19286	116888
1991	69025	39906	37209	2697	29119	2147	26972	131849	18446	113403
1992	73164	42429	38033	4396	30735	2590	28145	134558	20400	114158
1993	64973	33745	28192	5553	31228	3120	28108	143696	25855	117841
1994	67420	31284	24059	7225	36136	2565	33571	144869	26583	118286
1995	74778	32132	24637	7495	42646	2084	40562	162609	27795	134814
1996	81067	33363	25471	7892	47704	1940	45764	172656	27791	144865
1997	91901	35407	26704	8703	56494	5157	51337	184889	30326	154563
1998	96872	33618	24319	9299	63254	3146	60108	192381	29223	163158
1999	94023	31332	24257	7075	62691	2747	59944	167880	19440	148440
2000	95076	33234	24180	9054	61842	3135	58707	167841	25695	142146
2001	89599	30877	23726	7151	58722	2285	56437	155720	27928	127792
2002	82361	30800	23474	7326	51561	2762	48799	142167	26696	115471
2003	75756	30151	22826	7325	45605	2121	43484	126660	27097	99563
2004	71526	29289	22382	6907	42237	3078	39159	125116	25652	99464
2005	67381	28319	21622	6697	39062	1783	37279	102023	23530	78493
2006	47059	21152	15256	5897	25907	1062	24845	71745	6345	65400
2007	47292	21637	15992	5645	25655	857	24797	71100	5925	65175
2008	72282	21297	14322	6975	50985	512	50473	137718	17559	120159
2009	73323	19034	13205	5829	54289		54289	129136	4197	124939
2010	76268	19300	13257	6043	56968	1563	55405	132960	4147	128813
2011	78229	17816	12255	5561	60413	1801	58612	118676	3473	115203

3-20 主要农产品产量与最高年份比较（2011年）

Output of Main Agricultural Products in Comparison with Peak Year (2011)

指　　标	单位	2011年	建国以来最高年份		
			年　份	产　量	2011年为最高年份的%
一、粮食总产量	吨	12890	1977	563463	2.3
#稻　谷	吨	9137	1973	548073	1.7
#早　稻	吨	4367	1983	279723	1.6
晚　稻	吨	4770	1984	279898	1.7
二、大　　豆	吨	53	1954	2790	1.9
三、经济作物					
#甘　蔗	吨	14239	1982	707764	2.0
#糖　蔗	吨	845	1982	699174	0.1
花　生	吨	78	1981	35506	0.2
四、其他作物					
#蔬　菜	吨	389014	2001	706775	55.0
五、水果总产量	吨	73866	1987	363085	20.3
#香(大)蕉	吨	55291	1987	222826	24.8
荔　枝	吨	11032	2002	45339	24.3
六、水产品	吨	78229	1998	96872	80.8
七、生猪年末存栏量	头	176805	2001	1079397	16.4
生猪年出栏头数	头	279070	2005	2273842	12.3
猪肉产量	吨	19074	2001	168353	11.3
八、三鸟饲养量	万只	706	2000	2362	29.9
三鸟出栏量	万只	547	2000	1784	30.7
禽蛋产量	吨	643	1989	7109	9.0

主要统计指标解释

Explanatory Notes on Main Statistical Indicators

耕地面积 指可以用来种植农作物、经常进行耕锄的田地，包括熟地、当年新开荒地、连续撂荒未满三年的耕地和当年的休闲地(轮歇地)，还包括以种植农作物为主并附带种植桑树、茶树、果树和其他林木的土地，以及沿海、沿湖地区已围垦利用的“海涂”、“湖田”等面积。不包括属于专业性的桑园、茶园、果园、果木苗圃、林地、芦苇地、天然或人工草地面积。

农作物播种面积 指实际播种或移植有农作物的面积。凡是实际种植有农作物的面积，不论种植在耕地上还是种植在非耕地上，均包括在农作物播种面积中。在播种季节基本结束后，因遭灾而重新改种和补种的农作物面积，也包括在内。

粮食产量 指全社会的产量。包括国有经济经营的、集体统一经营的和农民家庭经营的粮食产量，还包括工矿企业办的农场和其他生产单位的产量。粮食除包括稻谷、小麦、玉米、高粱、谷子及其他杂粮外，还包括薯类和豆类。其产量计算方法，豆类按去豆荚后的干豆计算；薯类(包括甘薯和马铃薯，不包括芋头和木薯)1963年以前按每4公斤鲜薯折1公斤粮食计算，从1964年开始改为按5公斤鲜薯折1公斤粮食计算。城市郊区作为蔬菜的薯类(如马铃薯等)按鲜品计算，并且不作粮食统计。其他粮食一律按脱粒后的原粮计算。

水产品产量 指人工养殖的水产品和天然生长的水产品的捕捞量。包括海水的鱼类、虾蟹类、贝类和藻类以及内陆水域的鱼类、虾蟹类和贝类，不包括淡水生植物。

猪、牛、羊肉产量 指当年出栏并已屠宰、除去头蹄下水后带骨肉(即胴体重)的重量。

期初(末)畜禽存栏头(只)数 指报告期初(末)农村各种合作经济组织和国营农场、农民个人、机关、团体、学校、工矿企业、部队等单位以及城镇居民饲养的大牲畜、猪、羊、家禽等畜禽的存栏数。

农林牧渔业总产值 指以货币表现的农、林、牧、渔业全部产品的总量，它反映一定时期内农业生产总规模和总成果。农业总产值的计算方法通常是按农林牧渔业产品及其副产品的产量分别乘以各自单位产品价格求得；少数生产周期较长，当年没有产品或产品产量不易统计的，则采用间接方法匡算其产值；然后将四业产品产值相加即为农业总产值。

农业机械总动力 指主要用于农、林、牧、渔业的各种动力机械的动力总和。包括耕作机械、排灌机械、收获机械、农用运输机械、植物保护机械、牧业机械、林业机械、渔业机械和其他农业机械〔内燃机按引擎马力折成瓦(特)计算、电动机按功率折成瓦(特)计算〕。不包括专门用于乡、镇、村、组办工业、基本建设、非农业运输、科学试验和教学等非农业生产方面用的动力机械与作业机械。

农民人均纯收入 **纯收入**指农村住户当年从各个来源得到的总收入相应地扣除所发生的费用后的收入总和。**“农民人均纯收入”**按人口平均的纯收入水平，反映的是一个地区农村居民的平均收入水平。计算方法：纯收入=总收入（包括现金形态和实物形态折算款）-家庭经营费用支出-税费支出-生产性固定资产折旧-赠送农村外部亲友支出

四、工　业

Industry

4-1 主要年份工业主要指标

Main Indicators of Industry in Main Years

指　　标	单位	1998年	2000年	2001年	2005年	2010年	2011年
全市企业单位数	个	16406	16975	18094	21868	38273	46413
全市工业增加值	万元	2906904	4304525	5170314	11732288	20784479	22884117
规模以上工业:							
企业单位数	个	1500	1663	1680	4505	5899	4243
年末固定资产原值合计	万元	6257040	7288486	8259152	18560858	32162507	33049643
年末固定资产	万元	4392164	4701886	5354719	11052566	17836928	19882642
年末流动资产	万元	3798813	5298239	5629510	18732801	37888251	41732138
年末资产总额	万元	9267121	11225950	11730032	33453291	60017098	66127123
年末负债总额	万元	4752964	5630399	5796530	18580908	35252952	38770617
所有者权益	万元	4514157	5595551	5933502	14872383	24750103	27263562
工业增加值	万元	1687134	2594352	2906664	10624190	17083110	16424508
主营业务收入	万元	6399088	9889058	11312944	39121487	77081695	84549238
利税总额	万元	447544	841047	789734	1830988	4695854	4833042
#利润总额	万元	255715	503589	433640	1243516	3523632	3165403
全员劳动生产率(按增加值计算)	元/人	26688	36101	39438	53340	60854	65087
综合效益指数	%	94.1	114.0	109.5	119.9	130.3	128.3

注：1. 2005年以前数据根据东莞市第一次经济普查取得，2008年数据根据第二次经济普查取得，下同。
2. 规模以上工业企业1997年及以前年份为独立核算工业企业口径,1998-2005年为全部国有工业及年销售收入500万元以上非国有工业企业口径，2006-2010年为年主营业务收入500万元及以上工业企业口径，2011年起为年主营业务收入2000万元及以上的工业企业口径,下同。

4-2 历年工业企业单位数（按经济成份分）

Number of Industrial Enterprises over Years (by Ownership)

单位：个

年 份	全市工业企业单位数	国有	集体企业	港澳台投资企业	外商投资企业	其他类型企业
1949	1	1				
1952	23	20	3			
1957	262	76	186			
1962	280	57	223			
1965	260	61	199			
1970	220	57	163			
1975	324	61	263			
1978	1290	64	1226			
1979	1250	63	1187			
1980	1293	64	1229			
1981	1479	64	1415			
1982	1862	66	1796			
1983	1964	68	1896			
1984	2329	69	2109			151
1985	4187	73	2990	79		1045
1986	5949	81	4263	89		1516
1987	8106	74	5123	175		2734
1988	8408	72	5424	241		2671
1989	8757	76	5835	323		2523
1990	9892	78	6165	521	4	3124
1991	10094	77	6404	754	4	2855
1992	11639	72	6400	932	4	4231
1993	12449	75	7129	1388	24	3833
1994	14086	45	7185	2002	191	4663
1995	15215	70	9345	2631	210	2959
1996	15326	40	8958	2128	253	3947
1997	16857	41	9949	2064	315	4488
1998	16406	29	8814	2050	461	5052
1999	16877	29	10325	2627	731	3165
2000	16975	23	10184	2717	893	3158
2001	18094	20	9978	3605	1186	3305
2002	21313	19	198	10830	907	9359
2003	21935	19	200	10969	958	9789
2004	22156	13	211	9450	1422	11060
2005	21868	10	220	10141	2093	9404
2006	22447	10	211	10271	2190	9765
2007	22587	16	151	10041	2528	9851
2008	26372	35	484	5122	2489	18242
2009	31160	26	313	5141	2439	23241
2010	38273	21	262	5417	2447	30126
2011	46413	20	215	6114	2562	37502

注：本表2002年起集体企业不包括“三来一补”企业。

4-3 主要年份工业企业单位数（按不同类型分）

Number of Industrial Enterprises in Main Years (by Ownership)

单位：个

指　　标	1998年	2000年	2004年	2005年	2010年	2011年
全市企业单位数	16406	16975	22156	21868	38273	46413
轻工业	14389	14440	15270	12651	20651	24787
重工业	2017	2535	6886	9217	17622	21626
在总计中:						
(一)规模以上工业企业	1500	1663	4224	4505	5899	4243
按轻重工业分						
轻工业	1082	1124	2405	2569	3183	2266
重工业	418	539	1819	1936	2716	1977
按登记注册类型分						
国有	29	16	4	5	10	9
集体	204	248	162	162	151	81
私营	24	44	557	621	1159	736
联营	5	6	4	2	5	1
股份合作	9	6		1	2	1
股份有限公司	6	3	19	18	20	24
外商投资	134	201	787	820	1321	1073
港澳台投资	1082	1119	2367	2481	2564	1823
其他	7	20	324	395	667	495
按企业规模分						
大型企业	16	28	40	39	84	206
中型企业	27	19	592	579	1327	1677
小型企业	1457	1616	3592	3887	4488	2256
微型企业						104
(二)规模以下工业企业	14906	15312	20107	17363	32374	42170

注：2011年起采用新的企业规模划分标准，共分大型、中型、小型、微型四类企业规模，下同。

4-4 历年工业增加值

Value-added of Industry over Years

年 份	工业增加值	
	绝对值 （万元）	增速 （%）
1986	105398	
1987	142357	25.8
1988	250456	51.4
1989	272185	6.4
1990	391840	30.6
1991	483441	21.8
1992	566316	13.7
1993	828934	38.5
1994	1107729	24.3
1995	1541922	35.3
1996	1878517	16.2
1997	2307863	20.1
1998	2906904	22.2
1999	3495304	20.7
2000	4304525	20.9
2001	5170314	22.0
2002	6218553	23.0
2003	7571849	21.4
2004	9680128	26.5
2005	11732288	20.2
2006	14416864	22.0
2007	16818293	15.0
2008	18192243	6.4
2009	17415347	-0.6
2010	20784479	17.5
2011	22884117	7.7

注：本表工业增加值绝对值为当年价，增速按可比价计算。

4-5 规模以上工业企业单位数（2011年）

Number of Industrial Enterprises above Designated Size (2011)

单位：个

项　　目	工业单位数	按登记注册类型分		
		国有及国有控股工业	集体工业	港澳台及外商投资工业
总　　计	4243	28	81	2896
按轻重工业分				
轻工业	2266	13	62	1494
重工业	1977	15	19	1402
按企业规模分				
大型企业	206	5	2	168
中型企业	1677	12	29	1324
小型企业	2256	11	40	1344
微型企业	104		10	60
按工业行业分(大类)				
煤炭开采和洗选业				
石油和天然气开采业				
黑色金属矿采选业				
有色金属矿采选业				
非金属矿采选业				
开采辅助活动				
其他采矿业				
农副食品加工业	38	2	1	12
食品制造业	32			14
酒、饮料和精制茶制造业	10	3		7
烟草制品业				
纺织业	183			127
纺织服装、服饰业	247	1	4	106
皮革、毛皮、羽毛及其制品和制鞋业	267	1	7	222
木材加工和木、竹、藤、棕、草制品业	24			13
家具制造业	192			117
造纸和纸制品业	219		12	93
印刷和记录媒介复制业	74	1	1	51
文教、工美、体育和娱乐用品制造业	186	1	1	163
石油加工、炼焦和核燃料加工业	6			3
化学原料和化学制品制造业	145	2	1	91
医药制造业	11			6
化学纤维制造业	6			4
橡胶和塑料制品业	459		6	336
非金属矿物制品业	84	1	1	47
黑色金属冶炼和压延加工业	36			26
有色金属冶炼和压延加工业	53			32
金属制品业	243	1		154
通用设备制造业	176	2		128
专用设备制造业	138	1		102
汽车制造业	40			30
铁路、船舶、航空航天和其他运输设备制造业	12	1		9
电气机械和器材制造业	439		8	313
计算机、通信和其他电子设备制造业	762	4	12	592
仪器仪表制造业	61		1	48
其他制造业	46			38
废弃资源综合利用业	1			
金属制品、机械和设备修理业	2			1
电力、热力生产和供应业	14	5	1	8
燃气生产和供应业	5			3
水的生产和供应业	32	2	25	

注：2011年起，行业分类采用2011年新发布的《国民经济行业分类》，下同。

4-6 规模以上工业增加值（2011年）

Value-added of Industrial Enterprises above Designated Size(2011)

单位：万元

项　　　目	工业增加值	按登记注册类型分		
		国有及国有控股工业	集体工业	港澳台及外商投资工业
总　　计	16424508	1477919	254458	12098766
按轻重工业分				
轻工业	7590143	154715	165523	5656203
重工业	8834365	1323204	88935	6442564
按企业规模分				
大型企业	7162882	1111282	65988	5195455
中型企业	6533311	323498	128536	5186475
小型企业	2688732	43139	57128	1691334
微型企业	39583		2805	25502
按工业行业分(大类)				
煤炭开采和洗选业				
石油和天然气开采业				
黑色金属矿采选业				
有色金属矿采选业				
非金属矿采选业				
开采辅助活动				
其他采矿业				
农副食品加工业	259003	71318	948	119774
食品制造业	253360			227065
酒、饮料和精制茶制造业	246989	11324		238790
烟草制品业				
纺织业	499331			418888
纺织服装、服饰业	775242	2343	8656	278807
皮革、毛皮、羽毛及其制品和制鞋业	981029	4483	22766	851334
木材加工和木、竹、藤、棕、草制品业	37040			25230
家具制造业	502381			302677
造纸和纸制品业	731410		31415	521094
印刷和记录媒介复制业	360342	985	1821	316103
文教、工美、体育和娱乐用品制造业	580663	1047	1068	531055
石油加工、炼焦和核燃料加工业	2434			622
化学原料和化学制品制造业	452011	21610	594	336459
医药制造业	46556			7476
化学纤维制造业	6663			4238
橡胶和塑料制品业	949486		54821	756860
非金属矿物制品业	327597	1663	279	248142
黑色金属冶炼和压延加工业	47988			34080
有色金属冶炼和压延加工业	70192			49457
金属制品业	477973	1296		328895
通用设备制造业	577610	7633		499934
专用设备制造业	313261	3587		259826
汽车制造业	232353			209575
铁路、船舶、航空航天和其他运输设备制造业	127391	91004		122475
电气机械和器材制造业	1513610		42432	1206665
计算机、通信和其他电子设备制造业	4336666	100526	32782	3617763
仪器仪表制造业	266952		10415	211399
其他制造业	115101			110989
废弃资源综合利用业	3556			
金属制品、机械和设备修理业	1433			1433
电力、热力生产和供应业	1194292	1122976	214	221100
燃气生产和供应业	42172			40563
水的生产和供应业	92422	36124	46246	

4-7 规模以上工业企业主要财务指标（2011年）

Main Financial Indicators of Industrial Enterprises above Designated Size (2011)

单位：万元

指　　标	全市总计	按登记注册类型分			按轻重工业分	
		内资企业	港澳台商投资企业	外商投资企业	轻工业	重工业
一、企业单位数(个)	4243	1347	1823	1073	2266	1977
二、年末资产						
流动资产合计	41732138	10371657	18063698	13296783	19332307	22399831
#产成品存货	3526442	885346	1554479	1086617	1722977	1803465
固定资产净值	18237651	5818377	7932663	4486610	7248268	10989383
年末资产总额	66127123	18518963	28141247	19466913	29023172	37103951
三、年末负债及所有者权益						
年末负债总额	38770617	12011269	15822851	10936497	17331840	21438777
所有者权益合计	27263562	6508046	12275741	8479776	11618647	15644915
四、损益及分配						
主营业务收入	84549238	23074567	34360045	27114627	35576518	48972721
主营业务成本	75478078	20390102	30754217	24333759	31231154	44246925
主营业务税金及附加	201987	64245	72714	65029	113833	88155
主营业务利润	8869173	2620220	3533114	2715839	4231531	4637641
销售费用	4193616	540982	3050792	601842	3477832	715784
管理费用	3933108	903588	1769008	1260513	1821837	2111271
财务费用	201479	193776	27904	-20201	87168	114311
#利息支出	440878	236729	135900	68249	205930	234948
利税总额	4833042	1572015	1822378	1438649	2142095	2690946
利润总额	3165403	888125	1319747	957531	1362706	1802697
亏损企业亏损总额	407800	63380	190517	153903	204689	203112

4-8 规模以上工业企业主要指标（2011年）

Main Indicators of Industrial Enterprises above Designated Size (2011)

单位：万元

项　　目	企业单位数(个)	#亏损企业	工业销售产值	工业增加值	全部从业人员平均人数(人)
总　　计	4243	679	84357680	16424508	2523487
按轻重工业分					
轻工业	2266	380	35544028	7590143	1362801
重工业	1977	299	48813651	8834365	1160686
按企业规模分					
大型企业	206	16	38188889	7162882	816904
中型企业	1677	255	28847483	6533311	1333602
小型企业	2256	383	17114991	2688732	366696
微型企业	104	25	206317	39583	6285
按工业行业分(大类)					
煤炭开采和洗选业					
石油和天然气开采业					
黑色金属矿采选业					
有色金属矿采选业					
非金属矿采选业					
开采辅助活动					
其他采矿业					
农副食品加工业	38	5	2982952	259003	6760
食品制造业	32	3	833623	253360	14508
酒、饮料和精制茶制造业	10	1	1782961	246989	13810
烟草制品业					
纺织业	183	33	2352584	499331	102684
纺织服装、服饰业	247	25	3050921	775242	141911
皮革、毛皮、羽毛及其制品和制鞋业	267	48	2871637	981029	287829
木材加工和木、竹、藤、棕、草制品业	24	9	153426	37040	6639
家具制造业	192	42	1969572	502381	90951
造纸和纸制品业	219	23	4850192	731410	65845
印刷和记录媒介复制业	74	7	973099	360342	37758
文教、工美、体育和娱乐用品制造业	186	40	2178091	580663	164597
石油加工、炼焦和核燃料加工业	6		212192	2434	523
化学原料和化学制品制造业	145	19	2483944	452011	27712
医药制造业	11	1	111942	46556	2563
化学纤维制造业	6	2	41707	6663	908
橡胶和塑料制品业	459	76	3880355	949486	196212
非金属矿物制品业	84	6	1228434	327597	27776
黑色金属冶炼和压延加工业	36	10	558080	47988	6573
有色金属冶炼和压延加工业	53	11	715795	70192	8848
金属制品业	243	28	2295960	477973	86118
通用设备制造业	176	19	4574020	577610	93358
专用设备制造业	138	13	1217882	313261	51943
汽车制造业	40	5	848839	232353	16416
铁路、船舶、航空航天和其他运输设备制造业	12	2	459668	127391	7161
电气机械和器材制造业	439	72	8530577	1513610	255620
计算机、通信和其他电子设备制造业	762	143	25796459	4336666	707057
仪器仪表制造业	61	10	751085	266952	48757
其他制造业	46	9	885819	115101	25651
废弃资源综合利用业	1		24730	3556	314
金属制品、机械和设备修理业	2		6942	1433	175
电力、热力生产和供应业	14	3	5210596	1194292	21230
燃气生产和供应业	5		271800	42172	655
水的生产和供应业	32	14	251798	92422	4625

4-8 续表 1

(2011年)

单位：万元

项目	年末资产合计	#流动资产年合计	#产成品	固定资产合计	年末负债合计
总计	66127123	41732138	3526442	19882642	38770617
按轻重工业分					
轻工业	29023172	19332307	1722977	7748013	17331840
重工业	37103951	22399831	1803465	12134629	21438777
按企业规模分					
大型企业	27785580	15616536	1186263	10595509	16033825
中型企业	24363925	16116610	1436006	6077266	13749426
小型企业	13681671	9813861	890209	3133432	8802913
微型企业	295947	185132	13963	76436	184453
按工业行业分(大类)					
煤炭开采和洗选业					
石油和天然气开采业					
黑色金属矿采选业					
有色金属矿采选业					
非金属矿采选业					
开采辅助活动					
其他采矿业					
农副食品加工业	2021180	1667000	105027	267971	1667070
食品制造业	911169	517085	21686	216798	313869
酒、饮料和精制茶制造业	1029285	605360	56243	337115	623491
烟草制品业					
纺织业	2005943	1416525	127281	509979	1129403
纺织服装、服饰业	2475310	1981845	173219	381077	1503937
皮革、毛皮、羽毛及其制品和制鞋业	1785484	1350995	118012	342659	1158143
木材加工和木、竹、藤、棕、草制品业	176629	125148	10417	31890	111057
家具制造业	1623974	1182499	128650	331592	954503
造纸和纸制品业	5366158	2637152	282567	2343586	3141897
印刷和记录媒介复制业	1012782	714621	46931	240017	451055
文教、工美、体育和娱乐用品制造业	1560050	1106196	184645	324709	926605
石油加工、炼焦和核燃料加工业	132346	116980	27895	9963	99276
化学原料和化学制品制造业	2089343	1547487	110772	404401	1174798
医药制造业	221017	146027	4847	42211	53527
化学纤维制造业	22141	18208	1675	3497	16283
橡胶和塑料制品业	3234901	2230828	226390	828929	1856693
非金属矿物制品业	1730094	918380	83255	624195	932840
黑色金属冶炼和压延加工业	432144	361925	32068	56443	287936
有色金属冶炼和压延加工业	474280	382367	33912	71382	301254
金属制品业	1939038	1422400	102994	439377	1160487
通用设备制造业	2926743	2018045	114548	543126	1870184
专用设备制造业	1213438	826042	72244	299925	629208
汽车制造业	1295622	1047868	22763	215418	738867
铁路、船舶、航空航天和其他运输设备制造业	438376	233969	23152	155212	282071
电气机械和器材制造业	6345934	4393407	479107	1252787	3495013
计算机、通信和其他电子设备制造业	15622253	10602097	876579	4261790	9494863
仪器仪表制造业	830085	353717	26932	224795	330152
其他制造业	606116	431010	28972	141421	337039
废弃资源综合利用业	13270	8211	1095	2842	6024
金属制品、机械和设备修理业	13638	4292		9089	10857
电力、热力生产和供应业	5448225	1036524	13	4308879	2937967
燃气生产和供应业	202617	57323	560	99831	116989
水的生产和供应业	927540	270603	1994	559739	657262

4-8 续表 2

(2011年)

单位：万元

项目	主营业务收入	主营业务税金及附加	成本费用总额	本年应交增值税	亏损企业亏损总额
总计	84549238	201987	83806281	1433149	407800
按轻重工业分					
轻工业	35576518	113833	36617990	656589	204689
重工业	48972721	88155	47188291	776559	203112
按企业规模分					
大型企业	38080754	82881	36480072	598038	100340
中型企业	28839426	73336	27598706	484318	164447
小型企业	17233697	44401	16876434	346732	133266
微型企业	395361	1369	2851069	4061	9747
按工业行业分(大类)					
煤炭开采和洗选业					
石油和天然气开采业					
黑色金属矿采选业					
有色金属矿采选业					
非金属矿采选业					
开采辅助活动					
其他采矿业					
农副食品加工业	3023388	1645	2863661	42936	6602
食品制造业	833208	4917	719701	46822	588
酒、饮料和精制茶制造业	1743545	9564	1633338	56774	633
烟草制品业					
纺织业	2330881	5652	2283320	37980	20731
纺织服装、服饰业	3056066	9799	2879675	74055	18138
皮革、毛皮、羽毛及其制品和制鞋业	2894396	8952	2840561	39919	40393
木材加工和木、竹、藤、棕、草制品业	154402	899	151606	4636	2145
家具制造业	1972142	20076	1922676	40363	22819
造纸和纸制品业	4827662	13258	4688162	98299	2807
印刷和记录媒介复制业	982314	3956	873626	29336	3634
文教、工美、体育和娱乐用品制造业	2170259	6650	2089886	16870	17080
石油加工、炼焦和核燃料加工业	211032	414	207271	2021	
化学原料和化学制品制造业	2479834	7166	2360721	109655	28682
医药制造业	112359	945	92702	10066	231
化学纤维制造业	41087	123	40192	993	168
橡胶和塑料制品业	3914642	9787	6248415	59568	21228
非金属矿物制品业	1256497	3374	1145995	36577	5587
黑色金属冶炼和压延加工业	569268	658	574113	5708	6509
有色金属冶炼和压延加工业	716737	837	705009	5887	2223
金属制品业	2341030	7117	2281972	40981	5968
通用设备制造业	4581433	6705	4466038	37807	14512
专用设备制造业	1204475	3422	1137721	33363	750
汽车制造业	848048	2942	773098	45334	1189
铁路、船舶、航空航天和其他运输设备制造业	462764	1608	431763	1057	445
电气机械和器材制造业	8571613	16947	8286625	70016	32141
计算机、通信和其他电子设备制造业	25834791	43677	25148835	242769	126784
仪器仪表制造业	770757	1939	727790	5906	2891
其他制造业	899529	1409	889541	6072	6628
废弃资源综合利用业	25262	16	24457		
金属制品、机械和设备修理业	11864	8	11220	22	
电力、热力生产和供应业	5185043	5292	4813940	213948	5154
燃气生产和供应业	271788	143	238691	4815	
水的生产和供应业	251125	2093	253960	12595	11140

4-8 续表 3

(2011年)

项目	利税总额(万元)	人均税收(元)	利润总额(万元)	人均利润(元)
总计	4833042	6608	3165403	12544
按轻重工业分				
轻工业	2142095	5719	1362706	9999
重工业	2690946	7653	1802697	15531
按企业规模分				
大型企业	2282897	8634	1577542	19311
中型企业	1745187	4233	1180643	8853
小型企业	803939	10698	411635	11226
微型企业	1018	8649	-4417	-7028
按工业行业分(大类)				
煤炭开采和洗选业				
石油和天然气开采业				
黑色金属矿采选业				
有色金属矿采选业				
非金属矿采选业				
开采辅助活动				
其他采矿业				
农副食品加工业	188376	65949	143794	212713
食品制造业	162155	36339	109435	75431
酒、饮料和精制茶制造业	180795	51226	110053	79690
烟草制品业				
纺织业	92504	4271	48652	4738
纺织服装、服饰业	228249	5920	144241	10164
皮革、毛皮、羽毛及其制品和制鞋业	84730	1725	35086	1219
木材加工和木、竹、藤、棕、草制品业	6281	8392	710	1069
家具制造业	101154	6661	40573	4461
造纸和纸制品业	275900	16972	164149	24930
印刷和记录媒介复制业	154684	8841	121300	32126
文教、工美、体育和娱乐用品制造业	90326	1477	66011	4010
石油加工、炼焦和核燃料加工业	8402	46549	5967	114094
化学原料和化学制品制造业	221797	42160	104964	37877
医药制造业	30339	43089	19295	75284
化学纤维制造业	2088	12295	971	10698
橡胶和塑料制品业	179922	3552	110219	5617
非金属矿物制品业	153822	14545	113421	40834
黑色金属冶炼和压延加工业	10416	9685	4051	6162
有色金属冶炼和压延加工业	22130	7603	15404	17409
金属制品业	120276	5623	71852	8343
通用设备制造业	194902	4791	150175	16086
专用设备制造业	105960	7096	69099	13303
汽车制造业	124910	29408	76634	46682
铁路、船舶、航空航天和其他运输设备制造业	35438	3761	32745	45727
电气机械和器材制造业	410305	3420	322892	12632
计算机、通信和其他电子设备制造业	1000514	4074	712492	10077
仪器仪表制造业	49596	1647	41566	8525
其他制造业	25817	2916	18336	7148
废弃资源综合利用业	1172	519	1156	36815
金属制品、机械和设备修理业	151	1749	121	6897
电力、热力生产和供应业	520562	112759	281173	132441
燃气生产和供应业	38393	86521	32726	499629
水的生产和供应业	10978	32073	-3856	-8337

4-9 规模以上工业企业主要经济效益指标（2011年）

Main Indicators on Economic Benefit of Industrial Enterprises above Designated Size (2011)

项　　　目	工业增加值率(%)	总资产贡献率(%)	资　产负债率(%)	流动资产周转率(次/年)	成本费用利润率(%)	全员劳动生产率(元/人)	产　品销售率(%)
总　计	19.4	7.8	58.6	2.1	3.7	65087	99.6
按轻重工业分							
轻工业	21.4	7.9	59.7	1.9	3.6	55695	100.3
重工业	17.9	7.7	57.8	2.2	3.8	76113	99.1
按企业规模分							
大型企业	18.7	8.6	57.7	2.5	4.3	87683	99.6
中型企业	22.5	7.5	56.4	1.8	4.2	48990	99.3
小型企业	15.7	6.7	64.3	1.8	2.4	73323	100.2
微型企业	18.4	0.4	62.3	2.0	-0.2	62980	95.7
按工业行业分(大类)							
煤炭开采和洗选业							
石油和天然气开采业							
黑色金属矿采选业							
有色金属矿采选业							
非金属矿采选业							
开采辅助活动							
其他采矿业							
农副食品加工业	8.6	10.0	82.5	1.9	4.9	383140	99.5
食品制造业	32.2	17.5	34.5	1.6	15.2	174634	105.9
酒、饮料和精制茶制造业	14.2	18.4	60.6	2.9	6.7	178848	102.4
烟草制品业							
纺织业	21.3	4.8	56.3	1.7	2.1	48628	100.5
纺织服装、服饰业	25.3	9.5	60.8	1.6	5.0	54629	99.7
皮革、毛皮、羽毛及其制品和制鞋业	33.9	4.9	64.9	2.2	1.2	34084	99.2
木材加工和木、竹、藤、棕、草制品业	24.9	4.7	62.9	1.3	0.5	55791	103.3
家具制造业	25.4	6.6	58.8	1.7	2.1	55236	99.5
造纸和纸制品业	15.0	6.1	58.6	2.0	3.2	111081	99.6
印刷和记录媒介复制业	38.1	15.2	44.5	1.4	13.7	95435	102.8
文教、工美、体育和娱乐用品制造业	26.7	6.2	59.4	2.0	3.1	35278	100.2
石油加工、炼焦和核燃料加工业	1.2	7.5	75.0	1.8	2.9	46535	102.5
化学原料和化学制品制造业	18.0	10.9	56.2	1.6	4.4	163110	99.0
医药制造业	43.2	13.1	24.2	0.8	20.6	181646	103.8
化学纤维制造业	16.8	9.9	73.5	2.3	2.4	73384	105.0
橡胶和塑料制品业	24.3	5.8	57.4	1.8	1.8	48391	99.3
非金属矿物制品业	25.5	9.3	53.9	1.4	9.8	117943	95.7
黑色金属冶炼和压延加工业	8.2	3.6	66.6	1.6	0.7	73007	95.7
有色金属冶炼和压延加工业	9.7	5.4	63.5	1.9	2.2	79331	99.1
金属制品业	20.6	6.6	59.9	1.7	3.1	55502	98.8
通用设备制造业	12.6	6.8	63.9	2.3	3.4	61870	99.8
专用设备制造业	25.7	9.0	51.9	1.5	6.0	60309	99.9
汽车制造业	27.6	9.9	57.0	0.8	9.9	141541	100.8
铁路、船舶、航空航天和其他运输设备制造业	27.6	8.2	64.3	2.0	7.6	177896	99.5
电气机械和器材制造业	17.7	6.9	55.1	2.0	3.9	59213	99.5
计算机、通信和其他电子设备制造业	16.7	6.5	60.8	2.5	2.8	61334	99.2
仪器仪表制造业	35.3	6.2	39.8	2.2	5.7	54752	99.4
其他制造业	14.0	4.4	55.6	2.1	2.1	44872	107.6
废弃资源综合利用业	13.1	10.7	45.4	3.2	4.7	113236	90.7
金属制品、机械和设备修理业	20.6	1.1	79.6	2.8	1.1	81874	100.0
电力、热力生产和供应业	22.8	11.2	53.9	5.1	5.7	562549	99.6
燃气生产和供应业	15.6	20.0	57.7	4.7	13.7	643847	100.3
水的生产和供应业	35.2	3.8	70.9	0.9	-1.5	199830	95.8

4-10 规模以上国有及国有控股工业企业主要经济指标（2011年）

Main Indicators of State-owned and State-holding Industrial Enterprises above Designated Size (2011)

项目	企业单位数(个)	#亏损企业	工业增加值(万元)	主营业务收入(万元)	亏损企业亏损总额(万元)
总计	28	4	1477919	6490578	21206
按轻重工业分					
轻工业	13	2	154715	730388	8352
重工业	15	2	1323204	5760190	12855
按企业规模分					
大型企业	5	1	1111282	4818705	12753
中型企业	12	2	323498	1273159	7821
小型企业	11	1	43139	398714	633
微型企业					
按销售收入分					
10亿元以上	9	1	1370318	6064267	12753
5-10亿元	3		48695	230404	
1-5亿元	7	2	42317	147073	8352
1亿元以下	9	1	16590	48834	102
按工业行业分(大类)					
煤炭开采和洗选业					
石油和天然气开采业					
黑色金属矿采选业					
有色金属矿采选业					
非金属矿采选业					
开采辅助活动					
其他采矿业					
农副食品加工业	2		71318	523412	
食品制造业					
酒、饮料和精制茶制造业	3	1	11324	53854	633
烟草制品业					
纺织业					
纺织服装、服饰业	1		2343	10005	
皮革、毛皮、羽毛及其制品和制鞋业	1		4483	4631	
木材加工和木、竹、藤、棕、草制品业					
家具制造业					
造纸和纸制品业					
印刷和记录媒介复制业	1		985	2531	
文教、工美、体育和娱乐用品制造业	1		1047	4218	
石油加工、炼焦和核燃料加工业					
化学原料和化学制品制造业	2	1	21610	105591	12753
医药制造业					
化学纤维制造业					
橡胶和塑料制品业					
非金属矿物制品业	1		1663	6549	
黑色金属冶炼和压延加工业					
有色金属冶炼和压延加工业					
金属制品业	1		1296	5607	
通用设备制造业	2		7633	99516	
专用设备制造业	1		3587	9003	
汽车制造业					
铁路、船舶、航空航天和其他运输设备制造业	1		91004	300060	
电气机械和器材制造业					
计算机、通信和其他电子设备制造业	4	1	100526	406694	102
仪器仪表制造业					
其他制造业					
废弃资源综合利用业					
金属制品、机械和设备修理业					
电力、热力生产和供应业	5		1122976	4858786	
燃气生产和供应业					
水的生产和供应业	2	1	36124	100121	7719

4-10 续表 1

(2011年)

项　　目	利税总额(万元)	人均税收(元)	利润总额(万元)	人均利润(元)
总　　计	636088	76060	372227	107298
按轻重工业分				
轻工业	80280	25818	62858	93151
重工业	555808	88193	309369	110714
按企业规模分				
大型企业	389284	80971	183246	72013
中型企业	232555	68075	181989	245004
小型企业	14248	39932	6993	38484
微型企业				
按销售收入分				
10亿元以上	609832	91979	366346	138390
5-10亿元	9346	57785	3105	28753
1-5亿元	12668	24218	1188	2507
1亿元以下	4242	11065	1588	6619
按工业行业分(大类)				
煤炭开采和洗选业				
石油和天然气开采业				
黑色金属矿采选业				
有色金属矿采选业				
非金属矿采选业				
开采辅助活动				
其他采矿业				
农副食品加工业	61158	4401	60921	1132357
食品制造业				
酒、饮料和精制茶制造业	7820	78477	2091	28648
烟草制品业				
纺织业				
纺织服装、服饰业	262		262	5452
皮革、毛皮、羽毛及其制品和制鞋业	837	10283	26	323
木材加工和木、竹、藤、棕、草制品业				
家具制造业				
造纸和纸制品业				
印刷和记录媒介复制业	826	17858	599	47197
文教、工美、体育和娱乐用品制造业	287	14114	15	756
石油加工、炼焦和核燃料加工业				
化学原料和化学制品制造业	-8369	31624	-12670	-93161
医药制造业				
化学纤维制造业				
橡胶和塑料制品业				
非金属矿物制品业	227	5275	115	5464
黑色金属冶炼和压延加工业				
有色金属冶炼和压延加工业				
金属制品业	687	32278	455	63139
通用设备制造业	3496	34189	1175	17302
专用设备制造业	282		282	7552
汽车制造业				
铁路、船舶、航空航天和其他运输设备制造业	28460	4332	27541	129847
电气机械和器材制造业				
计算机、通信和其他电子设备制造业	57291	10024	50936	80341
仪器仪表制造业				
其他制造业				
废弃资源综合利用业				
金属制品、机械和设备修理业				
电力、热力生产和供应业	483124	120456	247536	126565
燃气生产和供应业				
水的生产和供应业	-299	60319	-7055	-62988

4-11 规模以上国有及国有控股工业企业主要经济效益指标（2011年）

Main Indicators on Economic Benefit of State-owned and State-holding Industrial Enterprises above Designated Size (2011)

项　　目	工业增加值率 (%)	总资产贡献率 (%)	资　产负债率 (%)	流动资产周转率 (次/年)	成本费用利润率 (%)	全员劳动生产率 (元/人)	产　品销售率 (%)
总　　计	22.4	10.9	53.6	4.1	6.0	426024	98.5
按轻重工业分							
轻工业	19.1	13.2	73.0	3.3	8.8	229275	89.2
重工业	22.9	10.7	51.3	4.2	5.7	473537	99.8
按企业规模分							
大型企业	23.1	9.2	54.4	5.9	4.0	436722	100.2
中型企业	23.5	18.3	45.4	2.0	15.9	435511	92.2
小型企业	10.9	7.7	80.7	3.5	1.8	237420	100.3
微型企业							
按工业行业分(大类)							
煤炭开采和洗选业							
石油和天然气开采业							
黑色金属矿采选业							
有色金属矿采选业							
非金属矿采选业							
开采辅助活动							
其他采矿业							
农副食品加工业	12.3	35.3	72.1	5.1	12.1	1325619	88.0
食品制造业							
酒、饮料和精制茶制造业	17.2	10.8	69.6	2.5	4.0	155118	81.8
烟草制品业							
纺织业							
纺织服装、服饰业	26.8	2.0	35.8	1.3	2.7	48821	114.6
皮革、毛皮、羽毛及其制品和制鞋业	96.8	11.0	16.1	1.2	0.6	56817	100.0
木材加工和木、竹、藤、棕、草制品业							
家具制造业							
造纸和纸制品业							
印刷和记录媒介复制业	36.3	19.3	28.2	0.8	31.4	77520	100.0
文教、工美、体育和娱乐用品制造业	24.2	8.3	4.7	2.4	0.3	54269	97.7
石油加工、炼焦和核燃料加工业							
化学原料和化学制品制造业	20.3	-3.0	73.0	0.7	-12.1	158899	101.9
医药制造业							
化学纤维制造业							
橡胶和塑料制品业							
非金属矿物制品业	23.9	4.9	73.6	2.3	1.5	78791	94.1
黑色金属冶炼和压延加工业							
有色金属冶炼和压延加工业							
金属制品业	21.2	10.3	64.1	0.7	8.6	180042	91.6
通用设备制造业	8.0	10.4	58.8	3.9	1.2	112418	104.0
专用设备制造业	29.8	0.5	54.1	0.5	3.2	96177	100.0
汽车制造业							
铁路、船舶、航空航天和其他运输设备制造业	31.4	9.2	65.8	2.2	10.0	429059	102.0
电气机械和器材制造业							
计算机、通信和其他电子设备制造业	24.1	9.7	31.3	1.5	13.4	158558	100.6
仪器仪表制造业							
其他制造业							
废弃资源综合利用业							
金属制品、机械和设备修理业							
电力、热力生产和供应业	23.0	11.6	51.6	6.3	5.4	574177	99.6
燃气生产和供应业							
水的生产和供应业	33.3	3.8	84.8	1.5	-6.6	322535	92.2

4-12 规模以上集体工业主要经济指标（2011年）

Main Indicators of Collective-owned Industrial Enterprises above Designated Size (2011)

项目	企业单位数（个）	#亏损企业	工业增加值（万元）	主营业务收入（万元）	亏损企业亏损总额（万元）
总计	81	25	254458	747127	22208
按轻重工业分					
轻工业	62	20	165523	584535	19545
重工业	19	5	88935	162592	2662
按企业规模分					
大型企业	2		65988	199491	
中型企业	29	9	128536	340604	14077
小型企业	40	14	57128	176669	7563
微型企业	10	2	2805	30364	568
按销售收入分					
10亿元以上	1		21840	147454	
5-10亿元	1		44149	52037	
1-5亿元	14	2	94758	280375	4187
1亿元以下	65	23	93712	267261	18021
按工业行业分(大类)					
煤炭开采和洗选业					
石油和天然气开采业					
黑色金属矿采选业					
有色金属矿采选业					
非金属矿采选业					
开采辅助活动					
其他采矿业					
农副食品加工业	1		948	3655	
食品制造业					
酒、饮料和精制茶制造业					
烟草制品业					
纺织业					
纺织服装、服饰业	4		8656	20273	
皮革、毛皮、羽毛及其制品和制鞋业	7	4	22766	58734	12598
木材加工和木、竹、藤、棕、草制品业					
家具制造业					
造纸和纸制品业	12	2	31415	244656	103
印刷和记录媒介复制业	1		1821	4440	
文教、工美、体育和娱乐用品制造业	1	1	1068	2990	2447
石油加工、炼焦和核燃料加工业					
化学原料和化学制品制造业	1		594	2022	
医药制造业					
化学纤维制造业					
橡胶和塑料制品业	6	1	54821	83062	156
非金属矿物制品业	1		279	2541	
黑色金属冶炼和压延加工业					
有色金属冶炼和压延加工业					
金属制品业					
通用设备制造业					
专用设备制造业					
汽车制造业					
铁路、船舶、航空航天和其他运输设备制造业					
电气机械和器材制造业	8		42432	129088	
计算机、通信和其他电子设备制造业	12	4	32782	63920	2619
仪器仪表制造业	1	1	10415	10429	1360
其他制造业					
废弃资源综合利用业					
金属制品、机械和设备修理业					
电力、热力生产和供应业	1	1	214	3217	43
燃气生产和供应业					
水的生产和供应业	25	11	46246	118101	2881

4-12 续表 1

(2011年)

项　　目	利税总额(万元)	人均税收(元)	利润总额(万元)	人均利润(元)
总　计	28488	2683	5629	661
按轻重工业分				
轻工业	19603	4477	-559	-124
重工业	8885	672	6188	1541
按企业规模分				
大型企业	17306	7157	6170	3965
中型企业	4823	728	382	63
小型企业	6319	10588	-832	-1232
微型企业	41	688	-91	-472
按销售收入分				
10亿元以上	15054	63596	5514	36761
5-10亿元	2252	1136	656	466
1-5亿元	10548	1147	6458	1811
1亿元以下	635	2247	-6999	-2060
按工业行业分(大类)				
煤炭开采和洗选业				
石油和天然气开采业				
黑色金属矿采选业				
有色金属矿采选业				
非金属矿采选业				
开采辅助活动				
其他采矿业				
农副食品加工业	69	3613	35	3753
食品制造业				
酒、饮料和精制茶制造业				
烟草制品业				
纺织业				
纺织服装、服饰业	580	785	346	1162
皮革、毛皮、羽毛及其制品和制鞋业	-11318	78	-11475	-5659
木材加工和木、竹、藤、棕、草制品业				
家具制造业				
造纸和纸制品业	17822	36235	6339	20004
印刷和记录媒介复制业	12		12	2054
文教、工美、体育和娱乐用品制造业	-2446	3	-2447	-8545
石油加工、炼焦和核燃料加工业				
化学原料和化学制品制造业	71	6359	31	4781
医药制造业				
化学纤维制造业				
橡胶和塑料制品业	5089	1053	3142	1699
非金属矿物制品业	85	1293	78	13362
黑色金属冶炼和压延加工业				
有色金属冶炼和压延加工业				
金属制品业				
通用设备制造业				
专用设备制造业				
汽车制造业				
铁路、船舶、航空航天和其他运输设备制造业				
电气机械和器材制造业	7654	348	7214	5698
计算机、通信和其他电子设备制造业	2721	1105	532	268
仪器仪表制造业	-1360		-1360	-7556
其他制造业				
废弃资源综合利用业				
金属制品、机械和设备修理业				
电力、热力生产和供应业	-17	17133	-43	-28533
燃气生产和供应业				
水的生产和供应业	9527	22114	3226	11324

4-13 规模以上集体工业企业主要经济效益指标（2011年）

Main Indicators on Economic Benefit of Collective-owned Industrial Enterprises above Designated Size (2011)

项目	工业增加值率(%)	总资产贡献率(%)	资产负债率(%)	流动资产周转率(次/年)	成本费用利润率(%)	全员劳动生产率(元/人)	产品销售率(%)
总计	35.4	4.1	66.5	2.2	0.8	29868	100.5
按轻重工业分							
轻工业	29.0	3.9	71.4	2.0	-0.1	36751	99.3
重工业	59.9	4.9	50.9	3.9	3.9	22148	105.3
按企业规模分							
大型企业	32.7	12.6	69.1	2.4	3.3	42412	99.5
中型企业	39.8	2.2	55.5	4.9	0.1	21086	102.5
小型企业	31.6	3.0	72.6	1.1	-0.5	84584	98.2
微型企业	22.1	0.2	73.9	1.6	-0.3	14580	99.7
按工业行业分(大类)							
煤炭开采和洗选业							
石油和天然气开采业							
黑色金属矿采选业							
有色金属矿采选业							
非金属矿采选业							
开采辅助活动							
其他采矿业							
农副食品加工业	23.6	7.9	46.2	8.9	0.9	101957	91.1
食品制造业							
酒、饮料和精制茶制造业							
烟草制品业							
纺织业							
纺织服装、服饰业	42.7	3.5	56.0	2.3	2.2	29036	100.0
皮革、毛皮、羽毛及其制品和制鞋业	46.5	-50.3	204.2	2.9	-16.4	11226	99.9
木材加工和木、竹、藤、棕、草制品业							
家具制造业							
造纸和纸制品业	12.7	10.7	59.7	2.6	2.7	99133	99.4
印刷和记录媒介复制业	36.3	0.1	24.8	2.1	0.2	325107	100.0
文教、工美、体育和娱乐用品制造业	35.7	-140.9	15.8	1.9	-45.0	3728	100.0
石油加工、炼焦和核燃料加工业							
化学原料和化学制品制造业	28.2	5.9	83.7	1.6	1.5	92859	95.8
医药制造业							
化学纤维制造业							
橡胶和塑料制品业	76.3	9.6	92.5	3.9	4.0	29644	101.1
非金属矿物制品业	11.2	15.1	82.2	27.4	3.2	48103	102.4
黑色金属冶炼和压延加工业							
有色金属冶炼和压延加工业							
金属制品业							
通用设备制造业							
专用设备制造业							
汽车制造业							
铁路、船舶、航空航天和其他运输设备制造业							
电气机械和器材制造业	36.9	5.1	36.6	7.5	5.8	33514	106.8
计算机、通信和其他电子设备制造业	51.3	12.3	111.5	6.5	0.8	16547	99.5
仪器仪表制造业	99.9	-26.0	136.4	3.9	-11.5	57863	100.0
其他制造业							
废弃资源综合利用业							
金属制品、机械和设备修理业							
电力、热力生产和供应业	6.7	0.3	101.2	0.8	-1.3	142800	100.0
燃气生产和供应业							
水的生产和供应业	38.1	4.0	67.4	0.8	2.8	162325	97.9

4-14 规模以上外商投资工业企业主要经济指标（2011年）

Main Indicators of Industrial Enterprises above Designated Size with Foreign Funds (2011)

项目	企业单位数（个）	#亏损企业	工业增加值（万元）	主营业务收入（万元）	亏损企业亏损总额（万元）
总计	1073	231	4808731	27114627	153903
按轻重工业分					
轻工业	477	109	1962672	9271460	55852
重工业	596	122	2846059	17843167	98052
按企业规模分					
大型企业	75	5	2256880	14039896	40430
中型企业	453	91	1730524	7770816	56337
小型企业	525	130	807359	5204656	55609
微型企业	20	5	13968	99260	1527
按销售收入分					
10亿元以上	43	4	1832444	13849229	14783
5-10亿元	49	5	689304	3271971	30985
1-5亿元	331	60	1508137	6835384	69796
1亿元以下	650	162	778846	3158043	38340
按工业行业分(大类)					
煤炭开采和洗选业					
石油和天然气开采业					
黑色金属矿采选业					
有色金属矿采选业					
非金属矿采选业					
开采辅助活动					
其他采矿业					
农副食品加工业	6	2	72647	824001	6136
食品制造业	4		174847	500304	
酒、饮料和精制茶制造业	2		112283	424625	
烟草制品业					
纺织业	22	4	57736	383545	389
纺织服装、服饰业	22	3	69603	243131	163
皮革、毛皮、羽毛及其制品和制鞋业	85	15	306198	1067039	3069
木材加工和木、竹、藤、棕、草制品业	4	3	3472	15656	814
家具制造业	49	11	145214	594696	12564
造纸和纸制品业	13	1	107740	582781	204
印刷和记录媒介复制业	10	1	90589	191812	390
文教、工美、体育和娱乐用品制造业	53	13	143642	449270	5047
石油加工、炼焦和核燃料加工业					
化学原料和化学制品制造业	43	8	189937	990414	10377
医药制造业	1	1	1880	5961	231
化学纤维制造业					
橡胶和塑料制品业	124	29	277947	1166815	5957
非金属矿物制品业	16	4	40135	194470	2901
黑色金属冶炼和压延加工业	11	3	11610	175502	1152
有色金属冶炼和压延加工业	16	3	20034	269004	516
金属制品业	51	13	107346	656634	2477
通用设备制造业	55	9	228040	1538030	10773
专用设备制造业	39	3	124525	552078	198
汽车制造业	15	3	147453	526533	897
铁路、船舶、航空航天和其他运输设备制造业	6	2	18309	89520	445
电气机械和器材制造业	127	29	502771	3264078	10989
计算机、通信和其他电子设备制造业	256	62	1654956	11269748	71049
仪器仪表制造业	18	2	102188	276293	268
其他制造业	18	5	30335	484473	1787
废弃资源综合利用业					
金属制品、机械和设备修理业					
电力、热力生产和供应业	4	2	26735	124477	5111
燃气生产和供应业	3		40563	253738	
水的生产和供应业					

4-14 续表 1

(2011年)

项目	利税总额(万元)	人均税收(元)	利润总额(万元)	人均利润(元)
总计	1438649	6737	957531	13408
按轻重工业分				
轻工业	619918	6867	394938	12055
重工业	818730	6626	562593	14554
按企业规模分				
大型企业	795059	7961	577836	21178
中型企业	372467	3596	245947	6990
小型企业	270898	15632	134354	15381
微型企业	225	3949	-606	-2881
按销售收入分				
10亿元以上	798414	14857	564716	35900
5-10亿元	232171	9390	139960	14253
1-5亿元	295493	3489	201123	7435
1亿元以下	112570	3234	51732	2750
按工业行业分(大类)				
煤炭开采和洗选业				
石油和天然气开采业				
黑色金属矿采选业				
有色金属矿采选业				
非金属矿采选业				
开采辅助活动				
其他采矿业				
农副食品加工业	33713	43938	27079	179328
食品制造业	124582	56293	87614	133415
酒、饮料和精制茶制造业	96631	42606	59483	68222
烟草制品业				
纺织业	7991	1892	5609	4456
纺织服装、服饰业	10568	2077	7378	4802
皮革、毛皮、羽毛及其制品和制鞋业	31058	1515	18120	2122
木材加工和木、竹、藤、棕、草制品业	-470	4106	-750	-10991
家具制造业	37379	11998	4739	1742
造纸和纸制品业	42201	15428	32330	50532
印刷和记录媒介复制业	58235	12020	51878	98086
文教、工美、体育和娱乐用品制造业	15720	2471	5572	1357
石油加工、炼焦和核燃料加工业				
化学原料和化学制品制造业	106107	79221	31133	32896
医药制造业	-225	272	-231	-10840
化学纤维制造业				
橡胶和塑料制品业	55851	3515	38185	7597
非金属矿物制品业	7565	6546	4788	11284
黑色金属冶炼和压延加工业	2950	11486	1770	17236
有色金属冶炼和压延加工业	5854	9648	3390	13272
金属制品业	21204	3471	15770	10073
通用设备制造业	58390	3466	46922	14180
专用设备制造业	45263	7919	28542	13517
汽车制造业	92635	49761	57583	81748
铁路、船舶、航空航天和其他运输设备制造业	5203	3628	4320	17749
电气机械和器材制造业	93883	2181	75067	8702
计算机、通信和其他电子设备制造业	397853	4903	276123	11123
仪器仪表制造业	25500	1411	23622	17757
其他制造业	11534	6407	6811	9239
废弃资源综合利用业				
金属制品、机械和设备修理业				
电力、热力生产和供应业	14886	29950	13442	278878
燃气生产和供应业	36590	88200	31245	515594
水的生产和供应业				

4-15 规模以上外商投资工业企业主要经济效益指标（2011年）

Main Indicators on Economic Benefit of Industrial Enterprises above Designated Size with Foreign Funds (2011)

项　　目	工业增加值率(%)	总资产贡献率(%)	资产负债率(%)	流动资产周转率(次/年)	成本费用利润率(%)	全员劳动生产率(元/人)	产品销售率(%)
总　计	17.7	7.6	56.2	2.1	3.6	67335	99.7
按轻重工业分							
轻工业	21.5	8.7	53.4	2.0	4.4	59910	101.7
重工业	15.8	6.9	57.8	2.1	3.2	73628	98.6
按企业规模分							
大型企业	16.0	9.0	58.0	2.3	4.3	82717	99.7
中型企业	22.0	5.9	52.4	1.9	3.2	49183	99.0
小型企业	15.8	7.3	58.2	1.8	2.6	92430	100.7
微型企业	23.3	0.3	64.4	2.5	-0.6	66451	98.3
按工业行业分(大类)							
煤炭开采和洗选业							
石油和天然气开采业							
黑色金属矿采选业							
有色金属矿采选业							
非金属矿采选业							
开采辅助活动							
其他采矿业							
农副食品加工业	9.2	8.5	72.5	2.3	3.4	481104	101.6
食品制造业	38.2	20.6	25.9	1.7	21.4	266252	109.4
酒、饮料和精制茶制造业	26.1	32.2	41.7	2.0	16.3	128780	107.7
烟草制品业							
纺织业	14.9	4.0	60.4	1.9	1.5	45866	100.9
纺织服装、服饰业	29.8	4.5	73.2	1.4	3.1	45306	100.3
皮革、毛皮、羽毛及其制品和制鞋业	28.5	4.5	58.5	2.2	1.7	35865	100.2
木材加工和木、竹、藤、棕、草制品业	22.3	1.3	56.2	0.6	-4.0	50912	101.7
家具制造业	24.5	7.7	55.0	1.6	0.8	53376	100.1
造纸和纸制品业	18.4	5.2	35.3	1.7	5.8	168396	99.6
印刷和记录媒介复制业	47.6	25.2	28.8	1.1	36.8	171277	99.9
文教、工美、体育和娱乐用品制造业	31.4	4.2	49.4	1.8	1.3	34979	101.0
石油加工、炼焦和核燃料加工业							
化学原料和化学制品制造业	19.0	14.3	62.6	1.8	3.2	200694	98.9
医药制造业	31.5	-10.3	113.9	3.1	-3.7	88254	100.0
化学纤维制造业							
橡胶和塑料制品业	23.8	5.7	55.8	1.8	3.3	55296	99.9
非金属矿物制品业	19.0	2.8	47.1	1.4	2.5	94590	91.7
黑色金属冶炼和压延加工业	6.4	3.2	56.0	1.5	1.0	113044	87.8
有色金属冶炼和压延加工业	7.4	4.1	56.7	2.2	1.3	78441	98.9
金属制品业	16.6	4.4	56.9	1.8	2.5	68565	97.0
通用设备制造业	14.7	4.9	59.3	2.0	3.1	68913	99.0
专用设备制造业	22.4	9.4	50.8	1.5	5.4	58972	99.8
汽车制造业	28.6	9.4	57.1	0.6	12.2	209331	101.7
铁路、船舶、航空航天和其他运输设备制造业	19.5	7.4	60.2	1.6	5.1	75220	96.6
电气机械和器材制造业	15.4	4.3	51.2	2.2	2.3	58285	99.8
计算机、通信和其他电子设备制造业	14.5	6.5	62.7	2.6	2.5	66664	98.6
仪器仪表制造业	36.7	12.6	54.3	2.6	9.3	76816	99.7
其他制造业	7.4	5.0	57.1	2.9	1.4	41149	114.9
废弃资源综合利用业							
金属制品、机械和设备修理业							
电力、热力生产和供应业	20.8	9.6	61.5	1.6	10.9	554658	100.0
燃气生产和供应业	16.0	20.0	58.0	4.7	14.1	669363	100.3
水的生产和供应业							

4-16 规模以上港澳台商投资工业企业主要经济指标（2011年）

Main Indicators of Industrial Enterprises above Designated Size with Hong Kong, Macao and Taiwan Funds(2011)

项　　　目	企　业 单位数 (个)	#亏 损 企 业	工　业 增加值 (万元)	主营业 务收入 (万元)	亏损企业 亏损总额 (万元)
总　　计	1823	339	7290036	34360045	190517
按轻重工业分					
轻工业	1017	199	3693531	16267436	110297
重工业	806	140	3596504	18092609	80220
按企业规模分					
大型企业	93	10	2938575	14496695	47157
中型企业	871	136	3455952	14073066	74032
小型企业	819	179	883975	5644592	61886
微型企业	40	14	11534	145692	7443
按销售收入分					
10亿元以上	49	2	2415175	14211002	29223
5-10亿元	58	10	860509	3993878	22038
1-5亿元	515	71	2663539	10706526	60930
1亿元以下	1201	256	1350813	5448639	78327
按工业行业分(大类)					
煤炭开采和洗选业					
石油和天然气开采业					
黑色金属矿采选业					
有色金属矿采选业					
非金属矿采选业					
开采辅助活动					
其他采矿业					
农副食品加工业	6	1	47127	440647	305
食品制造业	10	1	52218	189450	176
酒、饮料和精制茶制造业	5	1	126506	1250552	633
烟草制品业					
纺织业	105	22	361152	1532959	18421
纺织服装、服饰业	84	18	209204	699116	17901
皮革、毛皮、羽毛及其制品和制鞋业	137	28	545137	1421707	24720
木材加工和木、竹、藤、棕、草制品业	9	4	21758	69777	1151
家具制造业	68	20	157463	634700	9771
造纸和纸制品业	80	13	413354	2609139	1936
印刷和记录媒介复制业	41	5	225515	649120	3218
文教、工美、体育和娱乐用品制造业	110	24	387414	1245911	9532
石油加工、炼焦和核燃料加工业	3		622	55038	
化学原料和化学制品制造业	48	7	146522	779592	5346
医药制造业	5		5596	18470	
化学纤维制造业	4	1	4238	29782	146
橡胶和塑料制品业	212	43	478913	1975309	15088
非金属矿物制品业	31	2	208007	729680	2686
黑色金属冶炼和压延加工业	15	6	22470	266292	5167
有色金属冶炼和压延加工业	16	7	29424	208447	1605
金属制品业	103	12	221549	1004225	2798
通用设备制造业	73	8	271894	2631030	1351
专用设备制造业	63	8	135301	428491	469
汽车制造业	15	2	62122	203309	292
铁路、船舶、航空航天和其他运输设备制造业	3		104166	359833	
电气机械和器材制造业	186	33	703894	3684520	20131
计算机、通信和其他电子设备制造业	336	64	1962807	9872736	45999
仪器仪表制造业	30	6	109211	295335	1184
其他制造业	20	3	80654	348793	496
废弃资源综合利用业					
金属制品、机械和设备修理业	1		1433	6939	
电力、热力生产和供应业	4		194366	719145	
燃气生产和供应业					
水的生产和供应业					

4-16 续表 1

(2011年)

项目	利税总额(万元)	人均税收(元)	利润总额(万元)	人均利润(元)
总计	1822378	3934	1319747	10329
按轻重工业分				
轻工业	809000	3719	535575	7285
重工业	1013379	4225	784172	14456
按企业规模分				
大型企业	751695	3633	604336	14898
中型企业	881319	3674	613945	8437
小型企业	193980	6075	107460	7545
微型企业	-4616	7182	-5994	-31234
按销售收入分				
10亿元以上	897985	6836	724430	28534
5-10亿元	235339	6547	165709	15580
1-5亿元	515050	3014	356305	6765
1亿元以下	174004	2577	73303	1876
按工业行业分(大类)				
煤炭开采和洗选业				
石油和天然气开采业				
黑色金属矿采选业				
有色金属矿采选业				
非金属矿采选业				
开采辅助活动				
其他采矿业				
农副食品加工业	36126	356172	5851	68838
食品制造业	27461	24614	16766	38587
酒、饮料和精制茶制造业	78670	68594	47844	106462
烟草制品业				
纺织业	61700	4006	32338	4412
纺织服装、服饰业	18233	2645	4238	801
皮革、毛皮、羽毛及其制品和制鞋业	28309	898	13847	860
木材加工和木、竹、藤、棕、草制品业	4304	9342	1050	3014
家具制造业	19528	3460	8083	2443
造纸和纸制品业	145704	15012	95405	28474
印刷和记录媒介复制业	87783	8332	65170	24013
文教、工美、体育和娱乐用品制造业	53984	843	44545	3977
石油加工、炼焦和核燃料加工业	5289	77449	3617	167431
化学原料和化学制品制造业	81371	21467	59952	60084
医药制造业	2478	15519	1709	34531
化学纤维制造业	1536	15347	779	15807
橡胶和塑料制品业	75889	2527	48573	4493
非金属矿物制品业	116187	17304	91548	64294
黑色金属冶炼和压延加工业	2877	9959	-55	-188
有色金属冶炼和压延加工业	9095	3736	7831	23133
金属制品业	44790	3206	29558	6222
通用设备制造业	103202	4635	83580	19742
专用设备制造业	39038	6002	25528	11340
汽车制造业	22802	13479	13041	18007
铁路、船舶、航空航天和其他运输设备制造业	29036	2468	27968	64635
电气机械和器材制造业	200804	2570	170304	14348
计算机、通信和其他电子设备制造业	349571	2098	277699	8105
仪器仪表制造业	8554	894	5958	2051
其他制造业	15733	866	14288	8566
废弃资源综合利用业				
金属制品、机械和设备修理业	86	629	75	4269
电力、热力生产和供应业	152240	624046	122660	2587757
燃气生产和供应业				
水的生产和供应业				

4-17 规模以上港澳台商投资工业企业主要经济效益指标（2011年）

Main Indicators on Economic Benefit of Industrial Enterprises above Designated Size with Hong Kong, Macao and Taiwan Funds(2011)

项目	工业增加值率(%)	总资产贡献率(%)	资产负债率(%)	流动资产周转率(次/年)	成本费用利润率(%)	全员劳动生产率(元/人)	产品销售率(%)
总计	21.1	6.8	56.2	2.0	3.6	57058	99.6
按轻重工业分							
轻工业	22.7	6.2	57.1	1.9	2.9	50239	100.0
重工业	19.8	7.3	55.4	2.0	4.5	66299	99.3
按企业规模分							
大型企业	20.1	6.9	57.7	2.3	4.2	72443	99.8
中型企业	24.4	7.8	52.9	1.8	4.5	47494	99.5
小型企业	15.6	4.5	61.0	1.5	1.9	62064	99.5
微型企业	11.7	-3.1	41.5	1.5	-0.2	60105	91.9
按工业行业分(大类)							
煤炭开采和洗选业							
石油和天然气开采业							
黑色金属矿采选业							
有色金属矿采选业							
非金属矿采选业							
开采辅助活动							
其他采矿业							
农副食品加工业	10.0	15.7	72.6	2.5	1.4	554433	93.3
食品制造业	27.3	13.9	36.3	1.5	9.6	120178	99.6
酒、饮料和精制茶制造业	10.3	12.7	68.5	3.4	4.0	281500	101.7
烟草制品业							
纺织业	23.1	4.0	50.3	1.5	2.1	49269	99.2
纺织服装、服饰业	30.5	2.7	50.9	1.4	0.6	39543	100.6
皮革、毛皮、羽毛及其制品和制鞋业	38.2	3.3	66.4	2.0	1.0	33847	98.5
木材加工和木、竹、藤、棕、草制品业	31.2	5.5	57.7	1.1	1.5	62468	101.2
家具制造业	24.8	3.5	53.7	1.5	1.3	47598	99.9
造纸和纸制品业	15.7	5.2	59.4	1.8	3.2	123367	100.4
印刷和记录媒介复制业	36.2	13.0	45.8	1.5	10.8	83093	104.2
文教、工美、体育和娱乐用品制造业	31.2	5.9	62.5	1.8	3.7	34585	100.1
石油加工、炼焦和核燃料加工业	1.2	12.6	55.1	1.2	6.9	28810	103.9
化学原料和化学制品制造业	18.6	12.3	42.6	1.5	8.3	146845	99.3
医药制造业	30.8	6.8	83.7	0.8	10.2	113051	99.3
化学纤维制造业	14.7	11.1	64.6	2.4	2.7	85953	106.9
橡胶和塑料制品业	24.1	4.4	53.5	1.6	1.1	44299	98.5
非金属矿物制品业	27.8	10.9	49.5	1.4	14.2	146083	96.7
黑色金属冶炼和压延加工业	8.3	2.7	66.8	1.7	-0.02	76326	99.6
有色金属冶炼和压延加工业	13.7	6.2	57.2	1.8	3.8	86923	97.2
金属制品业	22.6	5.2	56.6	1.7	2.8	46633	101.7
通用设备制造业	10.4	7.2	67.3	2.5	3.3	64223	99.9
专用设备制造业	31.1	8.4	43.4	1.5	6.2	60104	100.6
汽车制造业	30.0	12.3	42.8	1.8	6.8	85781	98.9
铁路、船舶、航空航天和其他运输设备制造业	29.5	8.3	65.1	2.2	8.4	240736	100.4
电气机械和器材制造业	19.0	8.1	58.7	2.0	4.8	59301	99.5
计算机、通信和其他电子设备制造业	19.8	5.3	57.4	2.3	2.9	57289	99.5
仪器仪表制造业	37.3	1.8	28.2	2.0	2.0	37603	101.2
其他制造业	23.2	5.3	35.9	1.8	4.3	48354	100.3
废弃资源综合利用业							
金属制品、机械和设备修理业	20.6	1.7	58.9	2.0	1.1	81874	100.0
电力、热力生产和供应业	26.6	21.5	54.1	1.9	19.6	4100544	98.6
燃气生产和供应业							
水的生产和供应业							

4-18 规模以上私营工业企业主要经济指标（2011年）

Main Indicators of Private Industrial Enterprises above Designated Size (2011)

项　　目	企　业 单位数 (个)	#亏 损 企 业	工　业 增加值 (万元)	主营业 务收入 (万元)	亏损企业 亏损总额 (万元)
总　　计	736	39	1422436	7616185	9152
按轻重工业分					
轻工业	430	25	876465	4555638	2181
重工业	306	14	545971	3060547	6971
按企业规模分					
大型企业	13		346452	1395533	
中型企业	177	9	533538	2736574	7889
小型企业	517	26	536083	3395780	1054
微型企业	29	4	6363	88298	209
按销售收入分					
10亿元以上	6		242645	1124949	
5-10亿元	15	1	148267	1013846	123
1-5亿元	158	8	522806	2974545	7141
1亿元以下	557	30	508718	2502844	1888
按工业行业分(大类)					
煤炭开采和洗选业					
石油和天然气开采业					
黑色金属矿采选业					
有色金属矿采选业					
非金属矿采选业					
开采辅助活动					
其他采矿业					
农副食品加工业	11	1	20969	309950	31
食品制造业	10	1	12715	85987	411
酒、饮料和精制茶制造业	1		368	27888	
烟草制品业					
纺织业	31	3	38674	226518	987
纺织服装、服饰业	112	2	409275	1792077	19
皮革、毛皮、羽毛及其制品和制鞋业	20		53750	187575	
木材加工和木、竹、藤、棕、草制品业	8	2	5808	44054	181
家具制造业	46	8	76132	370788	339
造纸和纸制品业	70	2	101989	781896	164
印刷和记录媒介复制业	10	1	23100	74868	27
文教、工美、体育和娱乐用品制造业	13	1	12873	70753	2
石油加工、炼焦和核燃料加工业	1		60	5106	
化学原料和化学制品制造业	24	1	46194	252990	6
医药制造业					
化学纤维制造业	1		1960	8529	
橡胶和塑料制品业	78	3	82900	414766	27
非金属矿物制品业	18		56765	214643	
黑色金属冶炼和压延加工业	6		11155	67951	
有色金属冶炼和压延加工业	12	1	12493	128028	102
金属制品业	49		41700	268059	
通用设备制造业	20		40312	177125	
专用设备制造业	22	2	20974	111587	83
汽车制造业	2		5455	28419	
铁路、船舶、航空航天和其他运输设备制造业	3		4916	13411	
电气机械和器材制造业	79	7	128303	908366	897
计算机、通信和其他电子设备制造业	75	3	167832	853200	5799
仪器仪表制造业	9	1	42362	166784	79
其他制造业	4		3403	19941	
废弃资源综合利用业					
金属制品、机械和设备修理业	1			4925	
电力、热力生产和供应业					
燃气生产和供应业					
水的生产和供应业					

4-18 续表 1

(2011年)

项　　目	利税总额(万元)	人均税收(元)	利润总额(万元)	人均利润(元)
总　计	537388	9953	328643	15670
按轻重工业分				
轻工业	346752	9999	214002	16120
重工业	190636	9873	114641	14894
按企业规模分				
大型企业	181657	13075	134514	37308
中型企业	167483	7488	93988	9577
小型企业	186496	11521	99865	13281
微型企业	1751	43421	275	8091
按销售收入分				
10亿元以上	150583	18819	111834	54315
5-10亿元	61023	10412	46153	32313
1-5亿元	191948	9743	113227	14014
1亿元以下	133834	8123	57430	6106
按工业行业分(大类)				
煤炭开采和洗选业				
石油和天然气开采业				
黑色金属矿采选业				
有色金属矿采选业				
非金属矿采选业				
开采辅助活动				
其他采矿业				
农副食品加工业	15851	17038	13950	124997
食品制造业	4037	13957	1345	6971
酒、饮料和精制茶制造业	11	754	2	115
烟草制品业				
纺织业	12868	6220	6979	7371
纺织服装、服饰业	186758	11348	125534	23269
皮革、毛皮、羽毛及其制品和制鞋业	22085	12538	10592	11554
木材加工和木、竹、藤、棕、草制品业	1352	10454	69	563
家具制造业	19259	5375	11711	8339
造纸和纸制品业	44631	16471	23852	18906
印刷和记录媒介复制业	3335	5710	1608	5320
文教、工美、体育和娱乐用品制造业	2428	3527	1209	3499
石油加工、炼焦和核燃料加工业	286	51047	67	15465
化学原料和化学制品制造业	23131	21829	15988	48864
医药制造业				
化学纤维制造业	504	9298	214	6862
橡胶和塑料制品业	20571	10074	9051	7914
非金属矿物制品业	19359	13876	10639	16931
黑色金属冶炼和压延加工业	3461	5904	2293	11591
有色金属冶炼和压延加工业	3918	16112	2054	17752
金属制品业	10953	8628	4150	5264
通用设备制造业	19845	17622	12486	29900
专用设备制造业	9078	8456	6050	16894
汽车制造业	2626	27091	1407	31256
铁路、船舶、航空航天和其他运输设备制造业	1200	18553	457	11435
电气机械和器材制造业	41923	9961	21487	10474
计算机、通信和其他电子设备制造业	50784	5509	32427	9732
仪器仪表制造业	16301	8266	12816	30398
其他制造业	769	10408	162	2784
废弃资源综合利用业				
金属制品、机械和设备修理业	66		46	
电力、热力生产和供应业				
燃气生产和供应业				
水的生产和供应业				

4-19 规模以上私营工业企业主要经济效益指标（2011年）

Main Indicators on Economic Benefit of Private Industrial Enterprises above Designated Size (2011)

项　　目	工业增加值率(%)	总资产贡献率(%)	资　产负债率(%)	流动资产周转率(次/年)	成本费用利润率(%)	全员劳动生产率(元/人)	产　品销售率(%)
总　　计	18.7	11.3	69.8	1.9	4.5	67822	99.2
按轻重工业分							
轻工业	19.2	13.0	68.9	2.1	4.9	66020	99.4
重工业	17.8	9.2	70.9	1.8	3.9	70930	98.9
按企业规模分							
大型企业	23.6	17.6	53.5	1.6	10.7	96090	94.9
中型企业	19.5	9.3	70.6	2.0	3.6	54363	99.0
小型企业	15.8	10.2	76.9	2.1	3.0	71295	101.2
微型企业	22.0	4.2	78.4	4.3	0.4	187138	98.7
按工业行业分(大类)							
煤炭开采和洗选业							
石油和天然气开采业							
黑色金属矿采选业							
有色金属矿采选业							
非金属矿采选业							
开采辅助活动							
其他采矿业							
农副食品加工业	7.0	12.3	77.8	2.7	4.3	187895	101.3
食品制造业	15.4	6.9	86.0	1.9	1.6	65917	103.8
酒、饮料和精制茶制造业	1.3	3.9	74.4	239.8		28331	98.8
烟草制品业							
纺织业	18.2	11.3	80.3	2.3	3.2	40847	108.4
纺织服装、服饰业	22.6	16.0	61.2	1.8	7.6	75863	99.5
皮革、毛皮、羽毛及其制品和制鞋业	28.5	20.9	60.1	3.2	6.0	58634	97.9
木材加工和木、竹、藤、棕、草制品业	15.6	5.0	84.8	2.3	0.2	47331	110.3
家具制造业	20.4	7.5	70.3	1.7	3.3	54213	97.7
造纸和纸制品业	12.8	12.1	73.5	2.8	3.2	80841	96.9
印刷和记录媒介复制业	34.8	7.3	77.6	1.8	2.2	76415	99.4
文教、工美、体育和娱乐用品制造业	18.5	8.1	78.5	2.6	1.8	37247	101.9
石油加工、炼焦和核燃料加工业	1.2	13.9	63.3	3.8	1.3	13953	100.0
化学原料和化学制品制造业	17.6	13.4	57.4	1.8	6.8	141178	98.1
医药制造业							
化学纤维制造业	24.3	11.7	86.6	3.0	2.6	62821	100.0
橡胶和塑料制品业	20.4	10.2	78.2	2.3	2.3	72490	99.6
非金属矿物制品业	26.1	10.6	77.1	1.5	5.1	90333	98.4
黑色金属冶炼和压延加工业	16.3	7.7	84.9	2.0	3.5	56396	100.2
有色金属冶炼和压延加工业	10.0	5.7	77.7	1.6	1.6	107974	102.4
金属制品业	15.3	6.1	82.5	1.4	1.6	52892	99.3
通用设备制造业	23.0	15.1	66.9	1.7	7.5	96532	100.3
专用设备制造业	18.4	10.8	77.4	1.6	5.7	58569	97.1
汽车制造业	20.4	8.3	79.1	0.8	5.2	121227	106.2
铁路、船舶、航空航天和其他运输设备制造业	33.9	9.9	66.1	1.4	3.6	122910	97.6
电气机械和器材制造业	14.1	7.8	71.0	1.8	2.4	62541	97.4
计算机、通信和其他电子设备制造业	19.5	8.7	69.6	2.0	4.0	50371	99.5
仪器仪表制造业	26.2	13.4	52.1	1.9	8.4	100480	95.4
其他制造业	16.7	8.2	64.4	2.4	0.8	58369	103.1
废弃资源综合利用业							
金属制品、机械和设备修理业		0.8	91.6	6.8	1.1		
电力、热力生产和供应业							
燃气生产和供应业							
水的生产和供应业							

4-20 大中型工业企业主要经济指标（2011年）

Main Indicators of Large and Medium-sized Industrial Enterprises (2011)

项目	企业单位数（个）	#亏损企业	工业增加值（万元）	主营业务收入（万元）	亏损企业亏损总额（万元）
总计	1883	271	13696194	66920180	264787
按轻重工业分					
轻工业	1081	165	6288616	27587985	133382
重工业	802	106	7407578	39332196	131405
按企业规模分					
大型企业	206	16	7162882	38080754	100340
中型企业	1677	255	6533311	28839426	164447
按工业行业分(大类)					
煤炭开采和洗选业					
石油和天然气开采业					
黑色金属矿采选业					
有色金属矿采选业					
非金属矿采选业					
开采辅助活动					
其他采矿业					
农副食品加工业	7		139931	1586159	
食品制造业	12	1	227907	713272	411
酒、饮料和精制茶制造业	6		235297	1661804	
烟草制品业					
纺织业	82	8	423518	1873928	9733
纺织服装、服饰业	139	15	681942	2618057	16885
皮革、毛皮、羽毛及其制品和制鞋业	174	27	898591	2534240	32589
木材加工和木、竹、藤、棕、草制品业	3	1	17858	52649	100
家具制造业	89	15	411416	1520134	19227
造纸和纸制品业	62	9	564613	3563148	1159
印刷和记录媒介复制业	35	4	303703	803922	2553
文教、工美、体育和娱乐用品制造业	126	24	512277	1927407	11627
石油加工、炼焦和核燃料加工业	1		214	18265	
化学原料和化学制品制造业	25	6	185344	884070	21358
医药制造业	2		34779	75500	
化学纤维制造业	1		1960	8529	
橡胶和塑料制品业	158	19	639642	2287741	8200
非金属矿物制品业	30	1	262694	938646	5
黑色金属冶炼和压延加工业	4		22276	81957	
有色金属冶炼和压延加工业	7		24232	148289	
金属制品业	72	13	316298	1344769	3597
通用设备制造业	50	6	443785	3688819	12411
专用设备制造业	48	4	211144	814265	225
汽车制造业	18	2	195600	720329	867
铁路、船舶、航空航天和其他运输设备制造业	6		117322	429841	
电气机械和器材制造业	213	32	1266692	6420299	18518
计算机、通信和其他电子设备制造业	448	75	4002102	23906895	94794
仪器仪表制造业	39	6	240047	662955	2594
其他制造业	17	2	95169	395718	214
废弃资源综合利用业					
金属制品、机械和设备修理业					
电力、热力生产和供应业	5		1143577	4897101	
燃气生产和供应业	1		38902	237824	
水的生产和供应业	3	1	37365	103646	7719

4-20 续表 1

(2011年)

项 目	利税总额(万元)	人均税收(元)	利润总额(万元)	人均利润(元)
总 计	4028085	5905	2758186	12826
按轻重工业分				
轻工业	1800681	5232	1190789	10215
重工业	2227404	6702	1567397	15917
按企业规模分				
大型企业	2282897	8634	1577542	19311
中型企业	1745187	4233	1180643	8853
按工业行业分(大类)				
煤炭开采和洗选业				
石油和天然气开采业				
黑色金属矿采选业				
有色金属矿采选业				
非金属矿采选业				
开采辅助活动				
其他采矿业				
农副食品加工业	128885	114103	96822	344561
食品制造业	153000	42115	104226	89998
酒、饮料和精制茶制造业	172964	50196	107960	83367
烟草制品业				
纺织业	85903	4216	49454	5720
纺织服装、服饰业	211017	5794	139728	11356
皮革、毛皮、羽毛及其制品和制鞋业	80873	1648	36702	1370
木材加工和木、竹、藤、棕、草制品业	2581	2527	1735	5181
家具制造业	89408	7330	37089	5197
造纸和纸制品业	215058	17030	140234	31917
印刷和记录媒介复制业	145474	8917	116956	36569
文教、工美、体育和娱乐用品制造业	63934	1363	43176	2835
石油加工、炼焦和核燃料加工业	2232	10200	2028	101415
化学原料和化学制品制造业	80902	23349	47606	33384
医药制造业	26800	71538	17500	134615
化学纤维制造业	504	9298	214	6862
橡胶和塑料制品业	121142	2248	86848	5692
非金属矿物制品业	134242	14448	104635	51061
黑色金属冶炼和压延加工业	6335	6583	4299	13903
有色金属冶炼和压延加工业	8292	2745	7042	15471
金属制品业	69464	4686	40584	6585
通用设备制造业	141210	3049	118673	16054
专用设备制造业	66971	5489	45994	12036
汽车制造业	110026	31251	68077	50716
铁路、船舶、航空航天和其他运输设备制造业	33167	2884	31406	51443
电气机械和器材制造业	348739	2635	291694	13475
计算机、通信和其他电子设备制造业	933322	3919	679156	10471
仪器仪表制造业	41738	1303	35866	7960
其他制造业	17611	916	15724	7632
废弃资源综合利用业				
金属制品、机械和设备修理业				
电力、热力生产和供应业	500566	118479	263135	131305
燃气生产和供应业	35539	99409	30439	593357
水的生产和供应业	187	50927	-6816	-49568

4-21 大中型工业企业主要经济效益指标（2011年）

Main Indicators on Economic Benefit of Large and Medium-sized Industrial Enterprises (2011)

项目	工业增加值率(%)	总资产贡献率(%)	资产负债率(%)	流动资产周转率(次/年)	成本费用利润率(%)	全员劳动生产率(元/人)	产品销售率(%)
总计	20.3	8.1	57.1	2.1	4.2	63688	99.5
按轻重工业分							
轻工业	22.7	8.2	58.3	1.9	4.4	53943	99.8
重工业	18.7	8.0	56.2	2.4	4.1	75225	99.3
按企业规模分							
大型企业	18.7	8.6	57.7	2.5	4.3	87683	99.6
中型企业	22.5	7.5	56.4	1.8	4.2	48990	99.3
按工业行业分(大类)							
煤炭开采和洗选业							
石油和天然气开采业							
黑色金属矿采选业							
有色金属矿采选业							
非金属矿采选业							
开采辅助活动							
其他采矿业							
农副食品加工业	8.6	10.1	86.7	1.4	6.5	497977	96.6
食品制造业	34.1	19.1	33.1	1.7	17.1	196794	106.8
酒、饮料和精制茶制造业	14.3	19.0	59.9	2.9	6.9	181697	103.3
烟草制品业							
纺织业	22.3	5.3	56.4	1.6	2.7	48987	99.9
纺织服装、服饰业	25.5	10.0	59.2	1.5	5.7	55422	98.1
皮革、毛皮、羽毛及其制品和制鞋业	35.3	5.4	64.2	2.2	1.5	33532	99.3
木材加工和木、竹、藤、棕、草制品业	32.9	5.0	58.6	1.3	3.4	53323	99.2
家具制造业	26.8	7.4	54.9	1.7	2.5	57644	99.0
造纸和纸制品业	15.6	5.7	57.3	1.9	3.6	128505	99.9
印刷和记录媒介复制业	39.0	17.2	43.2	1.4	16.5	94961	103.0
文教、工美、体育和娱乐用品制造业	26.6	5.4	60.1	2.1	2.3	33639	100.6
石油加工、炼焦和核燃料加工业	1.2	14.1	56.3	1.5	11.8	10680	106.9
化学原料和化学制品制造业	20.7	8.0	57.9	1.2	5.8	129974	99.0
医药制造业	48.3	15.3	5.7	0.7	30.4	267529	104.9
化学纤维制造业	24.3	11.7	86.6	3.0	2.6	62821	100.0
橡胶和塑料制品业	27.7	6.1	53.6	1.7	3.9	41925	99.3
非金属矿物制品业	27.0	10.0	51.1	1.3	12.4	128193	95.5
黑色金属冶炼和压延加工业	26.1	13.0	72.9	2.4	5.5	72044	99.0
有色金属冶炼和压延加工业	16.3	7.5	63.8	1.4	4.9	53233	100.6
金属制品业	23.6	7.1	58.5	2.0	3.1	51320	100.0
通用设备制造业	12.0	6.4	65.2	2.5	3.3	60037	99.6
专用设备制造业	25.4	8.5	51.0	1.5	5.9	55252	100.2
汽车制造业	27.4	9.4	57.5	0.7	10.4	145720	101.0
铁路、船舶、航空航天和其他运输设备制造业	27.5	8.3	64.8	2.1	7.8	192174	99.9
电气机械和器材制造业	19.6	7.5	49.8	2.1	4.7	58514	99.6
计算机、通信和其他电子设备制造业	16.6	6.8	60.8	2.6	2.9	61702	99.1
仪器仪表制造业	36.6	5.8	38.5	2.2	5.7	53277	99.5
其他制造业	23.9	5.6	33.1	1.9	4.1	46194	96.2
废弃资源综合利用业							
金属制品、机械和设备修理业							
电力、热力生产和供应业	23.2	11.8	51.0	6.0	5.7	570647	99.7
燃气生产和供应业	16.4	20.8	57.3	4.6	14.7	758316	100.0
水的生产和供应业	33.3	3.7	84.3	1.3	-6.2	271746	92.5

4-22 主要年份规模以上工业企业经济效益指标

Main Indicators on Economic Benefit of Industrial Enterprises above Designated Size in Main Years

项　　目	单位	1985年	1990年	1995年	2000年	2004年	2005年	2010年	2011年
产品销售率	%	85.6	94.7	98.7	99.8	99.6	99.5	99.9	99.6
成本费用利润率	%	6.5	1.5	5.0	5.4	3.4	3.3	4.8	3.7
产值利税率	%	6.9	6.4	9.8	9.2	5.6	4.6	6.1	5.7
资金利税率	%	9.0	6.3	6.9	7.5	3.6	5.5	7.8	7.3
销售利税率	%	8.2	6.7	9.1	9.2	5.7	4.7	6.1	5.7
每百元固定资产原值实现的产值	元	174.9	133.6	108.7	125.5	220.3	212.4	240.6	256.3
每百元固定资产原值实现的利税	元	14.2	8.5	10.7	11.5	9.8	9.9	14.6	14.6
每百元固定资产原值实现的利润	元	4.4	1.8	5.5	6.9	6.8	6.7	11.0	9.6
每百元流动资产实现的产值	元	210.2	247.8	169.4	178.6	227.3	216.3	204.3	203.0
每百元流动资产实现的利税	元	17.1	15.7	16.6	16.4	10.2	10.0	12.4	11.6
每百元流动资产实现的利润	元	4.9	3.3	8.6	9.8	7.0	6.8	9.3	7.6
亏损企业亏损面	%	7.2	11.1	25.9	31.3	33.7	30.1	16.2	16.0
全部流动资产周转天数	天	173.7	155.6	201.1	189.0	170.6	169.8	179.4	177.6
增加值全员劳动生产率	元/人	2906	6439	13778	36101	52464	53340	60854	65087
平均每个职工提供利税	元	626	1519	5351	11703	12192	9193	16728	19152

注：由于1993年财务会计制度改革，本表中有关财务指标1993年起数字与往年不可比；全员劳动生产率1993年起按增加值计算，以前年份按净产值计算；1993年以前的流动资产按定额资金计算。下同。

4-23 主要年份规模以上国有经济工业企业经济效益指标

Main Indicators on Economic Benefit of State-owned and State-holding Industrial Enterprises above Designated Size in Main Years

项　　目	单位	1985年	1990年	1995年	2000年	2004年	2005年	2010年	2011年
产品销售率	%	89.6	102.0	100.8	98.3	99.9	100.0	99.8	100.0
成本费用利润率	%	8.0	-0.8	15.5	7.0	6.8	5.8	3.2	2.7
产值利税率	%	13.2	9.2	40.6	69.4	98.7	11.3	7.3	7.3
资金利税率	%	20.4	8.3	14.9	21.6	40.8	10.6	6.7	7.1
销售利税率	%	14.8	9.0	20.6	19.2	98.7	11.3	7.3	7.3
每百元固定资产原值实现的产值	元	142.9	85.5	61.1	63.4	44.2	105.0	79.0	79.4
每百元固定资产原值实现的利税	元	21.1	7.8	24.8	44.0	12.2	11.8	5.7	5.8
每百元固定资产原值实现的利润	元	9.6	-0.6	10.8	14.5	8.7	5.6	2.4	2.1
每百元流动资产实现的产值	元	445.1	397.8	96.3	73.4	215.4	443.4	794.5	796.5
每百元流动资产实现的利税	元	65.7	36.4	39.1	50.9	59.3	50.0	57.7	58.2
每百元流动资产实现的利润	元	27.5	-2.4	17.0	16.7	42.3	23.8	24.6	20.8
亏损企业亏损面	%	9.9	16.7	20.9		25.0	20.0		
全部流动资产周转天数	天	80.9	88.7	299.8	137.7	56.2	83.0	46.1	45.8
增加值全员劳动生产率	元/人	3641	11253	73910	456736	1694891	2320312	405232	450003
平均每个职工提供利税	元	1757	5325	55113	303960	1603751	1197862	144620	152273

4-24 主要年份规模以上集体经济工业企业经济效益指标

Main Indicators on Economic Benefit of Collective-owned Industrial Enterprises above Designated Size in Main Years

项　　目	单位	1985年	1990年	1995年	2000年	2004年	2005年	2010年	2011年
产品销售率	%	85.1	92.2	98.0	97.0	101.2	100.5	97.4	100.5
成本费用利润率	%	5.9	3.3	5.2	2.7	4.5	3.3	9.7	0.8
产值利税率	%	9.3	6.9	9.0	5.1	7.6	5.8	10.4	4.0
资金利税率	%	15.1	9.7	6.0	2.9	5.8	3.2	9.7	3.2
销售利税率	%	11.0	7.5	8.7	5.2	7.6	5.8	10.7	3.8
每百元固定资产原值实现的产值	元	236.7	159.4	128.0	99.3	106.1	98.1	131.1	139.1
每百元固定资产原值实现的利税	元	22.1	11.0	11.5	5.0	7.8	5.7	13.6	5.5
每百元固定资产原值实现的利润	元	10.8	4.5	6.4	2.4	3.8	3.0	11.5	1.1
每百元流动资产实现的产值	元	509.0	225.7	179.5	113.8	194.2	157.7	214.9	210.5
每百元流动资产实现的利税	元	47.5	15.6	16.1	5.7	14.3	9.1	22.4	8.3
每百元流动资产实现的利润	元	23.2	6.4	9.0	2.8	6.9	4.8	18.8	1.6
亏损企业亏损面	%	6.6	8.8	12.8	18.6	19.5	25.9	22.5	30.9
全部流动资产周转天数	天	84.3	175.3	197.4	340.1	207.4	241.7	175.1	165.8
增加值全员劳动生产率	元/人	2664	5437	5820	16344	21711	28414	31412	29868
平均每个职工提供利税	元	715	1058	1533	3135	5702	5241	8428	3344

4-25 主要年份大中型工业企业经济效益指标

Main Indicators on Economic Benefit of Large and Medium-sized Industrial Enterprises in Main Years

项　　目	单位	1985年	1990年	1995年	2000年	2004年	2005年	2010年	2011年
产品销售率	%	104.3	103.5	99.7	98.6	99.5	99.5	100.6	99.5
成本费用利润率	%	14.3	2.2	12.9	12.0	3.9	3.8	5.1	4.2
产值利税率	%	16.1	8.7	19.9	21.4	5.2	4.7	6.4	6.0
资金利税率	%	14.8	6.5	14.0	15.3	6.4	6.1	8.4	7.7
销售利税率	%	15.5	8.4	19.8	21.7	5.3	4.7	6.4	6.0
每百元固定资产原值实现的产值	元	106.0	87.1	112.8	98.4	227.2	229.8	221.6	243.6
每百元固定资产原值实现的利税	元	17.1	7.6	22.4	21.1	11.7	10.7	14.2	14.6
每百元固定资产原值实现的利润	元	11.5	1.7	13.1	13.0	8.8	8.4	10.9	10.0
每百元流动资产实现的产值	元	758.8	329.3	174.3	183.4	242.9	227.4	220.6	212.4
每百元流动资产实现的利税	元	122.4	28.6	34.6	39.2	12.5	10.6	14.2	12.7
每百元流动资产实现的利润	元	82.3	6.4	20.2	24.2	9.4	8.3	10.9	8.7
亏损企业亏损面	%		17.2	22.2	12.8	24.6	20.1	12.2	14.4
全部流动资产周转天数	天	46.1	107.1	209.5	210.2	156.7	160.8	164.8	170.3
增加值全员劳动生产率	元/人	6202	16492	81787	280810	65573	72657	66101	63688
平均每个职工提供利税	元	2601	7883	52997	165448	14187	11918	18679	18731

4-26 主要年份规模以上港澳台商投资工业企业经济效益指标

Main Indicators on Economic Benefit of Industrial Enterprises above Designated Size with Hong Kong, Macao and Taiwan Funds in Main Years

项　　目	单位	1990年	1995年	2000年	2004年	2005年	2010年	2011年
产品销售率	%	94.2	99.6	100.8	99.9	99.4	99.7	99.6
成本费用利润率	%	-11.5	2.1	4.6	2.5	3.2	5.4	3.6
产值利税率	%	-9.3	4.9	6.6	3.3	4.0	6.3	5.3
资金利税率	%	-14.3	3.8	5.4	3.5	4.6	7.6	6.5
销售利税率	%	-9.9	4.9	6.5	3.3	4.1	6.3	5.3
每百元固定资产原值实现的产值	元	104.9	114.8	114.5	178.6	198.1	216.6	232.0
每百元固定资产原值实现的利税	元	-9.7	5.6	7.5	8.2	8.0	13.6	12.3
每百元固定资产原值实现的利润	元	-12.6	2.6	5.1	5.5	6.0	11.1	8.9
每百元流动资产实现的产值	元	154.3	165.2	182.2	209.0	192.3	189.1	191.0
每百元流动资产实现的利税	元	-14.3	8.1	12.0	9.5	7.8	11.8	10.1
每百元流动资产实现的利润	元	-18.5	3.7	8.1	6.5	5.8	9.7	7.3
亏损企业亏损面	%	25.0	46.4	36.1	39.9	35.1	20.2	18.6
全部流动资产周转天数	天	251.1	199.1	199.9	207.4	191.1	194.1	187.5
增加值全员劳动生产率	元/人	16962	17478	28933	42634	41933	54793	57058
平均每个职工提供利税	元	-8238	4232	7026	5612	6244	14293	14263

4-27 主要年份规模以上外商投资工业企业经济效益指标

Main Indicators on Economic Benefit of Foreign-funded Industrial Enterprises above Designated Size in Main Years

项　　目	单位	1990年	1995年	2000年	2004年	2005年	2010年	2011年
产品销售率	%	94.2	91.0	99.2	98.8	99.4	100.1	99.7
成本费用利润率	%	-11.5	-2.6	4.7	3.2	2.8	4.4	3.6
产值利税率	%	-9.3	-0.6	5.7	3.3	3.2	5.3	5.3
资金利税率	%	-14.3	-0.5	7.4	5.0	4.1	7.5	7.4
销售利税率	%	-9.9	-0.6	5.7	3.3	3.2	5.3	5.3
每百元固定资产原值实现的产值	元	104.9	155.5	231.2	307.9	285.2	286.9	332.4
每百元固定资产原值实现的利税	元	-9.7	-0.9	13.1	9.8	9.2	15.3	17.6
每百元固定资产原值实现的利润	元	-12.6	-1.9	10.3	8.0	7.6	12.1	11.7
每百元流动资产实现的产值	元	154.3	94.3	251.0	252.2	223.6	211.1	204.1
每百元流动资产实现的利税	元	-14.3	-1.5	14.2	8.0	7.2	11.2	10.8
每百元流动资产实现的利润	元	-18.5	5.5	11.1	6.5	5.9	8.9	7.2
亏损企业亏损面	%	25.0	38.2	31.3	29.5	34.5	18.8	21.5
全部流动资产周转天数	天	251.1	174.1	148.4	156.0	164.4	173.0	177.3
增加值全员劳动生产率	元/人	16962	3646	50318	70718	70722	66212	67335
平均每个职工提供利税	元	-8238	-700	13714	12328	8288	16893	20145

4-28 主要年份规模以上工业产品产量

Output of Main Industrial Products of Industrial Enterprises above Designated Size in Main Years

产品名称	单位	1985年	1990年	1995年	2000年	2005年	2010年	2011年
食用植物油	吨	5571	4431	6824	5180	181869	1135677	1293312
糖	吨	51858	61016	7841	17869			
饼干	吨		45158	26252	21262	38859	142126	
罐头	吨	924	1352	5982			12890	
饮料酒	千升	4034	2441	1720			493644	595920
软饮料	吨		44061	71566	158599	861853	3142076	3737047
棉纱	吨		321	9902	3048	49383	11252	3411
布	万米		82	31045	28139	65669	15794	9958
服装	万件	108	1835	112177	85635	70054	140556	107297
#衬衫	万件			2518	3624	2210	6372	8869
西服	万件			205	1761	555	204	462
轻革	万平方米		5	1076	378	1391	744	574
皮鞋	万双	17	457	27184	23474	31942	43062	31905
人造板	立方米		7100	40666		167088	266113	98777
家具	万件	815	8657	77501	151374	7974	7390	6413
机制纸及纸板	吨	30241	106535	339742	618000	4081761	9331823	10213204
玩具	万元			657936	469792	1354386	827916	
火柴	万件	19	22	9				
中成药	吨		216	6268	2354	1759	2478	2154
塑料制品	吨	3089	17335	624476	571900	1265865	3998208	2015355
#塑料薄膜	吨		1928	59128	71394	83954	134737	152599
水泥	万吨	41	140	283	435	305	249	251
砖	万块	159305	296962	252783		2903		
日用陶瓷	万件	561	480	2414	1860	5745	2426	
耐火材料制品	吨	7600	9928	9144			62512	52162
钢材	吨	4678	1730	19690	14550	1087242	191656	
铝材	吨		881	3536	4080	61510	69933	14808
输送机械	吨		8622	3736		33200		

注：2000年以前家具的计量单位为“万元”，输送机械的计量单位为“吨”。

4-28　续表

产 品 名 称	单 位	1985年	1990年	1995年	2000年	2005年	2010年	2011年
电动工具	万台		1.89	471	357	6	1520	585
滚动轴承	万套	36	373	691	594	1333	4232	10183
民用钢质船	载重吨	1916	841	3620	2894		18186	17934
交流电动机	万千瓦	23	19	43	87		193	163
变压器	千伏安				6730	816409	2980343	1705625
电力电缆	公里		15091	20694	61996	78266	383829	367142
原电池(折干电池)	万只	12354	7607	63237	69401	214507	417215	390496
吸尘器	万台	0.13	7.35	483	67	464	428	918
电风扇	万台		106	474	436	964	2081	1811
房间空调器	台	31		26480	39582	4941		239260
排油烟机	台			57551				
缝纫机	台			190		504	440	
自行车	辆			95439	185608	885211	1014533	975192
家用电冰箱	台			35336		19360		2707
白炽灯泡	万只			5778	8560	45164	13198	16
灯　具	万件		87	42407	25135	14017	22819	18770
电话单机	万部		17	877	1074	3651	4809	4443
移动电话机	万部				619	639	1995	4336
电子计算机	万台				27	180	44	44
彩色显像管	万只			210	394			
电子元件	万只	1422	20487	719259	1039500	46416689	91845708	101254508
显示器	万台						157	1
打印机	万台						57	77
硬盘存储器	万台						30	2
半导体分立器件	万只			2484814	32256	2203170	4044448	4756592
彩色电视机	万台		1.04	81	134	135	536	541
组合音响	万台			1136	1572	2446	3637	2827
照相机	万台		3	374	122	1355	210	185
手　表	万只		15	8514	954	1370	2168	1670
钟	万只			1986	984	1193	3776	3656
发电量	亿千瓦时	0.29	93	139	269	344	356	376
自来水生产量	万吨			21070	102083	94962	179639	174538

4-29 规模以上五大支柱产业及四个特色产业主要经济指标(2011年)

Main Indicators of Five Pillar Industries & Four Characteristic Industries above Designated Size (2011)

项　　目	企业单位数(个)	#亏损企业	工业增加值(万元)	主营业务收入(万元)	亏损企业亏损总额(万元)
总　计	3227	510	13012038	68798606	340821
按轻重工业分					
轻工业	1840	304	6626436	31695456	174960
重工业	1387	206	6385602	37103150	165861
按企业规模分					
大型企业	185	15	5772495	32362020	100011
中型企业	1395	219	5288948	23985789	144942
小型企业	1563	258	1915830	12131140	87131
微型企业	84	18	34766	319658	8737
按工业行业分(大类)					
五大支柱产业	2624	402	11114208	60983026	268605
1. 电子信息制造业	762	143	4336666	25834791	126784
2. 电气机械及设备制造业	866	121	3031178	16439090	51929
3. 纺织服装鞋帽制造业	697	106	2255603	8281343	79262
4. 食品饮料加工制造业	80	9	759351	5600141	7822
5. 造纸及纸制品业	219	23	731410	4827662	2807
四个特色产业	603	108	1897830	7815580	72216
1. 玩具及文体用品制造业	186	40	580663	2170259	17080
2. 家具制造业	192	42	502381	1972142	22819
3. 化工制品制造业	151	19	454445	2690866	28682
4. 包装印刷业	74	7	360342	982314	3634

4-29　续表 1

(2011年)

项　　目	利税总额(万元)	人均税收(元)	利润总额(万元)	人均利润(元)
总　计	3710695	5671	2499825	11708
按轻重工业分				
轻工业	1922554	5876	1230798	10454
重工业	1788141	5419	1269028	13248
按企业规模分				
大型企业	1842882	6536	1363898	18612
中型企业	1261940	3839	828948	7350
小型企业	604837	10956	310791	11580
微型企业	1036	7914	-3812	-6223
按工业行业分(大类)				
五大支柱产业	3134332	5367	2161011	11915
1. 电子信息制造业	1000514	4074	712492	10077
2. 电气机械及设备制造业	921111	4818	693110	14646
3. 纺织服装鞋帽制造业	405482	3334	227979	4282
4. 食品饮料加工制造业	531326	47906	363281	103564
5. 造纸及纸制品业	275900	16972	164149	24930
四个特色产业	576363	7388	338815	10537
1. 玩具及文体用品制造业	90326	1477	66011	4010
2. 家具制造业	101154	6661	40573	4461
3. 化工制品制造业	230198	42241	110931	39288
4. 包装印刷业	154684	8841	121300	32126

4-30 规模以上电子信息、电气机械及仪器仪表制造业主要指标(2010-2011年)

Main Indicators of Electronic Information，Machinery and Instrument Manufacturing above Designated Size(2010-2011)

指　　标	单位	2010年	2011年
企业单位数	个	1616	1292
#亏损企业单位数	个	289	231
工业增加值	亿元	624.72	633.84
主营业务收入	亿元	3219.91	3754.40
成本费用总额	亿元	3110.48	3647.55
#销售成本及费用	亿元	2955.35	3476.10
管理费用	亿元	153.14	171.69
财务费用	亿元	1.99	-0.24
利税总额	亿元	146.17	152.61
#利润总额	亿元	122.56	113.66
应交增值税	亿元	21.11	32.39
亏损企业亏损总额	亿元	10.19	16.72
企业资产总额	亿元	2026.27	2390.82
#流动资产	亿元	1390.37	1622.67
#应收帐款余额	亿元	580.85	663.92
产成品存货	亿元	103.57	141.08
企业负债总额	亿元	1209.40	1406.50
企业资产负债率	%	59.69	58.83
成本费用利润率	%	3.94	3.10

注：本表统计范围为规模以上计算机、通信和其他电子设备制造业、电气机械和器材制造业、仪器仪表及文化办公用机械制造业。

4-31 规模以上先进制造业企业主要经济指标（2011年）

Main Indicators of Advanced Manufacturing Enterprises above Designated Size (2011)

项目	企业单位数（个）	#亏损企业	工业增加值（万元）	主营业务收入（万元）	亏损企业亏损总额（万元）
总计	1706	257	6874944	40341453	192444
按企业规模分					
大型企业	107	11	3175136	20982964	68653
中型企业	610	90	2527655	11384434	63524
小型企业	947	147	1150624	7774930	54872
微型企业	42	9	21529	199125	5390
按工业行业分					
装备制造业	1489	223	6353926	36937323	155075
金属制品业	196	23	327933	1900047	4602
通用设备制造业	146	13	356467	2214582	9119
专用设备制造业	129	12	293625	1150713	689
汽车制造业	40	5	232353	848048	1189
铁路、船舶、航空航天和其他运输设备制造业	7	2	104029	333311	445
电气机械和器材制造业	270	44	933805	5906864	21790
计算机、通信和其他电子设备制造业	667	120	3989128	24158557	116479
仪器仪表制造业	34	4	116585	425200	762
船舶、航空航天器修理					
钢铁冶炼及加工	27	9	22437	443902	6448
炼铁	2	2	541	4978	1109
炼钢					
钢压延加工	24	7	20744	435565	5339
铁合金冶炼	1		1152	3359	
石油及化学	190	25	498581	2960229	30920
石油和天然气开采业					
石油加工、炼焦及核燃料加工业	6		2434	211032	
化学原料和化学制品制造业	145	19	452011	2479834	28682
橡胶制品业	39	6	44137	269363	2238

4-31 续表 1

项　　目	利税总额(万元)	人均税收(元)	利润总额(万元)	人均利润(元)	工业增加值率(%)
总　计	1907739	5581	1328554	12801	17.0
按企业规模分					
大型企业	843067	4160	670587	16175	15.0
中型企业	675731	4393	468577	9938	22.1
小型企业	389634	13477	192028	13096	14.7
微型企业	-693	3818	-2638	-5177	19.1
按工业行业分					
装备制造业	1668974	4543	1216670	12221	17.1
金属制品业	77410	5183	47838	8385	17.5
通用设备制造业	129249	8028	90533	18773	16.0
专用设备制造业	101365	7327	66342	13879	25.3
汽车制造业	124909	29408	76634	46683	27.6
铁路、船舶、航空航天和其他运输设备制造业	30901	5363	28941	79203	31.9
电气机械和器材制造业	246884	3170	197612	12713	15.8
计算机、通信和其他电子设备制造业	922425	3756	678875	10471	16.4
仪器仪表制造业	35831	3187	29896	16053	27.8
船舶、航空航天器修理					
钢铁冶炼及加工	2381	8878	-960	-2550	5.0
炼铁	-1074	1318	-1109	-41543	10.6
炼钢					
钢压延加工	2782	9361	-411	-1205	4.7
铁合金冶炼	673	13224	561	65965	34.3
石油及化学	236384	32090	112844	29312	16.8
石油和天然气开采业					
石油加工、炼焦及核燃料加工业	8402	46549	5967	114094	1.2
化学原料和化学制品制造业	221797	42160	104964	37877	18.0
橡胶制品业	6185	4163	1913	1864	17.1

4-31 续表 2

项目	总资产贡献率(%)	资产负债率(%)	流动资产周转率(次/年)	成本费用利润率(%)	全员劳动生产率(元/人)	产品销售率(%)
总计	7.0	59.0	2.1	3.4	66243	99.2
按企业规模分						
大型企业	7.1	62.7	2.6	3.3	76586	99.4
中型企业	7.0	52.5	1.8	4.3	53606	99.3
小型企业	6.9	62.3	1.6	2.5	78472	98.3
微型企业	-0.4	60.3	2.7	-1.4	42247	98.5
按工业行业分						
装备制造业	6.8	59.0	2.1	3.4	63822	99.3
金属制品业	5.3	60.5	1.6	2.6	57478	99.1
通用设备制造业	7.4	61.9	1.9	4.2	73917	99.3
专用设备制造业	9.2	51.7	1.5	6.1	61428	99.9
汽车制造业	9.9	57.0	0.8	9.9	141541	100.8
铁路、船舶、航空航天和其他运输设备制造业	9.0	65.3	2.0	9.4	284700	100.8
电气机械和器材制造业	6.4	57.6	2.1	3.4	60075	99.3
计算机、通信和其他电子设备制造业	6.4	60.5	2.4	2.9	61526	99.2
仪器仪表制造业	6.8	30.5	2.1	7.5	62603	98.5
船舶、航空航天器修理						
钢铁冶炼及加工	2.1	68.6	1.5	-0.2	59624	95.0
炼铁	-10.3	18.5	1.0	-9.9	20255	99.8
炼钢						
钢压延加工	2.3	69.9	1.5	-0.1	60814	94.9
铁合金冶炼	17.4	83.5	1.6	20.1	135541	100.0
石油及化学	10.1	57.8	1.6	4.0	129508	99.1
石油和天然气开采业						
石油加工、炼焦及核燃料加工业	7.5	75.0	1.8	2.9	46535	102.5
化学原料和化学制品制造业	10.9	56.2	1.6	4.4	163110	99.0
橡胶制品业	3.2	63.1	1.7	0.7	43006	98.0

4-32 规模以上IT制造业企业主要经济指标（2011年）

Main Indicators of IT Manufacturing Enterprises above Designated Size (2011)

项　　目	企业单位数(个)	#亏损企业	工业增加值(万元)	主营业务收入(万元)	亏损企业亏损总额(万元)
总　计	959	176	4982063	30279789	143528
按企业规模分					
大型企业	85	6	2697284	18461165	42014
中型企业	461	88	1839447	8134618	68817
小型企业	384	76	432624	3576318	27749
微型企业	29	6	12708	107688	4948
按工业行业分(小类)					
训练健身器材制造	3		4940	23086	
玩具制造	84	21	278429	776060	11203
信息化学品制造	2		2546	6975	
照相机及器材制造	11	6	34213	205156	5393
复印和胶印设备制造	12		120274	1188289	
计算器及货币专用设备制造	5		66155	966675	
医疗诊断、监护及治疗设备制造					
微电机及其他电机制造	17	1	137494	550424	47
电线、电缆制造	127	21	270490	2356106	7200
光纤、光缆制造					
锂离子电池制造	8	2	24445	145566	401
镍氢电池制造	3		6355	32733	
其他电池制造	16	3	185506	814919	2624
计算机整机制造	18	3	265914	1600378	2677
其他计算机制造	9	3	38893	380263	165
通信系统设备制造	14	1	116503	971901	28
通信终端设备制造	24	4	338454	3444009	8181
电视机制造	10	4	54300	153700	3130
音响设备制造	62	15	219517	933658	5850
影视录放设备制造	23	4	73721	588876	1326
电子真空器件制造	3		132536	1519989	
集成电路制造	17	5	177534	1524926	7086
光电子器件及其他电子器件制造	64	13	354400	1672086	17226
电子元件及组件制造	306	46	1652170	8234027	52024
印制电路板制造	40	10	174629	863835	15217
其他电子设备制造	59	10	229469	791882	1788
电子测量仪器制造	1		2146	10487	
其他未列明制造业	21	4	21028	523782	1963

4-32 续表 1

项　　目	利　税 总　额 (万元)	人　均 税　收 (元)	利　润 总　额 (万元)	人　均 利　润 (元)	工业增 加值率 (%)
总　　计	1184276	3810	858441	10038	16.4
按企业规模分					
大型企业	732655	4596	567479	15789	14.5
中型企业	338303	2600	228560	5414	22.3
小型企业	112174	6832	63609	8949	12.4
微型企业	1144	9398	-1207	-4825	26.3
按工业行业分(小类)					
训练健身器材制造	1059	6608	193	1473	22.2
玩具制造	7153	646	1016	107	35.7
信息化学品制造	486	904	421	5853	32.3
照相机及器材制造	2183	711	730	357	16.1
复印和胶印设备制造	45982	2167	42577	27095	10.2
计算器及货币专用设备制造	15514	453	15119	17338	6.9
医疗诊断、监护及治疗设备制造					
微电机及其他电机制造	42235	1186	40001	21237	25.2
电线、电缆制造	59156	5058	33726	6708	11.3
光纤、光缆制造					
锂离子电池制造	10249	5100	7600	14631	17.3
镍氢电池制造	1915	5735	1317	12623	17.4
其他电池制造	77849	4743	68800	36064	22.8
计算机整机制造	73995	11140	45039	17327	16.7
其他计算机制造	7016	2617	5338	8325	10.7
通信系统设备制造	27817	2406	23614	13516	11.8
通信终端设备制造	93675	9048	45723	8628	9.7
电视机制造	10412	3156	6963	6369	35.0
音响设备制造	55943	9887	19600	5332	23.9
影视录放设备制造	11733	4250	7055	6409	11.8
电子真空器件制造	74762	375	74476	97738	8.6
集成电路制造	46658	16216	14781	7520	11.5
光电子器件及其他电子器件制造	63085	1365	53274	7413	20.5
电子元件及组件制造	385958	3062	300678	10795	20.0
印制电路板制造	22295	4185	12845	5688	20.5
其他电子设备制造	33334	1010	28239	5596	29.1
电子测量仪器制造	504		504	15036	20.8
其他未列明制造业	13309	7281	8815	14279	4.7

4-32 续表 2

项　　目	总资产贡献率(%)	资　产负债率(%)	流动资产周 转 率(次/年)	成本费用利 润 率(%)	全员劳动生 产 率(元/人)	产　品销售率(%)
总　　计	6.6	61.5	2.4	2.9	58259	99.7
按企业规模分						
大型企业	7.6	62.6	2.8	3.2	75049	99.5
中型企业	5.7	58.4	1.9	2.9	43572	99.0
小型企业	5.1	64.2	1.8	1.8	60864	102.4
微型企业	1.4	80.6	2.5	-1.2	50791	102.1
按工业行业分(小类)						
训练健身器材制造	6.9	60.2	1.7	0.8	37709	105.8
玩具制造	1.3	63.6	1.6	0.1	29308	99.4
信息化学品制造	8.0	10.0	1.4	6.2	35416	88.5
照相机及器材制造	1.8	45.4	2.0	0.4	16731	96.8
复印和胶印设备制造	10.6	58.4	3.5	3.7	76540	100.8
计算器及货币专用设备制造	2.9	80.0	2.3	1.6	75866	100.1
医疗诊断、监护及治疗设备制造						
微电机及其他电机制造	12.9	43.5	2.2	7.7	72996	99.0
电线、电缆制造	4.5	70.7	1.8	1.4	53798	98.9
光纤、光缆制造						
锂离子电池制造	9.6	84.2	1.6	5.5	47063	102.2
镍氢电池制造	7.3	73.7	1.4	4.2	60928	89.8
其他电池制造	13.0	53.2	2.0	9.2	97241	100.1
计算机整机制造	14.4	55.5	5.0	3.0	102298	100.5
其他计算机制造	3.8	71.3	2.3	1.4	60657	104.4
通信系统设备制造	6.4	65.0	3.2	2.5	66684	98.8
通信终端设备制造	5.6	83.1	2.3	1.3	63865	99.1
电视机制造	8.9	76.1	1.4	4.7	49676	102.0
音响设备制造	9.1	57.3	2.3	2.1	59721	101.7
影视录放设备制造	4.9	78.4	3.1	1.2	66971	93.7
电子真空器件制造	16.6	73.7	4.7	5.2	173931	99.1
集成电路制造	7.6	74.4	4.0	1.0	90316	99.2
光电子器件及其他电子器件制造	5.0	62.9	2.0	3.2	49314	99.1
电子元件及组件制造	6.7	53.0	2.2	3.8	59314	99.3
印制电路板制造	3.1	39.9	1.9	1.5	77331	100.3
其他电子设备制造	5.0	50.1	1.8	3.7	45473	99.8
电子测量仪器制造	18.7	52.0	4.6	5.2	64051	100.0
其他未列明制造业	6.0	64.7	3.0	1.7	34064	118.0

主要统计指标解释

Explanatory Notes on Main Statistical Indicators

工业　指从事自然资源的开采，对采掘品和农产品进行加工和再加工的物质生产部门。具体包括：对自然资源的开采，如采矿、晒盐、森林采伐等（但不包括禽兽捕猎和水产捕捞）；对农副产品的加工、再加工，如粮油加工、食品加工、轧花、缫丝、纺织、制革等；对采掘品的加工、再加工，如炼铁、炼钢、化工生产、石油加工、机器制造、木材加工等，以及电力、自来水、煤气的生产和供应等；对工业品的修理、翻新，如机器制造设备的修理、交通运输工具（包括小卧车）的修理等。

轻工业　是指主要提供生活消费品和制作手工工具的工业。按其所使用的原料不同，可分为两大类：以农产品为原料的轻工业，是指直接或以农产品为基本原料的轻工业，主要包括食品制造、饮料制造、烟草加工、纺织、缝纫、皮革和毛皮制作、造纸以及印刷等工业；以非农产品为原料的轻工业，是以工业品为原料的轻工业，主要包括文教体育用品、化学药品制造、合成纤维制造、日用化学制品、日用玻璃制品、日用金属制品、手工工具制造、医疗器械制造、文化和办公用机械制造等工业。

重工业　是指为国民经济各部门提供物质技术基础的主要生产资料的工业。按其生产性质和产品用途，可以分为下列三类：采掘（伐）工业，是对自然资源的开采，包括石油开采、煤炭开采、金属矿开采等工业；原材料工业，指向国民经济各部门提供基本材料、动力和燃料的工业，包括金属冶炼及加工、炼焦及焦炭化学、化学原料、水泥、人造板以及电力、石油和煤炭加工等工业；加工工业，是指对工业原材料进行再加工制造的工业，包括装备国民经济各部门的机械设备制造工业、金属结构、水泥制造等工业，以及为农业提供的生产资料如化肥、农药等工业。

资产总额　是指企业拥有或控制的能以货币计量的经济资源，包括各种财产、债权和其他权利。资产按其流动性（即资产的变现能力和支付能力）划分为：流动资产、长期投资、固定资产、无形资产、递延资产和其他资产，即为企业资产负债表中的资产总计项。

流动资产　是企业资产的重要组成部分，通常是指一年内或超过一年的一个营业周期内可以变现或耗用的资产。其特点是在企业的生产经营或者业务活动中不断地在生产循环中周转，不断改变其形态。其价值一次性消耗、转移或者实现。包括：货币资金、短期投资、应收票据、应收账款、预付账款、其他应收款、存货、待摊费用、待处理流动资产损失、一年内到期的本期债券投资及其他流动资产。

固定资产原价　是指企业在建造、购置、安装、改建、扩建、技术改造某项固定资产时实际支出的全部货币总额。它一般包括买价、包装费、运杂费和安装费等。

固定资产合计　包括固定资产净值、固定资产清理、在建工程、待处理固定资产净损失所占用的资金合计。

固定资产净值　是指固定资产原价减去历年已提折旧额后的净额。

负债　是指企业所承担的能以货币计量，将以资产或劳务偿付的债务。其偿还形式可以用货币，也可以用资产或提供劳务的方式进行。包括流动负债、长期负债和递延税款贷项等，即为企业资产负债表的负债合计项。

实收资本　是指企业实际收到的投资人投入的资本。包括有国家资本、集体资本、法人资本、个人资本、外商资本、港澳台资本等。

主营业务收入　是企业在销售商品、提供劳务及让渡资产使用权等日常活动中所产生的收入。

主营业务税金及附加　是指企业日常活动应负担的税金及附加，包括营业税、消费税、城市维护建设税、资源税、土地增值税和教育费附加等。

主营业务成本　是指企业因销售商品、提供劳务或让渡资产使用权等日常活动而发生的实际成本。

营业利润　是企业生产经营活动所取得的利润，包括主营业务利润和其他业务利润。

利润总额　是指企业在一定时期内生产经营活动的最终的财务成果，是企业的收入减去有关成本与费用后的差额，收入大于相关的成本费用，企业就盈利，反之则亏损。包括营业利润、补贴收入、投资净收益、营业外收支净额、以前年度损失调整。

应交增值税　是指企业按税法规定，从事货物销售或提供加工、修理修配劳务等增加货物价值的活动本期应交纳的税金，即企业在报告期应交的增值税额。计算公式为：

应交增值税 ＝ 销项税额-(进项税额-进项税额转出)-出口抵减内销产品应纳税额-减免税款+出口退税

从业人员平均人数　从业人员指企业工作并取得劳动报酬的全部人员数。包括在岗职工、再就业的离退休人员、民办教师及在企业工作的外方人员和港澳台方人员、兼职人员、借用的外单位人员和第二职业者。不包括离开本单位但仍保留劳动关系的职工。而从业人员平均人数指报告期内每天平均拥有的从业人员人数。其计算公式为：

月平均人数=报告月内每天实有人数之和÷报告月日历日数

季平均人数=季内各月平均人数之和÷3

年平均人数=全年各月平均人数之和÷12

资产利税率　是在一定时期内已实现的利润、税金总额与同期的资产总额之比。计算公式：

$$资产利税率（\%）= \frac{报告期累计实现利税总额}{资产总额} \times 100\%$$

资产利税率反映每单位（通常是每万元）资产所提供的利税金额。它是考察和评价部门或企业资金运用的经济效益，分析资金投入效果的主要分析指标。

产值利税率　是报告期已实现的利润、税金总额（包括利润总额、产品销售税金及附加和应交增值税）占同期全部工业总产值的百分比，计算公式为：

$$产值利税率（\%）= \frac{利税总额}{工业总产值（现价）} \times 100\%$$

工业经济效益综合指数　是现行综合评价工业经济效益总体水平及工业经济运行质量的指数，它是以若干项代表性经济效益指标，分别除以各项指标的标准值，再乘以各自的权数，加总后除以总权数求得。其计算公式为：

$$工业经济效益综合指数= \Sigma（\frac{某项经济效益指标报告期数值}{该项指标标准值} \times 权数）\div 总权数$$

上式总权数为100。

工业产品销售率　是反映工业产品已实现销售的程度，是分析工业产销衔接情况、研究工业产品满足社会需求的指标。计算公式是：

$$产品销售率（\%）= \frac{现价工业销售产值}{现价工业总产值} \times 100\%$$

总资产贡献率　是指企业一定时期内全部资产获利能力，是企业经营业绩和管理水平的集中体现，是评价和考核企业盈利能力的核心指标。计算公式为：

$$总资产贡献率（\%）= \frac{利润总额+税金总额+利息支出}{平均资产总额} \times 100\% \times \frac{12}{累计月数}$$

注：税金总额为主营业务税金及附加与应交增值税之和，平均资产总额为期初、期末资产总计的算术平均值。

资本保值增值率 是反映企业净资产变动状况的一个重要指标，是企业发展能力的集中体现。是指期末所有者权益总额与期初所有者权益总额的比率。计算公式为：

$$资本保值增值率（\%）= \frac{期末所有者权益}{期初所有者权益} \times 100\%$$

所有者权益等于资产总计减负债总计。

资产负债率 是指反映企业经营风险的大小，反映企业利用债权人提供的资金从事经营活动的能力。计算公式为：

$$资产负债率（\%）= \frac{负债总额}{资产总额} \times 100\%$$

资产及负债均为报告期期末数。

流动资产周转率 是指一定时期内流动资产完成的周转次数，反映投入工业企业流动资金的周转速度，一般以一年内周转多少次表示。计算公式为：

$$流动资产周转率（次）= \frac{产品销售收入}{流动资产平均余额} \times \frac{12}{累计月数}$$

成本费用利润率 是指工业企业投入的生产成本及费用的经济效益，同时也反映企业降低成本所取得的经济效益。计算公式为：

$$成本费用利润率（\%）= \frac{利润总额}{成本费用总额} \times 100\%$$

注：成本费用总额为产品销售成本、销售费用、管理费用、财务费用之和。

全员劳动生产率 是指反映企业的生产效率和劳动投入的经济效益。一般用平均每人一年创造的工业增加值表示。计算公式为：

$$全员劳动生产率（元/人）= \frac{工业增加值}{全部职工平均人数} \times \frac{12}{累计月数}$$

五、固定资产投资与建筑业

Investment in Fixed Assets and Construction

5-1 主要年份固定资产投资与建筑业主要指标

Main Indicators of Investment in Fixed Assets and Construction in Main Years

项　　目	单　位	1985年	1990年	1995年	2000年	2005年	2010年	2011年
固定资产投资总额	万元	70600	75052	631355	1028914	5972443	11149822	10797662
#国有单位	万元	16914	50658	106935	197658	686333	1479886	923083
私营个体经济	万元					1027969	2077250	1988277
港澳台投资经济	万元			10281	130501	1246450	1326063	1460388
外商投资经济	万元			230409	92699	507322	938943	747677
新增固定资产	万元					1732967	5778616	5788944
固定资产交付使用率	%					29.02	51.83	53.61
房屋竣工面积	万平方米					696.99	686.22	441.43
房屋面积竣工率	%					21.62	20.65	12.85
计划总投资	万元					13905355	45000174	48292866
固定资产投资建设周期	年					2.32	4.04	4.47
固定资产投资资金来源	万元	17000	50100	480875	1047861	6717711	18550102	17030960
#国家预算内资金	万元	1100	3600	10858	10490	536	130717	47949
国内贷款	万元	2800	2900	27439	122561	651723	1882278	1401681
利用外资	万元		17000	194486	207444	940432	1400920	1237319
自筹资金	万元	13100	25400	163090	587176	3901138	8390847	8087349
房地产开发投资	万元			85163	112498	1444277	2989853	3737580
房地产开发当年房屋施工面积	万平方米			160.74	315.45	1160.17	2060.54	2396.55
房地产开发当年房屋竣工面积	万平方米			76.78	103.20	132.88	296.59	242.28
#住宅	万平方米			68.36	77.97	115.23	256.09	210.85
商品房销售面积	万平方米			25.42	63.21	321.85	511.25	595.61
#住宅	万平方米			20.49	51.02	297.19	469.90	540.68
建筑企业(单位)个数	个		8	8	99	361	431	448
建筑企业平均人数	人		6803	22200	64300	79965	57473	59013
建筑企业总产值	万元		12678	94941	404493	843540	1220569	1308530
劳动生产率(按总产值计算)	元/人		18636	42766	60849	108136	218076	207555
建筑业房屋施工面积	万平方米		66.30	278.72	1218.00	1234.98	733.44	756.01
建筑业房屋竣工面积	万平方米		29.95	94.99	53.76	707.77	311.94	403.94

注：1. 本表固定资产投资资金来源1990年前是国有单位数，1995年以后是城镇集体以上单位数；1995年固定资产投资含沙角C厂完成的126374万元，2005年起是全社会固定资产投资单位数。
2. 从2011年起，固定资产投资统计起点由计划投资50万元提高到计划投资500万元，下同。

5-2 历年固定资产投资

Total Investment in Fixed Assets over Years

单位：万元

年份	固定资产投资总额	#民营	#外资	#港澳台	#房地产开发
1978	2319				
1979	1641				
1980	2395				
1981	3756				
1982	18102				
1983	18370				
1984	30050				
1985	70600				
1986	115173				
1987	141856				
1988	165459				
1989	50135				
1990	75052				
1991	137464				
1992	188824				
1993	327630		62600		52110
1994	1407621		1038599		78392
1995	631355		240690		85163
1996	676185		259705		86258
1997	658941		69055		86662
1998	769953		91719	35868	95451
1999	883201		188036	116708	104411
2000	1028914		146887	96112	112498
2001	1254945		224812	181822	148544
2002	1915741		466569	213458	268350
2003	3193889		888664	619193	551184
2004	4548691		1094045	716611	1144195
2005	5972443		1753772	1246450	1444277
2006	7054511	2410417	2297486	1584104	1642398
2007	8412074	2841860	2356983	1136955	2094187
2008	9443426	3240949	2710398	1469186	2714197
2009	10940753	4279669	2038232	1114631	2776623
2010	11149822	4847208	2265006	1326063	2989853
2011	10797662	4418315	2208065	1460388	3737580

注：1994、1995、1996年全社会投资总额分别含沙角C厂投资额956758万元、126374万元、102760万元。

5-3 按登记类型和行业分的固定资产投资(2011年)

Total Investment in Fixed Assets by Registration Status and Sector (2011)

单位：万元

项　　目	全市合计	城镇	#房地产	农村
合　　计	10797662	8942813	3737580	1854849
按登记注册类型分				
内资	8589597	7161601	3469952	1427996
国有	923083	908511	38188	14572
集体	1172394	696882	52871	475512
股份合作	17111	12611		4500
国有联营				
集体联营	3890			3890
国有与集体联营				
其他联营	10455	10455	10455	
国有独资公司	340513	340513	144076	
其他有限责任公司	3781660	3245048	1974172	536612
股份有限公司	111724	101338	28898	10386
私营	1782611	1594934	1201568	187677
其他	240490	187758	19724	52732
个体经营：个体户	185682	62051		123631
个人合伙	19984	1500		18484
港澳台商投资	1460388	1203785	172426	256603
合资经营	313274	292307	43701	20967
合作经营	76558	76022	64392	536
独资	1021088	787640	64103	233448
股份有限	49468	47816	230	1652
外商投资	747677	577427	95202	170250
合资经营	129999	126537	85391	3462
合作经营	5631			5631
独资	606004	450098	9811	155906
股份有限	6043	792		5251
按国民经济行业分				
第一产业	5994	5094		900
第二产业	3511671	2471752		1039919
制造业	3021838	2053886		967952
电力、燃气及水的生产和供应业	487845	416778		71067
建筑业	1468	1088		380
第三产业	7279997	6465967	3737580	814030
交通运输、仓储和邮政业	1093310	1011389		81921
信息传输、计算机服务和软件业	199193	194943		4250
批发和零售业	264068	194798		69270
住宿与餐饮业	46117	24135		21982
金融业	19395	16595		2800
房地产业	4041821	3875291	3737580	166530
租赁和商务服务业	74593	14199		60394
科学研究、技术服务和地质勘查业	77528	65487		12041
水利、环境和公共设施管理业	1025426	806322		219104
居民服务和其他服务业	17109	7168		9941
教育	235049	117390		117659
卫生、社会保障和社会福利业	73711	61054		12657
文化、体育和娱乐业	70148	44448		25700
公共管理和社会组织	42529	32748		9781

5-4 固定资产投资主要指标（2011年）

Main Indicators of Total Investment in Fixed Assets (2011)

单位：万元

项　　目	计　划总投资	本年完成投资	建　筑工　程	安　装工　程	设备工器具购置	其　他费　用
合　　计	24546214	7060082	3827609	251840	2397573	583060
按登记注册类型分						
内资	21188126	5119645	3389211	225620	948979	555835
国有	5100988	884895	725855	44847	36530	77663
集体	3680058	1119523	950060	48148	15607	105708
股份合作	116992	17111	16406	617		88
国有联营						
集体联营	4000	3890	3700	190		
国有与集体联营						
其他联营						
国有独资公司	1882483	196437	157537			38900
其他有限责任公司	8241166	1807488	951932	90284	543857	221415
股份有限公司	242073	82826	38051	1635	27903	15237
私营个体	1414095	786709	418133	35830	263262	69484
其他	506271	220766	127537	4069	61820	27340
港澳台商投资	2383327	1287962	347646	17598	903055	19663
外商投资	974761	652475	90752	8622	545539	7562
按国民经济行业分						
第一产业	6294	5994	1827	1340	2827	
第二产业	7169554	3511671	1121092	70929	2152325	167325
制造业	5046868	3021838	752140	45308	2083843	140547
电力、燃气及水的生产和供应业	2118136	487845	368552	25621	66894	26778
建筑业	3900	1468	400		1068	
第三产业	17370366	3542417	2704690	179571	242421	415735
交通运输、仓储和邮政业	9589085	1093310	856248	2055	35717	199290
信息传输、计算机服务和软件业	204823	199193	9613	75636	113794	150
批发和零售业	480000	264068	204541	14926	34897	9704
住宿与餐饮业	141934	46117	22817	6129	11768	5403
金融业	70300	19395	16328	567	1000	1500
房地产业	1520261	304241	244945	19739	1380	38177
租赁和商务服务业	131135	74593	33429	7624	3043	30497
科学研究、技术服务和地质勘查业	488255	77528	49898	2000	9137	16493
水利、环境和公共设施管理业	3123629	1025426	912450	23669	6008	83299
居民服务和其他服务业	48147	17109	7485	500	7959	1165
教育	599941	235049	196635	10349	4279	23786
卫生、社会保障和社会福利业	468638	73711	56913	3459	9500	3839
文化、体育和娱乐业	275116	70148	58309	7938	2139	1762
公共管理和社会组织	229102	42529	35079	4980	1800	670
按建设性质分						
新建	18792496	4121508	3068467	201943	327178	523920
扩建	1135401	300403	217686	7964	64932	9821
改建	2328567	797287	527520	39816	180632	49319
单纯建造生活设施	1500	1171		1171		
迁建	182500	3155	3075	80		
恢复	79017	12827	10861	866	1100	
单纯购置	2026733	1823731			1823731	

注：本表不含房地产开发投资。

5-4 续表 1

(2011年)

单位：万元

项目	本年新增固定资产	本年施工房屋面积(万平方米)	本年竣工房屋面积(万平方米)	本年资金来源合计	#上年末结余资金
合计	4618853	1039.69	199.14	9153107	809448
按登记注册类型分					
内资	3058810	899.49	166.18	6623575	516492
国有	415877	26.17		941749	37038
集体	841787	248.77	22.65	1503742	209339
股份合作	15961	8.36		17111	
国有联营					
集体联营	2700	2.56	2.18	4000	
国有与集体联营					
其他联营					
国有独资公司	52835			196437	
其他有限责任公司	932080	229.05	65.89	2599347	209601
股份有限公司	50402	20.41	0.66	138986	13432
私营个体	673251	290.14	61.13	955539	38503
其他	73917	74.04	13.66	266664	8579
港澳台商投资	1080922	110.00	16.58	1816193	267503
外商投资	479121	30.20	16.38	713339	25453
按国民经济行业分					
第一产业	5994	2.90		7141	
第二产业	2464061	501.90	144.35	4301111	375305
制造业	2265775	498.04	142.17	3764047	319978
电力、燃气及水的生产和供应业	196298	3.86	2.18	534976	55327
建筑业	1468			1568	
第三产业	2148798	534.89	54.79	4844855	434143
交通运输、仓储和邮政业	217067	52.09		1357672	92957
信息传输、计算机服务和软件业	195772	0.80		199943	9380
批发和零售业	259596	57.24	12.27	378873	61291
住宿与餐饮业	27608	18.68	4.26	99353	
金融业	8162	14.91		19397	
房地产业	236356	181.99	16.84	712094	98349
租赁和商务服务业	30587	30.19	2.31	100101	2448
科学研究、技术服务和地质勘查业	33842	3.75		78523	587
水利、环境和公共设施管理业	797704	5.60	0.45	1205991	54929
居民服务和其他服务业	13125	6.93	6.21	36079	11604
教育	168266	101.72	3.31	330099	16882
卫生、社会保障和社会福利业	67644	52.09	7.20	101848	20250
文化、体育和娱乐业	67142	5.82	1.93	93764	4283
公共管理和社会组织	25927	3.09		131118	61183
按建设性质分					
新建	2471440	884.44	177.59	5629381	507555
扩建	200293	43.14	7.55	352710	15685
改建	503585	74.82	14.00	992946	126738
单纯建造生活设施	1171			1171	
迁建	3155	5.30		3180	2600
恢复	12827	32.00		13450	
单纯购置	1426382			2160269	156870

5-4 续表 2

(2011年)

单位：万元

项目	#本年资金来源小计	本年资金来源 国家预算内资金	国内贷款	利用外资	自筹资金	其他资金来源
合 计	8343659	47949	615554	1233669	5860078	586409
按登记注册类型分						
内资	6107083	47949	587568	6710	4981133	483723
国有	904711	3283	85524		756411	59493
集体	1294403	27396	34413	4110	1057011	171473
股份合作	17111		7507		9312	292
国有联营						
集体联营	4000				4000	
国有与集体联营						
其他联营						
国有独资公司	196437		27590		168847	
其他有限责任公司	2389746	900	297162	2000	1898569	191115
股份有限公司	125554		7500		118054	
私营个体	917036		127872	600	747280	41284
其他	258085	16370			221649	20066
港澳台商投资	1548690		27986	744655	702886	73163
外商投资	687886			482304	176059	29523
按国民经济行业分						
第一产业	7141				6641	500
第二产业	3925806	900	77893	1177103	2457656	212254
制造业	3444069	900	52428	1177103	2004523	209115
电力、燃气及水的生产和供应业	479649		25465		451045	3139
建筑业	1568				1568	
第三产业	4410712	47049	537661	56566	3395781	373655
交通运输、仓储和邮政业	1264715		350222		825644	88849
信息传输、计算机服务和软件业	190563		3000		187563	
批发和零售业	317582		12600	15059	249061	40862
住宿与餐饮业	99353			4900	94453	
金融业	19397				19397	
房地产业	613745	5434	85183		499707	23421
租赁和商务服务业	97653				95022	2631
科学研究、技术服务和地质勘查业	77936	680			77256	
水利、环境和公共设施管理业	1151062	13908	77061	19413	909852	130828
居民服务和其他服务业	24475	1019		444	21212	1800
教育	313217	8938		3000	239436	61843
卫生、社会保障和社会福利业	81598		7507	13750	54369	5972
文化、体育和娱乐业	89481	15700	2088		57043	14650
公共管理和社会组织	69935	1370			65766	2799
按建设性质分						
新建	5121826	39919	454962	114714	4102939	409292
扩建	337025	4646	22448	2878	292069	14984
改建	866208	900	129330	64129	558622	113227
单纯建造生活设施	1171				1171	
迁建	580				580	
恢复	13450				13450	
单纯购置	2003399	2484	8814	1051948	891247	48906

5-5　固定资产投资分类情况(2011年)

Basic Statistics on Total Investment in Fixed Assets by Type (2011)

单位：万元

项　　目	计　划 总投资	自开始建设 累计完成投资	本年完 成投资	#住宅	本年新增 固定资产
固定资产投资总额	24546214	13268267	7060082	92762	4618853
#基础设施	14525161	6500427	2704124	30	1400091
#基础产业	14623056	6561865	2765262	30	1424614
#城市建设	7557673	3114738	1471637	30	828900
#原材料	257795	190767	144018		52710
#能源	1330071	744164	377788		167830
#工业合计	7165654	5106262	3510203	21042	2462593
#工业九大产业	3898936	2796496	2278175	2590	1656797
#电子信息业	1451858	1166234	989625	2590	767343
电气机械及专用设备	1129898	620341	483113		355629
石油及化学	131807	104897	76340		23781
纺织及服装	305389	263182	235984		210354
食品饮料	298297	172248	114353		52100
建筑材料	128315	88482	70740		33783
森工造纸	370959	323998	252236		177952
医药	25303	14634	14634		41
汽车	57110	42480	41150		35814

注:本表不含房地产开发投资。

5-6　房地产开发主要指标

Main Indicators of Real Estate Development

项　　目	单位	2005年	2006年	2007年	2008年	2009年	2010年	2011年
一、土地购置								
本年土地购置面积	万平方米	44.9	73	57.7	69.45	92.02	135.74	151.9
二、本年完成投资额	万元	1444277	1642398	2094187	2714197	2776623	2989853	3737580
#住宅	万元	1197154	1475181	1860580	2213498	2513852	2504525	3229200
三、资金来源	万元	1632570	2120240	2900238	4049833	4281021	6533564	7877853
#国内贷款	万元	114755	292488	446710	1079194	544169	1271530	786127
利用外资	万元	2075	10140		27053	105397	75182	3650
自筹资金	万元	867824	677095	905912	1067823	1840753	2025670	2227271
四、房屋建筑面积								
施工面积	万平方米	1160.2	1437.6	1521.6	1998.0	2333.9	2060.5	2396.5
#住宅	万平方米	889.9	1229.4	1371	1680.8	2050.1	1686.6	1999.6
竣工面积	万平方米	132.9	166.3	137.3	478.0	310.2	296.6	242.3
#住宅	万平方米	115.2	114.1	111.9	395.2	268.1	256.1	210.8
五、商品房屋销售额	万元	1193991	1612449	2949939	2885975	3530040	3737742	4596123
#住宅	万元	1091095	1460425	2736729	2461024	3342466	3341485	4133322
六、商品房屋销售面积	万平方米	321.9	382	573	511.59	600.27	511.3	595.6
#住宅	万平方米	297.2	353	541.1	467.98	578.82	469.9	540.7

5-7　房地产开发企业主要经济指标（2011年）

Main Indicators of Real Estate Enterprises (2011)

单位：万元

项　　目	资产总计	负债总计	主营业务收入	主营业务税金及附加	利润总额	全部从业人员年平均人数（人）
合　　计	17926375	14285664	3517723	354872	999541	11356
按登记注册类型分						
#内源型经济	15829552	12749211	3172973	325766	956216	9669
#民营经济	12402791	9926646	2646437	258815	766468	7477
#国有经济	650486	551261	89230	14762	55643	109
集体经济	556023	373775	109712	18139	14350	763
私营个体经济	6303927	4938200	1149468	120976	511183	3846
外源型经济	2096823	1536453	344750	29106	43325	1687
#港澳台商投资	1423646	1129856	265818	21217	43915	1128
外商投资	673177	406597	78932	7889	-589	559
按控股情况分						
国有控股	650486	551261	89230	14762	55643	116
集体控股	658964	455658	110453	18229	15287	737
私人控股	12402791	9926646	2646437	258815	766468	7511
港澳台控股	1424646	1129856	265818	21217	43915	1130
外商控股	733409	426040	82554	8895	4947	539
其他控股	2056079	1796202	323231	32954	113282	1323
按资质等级分						
一级	2116228	1318959	264951	54932	511658	659
二级	2308766	1804592	495031	41379	99235	1888
三级	3992536	3276318	890439	97448	95026	2430
四级	5337500	4293080	1319034	108054	178944	4343
暂定	3210246	2800099	423041	44817	114061	1333
其他	961101	792616	125228	8242	618	703

5-8 房地产开发投资情况（2011年）

Investment in Real Estate Development (2011)

项　　目	房地产开发投资（万元）	住宅
合　　计	3737580	3229200
内资	3469952	3017666
国有	38188	30322
集体	52871	45698
国有独资公司	144076	137605
其他有限责任公司	1974172	1787205
私营独资	131715	122741
私营有限责任公司	1022016	797132
私营股份有限公司	28573	27805
其他内资企业	19724	13943
港澳台商投资	172426	117385
外商投资	95202	94149

5-9 房地产开发企业、房屋建筑面积及价值（2011年）

Floor Space and Value of Buildings in Real Estate Development (2011)

项　　目	房屋建筑面积（平方米）		竣工房屋价值（万元）
	施工面积	竣工面积	
合　　计	23965497	2422825	1112723
内资	21802171	2363626	1078537
国有	798983		
集体	571255	87097	46134
国有独资公司	388859		
其他有限责任公司	10245839	948612	438179
私营独资	432352	98102	46391
私营有限责任公司	8949107	1186300	511667
私营股份有限公司	114106		
其他内资企业	117949	18008	9004
港澳台商投资	1849928	59199	34186
外商投资	313398		

5-10 商品房屋销售情况（2011年）

Sale of Commercialized Buildings (2011)

项目	商品房屋销售建筑面积（平方米）	#住宅	商品房屋销售额（万元）	#住宅
合计	5956139	5406769	4596123	4133322
内资	5326091	4852807	4122721	3776470
国有	33252	33252	34828	34828
集体	197718	183292	114462	97852
国有独资公司	137370	130515	143058	136058
其他有限责任公司	3095521	2845453	2358925	2153669
私营独资	64864	64564	33571	33174
私营有限责任公司	1616305	1419762	1244874	1134718
私营股份有限公司	75038	70574	43415	37022
其他内资企业	24983	24983	15864	15864
港澳台商投资	412124	345296	333940	226886
外商投资	217924	208666	139462	129966

5-11 建筑施工企业主要指标（2010-2011年）

Main Indicators of Construction Enterprises (2010-2011)

指标	单位	2010年 合计	2010年 #国有单位	2011年 合计	2011年 #国有单位
企业单位数	个	431	1	448	1
年平均人数	人	57473	1841	59013	1539
自有固定资产原价	万元	262771	14485	266362	15518
自有固定资产净值	万元	150269	6921	145481	7331
自有施工机械设备年末总台数	台	17596	413	15645	375
自有施工机械设备年末净值	万元	58404	1503	57644	2384
自有施工机械设备年末总功率	万千瓦	17	1	21	1
建筑业总产值	万元	1220569	197246	1308530	211649
建筑工程产值	万元	994608	197246	1048214	211527
安装工程产值	万元	172772		191160	122
其他产值	万元	53189		69156	
建筑业竣工产值	万元	799524	80081	866997	130724
建筑业增加值	万元	823674		777901	
房屋建筑施工面积	万平方米	733	15	756	11
房屋建筑竣工面积	万平方米	312	5	404	2
利润总额	万元	57835	1039	49397	1310
利税总额	万元	99072	8669	97110	8981
劳动生产率(按总产值计算)	元/人	218076	1071407	207555	1812063
劳动生产率(按增加值计算)	元/人	147163		130949	
技术装备率	元/人	10162	8164	9768	15491
动力装备率	千瓦/人	3.0	5.0	3.5	8.1
房屋建筑面积竣工率	%	42.6	33.3	53.4	21.7
产值利润率	%	4.7	0.5	3.8	0.5
产值利税率	%	8.1	4.4	7.4	4.2

主要统计指标解释

Explanatory Notes on Main Statistical Indicators

固定资产投资额 是以货币形式表现的在一定时期内建造和购置固定资产的工作量以及与此有关的费用的总称。按构成可分为建筑工程、安装工程、设备工器具购置和其他费用。

房屋建筑施工面积 指报告期内施工的全部房屋建筑面积。包括本期新开工的面积和上期开工跨入本期继续施工的房屋面积，以及上期已停建在本期复工的房屋面积。本期竣工和本期施工后又停缓建的房屋，其建筑面积仍计入本期施工房屋面积中。

房屋建筑新开工面积 指报告期内新开工的全部房屋建筑面积，以单位工程为核算对象。房屋新开工面积指整栋房屋的全部建筑面积，不能分割计算。

房屋建筑竣工面积 指在报告期内房屋建筑按照设计要求已全部完工，达到住人和使用条件，经验收鉴定合格(或达到竣工验收标准)，可正式移交使用的各栋房屋建筑面积的总和。

房屋建筑面积竣工率 指一定时期内房屋竣工面积占同期房屋施工面积的比率。它是从房屋建筑施工速度的角度反映投资效果和建筑业经济效益的指标。

固定资产交付使用率 指一定时期新增固定资产与同期完成投资额的比率。它反映各个时期固定资产动用速度、衡量建设过程中投资效果的一个综合性指标。

六、运输邮电

Transport, Postal and Telecommunication Services

6-1 主要年份运输邮电主要指标

Main Indicators of Transport, Postal and Telecommunication Services in Main Years

项　　目	单　位	1985年	1990年	1995年	2000年	2005年	2010年	2011年
公路通车里程	公里	1240	1325	2327	2519	2871	4751	4828
#高速公路	公里				89	154	217	251
一级公路	公里		6	679	782	1315	2394	2420
内河通航里程	公里	532	598	598	798	664	643	643
公路桥梁	座	211	267	338	538	826	1211	1395
民用汽车	辆	7897	19394	88311	153684	406577	920766	1061373
#载客	辆	1878	7225	25366	69658	268918	772701	906454
载货	辆	5980	12087	52242	80405	129298	143005	149635
摩托车	辆	11786	47881	255591	482636	775838	423766	352553
机动船	艘	2883	5885	5292	806	467	286	312
机动船净载重	吨位	80324	186056	259329	152661	148737	557846	1083217
邮电局(所)	处	52	53	273	594	702	555	626
邮路长度	公里	790	459	685	3550	6835	4667	4283
长途自动交换机容量	路端		2100	15000	42182	510045	419110	419237
局用交换机容量	万门	1.14	6.98	52.29	103.13	286.25	365.02	357.00
移动电话交换机总容量	万户			4.8	154.2	1059.1	1657.0	2066.0
本地电话用户	万户	0.77	4.90	31.58	78.12	384.52	332.42	319.55
移动电话用户(含充值卡)	万户		0.05	4.77	123.68	1016.41	1607.60	1677.77
互联网用户	万户			0.05	13.78	52.90	153.92	190.72
邮政业务收入	万元						63178	73686
电信业务收入	万元						1490174	1574893
客运量	万人	2072	5758	10237	30697	33551	77446	80337
#公路	万人	1940	5728	10210	30680	33510	77415	80306
旅客周转量	万人公里	95237	322236	446230	1001906	1185290	1290692	1458811
#公路	万人公里	90950	320690	444293	1000492	1182000	1288675	1456782
货运量	万吨	2913	2701	4266	5431	6400	9312	10165
#公路	万吨	1922	1571	2377	3440	4586	7640	8210
货物周转量	万吨公里	171591	184700	264605	404678	424829	1090340	1874802
#公路	万吨公里	113038	72162	128026	246046	272500	510801	531304
港口货物吞吐量	万吨	276	233	201	746	2280	5657	6848

注：1. 2006年起公路通车里程含专用公路和村道，下同。
2. 2010年起，长途自动交换机容量统计口径有变，与往年不可比，下同。
3. 2010年起，邮政业务相关指标不包括速递物流及邮政储蓄银行独立运营部分，下同。

6-2 历年运输线路长度与公路密度

Length of Transportation Routes and Road Density over Years

年份	公路通车里程(公里)	#等级公路	#一级	等外公路	高级、次高级路面通车里程(公里)	内河通航里程(公里)	公路密度(公里/百平方公里)
1978	1259	287		972		530	51.08
1979	1225	355		870		603	49.70
1980	1225	355		870		603	49.70
1981	1225	845		380		415	49.70
1982	1225	845		380		115	49.70
1983	1225	872		353		132	49.70
1984	1240	896		344		132	50.30
1985	1240	490		750	488	132	50.30
1986	1248	977		271		274	50.63
1987	1261	991		270		598	51.15
1988	1302	1068	6	234		598	52.82
1989	1325	1091	6	234		598	53.75
1990	1325	1102	6	223	750	598	53.75
1991	1759	1226	6	533	1137	598	71.36
1992	2055	1431	151	624	1442	599	83.37
1993	2260	1673	315	587	1675	598	91.68
1994	2292	1868	599	424	1773	598	92.98
1995	2327	1930	679	397	1650	598	94.40
1996	2330	2087	689	243	1653	598	94.50
1997	2330	2087	690	243	1563	598	94.50
1998	2429	1897	714	480	1958	598	98.52
1999	2467	1935	717	480	2048	798	100.06
2000	2519	2339	782	91	2253	798	102.15
2001	2570	2393	845	78	2321	798	104.26
2002	2641	2464	908	78	2406	798	107.14
2003	2688	2508	967	75	2472	716	109.05
2004	2759	2609	1148	37	2637	798	111.93
2005	2871	2686	1315	31	2774	664	116.47
2006	3891	3619	1585	117	3823	664	157.85
2007	3924	3650	1591	116	3860	535	159.19
2008	4001	3884	1639	117	3864	643	162.31
2009	4713	4598	2389	115	4643	643	191.21
2010	4751	4637	2394	114	4681	643	192.74
2011	4828	4716	2420	112	4759	643	196.24

注：公路密度数据来源于交通运输局，下同。

6-3 主要年份运输线路长度

Length of Transport Routes in Main Years

项　　目	单　位	1980年	1985年	1990年	1995年	2000年	2005年	2010年	2011年
一、公路通车里程合计	公里	1225	1240	1325	2327	2519	2871	4751	4828
#按等级分									
等级公路	公里	355	490	1102	1930	2339	2686	4637	4716
高速公路	公里					89	154	217	251
一　级	公里			6	679	782	1315	2394	2420
二　级	公里		58	65	361	684	703	1317	1335
三　级	公里		61	60	135	310	297	178	182
四　级	公里	355	371	971	755	563	371	532	528
等外公路	公里	870	750	223	397	91	31	114	112
#按路面分									
有路面里程	公里		622	800	1808	2508	2858	4689	4767
#高级、次高级	公里		488	750	1650	2253	2774	4681	4759
无路面里程	公里		618	524	519	11	13	62	61
二、桥梁合计	座		211	267	338	538	826	1211	1395
	延米					39956	112385	162767	224548
三、公路密度	公里/百平方公里	49.70	50.30	53.75	94.40	102.15	116.47	192.74	196.24
#等级公路密度	公里/百平方公里	14.40	19.88	44.71	78.30	94.89	108.97	188.12	191.70
四、内河通航里程	公里	603	532	598	598	798	664	643	643

6-4 主要年份客货运输量

Passenger and Freight Traffic in Main Years

年　份	客运量（万人）	旅客周转量（万人公里）	货运量（万吨）	货物周转量（万吨公里）	港口货物吞吐量（万吨）
1952	86	1350	7	139	
1957	120	2100	10	195	
1962	187	4120	14	293	
1965	193	4725	22	457	
1970	118	2800	36	900	
1975	169	3890	30	694	
1978	403	9425	394	15148	293
1980	572	13584	349	16353	295
1985	2072	95237	2913	171591	276
1990	5758	322236	2701	184700	233
1995	10237	446230	4266	264605	201
1996	10749	477466	4451	267193	289
1997	11300	511592	4644	278649	338
1998	17485	577452	4776	285889	516
1999	25404	804278	5016	300410	654
2000	30697	1001906	5431	404678	746
2001	31220	1031579	5527	406247	883
2002	32100	1091821	5857	420684	1611
2003	32588	1126964	5877	422822	2352
2004	33240	1166262	6054	423669	2600
2005	33551	1185290	6400	424829	2280
2006	35182	1213809	5481	336783	1951
2007	37182	1264982	5676	356677	2017
2008	122468	2248521	9273	1747489	3208
2009	73324	1053469	8733	1016490	3530
2010	77446	1290692	9312	1090340	5657
2011	80337	1458811	10165	1874802	6848

6-5 客货运输量

Passenger and Freight Traffic

项　　目	单　位	1980年	1985年	1990年	1995年	2000年	2005年	2010年	2011年
一、客运量	万人	572	2072	5758	10237	30697	33551	77446	80337
公　路	万人	362	1940	5728	10210	30680	33510	77415	80306
水　运	万人	210	132	30	27	17	41	31	31
二、旅客周转量	万人公里	13584	95237	322236	446230	1001906	1185290	1290692	1458811
公　路	万人公里	8285	90950	320690	444293	1000492	1182000	1288675	1456782
水　运	万人公里	5299	4287	1546	1937	1414	3290	2017	2029
三、货运量	万吨	349	2913	2701	4266	5431	6400	9312	10165
公　路	万吨	51	1922	1571	2377	3440	4586	7640	8210
#个体及联户	万吨		1906	1557	2368	3440	4586	2080	2155
水　运	万吨	298	991	1130	1889	1991	1814	1672	1955
#个体及联户	万吨		617	837	1599	1660	1484	158	133
四、货物周转量	万吨公里	16353	171591	184700	264605	404678	424829	1090340	1874802
公　路	万吨公里	1479	113038	72162	128026	246046	272500	510801	531304
#个体及联户	万吨公里		113002	72141	127928	246046	272500	131929	138976
水　运	万吨公里	14874	58553	112538	136579	158632	152329	579539	1343498
#个体及联户	万吨公里		31784	83094	105099	119855	113249	9399	9606

6-6 主要年份运输工具拥有量

Possession of Main Means of Transport in Main Years

项　　目	单　位	1980年	1985年	1990年	1995年	2000年	2005年	2010年	2011年
一、民用车辆拥有量									
(一)汽车	辆	2009	7897	19394	88311	153684	406577	920766	1061373
1. 载客汽车	辆	516	1878	7225	25366	69658	268918	772701	906454
	客位	1909	23462	66361	302844	560155	2420591	5101240	5810047
2. 载货汽车	辆	1457	5980	12087	55000	81623	129298	143005	149635
	吨位	3368	20428	38010	133757	332621	243390	253879	270309
3. 其他汽车	辆	36	39	82	7945	2403	8361	5060	5284
(二)摩托车	辆	170	11786	47881	255591	482636	775838	423766	352553
(三)挂车	辆					8	2222	2983	3196
二、民用运输船舶拥有量									
机动船	艘	1948	2883	5885	5292	806	467	286	312
	净载重吨位	42473	80323	186056	259329	152661	148737	557846	1083217
	客位	2107	2056	776	1881	1054	604	902	902
#货船	艘		2866	5875	5259	796	465	283	309
	净载重吨位		80285	186038	259314	152661	148431	557236	1082607
客船	艘				26	10	2	3	3
	客位				1295	1054	604	902	902
三、期末机动车驾驶员	人		44186	118229	351947	563564	798086	1287738	1486810
#汽车驾驶员	人		10661	28768	94778	173865	428912	1110932	1334243

注：2002年起民用汽车拥有量按新的口径分类，部分指标数值与往年不可比。

6-7 历年主要运输工具年末拥有量

Possession of Main Means of Transport at Year-end over Years

年 份	民用汽车 (辆)	#客车	#货车	摩托车 (辆)	机动船 (艘)
1978	623	78	506	134	2169
1979	1115	178	1089	156	2034
1980	2009	516	1457	170	1948
1981	3039	751	2031	517	2107
1982	3419	791	2724	1168	2285
1983	4473	854	3580	1636	2313
1984	6059	1243	4822	7060	2563
1985	7897	1878	5980	11786	2883
1986	8632	2245	6334	18006	4368
1987	9983	2954	6973	21308	4884
1988	13581	3456	8690	26995	4911
1989	16340	4214	10434	36820	4901
1990	19394	7225	12087	47881	5885
1991	20734	5206	15423	65770	4405
1992	32625	5753	25048	106013	4351
1993	48145	8710	35421	153014	4379
1994	61572	11550	43925	200543	4562
1995	88311	25366	55000	255591	5292
1996	90793	29430	54870	249492	5313
1997	103425	40101	62507	287076	5064
1998	113435	47769	64434	382010	456
1999	127007	55715	69470	399324	690
2000	153684	69658	82841	482636	806
2001	183638	89677	91304	560310	536
2002	220134	116783	102253	642034	483
2003	255603	155206	97047	692562	392
2004	319725	210531	105050	687651	417
2005	406577	268918	129298	775838	467
2006	489306	351265	131704	697175	440
2007	608933	466999	134825	567002	393
2008	701600	557359	136295	521118	326
2009	795554	653273	137334	470818	293
2010	920766	772701	143005	423766	286
2011	1061373	906454	149635	352553	312

6-8 主要年份邮电通信业务基本情况

Basic Statistics on Postal and Telecommunication Services in Main Years

项　　目	单位	1978年	1985年	1990年	1995年	2000年	2005年	2010年	2011年
一、邮电通信网									
邮电局、所	处	50	52	53	273	594	702	555	626
邮路长度	公里	513	790	459	685	3550	6835	4667	4283
农村投递线路长度	公里	1985	2302	1812	2057	8865	19722	13261	12875
二、邮电通信工具									
邮政汽车	辆		2	7	10	35	192	131	151.0
长途自动交换机容量	路端			2100	15000	42182	510045	419110	419237
移动电话交换机总容量	万户				4.8	154.2	1059.1	1657.0	2066.00
移动电话用户(含充值卡)	万户					123.68	1016.41	1607.60	1677.77
移动电话用户(不含充值卡)	万户			0.05	4.77	80.97	176.83	174.04	244.78
局用交换机容量	万门		1.14	6.98	52.29	103.13	286.25	365.02	357.00
#市话交换机	万门		0.22	2.10	16.82	21.84	67.68	94.28	56.43
本地电话用户	万户	0.20	0.77	4.90	31.57	78.12	384.52	332.42	319.55
市内电话用户	万户	0.04	0.16	1.50	9.78	19.69	68.30	85.76	73.37
农村电话用户	万户	0.16	0.61	3.40	21.80	58.43	316.22	246.66	246.18
数字数据用户(DDN)	端口					2741	2170	1098	388.00
互联网用户	万户				0.05	13.78	52.90	153.92	190.72
三、邮电业务量									
邮电业务收入	亿元							155.34	164.86
#电信业务	亿元							149.02	157.49
#移动通信业务	亿元							105.78	116.34
邮政特快专递	万件						292.17	183.00	167.00
函件	万件		805	3372	10407	8124	9430	4507	5148
长途电话	万次		89	1739	21287	66419	159762	135811	152131

6-9 历年邮电通信业务主要指标

Main Indicators of Postal and Telecommunication Services over Years

年 份	邮 电 局、所 (处)	长途自动交换机容量 (路端)	局用交换机容量 (万门)	本地电话用户 (万户)	移动电话用户 (万户)	邮电业务收入 (亿元)
1978	50			0.20		
1979	50			0.21		
1980	50		0.50	0.31		
1981	50			0.34		
1982	51			0.35		
1983	51			0.39		
1984	52			0.48		
1985	52		1.14	0.77		
1986	53			0.88		
1987	45			1.63		
1988	48			2.52		
1989	50			4.30	0.02	
1990	53	2100	6.98	4.90	0.05	
1991	60		9.82	7.50	0.11	
1992	91	3510	11.07	9.70	0.30	
1993	161	3510	21.24	14.98	0.72	
1994	216	11410	36.37	23.19	2.41	
1995	273	15000	52.29	31.57	4.77	
1996	310	15000	52.79	36.91	8.24	
1997	339	15000	57.76	42.65	15.29	
1998	397	25000	73.09	50.13	26.17	
1999	458	40000	84.79	60.87	51.01	
2000	594	42182	103.13	78.12	123.68	
2001	689	59000	155.29	98.96	295.76	
2002	696	59000	176.94	127.93	412.39	90.56
2003	846	129000	220.28	206.11	660.86	105.12
2004	854	200985	265.66	281.35	856.09	120.78
2005	702	510045	286.25	384.52	1016.41	132.82
2006	560	563071	299.19	461.31	1216.34	146.69
2007	567	713290	329.50	469.17	1408.23	161.90
2008	547	766946	340.71	439.41	1454.29	172.38
2009	546	864970	347.15	378.40	1409.29	156.31
2010	555	419110	365.02	332.42	1607.60	155.34
2011	626	419237	357.00	319.55	1677.77	164.86

注：本地电话用户含小灵通用户。

6-10　历年邮电通信企业财务指标

Main Financial Indicators of Postal and Telecommunication Enterprises over Years

单位：万元

指　　标	2002年	2003年	2004年	2005年	2006年	2007年	2010年	2011年
职工人数(人)	5035	5269	9485	10730	10881	11309	10050	10276
#固定工	4038	4277	7941	4803	4498	4528	4375	4575
年末资产总额	1211054	1211056	1342540	1465629	1548349	1623628	1615528	1598573
年末流动资产合计	224550	146908	133768	181039	228697	279043	261091	157213
#应收帐款净额	63042	57368	53062	67608	56478	62631	53749	60994
年末固定资产合计	947924	998057	1151720	1238276	1280974	1258143	1118833	1198064
年末固定资产原值合计	1157237	1402762	1534094	1790159	2018571	2252314	2835390	3130717
#生产用	1122155	1386056	1516466	1770843	2006747	2163153	2827527	3121472
累计折旧	348785	472350	531081	664786	860633	1077754	1647586	1865640
#当年折旧	115935	122390	154417	177293	197314	230146	112848	218732
年末固定资产净值合计	808453	930412	1003012	1125360	1157926	1174540	1187804	1265077
无形资产及递延资产	15635	25839	57051	42582	38777	81176	63073	63960
其它资产	12707	11056		2198	2551	5265	172531	179336
负债及所有者权益总计	1211054	1211056	1342540	1465629	1548349	1623628	1615528	1598573
年末流动资产负债合计	244828	194474	202929	365735	451449	465033	570387	597492
#未交税金	19870	17729	29345	39447	42265	33785	17248	29965
短期借款				3000		8000		
年末长期负债合计	95	14175	9932				-2635	31522
期末所有者权益合计	966131	1002408	1129679	1099894	1096900	1158595	1047776	969559
主营业务收入	890138	1036123	1174265	1326686	1446601	1603151	1155820	1723350
#营业成本	236322	278125	303464	406999	471863	552168	468110	644909
营业税金及附加	26517	34307	36790	41122	41635	48758	32063	51978
其他业务利润	-855	266223	11911	-11316	-15355	1230	-1721	-2868
管理费用	24375	214051	84868	99425	56157	54236	34802	53001
财务费用	3910	447	37848	539	897	898	2718	735
营业外收入	874	1088	1676	879	1809	2135	6093	2679
营业外支出	10122	2424	8424	2838	3325	6132	3281	2962
利润总额	548341	580729	676902	716380	805496	877893	496456	748937
利税总额	576501	627697	713700	756757	835548	926720	520173	780934

主要统计指标解释

Explanatory Notes on Main Statistical Indicators

公路里程 指在一定时点上实际达到交通部规定的公路技术等级标准，并经公路主管部门正式验收交付使用的公路里程数。包括大、中城市的郊区公路以及公路通过城镇（指县城、集镇）街道的里程数。但不包括大、中城市街道，厂矿、林区内部生产用道、农业生产用道，以及新建公路尚未进行验收交付使用的路段里程。公路按工程技术等级分为高速、一、二、三、四级公路；按公路是否铺设路面分为有路面和无路面公路；按公路通车情况分为晴雨通车里程和晴通雨阻里程。计量单位为公里。

货（客）运量 在一定时期内，各运输部门实际运送的货物（旅客）数量。货运按吨计算，客运按人计算。货物不论运输距离长短，货物类型，均按实际重量统计；旅客不论行程远近或票价多少，均按一人一次作为客运量统计。半价票，小孩票也按一人统计。货（客）运量反映运输业为国民经济和人民生活服务的数量，也是制定和检查运输生产计划，研究运输发展规模和速度的重要指标。

货物（旅客）周转量 指在一定时期内，由各种运输工具运输业运送的货物（旅客）数量与其相应运输距离的乘积，通常以吨公里和人公里为计算单位。计算货物周转量通常按发出站与到达站之间的最短距离，也就是计费距离计算。它是反映运输业生产总成果的重要指标，也是编制和检查运输生产计划，计算运输效率，劳动生产率以及核算运输单位成本的主要基础资料。

货物吞吐量 是指经由水运运进、运出港区范围，并经过装卸的货物数量。货物吞吐量分别按国内进口（装卸）、出口（装船），外贸进口、出口统计。货物吞吐量按货物实际重量吨统计，以货物交接清单或货单上记载的重量吨为准。如无实际重量吨，可根据船舶装载情况来推算。在本港区内的水运转口分别按进口和出口各计算一次吞吐量。货物吞吐量是衡量港口生产规模的一个主要数量指标。

邮电业务收入 是指邮电营运企业从事邮政、电信、移动及其他邮电业务所取得的营业收入。

局用电话交换机容量 指安装在本地电信运营商内用于接读本地固定电话的电话交换机容量，有倍增设备按倍增后的数量计数。包括现用和备用的人工或自动交换全部容量。

本地电话用户 是指接入本地电信运营商固定电话网上的电话用户。包括：住宅电话、单位用户、公用电话用户等。

移动电话用户 是指在移动通信部门办理登记手续，通过移动电话交换机进入移动电话网，占用移动电话号码的电话用户。

邮电局所 是指对外营业、直接为用户办理邮电业务的服务机构。一个邮电局所，必须同时具备以下三个条件：①有固定的局所地址；②领有上级发给的日戳或戳记；③至少办理出售邮票和收寄挂号信两种邮政业务或办理一种电信业务。凡是具备上述三个条件的，均按邮电局所统计，计量单位为“处”。邮电局所按经营方式分为自办局所和代办所。

邮电服务网点 指为用户进行邮电服务的地点，包括邮电局所、报刊亭等。

七、国内贸易

Domestic Trade

7-1 历年社会消费品零售总额

Total Retail Sales of Consumer Goods over Years

年　　份	社会消费品零售总额	
	绝对值（万元）	增速（%）
1978	21269	
1979	24956	17.3
1980	31595	26.6
1981	40201	27.2
1982	48126	19.7
1983	52255	8.6
1984	73930	41.5
1985	93640	26.7
1986	122420	30.7
1987	150511	23.0
1988	246518	63.8
1989	270354	9.7
1990	319738	18.3
1991	364972	14.2
1992	443464	21.5
1993	636882	43.6
1994	851556	33.7
1995	1130081	32.7
1996	1255311	11.1
1997	1460396	16.3
1998	1751551	19.9
1999	2023008	15.5
2000	2351634	16.2
2001	2757143	17.2
2002	3212436	16.5
2003	3697814	15.1
2004	4264704	15.3
2005	5062917	18.7
2006	5993201	18.4
2007	7224491	20.5
2008	8811519	22.0
2009	9590727	8.8
2010	11080592	15.9
2011	12663109	15.0

注：本表1979-2003年数据根据东莞市第一次全国经济普查结果重新核定，2005-2008年数据根据东莞市第二次全国经济普查结果重新核定，2010年、2011年统计口径均有调整，增长速度按同口径计算。

7-2 历年批发零售贸易企业与个体户数

Wholesale and Retail Trades Enterprises and Self-employed Individuals over years

单位：个

年　份	单位数合计	国有经济	集体经济	其他经济	
					私营个体经济
1979	2459	406	1918	135	135
1980	2613	395	1679	539	537
1981	4603	371	1954	2278	2274
1982	3323	373	1838	1112	1107
1983	8723	401	1539	6783	6783
1984	18917	431	6720	11766	11766
1985	16885	670	4543	11672	11671
1986	18547	823	3063	14661	14660
1987	23468	739	4102	18627	18626
1988	26247	665	4405	21177	21176
1989	28453	695	4196	23562	23561
1990	27931	709	3512	23710	23709
1991	29474	678	3934	24862	24862
1992	34465	803	4193	29469	29469
1993	43511	886	7640	34985	34985
1994	49706	633	11396	37677	37677
1995	56339	745	14492	41102	41101
1996	60078	670	15183	44225	44224
1997	48910	811	8477	39622	39546
1998	52543	1064	4046	47433	46615
1999	55925	1056	3843	51026	50172
2000	57474	1024	3581	5289	51914
2001	68909	866	2960	65083	63760
2002	89246	748	2424	86078	84614
2003	113531	530	2068	110933	109236
2004	149067	539	1941	146587	144304
2005	192525	393	1451	190681	188082
2006	236124	283	1090	234751	231930
2007	284109	268	930	282911	279524
2008	301996	288	833	300875	296613
2009	300088	256	744	299088	294753
2010	300668	239	654	299775	295166
2011	288904	223	629	288052	283209

7-3 批发零售业商品销售总额（2011年）

Total Sales of Commodities in Wholesale and Retail Trades(2011)

单位：万元

项　目	商品销售总额	批发额	零售额
合　计			
按行业分	23461849	11955784	11506066
批发业	11260188	10732759	527429
零售业	12201661	1223024	10978637
按规模分			
限额以上企业和个体户	16016725	10275525	5741200
粮油、食品、饮料、烟酒类	1863114	1471150	391964
粮油类	325431	225560	99871
肉禽蛋类	60094	27583	32511
水产品类	15151	1459	13692
蔬菜类	31463	679	30784
干鲜果品类	44088	7231	36857
饮料类	156792	92367	64425
烟酒类	756328	719275	37053
服装鞋帽、针纺织品类	1198262	899007	299256
服装类	684952	516953	167999
鞋帽类	248858	146526	102332
针、纺织品类	264452	235528	28924
化妆品类	55631	6542	49089
金银珠宝类	33576	17866	15710
日用品类	366151	267492	98659
洗涤用品类	176710	117854	58856
儿童玩具类	45778	38943	6835
五金、电料类	275045	261009	14036
体育、娱乐用品类	33264	21416	11848
书报杂志类	17249	7195	10054
电子出版物及音像制品类	3545	177	3368
家用电器和音像器材类	682441	361297	321144
中西药品类	369427	222108	147319
西药	221130	114600	106530
中草药及中成药	72278	42320	29958
文化办公用品类	184407	74271	110135
家具类	548199	543158	5041
通讯器材类	524970	417825	107146
煤炭及制品类	632672	631844	828
木材及制品类	3860	3860	
石油及制品类	3432768	1838368	1594400
化工材料及制品类	1326968	1326968	
化肥类	1072	1072	
金属材料类	524909	524909	
建筑及装潢材料类	63546	40800	22746
机电产品及设备类	253726	237714	16012
农机类	637	637	
汽车类	2642757	165062	2477695
种子饲料类	851	851	
棉麻类	144	144	
其它	979245	934493	44751
限额以下企业和个体户	7445125	1680259	5764866

7-4 限额以上住宿业和餐饮业经营情况（2011年）

Business of Hotels and Catering Services above Designated Size (2011)

项　　目	法人企业（个）	从业人数（人）	营业额（万元）	客房收入	餐费收入	商品销售收入	其它收入
总　计	315	68771	830295	190584	541547	5556	92608
一、住宿业	169	45015	525744	176847	261281	3199	84417
（一）按登记注册类型分							
内资企业	156	40691	469432	158803	228631	2851	79147
港、澳、台商投资企业	8	2480	33487	11349	18931	347	2860
外商投资企业	5	1844	22826	6696	13718	1	2411
（二）按国民经济行业分							
旅游饭店	136	41383	493565	163946	247557	3105	78955
一般旅馆	30	3482	30524	11540	13486	93	5404
其它住宿服务业	3	150	1656	1361	238		57
二、餐饮业	146	23756	304551	13736	280266	2357	8191
（一）按登记注册类型分							
内资企业	129	16218	169017	8893	152871	2147	5105
港、澳、台商投资企业	10	2895	50846	4844	42707	210	3085
外商投资企业	7	4643	84688		84688		
（二）按国民经济行业分							
正餐服务业	127	13815	172841	13736	149495	1419	8191
快餐服务业	9	8933	120887		120887		
饮料及冷饮服务业	1	451	1008		69	939	
其他餐饮服务业	9	557	9815		9815		

7-5 限额以上批发和零售企业财务状况（2011年）

Main Financial Indicators of Enterprises above Designated Size in Wholesale and Retail Trade (2011)

单位:万元

项目	法人企业数（个）	年末资产负债				
		流动资产合计	存货	固定资产原价	累计折旧	本年折旧
总计	804	6030245	1163662	842333	289508	63771
一、批发企业	335	4203509	570563	300942	109170	23244
（一）按登记注册类型分						
内资企业	318	4032569	532445	290627	104964	22449
港、澳、台商投资企业	13	132161	33086	7035	2408	639
外商投资企业	4	38779	5032	3280	1798	156
（二）按国民经济行业分						
农畜产品批发业	1	89	83	55	46	2
食品、饮料及烟草制品批发业	34	423398	85470	42771	15977	4444
纺织、服装及日用品批发业	32	438287	27378	40000	16072	1877
文化、体育用品及器材批发业	10	104180	18471	7149	2523	798
医药及医疗器材批发业	12	110586	29610	6551	2557	702
矿产品、建材及化工产品批发业	140	2150866	259984	116986	42665	9321
机械设备、五金交电及电子产品批发业	67	654469	100672	60531	18908	4449
贸易经纪与代理	10	48638	3621	12444	4841	549
其他批发业	29	272995	45275	14456	5581	1101
二、零售企业	469	1826736	593099	541391	180339	40527
（一）按登记注册类型分						
内资企业	433	1654523	529054	459528	154791	32633
港、澳、台商投资企业	13	102288	44597	41354	10804	3712
外商投资企业	23	69924	19449	40509	14744	4182
（二）按国民经济行业分						
综合零售业	83	257593	66244	165255	45932	14476
食品、饮料及烟草制品专门零售业	10	36509	17558	3113	1738	817
纺织、服装及日用品专门零售业	8	13310	8635	925	574	72
文化、体育用品及器材专门零售业	4	11729	7129	292	239	85
医药及医疗器材专门零售业	27	58167	17790	10346	4284	515
汽车、摩托车、燃料及零配件专门零售业	273	1045133	329427	319404	109945	21797
家用电器及电子产品专门零售业	27	348900	133193	10502	4031	1056
五金、家具及室内装修材料专门零售业	11	8068	3437	6663	4895	74
无店铺及其他零售业	26	47327	9686	24891	8699	1636

7-5　续表 1

(2011年)

单位: 万元

项　目	年末资产负债				损益及分配	
	资产总计	负债合计	所有者权益合计	实收资本	营业收入合计	主营业务收入
总　计	8574437	6442761	2131675	705462	16091994	15955577
一、批发企业	5118746	4330479	788267	396370	9925588	9869485
(一)按登记注册类型分						
内资企业	4936231	4190438	745793	371641	9535687	9481288
港、澳、台商投资企业	136953	108953	28001	17705	257729	256025
外商投资企业	45562	31088	14473	7025	132172	132172
(二)按国民经济行业分						
农畜产品批发业	98	31	67	50	812	812
食品、饮料及烟草制品批发业	897462	558538	338924	72942	1369392	1368839
纺织、服装及日用品批发业	484209	428469	55739	30009	2020073	2018982
文化、体育用品及器材批发业	117934	95927	22008	15916	141471	141471
医药及医疗器材批发业	118352	104425	13926	9345	205978	205978
矿产品、建材及化工产品批发业	2425088	2187218	237870	211494	4242837	4240883
机械设备、五金交电及电子产品批发业	722896	643786	79110	30767	1059414	1007645
贸易经纪与代理	59294	52898	6396	5618	334104	333664
其他批发业	293413	259186	34227	20230	551506	551210
二、零售企业	3455691	2112283	1343408	309092	6166405	6086092
(一)按登记注册类型分						
内资企业	3206253	1928257	1277995	234708	5457087	5387430
港、澳、台商投资企业	136514	90129	46385	28221	351301	346782
外商投资企业	112924	93897	19028	46163	358018	351880
(二)按国民经济行业分						
综合零售业	412007	331978	80029	57991	798710	778596
食品、饮料及烟草制品专门零售业	38859	30255	8604	5397	39965	39369
纺织、服装及日用品专门零售业	14845	14253	592	1250	75035	70440
文化、体育用品及器材专门零售业	15487	13614	1873	2420	9122	9122
医药及医疗器材专门零售业	67084	52050	15034	3874	130329	129559
汽车、摩托车、燃料及零配件专门零售业	2459203	1301571	1157632	181302	4118942	4079989
家用电器及电子产品专门零售业	368512	310761	57751	25020	748305	738150
五金、家具及室内装修材料专门零售业	10935	17603	-6668	7749	30289	30289
无店铺及其他零售业	68761	40198	28562	24089	215708	210579

7-5 续表 2

(2011年)

单位: 万元

项目	损益及分配					
	主营业务成本	营业税金及附加	其他业务利润	销售费用	管理费用	税金
总计	14651231	61210	134720	625392	225775	7649
一、批发企业	9284443	43948	33592	252068	101536	4202
(一)按登记注册类型分						
内资企业	8961832	43110	32709	214926	94741	3704
港、澳、台商投资企业	203119	704	770	32522	5264	205
外商投资企业	119492	134	113	4619	1531	293
(二)按国民经济行业分						
农畜产品批发业	762			13	19	2
食品、饮料及烟草制品批发业	1164659	36446	11584	42307	27004	787
纺织、服装及日用品批发业	1969172	524	5100	23360	9909	472
文化、体育用品及器材批发业	129461	173	114	6462	3416	163
医药及医疗器材批发业	190815	277	62	7907	3218	172
矿产品、建材及化工产品批发业	4032795	3066	10677	119531	28928	1411
机械设备、五金交电及电子产品批发业	951164	1411	3678	33295	17611	339
贸易经纪与代理	327768	1245	967	1854	3251	262
其他批发业	517848	806	1410	17339	8181	593
二、零售企业	5366788	17262	101128	373324	124240	3447
(一)按登记注册类型分						
内资企业	4749930	15624	85061	313487	109522	3054
港、澳、台商投资企业	303184	887	5693	25807	7701	338
外商投资企业	313675	751	10375	34030	7017	55
(二)按国民经济行业分						
综合零售业	650877	5154	40313	130617	19236	612
食品、饮料及烟草制品专门零售业	36313	177	415	1259	1076	20
纺织、服装及日用品专门零售业	28313	2485	108	26485	11856	28
文化、体育用品及器材专门零售业	7309	104	305	1718	501	34
医药及医疗器材专门零售业	110630	272	471	9877	7042	90
汽车、摩托车、燃料及零配件专门零售业	3647224	6370	36266	120436	66815	2561
家用电器及电子产品专门零售业	670999	2032	16948	62481	11842	32
五金、家具及室内装修材料专门零售业	25102	189	1443	5395	398	14
无店铺及其他零售业	190020	480	4859	15058	5475	57

7-5 续表 3

(2011年)

单位: 万元

项目	损益及分配				应付职工薪酬	应交增值税
	财务费用	营业利润	利润总额	应交所得税		
总计	116215	488392	271440	64132	266091	169251
一、批发企业	79365	217585	217542	39292	94257	90263
(一)按登记注册类型分						
内资企业	79720	190484	190360	35778	79354	81353
港、澳、台商投资企业	-561	15746	15741	1983	12086	7495
外商投资企业	205	11355	11441	1531	2816	1411
(二)按国民经济行业分						
农畜产品批发业		18	18	5	41	
食品、饮料及烟草制品批发业	18703	153991	154593	26309	26993	33240
纺织、服装及日用品批发业	6770	14473	15041	2381	12435	4180
文化、体育用品及器材批发业	665	1409	-1275	194	4931	1589
医药及医疗器材批发业	2470	1349	1521	447	4526	2274
矿产品、建材及化工产品批发业	44691	35070	35726	5924	20081	35751
机械设备、五金交电及电子产品批发业	3798	4406	4969	2035	15723	7909
贸易经纪与代理	474	38	84	144	1611	562
其他批发业	1793	6830	6867	1854	7917	4759
二、零售企业	36850	270808	53899	24840	171834	78987
(一)按登记注册类型分						
内资企业	33425	252439	59589	20528	145408	69232
港、澳、台商投资企业	2048	13047	-10578	2406	13326	7350
外商投资企业	1378	5322	4888	1906	13101	2405
(二)按国民经济行业分						
综合零售业	3323	10266	-13479	4623	45622	15549
食品、饮料及烟草制品专门零售业	210	796	795	121	1439	1284
纺织、服装及日用品专门零售业	108	1302	1522	432	3019	1704
文化、体育用品及器材专门零售业	90	-295	-296	9	704	269
医药及医疗器材专门零售业	1110	1117	930	460	8841	1736
汽车、摩托车、燃料及零配件专门零售业	28531	248192	54788	16433	74028	47698
家用电器及电子产品专门零售业	2485	5275	5741	1532	28132	7756
五金、家具及室内装修材料专门零售业	444	204	159	75	2243	690
无店铺及其他零售业	549	3950	3738	1154	7805	2303

7-6 限额以上住宿和餐饮企业财务状况（2011年）

Main Financial Indicators of Enterprises above Designated Size in Hotels and Catering Services (2011)

单位：万元

项　　目	法人企业数（个）	年末资产负债				
		流动资产合计	存货	固定资产原价	累计折旧	本年折旧
总　　计	315	544293	48887	1065488	505206	56666
一、住宿业	169	456594	31439	883654	407452	46664
（一）按登记注册类型分						
内资企业	156	369624	28733	744803	320192	41758
港、澳、台商投资企业	8	69155	1815	92773	66817	3675
外商投资企业	5	17815	891	46078	20444	1230
（二）按国民经济行业分						
旅游饭店	136	436245	30170	841842	390999	44777
一般旅馆	30	20221	1248	40996	15916	1690
其它住宿服务业	3	129	21	816	537	197
二、餐饮业	146	87699	17449	181834	97754	10002
（一）按登记注册类型分						
内资企业	129	48104	12355	78418	35285	5888
港、澳、台商投资企业	10	24747	1380	83874	52631	2710
外商投资企业	7	14847	3714	19542	9838	1404
（二）按国民经济行业分						
正餐服务业	127	63435	5733	147955	79705	6489
快餐服务业	9	19973	11181	33492	17855	3479
饮料及冷饮服务业	1	55	52	32	2	1
其他餐饮服务业	9	4236	482	355	192	32

7-6 续表 1

(2011年)

单位: 万元

项目	年末资产负债				损益及分配	
	资产总计	负债合计	所有者权益合计	实收资本	营业收入	主营业务收入
总计	1461509	1315355	146154	357807	831168	830308
一、住宿业	1230785	1085174	145611	247055	526561	525756
(一)按登记注册类型分						
内资企业	1081853	966674	115180	185838	472211	471476
港、澳、台商投资企业	102181	81220	20961	39710	33437	33437
外商投资企业	46751	37280	9471	21507	20912	20843
(二)按国民经济行业分						
旅游饭店	1178121	1063293	114828	228796	494380	493605
一般旅馆	52127	20909	31218	18009	30500	30471
其它住宿服务业	537	971	-434	250	1681	1681
二、餐饮业	230724	230182	543	110752	304607	304551
(一)按登记注册类型分						
内资企业	117737	71628	46109	61359	169069	169013
港、澳、台商投资企业	72545	142168	-69623	37777	50850	50850
外商投资企业	40442	16386	24057	11617	84688	84688
(二)按国民经济行业分						
正餐服务业	166691	216739	-50048	83154	172824	172768
快餐服务业	59431	12250	47181	24483	120961	120961
饮料及冷饮服务业	85	11	74	24	1008	1008
其他餐饮服务业	4517	1182	3336	3092	9815	9815

7-6 续表 2

(2011年)

单位: 万元

项　　　目	损益及分配					
	主营业务成本	主营业务税金及附加	其他业务利润	销售费用	管理费用	税　金
总　　计	318848	51003	3484	284249	160186	4189
一、住宿业	167041	33439	3090	193359	122621	1998
(一)按登记注册类型分						
内资企业	149164	30164	2988	172977	107236	1770
港、澳、台商投资企业	10128	1962	29	12277	10591	201
外商投资企业	7750	1312	73	8105	4794	28
(二)按国民经济行业分						
旅游饭店	156960	31077	2817	180890	116206	1970
一般旅馆	9617	2263	273	11591	6258	26
其它住宿服务业	464	100		878	157	2
二、餐饮业	151807	17564	395	90890	37565	2191
(一)按登记注册类型分						
内资企业	94260	9893	328	41993	23382	1048
港、澳、台商投资企业	18212	2968	8	18283	9685	75
外商投资企业	39335	4703	58	30614	4498	1069
(二)按国民经济行业分						
正餐服务业	84286	10415	251	50894	27220	1075
快餐服务业	60042	6559	7	39273	8472	1114
饮料及冷饮服务业	628	53		283	2	1
其他餐饮服务业	6850	537	137	440	1870	2

7-6 续表 3

(2011年)

单位: 万元

项　　目	损益及分配				应付职工薪酬
	财务费用	营业利润	利润总额	应交所得税	
总　计	25976	-6201	-6263	4592	170941
一、住宿业	24692	-12041	-11103	1871	116879
(一)按登记注册类型分					
内资企业	22849	-7660	-6784	1870	104710
港、澳、台商投资企业	881	-2374	-2337		7351
外商投资企业	962	-2007	-1982	1	4819
(二)按国民经济行业分					
旅游饭店	24082	-12526	-11430	1657	109723
一般旅馆	595	419	261	199	6876
其它住宿服务业	16	66	66	15	281
二、餐饮业	1283	5840	4840	2721	54062
(一)按登记注册类型分					
内资企业	817	-1004	-1207	986	32256
港、澳、台商投资企业	495	1215	1092	404	8410
外商投资企业	-29	5629	4955	1332	13397
(二)按国民经济行业分					
正餐服务业	1754	-1550	-1976	910	33385
快餐服务业	-474	7094	6521	1737	18851
饮料及冷饮服务业	1	41	41	17	665
其他餐饮服务业	2	255	255	57	1162

7-7 历年住宿餐饮企业与个体户数

Enterprises and Self-employed Individuals in Hotels and Catering Services over Years

单位：个

年 份	单位数合 计	国有经济	集体经济	其他经济	#私营个体经济
1979	147	22	115	10	10
1980	182	23	121	38	38
1981	622	24	283	315	315
1982	308	24	102	182	182
1983	2069	31	98	1940	1940
1984	4012	31	445	3536	3536
1985	2982	36	389	2557	2557
1986	3268	38	270	2960	2956
1987	2281	35	308	1938	1934
1988	2265	31	296	1938	1934
1989	2850	32	276	2542	2538
1990	3387	30	439	2918	2914
1991	3438	44	225	3169	3165
1992	4456	25	320	4111	4106
1993	7119	12	1851	5256	5232
1994	7819	12	1748	6059	6051
1995	8918	26	1802	7090	7082
1996	9708	9	1900	7799	7789
1997	9968	28	606	9334	9210
1998	11069	102	368	10599	10532
1999	11904	80	337	11487	11392
2000	8335	78	361	7896	7831
2001	9776	67	343	9366	9318
2002	15128	74	265	14789	14740
2003	17615	64	229	17322	17276
2004	19802	39	424	19339	19224
2005	25972	28	315	25629	25522
2006	27108	16	247	26845	26747
2007	38435	11	219	38205	38094
2008	40154	9	177	39968	39687
2009	38220	5	130	38085	37795
2010	36156	4	113	36039	35728
2011	29280	4	91	29185	28825

7-8 历年限额以上企业商品购进、销售、库存总额

Total Purchases, Sales and Stock of Commercial Enterprises above Designated Size over Years

单位：万元

年 份	商品购进总额	商品销售总额	批 发	零 售	年末库存总额
1978	82347	74936	50207	24729	7576
1979	91074	82878	55528	27350	8378
1980	109147	99324	66547	32777	10041
1981	131797	119936	80357	39579	12125
1982	156730	142615	95552	47063	14413
1983	160485	146042	97848	48194	14764
1984	214364	195072	130698	64374	19721
1985	254458	231557	155143	76414	23410
1986	630988	283945	190243	93702	28706
1987	380242	346021	231834	114187	34982
1988	714661	650342	435729	214613	65749
1989	729163	663539	444570	218969	67083
1990	766549	697560	467365	230195	70523
1991	796488	672666	433991	238675	74092
1992	881697	743990	473014	270976	64939
1993	1141163	1063567	725979	337588	92249
1994	1323263	1296363	912457	383906	177377
1995	1584470	1556882	1044334	512548	143404
1996	1694496	1737121	1117111	620010	166267
1997	1857884	1922001	1212399	709602	175715
1998	779319	863214	696921	166293	91640
1999	1064070	1106048	875799	230249	73620
2000	1232026	1354640	1072929	281711	58304
2001	1312924	1405409	1080688	324721	67415
2002	1588853	1682579	1188961	493618	102657
2003	1712564	1805840	1138496	667344	107996
2004		5406921	3479209	1927712	251427
2005	4798504	5683548	3882222	1801326	322445
2006	5324450	6487742	4215562	227179	335108
2007	6706290	8102415	4875668	3226748	485401
2008	8349926	10772768	6604662	4168106	790691
2009	8689984	10167222	6137228	4029994	839175
2010	12846503	14271362	9046899	5224463	1002940
2011	15777469	18129917	11738336	6391581	1401733

7-9 市场分类基本情况(2011年)

Basic Statistics on Market Classification (2011)

单位：个

项　　目	合　计	城　市	农　村
合　　计	812	181	631
一、消费品市场	765	167	598
（一）消费品综合市场	162	42	120
（二）农副产品市场	496	100	396
1. 农副产品综合市场	465	96	369
2. 农副产品专业市场	31	4	27
（三）工业品消费市场	72	18	54
1. 工业消费品综合市场	32	11	21
2. 工业消费品专业市场	40	7	33
（四）其他消费品市场	35	7	28
二、生产资料市场	47	14	33
（一）生产资料综合市场	6	2	4
（二）工业生产资料市场	23	4	19
1. 机动车交易市场	6	2	4
2. 钢材交易市场	2		2
3. 煤炭交易市场			
4. 木材交易市场	5	1	4
5. 其他工业生产资料市场	10	2	8
（三）农业生产资料市场			
1. 农业生产资料综合市场			
2. 农业生产资料专业市场			
（四）其他生产资料市场	18	8	10

注：本表数据来源于市工商局。

7-10 历年城乡集市贸易

Statistics on Urban and Rural Trade Fairs over Years

单位：个

年　份	集贸市场 总　数	城　市	农　村
1978	35		35
1979	35		35
1980	35		35
1981	38		38
1982	40		40
1983	41		41
1984	43		43
1985	48		48
1986	57	7	50
1987	63	10	53
1988	66	12	54
1989	69	11	58
1990	73	10	63
1991	75	10	65
1992	53	7	46
1993	155	13	142
1994	162	12	150
1995	189	17	172
1996	219	20	199
1997	241	23	218
1998	252	25	227
1999	286	36	250
2000	308	29	279
2001	375	31	344
2002	495	28	467
2003	576	34	542
2004	610	35	575
2005	665	36	629
2006	812	39	773
2007	845	36	809
2008	871	228	643
2009	883	225	658
2010	792	194	598
2011	812	181	631

注：1995年前为工商系统口径，从1996年起为全市口径。2008年以前的城市集贸市场数只包括莞城的集贸市场，2008年起包括莞城、东城、南城和万江四大街道办的市场数。

主要统计指标解释

Explanatory Notes on Main Statistical Indicators

社会消费品零售总额 指企业（单位、个体户）通过交易直接售给个人、社会集团非生产、非经营用的实物商品金额，以及提供餐饮服务所取得的收入金额。个人包括城乡居民和入境人员，社会集团包括机关、社会团体、部队、学校、企事业单位、居委会或村委会等。

商品购进总额 指从本企业以外的单位和个人购进（包括从国外直接进口）作为转卖或加工后转卖的商品金额（含增值税）。本指标反映批发和零售业从国内外市场上购进商品的总价。

商品销售总额 指对本单位以外的单位和个人出售的商品金额（包括售给本单位消费用的商品，含增值税），本指标反映批发和零售业在国内市场上销售商品以及出口商品的总量。

期末库存 对于批发和零售业法人企业和个体经营户，是指取得所有权的全部商品金额（含增值税）；对于批发和零售业产业活动单位，是指期末实际在库且归属法人具有所有权的全部商品金额（含增值税）。这个指标反映批发和零售业的商品库存情况，以及对市场商品供应的保证程度。

批发额 指售给国民经济各行业企业（单位）用于生产、经营用的商品金额。

零售额 指售给城乡居民用于生活消费和社会集团用于公共消费的商品金额。

住宿和餐饮业零售额 指住宿和餐饮业单位因为提供就餐服务或销售商品取得的全部收入，包括餐费收入和商品销售收入（含增值税）。

流动资产合计 资产满足以下条件之一应归为流动资产：（1）预计在一个正常营业周期中变现、出售或耗用，主要包括存货、应收帐款等；（2）主要为交易目的而持有；（3）预计在资产负债表日起一年内（含一年）变现；（4）自资产负债日起一年内，交换其他资产或清偿负债的能力不受限制的现金或现金等价物。包括货币资金、应收票据、应收账款、存货等项目。根据会计“资产负债表”中“流动资产合计”项目的期末余额数填报。

固定资产合计 指企业为生产商品、提供劳务、出租或经营管理而持有的，使用寿命超过一个会计年度的有形资产。包括使用期限超过一年的房屋、建筑物、机器、机械、运输工具以及其他与生产、经营有关的设备、器具、工具等。固定资产合计是时点指标，表示固定资产经过扣减折旧、减值准备等后的期末余额。根据会计“资产负债表”中“固定资产”项目的期末余额数填报。

所有者权益合计 指企业资产扣除负债后由所有者享有的剩余权益。公司的所有者权益又称股东权益。包括实收资本、资本公积、盈余公积、未分配利润等。根据会计“资产负债表”中“所有者权益合计”项目的期末余额数填报。

营业税金及附加 指企业因从事生产经营活动按税法规定缴纳的应从经营收入中抵扣的税金和附加，包括营业税、消费税、城市维护建设税、教育费附加等。根据会计“利润表”中“营业税金及附加”项目的本期金额数填报。

利润总额 指企业在一定会计期间的经营成果，是生产经营过程中各种收入扣除各种耗费后的盈余，反映企业在报告期内实现的亏盈总额。根据会计“利润表”中“利润总额”项目的本期金额数填报。执行2006 年《企业会计准则》的企业，利润总额为营业利润加上营业外收入，减去营业外支出后的金额；未执行 2006 年《企业会计准则》的企业，利润总额为营业利润加上投资收益、补贴收入、营业外收入，再减去营业外支出后的金额。

应交增值税 指企业按税法规定，从事货物销售或提供加工、修理修配劳务等增加货物价值的活动本期应交纳的税金。指企业在报告期应交增值税额。

计算公式 本年应交增值税＝销项税额－（进项税额-进项税额转出）－出口抵减内销产品应纳税额－减免税款＋出口退税

批发零售贸易、餐饮业统计限额标准

行业类别	统计指标名称	限额标准
批发业	年主营业务收入	2000万元
零售业	年主营业务收入	500万元
住宿业、餐饮业	年主营业务收入	200万元

说明：

1. 外贸企业包括在批发业中，其年销售额以外币计量的，应折合成人民币，按批发业标准执行。

2. 本限额标准对象为批发和零售业、住宿和餐饮业法人企业和个体经营户、非批发和零售业、住宿和餐饮业法人单位附营的批发和零售业、住宿和餐饮业产业活动单位。

八、价格指数

Price Indices

8-1 历年物价总指数（以上年价格为100）

General Price Indices over Years (Preceding Year=100)

年　份	商品零售价格总指数	#食品	#家用电器及音像器材	居民消费价格总指数	#食品	#服务项目
1978	100.4	101.6				
1979	102.6	107.1				
1980	110.9	114.5				
1981	109.3	110.3				
1982	101.2	100.8				
1983	99.6	99.5				
1984	98.6	97.5		99.3	97.5	102.0
1985	106.9	108.7		106.5	108.7	103.3
1986	104.4	105.0		104.2	105.0	102.3
1987	112.2	113.6		112.0	113.6	109.6
1988	132.8	133.9		136.0	133.9	168.0
1989	122.4	125.7		122.0	127.5	118.8
1990	94.9	92.8		96.6	92.8	111.0
1991	101.4	101.1		102.4	101.1	109.8
1992	107.7	109.0		109.2	109.0	117.9
1993	119.5	123.7		121.8	123.7	134.6
1994	118.4	125.9	99.6	123.5	126.4	141.2
1995	109.7	119.5	95.6	113.9	119.1	128.9
1996	104.7	108.1	94.5	106.8	107.8	115.0
1997	99.7	100.0	92.7	101.5	99.4	113.1
1998	98.7	99.9	93.3	99.9	99.5	108.4
1999	95.9	95.6	94.9	97.9	95.7	109.5
2000	100.1	100.3	97.2	101.5	100.4	112.8
2001	97.8	99.1	97.0	96.6	98.9	101.1
2002	99.1	100.9	98.0	98.1	99.0	98.7
2003	101.7	103.6	99.0	100.7	103.5	97.8
2004	103.2	108.6	98.7	103.0	108.6	99.7
2005	103.0	106.5	101.1	102.4	106.5	100.4
2006	102.8	100.1	100.5	101.2	100.1	101.6
2007	104.2	108.3	98.2	103.1	108.0	100.2
2008	107.9	115.6	100.4	105.5	115.1	100.1
2009	95.3	97.9	95.6	96.9	98.1	96.3
2010	103.2	104.8	95.6	102.8	104.6	102.6
2011	104.7	111.1	99.3	104.9	111.1	103.0

8-2 居民消费价格分类指数(2011年，以上年价格为100)

Consumer Price Indices by Category (2011, Preceding Year=100)

项　　　目	指 数	项　　　目	指 数
居民消费价格总指数	104.9	袜子	95.0
非食品价格指数	102.2	帽子	95.1
服务项目价格指数	103.0	衣着加工服务费	113.9
扣除鲜菜鲜果总指数	105.0	四、家庭设备用品及维修服务	105.5
消费品价格指数	105.7	耐用消费品	101.5
一、食　品	111.1	家具	100.6
粮食	114.6	家庭设备	102.0
大米	118.3	室内装饰品	103.0
粮食制品	105.8	床上用品	104.9
淀粉及制品	101.6	家庭日用杂品	101.1
干豆类及豆制品	98.8	家庭服务及加工维修服务	120.5
油脂	110.3	五、医疗保健和个人用品	102.4
肉禽及其制品	114.5	医疗保健	101.7
蛋	118.0	中药材及中成药	104.4
水产品	122.0	西药	101.6
菜	96.7	医疗保健服务	100.0
鲜菜	95.3	个人用品及服务	103.7
干菜及菜制品	102.6	化妆美容用品	97.5
调味品	106.7	清洁类化妆品	105.8
糖	103.1	个人饰品	118.6
食糖	105.7	个人服务	100.3
糖果	99.5	六、交通和通信	100.1
茶及饮料	102.0	交通	102.5
干鲜瓜果	113.5	交通工具	98.2
鲜瓜果	112.9	市区公共交通费	101.8
糕点饼干面包	103.3	城市间交通费	101.1
液体乳及乳制品	102.8	通信	96.4
在外用膳食品	110.7	通信工具	86.8
主食	110.0	通信服务	98.3
炒菜	113.7	七、娱乐教育文化用品及服务	100.3
地方小吃	104.0	文娱用耐用消费品及服务	96.8
其他食品	100.4	教育	103.3
二、烟酒	101.5	教材及参考书	100.6
烟草	100.0	学前教育	115.2
酒	103.8	文化娱乐类	100.8
三、衣着	101.4	文化娱乐用品	101.4
服装	101.0	书报杂志	100.0
衣着材料	108.6	文娱费	100.6
棉布	113.5	旅游	99.1
化纤布	118.6	八、居住	104.3
毛线	100.0	建房及装修材料	99.8
其他	98.1	住房租金	102.3
鞋袜帽	100.3	自有住房	106.1
鞋	101.6	水、电、燃料	104.8

8-3 居民消费价格分月指数（2011年，以上年同月价格为100）

Consumer Price Indices by Month (2011, Same Month of Preceding Year=100)

项　　目	1 月	2 月	3 月	4 月	5 月	6 月
居民消费价格总指数	104.7	103.0	105.5	105.2	103.7	104.1
非食品价格指数	103.4	101.6	102.7	102.3	101.6	101.8
服务项目价格指数	105.7	102.2	104.9	103.2	101.6	101.5
扣除鲜菜鲜果总指数	104.2	103.0	104.9	104.7	104.0	104.7
消费品价格指数	104.4	103.4	105.7	106.0	104.6	105.2
一、食品	107.8	106.2	111.8	112.0	108.7	109.7
#粮食	112.2	113.1	114.0	113.5	111.9	115.4
肉禽及制品	103.5	100.9	109.9	112.2	113.3	116.9
蛋	117.8	112.1	115.4	114.5	115.6	118.4
水产品	114.2	119.4	129.6	128.3	123.0	126.2
菜	106.6	92.2	104.3	102.2	86.7	87.5
二、烟酒	100.8	101.0	101.0	101.4	101.4	101.7
#烟草	100.0	100.0	100.0	100.0	100.0	100.0
酒	102.0	102.4	102.4	103.5	103.5	104.1
三、衣着	99.4	98.1	97.0	100.1	102.0	102.5
#服装	101.6	99.2	99.5	100.9	101.1	101.3
四、家庭设备用品及维修服务	106.9	105.5	107.4	109.1	107.0	104.2
#耐用消费品	100.8	100.5	100.1	100.4	99.0	99.1
五、医疗保健和个人用品	103.4	102.6	102.6	102.4	102.6	102.8
#医疗保健	104.6	103.7	103.8	102.9	102.3	101.3
个人用品及服务	101.1	100.4	100.3	101.5	103.1	105.6
六、交通和通信	100.1	99.1	100.1	100.5	100.3	100.2
#交通	101.2	99.8	101.4	102.2	102.1	103.1
通信	98.5	98.0	98.1	98.0	97.5	95.8
七、娱乐教育文化用品及服务	103.1	101.8	100.9	99.7	95.8	97.2
#文娱用耐用消费品及服务	97.0	97.3	98.5	98.2	96.4	96.3
教育	99.9	100.3	100.3	100.1	100.1	100.2
文化娱乐类	100.4	99.0	99.8	100.1	100.1	101.2
旅游类	117.0	110.5	105.0	100.0	87.4	91.5
八、居住	106.7	102.9	106.5	103.7	104.0	104.6
#建房及装饰材料	105.3	101.6	102.9	95.8	96.9	98.7
住房租金	100.0	98.4	101.6	101.6	103.3	103.3
自有住房	110.3	103.4	110.4	106.5	105.5	105.7
水、电、燃料	105.6	104.5	105.3	104.8	105.7	106.3

8-3 续表

项目	7月	8月	9月	10月	11月	12月
居民消费价格总指数	105.1	105.8	105.9	105.5	105.7	104.6
非食品价格指数	102.2	102.5	102.8	102.3	102.6	101.2
服务项目价格指数	101.8	101.9	102.7	102.8	104.7	102.9
扣除鲜菜鲜果总指数	105.7	106.3	106.5	106.0	105.8	104.3
消费品价格指数	106.4	107.5	107.2	106.6	106.1	105.3
一、食品	111.8	113.5	113.1	112.9	112.9	112.6
#粮食	117.7	118.0	117.6	117.5	113.7	110.7
肉禽及制品	121.5	120.6	121.8	121.4	117.3	114.6
蛋	121.0	122.2	123.5	123.9	120.7	110.9
水产品	127.1	126.4	122.7	118.4	116.8	113.9
菜	93.2	95.4	91.0	89.0	100.1	118.2
二、烟酒	101.8	101.3	101.4	101.5	102.5	102.5
#烟草	100.0	100.0	100.0	100.0	100.0	100.0
酒	104.5	103.1	103.4	103.6	106.2	106.2
三、衣着	102.6	102.0	103.9	103.9	103.4	102.1
#服装	101.5	100.3	102.3	102.3	102.3	99.9
四、家庭设备用品及维修服务	104.9	105.5	106.2	104.9	105.2	100.3
#耐用消费品	101.2	103.0	103.5	103.1	103.9	103.0
五、医疗保健和个人用品	102.3	102.9	102.3	102.0	101.8	100.8
#医疗保健	100.7	101.1	100.7	100.2	99.7	99.2
个人用品及服务	105.4	106.3	105.6	105.4	105.7	103.8
六、交通和通信	100.5	101.0	100.8	99.8	99.4	99.4
#交通	103.6	104.7	104.6	103.2	102.4	102.2
通信	95.8	95.4	95.1	94.6	94.6	95.1
七、娱乐教育文化用品及服务	97.1	97.4	100.1	100.6	105.6	105.3
#文娱用耐用消费品及服务	96.4	96.7	96.4	96.2	96.7	96.0
教育	100.4	100.4	109.6	109.5	109.5	109.5
文化娱乐类	100.9	102.2	101.4	101.4	101.4	101.3
旅游类	91.4	91.4	91.6	93.6	111.7	111.6
八、居住	106.0	106.2	104.8	104.0	102.3	100.0
#建房及装饰材料	98.0	98.2	99.7	101.6	101.3	98.5
住房租金	104.3	104.3	104.3	105.2	102.7	99.3
自有住房	107.1	107.1	105.7	104.6	104.8	102.2
水、电、燃料	108.8	109.5	106.1	103.9	99.9	98.3

8-4 居民消费价格分月指数（2011年，以上月价格为100）

Consumer Price Indices by Month (2011, Preceding Month=100)

项　　目	1 月	2 月	3 月	4 月	5 月	6 月
居民消费价格总指数	101.5	100.4	100.6	100.6	99.5	100.3
非食品价格指数	100.5	99.7	99.9	100.6	100.5	100.1
服务项目价格指数	100.7	100.3	100.4	100.0	100.6	100.0
扣除鲜菜鲜果总指数	100.9	100.4	100.3	100.6	100.1	100.5
消费品价格指数	101.8	100.5	100.7	100.9	99.0	100.4
一、食品	103.8	102.1	102.2	100.7	97.3	100.8
#粮食	103.6	101.0	100.5	99.9	98.6	103.8
肉禽及制品	99.2	103.2	100.7	101.7	100.9	103.1
蛋	102.5	98.9	101.1	99.3	100.9	102.5
水产品	104.3	109.0	103.0	101.3	94.3	101.5
菜	120.3	97.1	107.9	97.1	86.8	99.7
二、烟酒	100.0	100.1	100.1	100.4	100.0	99.8
#烟草	100.0	100.0	100.0	100.0	100.0	100.0
酒	100.0	100.2	100.3	100.9	100.0	99.6
三、衣着	100.5	97.2	99.2	103.1	101.5	100.1
#服装	99.8	97.2	100.3	101.3	100.3	100.2
四、家庭设备用品及维修服务	100.8	100.0	99.7	100.1	99.6	99.3
#耐用消费品	100.5	99.6	99.8	99.9	100.1	99.8
五、医疗保健和个人用品	100.4	99.4	99.5	100.5	101.1	100.0
#医疗保健	100.6	99.8	100.0	100.2	100.2	99.1
个人用品及服务	100.1	98.9	98.7	100.9	103.0	101.7
六、交通和通信	100.7	99.9	100.0	100.5	99.9	99.6
#交通	101.3	100.2	100.2	100.9	100.3	100.4
通信	99.8	99.5	99.8	99.8	99.4	98.3
七、娱乐教育文化用品及服务	100.8	101.6	98.7	100.0	100.2	100.8
#文娱用耐用消费品及服务	100.0	99.9	100.2	99.4	98.1	99.6
教育	99.9	100.4	100.0	99.9	100.0	100.1
文化娱乐类	100.0	99.8	100.1	100.0	100.2	101.1
旅游类	103.5	106.1	94.7	100.5	102.4	102.4
八、居住	100.0	99.1	100.9	100.6	100.8	100.3
#建房及装饰材料	100.1	98.8	97.7	98.2	99.7	104.9
住房租金	100.0	98.4	103.3	100.0	101.7	100.0
自有住房	100.0	99.2	103.3	100.0	100.7	100.0
水、电、燃料	100.0	99.4	98.9	102.4	101.0	98.8

8-4 续表

项目	7月	8月	9月	10月	11月	12月
居民消费价格总指数	101.1	100.5	100.5	100.4	99.5	99.6
非食品价格指数	100.5	99.9	100.3	100.0	99.7	99.5
服务项目价格指数	101.3	100.2	100.8	100.7	98.7	99.1
扣除鲜菜鲜果总指数	101.0	100.6	100.5	100.2	99.5	99.6
消费品价格指数	101.0	100.7	100.3	100.3	99.8	99.8
一、食品	102.3	101.8	100.8	101.2	99.1	99.7
#粮食	102.0	100.4	99.9	100.3	100.0	100.2
肉禽及制品	104.2	101.2	102.8	100.6	97.4	98.9
蛋	102.1	105.2	101.7	100.4	97.4	98.8
水产品	98.8	100.5	100.0	101.1	99.6	100.5
菜	110.8	99.8	98.4	106.1	95.1	101.5
二、烟酒	100.7	100.0	100.0	100.4	101.0	100.0
#烟草	100.0	100.0	100.0	100.0	100.0	100.0
酒	101.7	100.0	100.0	101.0	102.4	100.0
三、衣着	100.1	98.9	101.0	100.1	100.3	100.1
#服装	100.2	98.7	101.8	100.0	100.0	100.2
四、家庭设备用品及维修服务	100.6	99.9	100.5	99.1	100.7	100.0
#耐用消费品	101.1	100.1	101.4	99.2	100.6	100.8
五、医疗保健和个人用品	99.7	100.4	99.7	99.9	100.2	100.0
#医疗保健	99.7	100.4	99.7	99.6	100.0	100.0
个人用品及服务	99.8	100.5	99.7	100.4	100.4	99.8
六、交通和通信	100.1	99.8	99.8	99.4	99.8	99.8
#交通	100.1	100.0	99.9	99.4	99.7	99.9
通信	100.0	99.6	99.7	99.5	100.0	99.7
七、娱乐教育文化用品及服务	102.1	100.0	102.0	100.9	98.9	99.4
#文娱用耐用消费品及服务	100.3	99.8	99.7	99.8	99.9	99.3
教育	100.1	100.0	109.2	99.9	100.0	100.0
文化娱乐类	100.0	100.1	100.0	100.0	100.0	100.0
旅游类	107.5	100.0	97.1	103.9	95.9	98.0
八、居住	100.4	100.1	99.7	100.3	99.1	98.8
#建房及装饰材料	98.6	100.0	100.5	99.1	102.4	98.8
住房租金	101.0	100.0	100.0	100.8	97.6	96.7
自有住房	101.7	100.7	100.0	100.8	97.7	98.3
水、电、燃料	99.6	99.5	98.8	100.0	100.0	100.0

8-5 居民消费价格分月指数(2011年，以上年12月价格为100)

Consumer Price Indices by Month (2011, December of Preceding Year=100)

项　　目	1 月	2 月	3 月	4 月	5 月	6 月
居民消费价格总指数	101.5	101.9	102.6	103.2	102.7	102.9
非食品价格指数	100.5	100.2	100.0	100.6	101.1	101.2
服务项目价格指数	100.7	101.0	101.3	101.3	102.0	102.0
扣除鲜菜鲜果总指数	100.9	101.3	101.6	102.2	102.3	102.9
消费品价格指数	101.8	102.3	103.1	104.0	102.9	103.3
一、食品	103.8	106.0	108.4	109.2	106.3	107.1
#粮食	103.6	104.7	105.3	105.2	103.7	107.6
肉禽及制品	99.2	102.5	103.2	105.0	105.9	109.2
蛋	102.5	101.3	102.4	101.7	102.6	105.1
水产品	104.3	113.7	117.1	118.6	111.8	113.4
菜	120.3	116.8	126.0	122.3	106.3	106.0
二、烟酒	100.0	100.1	100.2	100.6	100.6	100.4
#烟草	100.0	100.0	100.0	100.0	100.0	100.0
酒	100.0	100.2	100.5	101.4	101.4	101.0
三、衣着	100.5	97.7	96.9	99.9	101.4	101.5
#服装	99.8	97.0	97.3	98.6	99.0	99.1
四、家庭设备用品及维修服务	100.8	100.8	100.5	100.6	100.2	99.5
#耐用消费品	100.5	100.2	100.0	99.9	100.0	99.8
五、医疗保健和个人用品	100.4	99.9	99.4	99.8	100.9	101.0
#医疗保健	100.6	100.3	100.3	100.5	100.7	99.8
个人用品及服务	100.1	98.9	97.6	98.5	101.5	103.2
六、交通和通信	100.7	100.6	100.6	101.1	101.0	100.6
#交通	101.3	101.4	101.6	102.5	102.8	103.2
通信	99.8	99.3	99.1	98.9	98.3	96.6
七、娱乐教育文化用品及服务	100.8	102.4	101.0	101.0	101.2	102.0
#文娱用耐用消费品及服务	100.0	99.9	100.1	99.5	97.6	97.2
教育	99.9	100.3	100.3	100.1	100.1	100.2
文化娱乐类	100.0	99.8	99.9	99.9	100.1	101.2
旅游类	103.5	109.9	104.0	104.5	107.0	109.5
八、居住	100.0	99.1	100.0	100.6	101.4	101.6
#建房及装饰材料	100.1	98.9	96.6	94.9	94.6	99.2
住房租金	100.0	98.4	101.6	101.6	103.3	103.3
自有住房	100.0	99.2	102.5	102.5	103.2	103.2
水、电、燃料	100.0	99.4	98.3	100.7	101.7	100.5

8-5 续表

项目	7月	8月	9月	10月	11月	12月
居民消费价格总指数	104.1	104.6	105.1	105.6	105.1	104.6
非食品价格指数	101.7	101.6	102.0	102.0	101.7	101.2
服务项目价格指数	103.4	103.6	104.5	105.2	103.9	102.9
扣除鲜菜鲜果总指数	103.9	104.5	105.0	105.2	104.7	104.3
消费品价格指数	104.4	105.1	105.4	105.8	105.6	105.3
一、食品	109.6	111.6	112.5	113.9	112.9	112.6
#粮食	109.8	110.2	110.2	110.5	110.5	110.7
肉禽及制品	113.8	115.1	118.4	119.1	116.0	114.6
蛋	107.3	112.9	114.8	115.3	112.3	110.9
水产品	112.0	112.6	112.6	113.9	113.4	113.9
菜	117.4	117.2	115.3	122.3	116.4	118.2
二、烟酒	101.1	101.1	101.1	101.5	102.5	102.5
#烟草	100.0	100.0	100.0	100.0	100.0	100.0
酒	102.6	102.6	102.6	103.6	106.2	106.2
三、衣着	101.6	100.6	101.6	101.7	102.0	102.1
#服装	99.4	98.0	99.8	99.7	99.7	99.9
四、家庭设备用品及维修服务	100.1	100.0	100.5	99.5	100.3	100.3
#耐用消费品	100.9	100.9	102.4	101.5	102.2	103.0
五、医疗保健和个人用品	100.7	101.1	100.8	100.7	100.8	100.8
#医疗保健	99.5	99.9	99.6	99.2	99.2	99.2
个人用品及服务	102.9	103.4	103.1	103.5	104.0	103.8
六、交通和通信	100.7	100.5	100.3	99.8	99.6	99.4
#交通	103.3	103.3	103.2	102.6	102.3	102.2
通信	96.6	96.2	95.9	95.4	95.4	95.1
七、娱乐教育文化用品及服务	104.1	104.1	106.2	107.2	106.0	105.3
#文娱用耐用消费品及服务	97.5	97.3	97.0	96.8	96.7	96.0
教育	100.4	100.4	109.6	109.5	109.5	109.5
文化娱乐类	101.2	101.3	101.3	101.3	101.3	101.3
旅游类	117.8	117.7	114.3	118.7	113.8	111.6
八、居住	102.1	102.2	101.8	102.1	101.2	100.0
#建房及装饰材料	97.7	97.7	98.3	97.4	99.7	98.5
住房租金	104.3	104.3	104.3	105.2	102.7	99.3
自有住房	104.9	105.6	105.6	106.5	104.0	102.2
水、电、燃料	100.0	99.5	98.3	98.3	98.3	98.3

8-6 商品零售价格分类指数（2011年，以上年价格为100）

Retail Price Indices by Category (2011, Preceding Year=100)

项　　目	指　数	项　　目	指　数
商品零售价格总指数	104.7	3. 专业音像器材	98.7
一、食品类	111.1	六、文化办公用品	97.1
1. 粮食	114.6	七、日用品	103.2
2. 淀粉及制品	101.6	1. 日用百货	103.9
3. 干豆类及豆制品	98.8	2. 日用杂品	97.7
4. 油脂	110.3	3. 洗涤用品	106.9
5. 肉禽及其制品	114.5	4. 其他日用品	99.6
6. 蛋	118.0	八、体育娱乐用品	95.5
7. 水产品	122.0	1. 体育用品	87.8
8. 菜	96.7	2. 娱乐用品	103.7
9. 调味品	106.7	九、交通、通信用品	93.5
10.糖	103.1	1. 交通运输机械	98.7
11.干鲜瓜果	113.5	2. 通信器材类	87.1
12.糕点饼干面包	103.3	十、家具	100.6
13.液体乳及乳制品	102.8	十一、化妆品类	101.1
14.在外用膳食品	110.7	十二、金银珠宝类	116.6
15.其他食品	100.4	十三、中西药品及医疗保健用品类	102.3
二、饮料、烟酒	101.8	1. 医疗器具及用品	107.3
1. 茶及饮料	102.0	2. 中药材及中成药	104.4
2. 烟草	100.0	3. 西药	101.6
3. 酒	103.8	4. 保健器具及用品	99.7
三、服装、鞋帽类	100.8	十四、书报杂志及电子出版物类	100.3
1. 服装	101.0	1. 教材及参考书	100.6
2. 鞋袜帽	100.3	2. 书报杂志	100.0
3. 其他	100.3	3. 电子音像制品	100.0
四、纺织品类	108.4	十五、燃料类	113.2
1. 衣着材料	108.6	1. 煤炭及制品类	100.0
2. 床上用品	108.3	2. 石油及制品类	113.2
五、家用电器及音像器材	99.3	十六、建筑材料及五金电料类	102.3
1. 家庭设备	101.8	1. 建筑装璜材料	102.1
2. 文娱用耐用消费品	96.2	2. 五金电料类	102.8

8-7 主要年份食品全社会综合平均价格

Comprehensive Average Prices of Food in Main Years

项 目	规 格 等 级	单 位	价 格（元）						
			1985年	1990年	1995年	2000年	2005年	2010年	2011年
大 米	标 二	千克	0.39	0.85	2.93	2.16	2.90	3.57	4.46
面 粉	南 方	千克	0.74	1.70	3.11	3.65	2.53	6.36	5.17
豆 类	一等大豆	千克	1.07	2.94	3.77	3.99	5.57	7.18	6.97
植物油	一级花生油	千克	3.55	7.36	12.53	10.62	11.95	18.50	22.74
猪 肉	鲜 上 肉	千克	3.55	9.50	15.98	13.78	18.53	21.89	27.30
瘦猪肉	鲜 肉	千克	7.20	13.35	23.73	18.04	25.00	29.40	34.76
牛 肉	去骨统肉	千克	5.60	11.22	22.40	18.61	25.73	44.00	43.13
白条鸡	开 膛	千克		9.21	13.80	14.61	21.82	27.82	23.61
鸡	上等竹丝鸡	千克	7.20	13.04	22.31	15.77	14.99	17.38	19.29
鸭	上等番鸭	千克	3.17	5.81	11.65	14.28	14.33	17.01	19.78
鸡 蛋	新鲜鸡蛋	千克	3.63	6.70	7.91	6.21	7.73	12.84	15.54
再制蛋	皮 蛋	千克	2.40	4.52	6.40	5.85	7.05	8.82	10.59
香 肠	本地产中等	千克	11.60	23.75	52.13	53.67	31.67	90.00	91.50
烧 鹅	本 地 产	千克	8.53	14.41	32.54	30.67	44.49	58.20	62.95
胖头鱼	中等0.5公斤以上一条	千克	2.91	4.81	9.56	8.80	11.79	14.32	16.52
红三鱼	冰 鲜	千克			9.13	16.20	24.85	34.30	42.88
虾	罗 氏 虾	千克				40.06	37.18	74.68	86.68
草 鱼	中等1公斤以上一条	千克	2.69	6.67	13.30	10.18	14.25	20.50	18.02
精 盐	再 制 盐	千克		0.49	1.20	1.60	1.27	3.25	3.25
白砂糖	国家机制一级	千克	1.36	2.71	6.10	4.32	5.23	6.50	8.50
红 糖	一级冰片糖	千克		2.95	6.55	4.95	5.70	9.50	10.52
卷 烟	广州双喜	盒	1.12	1.40	4.87	5.92	6.62	6.50	6.50
白 酒	0.5千克装	瓶	2.30	2.40	5.55	6.58	7.25	6.25	6.67
啤 酒	热 12 度	瓶		1.60	6.40	4.92	4.66	5.00	5.50
红 茶	一 级	千克	3.98	12.76	28.95	64.68	6.91	127.50	133.38
绿 茶	一 级	千克	8.00	10.34	15.40	59.21	27.40	123.00	123.00
苹 果	一 级	千克	2.14	4.89	6.54	5.80	6.44	11.18	11.88
梨	一 级	千克	1.86	4.40	5.46	3.99	3.74	5.18	6.28
柑	一 级	千克	1.75	1.97	3.28	3.27	3.54	4.84	6.96
香 蕉	一 级	千克	1.24	2.22	3.90	3.18	3.04	4.68	5.77
荔 枝	桂味/糯米糍	千克	2.57	7.95	20.50	14.93	11.75	14.88	11.94
面 包	中 等	千克	2.00	5.09	4.39	15.25	7.39	16.70	17.65
饼 干	一 级	千克	2.48	7.88	9.03	22.97	8.80	22.00	22.00
奶 粉	国 产	千克	4.80	5.27	25.12	24.55	22.33	32.00	56.98

注：2000年起茶叶的档次提高。

8-8 工业生产者出厂价格指数(2005－2011年，以上年价格为100)

Producer Price Index (PPI) for Manufactured Goods (2005-2011,Preceding Year=100)

项目	2005年	2006年	2007年	2008年	2009年	2010年	2011年
工业生产者出厂价格指数	100.4	100.7	101.4	101.7	96.8	102.6	102.9
#轻工业	99.9	100.2	101.4	102.6	97.7	101.8	103.2
重工业	100.6	101.1	101.5	101.0	96.1	103.1	102.7
#非金属矿采选业	97.0	100.1	101.3	101.7	103.9	102.9	99.4
农副食品加工业	107.5	99.2	106.8	119.1	93.2	107.8	111.8
食品制造业	100.3	100.2	101.5	101.7	97.2	102.7	102.7
饮料制造业	99.2	100.8	99.9	103.0	102.2	100.6	101.5
纺织业	101.5	102.2	101.5	104.2	99.3	100.8	106.5
纺织服装、鞋、帽制造业	100.9	100.5	100.9	100.5	98.3	101.6	104.2
皮革、皮毛、羽毛(绒)及其制品业	101.1	101.0	105.6	103.7	100.8	101.7	104.6
木材加工及木、竹、藤、棕、草制品业	100.5	102.6	101.6	106.3	100.4	102.3	100.3
家具制造业	100.7	102.2	101.8	103.1	100.9	102.4	102.3
造纸及纸制品业	100.8	101.8	101.4	104.3	94.3	113.1	100.3
印刷业和记录媒介的复制	99.6	98.2	100.4	103.7	100.4	101.6	104.0
文教体育用品制造业	101.8	103.9	103.3	101.6	100.4	99.4	102.9
石油加工、炼焦及核燃料加工业	122.8	117.0	104.6	120.1	88.5	119.7	115.6
化学原料及化学制品制造业	103.5	101.2	106.7	104.8	92.7	109.1	111.2
医药制造业	101.1	100.4	105.7	102.3	97.5	101.7	97.5
化学纤维制造业	104.4	101.0	101.6	95.1	87.1	120.2	125.7
橡胶制品业	101.0	104.1	99.8	100.2	97.5	101.5	104.3
塑料制品业	107.4	101.7	101.0	102.0	96.7	102.9	105.3
非金属矿物制品业	96.7	100.3	102.2	104.7	99.0	105.1	101.7
黑色金属冶炼及压延加工业	101.2	94.2	113.4	130.1	79.1	109.1	114.0
有色金属冶炼及压延加工业	106.8	136.6	110.0	98.7	87.3	122.1	115.5
金属制品业	100.8	103.0	104.9	105.9	96.2	102.8	103.4
通用设备制造业	104.0	102.8	100.1	103.8	99.2	103.0	101.5
专用设备制造业	101.6	100.9	99.7	103.6	99.1	98.3	102.7
交通运输设备制造业	99.2	96.7	95.7	99.7	100.2	100.4	99.6
电气机械及器材制造业	103.7	106.6	104.3	99.7	93.0	103.9	104.0
通信设备、计算机及其他电子设备制造业	96.9	95.9	98.3	97.6	96.1	100.0	100.7
仪器仪表及文化、办公用机械制造业	100.6	102.2	100.4	100.5	99.1	99.7	97.6
工艺品及其他制造业	101.6	106.0	102.2	103.9	103.0	103.7	101.0
电力、热力的生产和供应业	102.3	101.7	101.4	103.4	102.4	98.8	100.7
燃气生产和供应业						112.1	108.1
水的生产和供应业	100.8	103.4	104.1	102.8	101.3	103.1	102.7

注：2011年起，工业品出厂价格总指数改名为工业生产者出厂价格指数。

主要统计指标解释

Explanatory Notes on Main Statistical Indicators

居民消费价格指数 是度量消费商品及服务项目价格水平随着时间而变动的相对数，反映居民家庭购买的消费品及服务价格水平的变动情况。它是宏观经济分析、决策、调控和价格总水平监测以及国民经济核算的重要指标。其按年度计算的变动率通常被用来作为反映通货膨胀(或紧缩)程度的指标。

商品零售价格指数 是度量市场商品零售价格水平变动趋势和变动程度的相对数，反映商品在流通过程中最后一个环节的价格即工业、商业、餐饮业和其他零售企业向城乡居民、机关团体出售生活消费品和办公用品价格水平的变动趋势。它可以为国家宏观调控和国民经济核算提供参考依据，并在此基础上派生其他价格指数。

九、对外经济贸易与旅游

Foreign Trade and Tourism

9-1 主要年份对外经济与旅游业主要指标

Main Indicators of Foreign Trade and Economic Cooperation and Tourism in Main Years

指　　标	单 位	1979年	1985年	1990年	1995年	2000年	2005年	2010年	2011年
进出口总额	万美元			108229	1539112	3204526	7437150	12133773	13522382
出口总额	万美元	5382	17545	56828	779867	1715927	4092905	6959751	7832871
进口总额	万美元			51401	759245	1488599	3344245	5174022	5689511
新签利用外资协议(合同)数	宗	184	625	1267	3077	1276	992	875	1325
#增资项目	宗						1138	1059	892
#“三来一补”项目	宗	184	514	1075	2094	871	219	6	1
“三资”项目	宗		111	192	983	405	773	869	1324
合同规定外商投资额	万美元	476	6815	30180	330920	183633	475238	307282	370189
#增资项目	万美元						187422	180723	181800
#“三来一补”项目	万美元	476	1870	12346	97428	69302	166363	47542	19353
“三资”项目	万美元		4945	17834	233492	114331	308875	259740	350836
实际利用外资(不含对外借款)	万美元	173	2894	24319	105665	164712	375139	316287	321821
“三来一补”项目	万美元	173	1511	14309	38418	55975	93023	43116	16769
“三资”项目	万美元		1383	10010	67247	108737	282116	273171	305052
本年止累计“三来一补”企业投产宗数	宗	140	1592	3880	8447	9917	8997	5688	3196
年末“三来一补”企业从业人员	万人	1.15	9.82	21.48	59.44	72.89	126.49	81.00	61.66
本年止累计“三资”企业投产数	宗		51	454	2629	3908	6657	8338	8961
年末“三资”企业从业人员	万人		0.64	3.81	25.01	87.17	145.50	163.53	175.97
当年来料加工企业转为三资或民营企业	家							1250	1122
合同规定外商投资额(新口径)	万美元						298029	259740	350836
实际利用外资(新口径)	万美元						146796	273171	305052
全年接待旅游人数	万人次			125	89	291	1156	2251	2615
#国际及港澳台旅游者	万人次			27	27	106	169	327	357
#外国人	万人次			1	6	15	70	109	121
国内旅客	万人次			98	62	185	987	1924	2258
国际旅游收入	万美元			1025	5679	7617	28189	67592	90975
星级以上宾馆酒店客房数	间			3793	7568	18024	18258	16631	17899
宾馆酒店客房开房率	%			60.19	68.80	61.88	58.90	58.12	60.01

注：1. 对外经济部分除有注明新口径的以外均为旧口径，旧口径包括“三资”和“三来一补”,新口径不含“三来一补”且以验资作为统计标准，后同。
2. 2002年起旅游业指标采用旅游局口径，与往年数不可比。

9-2 主要年份进出口贸易

Total Imports and Exports in Main Years

单位：万美元

项　　目	1995年	2000年	2001年	2002年	2003年	2004年	2005年	2010年	2011年
进出口总额	1539112	3204526	3445457	4424706	5210623	6451775	7437150	12133773	13522382
出口总额	779867	1715927	1898924	2373646	2800227	3519237	4092905	6959751	7832871
按贸易方式分									
#一般贸易	23180	20937	25945	34848	48988	85056	175502	954098	1341146
来料加工装配	434646	834347	940908	1171688	1257934	1503757	1611676	1955379	1693479
进料加工	320186	858409	931766	1167047	1492723	1929967	2304325	3946227	4654300
其他	1855	2234	305	63	582	457	1402	104047	143947
按经济类型分									
#国有企业	474304	867501	972541	1189726	991762	1086698	1139776	1102678	702978
三资企业	305061	835611	908388	1153178	1498993	1948473	2353253	4426236	5428116
集体企业	122	12259	17584	25798	27072	30229	37893	141561	142343
民营企业			143	4905	282079	453457	561650	1285124	1556283
进口总额	759245	1488599	1546533	2051060	2410396	2932538	3344245	5174022	5689511
按贸易方式分									
#一般贸易	5394	72475	68392	83522	144235	222262	236133	755349	988370
来料加工装配	353138	645562	684323	922916	962367	1090197	1216566	1424118	1174341
进料加工	259397	616319	656910	886699	1127404	1402413	1625629	2457194	2881689
其他	141316	154243	5513	4112	5551	217666	265917	537362	645110
按经济类型分									
#国有企业	419827	764945	795407	1019994	832593	855107	987421	1076821	723370
三资企业	329164	706145	733492	1002467	1308831	1655308	1882393	3028036	3651145
集体企业	243	10267	12101	17930	19408	24151	32167	78053	85574
民营企业			21	6521	244005	391706	439521	967472	1172126
贸易顺差	20622	227328	352391	322586	389831	586699	748660	1785728	2143361

9-3 历年进出口总额

Total Value of Imports and Exports over Years

单位：万美元

年 份	进出口总额	出口总额	#一般贸易	来料加工装配	进料加工	进口总额	#一般贸易	来料加工装配	进料加工
1978		3938							
1979		5382							
1980		7737							
1981		9173							
1982		10879							
1983		11890							
1984		12966							
1985		17545							
1986		23280							
1987		26755							
1988		31781							
1989		34868							
1990	108229	56828				51401			
1991	317463	165159				152304			
1992	509007	260272				248735			
1993	675647	321137				354510			
1994	882997	429416				453581			
1995	1539112	779867	23180	434646	320186	759245	5394	353138	259397
1996	1784222	918683	16377	496833	405066	865539	8956	383988	309710
1997	2129885	1136768	18020	582863	535708	993117	7598	445237	420014
1998	2327324	1306055	15409	652853	636822	1021269	10406	462194	463450
1999	2846291	1515391	16347	759638	738191	1330900	51726	584224	582721
2000	3204526	1715927	20937	834347	858409	1488599	72475	645562	616319
2001	3445457	1898924	25945	940908	931766	1546533	68392	684323	656910
2002	4424706	2373646	34848	1171688	1167047	2051060	83522	922916	886699
2003	5210623	2800227	48988	1257934	1492723	2410396	144235	962367	1127404
2004	6451775	3519237	85056	1503757	1929967	2932538	222262	1090197	1402413
2005	7437150	4092905	175502	1611676	2304325	3344245	236133	1216566	1625629
2006	8422107	4737640	265784	1661399	2806910	3684467	259709	1265725	1879233
2007	10687290	6023212	357941	2235125	3398212	4664078	371073	1702595	2196521
2008	11329947	6553738	487193	2428365	3585619	4776209	455447	1712939	2206139
2009	9415458	5516861	571682	1823160	3055047	3898597	456075	1297315	1820882
2010	12133773	6959751	954098	1955379	3946227	5174022	755349	1424118	2457194
2011	13522382	7832871	1341146	1693479	4654300	5689511	988370	1174341	2881689

注：出口总额1990年以前为外经贸口径，1990年起为海关口径。

9-4 分国别(地区)进出口总值（2010-2011年）

Total Value of Imports and Exports by Countries (Regions)(2010-2011)

单位：亿美元

国别(地区)	实际出口		进口到货	
	2011年	2010年	2011年	2010年
亚洲	408.65	354.36	483.79	447.88
东南亚联盟	35.24	27.68	81.81	77.04
非洲	4.98	4.27	1.50	1.60
欧洲	135.86	121.37	31.56	25.78
欧洲共同体	128.17	115.64	29.90	24.50
拉美洲	24.38	17.50	20.40	14.00
北美洲	199.75	189.88	27.32	24.81
大洋洲	9.66	8.60	3.14	3.20
美国	189.20	179.78	21.88	20.31
香港	232.82	219.75	9.05	7.03
日本	69.07	60.88	85.07	88.33
荷兰	26.69	22.90	3.01	2.53
德国	30.30	26.01	8.21	7.71
英国	19.21	18.54	3.65	2.69
韩国	36.26	18.17	63.60	44.83
台湾	11.58	10.04	95.98	96.17
法国	10.71	10.13	1.51	1.35
加拿大	10.52	10.09	5.45	4.50
澳大利亚	8.81	7.96	2.45	2.53
新加坡	7.54	6.31	11.48	11.89
马来西亚	5.44	4.44	23.63	23.00

9-5 主要商品类别出口总值（2008-2011年）

Total Export Value by Category of Main Commodities (2008-2011)

单位：亿美元

商品名称	2008年	2009年	2010年	2011年
机电产品	483.66	387.52	494.83	556.16
高新技术产品	201.49	159.39	241.95	273.42
自动数据处理设备及其部件	65.86	42.26	52.82	61.21
服装及衣着附件	31.92	28.11	38.98	46.13
录、放像机	11.64	8.41	13.24	16.19
自动数据处理设备的零件	31.97	26.68	33.31	34.71
纺织纱线、织物及制品	14.69	13.68	15.21	16.43
玩具	14.69	12.28	16.32	17.20
鞋类	27.06	24.57	30.96	30.72
家具及其零件	27.79	24.26	32.09	34.00
录音机及收录(放)音组合机(包括整套散件)	10.62	7.46	8.85	9.42
塑料制品	10.74	9.10	11.37	12.71
静止式变流器	26.71	23.14	35.98	37.61
旅行用品及箱包	10.91	11.43	15.65	18.16
灯具、照明装置及类似品	8.87	7.84	10.37	11.74
电线和电缆	14.03	10.81	15.22	17.31
通断及保护电路装置	12.36	10.37	13.40	16.18
有线电话机	15.37	14.84	16.44	19.26
电视、收音机及无线电讯设备的零附件	16.21	12.59	16.12	14.42

9-6 主要商品进口数量与金额(海关口径，2009-2011年)

Main Import Commodities in Volume and Value (Custom Statistics) (2009-2011)

金额单位：万美元

商品名称	数量单位	2009年		2010年		2011年	
		数量	金额	数量	金额	数量	金额
谷物及谷物粉	万吨	3.18	1205	5.24	2039	5.01	2338
#小麦粉	吨	12	2				
食用植物油	万吨	3.50	2218	4.43	3524	4.08	4612
食糖	万吨	6.63	2187	6.27	2664	4.13	2852
天然橡胶(包括胶乳)	万吨	2.30	3612	2.26	4950	2.39	6747
合成橡胶(包括胶乳)	万吨	9.49	17575	10.09	21424	7.82	20953
原木	万立方	5.50	2664	9.95	4699	10.98	6413
锯材	万立方	32.17	8082	46.71	14312	41.33	13547
羊毛(包括羊毛条)	吨	1348	818	832	562	1072	962
纺织用合成纤维	万吨	1.81	3082	1.68	3299	1.50	3304
#聚酯纤维	万吨	1.15	1829	1.00	1566	0.91	1521
人造纤维短纤	吨	40.92	13	17.47	5	8.44	2
成品油	万吨	0.36	835	0.92	1769	5.17	6636
合成有机染料	吨	1471.71	1053	1886.80	1213	3116.70	1910
初级形状的塑料	万吨	191.68	308584	216.71	390243	190.50	378111
#初级形状的聚乙烯	万吨	16.66	21793	17.31	24156	15.68	23223
初级形状的聚丙烯	万吨	29.74	39425	34.10	49226	28.66	45219
初级形状的苯乙烯聚合物	万吨	63.05	99175	69.04	119466	62.58	120047
初级形状的氯乙烯聚合物	万吨	24.08	21237	27.52	28931	24.03	26911
初级形状的聚酯	万吨	15.15	39344	20.22	58565	18.11	57769
牛皮革及马皮革	万吨	5.38	42245	7.18	56696	6.95	57310
纸及纸板(未切成形的)	万吨	59.26	34709	44.87	33999	36.15	32037
毛纱线	万吨	0.67	4483	0.76	5678	0.75	6349
合成纤维纱线	万吨	4.86	15035	5.54	18795	4.60	18891
棉机织物	万米	13525.38	19178	13572.82	20279	12674	20175
涂覆浸渍塑料的织物	万吨	3.16	9184	3.59	12218	2.94	11515
针织或钩编织物	万米	25197.31	27452	24854.37	27468	20028	26893
钢材	万吨	110.17	109430	141.82	152727	108.79	133356
#钢铁板材	万吨	100.54	94963	126.45	128706	97.58	110644
未锻造的铜及铜材	万吨	24.12	130340	25.18	174812	20.49	171532
#铜材	万吨	17.24	96339	18.19	122608	13.44	108623
未锻造的铝及铝材	万吨	8.92	29377	8.40	33203	6.98	30002
#铝材	万吨	4.41	20253	4.58	24723	3.76	22133

9-6 续表

金额单位：万美元

商品名称	数量单位	2009年		2010年		2011年	
		数量	金额	数量	金额	数量	金额
钢材或铝制结构体及其部件	吨	934	285	955	377	834	346
蒸汽锅炉及过热水锅炉	台	7	18	2	8		
液泵及液体提升机	台	1362113	1155	1108302	1417	899529	1419
冷冻机和制冷设备	台		90		283		370
机械提升搬运装卸设备及零件	台		2892		5335		4556
制造纸及纸制品用机械及零件	金额		11023		15077		9448
印刷、装订机械及零件	金额		44739		79242		95620
纺织机械及零件	金额		8668		12500		15344
#针织机及缝编机	台	1764	5834	2248	10785	3035	12536
纱线织物等后整理机器	台	974	690	279	829	204	531
工业用缝纫机	台	2262	343	3521	1135	2026	795
金属加工机床	台	1635	7283	3687	20131	2426	16884
橡胶或塑料加工机械及零件	金额		5487		11352		9957
型模及金属铸造用型箱	吨		4547		6458		7861
自动数据处理设备及其部件	万台	2744	59580	2646	59022	2430	57192
自动数据处理设备的零件	吨	17967	73356	22515	107192	21254	119062
电动机及发电机	万台	32351	22938	39427	29339	44420	31748
发电机组及旋转式变流机	台	80	961	28	471	54	3267
电视、收音机及无线电讯设备	吨	8153	60863	7731	85203	7058	88685
通断及保护电路装置及零件	万吨		89996		130794		152710
电视显像管	万只	2.98	23	0.79	7		
#彩色显像管	万只	0.75	19	0.50	6		
二极管、晶体管及类似半导体	亿个	419.24	147379	512.09	196257	489.63	191639
电线和电缆	吨	28328	27093	33507	36761	31479	43402
计量检测分析自控仪器及器具	金额		19697		28444		31634
塑料制品	吨	22961	10870	24384	13805	22345	16460

9-7 主要商品出口数量与金额（海关口径，2009-2011年）

Main Export Commodities in Volume and Value (Custom Statistics) (2009-2011)

金额单位：万美元

商品名称	数量单位	2009年		2010年		2011年	
		数　量	金　额	数　量	金　额	数　量	金　额
活猪(种猪除外)	万头	1.13	217		157	121.66	225
水海产品	万吨	0.04	253	0.02	245	0.04	483
谷物及谷物粉	万吨		1		1		
蔬菜	万吨	0.02	19	0.16	173	0.72	687
鲜、干水果及坚果	万吨		2		7		3
食用植物油(包括棕榈油)	吨	24.75	9	324.35	127	535.75	226
药材	吨			44.37	8	44.18	9
锯材	立方米	200	10		1		
成品油	万吨	0.03	50	0.03	54	0.18	259
合成有机染料	吨	319.02	315	198.91	70	165.81	77
医药品	吨	2480.77	1425	1437.78	779	965.72	692
美容化妆品及护肤品	吨	2888.88	1226	3476.26	1449	3856.03	1955
洗衣粉	吨	11106.46	687	17887.35	1098	25060.74	1696
烟花、爆竹	吨	998.44	95	416.28	63	353.47	60
初级形状的聚氯乙烯	吨	3500.00	533	6000	900	7500	1134
家用或装饰用木制品	吨	8900.00	1321	9500	1828	10900	2495
纸及纸板(未切成形的)	万吨	5.09	2773	3.37	2675	3.07	2479
纺织纱线、织物及制品	金额		136789		152070		164309
#棉纱线	吨	25499.61	9265	25927.56	10422	17615.81	9831
亚麻及苎麻纱线	万米			43.25	116	36.27	104
棉机织物	万米	2093.69	2870	2349.16	4058	1804.53	4299
玻璃制品	金额		2616		3790		4890
家用陶瓷器皿	吨	20900.00	2335	26100	4312	23900	5100
钢材	万吨	2.39	2839	4.40	5098	4.82	6718
未锻造的铜及铜材	吨	24790.85	15726	28597.01	22750	21625.06	19640
未锻造的铝及铝材	吨	4800.00	1874	7600	3191	8700	3971
手用或机用工具	吨	9200.00	6544	10300	9527	9400	12220

9-7 续表

金额单位：万美元

商品名称	数量单位	2009年		2010年		2011年	
		数量	金额	数量	金额	数量	金额
锁	吨						
电扇	万台	9316.9	25552	11169.8	31980	11320.8	36244
纺织机械及零件	金额		1928		2005		2002
金属加工机床	万台	0.8	1068	0.2	1488	0.2	2432
电子计算器	亿台	0.4	11829	0.5	12682	0.5	14440
电动机及发电机	亿台	6.1	41501	7.2	60650	6.0	63485
静止式变流器	亿个	4.4	231369	6.9	359806	7.3	376054
原电池	亿个	11.5	11942	13.7	16375	12.4	14580
蓄电池	亿个	2.2	27656	2.4	31218	1.8	38253
电话机	万个	4240.1	148365	5011.5	164438	5183.6	192614
扬声器	亿个	1.4	34594	1.8	50717	1.9	66479
收音设备（包括收录音组合机）	万台	3337.9	74636	4124.6	88472	4350.9	94214
电视机	万台	568.7	101880	518.0	96536	452.5	96155
＃彩色电视机	万台	568.7	101880	517.5	96529	452.5	96155
电视、收音机及无线电讯零附件	万吨	6.9	125973	7.2	161166	6.0	144218
电容器	吨	11598	49340	14790	72468	13565.5	80327
通断及保护电路装置	亿个		103732		133965		161770
二极管及类似半导体器件	亿个	350.8	36080	479.4	54844	553.8	55606
电线和电缆	万吨	17.5	108069	20.8	152169	19.3	173136
照相机	万架	2144	127230	2582	160905	2224.0	129006
医疗仪器及器械	金额		8573		12824		14739
手表	亿只	0.6	8562	0.5	11268	0.5	13635
＃电动手表	亿只	0.6	8306	0.5	11028	0.5	13311
家具	金额		242625		320917		339959
灯具、照明装置及类似品	金额		78441		103738		117380
箱包及类似容器	金额		114374		156455		181550
服装及衣着附件	金额		281057		389784		461285
＃织物制服装	金额		242454		342793		412029
裘皮服装	吨	157	2013	145	1857	124.4	1341
帽类	万个	9939.9	8992	15532.2	11470	13635.0	12383
鞋	亿双	2.4	237001	2.7	297056	2.2	293536
塑料制品	万吨	44.6	90913	51.1	113700	50.6	127124
玩具	金额		122821		163174		172040
贵金属或包贵金属的首饰	金额		5934		15089		19720

9-8 历年新签利用外资协议(合同)宗数

Number of Signed Agreements or Contracts of Utilization of Foreign Capital over Years

单位：宗

年 份	新签协议(合同)数	“三来一补”企业	“三资”企业
1979	184	184	
1980	415	415	
1981	555	553	2
1982	470	468	2
1983	454	447	7
1984	551	508	43
1985	625	514	111
1986	618	559	59
1987	824	729	95
1988	2048	1839	209
1989	939	779	160
1990	1267	1075	192
1991	1636	1268	368
1992	2232	1374	858
1993	3118	1773	1345
1994	2678	1521	1157
1995	3077	2094	983
1996	1678	1343	335
1997	1685	1492	193
1998	1383	1051	332
1999	1362	1135	227
2000	1276	871	405
2001	1395	705	690
2002	1391	524	867
2003	1524	392	1132
2004	1423	391	1032
2005	992	219	773
2006	786	177	609
2007	790	82	708
2008	588	35	553
2009	601	22	579
2010	875	6	869
2011	1325	1	1324

9-9 历年新签利用外资协议(合同)规定外商投资额

Amount of Signed Agreements or Contracts of Utilization of Foreign Capital over Years

单位：万美元

年　份	协议(合同)规定外商投资额	“三来一补”企业	“三资”企业
1979	476	476	
1980	1055	1055	
1981	806	784	22
1982	787	771	16
1983	1616	841	775
1984	3217	1013	2204
1985	6815	1870	4945
1986	3398	1593	1805
1987	18513	14082	4431
1988	62173	42507	19666
1989	23365	9268	14097
1990	30180	12346	17834
1991	64483	19348	45135
1992	208825	29720	179105
1993	355515	54823	300692
1994	349703	47700	302003
1995	330920	97428	233492
1996	208861	62811	146050
1997	121351	62114	59237
1998	163677	58709	104968
1999	147247	69756	77491
2000	183633	69302	114331
2001	209779	56833	152946
2002	248914	47285	201629
2003	325633	59538	266095
2004	413216	124089	289127
2005	475238	166363	308875
2006	552758	197836	354922
2007	625088	176903	448185
2008	393701	134952	258749
2009	203040	41420	161620
2010	307282	47542	259740
2011	370189	19353	350836

9-10 历年实际利用外资

Foreign Capital Actually Utilized over Years

单位：万美元

年 份	累计实际利用外资	当年实际利用外资	“三来一补”企业	“三资”企业
1979	173	173	173	
1980	1107	934	934	
1981	1642	535	528	7
1982	2357	715	668	47
1983	3258	901	871	30
1984	5175	1917	1233	684
1985	8069	2894	1511	1383
1986	11111	3042	1553	1489
1987	22370	11259	9185	2074
1988	46496	24126	17717	6409
1989	71445	24949	16559	8390
1990	95764	24319	14309	10010
1991	121918	26154	11478	14676
1992	168510	46592	13716	32876
1993	261938	93428	14181	79247
1994	366750	104812	26938	77874
1995	472415	105665	38418	67247
1996	579979	107564	38061	69503
1997	701406	121427	33467	87960
1998	835219	133813	40780	93033
1999	980951	145732	48620	97112
2000	1145663	164712	55975	108737
2001	1327225	181562	66841	114721
2002	1542073	214848	68980	145868
2003	1798409	256336	80936	175400
2004	2101839	303430	89555	213875
2005	2476978	375139	93023	282116
2006	2910751	433773	98543	335230
2007	3415146	504395	94365	410030
2008	3737716	322570	77902	244668
2009	4031873	294157	34758	259399
2010	4348160	316287	43116	273171
2011	4669981	321821	16769	305052

注：本表数据不含对外借款。

9-11 主要年份“三资”企业利用外资

Utilization of Foreign Capital of Enterprises with Foreign Investment in Main Years

项　　目	计量单位	1985年	1990年	1995年	2000年	2005年	2010年	2011年
一、全部“三资”企业利用外资情况								
当年新签协议宗数	宗	111	192	983	405	773	869	1324
本年止累计执行宗数	宗	51	591	2807	4012	6657	8338	8961
#已投产	宗	47	454	2629	3908	5870	7469	7636
项目(协议)终止宗数	宗	3	24	48	338	193	471	707
实际投资总额	万美元	2565	18642	75853	115801	290553	277547	315609
境内资金总额	万美元	1182	8632	8606	7064	8437	4376	10557
中方实际投资	万美元	1182	5515	6448	4445	8337	4376	10557
企业境内借款	万美元		3117	2158	2619	100		
境外资金总额	万美元	1383	10010	67247	108737	282959	273171	305052
外商实际投资	万美元	1383	8934	65416	108468	282116	273171	305052
企业境外借款	万美元		1076	1831	269	842		
引进设备价值	万美元	995	6619	50267	80215	118401	63822	44106
出口总值	万美元	799	13439	178351	835600	2353253	4426236	5428116
期末职工人数	万人	0.54	3.81	25.01	87.17	145.50	163.53	175.97
二、中外合作企业利用外资情况								
当年新签协议宗数	宗	86	72	195	19	2		
本年止累计执行宗数	宗	43	237	730	705	337	184	138
#已投产	宗	41	177	682	700	299	184	138
项目(协议)终止宗数	宗	3	15	12	130	25	23	46
实际投资总额	万美元	1301	5072	15159	10045	13529	1345	2836
境内资金总额	万美元	423	1427	176	1731	860	169	1427
中方实际投资	万美元	423	651	136	1486	860	169	1427
企业境内借款	万美元		776	40	245			
境外资金总额	万美元	878	3645	14983	8314	12669	1176	1409
外商实际投资	万美元	878	3642	14981	8314	12669	1176	1409
企业境外借款	万美元		3	2				
引进设备价值	万美元	290	2411	9320	5033	4060	651	266
出口总值	万美元	534	2423	35718	92100	116157	117188	105642
期末职工人数	万人	0.33	1.02	5.82	13.57	10.38	3.50	2.84

注：本表2000年起出口总值是海关口径。

9-11 续表

项目	计量单位	1985年	1990年	1995年	2000年	2005年	2010年	2011年
三、中外合资企业利用外资情况								
当年新签协议宗数	宗	25	93	378	29	31	18	24
本年止累计执行宗数	宗	8	338	1590	1690	712	507	447
#已投产	宗	6	251	1498	1650	668	489	423
项目(协议)终止宗数	宗		9	31	159	53	99	84
实际投资总额	万美元	1264	13070	39659	23966	25672	36342	39481
境内资金总额	万美元	759	7199	8345	5333	7477	4207	9130
中方实际投资	万美元	759	4864	6312	2959	7477	4207	9130
企业境内借款	万美元		2335	2033	2374			
境外资金总额	万美元	506	5871	31314	18633	18195	32135	30351
外商实际投资	万美元	506	4798	29496	18364	18195	32135	30351
企业境外借款	万美元		1073	1818	269			
引进设备价值	万美元	705	3920	25557	14365	4060	28850	17757
出口总值	万美元	265	10934	90357	248800	289344	348622	340366
期末职工人数	万人	0.20	2.69	13.51	24.68	17.95	11.60	12.48
四、外商独资企业利用外资情况								
当年新签协议宗数	宗		27	410	357	740	851	1300
本年止累计执行宗数	宗		16	487	1614	5607	7641	8364
#已投产	宗		8	449	1555	4903	6790	7064
项目(协议)终止宗数	宗			5	49	115	349	577
实际投资总额	万美元		500	21035	79113	252194	239860	272534
境内资金总额	万美元		6	85		100		
中方实际投资	万美元							
企业境内借款	万美元		6	85		100		
境外资金总额	万美元		494	20950	79113	252094	239634	272534
外商实际投资	万美元		494	20939	79113	251252	239634	272534
企业境外借款	万美元			11		842		
引进设备价值	万美元		288	15390	58140	91288	34321	26082
出口总值	万美元		82	52276	494700	1947751	3960425	4982107
期末职工人数	万人		0.10	5.67	48.92	117.17	148.43	160.65

9-12 主要年份分方式、分国别(地区)实际利用外资

Foreign Capital Actually Utilized by Type and Countries(Regions) in Main Years

单位：万美元

项　　目	1990年	1995年	2000年	2001年	2003年	2005年	2010年	2011年
一、按引进方式分								
总　计	10167	68438	164712	181562	256336	375139	316287	321821
外商直接投资	10010	67247	108737	114721	175400	282116	273171	305052
合资经营企业	5871	31314	18865	16413	12938	18195	32135	30351
合作经营企业	3645	14983	8305	6798	8608	12669	1176	1409
外资(独资)经营企业	494	20950	78890	88413	153854	251252	239634	272534
外商投资股份公司			2677	3097			226	758
外商其他投资	157	1191	55975	66841	80936	93023	43116	16769
国际租赁								
补偿贸易								
加工装配	157	1191	55975	66841	80936	93023	43116	16769
二、按国家和地区分								
总　计	10167	67247	164712	181562	256336	375139	316287	321821
香　港	10167	58333	88950	89559	122639	185214	182600	183124
澳　门		13				44	442	653
台　湾		3016	23722	32130	30005	130682	82674	84261
日　本		391	7476	6994	11037	25253	12861	18649
泰　国		96	33	108		20		4
新加坡		822	3511	5595	5003	3994	6094	3230
德　国		3	1884	1210	5265	487	1488	1373
法　国			89			20	688	1303
瑞　士			546	426			127	58
加拿大		46	15	142	56	99	568	296
美　国		3230	2391	2576	5987	8122	3309	5407
澳大利亚		56	14	118	252	48	61	1431
韩　国			2362	2792	5012	6958	5955	8907
利比亚			153					
英　国		79		570	194	12	277	500
其　他		1162	33566	39342	70886	14186	19143	12625

注：1995年分国别地区的外商投资额是外商直接投资额。

9-13 外商直接投资分行业情况（2011年）

Foreign Direct Investment by Sector (2011)

单位：万美元

行业	项目个数(个)	合同外资金额	实际投资金额
总计	1325	370189	305052
农、林、牧、渔业	1	1580	559
采矿业			
制造业	1172	293826	259790
#纺织业	55	12846	16659
化学原料及化学制品制造业	12	2637	2476
医药制造业			179
通用设备制造业	30	5808	8814
专用设备制造业	32	13806	19921
通信设备、计算机及其他电子设备制造业	211	83647	65660
电力、燃气及水的生产和供应业	2	2950	
建筑业			2
交通运输、仓储和邮政业		4064	4052
信息传输、计算机服务和软件业	3	200	1045
批发和零售业	102	28232	23568
住宿和餐饮业	3	536	764
金融业			
房地产业	4	13876	10163
#房地产开发经营	3	13825	8093
租赁和商务服务业	22	1954	1865
科学研究、技术服务和地质勘查业	10	779	741
居民服务和其他服务业	1	252	328
卫生、社会保障和社会福利业		1275	2012
公共管理和社会组织			15

9-14 主要年份宾馆酒店接待能力和接待人数

Capacity and Tourists Received by Hotels in Main Years

项目	单位	1990年	1995年	2000年	2005年	2010年	2011年
一、三星级以上宾馆(酒店)	家	3	16	30	63	82	77
三星级	家	3	16	23	27	35	31
四星级	家			6	22	25	25
五星级	家			1	14	22	21
二、客　房（已评1星以上）	间	3793	7568	18024	18258	16631	17899
床　位（已评1星以上）	张	8531	15136	30895	25014	24841	24348
开房率	%	60.2	68.8	61.9	58.9	58.1	60.0
三、全年接待人数	万人次	125	89	291	1156	2251	2615
（一）国际及港澳台旅游者	万人次	27	27	106	169	327	357
#外国人	万人次	1	6	15	70	109	121
港澳台同胞	万人次	26	21	89	99	219	236
（二）国内旅客	万人次	98	62	185	987	1924	2258
四、外出旅游人数	万人次					154	183
国内旅游人数	万人次					139	167
出国（境）游人数	万人次					15	16

9-15 历年旅游业情况

Basic Statistics on Tourism over Years

年 份	三星级以上宾馆(酒店)(家)	客 房(已评1星以上)(间)	床 位(已评1星以上)(张)	开房率(%)	全年接待人数(万人次)					国际旅游外汇收入(万美元)
						国际及港澳台旅游者	外国人	港澳台同胞	国内游客	
1978										
1979										
1980										
1981										
1982										
1983										
1984										
1985										
1986					80	11		10	69	554
1987					107	19	1	18	87	453
1988		6435	7641	65.8	125	20		19	105	710
1989		3324	7376	64.8	115	18		18	97	504
1990		3793	8531	60.2	125	27	1	26	98	1025
1991		4004	8701	64.9	155	37	1	36	118	2443
1992		4042	8770	72.6	172	47	2	46	125	2473
1993		4258	8517	75.1	169	52	2	50	117	2888
1994		3542	7443	77.6	119	44	4	40	75	3464
1995	16	7568	15136	68.8	89	27	6	21	62	5679
1996	16	13409	26818	50.3	175	36	6	29	139	6464
1997	19	10420	19142	50.6	171	59	5	54	112	6778
1998	20	17428	31987	53.3	216	75	11	63	141	6601
1999	20	17931	25482	63.5	253	97	17	77	156	7055
2000	30	18024	30895	61.9	291	106	15	89	185	7617
2001	48	20572	32789	62.0	327	110	22	88	217	8200
2002	53	9427	14652	69.0	930	108	22	86	822	11847
2003	52	8170	12599	65.0	1086	80	24	56	1006	13825
2004	60	10530	14934	61.2	1131	149	66	83	982	23437
2005	63	18258	25014	58.9	1156	169	70	99	987	28189
2006	71	18258	25014	60.1	1363	193	81	112	1170	33180
2007	74	19023	26132	63.4	1725	248	102	146	1477	42702
2008	77	19510	26864	58.9	1872	268	103	165	1604	45614
2009	80	16332	24389	58.0	2037	286	104	182	1751	51756
2010	82	16631	24841	58.1	2251	327	109	219	1924	67592
2011	77	17899	24348	60.0	2615	357	121	236	2258	90975

注：国际旅游外汇收入1995年以前单位为万元(外汇券)，1995年起为万美元。

主要统计指标解释

Explanatory Notes on Main Statistical Indicators

海关进出口总额 指实际进出我国国境的货物（包括贸易和非贸易）的价值总和。主要包括对外贸易实际进出口货物，来料加工装配、补偿贸易、进料加工进出口货物，国家间及国际组织无偿援助物资和赠送品，华侨、港澳台同胞和外籍华人捐赠品，租赁期满归承租人所有的租赁货物，边境地方贸易及边境地区小额贸易进出口货物（边民互市贸易除外），中外合资、合作经营企业、外商独资经营企业进出口货物和公用物品，到、离岸价格在规定限额以上的进出口货样和广告品（无商业价值、无使用价值和免费提供出口的除外），从保税仓库提取在中国境内销售的进出口货物，以及其他进出口货物。海关进出口总额反映一个国家在对外经济贸易方面实际进出口货物的总规模。

贸易出口 指由外贸进出口公司、工农贸易进出口公司和地方性的进出口公司由国家统一安排的出口、代理出口和自营、联营出口，其中包括进料加工出口，以及各进出口公司在国内以外汇结算方式售给友谊商店、华侨商店、出国人员服务公司和中外合资、合作经营和外资企业等的出口商品。

"三来一补"出口 指来料加工装配出口按工缴费计算，中小型补偿贸易按金额计算。

"三资"企业出口 指三资企业自己出口的本企业产品。不包括委托外贸进出口公司出口的商品。

利用外资 指我国各级政府、部门、企业和其他经济组织通过对外借款、吸收外商直接投资以及向境外发行债券、股票等方式筹措的境外资金。

外资的形式可以是现汇、实物、工业产权或专有技术等有形资本和无形资本。

我国自有外汇如国家外汇、中国银行等金融机构用自有资金发放的外汇贷款等，华侨、港澳同胞的捐赠，联合国或其他国际组织的无偿赠送资金、无偿援建的项目均不属于外资范围。

利用外资的方式有：对外借款，外国（或港澳地区）企业和经济组织或个人在我国境内开办独资企业，与我国境内的企业或组织共同开办合资企业合作经营（企业）项目或合作开发资源，以及补偿贸易、国际租赁等。

对外借款 指我国政府、部门、企业和中国银行等单位向国际金融组织、外国政府、企业等借用的长期、短期资本，到期需还本付息。借款按不同渠道划分为：1. 外国政府贷款；2. 国际金融组织贷款；3. 外国银行贷款；4. 出口信贷；5. 发行债券、股票。

外商直接投资 指外国企业和经济组织或个人（包括华侨、港澳同胞以及我在境外注册的企业）按我国有关政策、法规，在我国境内开办外商独资企业，与我国境内的企业或经济组织共同举办中外合资企业、合作经营企业或合作开发资源的投资以及外商从企业得到收益的再投资。

新口径合同利用外资 根据2003年修订的《利用外资统计制度》，明确指出合同外资的统计指外商直接投资（三资企业）企业设立时，根据合同（章程）规定，外方投资者应缴付的注册资本。

国际旅游（外汇）收入 指国内各部门为来我国旅游的外国人、华侨、港澳和台湾同胞提供商品和劳务而得到的外汇收入。包括供应商品、饮食和提供住宿、交通、邮电、文化娱乐、导游等各项服务所得的全部外汇收入。

十、财政、金融与保险

Finance, Banking and Insurance

10-1 主要年份财政收支主要指标

Main Indicators of Government Revenue and Expenditure in Main Years

单位：万元

项 目	1978年	1980年	1985年	1990年	2000年	2005年	2006年
一、财政收入							
来源于东莞的财政收入	6604	6710	11118	35719	1035561	3319079	4065412
中央财政收入					617151	1935069	2323977
#关税和海关代征税					273972	483327	526251
省级财政收入					113681	344330	451990
市财政一般预算收入	6604	6710	11118	35719	304730	1039680	1289445
二、工商税收							
工商税收总额					867584	2923001	3593704
国税(不含关税)					607216	1849818	2208722
地税					260368	1073183	1384982
三、财政支出							
市财政一般预算支出	1792	2015	4999	22779	336102	1170427	1478955
#基本建设支出					27426	276646	242829
企业挖潜改造支出		88	15	37	1584	9107	9691
科技三项费用支出		7		140	9963	31572	87397
农林水气部门事业费支出		304	1154	3261	40097	62181	64911
工交部门事业费支出		2	7	180	192	20499	18552
城市维护费支出		31	219	1350	41267	162370	205426
科教文卫体事业费支出		1051	2139	7357	86737	210620	291467
#科学事业费				404	936	3956	3874
教育事业费		760	1504	3786	68194	171055	244113
卫生事业费		185	262	743	12083	11469	12826
体育事业费		18	50	827	1517	2860	3266
抚恤和社会福利救济支出		75	132	368	2888	8335	34050
行政管理费支出		293	320	1324	29817	102296	119034
公检法司支出			92	740	46446	166055	225382

注：1. 1995年及以前年份，来源于东莞的财政收入不含关税。
2. 从2007年起财政收支按新的分类项目，在10-2表中反映。

10-2 财政收支主要指标（2006-2011年）

Main Indicators of Government Revenue and Expenditure (2006-2011)

单位：万元

指　　标	2006年	2007年	2008年	2009年	2010年	2011年
来源于东莞的财政收入	4065412	5395362	6010642	6278114	7851003	8385226
财政总收入	3358095	4574778	5234746	5402140	6542697	7665371
#中央	1638195	2151906	2476902	2392927	2940745	3422151
省级	430455	558404	665596	697658	823548	1112580
市财政一般预算收入	1289445	1864468	2092248	2311555	2778404	3130639
#增值税	347153	474288	552515	534382	626301	719263
营业税	291122	380958	422427	446884	458712	453341
企业所得税	145739	173566	184478	176786	247986	265919
个人所得税	60518	75765	87895	87313	110441	111982
房产税	51622	63228	65560	75806	92706	106267
契税	80793	355039	113509	157533	186994	230554
罚没收入	75238	81766	79104	72888	78400	83203
市财政一般预算支出	1478955	1930968	2182626	2326216	2898306	3519171
#一般公共服务	161657	220367	234172	259865	269505	326164
公共安全	233413	324714	365387	367266	388243	478295
教育	293000	412347	499978	553429	653090	832341
科学技术	10593	91232	93518	112506	79830	181369
社会保障和就业	27100	104264	232742	194637	264017	243839
农林水事务	77188	116452	143695	131828	229613	180411
交通运输	14439	54144	49759	73635	90609	252799
税收总额	3593704	4709341	5361733	5475100	6887249	8435699
#国税	2208722	3057525	3390812	3384667	4394366	5234084
地税	1384982	1651816	1970921	2090433	2492883	3201615

注：1. 2009及以前年份，国税不含海关代征税。
2. 2010年及以前年份，地税不含契税和耕地占用税。
3. 2011年起，来源于东莞的财政收入含政府性基金和出口退税。

10-3 历年财政收入

Government Revenue over Years

单位：万元

年份	来源于东莞的财政收入	财政总收入	中央财政收入	省级财政收入	市财政一般预算收入	各项税收	工商税收	专项收入	其他收入
1978	6604				6604	6595	5826		9
1979	6634				6634	6625	5725		9
1980	6710				6710	6699	5785		11
1981	6823				6823	6805	5942		18
1982	8103				8103	8068	7184		35
1983	8578				8578	8501	7599		77
1984	8469				8469	8385	7442		84
1985	11118				11118	10998	9708		120
1986	16053				16053	15865	14574	45	143
1987	20221				20221	19989	18551	50	182
1988	27076				27076	26837	25309	76	163
1989	31888				31888	30997	29331	116	775
1990	35719				35719	33544	31911	686	1489
1991	44374				44374	41659	39302	913	1802
1992	56204				56204	52620	48272	1351	2233
1993	93828				93828	88920	83462	1947	2961
1994	130531				76940	70451	60889	2697	3792
1995	180051				115618	106388	95463	4070	5160
1996	283506				96541	85648	74323	4470	6423
1997	335044				114069	96980	85245	4794	12295
1998	472422				151012	123816	106700	5693	21503
1999	717847				182577	159873	134852	8759	13945
2000	1035561				304730	265565	248159	14709	24456
2001	1259961				450163	402668	381660	18356	29139
2002	1678848				552933	489780	467998	26438	36715
2003	2064052				674461	575342	536390	30710	68409
2004	2591086				826389	707954	655571	35273	83162
2005	3319079				1039680	879653	797038	36423	123604
2006	4065412	3358095	1638195	430455	1289445	1077152	990029	49285	163008
2007	5395362	4574778	2151906	558404	1864468	1652620	1291335	55863	155985
2008	6010642	5234746	2476902	665596	2092248	1682270	1555499	60590	349388
2009	6278114	5402140	2392927	697658	2311555	1822650	1618514	60007	428899
2010	7851003	6542697	2940745	823548	2778404	2217675	1950773	72153	488576
2011	8385226	7665371	3422151	1112580	3130639	2433937	2171228	133951	562751

注：1. 1995年及以前年份，来源于东莞的财政收入不含关税。
2. 2011年起，来源于东莞的财政收入含政府性基金和出口退税。

10-4 历年财政支出

Government Expenditure over Years

单位：万元

年 份	预算内地方财政支出总额	#基本建设支出	#科技三项费用	#农林水气等部门事业费	#城市维护费	#科教文卫体育事业费	#教育事业费	#行政管理费
1978	1792							
1979	1908		20	451	74	852	618	202
1980	2015		7	304	31	1051	760	293
1981	2139		4	341	36	1182	818	246
1982	2612		1	359	141	1346	912	336
1983	2804		1	413	28	1672	1004	287
1984	3013			264	48	1868	1309	340
1985	4999			1154	219	2139	1504	320
1986	9916			2541	1431	2887	1793	330
1987	12512			3479	1624	4759	1871	510
1988	17475		100	4094	1614	6950	3339	888
1989	21623		103	3509	2286	7958	3733	1159
1990	22779		140	3261	1350	7357	3786	1324
1991	27499		30	4938	866	7956	4720	1484
1992	38162		50	5637	567	17505	7682	2348
1993	72910	5400	1289	8882	5737	25716	14427	4002
1994	88984	14575	1496	12835	5254	20725	13552	6158
1995	124173	13736	441	15798	9947	31021	23110	8433
1996	124059	17285	1332	14962	5199	28927	21237	10384
1997	148510	16923	1479	15349	6258	36614	23262	11691
1998	179064	26144	1164	19255	7264	36710	25578	11082
1999	212641	40681	1429	26648	12994	40863	30631	12979
2000	336102	27426	9963	40097	41267	86737	68194	29817
2001	478646	119692	4113	28957	43706	105990	85544	28961
2002	649606	165283	28013	37348	64483	143225	120195	43678
2003	765190	201077	30062	41164	44240	193138	163390	50022
2004	941554	179039	27110	53855	164770	162573	139337	84798
2005	1170427	276646	31572	62181	162370	210620	171055	102296
2006	1478955	242829	87397	64911	205426	291467	244113	119034

注：从2007年起财政支出按新的分类项目，在10-2表中反映。

10-5 税务登记情况及税种征收情况（2010-2011年）

Taxes (2010-2011)

指　　标	国税		地税	
	2010年	2011年	2010年	2011年
税务登记情况(户)	247277	268962	304204	735568
#国有企业	358	329	1334	1523
集体企业	5057	4202	7787	11982
私营企业	33986	37493	31641	39377
港澳台投资企业	5823	7032	8455	22781
外商投资企业	4010	4025	3843	8081
个体经营	157155	165318	183214	559939
工商税收总额(万元)	4394366	5234084	2492883	2938906
#国有企业	9933	10465	35701	42090
集体企业	41161	41910	245968	231496
私营企业	432581	518783	234451	242012
港澳台投资企业	902769	1087092	399846	479100
外商投资企业	713086	748870	341140	401668
个体经营	367881	421657	229409	271647
#增值税	3586480	4218072		
消费税	38528	43305		
营业税			919809	1054446
企业所得税	588256	752046	550874	604192
个人所得税	1484	663	460168	559247
房产税			92704	106267
印花税			89081	59703
城镇土地使用税			94552	95962
土地增值税			142003	204218
车船税			31869	35188
车辆购置税	177508	218200		
#第一产业	1113	146	1310	1642
第二产业	2478868	2946786	1022327	1200865
#采矿业	597	1201	1314	1926
制造业	2264031	2737250	711871	849824
农副食品加工业	9554	12528	8266	8727
食品制造业	72742	74627	37054	39578
饮料制造业	33733	40675	7793	11953
纺织业	93705	118609	16803	19718
纺织服装、鞋、帽制造业	149890	191676	28726	35730
皮革、毛皮、羽绒及其制品业	76543	88459	15626	24201
木材加工及竹、藤、棕草制品业	10646	12670	2762	3690
家具制造业	79142	101335	18627	21744
造纸及纸制品业	125648	144575	20058	22315

10-5 续表

单位：万元

指标	国税		地税	
	2010年	2011年	2010年	2011年
印刷业、记录媒介的复制	54974	73580	14419	15447
文教体育用品制造业	47221	65234	18048	19440
石油加工、及炼焦业及核燃业	7960	5793	3205	2848
化学原料及化学制品制造业	68698	73940	15444	19486
医药制造业	12690	17160	4825	5642
化学纤维制造业	3256	3703	172	274
橡胶制品业	22984	27814	7901	9499
塑料制品业	156955	175274	49300	54932
非金属矿物制品业	69141	74411	9436	12135
黑色金属冶炼及压延加工业	311	343	1636	1782
有色金属冶炼及压延加工业	5228	6748	1935	2658
金属制品业	132603	190794	39579	48181
通用设备制造业	86175	94238	24233	21884
专用设备制造业	81485	111724	20194	25667
交通运输设备制造业	46474	58926	12473	16273
电气机械及器材制造业	164802	207154	63890	78273
通信设备、计算机及其他电子设备制造业	476071	589655	220276	261655
仪器仪表及文化、办公用机械制造业	44861	59675	9280	16047
其他制造业	130539	115930	39910	50045
电力、燃气及水的生产和供应业	208102	201080	61702	49841
建筑业	6138	7255	247440	299274
房屋和土木工程建筑业	785	1109	66006	95382
建筑安装业	2045	1729	151391	163570
建筑装饰业	1468	1649	15103	18968
其他建筑业	1840	2768	14940	21354
第三产业	1914386	2287152	1469246	1736399
#交通运输、仓储及邮政业	6263	11933	84894	104704
信息传输、计算机服务和软件业	2349	4447	58352	59102
批发和零售业	501711	529282	124125	142149
住宿和餐饮业	1633	1774	78305	89879
金融业	109961	140358	224405	250794
房地产业	121515	108582	515796	649545
租赁和商务服务业	11259	14444	104598	125967
居民服务和其他服务业	18188	17341	174026	209639
教育	193	169	4082	5068
卫生、社会保险和社会福利业	414	282	5992	5185
文化、体育和娱乐业	256	240	21611	25804
公共管理和社会组织	10	12	25531	24682
其他行业	1140634	1458288	47529	43881

10-6 历年金融机构各项人民币存贷款余额

Balance of RMB Deposits and Loans over Years

单位：万元

年 份	各项存款余额	#企业存款余额	#城乡居民储蓄存款余额	#财政性存款余额	各项贷款余额	#短期贷款	#中长期贷款
1978	10497	1431	5409	963	19607	19607	
1979	14875	2319	7184	1028	21301	21301	
1980	26093	5107	11718	1481	30797	29669	403
1981	38003	6546	20339	1503	40243	38365	765
1982	45120	8169	27650	1937	45525	44081	690
1983	60547	10190	38597	3343	57618	56063	837
1984	110265	22510	61823	5060	121891	114522	3365
1985	134867	23367	91941	3488	142437	130716	6230
1986	195948	35422	131352	5801	206813	193501	9486
1987	284819	49618	189654	5321	312431	292104	7162
1988	380511	73733	249134	6724	415818	381957	12351
1989	468203	75491	325670	9202	493737	456504	12338
1990	680696	116074	455140	7953	630355	570324	13427
1991	949713	164519	614737	10313	783957	714848	17385
1992	1473354	319933	815404	19926	1059794	935064	23000
1993	1798346	423791	1071715	33016	1343103	923157	237985
1994	2497834	616328	1515445	60551	1734350	1246772	250806
1995	3836761	895021	2329685	83933	2548512	1645696	274157
1996	4896463	1114040	3180215	56860	3128076	2053343	353298
1997	6711687	1595280	4258238	48923	3826560	2737916	205486
1998	8640053	2515686	5337482	49729	4427394	3666563	155295
1999	10408377	3268530	6163430	35166	5243735	4628058	328875
2000	12286706	4385202	6720704	39949	6308405	5313933	469249
2001	14586491	5032045	7991768	57056	7501801	5341925	1436127
2002	17901799	5775722	10016909	78673	9334054	5731973	2312883
2003	21267775	6378486	12310616	110077	12067237	6918877	3730104
2004	24628693	7546584	14316777	164648	14052461	7118671	5222504
2005	29334026	8558552	17282760	259771	15005217	7341939	7007138
2006	33656508	10111005	20133979	298793	17305554	7792175	8684306
2007	37518345	11624537	21207413	568912	21547660	9245906	11427676
2008	43545340	11839005	26380433	495375	23803585	10132902	12052974
2009	49866108	14199448	29045704	524501	29037984	12604957	14519686
2010	59433885	15215577	33868535	465766	33298244	12340319	19675448
2011	66093904		37109919	313912	37160847	14804666	20698930

10-7 保险行业主要指标(2006-2011年)

Main Indicators of Insurance (2006-2011)

指　　标	单位	2006年	2007年	2008年	2009年	2010年	2011年
保险公司	家	26	30	35	37	37	38
保险业从业人员	人	11714	17846	24771	27386	27281	28064
保费收入	万元	473835	676062	902986	1150795	1597166	1636513
寿险类	万元	277769	397962	583983	797192	1129950	1085528
#传统寿险	万元	51772	57890	61255	63681	72494	72212
分红险	万元	157264	190521	355674	572703	867738	813006
万能险	万元	34050	51114	73233	85142	110035	18650
投连险	万元	1750	60993	38195	18481	18953	805
意外险	万元	12382	14490	17188	17143	18718	23730
健康险	万元	20477	22954	38438	40043	42012	57507
财险类	万元	196066	278100	319010	353602	467216	550985
#机动车险	万元	155067	231073	270082	301526	400405	460241
企财险	万元	17160	21254	22626	24276	32123	34107
家财险	万元	3228	3393	1373	1113	1832	1806
货运险	万元	1985	2514	2819	3648	4576	6917
责任险	万元	4179	5477	6571	7273	9772	10516
短健险	万元	1448	271	759	8058	4289	7222
短意险	万元	10536	12945	13145	6184	11073	10271
农业险	万元	23	43	17		55	35

主要统计指标解释

Explanatory Notes on Main Statistical Indicators

财政收入 国家财政参与社会产品分配所取得的收入，是实现国家职能的财力保证，主要包括：

（1）各项税收 包括增值税、营业税、消费税、土地增值税、城市维护建设税、资源税、城市土地使用税、印花税、个人所得税、企业所得税、关税、农牧业税和耕地占用税等。

（2）专项收入 包括征收排污费收入、征收城市水资源费收入，教育费附加收入等。

（3）其他收入 包括基本建设贷款归还收入、基本建设收入、捐赠收入等。

（4）国有企业计划亏损补贴 这项为负收入，冲减财政收入。

财政支出 国家财政将筹集起来的资金进行分配使用，以满足经济建设和各项事业的需要，主要包括：基本建设支出、企业挖潜改造资金、地质勘探费用、科技三项费用、支援农村生产支出、农林水利气象等部门的事业费用、工业交通商业等部门的事业费、文教科学卫生事业费、抚恤和社会福利救济费、国防支出、行政管理费、价格补贴支出等项目。

银行信贷存款 指企业、机关、团体或居民把货币资金存入银行或其他信用机构保管并取得一定利息的一种信用活动形式。根据存款对象的不同可划分为：企业存款、财政存款、机关团体存款、基本建设存款、城镇居民储蓄存款、农村存款等科目。它是银行信贷资金的主要来源。

银行信贷贷款 银行或其他信用机构根据必须归还的原则，按一定利率，为企业、个人等提供资金的一种信用活动形式。我国银行贷款，分流动资金贷款、固定资产贷款、城乡个体工商户贷款以及农业贷款等科目。

十一、人民生活

People's Living Conditions

11-1 主要年份人民生活主要指标

Basic Statistics on People's Living Conditions in Main Years

指　　标	单位	1985年	1990年	1995年	2000年	2005年	2010年	2011年
城镇职工年平均工资	元	1456	3552	9682	14051	28253	46576	50398
国有单位	元	1400	3600	9390	16371	37919	57275	61504
城镇集体单位	元	1501	3507	7507	10475	15958	27391	30549
其他各种单位	元	1571	3525	7891	14218	20882	37803	39591
城市居民家庭每一就业者负担人口	人	1.58	1.70	1.50	1.54	1.58	1.60	1.58
城市居民家庭人均可支配收入	元	791	2508	9588	14142	22882	35690	39513
城市居民家庭人均总支出	元	718	2152	10049	14193	25822	32140	34978
城市居民家庭人均消费性支出	元	689	2038	9220	12529	21768	25733	27495
食品	元	493	1295	3644	4048	6035	8732	9513
衣着	元	28	95	604	487	1285	1706	1806
家庭设备用品及服务	元	48	153	694	623	1165	1771	1902
医疗保健	元	14	42	258	431	811	1294	1251
交通和通讯	元	4	25	1562	3309	7482	5925	6035
教育文化娱乐服务	元	21	113	991	1517	3205	3443	3886
居住	元	58	184	1084	1218	1242	2089	2128
杂项商品和服务	元	23	131	383	896	543	773	974
城市居民家庭人均非消费性支出	元		12	829	1664	4054	6407	7483
农民人均纯收入	元	803	1542	4769	8484	13076	20486	22842
全市职工年平均工资	元				7765	10639	16108	21739

注：1. 职工年平均工资从2000年起是城镇在岗职工工资,不含乡镇及以下办企业职工，下同。
2. 全市职工年平均工资统计是根据中央、省、市属各类企事业机关单位，各镇街、村及村以下非农企业,个体私营非农企业以及“三资”、“三来一补”非农企业的在岗从业人员劳动报酬抽样调查计算所得。
3. 本表城市居民人均可支配收入1997年以前是生活费收入口径，1997年起是可支配收入口径。
4. 农民人均纯收入采用农村住户抽样调查口径，相应调整了往年数，下同。

11-2 历年城镇职工工资总额与平均工资

Total and Average Wage of Employed Persons in Urban Areas over Years

项 目	工资总额(万元)	国有单位	城镇集体单位	其他单位	平均工资(元)	国有单位	城镇集体单位	其他单位
1978	4485	2911	1574		474	630	325	
1979	5869	3611	2258		650	708	574	
1980	7255	4210	3045		750	867	632	
1981	9416	5000	4416		887	979	801	
1982	11839	6440	5399		1095	1089	1102	
1983	12808	6834	5974		1197	1138	1273	
1984	14963	7002	7961		1383	1333	1431	
1985	17260	7619	9238	403	1456	1400	1501	1571
1986	20980	10336	10026	618	2616	1698	1525	1940
1987	27610	12300	14159	1151	2067	2028	2094	2166
1988	35007	17931	14854	2222	2757	2942	2588	2574
1989	42947	20340	20808	1799	3320	3355	3295	3236
1990	46780	22321	21012	3447	3552	3600	3507	3525
1991	54002	24456	23268	6278	3777	3841	3674	3933
1992	68360	30469	28886	9005	4531	4610	4404	4696
1993	107088	47088	40171	19829	6228	7007	5583	6044
1994	131160	61869	49323	19968	8360	9390	7507	7891
1995	171543	75157	51398	44988	9682	10802	8007	10367
1996	178968	83372	52581	43015	10382	11623	8658	10775
1997	175156	87890	47185	40081	10691	12160	8774	10610
1998	187636	98109	50302	39225	11422	13123	9362	10959
1999	204550	109437	52217	42896	12557	14601	9966	12062
2000	229404	125711	53903	49790	14051	16371	10475	14218
2001	261645	152564	52645	56436	16183	19869	11001	15238
2002	291778	165611	58907	67260	17804	22228	11640	17348
2003	362935	230464	55866	76605	22598	29773	12940	19140
2004	432893	282512	62898	87483	25326	35163	13954	19223
2005	518216	349572	70872	97772	28253	37919	15958	20882
2006	608670	413718	74637	120315	31135	41457	17174	23032
2007	707007	487826	74408	144773	35284	46197	18807	26218
2008	809893	570134	82432	157327	39516	51441	20833	28838
2009	944243	639161	76001	229081	42585	56129	22077	31195
2010	1029873	678673	96664	254537	46576	57275	27391	37803
2011	1229001	826777	104824	297400	50398	61504	30549	39591

注：2000年起本表统计口径为城镇在岗职工工资总额和平均工资。

11-3 城镇在岗职工工资总额及平均工资(2011年，按经济类型、行业分)

Total and Average Wage of Fully Employed Persons in Urban Areas (2011,by Status of Registration and Sector)

项目	工资总额(万元)	国有单位	城镇集体单位	其他单位	平均工资(元)	国有单位	城镇集体单位	其他单位
总计	1229001	826777	104824	297400	50398	61504	30549	39591
一、按企业、事业和机关分								
企业	628203	229713	101090	297400	46249	84323	30203	39591
事业	344149	340415	3734		51504	51596	44293	
机关	256649	256649			62281	62281		
二、按国民经济行业分								
农、林、牧、渔业	4886	4886			50167	50167		
工业	274194	28869	53026	192299	33284	78834	24001	33961
建筑业	5076	4254	805	18	32497	34193	25961	22000
交通运输、仓储及邮政业	53263	20554	11581	21128	33950	40350	35800	28706
信息传输、计算机服务和软件业	28431	26319		2112	116568	118394		97782
批发和零售业	27255	5122	6154	15980	44506	31912	33922	59075
住宿和餐饮业	1554		497	1057	23658		24259	23385
金融业	238677	147379	28019	63280	89587	109372	50357	83230
房地产业	2976	2391	585		61490	72245	38222	
租赁和商务服务业	11764	7173	3065	1527	52732	51419	44745	101093
科学研究、技术服务和地质勘查业	11945	11734	212		58185	58757	37804	
水利、环境和公共设施管理业	3899	3641	258		57598	62889	26337	
居民服务和其他服务业	941	941			59924	59924		
教育	106538	106538			41166	41166		
卫生、社会保障和社会福利业	185657	185440	217		58145	58139	63765	
文化、体育和娱乐业	11374	10968	406		65900	66073	61561	
公共管理和社会组织	260567	260567			61665	61665		
国际组织								

11-4　主要年份各种分组的城镇职工平均工资

Average Wage of Employed Persons in Urban Areas by Item in Main Years

单位：元

项　　目	1980年	1985年	1990年	1995年	2000年	2005年	2010年	2011年
职工平均工资	750	1456	3552	9682	14051	28253	46576	50398
一、按企业事业和机关分								
企　业				9316	13501	24152	43121	46249
事　业				10872	15485	32203	46478	51504
机　关				12171	15383	38441	57300	62281
二、按经济类型分								
国有单位	867	1400	3600	10802	16371	37919	57275	61504
城镇集体单位	632	1501	3507	8007	10475	15958	27391	30549
其他单位		1571	3525	10367	14218	20882	37803	39591
三、按国民经济行业分								
农、林、牧、渔业	694	1312	3639	12412	14000	37046	61606	50167
工　业	769	1450	3481	8945	12316	18371	30418	33284
建筑业	1018	2052	3813	9125	9820	18385	31020	32497
交通运输、仓储及邮政业						31989	40809	33950
信息传输、计算机服务和软件业						71801	110207	116568
批发和零售业						28565	38986	44506
住宿和餐饮业						18257	21955	23658
金融业	685	1500	3303	13254	20560	40655	94569	89587
房地产业	577	1779	4414	11184	17993	34805	53939	61490
租赁和商务服务业						29824	47505	52732
科学研究、技术服务和地质勘查业						37423	51017	58185
水利、环境和公共设施管理业						34573	51426	57598
居民服务和其他服务业						44853	56776	59924
教　育						27255	37734	41166
卫生、社会保障和社会福利业						37991	52867	58145
文化、体育和娱乐业						37710	58317	65900
公共管理和社会组织	695	1519	3666	12347	15424	37888	56817	61665
国际组织								

注：2000年起本表统计口径为城镇在岗职工平均工资。

11-5 各种经济类型分行业职工工资总额、平均工资(2010-2011年)

Total and Average Wage of Employed Persons by Status of Registration and Sector (2010-2011)

项目	国有经济		城镇集体经济		其他经济类型	
	2010年	2011年	2010年	2011年	2010年	2011年
一、职工工资总额(万元)	678673	826777	96664	104824	254537	297400
农、林、牧、渔业	3709	4886				
工业	25894	28869	49470	53026	180041	192299
建筑业	4783	4254	1847	805	18	18
交通运输、仓储及邮政业	11586	20554	12054	11581	2804	21128
信息传输、计算机服务和软件业	24308	26319	60		1938	2112
批发和零售业	5370	5122	5352	6154	12749	15980
住宿和餐饮业			456	497	971	1057
金融业	108124	147379	23083	28019	54508	63280
房地产业	2214	2391	450	585		
租赁和商务服务业	6448	7173	2694	3065	1509	1527
科学研究、技术服务和地质勘查业	9616	11734	194	212		
水利、环境和公共设施管理业	3062	3641	307	258		
居民服务和其他服务业	608	941				
教育	97647	106538				
卫生、社会保障和社会福利业	136300	185440	431	217		
文化、体育和娱乐业	9572	10968	266	406		
公共管理和社会组织	229431	260567				
国际组织						
二、职工平均工资(元)	57275	61504	27391	30549	37803	39591
农、林、牧、渔业	61606	50167				
工业	73230	78834	21350	24001	31444	33961
建筑业	38451	34193	20725	25961	22000	22000
交通运输、仓储及邮政业	53639	40350	33115	35800	41238	28706
信息传输、计算机服务和软件业	114339	118394	13378		89708	97782
批发和零售业	30545	31912	30082	33922	51343	59075
住宿和餐饮业			22810	24259	21576	23385
金融业	118324	109372	52200	50357	89681	83230
房地产业	67920	72245	26810	38222		
租赁和商务服务业	46255	51419	39103	44745	94874	101093
科学研究、技术服务和地质勘查业	51507	58757	34679	37804		
水利、环境和公共设施管理业	56590	62889	26921	26337		
居民服务和其他服务业	56776	59924				
教育	37734	41166				
卫生、社会保障和社会福利业	52834	58139	66308	63765		
文化、体育和娱乐业	58473	66073	53180	61561		
公共管理和社会组织	56817	61665				
国际组织						

注：本表统计口径为城镇在岗职工工资总额和平均工资。

11-6 国有企、事业和机关单位从业人员工资总额及平均工资(2011年)

Total and Average Wage of Employed Persons in State-owned Enterprises, Institutions and Government Agencies (2011)

项目	单位从业人员劳动报酬(万元)	在岗职工工资总额	其他从业人员工资总额	在岗职工平均工资(元)
总计	835823	826777	9046	61504
一、按企事业机关分				
企业	230477	229713	764	84323
#地方	174262	173518	744	92711
事业	343678	340415	3264	51596
#地方	341846	338583	3264	51480
机关	261667	256649	5019	62281
#地方	261667	256649	5019	62281
二、按行业分				
农、林、牧、渔业	4900	4886	14	50167
工业	28889	28869	20	78834
建筑业	4254	4254		34193
交通运输、仓储及邮政业	20563	20554	9	40350
信息传输、计算机服务和软件业	26319	26319		118394
批发和零售业	5650	5122	528	31912
住宿和餐饮业				
金融业	147385	147379	7	109372
房地产业	2420	2391	29	72245
租赁和商务服务业	7270	7173	98	51419
科学研究、技术服务和地质勘查业	11849	11734	115	58757
水利、环境和公共设施管理业	3649	3641	8	62889
居民服务和其他服务业	942	941	1	59924
教育	106578	106538	40	41166
卫生、社会保障和社会福利业	188234	185440	2794	58139
文化、体育和娱乐业	11288	10968	320	66073
公共管理和社会组织	265633	260567	5066	61665
国际组织				

11-7 主要年份工业、建筑业职工工资总额和平均工资

Total and Average Wage of Employed Persons in Industrial and Construction Units in Main Years

项目	2010年		2011年	
	工资总额(万元)	平均工资(元)	工资总额(万元)	平均工资(元)
一、工业总计	255405	30418	274194	33284
(一) 按经济类型分				
国有单位	25894	73230	28869	78834
城镇集体单位	49470	21350	53026	24001
其他各种单位	180041	31444	192299	33961
(二) 按工业行业分(大类)				
非金属矿采选业	311	61000	339	61655
木材及竹材采运业				
食品加工业	1164	29628	1269	32285
食品制造业	315	19000	613	27379
饮料制造业	1851	13661	2409	17754
烟草加工业				
纺织业	1588	13159	1874	15125
服装及其他纤维制品制造业	8313	14007	14680	23071
皮革、毛皮、羽绒及其制品	244	14263	288	16446
木材加工及竹、藤、棕、草制品业				
家具制造业	21359	38708		
造纸及纸制品业	1894	17359	2587	25714
印刷业、记录煤介的复制	1518	16255	1347	16793
文教、体育用品制造业	459	15831	500	17255
石油加工及炼焦业				
化学原料及化学制品制造业	2564	21689	3131	25413
医药制造业	6572	36011	6398	34867
化学纤维制造业				
橡胶制品业				
塑料制品业	6541	26929	8768	33201
非金属矿物制品业	2281	19987	2576	20591
黑色金属冶炼及压延加工业				
有色金属冶炼及压延加工业	112	13802	127	15900
金属制品业	816	15877	1225	23291
通用设备制造业	4100	39380	4883	44755
专用设备制造业	4588	29715	5553	37956
交通运输设备制造业	7525	39113	8339	54292
电气机械及器材制造业	28457	23419	43398	26628
电子及通信设备制造业	78943	35391	76273	38253
仪器、仪表及文化办公用品制造业	28057	22242	37046	26157
其他制造业	967	14071	935	13636
电力蒸汽热水生产和供应业	37150	64834	39841	68573
煤气生产和供应业				
自来水生产和供应业	7654	46051	9722	51276
二、建筑业总计	6648	31020	5076	32497
国有单位	4783	38451	4254	34193
城镇集体单位	1847	20725	805	25961
其他单位	18	22000	18	22000

注：2000年起本表劳动工资统计口径为城镇在岗职工工资总额和平均工资。

11-8 历年居民收支、农民收入

Income and Expenditure of Urban Households and Net Income of Rural Households over Years

年 份	城市居民人均可支配收入(元)	城市居民人均消费性支出(元)	农民人均纯收入(元)
1978			149
1979			188
1980			272
1981			463
1982			567
1983			618
1984			691
1985	791	689	803
1986	1033	883	951
1987	1247	1174	1142
1988	1778	1583	1325
1989	2282	1980	1424
1990	2508	2038	1542
1991	3068	2481	1673
1992	4026	3901	2290
1993	5970	5533	2903
1994	8270	7270	3769
1995	9588	9220	4769
1996	10824	8585	5554
1997	11032	8309	6132
1998	11506	8644	6830
1999	12954	11348	7704
2000	14142	12529	8484
2001	16938	14669	9383
2002	16949	15157	10178
2003	18471	15446	11033
2004	20526	18426	11941
2005	22882	21768	13076
2006	25320	18995	14313
2007	27025	21545	15747
2008	30275	23208	16904
2009	33045	24270	18098
2010	35690	25733	20486
2011	39513	27495	22842

注：本表城市居民人均可支配收入1997年以前是生活费收入口径，1997年起是可支配收入口径，下同。

11-9 历年城市居民家庭户基本情况

Basic Conditions of Urban Households over Years

年 份	平均每户家庭人口（人）	平均每户家庭就业人口（人）	平均每户住房使用面积（平方米）	平均每户家庭可支配收入（元）	平均每户家庭消费性支出（元）
1985	3.89	2.30	42.79	3077	2680
1986	4.01	2.13	48.12	4142	3541
1987	4.02	2.09	52.26	5013	4719
1988	4.08	2.17	61.20	7254	6459
1989	3.88	2.01	65.96	8854	7682
1990	4.06	2.09	64.96	10182	8274
1991	4.08	2.14	65.28	12517	10122
1992	4.06	2.06	69.02	16346	15838
1993	3.86	2.68	77.20	23044	21357
1994	3.86	2.26	88.78	31922	28062
1995	3.94	2.18	78.80	37777	36327
1996	4.07	2.31	85.47	44054	34941
1997	4.02	2.30	84.42	44349	33402
1998	3.92	2.17	101.92	45104	33884
1999	4.05	2.38	120.29	52464	45959
2000	3.89	2.69	121.10	55012	48738
2001	3.75	2.30	149.59	63518	55009
2002	3.66	2.47	152.99	62033	55475
2003	3.57	2.11	147.73	65941	55142
2004	3.50	2.17	145.53	71841	64491
2005	3.38	2.14	144.26	77341	73576
2006	3.68	2.31	166.23	93178	69902
2007	3.41	2.09	147.11	92155	73468
2008	3.43	1.81	138.06	103843	79603
2009	3.38	2.00	136.59	111692	82033
2010	3.32	2.08	146.23	118491	85434
2011	3.39	2.14	167.59	133948	93209

注：平均每户住房使用面积2002年以前为平均每户居住面积口径。

11-10 历年人均总收入分类

Per Capita Total Income over Years

单位：元

年 份	年人均总收入	#工资性收 入	经营净收 入	财产性收 入	转移性收 入	可支配收入
1985	837	603				791
1986	1111	974				1033
1987	1364	989				1247
1988	1889	1097				1778
1989	2439	1185				2282
1990	2678	1459	46	30	417	2508
1991	3343	2160	226	55	534	3062
1992	4520	2560	411	175	709	4026
1993	6623	3684	749	889	319	5969
1994	9131	5758	840	553	994	8270
1995	10491	6260	1210	659	1329	9588
1996	11640	8428	1127	455	1273	10824
1997	11063	8024	625	349	1544	11032
1998	11551	8334	884	319	1207	11506
1999	13009	7910	1799	357	1541	12954
2000	14231	8702	2740	895	720	14142
2001	17062	11037	2643	895	1879	16933
2002	17711	13050	1662	1076	1923	16949
2003	19478	15282	1598	1210	1388	18471
2004	21875	17153	1634	1553	1535	20526
2005	24663	18524	2709	1894	1536	22882
2006	27157	18318	4389	2504	1946	25320
2007	29335	18930	3359	4849	2101	27025
2008	31967	20872	4521	3527	3047	30275
2009	35750	23723	4724	4209	3094	33045
2010	38961	26799	4171	4771	3220	35690
2011	43202	27272	4075	7481	4374	39513

注：1. 本表2007年以前采用50户抽样调查的统计口径,2007年起采用250户抽样调查的统计口径，下同。
2. 本表年人均总收入指标2002年以前采用年人均实际收入统计口径，2002年起采用年人均总收入统计口径，下同。

11-11 历年人均消费性支出分类

Per Capita Living Expenditure over Years

单位：元

年 份	年人均消费性支出	食 品	衣 着	家庭设备用品及服务	医 疗保 健	交 通与通讯	教育文化娱乐服 务	居 住	其 他商 品和服务	恩格尔系 数(%)
1985	689	493	28	48	14	4	21	58	23	71.6
1986	883	588	43	84	15	6	46	66	35	66.6
1987	1174	709	64	128	55	9	106	79	24	60.4
1988	1583	977	64	171	22	12	124	136	77	61.7
1989	1980	1235	101	196	55	24	115	156	98	62.4
1990	2038	1295	95	153	42	25	113	184	131	63.5
1991	2481	1476	188	122	47	47	211	254	136	59.5
1992	3901	1834	259	263	94	587	331	369	164	47.0
1993	5533	2615	373	583	133	855	389	333	252	47.3
1994	7270	3172	420	925	192	850	714	761	236	43.6
1995	9220	3644	604	694	258	1562	991	1084	383	39.5
1996	8585	3682	706	660	225	990	847	674	802	42.9
1997	8309	3681	594	435	415	916	939	880	449	44.3
1998	8644	3785	457	612	455	1025	1074	659	577	43.8
1999	11348	3712	400	601	371	3398	1043	898	923	32.7
2000	12529	4048	487	623	431	3309	1517	1218	896	32.3
2001	14669	4572	648	746	513	4258	1429	1173	1330	31.2
2002	15157	4818	748	611	529	4303	2660	1060	428	31.8
2003	15446	4804	921	1093	693	2062	2512	2966	395	31.1
2004	18426	5041	1134	925	811	4973	2673	2517	352	27.4
2005	21768	6035	1285	1165	811	7482	3205	1242	543	27.7
2006	18995	6321	1238	1229	809	3531	3001	2341	525	33.3
2007	21545	6966	1213	1342	860	5208	3515	1903	538	32.3
2008	23208	7778	1349	1539	1332	4462	3464	2585	699	33.5
2009	24270	7972	1492	1616	1400	5456	3326	2232	776	32.8
2010	25733	8732	1706	1771	1294	5925	3443	2089	773	33.9
2011	27495	9513	1806	1902	1251	6035	3886	2128	974	34.6

11-12 不同收入等级年人均可支配收入与消费性支出水平

Per Capita Annual Disposable Income and Consumption Expenditure by Level of Income

单位：元

年 份	年人均可支配收入	#最低收入户	低收入户	高收入户	最高收入户	年人均消费性支出	#最低收入户	低收入户	高收入户	最高收入户
1985	791					689				
1986	1033					883				
1987	1247					1174				
1988	1778					1583				
1989	2282					1980				
1990	2508	1391	1744	3774	4546	2038	1170	1539	2099	4156
1991	3068	1665	2286	4092	4592	2481	1725	1877	2699	3784
1992	4026	2053	2650	5988	7275	3901	1966	2648	4690	6070
1993	5970	2977	4203	8484	9852	5533	3046	3685	6691	6956
1994	8270	4157	5248	12217	14265	7270	4477	5762	10839	8378
1995	9588	4539	5867	13828	18771	9220	4362	6912	12194	19353
1996	11639	5627	7142	15377	19224	8585	5152	6278	11496	10498
1997	11032	5778	7214	16496	22069	8309	5298	5963	15265	12323
1998	11506	6136	7853	16660	21591	8644	4888	6259	11774	14733
1999	12954	5998	7944	18951	23447	11348	4777	7755	18118	26001
2000	14142	6826	7806	19104	28769	12529	6706	7211	10297	25896
2001	16938	7174	10365	25167	33526	14669	6990	7425	18880	29834
2002	16949	6374	9398	23342	45001	15157	7224	8974	29735	21807
2003	18471	4535	9146	27000	48849	15446	6436	7990	25065	26683
2004	20526	8548	11658	31923	39058	18426	8047	9190	30530	45944
2005	22882	9590	13348	35885	43010	21768	10038	8908	31542	31498
2006	25320	13551	15633	37559	51957	18995	8841	11781	32568	39862
2007	27025	12073	16207	39071	55821	21545	12862	14547	31653	36732
2008	30275	11172	17340	46744	66034	23208	10927	14275	37741	53404
2009	33045	13642	19311	47680	71031	24270	12793	13654	27597	42949
2010	35690	18466	23384	48582	69968	25733	14073	15412	39674	46282
2011	39513	18405	22992	56246	86527	27495	13381	14980	43798	54008

注：本表分组数据采用城镇住户抽样调查按相对收入不等距九组分户汇总资料，下同。

11-13 主要年份城市居民家庭基本情况

Basic Conditions of Urban Households in Main Years

项　　目	单 位	1985年	1990年	1995年	2000年	2005年	2010年	2011年
一、调查户数	户	50	50	50	50	50	250	250
二、平均每户家庭人口	人	3.90	4.06	3.94	3.89	3.38	3.32	3.39
三、平均每户家庭就业人口	人	2.30	2.09	2.18	2.69	2.14	2.08	2.14
四、平均每一就业者负担人口	人	1.58	1.70	1.50	1.54	1.58	1.60	1.58
五、平均每人每年可支配收入	元	791	2508	9588	14142	22882	35690	39513
#工薪收入	元	603	1459	6260	8702	18524	26799	27272
六、平均每人每年消费性支出	元	689	2038	9220	12529	21768	25733	27495
(一)食　品	元	493	1295	3644	4048	6035	8732	9513
(二)衣　着	元	28	95	604	487	1285	1706	1806
(三)家庭设备用品及服务	元	48	153	694	623	1165	1771	1902
#耐用消费品	元	21	93	368	18	425	460	510
(四)医疗保健	元	14	42	258	431	811	1294	1251
(五)交通与通讯	元	4	25	1562	3309	7482	5925	6035
(六)娱乐教育文化服务	元	21	113	991	1517	3205	3443	3886
#文化娱乐用品	元	13	36	521	532	610	687	698
文化娱乐服务	元	5	37	173	286	1112	1691	1673
教　育	元	3	40	297	699	1482	1065	1515
(七)居　住	元	58	184	1084	1218	1242	2089	2128
(八)其他商品和服务	元	23	131	383	896	543	773	974
七、平均每人住房使用面积	平方米	10.98	16.61	20.00	31.13	42.68	44.05	49.44
八、平均每人每年购买商品								
1.粮　食	元	106	109	74	66	65	466	582
2.油脂类	元	5	5	7	8	8	121	129
3.肉禽及其制品	元	37	48	40	50	72	1692	1898
4.蛋　类	元	6	6	10	9	8	77	96
5.水产品	元	23	29	25	29	22	660	712
6.鲜　菜	元	90	100	117	116	114	591	582
7.烟草类	元	3	18	52	94	53	192	231
8.酒和饮料	元	16	25	48	78	132	324	410
9.干鲜瓜果	元	11	84	258	298	344	628	681
10.糕点、奶及奶制品	元		13	42	105	264	484	567
11.服　装	元	28	95	434	356	944	1297	1368

注：1. 工薪收入2002年以前为基本工资收入口径，2002年起为工薪收入口径。
2. 平均每人住房使用面积2002年以前为平均每人居住面积口径。
3. 粮食、油脂类、肉禽及其制品、蛋类、水产品、鲜菜2008年以前以公斤为计量单位。

11-14 主要年份城市居民人均消费性支出及构成

Consumption Expenditure of Urban Households in Main Years

项　　目	单位	1985年	1990年	1995年	2000年	2005年	2010年	2011年
一、年人均消费性支出	元	689	2038	9220	12529	21768	25733	27495
(一)食　品	元	493	1295	3644	4048	6035	8732	9513
(二)衣　着	元	28	95	604	487	1285	1706	1806
(三)家庭设备用品及服务	元	48	153	694	623	1165	1771	1902
#耐用消费品	元	21	93	368	18	425	460	510
(四)医疗保健	元	14	42	258	431	811	1294	1251
#药品费	元			109	240	276	466	407
滋补保健品	元			46	178	207	434	414
(五)交通与通讯	元	4	25	1562	3309	7482	5925	6035
交通	元	4	25	1245	2154	6381	4473	4605
通讯	元			317	1155	1101	1452	1430
(六)娱乐教育文化服务	元	21	113	991	1517	3205	3443	3886
文化娱乐用品	元	13	36	521	532	610	687	698
文化娱乐服务	元	5	37	173	286	1112	1691	1673
教　育	元	3	40	297	699	1482	1065	1515
(七)居　住	元	58	184	1084	1218	1242	2089	2128
#住房	元	7	92	725	455	34	482	409
水电燃料	元	51	92	358	763	972	1299	1411
(八)其他商品和服务	元	23	131	383	896	543	773	974
二、消费性支出构成								
(一)食　品	%	71.55	63.54	39.52	32.31	27.72	33.93	34.60
(二)衣　着	%	4.06	4.66	6.55	3.89	5.90	6.63	6.57
(三)家庭设备用品及服务	%	6.97	7.51	7.53	4.97	5.35	6.88	6.92
#耐用消费品	%	43.76	60.78	53.03	2.89	1.95	1.79	1.85
(四)医疗保健	%	2.03	2.06	2.80	3.44	3.73	5.03	4.55
(五)交通与通讯	%	0.58	1.23	16.94	26.41	34.37	23.02	21.95
(六)娱乐教育文化服务	%	3.05	5.54	10.75	12.11	14.72	13.38	14.13
(七)居　住	%	8.42	9.03	11.76	9.72	5.71	8.12	7.74
(八)其他商品和服务	%	3.34	6.43	4.15	7.15	2.50	3.00	3.54

11-15 历年城市居民家庭平均每百户主要耐用消费品拥有量

Ownership of Durable Consumer Goods Owned per 100 Urban Households over Years

年 份	汽车 (辆)	电冰箱 (台)	洗衣机 (台)	空调器 (台)	组合音响 (套)	彩色电视机 (台)	电话机 (部)	移动电话 (部)	电脑 (台)
1985		22	56			22			
1986		26	66			40			
1987		42	72			52			
1988		52	86			66			
1989		72	96		4	84			
1990		84	54	16	14	92			
1991		98	106	16	14	100			
1992		96	112	12	18	98	64		
1993		108	108	28	34	102	60		
1994		110	114	60	52	114	72		
1995		110	108	82	54	138	82		
1996		104	110	128	68	132	98		
1997		106	108	100	68	116	98		22
1998	2	110	112	122	64	146	96	28	28
1999	10	116	118	130	84	178	100	72	34
2000	12	108	114	150	88	178	100	126	68
2001	16	118	110	184	76	176	100	186	98
2002	24	126	112	204	76	192	100	200	102
2003	26	134	108	226	82	194	104	224	96
2004	32	132	118	258	80	192	112	264	108
2005	42	124	110	264	72	200	112	294	114
2006	44	130	112	280	80	218	116	298	112
2007	54	115	110	271	82	206	115	272	111
2008	47	110	103	200	59	180	108	248	100
2009	63	113	105	233	69	184	105	261	112
2010	68	118	107	259	68	186	110	267	129
2011	80	117	112	272	72	187	106	280	136

11-16 按收入等级分的城市居民家庭基本情况(2011年)

Basic Conditions of Urban Households by Level of Income (2011)

项　　目	单位	总平均	最低收入户	低收入户	中等偏下户	中等收入户	中等偏上户	高收入户	最高收入户
调查户数	户	250	25	25	50	50	50	25	25
平均每户家庭人口	人	3.39	3.79	3.54	3.59	3.22	3.41	3.14	2.97
平均每户家庭就业人口	人	2.14	1.95	2.04	2.16	2.11	2.36	2.10	2.04
平均每一就业者负担人口	人	1.58	1.94	1.74	1.66	1.53	1.44	1.50	1.46
平均每户就业面	%	63.13	51.45	57.63	60.17	65.53	69.21	66.88	68.69
平均每人总收入	元	43202	20609	24894	31152	40287	51135	61647	93699
平均每人可支配收入	元	39513	18405	22992	28759	36516	46637	56246	86527
平均每人总支出	元	34978	15950	19308	22756	32454	42862	53557	77307
平均每人消费性支出	元	27495	13381	14980	19131	26021	33641	43798	54008
平均每一就业者总收入	元	68437	40056	43198	51775	61481	73886	92177	136415
平均每人住房建筑面积	平方米	65.75	57.14	53.26	66.03	59.23	67.95	79.95	85.32
平均每百户家庭年末主要耐用消费品拥有量									
家用汽车	辆	80	20	40	68	72	102	124	132
洗衣机	台	112	100	96	114	112	118	116	124
电冰箱	台	117	104	100	114	112	124	128	140
彩色电视机	台	187	144	164	176	174	208	192	256
家用电脑	台	136	112	104	132	126	142	168	176
组合音响	套	72	56	60	60	76	90	68	84
照相机	架	82	40	52	72	88	98	88	120
钢琴	架	4	4		4	2	4	8	8
空调器	台	272	196	204	248	246	310	312	396
淋浴热水器	台	138	116	132	146	122	138	148	176
消毒碗柜	台	80	72	64	74	68	100	76	100
健身器材	套	14	28		10	14	16	12	16
固定电话	部	106	100	100	106	104	112	100	116
移动电话	部	280	280	292	274	268	288	284	288

11-17 按收入等级分的城市居民家庭平均每人全年现金收入(2011年)

Per Capita Annual Cash Income of Urban Households by Level of Income (2011)

项目	单位	总平均	最低收入户	低收入户	中等偏下户	中等收入户	中等偏上户	高收入户	最高收入户
一、平均每户家庭就业人口	人	2.14	1.95	2.04	2.16	2.11	2.36	2.10	2.04
#国有单位职工人数	人	0.33	0.21	0.09	0.12	0.34	0.45	0.53	0.72
集体单位职工人数	人	0.47	0.51	0.32	0.55	0.48	0.54	0.30	0.45
其它各类经济类型单位职工人数	人	0.40	0.47	0.61	0.38	0.36	0.33	0.40	0.34
个体雇主与自营者人数	人	0.22	0.14	0.19	0.10	0.20	0.30	0.35	0.32
个体被雇人员数	人	0.54	0.49	0.80	0.68	0.58	0.57	0.32	0.12
其他就业人员人数	人	0.15	0.12	0.04	0.30	0.11	0.16	0.08	0.08
二、家庭总收入	元	43202	20609	24894	31152	40287	51135	61647	93699
#可支配收入	元	39513	18405	22992	28759	36516	46637	56246	86527
#工资性收入	元	27272	14307	15906	20990	26613	33089	35742	52576
#工资及补贴收入	元	27033	14231	15803	20683	26553	32921	35615	51459
经营净收入	元	4075	1241	2035	1239	3126	5721	8401	11221
财产性收入	元	7481	3003	3841	6116	5907	8760	12082	16869
#股息与红利收入	元	3009	1609	2815	2994	2614	3785	5009	2154
租金收入	元	3650	1349	851	2993	2866	4456	5786	9255
转移性收入	元	4374	2058	3112	2807	4641	3565	5422	13033
#离退休金	元	1963	1331	1797	1416	2694	1497	2211	3562
赠送收入	元	1210	235	433	643	1243	1171	1869	4161

11-18 城市居民家庭平均每人全年消费性支出（2011年）

Per Capita Annual Consumption Expenditure of Urban Households (2011)

项目	单位	总平均	最低收入户	低收入户	中等偏下户	中等收入户	中等偏上户	高收入户	最高收入户
平均每人年消费性支出	元	27495	13381	14980	19131	26021	33641	43798	54008
(一)食　品	元	9513	6144	7735	7802	8827	11546	12856	13722
粮油类	元	798	605	746	733	726	876	902	1150
肉禽蛋水产品类	元	2705	2072	2698	2576	2514	3047	3058	3146
#水产品	元	712	512	699	683	657	801	810	875
蔬菜类	元	654	510	657	641	593	740	760	697
调味品	元	85	64	88	88	74	87	101	110
糖烟酒饮料类	元	707	515	659	584	521	961	941	915
干鲜瓜果类	元	681	463	704	581	654	837	806	767
糕点、奶及奶制品	元	567	381	543	524	624	610	679	608
其他食品	元	52	37	49	40	45	58	75	84
在外用餐和饮食服务	元	3264	1497	1591	2035	3076	4330	5534	6245
(二)衣　着	元	1806	799	929	1155	1594	2319	3357	3490
#服　装	元	1368	608	766	857	1191	1807	2416	2663
(三)居　住	元	2128	1236	1430	1739	2227	2896	2623	2577
#住房	元	409	38	39	223	592	907	434	197
水电、燃料及其它	元	1411	1078	1303	1370	1361	1550	1675	1600
(四)家庭设备用品及服务	元	1902	1125	1211	1173	1706	2196	3203	3999
#耐用消费品	元	510	152	82	289	631	419	772	1698
(五)医疗保健	元	1251	703	631	1149	1269	1144	1784	2605
#药品费	元	407	306	181	329	527	354	500	754
滋补保健品	元	414	128	156	349	354	438	721	1021
(六)交通与通讯	元	6035	1351	1677	2921	6445	7524	10076	16580
交通	元	4605	424	716	1811	5163	5744	7875	14404
通讯	元	1430	927	961	1110	1282	1780	2201	2176
(七)教育文化娱乐服务	元	3886	1764	1119	2813	3253	4493	7359	9047
文化娱乐用品	元	698	270	203	589	714	738	1051	1613
文化娱乐服务	元	1673	295	365	921	1468	2312	4301	3197
教育	元	1515	1199	551	1303	1071	1443	2007	4237
(八)其他商品和服务	元	974	259	248	379	700	1523	2540	1988

11-19 农村居民人均实际收入与实际支出（2006-2011年）

Per Capita Actual Income and Expenditure of Rural Households (2006-2011)

单位：元

年 份	家庭现金收入	#纯收入	家庭现金支出	#生活消费现金支出	#食品消费支出
2006	17676	14313	12173	9370	3380
2007	19945	15747	13078	10771	3805
2008	20622	16904	13154	10887	3823
2009	22077	18098	14643	10598	3711
2010	22537	20486	16245	11842	4447
2011	26460	22842	18061	14055	5313

11-20 农村居民人均实际收入（2006-2011年）

Per Capita Actual Income of Rural Households (2006-2011)

单位：元

年 份	家庭现金收 入	#工资性收入	家庭经营收入	财产性收入	转移性收入
2006	17676	8522	4195	4171	789
2007	19945	9446	4388	5191	920
2008	20622	9876	4326	5531	889
2009	22077	10442	4517	6210	908
2010	22537	11201	3629	6402	1305
2011	26460	13254	4150	7232	1822

11-21 农村居民人均消费支出（2006-2011年）

Per Capita Consumption Expenditure of Rural Households (2006-2011)

单位：元

年　份	生活消费现金支　出	#食品	衣着	家庭设备及 服 务	医疗保健	交通通讯	教育文化娱乐服务	居住	杂项商品和 服 务
2006	9370	3380	448	474	510	1543	932	1458	625
2007	10771	3805	602	581	494	1953	1029	2001	306
2008	10887	3823	691	622	545	1799	1198	1500	709
2009	10598	3711	633	471	565	1764	1223	1485	746
2010	11842	4447	627	480	569	2120	1082	1877	640
2011	14055	5313	655	574	665	2698	1225	2345	580

11-22 每百户农村居民家庭主要耐用消费品拥有量（2006-2011年）

Ownership of Durable Consumer Goods Owned per 100 Rural Households (2006-2011)

项目	单位	2006年	2007年	2008年	2009年	2010年	2011年
洗衣机	台	101	105	107	103	106	107
电冰箱	台	108	111	111	109	110	112
空调机	台	210	223	234	209	218	223
微波炉	台	37	45	50	46	46	48
热水器	台	137	143	142	129	132	133
摩托车	辆	134	95	84	83	87	89
生活用汽车	辆	49	59	67	53	57	61
固定电话机	部	139	137	137	122	120	121
移动电话	部	240	251	261	257	268	276
彩色电视机	台	175	178	183	160	164	167
影碟机	台	92	95	95	74	71	69
摄像机	台	15	17	21	13	17	17
照相机	架	54	59	64	53	55	58
家庭计算机	台	84	97	107	98	104	108
中高档乐器	件	8	9	10	10	11	12

主要统计指标解释

Explanatory Notes on Main Statistical Indicators

城市居民家庭可支配收入 指调查户可用于最终消费支出和其它非义务性支出以及储蓄的总和，即居民家庭可以用来自由支配的收入。它是家庭总收入扣除交纳的个人所得税、个人交纳的社会保障支出以及调查户的记账补贴后的收入。计算公式为：

可支配收入=家庭总收入-交纳个人所得税-个人交纳的社会保障支出-记账补贴

城市居民家庭消费性支出 指调查户用于本家庭日常生活的全部支出，包括食品、衣着、家庭设备用品及服务、医疗保健、交通和通讯、娱乐教育文化服务、居住、其他商品和服务八大类等，均按商品（服务）的用途分类。

农村居民家庭总收入 是指农村住户年内从各种来源得到的全部实际收入（包括现金收入和实物收入）。由基本收入、转移性收入和财产性收入三部分组成。

农村居民家庭纯收入 是农村常住居民家庭总收入扣除相应的各项费用性支出后，归农民所有的收入。它既可以用于生产、非生产投资、改善物质和文化生活，以及用于再分配的支出和结余的收入。这个指标用来观察农民实际收入水平，以及农民扩大再生产和改善生活的能力。

农村居民家庭生活费支出 是指农民住户年内用于物质生活和精神生活方面的实际支出，直接反映农民的生活水平、研究农民消费结构变化的基本指标。生活消费支出包括食品，衣着、居住，家庭设备，用品及服务，医疗保健，交通和通讯，文化教育娱乐用品及服务，其他商品和服务等消费支出。

单位从业人员劳动报酬 指各单位在一定时期内直接支付给本单位在岗职工的工资总额和其他从业人员的劳动报酬。

在岗职工工资总额 指各单位在一定时期内直接支付给本单位在岗职工的劳动报酬总额。

职工工资总额 指各单位在一定时期内直接支付给本单位在岗职工的工资总额和不在岗职工（离岗职工）的生活费。

单位从业人员劳动报酬和职工工资总额的计算原则应以直接支付给职工的全部劳动报酬为根据。各单位支付给职工的劳动报酬以及其他根据有关规定支付的工资，不论是计入成本的还是不计入成本的，不论是按国家规定列入计征奖金税项目的，还是未列入计征奖金税项目的，不论是以货币形式支付的还是以实物形式支付的，均包括在内。

职工平均工资 指企业、事业、机关单位的职工在一定时期内平均每人所得的货币工资额。它表明一定时期职工工资收入的高低程度，是反映职工工资水平的主要指标。计算公式为：职工平均工资=报告期实际支付全部职工工资总额/报告期全部职工平均人数

职工平均实际工资 指扣除物价变动因素后职工平均工资。计算公式为：

职工平均实际工资=报告期职工平均工资/报告期城镇居民消费价格指数

十二、社会事业

Social Undertakings

12-1 主要年份社会事业主要指标

Main Indicators of Social Undertakings in Main Years

项　　目	单位	1985年	1990年	1995年	2000年	2005年	2010年	2011年
国有企事业单位科学技术人员数	人	9166	11629	16856		42593	40025	41370
三种专利申请量	件		34	325	1653	6694	21654	24455
三种专利授权量	件		30	262	1399	3114	20397	19353
各类技术合同签订项目数	项		5	46	110	50	90	163
各类技术合同签订项目金额	万元		12	1804	3469	4058	18366	31966
在校学生数								
普通高等学校	人			1628	3241	16645	38293	45081
成人高等学校	人	403	531	1254	3642	12665	21703	20497
中等职业技术学校	人	3363	8919	18737	23144	29487	47531	48159
普通中学	人	46596	61188	92481	112418	191044	258276	263076
小学	人	134421	162664	195063	272793	480923	552377	578279
学龄儿童入学率	%	99.8	99.9	100.0	100.0	100.0	100.0	100.0
小学毕业生升学率	%	79.5	95.4	99.2	99.8	99.9	100.0	100.0
初中毕业生升学率	%	38.5	43.6	85.4	90.3	94.1	97.9	98.0
普通高中毕业生升学率	%	26.5	31.2	64.9	70.5	96.5	95.1	94.5
高考省线入围人数	人	285	224	809	2646	11196	13761	15501
电影放映单位	个	60	114	218	192	70	46	52
艺术表演团体	个	1	7	2	1		4	5
文化馆(群众艺术馆)	个	1	1	1	1	1	1	1
公共图书馆(室)	个	3	5	15	18	473	505	622
博物馆	个	2	2	2	3	16	30	31
档案馆	个	1	1	1	1	1	1	1
《东莞日报》发行量	万份		177	987	1578	2751	4563	3132
广播电台	座		1	1	1	1	1	1
电视台	座	1	1	1	1	1	1	1
病床床位数	张	2323	3866	5798	7081	11972	19980	22814
卫生技术人员数	人	3305	3902	5290	6915	16608	37487	39582
#执业(助理)医师	人	1201	1721	2299	3309	6901	13214	13644
举办镇街级及以上体育运动会	次	72	114	14	5	8	58	57
参加运动会的运动员人数	万人次	3.60	6.38	5.15	1.70	1.36	10.18	9.19
执业律师人数	人	6	12	85	130	625	1366	1513
公证人员数	人	6	10	19	20	48	96	106
人民调解委员会调解人员数	人	3603	3664	3664	3644	4556	17438	20240
优抚收养单位收养人数	人		19	11	7	8	8	9
工业固体废物综合利用率	%	37.5	17.9	18.2	63.8	86.5	95.0	77.9
城市环境空气质量优良天数	天						357	358

注：1. 2010年起，国有企事业单位科学技术人员数只统计在编在岗人员数，因此与往年不可比。
2. 中等职业技术学校包含市技工学校，不含一般成人中专。
3. 2004年起，卫生方面包含诊所、卫生所、医务室及村卫生室的数据，与往年数不可比。

12-2 科技活动基本情况(2011年)

Basic Statistics on Scientific and Technological Activities (2011)

项　目	单位	2011年
一、科技企业		
企业数	个	3881
#国家高新技术企业	个	415
省创新型试点企业	个	19
省创新型企业	个	10
省创新百强企业	个	8
省民营科技企业	个	852
重点培育上市后备科技企业	个	69
市民营科技企业	个	2508
二、科技合作		
国际合作项目立项数	项	5
#国家立项数	项	2
省级立项数	项	3
国际科技合作示范基地	个	10
#国家级基地	个	2
省级基地	个	8
产学研项目立项数	项	85
#省部合作	项	74
省院合作	项	11
总投入	万元	88488
资助金额	万元	5445
市配套金额	万元	
省部产学研示范基地	个	30
省部产学研创新联盟	个	8
三、科技机构		
机构数	个	45
从业人员	人	5534
#科技活动人员	人	4543
#本科及以上	人	2853
#中级及以上职称	人	
科技经费筹集额	万元	110264
#政府拨款	万元	69597
企业自筹	万元	38177
科技经费内部支出	万元	111723
项目(课题)数	项	273
项目(课题)经费支出额	万元	40251
论文数	篇	182
科技专著数	篇	3
专利申请数	件	234
获专利授权数	件	98
营业收入	万元	135316
四、科技园区和基地		
国家级高新区	个	1
省级高新区	个	
专业镇	个	18
#工业总产值	万元	50006624
专业镇科技投入	万元	215666
国家高新技术企业数	家	185
火炬计划特色产业基地	个	8
#工业总产值	万元	13448779
国家高新技术企业数	家	96
科技企业孵化器/加速器	个	6
#建筑场地面积	万平方米	23.54
在孵企业数	个	367
毕业企业数	个	59
五、工程中心		
国家级工程中心	个	1
省级工程中心	个	42
#工程中心职工总数	人	8328
经费收入	万元	134145
研究开发课题(项目)	项	486
专利授权数	项	594
研究与发展(R&D)人员	人	5442
研究与发展经费	万元	98343
市级工程中心	个	80
#工程中心职工总数	人	11821
经费收入	万元	183111
研究开发课题(项目)	项	837
专利授权数	项	788
研究与发展(R&D)人员	人	11041
研究与发展经费	万元	174074
六、科技金融		
科技贷款机构	个	
上市后备企业	个	58
创业风险机构	个	14

12-3 研究与试验发展(R&D)基本情况(2009-2011年)

Basic Statistics on Research and Development (R&D)(2009-2011)

指标	单位	2009年	2010年	2011年
R&D活动单位数	个	496	492	495
#规上工业企业	个	439	436	428
R&D研究机构数	个	454	414	482
#规上工业企业办机构	个	429	376	468
R&D项目(课题)数	个	2508	2583	3208
#规上工业企业	个	1992	1955	2448
R&D活动人员数	人	31334	38330	45123
#规上工业企业	人	28974	36064	39400
#女性	人	6356	7148	7936
R&D人员折合全时当量合计	人年	18524	27809	36038
#研究人员	人年	3502	5161	6558
R&D经费内部支出	万元	413840	516701	716221
按执行部门分				
规上工业企业	万元	390728	495099	612516
科研机构	万元	14211	12166	92239
高等院校	万元	3542	3528	5556
其他企事业单位	万元	5358	5908	5909
按活动类型分				
基础研究	万元	501	691	50653
应用研究	万元	9572	18253	18719
试验发展	万元	403766	497757	646850
按资金来源分				
政府资金	万元	22055	31237	85894
企业资金	万元	374463	463927	613432
境外资金	万元	6703	10021	3083
其他资金	万元	10619	11516	13810
按使用项目分				
日常性支出	万元	363143	433603	539954
#人员劳务费	万元	150423	179325	225151
资产性支出	万元	50697	83097	176266
#仪器设备	万元	48888	76774	123662
R&D经费内部支出占GDP比重	%	1.10	1.22	1.51
R&D经费外部支出	万元	15362	12383	14921
R&D产出情况				
专利申请数	件	4932	4994	6060
#发明专利	件	911	1433	1323
专利授权数	件	164	205	112
#发明专利	件	16	25	25
有效发明专利数	件	828	2044	3457
专利所有权转让及许可数	件	228	170	552
专利所有权转让及许可收入	万元	3216	9572	16763
集成电路布图设计登记数	件			
植物新品种权授予数	项	1	2	
形成国家或行业标准数	项	141	181	63
发表科技论文数	篇	1242	1205	1266
出版科技著作数	种	32	26	31
工业新产品产值	万元	3041803	5501675	6945494
工业新产品销售收入	万元	3019395	5391190	6373687

12-4 主要年份国有企事业单位科学技术人员

Scientific and Technical Personnel in State-owned Enterprises and Institutions in Main Years

单位：人

项　　目	1990年	1995年	2002年	2004年	2005年	2010年	2011年
国有企事业单位科技人员数	11629	16856	28154	39398	42593	40025	41370
#工程技术人员	1084	1718	1651	1752	1839	1438	1427
农业技术人员	432	230	183	276	290	172	216
卫生技术人员	1430	1988	6155	14541	16188	11171	11117
科学研究人员	21	52	19	141	77	16	21
教学人员	7524	11553	18599	20905	21717	24010	25084
经济人员	278	329	555	561	636	1184	1393
会计人员	581	484	500	613	1299	1454	1426
统计人员	170	77	70	74	82	91	90

注：2010年国有企事业单位科技人员为在编在岗人员数。

12-5 主要年份三种专利申请量与授权量

Three Kinds of Patents Application Accepted and Granted in Main Years

单位：件

项　　目	1990年	1995年	1999年	2000年	2002年	2004年	2005年	2010年	2011年
一、申请量	34	325	1221	1653	3100	4325	6694	21654	24455
发　明	1	5	15	35	90	185	245	3143	4214
实用新型	5	70	305	386	937	1523	1971	7677	10822
外观设计	28	250	901	1232	2073	2617	4478	10834	9419
二、授权量	30	262	819	1399	2680	3167	3114	20397	19353
发　明	1	8	16	4	10	26	24	442	758
实用新型	4	41	157	344	669	919	1116	7529	7977
外观设计	25	213	646	1051	2001	2222	1974	12426	10618

12-6 主要年份各类技术合同签订情况

Basic Statistics on Technical Contracts Signed by Type in Main Years

项　　目	1990年	1995年	1999年	2000年	2002年	2004年	2005年	2010年	2011年
一、技术合同项目数(项)	5	46	20	110	91	69	50	90	163
#技术开发合同	3			1	5	62	41	79	126
技术咨询合同							2		1
技术转让合同	2	44	20	78	81	6	1	2	6
技术服务合同		2		31	5	1	6	9	30
二、技术合同金额(万元)	12	1804	1124	3469	766	4278	4058	18366	31966
#技术开发合同				1000	110	4175	1888	6878	14984
技术咨询合同			1124				80		8
技术转让合同	12	1656		2007	637	91	2000	11046	16403
技术服务合同		148		1362	19	13	90	442	572
三、技术合同实现金额(万元)	7	1623	1077	2398	730	2726	2522	17891	29923
#技术开发合同				700	110	2623	1427	6402	13962
技术咨询合同							35		8
技术转让合同	7	1535	1077	1260	601	91	1000	11046	15381
技术服务合同		88		438	19	13	60	442	572

12-7 主要年份高新科技发展情况

Basic Statistics on High-tech Development in Main Years

项　　目	单 位	1995年	1999年	2000年	2002年	2004年	2005年	2010年	2011年
一、高新技术企业									
企业数	个	11	53	66	102	201	247	334	412
总产值	亿元	30.55	215.00	274.41	405.32	690.00	925.07	1240.59	1214.43
总收入	亿元	26.76	213.00	266.49	409.93	691.00	927.72	1249.50	1261.27
出口总额	亿美元	0.54	14.40	7.34	20.16	45.00	71.59	99.08	94.71
从业人员数	人	6400	29840	36304	50955	107541	171812	246134	227920
#科技活动人员	人	832	6424	8663	14426	26885	34448	72833	53259
二、高新技术产品									
产品	个	27	159	177	619	668	947	1430	1250
总产值	亿元	31.43	144.00	186.00	430.23	711.11	1062.40	2353.70	2756.86
#电子与信息技术	亿元				289.99	355.63	726.92	1407.39	1650.06
生物技术	亿元				3.63	8.45	8.20	51.93	20.01
新材料技术	亿元				22.80	34.48	51.43	115.46	101.25
光机电一体化技术	亿元				54.05	91.36	146.94	153.74	149.51
新能源高效节能技术	亿元				4.80	11.40	32.71	95.52	124.77
环保技术	亿元				0.53	1.07	6.58	4.95	13.58
其他	亿元				54.43	208.71	89.63	524.70	697.67

注：1. 高新技术企业情况2009年以前为省级高新技术企业情况，2009年起为国家级高新技术企业情况。
2. 高新技术产品情况从2010年起，统计口径为规模以上工业企业。

12-8 主要年份科学技术成果项数

Achievements for Scientific and Technological Research in Main Years

单位：项

项 目	1985年	1990年	1995年	1999年	2000年	2002年	2004年	2005年	2010年	2011年
获省级科技进步奖		1	4	9	6	3	6	3	8	13
市级科技进步奖	68	31	22	39	47	47	60	75	87	84
1. 农业方面	30	8	3	11	13	4	10	9	7	7
一等奖	1	4		1	2		1	1	2	2
二等奖	3	3		3	5	3	2	3	2	2
三等奖	18	1	3	6	6	1	7	5	3	3
四等奖	8									
2. 工业方面	32	18	14	19	24	23	27	42	57	46
特等奖					1		1	2		
一等奖	1	3		3	5	4	4	7	13	12
二等奖	8	11	5	8	8	6	11	19	21	17
三等奖	10	4	9	8	10	13	11	14	23	17
四等奖	13									
3. 医药卫生方面	6	5	5	5	10	20	22	25	23	24
特等奖										
一等奖			1	1		3	1		5	7
二等奖		1			2	6	6	4	6	11
三等奖	2	4	4	4	8	11	15	19	12	6
四等奖	4									
市长奖									5	7
技术成果类									1	1
荣誉类									4	2
创新企业奖									4	4

12-9 科技创新平台情况（2010-2011年）

Basic Statistics on Technology Innovation Platform (2010-2011)

单位：个

项 目	2010年	2011年
科技创新平台合计	207	224
#公共科技创新平台	10	11
行业性科技创新平台	34	30
#行业性科技创新平台(企业研究院)	11	12
专业镇技术创新平台	15	12
科技行业技术联盟	8	6
企业创新平台	125	124
#企业工程技术研究开发中心	125	124
#国家级	1	2
省级	40	42
市级	84	80
实验室	28	59
#国家级		
省级	5	9
市级	23	50
#重点实验室		31
资助获中国合格评定国家认可委员会认可实验室	10	19

12-10 历年国有企事业单位科学技术人员数

Scientific and Technical Personnel in Enterprises and Institutions over Years

单位：人

年份	科学技术人员	工程技术人员	农业技术人员	卫生技术人员	科学研究人员	教学人员	经济人员	会计人员	统计人员
1980	6619	370	190	1076	19	4282		564	99
1981	7473	463	217	1166	23	4978		501	109
1982	7547	468	243	1241	28	4954		509	101
1983	8453	525	315	1699		5257		109	109
1984	9033	615	307	1791		5534		261	201
1985	9166	663	318	2319	6	5129		491	214
1986	9490	768	358	2398	5	5222		501	203
1987	10945	797	378	2426	6	6495		583	222
1988	12495	1014	359	3093	24	7064	72	590	197
1989	11306	960	388	1393	19	7394	281	632	181
1990	11629	1084	432	1430	21	7524	278	581	170
1991	15004	2170	405	3347	13	7843	308	558	153
1992	16809	2522	375	3690	18	8659	313	613	153
1993	18491	2871	264	4074	112	9511	290	916	141
1994	20198	3490	272	4513	57	9949	300	657	112
1995	23104	3944	255	4878	66	11613	329	750	171
1996	24693	4037	263	5356	51	12287	360	740	143
1997	26103	4258	294	5504	48	13371	418	882	280
1998	26582	4321	310	4862	48	14316	376	894	171
1999	28789	4620	288	5246	48	15604	416	946	152
2000									
2001	24677	795	121	5493	31	17309	252	273	40
2002	34168	5261	246	6538	28	18756	555	1319	184
2003	33070	996	159	11145	44	19614	314	741	57
2004	39398	1752	276	14541	141	20905	561	613	74
2005	42593	1839	290	16188	77	21717	636	1299	82
2006	46371	1913	462	18401	70	22434	763	1512	93
2007	49032	2037	492	19528	71	23364	892	1832	92
2008	51729	2375	343	20955	50	24063	1048	1827	100
2009	55097	2302	284	21679	43	26741	1129	1940	122
2010	40025	1438	172	11171	16	24010	1184	1454	91
2011	41370	1427	216	11117	21	25084	1393	1426	90

注：2010年起为在编在岗人员数。

12-11 历年三种专利与技术合同签订情况

Basic Statistics on Three Kinds of Patents and Technical Contracts Signed by Type over Years

年 份	三种专利申请量（件）	#发明	三种专利授权量（件）	#发明	技术合同签订项目数（项）	技术合同签订金额（万元）	技术合同实现金额（万元）
1990	34	1	30	1	5	12	7
1991	70	3	50	1	4	10	10
1992	102	5	78	2	3	23	10
1993	100	3	90	1	2	24	2
1994	104	4	100	2	14	2537	1756
1995	325	5	262	8	46	1804	1623
1996	333	3	312	4	133	4839	3756
1997	725	1	321		78	2036	800
1998					62	3048	2398
1999					20	1124	1077
2000	1653	35	1399	4	110	3469	2398
2001	2914	71	1753	5	89	1335	953
2002	3100	90	2680	10	91	766	730
2003	3865	93	2858	14	58	700	680
2004	4325	185	3167	26	69	4278	2726
2005	6694	245	3114	24	50	4058	2522
2006	9879	553	4872	28	25	13644	13402
2007	13842	876	6752	44	53	8510	8138
2008	14406	1188	8093	115	54	12838	3694
2009	19106	1593	12918	254	60	6996	6264
2010	21654	3143	20397	442	70	15760	15572
2011	24455	4214	19353	758	163	31966	29923

12-12 历年科学技术成果项数

Scientific and Technological Achievements over Years

单位：项

年 份	获国家级科技进步奖	获省级科技进步奖	获市级科技进步奖	特等奖	一等奖	二等奖	三等奖	四等奖
1979			25			5	4	16
1980			27			2	11	14
1981			35		2	4	11	18
1982			62		1	3	21	37
1983			38		2	6	11	19
1984			35			11	11	13
1985			68		2	11	30	25
1986			86		5	14	27	40
1987			59		2	19	25	13
1988		1	37		6	10	16	5
1989		1	32		4	6	22	
1990		1	31		7	15	9	
1991		4	35	1	3	18	13	
1992		3	19		4	7	8	
1993			18	1	3	8	6	
1994		6	23		4	9	10	
1995		4	22		1	5	16	
1996		3	32		7	6	19	
1997		4	32		7	6	19	
1998		6	38	1	2	11	24	
1999		9	39		6	11	22	
2000		6	47	1	7	15	24	
2001		4	51		4	23	24	
2002		3	47		7	15	25	
2003		4	50		7	14	29	
2004		6	60	1	6	19	34	
2005		3	75	2	10	25	38	
2006		3	70	1	8	24	37	
2007		4	83	1	18	26	38	
2008		10	83		19	28	36	
2009		19	85		22	24	39	
2010		4	87		20	29	38	
2011		13	77		21	30	26	

12-13 主要年份各类学校情况

Basic Statistics on Schools by Type in Main Years

项目	单位	1985年	1990年	1995年	2000年	2005年	2010年	2011年
一、普通高等专业学校								
学校数	所			1	1	4	5	6
毕业生数	人			395	985	1439	8105	9463
招生数	人			576	1440	7273	12660	16837
在校学生数	人			1628	3241	16645	38293	45081
教职工数	人			262	293	1761	3192	3542
#专任教师	人			119	161	1081	2174	2435
二、中等职业技术学校								
学校数	所	3	17	20	23	21	26	26
毕业生数	人	234	2210	4641	9554	9062	14028	14774
招生数	人	1508	3866	8697	8759	10971	18477	17812
在校学生数	人	3363	8919	18737	23144	29487	47531	48159
教职员工数	人	217	619	1134	1608	2230	2996	3048
#专任教师	人	150	434	859	1221	1621	2341	2403
三、普通中学								
学校数	所	106	64	69	77	134	190	199
毕业生数	人	12317	18688	24165	30261	48935	73810	76816
#高中生	人	2055	2527	3231	7120	12233	20816	22095
招生数	人	16978	20441	33086	41488	70843	93196	95155
#高中生	个	2915	3389	6099	9048	19540	24668	25647
在校学生数	人	46596	61188	92481	112418	191044	258276	263076
#高中生	人	6304	8572	13653	24677	52283	70398	73644
教职员工数	人	3266	4001	5900	6012	12177	16946	19563
#专任教师	个	2420	2963	4381	5027	9640	14572	15262
四、小学								
学校数	所	583	570	595	552	414	330	324
毕业生数	人	17901	18262	27257	33684	61173	77429	80463
招生数	人	20264	26158	36702	53786	84784	108900	114763
在校学生数	人	134421	162664	195063	272793	480923	552377	578279
教职员工数	人	7009	7797	9560	9131	21964	28298	28420
#专任教师	人	6017	6785	8060	7946	17478	23733	24787

注：中等职业技术学校包含市技工学校，不含一般成人中专，下同。

12-13 续表

项　　目	单位	1985年	1990年	1995年	2000年	2005年	2010年	2011年
五、成人高等专业教育								
当年招生人数	人				1697	6387	6086	6345
在校学生数	人	403	531	1254	3642	12665	21703	20497
#广播电视大学	人	403	531	1254	1362	4169		
六、学龄儿童入学								
学龄儿童总数	人	103460	133011	177791	247555	423058	511439	539286
已入学学龄儿童数	人	103282	132934	177787	247539	423058	511439	539286
学龄儿童入学率	%	99.8	99.9	100.0	100.0	100.0	100.0	100.0
七、小学毕业生升学								
小学毕业生人数	人	17901	18262	27257	33684	61173	77429	80463
已升学人数	人	14235	17413	27166	33627	61095	77429	80463
小学毕业生升学率	%	79.5	95.4	99.2	99.8	99.9	100.0	100.0
八、初中毕业生升学								
初中毕业生人数	人	10262	16161	20933	23141	36702	52994	54721
已升学人数	人	3955	7134	17876	20896	34536	51881	53626
初中毕业生升学率	%	38.5	43.6	85.4	90.3	94.1	97.9	98.0
九、普通高中毕业生升学								
高考省线入围人数	人	285	224	809	2646	6455	13761	15501
高考录取人数	人	543	759	2095	5017	12461	20099	21358
#高考升本科人数	人	274	250	697	1678	5161	11033	11901
普通高中毕业生升学率	%	26.5	31.2	64.9	70.5	96.5	95.1	94.5
十、幼儿园								
幼儿园数	所	83	86	258	452	511	727	749
在园幼儿数	人	31382	47040	84263	111763	111330	208373	227656
幼教职工数	人	984	1387	1427	7517	12567	22122	26242
#专任教师	人	841	1160	1160	4618	7002	13947	15232
十一、全国各类大中专院校招生人数								
国家各大(学)专院校在我市招生人数	人				11680	35831	40795	43161
国家各中专学校在我市招生人数	人				3359	2768		
全市教育经费投入总额	亿元				15.5	50.2	94.4	125.1

12-14 历年各类学校在校学生数

Number of Students Enrollment by Type of School over Years

单位：人

年份	普通高等学校	中等职业技术学校	#技工学校	普通中学	#高中	小学	幼儿园
1949		151		1960	318	52781	
1952		543		3394	296	70359	
1957		561		6652	848	88001	
1962		380		9736	1513	119998	
1965		358		10469	1397	160931	
1970				60150	9873	118128	
1975		689		49569	10847	168236	
1978		595		76025	12092	161114	18228
1979		450		62292	7010	158008	12774
1980		386		54829	6909	154871	7630
1981		450		43514	5755	150857	8103
1982		661		41683	4654	144754	14650
1983		967		42777	4798	135440	15436
1984		1070		46488	5766	134567	23702
1985		3363		46596	6304	134421	31382
1986		3891	60	49445	7880	140700	38195
1987		5847	117	54435	8367	144287	42569
1988		7120	229	59268	8201	150097	42845
1989		7878	293	61955	7687	155852	44110
1990		8919	582	61188	8572	162664	47040
1991		10938	915	60146	8725	170064	51051
1992		13161	1277	65171	9711	175203	57537
1993	1079	14176	1516	75305	10297	180114	65310
1994	1451	16084	2025	85827	11409	186244	72552
1995	1628	18737	2404	92481	13653	195063	84263
1996	1771	22614	2567	95150	16887	205957	85709
1997	2025	24821	2598	98005	20609	221838	100059
1998	2171	25588	2291	101202	22490	235787	103585
1999	2241	25073	2001	105518	23084	248759	109773
2000	3241	23144	1746	112418	24677	272793	111763
2001	3802	23638	2039	122115	28232	295384	112963
2002	5144	25363	2152	135256	32398	342804	108898
2003	6884	27664	2564	149656	38143	386890	104832
2004	9104	28487	2559	171336	45050	448296	112538
2005	16645	29487	2618	191044	52283	480923	111330
2006	22005	35403	2905	214638	57662	496828	118683
2007	25178	40429	3063	234578	61151	520684	130932
2008	28656	45419	3238	248442	63962	528644	156362
2009	33992	46538	3268	249464	66750	511160	176249
2010	38293	47531	2955	258276	70398	552377	208373
2011	45081	48159	2915	263076	73644	578279	227656

12-15 历年各类学校当年招收学生数

Number of New Students Enrollment by Type of School over Years

单位：人

年 份	普通高等学校	中等职业技术学校	#技工学校	普通中学	#高中	小 学
1949		102				
1952		285		1666	190	
1957		80		2516	259	
1962		45		3716	566	
1965		134		3656	476	
1970				45069	7919	
1975		188		28329	5930	
1978		250		29788	3436	30152
1979		200		25364	3900	28315
1980		186		24083	3906	26857
1981		266		16808	2594	26461
1982		162		17492	2317	23970
1983		573		18111	2344	19604
1984		1964		16609	2477	17644
1985		1508		16978	2915	20264
1986		1977	60	17944	2781	25867
1987		2883	64	21720	2665	28926
1988		2832	112	23280	2925	29437
1989		2966	124	21877	2686	27539
1990		3866	343	20441	3389	26158
1991		5008	445	21430	3266	27539
1992		5696	487	26161	3751	28804
1993	567	5835	633	29948	3944	31841
1994	569	7064	952	32229	4440	34495
1995	576	8697	996	33086	6099	36702
1996	711	10119	978	33576	7385	39689
1997	750	9718	798	35140	8273	42066
1998	750	9664	852	36423	8118	43802
1999	802	9060	665	38400	8199	47715
2000	1440	8759	527	41488	9048	53786
2001	1597	8850	1116	44729	10727	56521
2002	2190	9417	1153	49881	11852	65066
2003	3104	9809	874	55564	15147	71476
2004	3804	10618	1044	63085	17467	80525
2005	7273	10971	1100	70843	19540	84784
2006	8032	13357	1250	79985	20866	89663
2007	8519	16491	1297	85816	21146	92860
2008	10218	17475	1163	89808	22313	94641
2009	12863	15767	1598	88325	23631	92281
2010	12660	18477	2052	93196	24668	108900
2011	16837	17812	1180	95155	25647	114763

12-16 历年各类学校当年毕业生数

Number of Graduates by Type of School over Years

单位：人

年份	普通高等学校	中等职业技术学校	#技工学校	普通中学	#高中	小学
1949				414	83	
1952		48		588	44	14349
1957		87		1365	203	59056
1962		209		2680	468	28418
1965		44		2363	393	32508
1970				15081	1954	26187
1975		374		20842	4937	25009
1978		244		43035	8533	30480
1979		244		33554	8004	28925
1980		250		19578	3096	27294
1981		191		13308	3046	27215
1982				10483	3004	27348
1983		260		10752	1940	26723
1984		230		10969	1404	17870
1985		234		12317	2055	17901
1986		660		13527	1271	17533
1987		819		13895	2296	23183
1988		1323		15322	2966	23054
1989		1960	60	15310	2716	20315
1990		2210	57	18688	2527	18262
1991		2634	112	19820	2559	19185
1992		2126	123	19323	2643	23303
1993	30	2915	390	18363	3020	26893
1994	197	5035	445	20360	2787	28500
1995	395	4641	541	24165	3231	27257
1996	560	5813	753	27675	3483	27156
1997	484	6745	691	28729	3834	27992
1998	556	8316	918	29839	5448	29794
1999	714	9044	796	30109	6585	31426
2000	985	9554	634	31291	7120	33684
2001	1019	7748	684	32409	7553	37077
2002	753	7171	542	34204	8277	40611
2003	1350	7217	509	39031	8784	45599
2004	1506	8630	917	43471	10676	51831
2005	1439	9062	777	48935	12233	61173
2006	2269	9422	677	55856	15486	70474
2007	5096	10061	754	60436	17354	74681
2008	6486	10728	821	66594	19315	78037
2009	7292	11927	962	71811	20550	78027
2010	8105	14028	956	73810	20816	77429
2011	9463	14774	831	76816	22095	80463

12-17 历年各级各类学校专任教师数

Number of Full-time Teachers by Level and Type of School over Years

单位：人

年 份	普通高等学校	中等职业技术学校	#技工学校	普通中学	#高中	小 学	幼儿园
1978		34		3641	638	5641	
1979		31		3367	369	6136	
1980		29		2996	370	6022	
1981		32		2343	344	6433	
1982		38		2210	284	6186	
1983		61		2361	296	5830	
1984		63		2352	309	5971	
1985		150		2420	354	6017	841
1986		168	5	2463	407	6515	720
1987		208	7	2709	490	6878	941
1988		306	9	3007	540	7112	967
1989		422	11	2949	462	6743	980
1990		434	12	2963	488	6785	1160
1991		513	15	3019	500	6831	1470
1992		600	17	3198	479	7164	1569
1993	99	737	16	3583	610	7314	1773
1994	113	767	26	4001	710	7610	1920
1995	119	859	34	4381	733	8060	1160
1996	119	924	40	4310	886	7410	2175
1997	123	1151	89	4404	991	7518	2753
1998	125	1338	93	4632	1065	7912	3247
1999	133	1205	92	4699	1149	7198	3715
2000	161	1221	84	5027	1310	7946	4618
2001	231	1286	121	5348	1411	8693	4701
2002	290	1445	125	6373	1769	10880	5351
2003	312	1548	124	7069	1976	12490	5505
2004	560	1531	134	8437	2367	15512	6218
2005	1081	1621	150	9640	2817	17478	7002
2006	1357	1801	122	10953	3215	18717	7919
2007	1569	1965	156	12272	3678	20511	9279
2008	1691	2218	161	12995	3976	21203	11072
2009	1890	2321	160	13598	4178	21130	12419
2010	2174	2341	171	14572	4541	23733	13947
2011	2435	2403	167	15262	4851	24787	15232

12-18 历年各类学校入(升)学率与高考入围人数

Number of Passing College Entrance Examination and Proportion of Students Entering Schools over Years

年 份	学龄儿童入学率(%)	小学毕业生升学率(%)	初中毕业生升学率(%)	高中毕业生升学率(%)	高考入围人数(人)	省线入围人数
1978	98.36	85.80	14.30	8.14	846	250
1979	98.70	76.00	16.00	6.71	566	166
1980	98.85	73.40	25.40	7.15	222	140
1981	98.72	50.56	27.40	8.64	239	154
1982	99.06	54.40	34.40	8.04	252	115
1983	99.75	57.60	37.40	12.34	245	150
1984	99.65	70.80	29.86	43.32	619	220
1985	99.83	79.52	38.54	26.50	534	285
1986	99.90	84.71	33.89	43.69	595	228
1987	99.94	83.60	40.10	27.09	644	297
1988	99.93	89.88	42.00	30.63	925	315
1989	99.92	96.18	43.30	32.92	977	284
1990	99.94	95.35	43.60	31.20	759	224
1991	99.92	96.18	45.20	26.22	861	268
1992	99.94	97.58	56.00	35.59	994	312
1993	99.95	97.79	68.50	39.23	1102	423
1994	99.96	98.94	79.02	62.75	1823	586
1995	99.99	99.16	85.40	64.90	2095	809
1996	99.98	96.45	86.70	66.80	2160	1093
1997	99.99	99.90	87.35	60.00	2212	1215
1998	99.99	99.86	88.25	47.69	2348	1315
1999	99.99	99.87	89.80	53.15	3501	1790
2000	99.99	99.83	90.30	70.50	5017	2646
2001	100.00	99.77	90.50	74.82	5651	3225
2002	100.00	99.80	91.10	83.00	6873	3759
2003	100.00	99.80	92.10	93.60	9167	4509
2004	100.00	99.90	93.30	96.70	10756	5452
2005	100.00	99.90	94.10	96.50	11196	6455
2006	100.00	100.00	94.80	82.90	11359	7652
2007	100.00	100.00	95.20	89.10	13275	9185
2008	100.00	100.00	96.60	91.00	15047	9987
2009	100.00	100.00	97.00	87.50	17487	12569
2010	100.00	100.00	97.90	95.10	18845	13761
2011	100.00	100.00	98.00	94.50	19588	15501

12-19 历年文化艺术、文物事业机构数

Number of Institutions in Culture and Cultural Relics over Years

年 份	电影放映单位(个)	#影剧院	艺术表演团体(个)	群 众艺术馆(个)	文化站(广电文化中心)(个)	公 共图书馆(座)	公共图书馆藏书量(万册)	博物馆(座)	档案馆(座)
1949	5	2							
1952	8	3							
1957	14	5							
1962	28	4	2	1	4	1		2	1
1965	28	4	2	1	4	1		2	1
1970	28	4	3	1	33	1		2	1
1975	33	4	3	1	33	1		2	1
1978	167	5	1	1	33	1	11	2	1
1979	157	5	1	1	33	1	15	2	1
1980	65	5	1	1	33	1	16	2	1
1981	75	6	1	1	33	1	17	2	1
1982	53	6	1	1	33	1	19	2	1
1983	49	6	1	1	33	1	19	2	1
1984	65	6	1	1	33	1	24	2	1
1985	60	7	1	1	33	3	30	2	1
1986	61	9	2	1	33	3	30	2	1
1987	70	13	4	1	33	8	30	2	1
1988	78	15	5	1	33	3	30	2	1
1989	102	26	6	1	33	3	30	2	1
1990	114	26	7	1	33	5	30	2	1
1991	126	36	5	1	33	6	31	2	1
1992	150	50	2	1	33	8	37	2	1
1993	163	53	2	1	33	11	47	2	1
1994	193	63	2	1	33	14	58	2	1
1995	218	97	2	1	33	15	68	2	1
1996	225	111	4	1	33	16	73	2	1
1997	229	130	4	1	33	26	84	2	1
1998	233	147	4	1	32	26	106	3	1
1999	210	87	4	1	32	20	133	3	1
2000	192	87	1	1	32	18	97	3	1
2001	145	84	1	1	32	21	99	3	1
2002	162	81	2	1	32	24	109	3	2
2003	107	55	2	1	32	346	289	3	2
2004	88	78		1	32	397	631	6	2
2005	70	31		1	32	473	660	16	2
2006	51	34		1	33	1222	771	21	2
2007	51	34		1	33	1271	896	23	2
2008	40	34	1	1	33	387	515	23	1
2009	40		4	1	33	504	599	31	1
2010	46		4	1	33	505	701	30	1
2011	52		5	1	33	622	771	31	1

12-20 主要年份广播电视事业发展情况

Basic Statistics on Radio and Television Industry in Main Years

项 目	单位	1985年	1990年	1995年	1999年	2000年	2004年	2005年	2010年	2011年
广播电台	座		1	1	1	1	1	1	1	1
电视台	座	1	1	1	1	1	1	1	1	1
镇街文化广电服务中心	个								28	23

12-21 主要年份安全生产事故中火灾事故情况

Basic Statistics on Fire of Production Accidents in Main Years

项 目	单位	1995年	1998年	1999年	2000年	2002年	2004年	2005年	2010年	2011年
一、发生起数	起	24	24	33	60	25	13	13	13	7
二、受伤人数	人	8	15	22	34	15	7	7	8	11
三、死亡人数	人	12	18	40	31	24	18	18	15	14
四、损失折款	万元	1596	1111	1016	1022	592	208	22	21	56
五、平均每起事故损失	万元	66.50	46.29	30.79	17.03	23.68	15.98	1.67	1.63	8.00

注：本表数据来源于市安监局。

12-22 主要年份交通事故发生情况

Basic Statistics on Traffic Accidents in Main Years

项　　目	单位	1995年	1998年	1999年	2000年	2002年	2004年	2005年	2010年	2011年
一、发生起数	起	2015	4248	6619	7386	9393	8029	7124	4874	4491
二、受伤人数	人	2061	4681	6843	8217	10410	9655	8642	5355	4999
三、死亡人数	人	692	858	902	903	1263	978	921	528	496
四、损失折款	万元	685	1213	1418	1759	1538	1038	934	682	566
五、平均每起事故损失	元	3400	2855	2142	2382	1637	1293	1312	1400	1261

注：本表数据来源于市安监局，含道路和水上交通事故。

12-23 各类卫生事业机构及床位、人员数（2011年）

Number of Health Care Institutions, Beds and Employed Personnel by Type of Institution(2011)

项　　目	机构数（个）	实有床位数（张）	人员数（人）	卫生技术人员	执业(助理)医师
总　　计	2249	22814	48142	39582	13644
医疗机构	2245	22814	47778	39294	13563
县及县以上及其他医院	72	22276	35198	28570	9378
#综合医院	54	20002	32087	26253	8661
中医医院	2	754	1285	1060	334
专科医院	16	1520	1826	1257	383
社区卫生服务中心(站)	390		5046	3815	1441
村(社区)卫生站	1243		3561	3561	1406
门诊部	265		2123	1736	682
诊所、卫生所、医务室	272		761	720	366
妇幼保健院	1	455	834	706	228
专科疾病防治院	1	83	225	167	62
急救中心(站)	1		30	19	
采供血机构	1		108	87	11
疾病预防控制中心	1		160	131	70
卫生监督所	1		96	70	
健康教育所	1				
其他卫生机构					

12-24 主要年份卫生事业机构各类人员数

Number of Personnel in Health Institutions in Main Years

单位：人

项　　目	1980年	1985年	1990年	1995年	2000年	2002年	2005年	2010年	2011年
总　　计	3599	3945	4503	6149	9289	10692	22127	46102	48142
一、卫生技术人员	2960	3305	3902	5290	6915	9011	16608	37487	39582
执业(助理)医师	980	1177	1724	2326	2819	3523	5981	13214	13644
注册护士	584	643	1164	1751	2673	3462	6303	14689	16217
药剂人员	236	572	546	602	706	794	1281	2284	2352
检验人员	120	147	152	216	367	476	781	1412	1427
其　他	1040	766	316	395	350	756	2262	5888	5942
二、其他技术人员	8		13	96	174	215	786	1217	1191
三、管理人员	299	282	243	432	597	745	1080	2418	2391
四、工勤人员	332	358	345	331	453	721	1504	4980	4978

注：1. 从2002年起卫生技术人员按新口径分类。
　　2. 2004年起，卫生方面包含诊所、卫生所、医务室及村卫生室的数据，与往年数不可比。

12-25 医疗机构服务情况（2011年）

Services in Medical Institutions (2011)

指标名称	诊疗人数(人次)	门、急诊	入院人数(人)	治愈率(%)	病死率(%)	健康检查人数(人次)
总　　计	59717474	59528715	773426	69.2	0.47	3688735
医院	32804849	32677980	748255	69.0	0.48	3103364
#综合医院	30919583	30801412	699604	68.6	0.50	2995282
中医医院	1155469	1153532	19729	55.7	0.64	19679
专科医院	729797	723036	28922	87.7	0.07	88403
#民营医院	4539652	4501256	168840	75.0	0.50	955877
社区卫生服务中心(站)	14327889	14323966				542905
村卫生站	8021370	7969823				
门诊部(所)	3374155	3367735				4294
妇幼保健院(所、站)	1009917	1009917	24067	79.5	0.03	6725
专科疾病防治院(所、站)	179294	179294	1104	8.9		31447

12-26 历年卫生事业机构、床位、人员数

Number of Health Care Institutions, Beds and Personnel over Years

年份	机构（个）	床位（张）	卫生工作人员（人）	#卫生技术人员	#执业(助理)医师
1949	5	219	170	156	
1952	6	179	124	109	
1957	26	403	287	252	
1962	37	1376	1572	1262	
1965	38	1308	1932	1618	
1970	39	1476	2135	1678	
1975	40	1970	2840	2282	
1978	82	2257	3242	2636	768
1979	81	2271	3466	2863	971
1980	83	2207	3599	2960	1167
1981	83	2210	3724	3091	1102
1982	83	2292	3886	3253	1097
1983	83	2098	3985	3335	1088
1984	83	2231	4005	3351	1132
1985	87	2323	3945	3305	1201
1986	88	3054	4084	3454	1179
1987	88	3393	4475	3490	1304
1988	87	3640	4582	3829	1537
1989	87	3677	4522	3874	1620
1990	85	3866	4503	3902	1721
1991	85	4085	4578	3946	1755
1992	83	4517	4705	4127	1832
1993	99	4940	5247	4524	2023
1994	98	5365	5689	4930	2221
1995	99	5798	6149	5290	2299
1996	99	5288	6712	5766	2449
1997	151	5505	7286	6283	2605
1998	171	5892	8306	7139	2955
1999	176	6241	8697	7575	3080
2000	174	7081	9289	8065	3309
2001	173	7474	9323	8064	3429
2002	178	8641	10692	9011	3523
2003	172	9820	11584	9807	3758
2004	944	10797	15058	13053	4870
2005	874	11972	22127	18757	6901
2006	1210	13293	27128	22904	8629
2007	1649	15227	34151	28758	10446
2008	2106	16778	40449	33113	11869
2009	2106	18080	43561	35766	12884
2010	2229	19980	46102	37487	13214
2011	2249	22814	48142	39582	13644

注：2004年起本表包含诊所、卫生所、医务室及村卫生室的数据，与往年数不可比。

12-27 历年体育运动情况

Basic Statistics on Sports over Years

年　份	破（超）世界纪录（次）	破（超）亚洲纪录（次）	破（超）全国纪录（次）	在国际比赛中获得金牌总数（枚）	在全国比赛中获得金牌总数（枚）	在省级比赛中获得金牌总数（枚）	市级运动会参赛运动员人数（人）	为国家省输送运动员（人）
1978			9	1	7	26	2500	11
1979	2		2	1	7		2250	18
1980			12		2		2400	14
1981			11	4	19		2500	13
1982			14	4	30	15	2650	9
1983	1		7	5	6		2420	7
1984			1	16	5		2500	33
1985		2	1	5	2		1960	7
1986		7	4	7	4	52	2420	16
1987	1	1	8	35	9		2130	19
1988	3	1	4	14	25		2540	15
1989			27	5	43	92	6430	18
1990	13	5		4	6		2370	25
1991	2	1	8	12	14		4800	16
1992	2	3	21	10	6		15000	30
1993	2	8	5	12	9		10350	16
1994	34	2	24	6	23	157	2720	14
1995	10	1		5	37		1500	14
1996				3	16		7800	13
1997	10	9		1	6	36	6000	74
1998	2	4	28	4	28	87	1560	74
1999				4	33		6000	6
2000			3	4	91		4000	6
2001				13	22	48	8000	5
2002				2	35	58		11
2003		7		2	31	82		6
2004	3	4	4	49	34			18
2005				2	13	46	8564	44
2006				20	21	32	16000	
2007				3	25	46	2740	9
2008				3	16	49	630	17
2009		1	3	8	20	94	1550	17
2010				4	6	40	9895	16
2011				8	27	116	3300	25

12-28 主要年份体育比赛成绩

Basic Statistics on Sports Achievements in Main Years

项　　目	单位	1980年	1985年	1990年	1995年	2000年	2005年	2010年	2011年
破世界纪录	次			13	10				
获得国际赛冠军	个		5	4	5	4		4	
破亚洲纪录	次		2	5	1				
破全国纪录	次	12	1			3			
获国际比赛奖牌									
金牌	枚		5	4	5	4	2	4	8
银牌	枚			4	3	2	1	2	1
铜牌	枚						2		3
获全国比赛金牌	枚	2	2	6	37	91	13	6	27

注:“获得国际赛冠军”及“获国际比赛奖牌”含地区赛。

12-29 主要年份群众体育活动情况

Basic Statistics on Activities of Mass Sports in Main Years

项　　目	单位	1980年	1985年	1990年	1995年	2000年	2005年	2010年	2011年
举办市级运动会	次	5	4	9	4	2	4	16	2
市级运动会参赛运动员人数	人	2400	1960	2370	1500	4000	8564	9895	3300
举办镇街级运动会	次	57	68	105	10	3	4	58	55
镇街级运动会参赛运动员人数	人	17100	34300	61500	50000	13000	5000	101760	88597
为国家和省输送运动员人数	人	14	7	25	14	6	47	16	25

12-30 历年治安案件情况

Basic Statistics on Public Security Cases over Years

项　　目	单位	2005年	2006年	2007年	2008年	2009年	2010年	2011年
治安案件受理数	起	13760	17537	32293	42270	64506	44979	50877
扰乱公共秩序	起	2816	1525	741	645	514	198	203
妨害公共安全	起	243	445	496	598	592	630	923
侵犯人身、财产权利	起	6044	9328	20171	25446	25157	24551	25355
#盗窃	起	2599	2984	6229	11633	10192	10513	6909
妨害社会管理秩序	起	4296	6239	10885	15581	38243	19600	24396
#吸毒	起	2697	3214	4180	3850	4164	4455	5297
卖淫、嫖娼	起	153	376	351	386	481	663	582
赌博或为赌博提供条件	起	942	1431	3123	6312	30416	10464	13597
治安案件查处数	起	12490	16711	29533	36081	58868	37818	45133
扰乱公共秩序	起	2797	1523	729	623	503	186	193
妨害公共安全	起	237	418	476	592	569	583	713
侵犯人身、财产权利	起	4865	8538	17504	19438	19706	17687	19925
#盗窃	起	2007	2479	4559	7416	6241	5476	3574
妨害社会管理秩序	起	4246	6232	10824	15428	38090	19362	24297
#吸毒	起	2665	3211	4179	3805	4059	4317	5259
卖淫、嫖娼	起	147	376	349	382	481	659	580
赌博或为赌博提供条件	起	938	1430	3113	6260	30402	10408	13587
查处违法人员数	人	20692	24539	36382	36081	65351	42815	48230
扰乱公共秩序	人	4486	1696	909	1118	457	363	356
妨害公共安全	人	218	477	565	641	573	618	662
侵犯人身、财产权利	人	6769	12010	19598	19353	15748	14145	15578
#盗窃	人	2676	2969	4222	5967	4448	3802	3161
妨害社会管理秩序	人	8201	10356	15310	19736	48573	27689	31634
#吸毒	人	3922	3842	4675	4145	4442	4885	5967
卖淫、嫖娼	人	415	850	737	814	1143	1506	1348
赌博或为赌博提供条件	人	3179	4089	6395	9672	39732	17191	19339

注：本表数据来源于市公安局。

12-31 历年刑事案件情况

Basic Statistics on Criminal Cases over Years

单位：起

项　　目	2005年	2006年	2007年	2008年	2009年	2010年	2011年
刑事案件立案数	44641	35528	33837	33880	33309	36965	37831
危害公共安全	264	293	263	205	348	586	849
破坏市场经济秩序	451	373	531	418	492	577	451
侵犯公民人身权利	3748	3328	3658	3634	3365	3587	3107
#杀人	87	70	72	52	67	69	52
伤害	3071	2703	2873	2840	2509	2882	2525
强奸	266	229	293	263	270	336	288
侵犯财产	39657	31045	28909	29120	28298	31251	32156
#抢劫	9144	7862	7380	7331	6704	5045	5168
抢夺	3736	2563	2343	2181	2364	3250	3906
入室盗窃	4150	3038	3327	5804	6834	8779	7134
盗窃机动车	16050	10588	7876	7264	4962	3526	4189
诈骗	897	953	1136	1587	2513	3203	2681
妨害社会管理秩序	571	488	458	503	805	963	1266
#毒品犯罪	215	258	261	257	424	587	826
刑事案件破案数	13682	13477	12729	8342	12525	16271	17796
危害公共安全	161	191	131	103	301	550	829
破坏市场经济秩序	439	283	243	273	239	388	210
侵犯公民人身权利	2037	1896	2077	1732	1748	1933	1644
#杀人	73	52	65	40	60	61	48
伤害	1586	1472	1527	1282	1231	1449	1225
强奸	171	147	192	152	165	224	195
侵犯财产	10598	10672	9870	5856	9543	12534	13935
#抢劫	3582	3707	3527	2474	3136	2531	2797
抢夺	1525	1328	1113	610	929	1700	2076
入室盗窃	1081	864	891	796	2422	4182	3970
盗窃机动车	1880	1717	703	526	761	631	1064
诈骗	202	278	285	154	572	536	435
妨害社会管理秩序	490	429	387	378	693	866	1178
#毒品犯罪	210	247	239	243	412	569	815

注：本表数据来源于市公安局。

12-32 历年道路交通违法情况

Basic Statistics on Traffic Offense over Years

项目	单位	2005年	2006年	2007年	2008年	2009年	2010年	2011年
处理违法起数	万起	61.04	92.71	94.95	266.96	294.27	282.48	278.42
#机动车	万起		90.29	92.05	263.86	291.69	280.44	276.42
非机动车	万起		1.04	1.88	1.90	1.11	1.01	1.11
行人和乘车人	万起		1.15	1.03	1.19	1.48	1.03	0.88
教育人次	万人次		10.76	13.05	15.00	24.37	26.14	27.24
#机动车	万人次		8.76	11.17	13.27	22.51	25.38	26.48
非机动车	万人次		0.93	0.98	0.79	0.62	0.35	0.42
行人和乘车人	万人次		1.07	0.90	0.93	1.24	0.41	0.33
罚款总额	万元	9991.70	19072.80	19705.00	43761.11	24534.65	44359.52	45213.47
#机动车	万元		19069.10	19689.00	43744.65	24531.19	44355.07	45210.39
非机动车	万元		2.00	16.00	17.14	2.98	2.80	1.82
行人和乘车人	万元				0.32	0.48	1.65	1.26

注：本表数据来源于市公安局。

12-33 主要年份律师、公证、基层司法及普法教育

Basic Statistics on Lawyers, Notarization, Grassroots Judicial Work and Law Education in Main Years

项目	单位	1990年	1995年	2000年	2005年	2010年	2011年
一、律师工作							
律师事务所	个	2	8	22	46	115	130
律师	人	12	85	221	625	1366	1513
担任常年法律顾问	家	102	364	416	1426	2752	2839
民事诉讼代理	件	145	343	1203	6543	12041	15892
非诉讼法律事务	件	110	1162	2079	13391	19967	16366
刑事辩护及代理	件	295	235	438	2496	2776	2913
国内经济案件诉讼代理	件	107	348	1100	1801	1133	1198
涉外及港澳台经济案件诉讼代理	件	165	11	27	160	299	80
二、公证工作							
公证处	个	1	1	1	1	3	3
公证人员	人	10	19	20	48	96	106
办结公证总数	件	5347	11377	28910	60685	48296	57298
#国内民事公证	件	113	2795	19607	19627	35104	42708
国内经济公证	件	236	898	1776	34015	3536	4266
涉外公证（含港澳台）	件	4998	7684	4809	4607	9656	10324
三、基层司法工作							
法律服务所	个	24	29	32	32	32	32
法律工作人员	人	70	115	117	191	360	378
担任法律顾问	家	62	482	695	1208	724	758
民事诉讼代理	件	26	568	1221	1790	1090	1207
非诉讼代理	件	129	1045	3016	3837	1549	1298
四、调解工作							
人民调解委员会	个	904	813	750	814	1552	1494
调解人员	人	3664	3466	3644	4556	17438	20240
调解民间纠纷	件	2005	2632	2642	15210	15239	16216
五、参加普法教育人数	万人	79.9	170	79	571	288	587

12-34 历年计划生育情况

Basic Statistics on Family Planning over Years

年 份	已婚育龄妇女人数（人）	女性初婚人数（人）			落实各种节育措施	
			23周岁及以上	不足20周岁	育龄夫妇（对）	节育率（%）
1978	130438	10974			103414	79.28
1979	134483	11914			104612	77.79
1980	136742	9270	8920		101190	74.00
1981	141079	13714			112956	80.07
1982	142324	8729			115302	81.01
1983	149928	12664			129035	86.06
1984	156444	9579			138785	88.71
1985	159985	11208			142974	89.37
1986	168611	13983	11899		150545	89.30
1987	176868	13492	11252		158857	89.80
1988	183022	12419	10072		164889	90.10
1989	196042	13691	10228	15	172799	88.20
1990	202505	13264	9670	29	177425	87.60
1991	211544	13790	10834	12	184254	87.10
1992	224624	15295	10375	13	190151	84.70
1993	235150	13932	9793	6	200673	85.30
1994	243456	13213	9833	9	208234	85.50
1995	252627	13921	10430	26	215339	85.20
1996	258873	13556	10114	20	221805	85.70
1997	263646	12968	9623	9	226674	85.98
1998	267982	12366	9260	7	233007	86.95
1999	280455	12114	8999	4	249368	88.92
2000	285244	11122	7050	14	249741	87.55
2001	295395	10903	6755	14	260077	88.04
2002	303134	11635	7082	8	268243	88.49
2003	306157	12441	7767	5	266832	87.16
2004	312941	13957	9318	2	273387	87.36
2005	317062	13251	9057	5	275685	86.95
2006	323479	12460	9117	3	279246	86.33
2007	331556	13621	10333	1	293733	85.29
2008	343051	14485	11053	1	291049	84.84
2009	352115	14450	11157	5	297559	84.51
2010	367607	14265	11019	4	309054	84.07
2011	380570	14899	11820	1	320135	84.12

12-34 续表

年 份	领取独生子女证		人口出生率（‰）		政策生育率(%)	多孩率(%)
	累 计(人)	领证率(%)	省计划指 标	实 际完 成		
1978			13.0	18.73		
1979			12.0	24.13		
1980	423	1.84	13.0	24.41	69.72	23.38
1981			11.9	21.86		
1982			18.1	19.07		
1983			17.0	16.74		
1984			15.5	15.54		
1985	1954	1.22	15.3	15.37	88.94	4.27
1986	2029	1.20	16.5	16.44	92.45	2.93
1987	2257	1.28	16.0	16.11	93.16	1.97
1988	2408	1.32	17.0	16.75	93.58	2.14
1989	2116	1.10	17.0	17.06	92.35	2.54
1990	2288	1.13	17.5	17.07	89.08	3.71
1991	2514	1.19	20.0	17.91	89.55	3.65
1992	2335	1.04	19.8	19.31	86.08	4.44
1993	2905	1.24	20.0	18.38	87.29	4.50
1994	3245	1.33	19.2	17.88	86.50	4.71
1995	3389	1.34	19.3	17.76	85.09	4.33
1996	4028	1.63	18.3	17.05	83.83	4.87
1997	4514	1.71	18.0	16.50	83.98	4.68
1998	4971	1.85	16.6	15.31	90.01	2.92
1999	21228	7.57	15.8	14.55	89.31	2.92
2000	30921	10.84	15.3	12.11	90.17	1.77
2001	41636	14.10	14.9	11.16	91.75	1.57
2002	49188	16.23	14.3	10.35	91.80	1.31
2003	51814	16.92	12.5	10.34	92.45	1.24
2004	55425	17.71	12.5	10.86	93.48	1.14
2005	60426	19.06	11.5	10.62	94.32	0.80
2006	69507	21.49	11.6	10.14	94.69	0.71
2007	73766	22.25	11.0	10.39	95.48	0.63
2008	77919	22.71	11.0	10.77	96.28	0.54
2009	80738	22.93	11.0	10.67	96.75	0.75
2010	81736	22.23	11.5	10.90	96.97	0.99
2011	83312	21.89	12.5	10.92	98.65	0.90

注：领证率是期末已领取独生子女证人数除以全市已婚育龄妇女人数。

12-35 主要年份优抚和社会救济、福利事业

Basic Statistics on Special Care, Social Relief and Welfare in Main Years

项　　目	单位	1990年	1995年	2000年	2005年	2010年	2011年
一、优抚事业							
优抚收养性事业单位数	个	1	1	1	1	1	1
优抚收养性单位收养人数	人次	19	11	7	8	8	9
优抚事业费用	万元	340	213	412	2400	4555	2761
二、社会救济							
社会救济人数	人次	4433	7273	19914	23886	36516	32584
年末社会散居孤老残幼人数	人	2026	2444	1596	875	11	11
#定期救济对象	人	142	569	29	18	11	11
社会救济福利事业费	万元		190	993	6955	21199	21629
自然灾害生活救助费	万元	4.6	70	50	744	139	269
三、社会福利							
社会福利事业单位数	个	1	1	3	36	38	38
#民政部门办	个	1	1	3	4	3	3
社会福利事业单位收养人数	人	363	351	406	2240	2609	2689
#民政部门办	人	363	351	406	893	1715	1816
社会福利企业单位	个	9	15	20	20	10	9
安排“四残”人员就业人数	人	199	239	393	351	321	296
社会福利事业单位费用支出	万元					9770	10773
四、敬老院情况							
全市敬老院个数	个			32	31	35	35
年末敬老院供养人数	人			833	1347	894	873
五、“五保户”情况							
年末列入“五保户”户数	户			1545	1575	1254	1199
年末列入“五保户”人数	人			1587	1575	1263	1210
全年“五保户”费用支出	万元			2198	1594	1536	1724
六、城乡基层社会保障							
建立社会保障网络镇街数	个	33	24	32	32	32	32

注：“五保户”人数及费用支出含敬老院供养人数及费用支出。

12-36 主要年份婚姻登记情况

Basic Statistics on Marriage Registration in Main Years

项　　目	单位	1985年	1990年	1995年	2000年	2005年	2010年	2011年
准予登记结婚	对	11870	13668	14170	10535	14293	11415	7025
#涉外、华侨、港澳台同胞	对	638	709	510	213	113	79	144
准予登记离婚	对				448	1319	1856	1074
#涉外、华侨、港澳台同胞	对						9	16

12-37 主要年份环境保护基本情况

Basic Statistics on Environmental Protection in Main Years

项　　目	单 位	1985年	1990年	1995年	2000年	2005年	2010年	2011年
一、废水								
废水排放总量	万吨	3100	5259	9681	40703	69049	87953	102679
#工业废水	万吨	2686	4124	5511	11753	21355	29742	29091
工业废水排放达标率	%	55.0	46.1	85.4	72.0	92.1	96.3	
城镇生活废水处理率	%						71.5	84.2
二、废气								
工业废气排放量	亿标立方	34	307	556	1318	1695	2340	2686
三、工业固体废物								
固体废物产生量	万吨	16	112	108	149	284	313	558
固体废物处置量	万吨	8	2	1	5	12	15	122
固体废物处置率	%	48.2	1.8	0.9	66.9	99.8	4.8	22.1
固体废物综合利用率	%	37.5	17.9	18.2	63.8	86.5	95.0	77.9
四、城市环境质量及污染控制								
空气污染指数	范围值				21-87	24-123	14-108	18-110
交通干线噪声平均值	db				68.4	67.9	67.7	67.8
汽车尾气排放达标率	%				81.2	88.1	81.0	83.6
全市生活垃圾无害化处理率	%						37.3	41.2

12-38 主要年份社会保险事业情况

Basic Statistics on Social Insurance in Main Years

项　　目	单 位	1995年	2000年	2005年	2010年	2011年
参加各种社会保险人数	万人次	149.33	338.33	804.71	2726.37	2464.69
#失业保险	万人次	6.49	17.84	177.78	279.90	299.38
养老保险	万人次	8.46	82.95	182.49	421.84	481.05
地方养老保险	万人次				371.01	
医疗保险	万人次	7.60	88.21	189.40	592.27	602.41
工伤保险	万人次	126.78	136.53	235.10	469.08	479.44
社会保险基金总收入	万元	18155	127964	491540	1544112	1793980
#失业保险	万元	60	2732	28954	27008	32312
养老保险	万元	7697	85245	343429	976257	1248706
地方养老保险	万元				144699	
医疗保险	万元	2057	23488	82138	333342	415349
工伤保险	万元	8341	15891	35073	62806	97613
社会保险待遇总支出	万元	10520	40454	217413	547470	732642
#失业保险	万元	16	440	6676	9681	14015
养老保险	万元	7450	24130	135958	194055	229260
地方养老保险	万元				1849	
医疗保险	万元	1436	3694	51021	299975	426244
工伤保险	万元	1618	11703	22220	41910	63123

注：1. 1997年起养老保险因口径调整，与以前年份不可比。
　　2. 参加各种社会保险总人数包含生育保险人数。

12-39 主要年份最低生活保障情况

Basic Statistics on Minimum Income Relief in Main Years

项　　目	单 位	2005年	2006年	2007年	2008年	2009年	2010年	2011年
居民最低生活保障线	元/人月	320	320	320	400	400	440	440
村民最低生活保障线	元/人月	300	300	300	400	400	440	440
居民最低生活保障户数	户	1911	2433	3079	1531	1606	1599	3796
居民最低生活保障人数	人	4885	6091	7574	3653	3770	3643	9415
居民最低生活保障金支出	万元	789.5			1052.0	726.7	673.4	2001.2
村民最低生活保障户数	户	6705	7133	6844	12125	13106	12214	8744
村民最低生活保障人数	人	17426	19050	18534	33384	33549	30785	21959
村民最低生活保障金支出	万元	2318			9747	6295.3	5922.3	4298.9

12-40　主要年份市政建设情况

Basic Statistics on Municipal Construction in Main Years

项　　　目	单 位	1995年	1999年	2000年	2005年	2010年	2011年
水厂日供水能力	万吨	66	182	187	480	700	700
年末供水管道总长度	公里	1580	2011	2106	3680	16268	22553
全年供水量	万吨	18802	66268	70046	155100	165607	173433
#生活用水量	万吨	7361	29530	21433	51100	28560	39628
园林绿地面积	万平方米	800	1229	1396	10298	33092	36091
#公园绿地面积	万平方米					9075	9837
建成区绿化覆盖面积	万平方米	1885	1556	1364	9436	35571	38035
建成区土地面积	平方公里	82.00	126.14	147.68	657.17	798.48	854.3
公园数	个		249	273	931	1004	1039
公园面积	公顷		827	1423	2887	11130	10546

注：公园数和公园面积不含森林公园数及其面积。

12-41　主要年份液化石油气及天然气供应情况

Basic Statistics on Supply of Liquefied Petroleum Gas and Natural Gas in Main Years

项　　　目	单 位	1995年	2000年	2005年	2009年	2010年	2011年
年末液化石油气用户数	户	63419	110172	144797	892874	956018	1176076
#家庭用气户数	户	62246	106910	144035	873246	870921	1040167
全年液化石油气供气量	吨	25935	58287	161930	351893	344762	338089
#家庭用量	吨	18948	22104	24354	215357	188108	195508
年末天然气用户数	户			5027	112230	147047	178780
#家庭用气户数	户			5000	111501	116239	177279
全年天然气供气量	万立方米			350	29255	23414	36486
#家庭用量	万立方米			45	1078	1600	2047
年末汽车天然气加气站	个				8	10	15
年末汽车天然气加气站全年供气量	万立方米				1955	5324	7800

注：本表2000-2006年为市喜威液化石油气有限公司与市中液石油气有限公司的业务量,2007年起调整为市城市管理局统计口径。

12-42 历年环境保护基本情况

Basic Statistics on Environmental Protection over Years

年份	降水PH均值	酸雨PH均值	酸雨频率(%)	酸雨占总降水量(%)	交通干线噪声平均值(db)	工业废水排放量(万吨)	工业废水排放达标量(万吨)	工业废水排放达标率(%)
1982						1842	1381	74.97
1983						2068	1564	75.63
1984	6.53					2127	1203	56.56
1985						2686	1483	55.21
1986					76.8	2416	596	24.67
1987	6.64	5.38		38.4	78.9	3501	1843	52.64
1988	4.85	4.72	63.6	75.1	77.6	3029	2349	77.55
1989	5.44	5.21	31.0	31.8	74.1	3976	2473	62.21
1990	6.15	5.30	29.5	43.3	75.9	4124	1900	46.07
1991	5.24	4.78	35.4	30.4	72.2	5506	3560	64.70
1992	5.10	4.71	36.8	35.9	76.0	5849	3501	59.90
1993	4.93	4.41	22.5	29.1	75.8	6500	4175	64.23
1994	5.33	4.81	23.2	25.5	72.6	7057	5361	75.97
1995	5.89	5.49	9.2	13.7	70.3	5511	4706	85.40
1996	5.83	5.40	14.7	10.9	70.4	6033	4790	79.40
1997	4.94	4.84	56.6	76.4	70.6	8930	5697	63.80
1998	4.79	4.70	60.3	80.4	70.3	7989	3683	46.10
1999	4.97	4.68	40.0	50.5	69.1	11719	6258	53.40
2000	4.90	4.67	50.7	56.6	68.7	11753	8468	72.00
2001	5.06	4.74	31.6	43.9	68.2	11694	8168	69.90
2002	5.47	5.09	29.3	28.8	68.0	25587	23179	90.60
2003	4.55	4.44	60.5	77.2	67.9	23389	19761	84.49
2004	4.47	4.41	69.6	85.7	68.0	22501	20274	90.10
2005	4.07	4.00	65.7	86.2	67.9	21355	19667	92.10
2006	3.57-6.57	4.70	50.0	42.4	68.0	24134	22344	92.58
2007	5.21	4.36-7.59	54.2	59.2	67.9	91260	88072	96.51
2008	4.83	4.65	60.1	63.6	63.6	33359	31560	94.61
2009	5.03	4.88	51.8	67.3	63.8	29960	29309	97.82
2010	5.11	4.97	52.2	65.3	67.7	29742	28639	96.29
2011	5.02	4.59	47.6	31.9	67.8	29091		

注：1. 2007年工业废水排放量和工业废水排放达标量两个指标统计口径变更，与往年不可比。
2. 2011年取消了“达标率”指标，有关达标率指标的数据都无法统计。

主要统计指标解释

Explanatory Notes on Main Statistical Indicators

工程技术人员 指在国民经济各行业从事工程技术工作的自然科学技术专业人员，包括：高级工程师、工程师、助理工程师、技术员和未评定职称的技术人员。

农业技术人员 指在国民经济各行业从事农业技术工作的自然科学技术专业人员，包括：高级农艺师、农艺师、助理农艺师、技术员和未评定职称的技术人员。

科学研究人员 指在国民经济各行业从事科学技术活动的科学技术专业人员，包括：正副研究员、助理研究员、研究实习员、技术员和未评定职称的技术人员。

专利申请量 指企业当年向国家知识产权局提出专利申请并被受理项数。

专利授权量 指企业当年获国家知识产权局授予专利权的项数。

发明 专利法及其实施细则所称的发明是指对有关产品、方法或其改进所提出的新的技术方案。

实用新型 专利法及其实施细则所称的实用新型是指对产品的形状、构造或者其结合所提出的适于实用的新的技术方案。

外观设计 专利法及其实施细则所称的外观设计是指对产品的形状、图案、色彩或者其结合所作出的富有美感并适于工业上应用的新设计。

毕业生数 毕业生数是指上学年内，具有学籍的学生学完教学计划规定的全部课程，考试及格，实际毕业的学生数。不包括结业生和肄业生。

招生数 招生数是指新学年开始时，按规定实际招收入学的新生数，不包括重读生和复学生（高等教育包括春秋两季招收的学生）。

在校学生数 是指具有学籍的注册学生总数。

学龄儿童入学率 指调查范围内已入小学学习的学龄儿童占校内外学龄儿童总数（包括弱智儿童在内，但不包括盲聋哑儿童）的比重。

电影放映单位 指具有放映机器设备、固定或不固定的放映场所与专职或兼职的放映技术人员，经有关部门登记批准，经常为一定的观众对象放映电影的机构。包括经批准对外开放进行营业，并与电影发行放映管理机构分帐的专用放映单位和军委系统租片单位。

公共图书馆藏书量 是指本馆已编目的古籍、图书、期刊和报纸的合订本、小册子、手稿，以及缩徽制品、录像带、录音带、光盘等视听文献资料数量之和。

医疗机构 是指根据《医疗机构管理条例》的规定，经登记取得《医疗机构执业许可证》的机构。包括医院、社区卫生服务中心（站）、卫生院、门诊所、诊疗所、医务室、村卫生室、妇幼保健院（所、站）、专科疾病防治院（所、站）、急救中心、临床检验中心。

医院 指设有固定床位能收容病人住院并能为病人提供医疗、护理服务的医疗机构。包括县及县以上医院、农村乡卫生院、其他医院三部分。按所属性质分为卫生部门、工业及其他部门、集体经济单位三类。其中县及县以上医院按业务性质分为综合医院和专科医院。

实有床位 是指报告期末固定实有床位数，包括正规床、简易床、监护床、正在消毒和修理床位、因扩建或修理而停用的床位，不包括产科新生儿床、待产室待产床、库存床、观察床、临时加床和病人家属陪伴床。

诊疗人数 是指所有诊疗工作的总人数。包括病人来院就诊的门诊、急诊人次和出诊、下地段、赴家庭病床、到工厂、农村、工地、会议、集体活动等外出诊疗的人次数，以及外出进行的单项健康检查及健康咨询指导人次数。并包括本院职工的诊疗的人次数及局部的单项健康检查人数。

卫生技术人员 指卫生事业机构支付工资的全部固定职工和合同制职工中现任职务为卫生技术工作的专业人员。包括中医师、西医师、中西医结合高级医师、护师、中药师、西药师、检验师、其他技师、中医士、西医士、护士、助产士、中药剂士、西药剂士、检验士、其他技士、其他中医、护理员、中药剂员、西药剂员、检验员，其他初级卫生技术人员。

治愈率 是指年内治愈（并经治疗后，疾病症状消失，功能完全恢复。）出院病人数占年内出院人数的比例。

病死率 是指年内住院病人中死亡人数占出院人数的比例。

刑事案件立案 是指实施违反我国刑事法律的行为，构成犯罪的案件。根据《关于公安机关办理刑事案件程序规定》第一百六十二条，公安机关受理案件后，经过审查，认为有犯罪事实需要追究刑事责任，且属于自己管辖的，由接受单位制作《刑事案件立案报告书》，经县级以上公安机关负责人批准，予以立案。

刑事案件破案 根据《关于公安机关办理刑事案件程序规定》第一百六十六条的规定，刑事案件破案应当具备下列条件：（一）犯罪事实已有证据证明；（二）有证据证明犯罪事实是犯罪嫌疑人实施的；（三）犯罪嫌疑人或者主要犯罪嫌疑人已经归案。

治安案件查处 是指触犯了《中华人民共和国治安管理处罚条例》规定，给社会或个人造成一定危害，公安机关依照相关法律、法规和规定，应当给予处罚的行为事件。

律师 指受聘参加法律顾问处工作，担任法律顾问、刑（民）事代理人、刑事辩护人，办理非诉讼事件、解答法律询问，代写法律事务文书等主要从事律师业务的专职法律工作者和兼职律师。

公证人员 指在国家公证机关依法办理公证事务的司法人员。包括公证员、助理公证员和在公证处工作的其他人员。

调解人员 在人民调解委员会担负调解民间一般民事纠纷和轻微违法行为所引起的纠纷的工作人员。包括调解委员会的委员和调解小组的调解员。

社会保险基金收入 是指根据国家规定，由纳入基本社会保险范围的单位，按照国家规定的缴费基数和缴费比例缴纳的社会统筹基金，以及通过其他方式取得的形成基金来源的收入，包括：单位缴纳的社会统筹基金收入、财政补贴收入、利息收入、其他收入。

社会保险基金支出 是指按照国家政策规定的开支范围和开支标准从社会统筹基金中支付给参加基本社会保险人员个人的费用，以及由于保险关系转移、上下级之间调剂资金等原因而发生的支出。

社会福利事业单位 指集中收养社会孤老、残、幼的机构。包括由民政部门管理的社会福利院、儿童福利院、精神病人福利院和城镇集体办的福利院，以及农村集体举办的敬老院。

社会福利事业单位收养人数包括民政部门管理的和城镇及农村集体举办的社会福利事业单位中收养的老人、少年儿童、缺乏生活自理能力的残疾人员和精神病人。

废水排放总量 包括工业废水和生活污水。工业废水指工业企业在生产、科研过程中向企业外部排放的所有排放口的废水量总和。生活污水指居民或职工在饮用、洗涤、烹饪、清洁卫生等过程中排放的污水量。

十三、能　源

Energy

13-1 能源主要指标(2005-2011年)

Main Indicators of Energy (2005-2011)

项　　目	单　位	2005年	2006年	2007年	2008年	2009年	2010年	2011年
地区能源消费总量(等价值)	万吨标准煤	1885.78	2138.97	2393.92	2589.66	2603.52	2812.65	2896.05
地区能源消费总量(当量值)	万吨标准煤	1800.14	2010.20	2154.52	2280.31	2311.86	2438.84	2512.46
电力消耗	亿千瓦时	419.83	472.01	515.40	514.16	495.58	562.00	586.07
单位GDP能耗(等价值)	吨标准煤/万元	0.864	0.822	0.778	0.738	0.705	0.691	0.632
单位GDP能耗(当量值)	吨标准煤/万元	0.825	0.772	0.700	0.650	0.626	0.599	0.548
规模以上工业综合能源消费量(当量值)	万吨标准煤	1203.77	1329.05	1437.94	1452.85	1367.94	1496.06	1482.56
规模以上工业发电量	亿千瓦时	378.81	410.54	402.54	362.53	342.29	368.26	384.78
全社会用电量	亿千瓦时	419.83	472.01	515.40	514.16	495.58	562.00	586.07
火力发电转换效率	%	37.05	36.97	36.68	37.59	39.24	38.91	39.21
供热转换效率	%				87.75	89.74	91.18	86.72
能源消费比上年增长	%		13.43	11.92	8.18	0.54	8.03	2.97
电力消费比上年增长	%		12.43	9.19	-0.24	-3.61	13.40	4.28
地区生产总值比上年增长	%		19.22	18.26	14.00	5.25	10.27	7.95
能源消费弹性系数			0.70	0.65	0.58	0.10	0.78	0.37
电力消费弹性系数			0.65	0.50			1.30	0.54

注:单位GDP能耗(等价值)和单位GDP能耗(当量值)2006-2010年按2005年可比价计算；2011年开始按2010年可比价计算。

13-2 综合能源平衡表(2005-2011年)

Overall Energy Balance Sheet (2005-2011)

单位：万吨标准煤

项　　目	2005年	2006年	2007年	2008年	2009年	2010年	2011年
可供本地区消费的能源量	1885.78	2138.97	2393.92	2589.66	2603.52	2812.65	2896.05
年初库存量	77.54	67.21	77.91	87.19	158.56	133.72	115.00
一次能源生产量						31.61	17.79
回收能	1.31	5.51	13.81	13.67	13.31		
外省调入量	1866.72	2139.88	2328.67	2537.65	2493.23	2564.50	2361.06
进口量	9.31	1.71	60.72	100.59	83.79	205.75	509.50
境内轮船和飞机在境外加油量							
本省调出量(-)						-7.31	-4.47
出口量(-)							
境外轮船和飞机在境内加油量(-)							
年末库存量(-)	-69.11	-75.35	-87.19	-149.43	-145.37	-115.62	-102.83
加工转换投入(-)产出(+)量	-0.08					-15.28	-22.63
火力发电							
供热						-13.93	-21.36
洗选煤							
炼焦							
炼油							
制气							
损失量	63.74	63.40	84.93	65.64	34.59	42.12	39.90
运输和输配损失	63.74	63.40	84.93	65.64	33.77	42.12	39.90
终端消费量	1821.96	2075.57	2308.98	2524.02	2568.93	2755.25	2833.52
第一产业	5.04	6.61	6.46	4.74	6.17	6.86	7.42
农、林、牧、渔业	5.04	6.61	6.46	4.74	6.17	6.86	7.42
第二产业	1334.30	1491.65	1654.16	1782.54	1790.15	1952.34	1969.34
工业	1305.42	1459.54	1617.24	1742.08	1749.90	1913.74	1932.12
#用作原材料、燃料							
建筑业	28.88	32.11	36.92	40.46	40.25	38.59	37.21
第三产业	304.16	366.00	409.89	459.67	475.19	483.54	521.94
交通运输、仓储及邮政业	84.47	97.27	114.30	129.63	134.83	139.41	148.88
批发、零售业和住宿、餐饮业	137.35	172.82	178.02	193.99	200.60	198.74	214.63
其他	82.34	95.91	117.57	136.05	139.76	145.39	158.43
生活消费	178.45	211.31	238.48	277.07	297.42	312.51	334.83
城镇	178.45	211.31	238.48	277.07	297.42	312.51	334.83
乡村							
平衡差额							
消费量合计	1885.78	2138.97	2393.92	2589.66	2603.52	2812.65	2896.05

13-3 石油平衡表(2005-2011年)

Petroleum Balance Sheet (2005-2011)

单位：万吨

项　　目	2005年	2006年	2007年	2008年	2009年	2010年	2011年
一、可供量	413.06	461.36	444.13	460.89	445.10	401.11	385.84
生产量							
外省(区、市)调入量	408.02	462.31	448.20	472.40	442.12	394.75	379.21
进口量	1.82	1.20				0.03	
境内轮船和飞机在境外加油量							
本省(区、市)调出量(-)						2.09	
出口量(-)							
境外轮船和飞机在境内加油量(-)							
年初年末库存差额	3.22	-2.15	-4.07	-11.51	2.98	8.42	6.63
年初库存量	18.64	15.42	17.57	21.64	33.15	28.29	19.87
年末库存量(-)	15.42	17.57	21.64	33.15	30.17	19.87	13.24
二、消费量	413.06	461.36	444.13	460.89	445.10	401.11	385.84
消费量分组一							
农林牧渔业	1.23	2.36	2.22	1.10	2.21	2.47	2.42
工业	249.88	269.49	227.73	196.77	172.29	135.08	112.06
建筑业	14.49	16.17	16.18	14.89	16.69	14.55	14.32
交通运输、仓储和邮政业	54.93	63.34	73.81	83.33	85.93	85.15	88.21
批发、零售业和住宿、餐饮业	28.76	33.17	37.70	55.53	52.47	48.56	51.75
其他	21.91	25.00	27.44	34.45	33.86	33.18	34.61
生活消费	41.86	51.83	59.05	74.82	81.65	82.11	82.47
消费量分组二							
终端消费	266.62	286.63	320.59	381.24	414.02	389.49	385.20
＃工业	103.76	95.08	104.24	117.23	141.34	123.56	111.52
加工转换损失	146.12	174.41	123.49	79.54	30.93	11.53	0.54
火力发电	146.12	174.41	123.49	79.54	30.85	11.53	0.54
供热					0.08		
炼油损耗							
制气							
损失量	0.32	0.32	0.05	0.11	0.15	0.09	0.10
三、平衡差额							

13-4 煤炭平衡表(2005-2011年)

Coal Balance Sheet (2005-2011)

单位：万吨

项　　目	2005年	2006年	2007年	2008年	2009年	2010年	2011年
一、可供量	1596.99	1738.97	1849.66	1924.57	1916.83	2039.07	2147.51
生产量							
外省(区、市)调入量	1582.15	1746.25	1769.23	1847.82	1906.10	1750.92	1439.79
进口量	9.40		85.00	140.82		287.97	713.18
本省(区、市)调出量(-)						8.02	9.15
出口量(-)							
年初年末库存差额	5.44	-7.28	-4.57	-64.07	10.73	8.20	3.69
年初库存量	70.80	65.36	72.64	77.21	141.28	129.63	121.43
年末库存量(-)	65.36	72.64	77.21	141.28	130.55	121.43	117.74
二、消费量	1596.99	1738.97	1849.66	1924.57	1916.83	2039.07	2147.51
消费量分组一							
农林牧渔业							
工业	1596.99	1738.97	1849.66	1924.57	1914.73	2037.77	2146.13
建筑业							
交通运输、仓储和邮政业							
批发、零售业和住宿、餐饮业					2.10	1.20	1.28
其他							
生活消费							
消费量分组二							
终端消费	132.22	184.22	233.99	441.92	481.42	374.94	385.56
#工业	132.22	184.22	233.99	441.92	479.32	373.74	384.28
用于加工转换	1464.76	1554.75	1615.67	1482.65	1434.21	1664.03	1761.85
火力发电	1464.76	1554.75	1615.67	1459.21	1335.14	1448.61	1533.55
供热				23.44	101.71	217.88	235.74
洗煤损耗							
炼焦							
制气							
型煤加工损耗					-2.64	-2.46	-7.44
损失量	0.01				1.20	0.10	0.10
三、平衡差额							

13-5 全社会用电量（2005-2011年）

Total Consumption of Electricity (2005-2011)

单位：万千瓦时

项　　目	2005年	2006年	2007年	2008年	2009年	2010年	2011年
全社会用电量总计	4198289	4720112	5154025	5141578	4955750	5619996	5860652
#各行业用电量合计	3855742	4329080	4718336	4651348	4409908	5036303	5203144
#第一产业	9761	9514	9643	9584	9354	10279	12359
第二产业	3397588	3761186	4101528	4019849	3724455	4317267	4403326
第三产业	448393	558380	607165	621915	676099	708757	787459
城乡居民生活用电量合计	342547	391032	435689	490230	545842	583693	657508
各行业用电分类							
农、林、牧、渔业	9761	9514	9643	9584	9354	10279	12359
工业	3374306	3735651	4061784	3962669	3673716	4262339	4351290
#轻工业	1357858	1502077	1656565	1675707	1590781	1821542	1801345
重工业	2016448	2233574	2405219	2286962	2082935	2440797	2549945
#采矿业	8112	6024	8796	8607	6865	8044	6902
制造业	3044575	3381692	3625554	3567232	3382129	3953169	4040754
#电力、燃气及水的生产和供应业	321619	347935	427434	386830	284722	301126	303634
#电力、热力的生产和供应业	240737	272067	328413	268378	173866	183361	193762
#电厂生产全部耗用电量	41656	75606	75090	68094	67286	51096	67171
线路损失电量	190736	189347	253318	200284	106573	132265	126591
燃气生产和供应业	654	845	895	917	1433	1778	2158
水的生产和供应业	80228	75023	98126	117535	109423	115987	107714
建筑业	23282	25535	39744	57180	50739	54928	52036
交通运输、仓储和邮政业	14425	15508	19789	22453	23358	26524	31830
#交通运输业	8614	9387	12512	13868	13997	16173	19913
仓储业	2084	2300	3122	3890	4459	5774	6930
邮政业	3727	3821	4155	4695	4902	4577	4987
信息传输、计算机服务和软件业	15277	17376	22259	26429	31172	35085	40150
批发、零售业和住宿、餐饮业	282238	364478	356196	337296	364374	376037	412597
#批发和零售业	148555	193891	177435	162736	177608	194549	223703
住宿和餐饮业	130153	170587	178761	174560	186766	181488	188894
金融、房地产、商务及居民服务业	65223	79917	101327	110630	114305	117690	131271
#金融业	16158	16225	16870	16178	15073	14156	14977
房地产业	21976	25083	25846	23986	23111	23489	23941
租赁和商务服务、居民服务和其他服务	27089	38609	58611	70466	76121	80045	92353
公共事业及管理组织	71230	81101	107594	125107	142890	153421	171611
#科学研究、技术服务和地质勘查业	4550	3206	3012	2691	2675	2950	2945
#地质勘查业	248	23	17	15	30	45	10
水利、环境和公共设施管理业	26633	30069	33736	38338	49440	56514	67243
#水利管理业	12157	11650	6618	2443	4127	5208	10119
教育、文化、体育和娱乐业	13596	15417	21112	24582	27728	29655	33757
#教育	4793	4871	5988	6295	7208	8615	10548
卫生、社会保障和社会福利业	12151	15088	7522	4012	5889	8964	12051
公共管理和社会组织、国际组织	14300	17321	42212	55484	57158	55338	55615

13-6 规模以上工业综合能源消费量（2005-2011年）

Overall Energy Consumpiton of Industrial Enterprises above Designated Size (2005-2011)

单位：吨标准煤

指标	2005年	2006年	2007年	2008年	2009年	2010年	2011年
合　计	12037714	13290543	14379411	14528511	13679420	14960593	14825631
(一)采矿业	769	675	706	361	160	193	
煤炭开采和洗选业							
石油和天然气开采业							
黑色金属矿采选业							
有色金属矿采选业							
非金属矿采选业	769	675	706	114	160	193	
其他采矿业				247			
(二)制造业	5273612	6365772	7492792	8140697	7848902	8743936	8366992
农副食品加工业	59666	94383	139017	146621	169496	190698	231577
食品制造业	51949	75174	84197	85670	89657	100257	82668
饮料制造业	34764	48904	60046	59173	54740	62258	58523
烟草制品业							
纺织业	876658	842201	932175	856952	758755	809179	645197
纺织服装、鞋、帽制造业	165413	144783	138591	99994	83779	58020	47883
皮革、毛皮、羽毛(绒)及其制品业	92086	183236	203600	160892	142298	188284	159368
木材加工及木、竹、藤、棕、草制品业	8684	11324	12470	17024	17524	31901	24898
家具制造业	106972	105694	100380	99529	75372	96883	80582
造纸及纸制品业	1452027	2246173	2889078	3477439	3708558	4155618	4288929
印刷业和记录媒介的复制	38855	41457	49755	63425	58184	49990	43545
文教体育用品制造业	150581	138360	136963	143387	108321	116821	100126
石油加工、炼焦及核燃料加工业	67	29939	92308	56016	696	2306	2257
化学原料及化学制品制造业	149516	156848	162108	174693	165849	215692	204612
医药制造业	4950	6075	6443	7111	6932	6972	6460
化学纤维制造业	17288	25988	22388	4378	4179	8430	6896
橡胶制品业	42554	41997	41964	61100	51890	41861	34296
塑料制品业	326872	320924	342762	424140	383414	418696	333106
非金属矿物制品业	333262	409912	539683	612137	657556	716487	672580
黑色金属冶炼及压延加工业	22399	27459	28448	20815	10287	17037	14787
有色金属冶炼及压延加工业	26412	34052	41856	55869	33015	41801	36630
金属制品业	180098	171235	180663	138760	115815	133152	108392
通用设备制造业	45760	48845	57133	81424	57777	69724	67260
专用设备制造业	104801	80444	89690	112887	103566	74432	66827
交通运输设备制造业	14488	13571	16419	51812	38347	45462	47166
电气机械及器材制造业	283994	305746	318329	301393	252323	270507	236466
通信设备、计算机及其他电子设备制造业	578746	659829	702659	697227	585042	710090	676744
仪器仪表及文化、办公用机械制造业	78158	69880	72045	65574	62713	68411	56536
工艺品及其他制造业	26474	31338	31624	65255	52816	42966	32680
废弃资源和废旧材料回收加工业	117						
(三)电力、燃气及水的生产和供应业	6763334	6924096	6885913	6387453	5830358	6216464	6458639
电力、热力的生产和供应业	6728304	6859857	6817766	6323666	5775585	6162853	6406720
燃气生产和供应业				21	184	231	195
水的生产和供应业	35030	64238	68147	63766	54589	53380	51724

主要统计指标解释

Explanatory Notes on Main Statistical Indicators

能源生产总量 指一定时期内全国（地区）一次能源生产量的总和，是观察全国（地区）能源生产水平、规模、构成和发展速度的总量指标。一次能源生产量包括原煤、原油、天然气、水电、核能及其他动力能（如风能、地热能等）发电量。不包括低热值燃料生产量、生物质能、太阳能等的利用和由一次能源加工转换而成的二次能源产量。

能源消费总量 指一定时期内全国（地区）生产和生活消费的各种能源的总和，是观察能源消费水平、构成和增长速度的总量指标，能源消费总量包括原煤和原油及其制品、天然气、电力等。能源消费总量分为三部分，即终端能源消费量、能源加工转换损失量和损失量。

(1)终端能源消费量 指一定时期内全国（地区）生产和生活消费的各种能源在扣除了用于加工转换二次能源消费量和损失量以后的数量。

(2)能源加工转换损失量 指一定时期内全国（地区）投入加工转换的各种能源数量之和与产出各种能源产品之和的差额。它是观察能源在加工转换过程中损失量变化的指标。

(3)能源损失量 指一定时期内能源在输送、分配、储存过程中发生的损失和由客观原因造成的各种损失量。不包括各种气体能源放空、放散量。

能源生产弹性系数 是研究能源生产增长速度与国民经济增长速度之间关系的指标。计算公式：

$$\text{能源生产弹性系数}=\frac{\text{能源生产总量增长速度}}{\text{国民经济增长速度}}$$

国民经济增长速度，可根据不同的目的或需要，用国民生产总值，国内生产总值等指标来计算，本资料是采用国内生产总值指标计算的。

电力生产弹性系数 是研究电力生产增长速度与国民经济增长速度之间关系的指标。计算公式：

$$\text{电力生产弹性系数}=\frac{\text{电力生产量增长速度}}{\text{国民经济增长速度}}$$

能源消费弹性系数 是反映能源消费增长速度与国民经济增长速度之间比例关系的指标。计算公式：

$$\text{能源消费弹性系数}=\frac{\text{能源消费量增长速度}}{\text{国民经济增长速度}}$$

电力消费弹性系数 是反映电力消费增长速度与国民经济增长速度之间比例关系的指标。计算公式：

$$\text{电力消费弹性系数}=\frac{\text{电力消费量增长速度}}{\text{国民经济增长速度}}$$

能源加工转换效率 指一定时期内能源经过加工、转换后，产出的各种能源产品的数量与同期内投入加工转换的各种能源数量的比率。它是观察能源加工转换装置和生产工艺先进与落后、管理水平高低等的重要指标。计算公式：

$$\text{能源加工转换效率}=\frac{\text{能源加工、转换产出量}}{\text{能源加工、转换投入量}}\times 100\%$$

十四、镇街主要指标

Main Indicators of Towns

14-1 镇街生产总值

Gross Domestic Product by Town

单位：万元

镇街	(1991年)				(1992年)			
	地区生产总值	第一产业	第二产业	第三产业	地区生产总值	第一产业	第二产业	第三产业
全市	959073	134523	503220	321330	1108922	144115	592701	372106
莞城	22046	174	16612	5260	28881	108	22263	6510
石龙	25154	907	17669	6578	29467	1026	21163	7278
虎门	44900	10059	16412	18429	56539	10336	24781	21422
东城	23500	7179	13793	2528	32770	7362	21392	4016
万江	18518	3874	11653	2991	27997	3968	18928	5102
南城	13339	2219	8181	2939	18147	1973	12681	3493
中堂	14889	3300	9065	2524	19902	4360	10669	4873
望牛墩	11950	2794	7394	1762	13789	2854	8683	2252
麻涌	24449	10489	11478	2482	26907	9797	14294	2816
石碣	12556	2686	7660	2210	16967	2888	11140	2939
高埗	11546	3352	5163	3031	14295	4017	6503	3775
道滘	15659	4540	9542	1577	19009	4805	12003	2201
洪梅	6492	3879	1872	741	6906	2441	3435	1030
沙田	12616	6467	4552	1597	16779	6511	7850	2417
厚街	31303	5679	22403	3221	38272	6064	28528	3680
长安	24850	7961	13185	3704	36298	8980	21883	5435
寮步	23700	9030	8979	5691	30083	9256	12627	8200
大岭山	10557	5918	3123	1516	16175	6342	4928	4905
大朗	19481	11277	4870	3334	24694	10104	9836	4754
黄江	20403	2765	15888	1750	28355	3244	22864	2247
樟木头	10515	10515	2107	6426	13972	2212	8536	3224
清溪	8673	2076	4428	2169	12742	2405	6936	3401
塘厦	17826	6128	9049	2649	30454	6300	19988	4166
凤岗	8676	2698	5550	428	12119	3257	8146	716
谢岗	9472	2019	5197	2256	7178	2339	4236	603
常平	38008	13134	14511	10363	45046	11625	20103	13317
桥头	14030	4083	8114	1833	22099	5429	10336	6334
横沥	11125	2499	6349	2277	15673	2710	9342	3621
东坑	16245	3544	11393	1308	22332	3368	17294	1670
企石	16155	3731	9575	2849	21159	4699	13097	3363
石排	16123	2350	10727	3046	18091	2704	11839	3548
茶山	13328	3385	7146	2797	16377	4160	8782	3435

注：各镇街合计不等于全市数，下同。

14-1 续表 1

单位：万元

镇街	(1993年)				(1994年)			
	地区生产总值	第一产业	第二产业	第三产业	地区生产总值	第一产业	第二产业	第三产业
全市	1570491	143953	873114	553424	2170340	174796	1194928	800616
莞城	41307		32838	8469	55021		43120	11901
石龙	34182	582	21188	12412	48891	216	32738	15937
虎门	74808	11281	37710	25816	103070	14350	51597	37123
东城	37567	4379	25901	7287	44963	5223	30065	9675
万江	39317	4818	26939	7561	45953	5499	31186	9268
南城	23341	2767	16312	4262	46416	2811	38511	5094
中堂	31352	7282	16982	7089	34819	6271	19472	9076
望牛墩	15717	2642	10196	2879	18449	2796	11974	3679
麻涌	34553	9305	22223	3025	42676	9160	27917	5599
石碣	23877	2542	16311	5024	34401	2816	24582	7003
高埗	17843	4751	8347	4745	22368	5495	10877	5996
道滘	24306	5086	15471	3749	37062	5698	27835	14072
洪梅	8069	2265	4292	1512	9020	2406	4756	1858
沙田	24446	6574	14434	3438	31950	6196	20646	5107
厚街	57912	6707	44408	6796	101289	7615	77637	16037
长安	49862	9995	31962	7905	68914	11024	46939	10951
寮步	46311	9423	21926	14962	63089	12428	30205	20456
大岭山	22611	6717	7660	8234	27722	6725	11258	9739
大朗	32720	10237	15152	7331	46550	13958	21052	11540
黄江	37008	3021	30171	3816	47096	3254	39031	4811
樟木头	18265	1361	13994	2910	23438	1680	18008	3750
清溪	19533	3299	12076	4158	30510	4230	20391	5889
塘厦	41635	4353	31001	6281	80870	6396	65620	8854
凤岗	16961	3282	12778	901	24520	4166	19054	1300
谢岗	12063	2367	8997	699	16093	3365	11143	1585
常平	67921	12564	34518	20839	100294	13561	62109	24624
桥头	27654	5023	15085	7546	40632	6225	22445	11962
横沥	23825	23825	2604	13815	33565	3922	17444	12198
东坑	33565	4073	25007	4485	36161	4245	26665	5251
企石	28573	5167	17684	5722	34915	6545	21854	6516
石排	25462	2992	17949	4521	31920	3699	21172	7049
茶山	21196	4908	12096	4192	30233	6017	18221	5995

14-1 续表 2

单位：万元

镇街	(1995年)				(1996年)			
	地区生产总值	第一产业	第二产业	第三产业	地区生产总值	第一产业	第二产业	第三产业
全市	2962892	214306	1669723	1078863	3617502	248645	1994826	1374031
莞城	69318		52710	16608	72335		50523	21812
石龙	70501	318	46550	23633	72190	303	36303	35584
虎门	130282	18388	68784	43110	158257	25193	85444	47620
东城	85114	6208	57257	21649	100581	6744	66136	27701
万江	55648	6705	37884	11059	63649	8488	40934	14227
南城	83707	2938	63407	17362	103785	3667	79347	20771
中堂	41537	6593	23358	11585	50533	7418	28908	14206
望牛墩	21961	3197	14061	4703	25963	3440	16512	6011
麻涌	47340	11783	28584	6973	49764	15494	26884	7386
石碣	46831	3332	33206	10293	66081	3495	45532	17054
高埗	28324	6213	14403	7708	36274	6945	19348	9981
道滘	47605	5698	27835	14072	55596	6031	35931	13634
洪梅	15209	2667	6923	5619	16733	2908	7657	6168
沙田	42922	7741	29376	5806	49023	10655	32354	6015
厚街	118353	9670	90642	18041	140036	10906	83151	45979
长安	93323	12505	65233	15585	131672	12882	97066	21724
寮步	75398	14727	32311	28360	85876	15651	37022	33203
大岭山	39228	8485	17265	13478	49383	9773	21083	18527
大朗	66807	17319	25844	23644	78506	16982	29641	31883
黄江	61098	3708	46392	10998	63391	3929	46558	12904
樟木头	31914	2662	24710	4543	41323	3443	32232	5647
清溪	52550	5721	35627	11202	82953	6083	55419	21451
塘厦	112158	6909	90588	14661	139903	9900	112916	17087
凤岗	37051	4767	30135	2149	48015	5521	39670	2824
谢岗	18872	4356	12655	1861	25536	5213	18242	2081
常平	135315	18444	87856	29015	146594	19303	86033	41258
桥头	54012	7206	30626	16180	64694	8418	38393	17883
横沥	44663	4484	23559	16620	54922	4717	29045	21161
东坑	34654	5179	19727	9748	50965	5274	32218	13473
企石	44588	7760	28861	7967	54066	8947	35535	9584
石排	34349	4898	20547	8904	37946	5718	21459	10769
茶山	41484	6017	18221	5995	51339	7159	24892	9433

14-1 续表 3

单位：万元

镇街	(1997年)				(1998年)			
	地区生产总值	第一产业	第二产业	第三产业	地区生产总值	第一产业	第二产业	第三产业
全市	4485981	256388	2432816	1796777	5579965	259437	3056779	2263749
莞城	80298		49962	30336	110076		49677	60399
石龙	95560	293	48361	46906	133953	116	77910	55927
虎门	246823	25799	130963	90061	362826	29535	176729	156562
东城	125730	5850	78959	40921	161819	5246	105142	51431
万江	69516	8749	42333	18434	82239	9424	50075	22922
南城	130392	3490	103126	23776	160524	3933	128850	27741
中堂	61741	7610	35991	18140	76980	7727	45359	23894
望牛墩	30854	3780	19390	7684	36531	3941	22769	9821
麻涌	52217	15965	29345	6907	62531	16443	35485	10603
石碣	85990	3782	54674	27534	109255	3852	70872	34531
高埗	46630	7586	26579	12465	60242	8235	36383	15624
道滘	69424	6383	47525	15516	80887	6756	54039	20092
洪梅	20052	4501	7602	7949	23134	4607	9569	8958
沙田	54881	11342	36602	6936	71203	16829	42167	12207
厚街	184205	11448	96880	75877	247177	12150	146229	88798
长安	180377	13111	134235	33031	245676	13562	183031	49083
寮步	103656	17341	45112	41203	129731	18768	60452	50511
大岭山	65246	10538	31884	22824	83268	9134	45040	29094
大朗	95301	19093	38996	37212	122409	15008	53085	54316
黄江	67618	4139	47073	16406	83585	4244	58492	20849
樟木头	55682	4725	43020	7936	71299	5333	51615	14351
清溪	120961	7519	84276	29166	160483	7802	115314	37367
塘厦	178757	11467	140870	26420	230580	12121	177569	40890
凤岗	63066	5925	51486	5655	79286	6187	65440	7659
谢岗	29488	6379	20521	2588	34881	6958	24888	3035
常平	185390	20195	98068	67127	231059	19811	131252	79996
桥头	79685	8523	51919	19243	96661	9712	61140	25809
横沥	67894	6411	34892	26591	81263	5364	45427	30472
东坑	63718	4810	44682	14226	78576	5726	54359	18491
企石	62625	9562	42240	10823	72065	9827	47551	14687
石排	43477	6463	23530	13484	53842	6606	28932	18304
茶山	63955	9321	39524	15110	77319	9878	47785	19656

14-1 续表 4

单位：万元

镇街	(1999年) 地区生产总值	第一产业	第二产业	第三产业	(2000年) 地区生产总值	第一产业	第二产业	第三产业
全市	6672386	257863	3670519	2744004	8202531	259087	4507072	3436372
莞城	131005		58104	72901	184225		67030	117195
石龙	157715	349	86171	71195	184256	189	98240	85827
虎门	442633	31013	213607	198014	532946	30479	263928	238539
东城	207432	4126	125159	78147	262854	4233	153667	104954
万江	97379	9435	59636	28308	138724	11604	85526	41594
南城	198820	2756	149678	46386	233013	3119	171413	58481
中堂	94412	7001	57217	30194	123213	7032	76571	39610
望牛墩	43303	4012	26738	12553	51516	4072	31399	16045
麻涌	75449	12466	44768	18215	90816	12213	45965	32638
石碣	137148	3866	88152	45130	175180	4021	111038	60121
高埗	78709	8792	50131	19786	102516	9155	67888	25473
道滘	93751	7151	61687	24913	109999	7569	67841	34589
洪梅	26118	4162	11872	10084	29921	4383	14095	11443
沙田	86339	12167	53505	20667	109128	12714	71503	24911
厚街	300721	12412	171495	116814	405317	12705	221947	170665
长安	332335	13820	240690	77825	419347	14256	299650	105441
寮步	161782	19944	82582	59256	202379	20732	110577	71070
大岭山	108469	9238	67662	31569	138789	9742	89991	39056
大朗	156427	16699	69193	70535	201504	17826	94065	89613
黄江	97621	4410	67206	26005	123331	5243	83748	34340
樟木头	94385	4225	64138	26021	147697	4639	71921	71138
清溪	206524	8790	151219	46515	303131	9984	231303	61844
塘厦	288110	12783	217897	57430	363971	13486	272234	78251
凤岗	100753	6267	61392	33094	128298	6336	79138	42824
谢岗	42142	3610	29017	9515	50174	3975	35779	10420
常平	302805	15703	166347	120755	395318	16116	218229	160974
桥头	111892	9062	69595	33235	130380	9093	82261	39026
横沥	97209	6178	55276	35756	116749	8593	62314	45842
东坑	101287	5363	65010	30913	118430	6241	76250	35940
企石	85313	10000	51789	23524	99467	11339	58897	29231
石排	69030	6772	37874	24384	87817	6913	48532	32372
茶山	90250	9514	55468	25268	105432	10712	64726	29994

14-1 续表 5

单位：万元

镇街	(2001年)				(2002年)			
	地区生产总值	第一产业	第二产业	第三产业	地区生产总值	第一产业	第二产业	第三产业
全市	9918905	260968	5405092	4252845	11869374	248791	6488109	5132474
莞城	222233		80203	142030	312742		76890	235852
石龙	215738	150	115691	99897	248664	144	135163	113357
虎门	618557	30469	304781	283307	717425	26838	350636	339951
东城	342044	3785	188628	149631	466960	2110	232502	232348
万江	175693	13015	90857	71821	213919	11026	106945	95948
南城	286473	2929	211622	71922	350029	2711	262431	84887
中堂	153366	7155	95677	50533	194263	5908	122819	65536
望牛墩	60921	3540	36872	20509	73104	3591	43299	26214
麻涌	127061	12298	74806	39957	173557	1002	120426	43079
石碣	243163	4139	150613	88411	340162	4141	209830	126191
高埗	133362	9477	90730	33155	173004	9701	120415	42888
道滘	128327	8011	76692	43624	153201	8479	87039	57683
洪梅	34245	4587	16543	13115	41756	4793	21676	15287
沙田	142060	13641	92266	36153	182363	13912	119778	48673
厚街	483117	13088	253149	216880	583689	13976	297707	272006
长安	529219	14496	371263	143460	679022	14622	469032	195368
寮步	252526	21246	143824	87456	314871	20276	182688	111907
大岭山	194021	10089	133489	50443	251078	5741	178811	66526
大朗	264929	17764	128283	118882	341930	15525	181234	145171
黄江	154595	5176	98438	50981	199781	5288	122001	72492
樟木头	176062	4460	84195	87407	210845	5545	101237	104063
清溪	393471	10517	302613	80341	501941	11106	382584	108251
塘厦	457175	13796	335872	107507	573947	13603	425078	135266
凤岗	162854	6400	97540	58914	205006	2035	126903	76068
谢岗	58323	4115	41585	12623	71092	5665	40790	24637
常平	493419	16451	272983	203985	557039	16077	310537	230425
桥头	151979	8366	98054	45559	179442	7245	118564	53633
横沥	140251	9252	74148	56851	168932	9380	90576	68976
东坑	132805	6013	84256	42535	149147	5438	92587	51122
企石	115314	12403	63421	39490	127616	9088	68807	49721
石排	107585	6925	61859	38801	131394	6967	75798	48629
茶山	123931	9801	75341	38789	153215	9801	91916	51498

14-1 续表 6

单位：万元

镇街	(2003年)				(2004年)			
	地区生产总值	第一产业	第二产业	第三产业	地区生产总值	第一产业	第二产业	第三产业
全市	14525187	228165	7981954	6315068	18060258	227087	10160382	7672789
莞城	415993		80802	335191	552370		94035	458335
石龙	287713	116	167126	120471	317521	51	186652	130820
虎门	905165	27106	462105	415954	1139827	27168	598000	514659
东城	652408	1657	314094	336657	897727	900	411172	485655
万江	269593	9622	129625	130346	329849	5617	156431	167801
南城	452911	2743	314752	135416	741609	1869	349496	390244
中堂	256251	7013	162945	86292	338808	5956	206693	126159
望牛墩	87872	3520	50846	33506	106086	3550	59709	42827
麻涌	234612	8769	177540	48303	292911	8664	226131	58116
石碣	463023	4253	290495	168275	590604	3649	381862	205093
高埗	224078	9891	157949	56238	282716	9943	202317	70456
道滘	178954	8975	100566	69413	217400	9499	119688	88213
洪梅	53960	5113	29668	19179	76686	4770	41140	30776
沙田	236769	13944	155438	67387	310921	13975	202383	94563
厚街	721188	12275	374482	334431	878666	12341	454284	412041
长安	887947	14863	603308	269776	1162826	15040	759582	388204
寮步	394322	13167	234806	146349	498253	5327	303435	189491
大岭山	322872	4937	226565	91370	447412	4571	313857	128984
大朗	443891	10640	240983	192268	574604	6986	325826	241792
黄江	258682	4567	152903	101212	331432	3294	187369	140769
樟木头	250877	4863	119145	126869	291893	4350	139729	147814
清溪	645553	11218	495035	139300	848426	9610	660589	178227
塘厦	710030	13565	526730	169735	882099	13700	653816	214583
凤岗	284608	2048	170574	111986	373309	2015	220434	150860
谢岗	91482	4266	51312	35904	119007	4328	69024	45655
常平	657385	12627	377679	267079	796109	10792	468642	316674
桥头	213712	5419	134937	73356	264849	4495	144282	116072
横沥	205872	9602	117554	78716	253887	9075	153884	90928
东坑	181394	8423	113270	59701	230057	7943	145998	76116
企石	142717	5216	72284	65217	167279	3848	80461	82970
石排	157729	7144	92020	58565	190127	7259	109953	72915
茶山	195098	8607	118895	67596	268473	7413	161070	99990

14-1 续表 7

单位：万元

镇街	(2005年) 地区生产总值	第一产业	第二产业	第三产业	(2006年) 地区生产总值	第一产业	第二产业	第三产业
全市	21831961	205546	12278624	9347791	26279791	120089	15065985	11093717
莞城	617849		153367	464482	712319		230144	482174
石龙	349301	141	194749	154411	384329	35	213392	170902
虎门	1283052	22937	668632	591483	1492628	11446	763086	718096
东城	1049758	480	473888	575389	1264850	427	571728	692694
万江	375471	4209	164099	207164	440346	4711	187932	247702
南城	1016644	1900	440431	574313	1229016	1995	508223	718798
中堂	424212	6122	276399	141691	507968	6428	332766	168774
望牛墩	126751	3511	73191	50049	156949	3480	87638	65831
麻涌	387211	8588	310275	68348	494018	7106	398466	88445
石碣	728816	3782	491498	233535	868731	3091	588622	277018
高埗	366593	10020	254017	102556	456695	6552	320225	129918
道滘	255589	8753	143285	103551	301036	9568	174820	116648
洪梅	102660	3939	61138	37583	123863	4082	77274	42507
沙田	364800	13695	240822	110283	442784	12585	293854	136345
厚街	1033929	11722	531019	491188	1199117	6929	609223	582965
长安	1339428	9492	917732	412204	1539236	7505	1042139	489592
寮步	598969	7765	364261	226943	739610	1136	451671	286803
大岭山	547734	4102	370108	173524	675091	2329	431260	241502
大朗	707369	14112	411161	282096	850356	1491	499588	349277
黄江	364377	3065	220654	140658	441152	741	276062	164349
樟木头	330537	3463	157434	169640	393688	600	185556	207532
清溪	984943	9036	761281	214626	1097986	8012	828219	261755
塘厦	1057175	13661	771724	271790	1186644	12312	830537	343794
凤岗	517427	1762	320177	195488	623929	1750	373375	248804
谢岗	148917	4467	91026	53424	192841	4795	118714	69332
常平	951464	10062	556932	384470	1119659	6338	644544	468777
桥头	287240	4495	168473	114271	388604	1387	210763	176454
横沥	304870	8593	195659	100619	373304	7274	242406	123624
东坑	261238	11543	165441	84254	295233	5703	194653	94877
企石	200581	3129	102183	95269	244027	2266	129255	112506
石排	234709	7268	128132	99308	294009	7283	154259	132467
茶山	305183	6652	190620	107911	384988	3215	245078	136695

14-1 续表 8

单位：万元

镇街	(2007年) 地区生产总值	第一产业	第二产业	第三产业	(2008年) 地区生产总值	第一产业	第二产业	第三产业
全市	31600489	118991	17546573	13934924	37036004	148251	19016068	17871685
莞城	897597		298250	599347	1015311		294311	721000
石龙	427216	10	235821	191385	475742	7	239943	235792
虎门	1846638	10373	936639	899626	2153489	11940	1093014	1048535
东城	1559123	377	699730	859017	1816793	339	773623	1042831
万江	520636	3405	221314	295917	604659	3702	262498	338459
南城	1425257	2015	583496	839747	1632407	1285	618209	1012913
中堂	588085	6553	379181	202351	659949	6760	419455	233734
望牛墩	193635	3462	105983	84190	236495	3359	127759	105377
麻涌	651344	5985	537412	107947	834681	7564	693959	133158
石碣	994532	3096	670790	320646	1082524	2795	694349	385380
高埗	568276	6530	384637	177109	690604	6526	442377	241701
道滘	362268	8202	211240	142826	439328	7218	240510	191600
洪梅	163384	4281	110958	48145	206785	4381	147969	54435
沙田	515106	12403	327706	174997	588063	12863	337140	238060
厚街	1420026	7270	719643	693113	1616483	7971	797404	811108
长安	1770272	7746	1152474	610052	2029075	4979	1158887	865209
寮步	886584	1118	531815	353650	1038493	2141	584767	451585
大岭山	822554	2241	502679	317634	960138	2248	554712	403178
大朗	1025864	2098	592111	431655	1100875	877	688340	411658
黄江	556305	740	347972	207593	721414	724	438204	282486
樟木头	461719	505	228647	232567	507743	311	253050	254382
清溪	1266762	6207	924401	336153	1417816	5170	966538	446108
塘厦	1365736	11206	903107	451422	1602945	10447	980030	612468
凤岗	747757	1752	409163	336843	901696	1725	472782	427189
谢岗	239771	5178	143093	91500	273944	9273	160217	104454
常平	1311744	6665	747353	557726	1495652	6058	796227	693366
桥头	467790	1326	242928	223536	536868	2692	254438	279737
横沥	443014	4350	275399	163265	522130	6972	300380	214778
东坑	320991	4532	204804	111654	372361	4017	231268	137076
企石	291765	2868	150052	138844	320630	2314	159252	159064
石排	360806	7308	187787	165711	417073	7313	216033	193727
茶山	476010	3131	293991	178888	593265	4327	353036	235902

14-1 续表 9

单位：万元

镇街	(2009年) 地区生产总值	第一产业	第二产业	第三产业	(2010年) 地区生产总值	第一产业	第二产业	第三产业
全市	37639142	147877	18230836	19260428	42464527	165719	21608153	20690656
莞城	1054949		318447	736502	1138887		328434	810453
石龙	502973	6	249848	253119	559487	14	301186	258287
虎门	2437582	13180	1213679	1210723	2728626	17635	1299038	1411953
东城	1989067	386	742171	1246510	2282606	391	926086	1356129
万江	611916	3578	241005	367333	685201	3590	268049	413562
南城	1841809	1235	706141	1134433	2005491	1173	524640	1479678
中堂	662727	6965	396592	259170	669207	7035	396336	265836
望牛墩	288697	3395	162960	122342	306900	3498	166207	137195
麻涌	932351	8332	788621	135398	1070116	9248	895934	164934
石碣	1094432	2667	641983	449782	1001406	2954	656042	342410
高埗	609392	6228	387053	216111	697532	6350	452412	238770
道滘	449115	8024	234381	206710	515731	8181	289160	218390
洪梅	253003	4612	186637	61754	341015	4626	263103	73286
沙田	614104	12894	360064	241146	674850	12903	417895	244052
厚街	1695963	8373	880274	807316	1918700	9108	1000759	908833
长安	2083662	4532	1196987	882143	2371479	4959	1450285	916235
寮步	1120641	1866	630705	488070	1335015	2395	774425	558195
大岭山	975717	2255	505238	468224	1060202	2407	524440	533355
大朗	1160519	1242	675946	483331	1352689	1352	807882	543455
黄江	768073	720	419897	347456	860211	745	463492	395974
樟木头	524759	378	251340	273041	550388	404	234874	315110
清溪	1363307	5410	873074	484823	1438135	5864	907020	525251
塘厦	1713803	11448	1059192	643163	1790583	11713	1120627	658243
凤岗	1013446	1220	513090	499136	1114665	1222	543805	569638
谢岗	294969	9452	166712	118805	358653	8230	216560	133863
常平	1516942	6725	799850	710367	1615270	7102	790276	817892
桥头	535223	3546	251952	279725	583924	5738	277615	300571
横沥	538610	6294	326010	206306	576143	3982	321902	250259
东坑	387579	2118	237522	147939	416762	1760	250523	164479
企石	318197	1974	172565	143658	327900	1648	184444	141808
石排	438939	7500	243190	188249	507685	7520	299884	200281
茶山	620174	4327	360862	254985	641962	2878	346959	292125

14-1 续表 10

单位：万元

镇街	(2011年)			
	地区生产总值	第一产业	第二产业	第三产业
全市	47353949	178776	23662018	23513155
莞城	1288562		387954	900608
石龙	622168	13	329569	292586
虎门	3100010	17434	1352694	1729882
东城	2553050	400	978519	1574131
万江	769132	4034	296564	468534
南城	2328755	1170	597078	1730507
中堂	740823	7895	430871	302057
望牛墩	360982	3786	198059	159137
麻涌	1205818	11411	967151	227256
石碣	1098260	3008	717595	377657
高埗	798981	6351	519762	272868
道滘	582510	9247	316509	256754
洪梅	372907	5001	281752	86154
沙田	724112	15098	423611	285403
厚街	2170463	9736	1149481	1011246
长安	2564370	4522	1550789	1009059
寮步	1471407	2029	841514	627864
大岭山	1221652	2463	575529	643660
大朗	1469179	1555	855609	612015
黄江	962019	765	488300	472954
樟木头	623121	445	259066	363610
清溪	1522825	6550	899945	616330
塘厦	2025381	12255	1204708	808418
凤岗	1305676	1370	629700	674606
谢岗	416269	10748	255645	149876
常平	1823461	7851	892551	923059
桥头	651918	4900	296495	350523
横沥	638887	5177	339962	293748
东坑	519150	2236	329596	187318
企石	364218	1817	196388	166013
石排	527052	7558	289733	229761
茶山	722124	3341	360722	358061

14-2 镇街第三产业增加值（2011年）

Value-added of the Tertiary Industry by Town (2011)

单位：万元

镇街	第三产业增加值	#交通运输及仓储业	批发和零售业	住宿和餐饮业	金融业	房地产业
全市	**23513155**	1109497	4628747	1694750	1830659	4076705
莞城	**900608**	66325	228211	31412	168542	195285
石龙	**292586**	19951	65627	28863	36837	47771
虎门	**1729882**	66566	514246	138688	110361	157559
东城	**1574131**	62583	205582	134342	160123	443202
万江	**468534**	24401	75416	40868	37255	79275
南城	**1730507**	39731	227807	82593	306475	276306
中堂	**302057**	11059	79786	31229	26534	34800
望牛墩	**159137**	34986	24760	8665	14568	10263
麻涌	**227256**	50867	26852	10813	18776	17308
石碣	**377657**	15790	72637	27998	31371	49171
高埗	**272868**	28337	53202	29362	17894	45331
道滘	**256754**	11600	35755	19375	19689	75151
洪梅	**86154**	10402	12613	10272	5734	11473
沙田	**285403**	34610	47495	27829	18104	37904
厚街	**1011246**	29834	145889	115571	76148	157590
长安	**1009059**	19299	268694	111136	78863	97562
寮步	**627864**	46302	103700	66435	56031	109498
大岭山	**643660**	16532	231170	46818	37968	91810
大朗	**612015**	8830	104430	77227	48616	117584
黄江	**472954**	17833	88672	53789	40961	97661
樟木头	**363610**	10123	80283	33034	33464	79654
清溪	**616330**	16156	66801	60271	43313	133838
塘厦	**808418**	19571	94689	96356	57250	138026
凤岗	**674606**	12550	90350	78500	47775	174565
谢岗	**149876**	9445	29733	15880	13482	33281
常平	**923059**	30124	160515	148512	74125	189255
桥头	**350523**	9514	58224	41486	20135	44790
横沥	**293748**	4074	52024	41612	24589	59365
东坑	**187318**	1581	32536	21148	17191	40824
企石	**166013**	8154	16776	13805	11006	33741
石排	**229761**	9293	42892	24403	21892	42347
茶山	**358061**	28569	62211	35139	25494	72020

14-3 镇街户籍户数与人口数(2011年)

Population of Household by Town (2011)

单位：人

镇街	户数(户)	农业户	非农业户	人口数	按性别分 男	女	按农业、非农业分 农业人口	非农业人口	总人口中未落户籍的人口数
全市总计	539044	262105	276939	1847691	937618	910073	903139	944552	3926
莞城	38839	1	38838	174412	89513	84899	2131	172281	
石龙	21481	2385	19096	71183	35388	35795	8923	62260	870
虎门	35304		35304	129105	65199	63906	2	129103	2
东城	25209		25209	90116	45988	44128		90116	19
万江	24434		24434	78538	39967	38571		78538	257
南城	20599		20599	74532	38759	35773		74532	17
中堂	21952	15373	6579	75531	38445	37086	55995	19536	43
望牛墩	11821	10043	1778	46353	23084	23269	39958	6395	850
麻涌	21886	17649	4237	72889	36574	36315	62558	10331	372
石碣	15068	11284	3784	44806	22870	21936	37415	7391	50
高埗	11414	10695	719	38186	19272	18914	35275	2911	121
道滘	16990	12511	4479	56083	28106	27977	44308	11775	17
洪梅	6558	6022	536	22271	11269	11002	20932	1339	255
沙田	12775	11487	1288	41330	20790	20540	36727	4603	56
厚街	29505	23543	5962	98121	49272	48849	84685	13436	69
长安	13664		13664	44925	23173	21752		44925	
寮步	21097	13446	7651	70114	35474	34640	43142	26972	1
大岭山	13372	11618	1754	45325	22858	22467	39344	5981	
大朗	18930	16424	2506	71280	36824	34456	62536	8744	10
黄江	8251	5976	2275	25491	12876	12615	18540	6951	1
樟木头	8136		8136	28038	14196	13842		28038	5
清溪	11622	9199	2423	36307	18121	18186	29544	6763	
塘厦	17905		17905	47140	23831	23309		47140	77
凤岗	7145	5012	2133	25018	12178	12840	17629	7389	7
谢岗	5385	4237	1148	20661	10298	10363	17270	3391	145
常平	25082	18029	7053	74894	38579	36315	58145	16749	24
桥头	11892	4960	6932	36327	18240	18087	16436	19891	206
横沥	11738	8851	2887	37387	19153	18234	30697	6690	9
东坑	10861	9074	1787	30407	15622	14785	27203	3204	190
企石	13233	11110	2123	42345	21672	20673	36955	5390	22
石排	13072	11493	1579	43531	21932	21599	39377	4154	200
茶山	13550	11683	1867	45079	22704	22375	37412	7667	31
松山湖	274		274	9966	5391	4575		9966	

14-4 镇街户籍人口自然变动情况（2011年）

Population Household by Town (2011)

镇　　街	出　生		死　亡		自然增长	
	人　数（人）	出生率（‰）	人　数（人）	死亡率（‰）	人　数（人）	自然增长率（‰）
全市总计	19884	10.92	8728	4.79	11156	6.13
莞　　城	1426	8.38	1052	6.18	374	2.20
石　　龙	549	7.76	353	4.99	196	2.77
虎　　门	1283	10.02	715	5.58	568	4.44
东　　城	878	11.88	346	4.68	532	7.20
万　　江	485	10.62	207	4.53	278	6.09
南　　城	737	9.55	344	4.46	393	5.09
中　　堂	548	12.32	160	3.60	388	8.72
望 牛 墩	419	11.09	159	4.21	260	6.88
麻　　涌	861	11.92	386	5.35	475	6.58
石　　碣	467	10.58	205	4.64	262	5.94
高　　埗	544	12.82	216	5.09	328	7.73
道　　滘	494	8.85	347	6.21	147	2.63
洪　　梅	276	12.59	127	5.79	149	6.80
沙　　田	1228	12.61	378	3.88	850	8.73
厚　　街	1093	15.02	211	2.90	882	12.12
长　　安	818	9.33	262	2.99	556	6.34
寮　　步	794	11.57	326	4.75	468	6.82
大 岭 山	568	13.11	158	3.65	410	9.46
大　　朗	788	11.17	386	5.47	402	5.70
黄　　江	306	12.42	109	4.42	197	8.00
樟 木 头	315	11.36	149	5.37	166	5.99
清　　溪	416	11.60	182	5.08	234	6.53
塘　　厦	589	12.77	218	4.73	371	8.05
凤　　岗	262	10.42	56	2.23	206	8.19
谢　　岗	279	13.69	79	3.88	200	9.81
常　　平	739	10.00	382	5.17	357	4.83
桥　　头	456	12.72	189	5.27	267	7.45
横　　沥	467	12.66	191	5.18	276	7.48
东　　坑	297	9.86	171	5.68	126	4.18
企　　石	473	11.15	249	5.87	224	5.28
石　　排	494	11.55	212	4.96	282	6.59
茶　　山	480	10.69	203	4.52	277	6.17
松 山 湖	55	5.83			55	5.83

14-5 镇街人口迁移变动情况（2011年）

Population Migration by Town (2011)

单位：人

镇街	迁移总计	省内	省外	迁入总计	省内迁入	省外迁入	迁出总计	迁往省内	迁往省外
全市总计	36048	14516	21532	28623	11512	17111	7425	3004	4421
莞城	5586	1319	4267	3522	937	2585	2064	382	1682
石龙	959	505	454	714	392	322	245	113	132
虎门	1702	794	908	1482	696	786	220	98	122
东城	2114	667	1447	1857	596	1261	257	71	186
万江	1053	349	704	955	314	641	98	35	63
南城	3606	1380	2226	2752	1012	1740	854	368	486
中堂	467	259	208	403	217	186	64	42	22
望牛墩	255	124	131	237	115	122	18	9	9
麻涌	673	262	411	512	214	298	161	48	113
石碣	954	370	584	810	312	498	144	58	86
高埗	244	116	128	222	107	115	22	9	13
道滘	312	144	168	281	133	148	31	11	20
洪梅	194	87	107	174	84	90	20	3	17
沙田	436	179	257	392	163	229	44	16	28
厚街	980	454	526	888	424	464	92	30	62
长安	1486	474	1012	1254	408	846	232	66	166
寮步	1269	423	846	1159	403	756	110	20	90
大岭山	627	258	369	566	243	323	61	15	46
大朗	893	347	546	799	324	475	94	23	71
黄江	707	342	365	679	327	352	28	15	13
樟木头	738	269	469	640	240	400	98	29	69
清溪	809	314	495	666	281	385	143	33	110
塘厦	1964	889	1075	1678	818	860	286	71	215
凤岗	892	394	498	795	354	441	97	40	57
谢岗	200	106	94	172	96	76	28	10	18
常平	1077	421	656	946	360	586	131	61	70
桥头	417	155	262	376	135	241	41	20	21
横沥	520	179	341	477	169	308	43	10	33
东坑	319	113	206	257	98	159	62	15	47
企石	349	167	182	310	152	158	39	15	24
石排	519	265	254	476	262	214	43	3	40
茶山	429	164	265	356	149	207	73	15	58

注：本表按户籍人口统计。

14-6 镇街土地面积和人口密度（2011年）

Land Area and Population Density by Town (2011)

镇　　街	土地面积（平方公里）	人口密度（人/平方公里）	
		户籍人口	常住人口
莞　城	11.2	15573	14670
石　龙	13.8	5158	10319
虎　门	166.5	775	3848
东　城	105.1	857	4716
万　江	48.5	1619	5078
南　城	56.6	1317	5159
中　堂	59.9	1261	2344
望牛墩	31.6	1467	2699
麻　涌	87.2	836	1362
石　碣	36.2	1238	6851
高　埗	34.6	1104	6298
道　滘	54.3	1033	2641
洪　梅	33.2	671	1759
沙　田	78.8	524	2261
厚　街	125.7	781	3498
长　安	89.4	503	7447
寮　步	72.5	967	5799
大岭山	95.5	475	2936
大　朗	97.5	731	3202
黄　江	92.9	274	2501
樟木头	118.8	236	1124
清　溪	140.1	259	2237
塘　厦	128.2	368	3775
凤　岗	82.4	304	3883
谢　岗	91.0	227	1096
常　平	103.3	725	3756
桥　头	56.0	649	2988
横　沥	44.7	836	4597
东　坑	23.7	1283	5873
企　石	58.2	728	2101
石　排	48.7	894	3306
茶　山	45.4	993	3458
松山湖	58.1	172	659

14-7 镇街常住人口(2010-2011年)

Permanent Population by Town(2010-2011)

单位：万人

镇　　街	2010年	2011年	镇　　街	2010年	2011年
莞　　城	16.21	16.43	寮　　步	41.86	42.04
石　　龙	14.19	14.24	大 岭 山	27.94	28.04
虎　　门	63.87	64.07	大　　朗	31.09	31.22
东　　城	49.29	49.57	黄　　江	23.14	23.23
万　　江	24.48	24.63	樟 木 头	13.28	13.35
南　　城	28.93	29.20	清　　溪	31.26	31.34
中　　堂	13.96	14.04	塘　　厦	48.21	48.40
望 牛 墩	8.48	8.53	凤　　岗	31.90	32.00
麻　　涌	11.81	11.88	谢　　岗	9.94	9.97
石　　碣	24.70	24.80	常　　平	38.64	38.80
高　　埗	21.74	21.79	桥　　头	16.68	16.73
道　　滘	14.31	14.34	横　　沥	20.48	20.55
洪　　梅	5.81	5.84	东　　坑	13.88	13.92
沙　　田	17.75	17.82	企　　石	12.17	12.23
厚　　街	43.83	43.97	石　　排	16.02	16.10
长　　安	66.42	66.58	茶　　山	15.65	15.70

注：2010年镇街常住人口数为东莞市第六次全国人口普查数据，以2010年11月1日零时为标准时点。

14-8 镇街外来暂住人口数（2010-2011年）

Migrant Population by Town (2010-2011)

单位：人

镇　街	2010年			2011年		
	外来暂住人口	男	女	外来暂住人口	男	女
全市总计	4114745	2010869	2103876	4136177	2054179	2081998
莞　城	54037	26954	27083	56323	28555	27768
石　龙	56289	26242	30047	52046	24892	27154
虎　门	418140	205782	212358	415700	203170	212530
东　城	209982	114118	95864	211983	106339	105644
万　江	61928	32077	29851	65386	33670	31716
南　城	130877	71174	59703	133878	72898	60980
中　堂	48260	24351	23909	48370	25421	22949
望牛墩	35173	15932	19241	37165	17632	19533
麻　涌	34798	19145	15653	34843	19354	15489
石　碣	100760	42537	58223	100445	45561	54884
高　埗	129189	77513	51676	128551	76216	52335
道　滘	65833	29151	36682	53961	22197	31764
洪　梅	24050	12058	11992	24467	12052	12415
沙　田	65890	34489	31401	68568	36591	31977
厚　街	289037	135689	153348	297025	138609	158416
长　安	401157	182837	218320	388226	187817	200409
寮　步	181021	95214	85807	177889	96346	81543
大岭山	100485	55816	44669	99160	53390	45770
大　朗	130003	61428	68575	111964	52904	59060
黄　江	153006	72294	80712	148650	81245	67405
樟木头	100900	48987	51913	114395	65201	49194
清　溪	133927	50250	83677	136616	54094	82522
塘　厦	351027	164772	186255	362173	167486	194687
凤　岗	132568	69732	62836	148377	77990	70387
谢　岗	44025	20755	23270	44200	21005	23195
常　平	201978	95393	106585	207803	97350	110453
桥　头	61003	26591	34412	61808	26586	35222
横　沥	94048	52017	42031	100629	58113	42516
东　坑	72268	33556	38712	67751	34503	33248
企　石	36727	18078	18649	36742	18330	18412
石　排	94447	45281	49166	92018	44250	47768
茶　山	77380	36336	41044	77792	34891	42901
其他单位	24532	14320	10212	31273	19521	11752

14-9 镇街计划生育情况（2011年）

Basic Statistics on Family Planning by Town (2011)

镇街	已婚育龄妇女人数(人)	女性初婚人数(人)	#23周岁及以上	落实各种节育措施 育龄夫妇(对)	节育率(%)	领取独生子女证 累计(人)	领证率(%)	政策生育率(%)	多孩率(%)
全市总计	380570	14899	11820	320135	84.12	83312	21.89	98.65	0.90
莞城	36981	1092	1002	31224	84.43	9588	25.93	98.74	0.28
石龙	14634	445	375	12514	85.51	4065	27.78	98.36	1.28
虎门	25803	1000	798	20689	80.18	5193	20.13	98.52	1.17
东城	14401	616	497	12048	83.66	3262	22.65	98.75	1.25
万江	8436	360	285	7132	84.54	1696	20.10	98.35	0.41
南城	15614	649	531	13565	86.88	4606	29.50	98.37	1.22
中堂	8838	334	238	7370	83.39	2320	26.25	98.54	0.55
望牛墩	7053	308	224	6173	87.52	1400	19.85	98.81	0.72
麻涌	12745	647	538	9984	78.34	3191	25.04	99.19	0.35
石碣	9717	413	360	8172	84.10	1585	16.31	99.36	1.71
高埗	9140	477	333	7587	83.01	1991	21.78	99.26	0.55
道滘	10687	404	331	8956	83.80	2184	20.44	98.58	1.01
洪梅	4211	188	147	3565	84.66	926	21.99	98.55	1.09
沙田	19386	778	617	16428	84.74	3633	18.74	98.78	0.98
厚街	18862	919	819	15553	82.46	3351	17.77	99.09	0.73
长安	19695	534	450	16656	84.57	3434	17.44	99.02	0.61
寮步	14607	606	454	12508	85.63	2906	19.89	97.98	0.88
大岭山	9808	489	365	8376	85.40	1811	18.46	99.82	0.88
大朗	14613	594	415	12139	83.07	3374	23.09	99.11	1.78
黄江	6033	251	194	5133	85.08	1469	24.35	98.37	1.63
樟木头	6738	287	220	5611	83.27	1058	15.70	98.73	0.32
清溪	8415	293	214	7176	85.28	1438	17.09	98.56	0.72
塘厦	9139	424	333	7458	81.61	2200	24.07	98.13	0.85
凤岗	6037	247	194	5046	83.58	889	14.73	97.71	1.15
谢岗	4541	191	146	3871	85.25	855	18.83	98.21	1.08
常平	15700	488	379	13600	86.62	4064	25.89	98.92	0.95
桥头	7731	315	229	6614	85.55	2117	27.38	98.03	
横沥	7882	317	236	6641	84.26	1922	24.38	98.07	1.07
东坑	5848	209	157	4972	85.02	1332	22.78	97.98	0.67
企石	8836	369	241	7759	87.81	1794	20.30	97.89	0.42
石排	8736	355	263	7455	85.34	1762	20.17	97.98	1.21
茶山	9140	277	212	8056	88.14	1800	19.69	98.54	1.88
松山湖	563	23	23	104	18.47	96	17.05	100.00	1.82

14-10 镇街农业总产值（2011年）

Gross Output Value of Agriculture by Town (2011)

单位：万元

镇　　街	农业总产值	种植业	林业	牧业	渔业	农林牧渔服务业
石　　龙	37				37	
虎　　门	28059	9576	145	6428	11910	
东　　城	2375	1593	124		659	
万　　江	6382	5369	2		1011	
南　　城	2508	2410			98	
中　　堂	13897	10720		1537	1640	
望 牛 墩	6010	4751		716	543	
麻　　涌	18841	15453	19	250	3120	
石　　碣	4824	3785			478	562
高　　埗	10393	9307			1086	
道　　滘	16469	6033	4	7535	2832	65
洪　　梅	10713	2820		5660	2233	
沙　　田	26107	7411		3158	15539	
厚　　街	15281	12445	31	245	2560	
长　　安	7980	1117	77	1495	5290	
寮　　步	3191	1655	8	6	1511	10
大 岭 山	4662	3206	115	12	1329	
大　　朗	3016	2122	4	205	685	
黄　　江	1188	818	34		336	
樟 木 头	763	564	44	88		67
清　　溪	10540	7269	121		242	2908
塘　　厦	21609	9850	11	8102	755	2890
凤　　岗	2496	2243	11		243	
谢　　岗	18357	4826	80	7992	5459	
常　　平	20616	7156	24	11471	1964	
桥　　头	8373	3595	4	3157	1617	
横　　沥	8865	3050		4236	1579	
东　　坑	3530	2836			694	
企　　石	5022	3114	15	493	1401	
石　　排	10876	3980	1	3067	3625	202
茶　　山	5662	2297		1013	2352	

14-11 镇街主要农产品生产及产品产量（2011年）

Production and Output of Main Agricultural Products by Town (2011)

镇街	粮食播种面积（亩）	粮食总产量（吨）	稻谷播种面积（亩）	稻谷产量（吨）	蔬菜播种面积（亩）	蔬菜产量（吨）	水果总面积（亩）	水果总产量（吨）
石龙								
虎门	748	280	732	276	20610	28196	4953	2191
东城	1439	636	1439	636	2969	5090	256	308
万江	740	284	431	160	11479	18182	123	194
南城					180	164	1836	932
中堂	2851	878	2092	683	19005	30236	6087	5354
望牛墩	690	238	592	211	2912	4112	6315	9329
麻涌	10243	3405	9834	3337	11202	15906	22029	27370
石碣	500	167	200	85	10800	14720	301	458
高埗	1873	595	1143	461	22698	34038	90	180
道滘	2000	594	2000	594	11183	22812	31	82
洪梅	3200	1094	3112	1068	419	838	4077	6135
沙田	3439	1106	3417	1100	14143	15647	4695	4203
厚街	1239	360			40674	44404	11642	2681
长安	350	80			1100	977	2000	1004
寮步	92	24			2110	3653	2050	664
大岭山	626	178			7066	7979	6708	925
大朗	701	179			3807	3735	11623	1151
黄江	750	185			577	577	7650	863
樟木头	120	14			1005	1427	5129	176
清溪	898	186			12700	13614	11624	706
塘厦	575	133	48	24	27801	27801	13094	870
凤岗	720	175			4926	4928	13186	1004
谢岗	1620	385	185	65	5000	7880	9550	5325
常平	850	215			16720	25239	9600	469
桥头	1313	311	3	1	7061	10241	2069	426
横沥	860	210			7180	9178	3565	92
东坑	354	130			7200	9036	1308	87
企石	1120	385	840	290	5557	9436	2643	22
石排	774	279	344	146	12413	12188	206	189
茶山	776	184			7040	6780	3227	476

14-11 续表 1

(2011年)

镇街	香(大)蕉面积(亩)	香(大)蕉产量(吨)	荔枝面积(亩)	荔枝产量(吨)	林业用地面积(亩)	当年种植面积(亩)	生猪年末存栏量(头)	肉猪出栏量(头)
石龙					150			
虎门	250	200	3100	600	31484	430	15368	23278
东城			136	123	10914			
万江	88	168	7	7				
南城			1075	95	15618			
中堂	5967	5293	22	33			3520	6998
望牛墩	6200	9213					2970	3790
麻涌	20963	26230					237	154
石碣	250	450	51	8				
高埗								
道滘	31	82					31662	43875
洪梅	4077	6135					13412	32023
沙田	3394	3566	56	9	500		4042	6143
厚街	252	98	9235	2230	55370	1000		
长安			1802	901	19431	2284	14440	8218
寮步	35	63	1382	295	14172	1800		
大岭山			5820	599	54234	1200		
大朗	50	10	10769	975	33921			
黄江			6550	750	71448	2300		
樟木头			4470	132	54107	350		
清溪	80	4	9140	480	71772	3450		
塘厦	10	10	11500	615	35861	1000	9500	22000
凤岗			9890	813	41412	2600		
谢岗	1050	3600	8000	1600	61743	350	34747	40449
常平			7930	293	30059		18376	42326
桥头	40	40	800	40	10314		9660	18600
横沥	15	12	3400	65	6150		14000	24500
东坑	9	1	1038	46	5186			
企石			2323	4	9293	200	3063	3050
石排	28	61	68	21	767			
茶山	85	55	2894	298	9959		1808	3666

注：林业用地面积、当年种植面积指标采用林业局数据。

14-11 续表 2

(2011年)

镇街	三鸟年末存栏量(只)	三鸟出栏量(只)	畜牧总肉量(吨)	#猪肉	禽蛋产量(吨)	淡水养殖面积(亩)	水产品产量(吨)	#淡水产量
石龙						94	67	67
虎门	148138	592702	2718	1613	14	555	12175	5437
东城						1654	845	845
万江						1995	950	950
南城						322	112	112
中堂			623	483	1	3462	1922	1601
望牛墩	34200	20700	287	265	34	1250	620	620
麻涌	42050	79352	90	11	23	4057	2041	2041
石碣						900	560	560
高埗						3013	1362	1362
道滘	78118	95133	3126	3005	105	6081	2919	2919
洪梅	27700	34075	2371	2353	3	4230	2026	2026
沙田	222101	688871	1257	420	14	16931	13830	6981
厚街						6006	1905	1905
长安	13602	49141	618	571		2636	4350	442
寮步		2200	2			2121	1490	1490
大岭山						1875	1820	1820
大朗	29440	44227	49			3521	902	902
黄江						4515	399	399
樟木头	3500	31565	33					
清溪						805	273	273
塘厦	446333	1390900	3015	1524	400	4450	1300	1300
凤岗						442	360	360
谢岗	104350	753300	3556	2426		15705	9000	9000
常平	388540	1585332	4573	2963	35	4088	2480	2480
桥头	15220	25200	1328	1299	2	3811	2280	2280
横沥	21500	58000	1764	1700	8	2840	1704	1704
东坑						3120	723	723
企石			207	205		2925	1588	1588
石排						7494	4200	4200
茶山	8344	22624	398	238	5	4305	3125	3125

14-12 镇街农机总动力、机耕面积及农村用电量（2011年）

Basic Statistics on Total Power of Agricultural Machinery, Area of Tractor Ploughing and Electricity Consumption in Rural Areas by Town (2011)

镇　街	农机总动力（千瓦）			农村用电量（万千瓦时）	化肥施用实物量（吨）	农药使用量（吨）
		#耕作机械	排灌机械			
石　龙				1702		
虎　门	31004	147	936	429928	1691	70
东　城	8894	154		57645	224	2
万　江	550	26	215	105500	1435	9
南　城				8046	92	1
中　堂	7935	636	2723	138213	2852	33
望牛墩	2343	232	382	6734	1830	20
麻　涌	3853	1326	259	12724	6994	36
石　碣	2139	225	1393	157717	1083	29
高　埗	13059	4161	2004	135821	1325	67
道　滘	2028	292	463	116425	1870	9
洪　梅	561	125	99	935	1746	19
沙　田	45818	1772	1533	47908	5475	125
厚　街	708		285	328340	2846	115
长　安	1003		36	503411	74	2
寮　步	131	5	126	23163	402	7
大岭山	8935	3873	442	26358	539	19
大　朗	772	499	64	223650	1243	35
黄　江	122	23	2	68604	228	31
樟木头				94807	96	11
清　溪	2391	1075	1107	232951	963	77
塘　厦	838	152	282	324507	2292	50
凤　岗	376	108	190	200219	230	10
谢　岗	2499	585	1330	4800	550	12
常　平	150			181012	797	9
桥　头	2377	187	1785	133767	1981	16
横　沥	2063		2063	110013	406	5
东　坑				81639	503	1
企　石	440	360	80	77172	344	
石　排	2495	351	1128	111967	1260	31
茶　山	1179	13	1016	131220	936	7

14-13 镇街农村集体(经联社、经济社两级合计)经济收益分配(2011年)

Income Distribution of Rural Economy by Town (2011)

单位：万元

镇　　街	经营总收入	经营总费用	经营纯收入
全市总计	1484812	694716	790096
莞　　城	15890	5020	10870
石　　龙	17203	9397	7806
虎　　门	143578	65696	77883
东　　城	97924	48215	49709
万　　江	54625	25536	29089
南　　城	53244	25268	27976
中　　堂	41753	15567	26186
望 牛 墩	8661	3927	4734
麻　　涌	19140	9666	9474
石　　碣	63775	29788	33987
高　　埗	25081	9627	15453
道　　滘	22744	9655	13089
洪　　梅	5324	3437	1887
沙　　田	23522	10751	12771
厚　　街	114478	60686	53792
长　　安	158910	69502	89408
寮　　步	68310	33053	35257
大 岭 山	38546	16416	22129
大　　朗	56611	27985	28626
黄　　江	23092	8907	14186
樟 木 头	20149	17277	2872
清　　溪	51109	21833	29275
塘　　厦	61197	25201	35997
凤　　岗	64001	19154	44847
谢　　岗	8448	3383	5065
常　　平	69059	32187	36872
桥　　头	29666	15366	14300
横　　沥	24229	15736	8493
东　　坑	20962	11639	9323
企　　石	14921	9823	5098
石　　排	29523	13124	16399
茶　　山	39139	21896	17242

14-14　镇街规模以上工业企业主要经济指标（2011年）

Main Indicators of Industrial Enterprises above Designated Size by Town (2011)

单位：万元

镇　街	企业单位数（个）	亏损企业	工业销售产值	工业增加值
莞　城	33	3	1074656	254261
石　龙	53	9	1790058	313392
虎　门	324	34	4543786	962915
东　城	178	17	3102866	810501
万　江	93	9	995786	204260
南　城	56	15	2690019	411286
中　堂	95	10	1940071	239738
望牛墩	73	15	727709	169172
麻　涌	66	8	5281589	889635
石　碣	109	24	3664693	586403
高　埗	102	16	1556264	510339
道　滘	114	7	1193193	214755
洪　梅	55	13	1722089	209768
沙　田	94	17	1690708	303072
厚　街	218	37	5230551	934281
长　安	276	68	6347256	1327724
寮　步	194	33	4367229	742178
大岭山	179	29	2606540	486929
大　朗	239	27	2509114	498049
黄　江	123	29	2039813	394040
樟木头	81	15	868109	190682
清　溪	217	35	3607464	785232
塘　厦	324	59	4671414	1028191
凤　岗	143	24	1964427	459329
谢　岗	87	22	658017	129202
常　平	179	23	3121825	576912
桥　头	92	13	963868	213249
横　沥	90	16	1094903	253208
东　坑	56	11	1513748	260132
企　石	67	9	703957	127662
石　排	90	14	660026	168820
茶　山	110	14	1327866	249320
松山湖	27	4	3336641	396959

14-14　续表 1

(2011年)

单位：万元

镇　街	资产总额	流动资产	固定资产净值	负债总额
莞　城	1649472	1037915	450218	1053995
石　龙	1011555	765032	173904	513847
虎　门	3858605	2715228	834713	2192657
东　城	2633273	1561128	796840	1274616
万　江	825667	543095	173822	537208
南　城	2163919	1389714	401008	1290821
中　堂	1644471	950686	505453	1033923
望牛墩	471956	333235	111352	318232
麻　涌	5360576	2864088	2075728	3413555
石　碣	1934465	1358880	458762	1090546
高　埗	1186112	808683	303047	753912
道　滘	958642	737130	171625	456918
洪　梅	2183737	1438566	478707	1362034
沙　田	1023364	708276	241487	608881
厚　街	2737262	1974695	595124	1688788
长　安	4664130	2996977	1192143	2939136
寮　步	2304184	1678229	493412	1399059
大岭山	2158232	1529040	483652	1425360
大　朗	2112150	1591415	409415	1433602
黄　江	1699840	1161347	379866	1113500
樟木头	758779	510372	204647	423894
清　溪	2865933	1977051	643796	1481890
塘　厦	3255877	2325386	689440	1842355
凤　岗	1743737	1055287	504517	899681
谢　岗	787078	386680	155472	367525
常　平	2523409	1847256	549248	1433171
桥　头	788085	593564	162515	515758
横　沥	1082297	651628	178706	573024
东　坑	849368	575761	223478	547175
企　石	569410	443643	85675	374842
石　排	567357	411414	120207	312830
茶　山	1100064	745560	282821	606763
松山湖	1974996	1310099	433524	1116785

14-14 续表 2

(2011年)

单位：万元

镇　街	主营业务收入	主营业务税金及附加	利润总额	利税总额	本年应交增值税	全部从业人员平均人数（人）
莞　城	1079075	3240	69679	116982	43331	21755
石　龙	1782635	3778	101619	131197	25672	35760
虎　门	4670853	14455	180315	283143	86689	173123
东　城	3056369	16640	204120	292303	68513	109445
万　江	996036	3218	32459	61124	25227	31246
南　城	2661514	3109	105635	150326	40225	58060
中　堂	1912583	9326	49633	90401	31185	34811
望牛墩	718968	2657	57974	86866	26093	19311
麻　涌	5280685	6523	279536	387216	101121	41719
石　碣	3680750	5508	106297	156628	44462	89847
高　埗	1560484	2961	33944	54306	17194	116807
道　滘	1188260	2903	45371	70379	21996	43482
洪　梅	1727404	1230	58892	77846	17700	18844
沙　田	1677699	2997	40796	120515	76682	39663
厚　街	5267635	12919	217084	287104	56795	165371
长　安	6397636	27802	182246	313097	102934	225323
寮　步	4363662	5903	139482	187606	42054	137864
大岭山	2595198	6197	26522	67635	34615	93462
大　朗	2546992	4472	48668	89707	36363	90778
黄　江	2075601	2531	43558	68181	21093	85522
樟木头	866888	2419	26780	38206	8978	39488
清　溪	3651439	9395	163651	195810	22670	130080
塘　厦	4637283	11350	210266	292453	70549	186470
凤　岗	1947183	4138	50492	85363	30264	91192
谢　岗	653897	1425	7595	16791	7757	27020
常　平	3097718	6127	109240	141053	25466	110815
桥　头	991302	2966	30896	42839	8865	40361
横　沥	1116723	1962	35460	48353	10826	57671
东　坑	1509139	2091	40928	74441	31342	46374
企　石	702669	1400	12445	27239	13105	25895
石　排	671545	1507	20052	33739	12051	41258
茶　山	1330352	3955	40573	70836	26049	38771
松山湖	3346158	9679	147535	191302	34082	35369

14-15 镇街规模以上工业企业主要经济效益指标（2011年）

Main Indicators on Economic Benefit of Industrial Enterprises above Designated Size by Town (2011)

镇 街	工业增加值率 (%)	总资产贡献率 (%)	资 产 负债率 (%)	流动资产周 转 率 (次/年)	成本费用利 润 率 (%)	全员劳动生 产 率 (元/人)	产 品 销售率 (%)
莞 城	24.1	8.1	63.9	1.1	6.9	116875	101.7
石 龙	17.5	13.1	50.8	2.3	6.0	87637	99.7
虎 门	20.5	7.7	56.8	1.7	4.0	55620	96.8
东 城	26.4	11.3	48.4	2.0	7.1	74056	100.9
万 江	21.2	8.4	65.1	1.9	3.4	65372	103.3
南 城	16.0	7.7	59.7	1.9	4.1	70838	104.7
中 堂	13.1	7.0	62.9	2.1	2.6	68868	105.6
望 牛 墩	23.3	19.2	67.4	2.2	8.6	87604	100.2
麻 涌	16.4	7.8	63.7	2.0	5.1	213245	97.3
石 碣	16.0	8.1	56.4	2.7	3.0	65267	99.9
高 埗	32.6	5.4	63.6	2.0	2.2	43691	99.5
道 滘	18.0	7.6	47.7	1.6	4.0	49389	99.8
洪 梅	12.1	3.9	62.4	1.2	3.5	111318	99.5
沙 田	18.0	12.7	59.5	2.4	2.5	76412	100.6
厚 街	17.8	10.9	61.7	2.7	4.3	56496	99.5
长 安	21.0	6.8	63.0	2.2	2.1	58925	100.5
寮 步	16.9	8.6	60.7	2.6	3.3	53834	99.7
大 岭 山	18.4	3.7	66.0	1.7	1.0	52099	98.5
大 朗	19.5	4.8	67.9	1.6	2.0	54864	98.3
黄 江	19.2	4.2	65.5	1.8	2.1	46075	99.2
樟 木 头	21.7	6.0	55.9	1.7	3.2	48289	98.8
清 溪	21.6	6.8	51.7	1.9	4.7	60365	99.0
塘 厦	21.5	9.1	56.6	2.1	4.6	55140	97.9
凤 岗	23.4	5.2	51.6	1.9	2.6	50369	100.3
谢 岗	19.8	2.6	46.7	1.7	1.2	47817	100.6
常 平	18.4	5.7	56.8	1.7	3.6	52061	99.8
桥 头	22.0	5.9	65.4	1.7	3.2	52835	99.4
横 沥	22.5	4.7	53.0	1.7	3.3	43906	97.1
东 坑	17.4	9.0	64.4	2.6	2.8	56094	101.0
企 石	18.1	5.7	65.8	1.6	1.8	49300	99.9
石 排	26.2	6.5	55.1	1.6	3.1	40918	102.5
茶 山	18.7	7.1	55.2	1.8	3.1	64306	99.5
松 山 湖	11.8	9.8	56.6	2.6	4.6	112234	98.9

14-16 镇街规模以上工业企业R&D人员情况(2011年)

R&D Personnel of Industrial Enterprises above Designated Size by Town (2011)

镇　街	有R&D活动的工业企业数（个）	R&D人员合计（人）	#参加项目人员	#女性	#研究人员	#全时人员	非全时人员
全市总计	428	39400	35376	6588	5513	29825	9575
莞　城	7	477	411	104	226	366	111
石　龙	20	812	725	133	135	757	55
虎　门	33	2569	2364	705	351	2171	398
东　城	13	2216	2070	231	148	2144	72
万　江	14	1163	1056	212	202	905	258
南　城	11	696	619	117	127	516	180
中　堂	6	357	311	78	114	177	180
望牛墩	3	101	98	19	4	72	29
麻　涌	20	1733	1614	199	376	1388	345
石　碣	15	7657	7064	607	737	6494	1163
高　埗	11	277	265	50	36	102	175
道　滘	8	267	246	32	51	127	140
洪　梅	4	395	375	47	27	130	265
沙　田	13	384	335	82	75	253	131
厚　街	16	1098	874	203	185	971	127
长　安	23	2975	2829	571	286	1695	1280
寮　步	24	1129	1006	130	190	981	148
大岭山	19	555	505	59	142	382	173
大　朗	23	2156	1918	547	231	1990	166
黄　江	15	1098	970	189	149	598	500
樟木头	9	292	257	60	69	142	150
清　溪	10	1201	1098	238	81	898	303
塘　厦	31	4025	3307	765	454	2744	1281
凤　岗	10	770	613	140	104	639	131
谢　岗	6	266	250	34	54	201	65
常　平	10	1011	758	292	219	798	213
桥　头	10	261	249	20	78	173	88
横　沥	11	432	380	171	83	369	63
东　坑	3	71	67	3	6	61	10
企　石	8	629	609	125	129	149	480
石　排	5	245	226	51	66	188	57
茶　山	8	339	319	80	39	265	74
松山湖	9	1743	1588	294	339	979	764

14-17 镇街规模以上工业企业R&D人员全时当量情况(2011年)

R&D Personnel Full-time-equivalent of Industrial Enterprises above Designated Size by Town (2011)

镇　街	有R&D活动的工业企业数(个)	R&D人员全时当量(人年)	#研究人员	#应用研究人员	#试验发展人员
全市总计	428	31743	4421	305	31445
莞　城	7	329	142		329
石　龙	20	644	89		644
虎　门	33	2193	267	21	2172
东　城	13	1630	135	54	1580
万　江	14	898	149	1	896
南　城	11	516	79		516
中　堂	6	298	101		298
望牛墩	3	97	3		97
麻　涌	20	1211	326		1211
石　碣	15	7371	713	8	7363
高　埗	11	176	12		176
道　滘	8	134	38		134
洪　梅	4	342	23		342
沙　田	13	261	47		261
厚　街	16	734	142	16	719
长　安	23	2583	249	8	2575
寮　步	24	683	119		683
大岭山	19	460	109		460
大　朗	23	1762	204		1762
黄　江	15	589	107		589
樟木头	9	254	59		254
清　溪	10	1048	77		1048
塘　厦	31	3087	338	48	3041
凤　岗	10	483	64		483
谢　岗	6	184	38		184
常　平	10	807	188	45	763
桥　头	10	180	46		180
横　沥	11	304	68	13	291
东　坑	3	39	4		39
企　石	8	447	94		447
石　排	5	161	48		161
茶　山	8	193	28		193
松山湖	9	1644	314	90	1555

14-18 镇街规模以上工业企业R&D经费情况(2011年)

The R&D Funds of Industrial Enterprises above Designated Size by Town (2011)

镇街	R&D经费内部支出合计（万元）	按活动类型分组		按资金来源分组			R&D经费外部支出合计（万元）
		应用研究支出	试验发展支出	政府资金	企业资金	境外资金	
全市总计	612516	7790	604726	23729	576732	3045	13888
莞城	9977		9977	818	8958	200	234
石龙	12531		12531	1476	10708	83	4428
虎门	29717	126	29591	679	28771	137	71
东城	28917	1244	27673	845	28072		365
万江	22184	353	21832	1212	20783		190
南城	23721		23721	1928	21794		662
中堂	5620		5620	275	5346		17
望牛墩	898		898	15	883		5
麻涌	41150		41150	506	40525		498
石碣	86094	223	85871	268	85826		1547
高埗	4007		4007	547	3136		20
道滘	4082		4082	65	3938		3
洪梅	17738		17738	16	17722		367
沙田	9403		9403	772	8632		23
厚街	24700	172	24528	127	24491	82	33
长安	33692	49	33643	399	33181	58	2931
寮步	18515		18515	2307	16207		294
大岭山	11982		11982	216	11465		25
大朗	26239		26239	171	26068		192
黄江	11798		11798	262	10906		
樟木头	5222		5222	16	5206		
清溪	13346		13346	2475	10100		24
塘厦	49670	490	49179	1180	43145	636	264
凤岗	7356		7356	390	6604		6
谢岗	4007		4007	100	2690	1216	40
常平	15809	1007	14803	495	14433		159
桥头	3690		3690	1300	2391		2
横沥	5654	381	5274	389	5131		102
东坑	3596		3596		3596		20
企石	11694		11694	843	10356	495	195
石排	2848		2848	57	2730		
茶山	9882		9882	144	9737		60
松山湖	56779	3746	53033	3439	53202	138	1114

14-19 镇街规模以上工业企业全部R&D项目情况(2011年)

Basic Statistics on R&D Projects of Industrial Enterprises above Designated Size by Town (2011)

镇　街	项目数(个)	参加项目人员(人)	项目人员折合全时当量(人年)	全部项目经费内部支出(万元)
全市总计	2448	35376	28646	481843
莞　城	492	411	282	8828
石　龙	131	725	587	10197
虎　门	122	2364	2029	25012
东　城	71	2070	1519	26314
万　江	70	1056	809	12450
南　城	50	619	466	19496
中　堂	28	311	259	5218
望牛墩	6	98	94	681
麻　涌	89	1614	1108	35139
石　碣	78	7064	6836	71689
高　埗	28	265	171	3307
道　滘	51	246	126	3032
洪　梅	13	375	326	17730
沙　田	39	335	230	7132
厚　街	88	874	553	11851
长　安	170	2829	2453	30827
寮　步	98	1006	614	14448
大岭山	46	505	418	10798
大　朗	108	1918	1560	18764
黄　江	94	970	521	9627
樟木头	11	257	223	3402
清　溪	64	1098	954	8131
塘　厦	171	3307	2577	34439
凤　岗	31	613	384	6643
谢　岗	19	250	172	3198
常　平	49	758	627	9516
桥　头	21	249	172	1850
横　沥	54	380	275	4392
东　坑	11	67	37	3421
企　石	22	609	437	6963
石　排	16	226	153	2341
茶　山	17	319	180	7453
松山湖	90	1588	1497	47556

14-20 镇街规模以上工业企业办科技机构情况(2011年)

Basic Statistics on Scientific and Technological Institutions of Industrial Enterprises above Designated Size by Town (2011)

镇 街	有科技机构的工业企业数（个）	机构数（个）	机构人员合计（人）	#博士毕业	#硕士毕业	#本科毕业	机构经费支出（万元）
全市总计	351	468	29782	283	947	12966	395076
莞 城	5	5	417	2	14	289	5871
石 龙	12	13	496	9	22	239	7198
虎 门	23	32	2047	28	42	695	21071
东 城	13	19	2956	10	48	1070	34030
万 江	9	10	621	6	19	276	12494
南 城	12	19	1021	12	93	546	27219
中 堂	6	7	297	3	13	119	3259
望牛墩	5	5	154	3	3	65	1689
麻 涌	14	17	1267	12	62	495	19149
石 碣	15	16	3745	5	63	2326	50122
高 埗	6	9	337	1	8	97	2804
道 滘	8	8	333	2	17	132	4946
洪 梅	4	5	610	5	3	75	4255
沙 田	9	11	353	4	9	156	3664
厚 街	10	11	958	7	23	626	9379
长 安	20	22	1625	14	56	638	21410
寮 步	19	32	892	9	23	355	12790
大岭山	16	25	584	10	19	346	10516
大 朗	19	23	1071	6	21	781	10262
黄 江	12	19	927	8	42	319	8872
樟木头	9	9	253	1	7	124	2351
清 溪	15	27	1743	15	31	509	14605
塘 厦	23	33	2299	16	62	714	25978
凤 岗	8	12	614	5	27	256	3707
谢 岗	2	2	26			16	287
常 平	14	19	762	23	56	315	8526
桥 头	5	11	312	5	12	257	4388
横 沥	8	10	240	5	9	94	2962
东 坑	5	5	111		6	56	4331
企 石	6	8	389	9	16	178	7697
石 排	2	2	128	1	2	14	943
茶 山	8	9	269	6	10	143	2091
松山湖	9	13	1925	41	109	645	46212

14-21 镇街规模以上工业企业高新技术产品情况(2011年)

Basic Statistics on High-tech Products of Industrial Enterprises above Designated Size by Town (2011)

镇街	高新产品个数(个)	高新产品产值(万元)	高新产品销售收入(万元)	#高新产品出口销售收入	高新产品实现利税(万元)
全市总计	1250	27568561	26826444	16729302	1513063
莞城	18	432877	435950	108954	20363
石龙	44	1469781	1454934	1291525	76600
虎门	70	1006217	951098	469910	55194
东城	56	1006042	954249	187112	38545
万江	53	383985	396602	87998	25943
南城	54	883975	833695	603829	54545
中堂	8	17712	19365	539	2399
望牛墩	16	70192	70824	42554	2732
麻涌	22	354294	322532	192211	40651
石碣	98	2297709	2286758	2009104	102215
高埗	20	449871	447382	305397	37233
道滘	7	45567	46143	6542	2855
洪梅	2	25398	23002		1855
沙田	17	470655	461101	89512	8663
厚街	25	1950956	1921040	1820188	134481
长安	128	2386365	2394990	1065028	168348
寮步	65	2821750	2783633	2606184	63983
大岭山	76	1199803	1185585	537273	57057
大朗	51	508126	480787	343132	72289
黄江	21	1428902	1422349	517846	14809
樟木头	27	300277	273989	171584	24040
清溪	27	532504	264592	193185	28177
塘厦	90	1356568	1263688	882834	42487
凤岗	29	383694	385080	230196	20609
谢岗	19	135326	131588	93349	-6887
常平	71	1521440	1525634	1325065	67109
桥头	14	66995	67190	34452	4141
横沥	32	417324	410174	332018	19119
东坑	18	489844	489858	379707	108306
企石	10	46916	48658	7991	1775
石排	16	109646	110507	42701	7635
茶山	21	273077	264725	98165	30235
松山湖	25	2724773	2698742	653218	185555

14-22 镇街固定资产投资总额（2011年）

Total Investment in Fixed Assets by Town(2011)

单位：万元

镇　　街	固定资产投资	第二产业	#工　业	第三产业	民营
莞　　城	249020	60329	60329	188691	143010
石　　龙	173142	67697	67697	105445	37408
虎　　门	917940	136891	136891	781049	353651
东　　城	511720	93653	93653	418067	284607
万　　江	261089	73725	72925	187364	148570
南　　城	1215628	256291	256291	959337	511438
中　　堂	185220	137527	137527	47693	166945
望 牛 墩	116258	92509	92509	23749	84607
麻　　涌	296633	215092	215092	81541	175182
石　　碣	188735	91347	91347	97388	90473
高　　埗	203971	97352	97352	106619	102007
道　　滘	130781	65763	65763	64318	80721
洪　　梅	150560	103483	103483	47077	29695
沙　　田	199191	85135	84755	114056	126025
厚　　街	391163	190182	190182	200981	90580
长　　安	536135	174449	174449	361686	327754
寮　　步	226926	71740	71740	154286	140502
大 岭 山	271008	95244	95244	175764	149734
大　　朗	336669	156025	156025	180644	229868
黄　　江	309557	55579	55579	253978	197922
樟 木 头	175162	36316	36316	138846	16475
清　　溪	229144	162108	161820	62642	69850
塘　　厦	363852	41181	41181	322671	100577
凤　　岗	330900	48342	48342	282558	226435
谢　　岗	85031	67358	67358	17673	37680
常　　平	303585	100002	100002	203583	146048
桥　　头	122780	75087	75087	47693	36366
横　　沥	129794	47967	47967	81827	38956
东　　坑	125582	92170	92170	33412	29366
企　　石	66726	9570	9570	57156	19535
石　　排	118379	80463	80463	37916	59121
茶　　山	123239	63965	63965	59274	61172
松 山 湖	368245	139175	139175	229070	90716

14-23 镇街邮电局、所通信能力及服务网点(2010-2011年)

Communication Capacity and Service Establishments of Telecommunication Offices by Town (2010-2011)

镇街	邮电局(所、综合营业厅)(处)		服务网点(含报刊亭)(处)		固定电话用户(含小灵通)(户)	
	2010年	2011年	2010年	2011年	2010年	2011年
全市总计	555	626	2916	2970	3324166	3113665
市区	68	87	497	508	761545	578751
石龙	13	14	49	51	84263	69760
虎门	36	46	232	239	219265	242557
中堂	9	11	57	57	51254	59637
望牛墩	4	6	23	25	27283	28478
麻涌	6	8	21	22	36237	39573
石碣	26	27	87	89	78810	87882
高埗	12	14	50	55	39219	53555
道滘	7	8	40	41	44691	49052
洪梅	4	5	16	17	19523	19196
沙田	9	9	48	49	40998	48750
厚街	30	36	164	170	169658	188486
长安	42	47	257	265	221734	237493
寮步	19	24	98	101	104412	127669
大岭山	19	17	95	90	70008	83923
大朗	20	21	119	116	134157	136709
黄江	15	17	82	85	86574	80886
樟木头	16	17	83	83	64361	81121
清溪	21	27	116	120	95309	95081
塘厦	34	34	150	150	139256	145496
凤岗	23	24	83	86	88055	104682
谢岗	7	8	45	45	29659	37577
常平	37	41	176	179	160024	164472
桥头	13	14	67	68	56518	62205
横沥	17	17	56	57	58087	70272
东坑	11	11	38	41	36586	43492
企石	9	9	48	47	40267	46010
石排	12	12	65	64	53533	64510
茶山	14	15	52	50	74941	66390

注：市区指莞城、南城、东城、万江四个街道。

14-24 镇街社会消费品零售总额（2011年）

Total Retail Sales of Consumer Goods by Town (2011)

镇　街	社会消费品零售总额（万元）	限额以上批发零售和住宿餐饮业		
		企业数（个）	年末从业人员（人）	销售额/营业额（万元）
莞　城	979601	203	9219	2070289
石　龙	240109	68	2730	309292
虎　门	1213844	256	10483	653747
东　城	848446	234	11555	1870824
万　江	348180	95	4365	426357
南　城	1358292	213	18915	3352993
中　堂	187021	66	2574	584682
望牛墩	54023	38	556	146539
麻　涌	96259	17	705	103807
石　碣	195745	43	2154	801336
高　埗	160515	37	1458	203056
道　滘	106543	54	2371	179365
洪　梅	37674	8	820	19831
沙　田	128776	56	1475	899247
厚　街	794542	212	11027	613831
长　安	580506	178	8039	501332
寮　步	1269005	157	6980	1463474
大岭山	427058	78	2711	198858
大　朗	467500	134	5137	483040
黄　江	222663	53	3749	128376
樟木头	362763	86	4076	601827
清　溪	299187	74	1812	80623
塘　厦	528815	107	4954	479101
凤　岗	256097	97	3609	278922
谢　岗	85030	35	592	230006
常　平	686464	239	8678	434569
桥　头	164725	58	2191	67099
横　沥	174161	61	944	55170
东　坑	103331	46	725	49878
企　石	96957	46	794	26870
石　排	175309	48	898	68466
茶　山	193674	66	1485	188465
松山湖	11749	14	1601	706574

注：限额以上批发零售和住宿餐饮业企业数为产业活动单位数，不是法人企业数。

14-25 镇街注册工商企业及个体户数（2011年）

Registered Industrial & Commercial Enterprises and Self-employed Individuals by Town (2011)

单位：户

镇　　街	总户数					
		国有集体	三资企业	三来一补	私营企业	个体户
全市总计	504509	10092	15520	4021	104894	369982
莞　　城	15928	774	247	14	4196	10697
石　　龙	8554	239	139	24	968	7184
虎　　门	44704	545	971	191	7264	35733
东　　城	33807	1045	773	123	8810	23056
万　　江	17046	346	251	30	4367	12052
南　　城	25442	1241	580	30	9244	14347
中　　堂	8499	291	117	26	1449	6616
望 牛 墩	3210	125	119	16	621	2329
麻　　涌	4559	200	100	19	695	3545
石　　碣	13244	162	355	131	2307	10289
高　　埗	7639	181	202	39	1139	6078
道　　滘	6031	154	206	35	1390	4246
洪　　梅	2200	87	85	8	424	1596
沙　　田	7507	298	221	17	1397	5574
厚　　街	32885	409	775	155	5051	26495
长　　安	50565	313	1619	564	12030	36039
寮　　步	21085	483	550	108	5020	14924
大 岭 山	20979	322	421	71	3900	16265
大　　朗	20725	356	590	167	3742	15870
黄　　江	12204	196	500	145	2800	8563
樟 木 头	13665	251	334	88	2817	10175
清　　溪	13751	55	823	234	2401	10238
塘　　厦	23703	151	1271	371	5765	16145
凤　　岗	15960	-26	921	434	2696	11935
谢　　岗	4963	46	306	89	773	3749
常　　平	20783	484	905	263	4301	14830
桥　　头	8906	195	426	107	1602	6576
横　　沥	10688	142	517	155	1977	7897
东　　坑	5633	182	241	87	935	4188
企　　石	7251	213	236	72	1168	5562
石　　排	10676	202	336	105	1582	8451
茶　　山	10844	226	317	103	1641	8557
松 山 湖	873	204	66		422	181

注:本表数据来源于市工商局。

14-26 镇街集市贸易市场数及私营个体户注册资金额(2010-2011年)

Fair Trades and Registered Capital of Private Enterprises & Self-employed Individuals by Town (2010-2011)

镇街	集市贸易市场数(个)		个体工商户注册资金额(万元)		私营企业注册资金额(万元)	
	2010年	2011年	2010年	2011年	2010年	2011年
全市总计	792	812	851416	844417	12049270	12923645
莞城	28	28	19560	19675	902764	825275
石龙	13	12	11951	11817	168064	166174
虎门	77	78	90668	72813	773379	830717
东城	57	60	47339	44068	1344802	1369788
万江	33	33	22389	25361	473474	49214[illegible]
南城	31	30	23369	27980	1772515	1784213
中堂	22	27	18347	18699	215908	234739
望牛墩	7	7	6361	6698	84017	94050
麻涌	14	14	7637	8078	147227	168695
石碣	21	23	22517	22353	145934	173739
高埗	13	13	13627	13945	161587	173189
道滘	10	12	11559	11792	175758	194886
洪梅	4	4	3015	3220	78000	115503
沙田	21	21	13834	13419	209840	202082
厚街	50	50	53051	57759	649934	687918
长安	46	49	71128	74430	776228	856293
寮步	32	37	30255	32359	532916	597742
大岭山	17	18	33361	34889	250459	302663
大朗	25	24	44905	41876	342680	402316
黄江	26	27	18806	19605	203708	239116
樟木头	24	24	21536	22633	161989	190898
清溪	20	20	20086	21013	172901	223926
塘厦	27	26	34851	33736	530896	590987
凤岗	22	22	28448	27435	206664	242252
谢岗	8	8	10870	10393	64422	78688
常平	40	41	55223	51501	392536	445332
桥头	16	18	18606	17355	173397	177973
横沥	17	18	19766	20791	139932	158922
东坑	16	15	12002	11764	117178	127995
企石	14	14	15607	16644	153408	162085
石排	22	18	27294	27739	111860	131541
茶山	19	21	23000	21810	169827	180158
松山湖			449	768	245066	301649

注:本表数据来源于市工商局。

14-27 镇街来料加工装配签约宗数、出口值及引进设备价值(2011年)

Contracts of Processing and Assembling of Import Materials, Export Value and Value of Equipments Imported by Town (2011)

镇　街	新签协议宗数(宗)	累计投产宗数(宗)	出口值(万美元)	引进设备价值(万美元)
莞　城	7	63	77814	41
石　龙	6	65	193430	27
虎　门	84	689	281031	29
东　城	45	396	280171	12
万　江	17	168	37251	14
南　城	24	231	251096	1526
中　堂	8	100	25164	10
望牛墩	8	86	21950	20
麻　涌	5	62	186389	
石　碣	54	289	361745	77
高　埗	20	130	125537	532
道　滘	7	152	40812	4
洪　梅	6	60	29091	32
沙　田	8	143	85791	
厚　街	72	521	682056	467
长　安	139	1364	736354	9785
寮　步	48	345	551692	24
大岭山	37	290	257927	745
大　朗	47	511	229216	86
黄　江	51	454	420618	1176
樟木头	22	204	91218	144
清　溪	79	734	532103	728
塘　厦	108	944	406354	2658
凤　岗	95	752	207658	123
谢　岗	37	255	55770	97
常　平	89	474	395840	429
桥　头	33	366	164534	335
横　沥	36	398	133081	58
东　坑	22	202	164194	51
企　石	20	162	40008	
石　排	31	297	64004	20
茶　山	29	250	59300	102

注：本表为外经贸局口径。

14-28 镇街"三资"企业签约、实际利用外资及出口值(新口径)(2011年)

Contracts, Foreign Capital Actually Utilized and Export Value of Enterprises with Foreign Investment by Town (2011)

镇　街	签约宗数(宗)	投产企业宗数(宗)	协议(合同)规定外商投资总额(万美元)	外商实际投资总额(万美元)	出口值(万美元)
莞　城	7	58	2626	3932	35000
石　龙	6	55	7920	7649	189181
虎　门	84	613	9171	12166	224085
东　城	45	320	15513	14457	217601
万　江	17	147	7754	1765	23344
南　城	24	211	6412	8923	128696
中　堂	8	80	4778	2512	17656
望牛墩	8	83	2550	2697	15307
麻　涌	5	48	9890	21444	184403
石　碣	54	181	4018	5695	348490
高　埗	20	110	9996	3342	54149
道　滘	7	140	1926	2599	35623
洪　梅	6	57	11817	9240	26395
沙　田	8	134	4371	2497	77770
厚　街	72	439	17904	15121	603182
长　安	139	729	33004	25963	485929
寮　步	48	310	12530	10769	397063
大岭山	37	274	8220	6285	144141
大　朗	47	362	14300	12538	85458
黄　江	51	308	16073	12233	194409
樟木头	22	204	4374	6623	53984
清　溪	79	537	24293	17724	417836
塘　厦	108	729	21318	19390	335065
凤　岗	95	419	18361	17171	139477
谢　岗	37	187	5098	6297	48868
常　平	89	316	15000	11610	355197
桥　头	33	294	12994	4389	78491
横　沥	36	342	12810	9701	112797
东　坑	22	132	4944	6315	132598
企　石	20	123	3620	2780	35427
石　排	31	207	3868	3560	45237
茶　山	29	182	7151	7534	41336

注：本表为外经贸局口径。

14-29 镇街进出口总额（2010-2011年，海关口径）

Total Value of Exports and Imports by Town (2010-2011, Custom Statistics)

单位：万美元

镇街	2010年			2011年		
	进出口总额	进口	出口	进出口总额	进口	出口
莞城	112212	50754	61458	130292	52478	77814
石龙	272041	93465	178576	292834	99404	193430
虎门	369333	142234	227099	406401	125370	281031
东城	373441	154607	218834	440514	160343	280171
万江	44842	13774	31068	55402	18150	37251
南城	563209	350966	212243	605897	354801	251096
中堂	76507	47189	29318	79593	54429	25164
望牛墩	28343	9331	19012	34484	12534	21950
麻涌	363189	199176	164013	424246	237857	186389
石碣	550904	214570	336334	625090	263346	361745
高埗	198511	69848	128663	193181	67643	125537
道滘	72156	33568	38588	78317	37504	40812
洪梅	159488	135083	24405	183742	154650	29091
沙田	186453	106939	79514	201115	115324	85791
厚街	784427	277270	507157	1091690	409634	682056
长安	1149654	499704	649950	1293144	556790	736354
寮步	940627	403534	537093	936140	384449	551692
大岭山	353467	135691	217776	417185	159259	257927
大朗	273352	112295	161057	316273	122372	193901
黄江	704122	282814	421308	697213	276594	420618
樟木头	151400	58980	92420	144227	53010	91218
清溪	968780	393677	575103	877523	345420	532103
塘厦	591603	223821	367782	631511	225157	406354
凤岗	320932	137308	183624	339311	131653	207658
谢岗	72620	27053	45567	83831	28061	55770
常平	603192	249694	353498	669186	273346	395840
桥头	248480	95428	153052	274104	109570	164534
横沥	192652	64329	128323	200574	67492	133081
东坑	245115	103078	142037	272314	108121	164194
企石	53068	16299	36769	54998	14990	40008
石排	72626	19908	52718	85760	21756	64004
茶山	97605	43150	54455	106482	47181	59300

14-30 镇街实际利用外资（2010-2011年）

Foreign Capital Actually Utilized by Town (2010-2011)

单位：万美元

镇　街	2010年	2011年	镇　街	2010年	2011年
莞　城	2415	3932	寮　步	8563	10769
石　龙	6866	7649	大岭山	11274	6285
虎　门	11390	12166	大　朗	11442	12538
东　城	10923	14457	黄　江	11123	12233
万　江	1537	1765	樟木头	5564	6623
南　城	6755	8923	清　溪	15467	17724
中　堂	2087	2512	塘　厦	16043	19390
望牛墩	2254	2697	凤　岗	13367	17171
麻　涌	25469	21444	谢　岗	5022	6297
石　碣	5135	5695	常　平	6365	11610
高　埗	5608	3342	桥　头	3018	4389
道　滘	1242	2599	横　沥	8795	9701
洪　梅	10145	9240	东　坑	5198	6315
沙　田	3009	2497	企　石	2673	2780
厚　街	12120	15121	石　排	4207	3560
长　安	20509	25963	茶　山	6801	7534

14-31 镇街税收总额（2010-2011年）

Taxes by Town (2010-2011)

单位：万元

镇街	2010年			2011年		
	税收总额	国税	地税	税收总额	国税	地税
莞城	332872	159046	173826	292371	98065	194306
石龙	107372	55570	51802	123514	61653	61861
虎门	375602	227265	148337	459405	265608	193797
东城	468433	217508	250926	542514	234234	308280
万江	98898	55338	43560	131670	70341	61329
南城	491596	139932	351664	704044	177713	526331
中堂	93651	72187	21464	96315	70200	26115
望牛墩	49557	37803	11753	54623	42680	11943
麻涌	165502	106116	59387	200026	121792	78235
石碣	142838	88837	54001	159240	95436	63804
高埗	83324	57706	25619	100190	65170	35021
道滘	78408	55847	22561	98325	62386	35940
洪梅	41802	30467	11335	50354	33464	16890
沙田	82215	47759	34457	100419	52466	47953
厚街	245523	151094	94429	298739	175006	123733
长安	388497	254602	133895	475890	301728	174162
寮步	207707	129670	78037	257789	153564	104225
大岭山	150110	89818	60293	185403	108635	76768
大朗	139088	87125	51963	190037	108691	81345
黄江	108441	66151	42290	132963	73767	59196
樟木头	72119	42832	29288	100226	52396	47830
清溪	155687	96966	58721	199573	129846	69727
塘厦	295451	148998	146453	354541	182560	171981
凤岗	156927	80508	76419	198149	95729	102420
谢岗	35506	23457	12048	48026	32000	16025
常平	188201	93186	95015	231640	112911	118729
桥头	64461	40409	24053	76990	47495	29495
横沥	78913	53714	25199	96333	66896	29436
东坑	49934	29701	20234	68883	39957	28926
企石	42649	28817	13832	56114	38015	18099
石排	48281	33054	15227	59751	40945	18806
茶山	79876	54322	25555	94026	62403	31623
松山湖	145441	79715	65725	214408	94215	120193

注：2010年的税收总额不包含耕地占用税和契税。

14-32 镇街本级可支配财政收入和财政支出（2010-2011年）

Disposable Government Revenue and Expenditure by Town (2010-2011)

单位：万元

镇街	可支配财政收入		财政支出	
	2010年	2011年	2010年	2011年
莞城	57425	74397	58257	70110
石龙	52727	59100	52010	58700
虎门	169952	204919	143662	217572
东城	138353	156688	132646	156182
万江	54033	59429	55407	55840
南城	154062	182904	115563	160794
中堂	55757	61553	54023	59502
望牛墩	36270	36518	30808	42208
麻涌	55622	59049	55622	59049
石碣	42384	46618	42367	46773
高埗	39141	44580	38842	44440
道滘	50046	55149	49602	54923
洪梅	23020	31808	23039	31762
沙田	43942	46450	38545	47312
厚街	93565	111564	93660	111542
长安	131282	143187	125357	140384
寮步	87283	96075	86992	95620
大岭山	77270	85017	77056	84879
大朗	65386	92378	82435	103402
黄江	104843	109517	104466	109422
樟木头	55438	135913	82625	117988
清溪	60191	73694	60737	73623
塘厦	119438	144351	113770	133532
凤岗	80171	98898	79144	98582
谢岗	30808	33325	31067	34097
常平	94628	105796	93458	102758
桥头	43943	53844	38800	49908
横沥	42368	47857	42357	47213
东坑	73079	98220	72182	97569
企石	26006	37957	26000	37958
石排	36685	43625	70834	54835
茶山	44297	50299	44766	50257
松山湖	274004	322107	228803	203129

14-33 镇街资产负债总额（2010-2011年）

Total Assets and Liabilities by Town (2010-2011)

单位：万元

镇　　街	资产总额		负债总额	
	2010年	2011年	2010年	2011年
莞　　城	354189	345680	81422	88549
石　　龙	318373	320716	175421	153949
虎　　门	1113922	1363193	305923	496173
东　　城	518506	560597		
万　　江	292498	288370	179569	172694
南　　城	499658	545121	63100	29500
中　　堂	336504	364470	171279	181465
望 牛 墩	190694	225888	119232	131163
麻　　涌	260245	297008	111410	94631
石　　碣	465073	464453	231852	223737
高　　埗	270487	314721	154362	158030
道　　滘	223614	245832	100848	108648
洪　　梅	158173	161183	107788	110297
沙　　田	375694	368876	129298	104650
厚　　街	495587	586773	139420	163997
长　　安	856785	882359	154041	106953
寮　　步	652839	654380	197055	184964
大 岭 山	339575	380666	113503	130371
大　　朗	262659	378577	44922	82981
黄　　江	386234	417072	132529	128761
樟 木 头	282864	330991	168217	160193
清　　溪	590031	615378	243831	272175
塘　　厦	822961	995413	236325	351496
凤　　岗	431987	472454	176812	187447
谢　　岗	164725	183623	101575	107276
常　　平	672482	723404	216111	213935
桥　　头	241362	355750	174787	184400
横　　沥	285738	331174	157858	199321
东　　坑	237399	236824	122805	107406
企　　石	239961	259268	157691	164279
石　　排	354606	374235	298130	318498
茶　　山	362503	417809	104058	113974

14-34 镇街各项人民币存贷款余额与城乡居民储蓄存款余额（2010-2011年）

Balance of Deposits and Loans by Town and Savings Deposit of Urban and Rural Household (2010-2011)

单位：万元

镇街	年末各项存款余额		年末各项贷款余额		城乡居民储蓄存款余额	
	2010年	2011年	2010年	2011年	2010年	2011年
莞城	6836386	7992828	4975504	5563564	2266112	2381163
石龙	1390116	1478689	594022	702449	905687	967071
虎门	4695398	5095656	2082215	2287280	3590249	3786685
东城	4816053	4920611	2501542	2719125	2611030	2863771
万江	1250488	1390694	786033	950306	833149	947985
南城	9162540	11085024	7409222	8255747	2233097	2535995
中堂	834866	893370	581732	670244	574883	640589
望牛墩	395863	414961	162056	186087	281740	299294
麻涌	728228	752735	343243	338336	355550	396647
石碣	1360772	1443871	471764	510145	937744	1021382
高埗	695656	753088	159044	214772	502032	520735
道滘	640928	669816	214599	266967	436287	476429
洪梅	255573	267100	129454	163564	142493	163577
沙田	869695	903968	348131	400293	430431	485443
厚街	2937956	3275691	2044178	2378858	2143817	2337351
长安	4195678	4426131	1767091	1888415	2746995	2960784
寮步	1395674	1534544	693107	771382	969146	1092838
大岭山	1022520	1229280	589130	667149	743551	831686
大朗	1810578	2050908	936551	1038020	1317177	1461741
黄江	1081735	1159845	478777	485417	755117	856638
樟木头	979395	1075966	635996	688798	767445	842036
清溪	1241391	1355190	488079	512255	846646	935645
塘厦	2245018	2448716	1187364	1327144	1433273	1571874
凤岗	1396353	1519195	641814	782655	933126	1052569
谢岗	388859	422040	143019	166667	276067	306742
常平	2386186	2611639	1092646	1117455	1734354	1888320
桥头	721245	787852	339180	344831	578266	639719
横沥	724335	796707	291954	337889	569499	641452
东坑	518500	558823	179983	225108	384164	415415
企石	485141	536811	291320	339291	367920	418246
石排	698930	776940	241336	281036	522528	589370
茶山	870723	941346	267398	285467	625931	695206
松山湖	401105	523866	230760	294132	53031	85521

注：本表为人民银行东莞支行口径。

14-35　镇街普通中学情况（2011年）

Basic Statistics on Regular Secondary Schools by Town (2011)

镇　街	学校数(所)	毕业生数(人)	#普通高中	招生数(人)	#普通高中	在校学生数(人)	#普通高中	教职工数(人)	#专任教师
全市总计	199	76816	22095	95155	25647	263076	73644	19563	15262
莞　城									
石　龙	4	1535		1387		4443		316	271
虎　门	8	3866	348	4237	345	11793	1008	1257	819
东　城	10	2543		3654		9557		665	495
万　江	7	3584	749	3639	650	10436	2083	646	562
南　城	7	2649	650	3281	681	9458	2112	783	535
中　堂	7	1940	135	2513	185	7116	525	567	397
望牛墩	3	1447		1493		4286		268	232
麻　涌	2	1304		1046		3095		269	217
石　碣	8	1642	213	2168		6191	616	438	356
高　埗	5	977		1234		3378		247	203
道　滘	4	1840	494	1993	456	5800	1445	462	306
洪　梅	1	294		214		749		75	59
沙　田	4	1264	337	1588	350	4344	1170	488	328
厚　街	9	2252		2701		7684		630	446
长　安	5	1807		2801		7190		521	370
寮　步	7	2374		3176		8771		575	465
大岭山	6	1763	302	2274	311	6111	981	473	354
大　朗	7	2425	537	3522	515	9638	1573	627	508
黄　江	3	825		1049		2827		214	163
樟木头	3	845		1232		3062		234	168
清　溪	6	1210		1903		4528		336	262
塘　厦	4	1822		2995	400	7741	872	491	384
凤　岗	9	1759	281	2900	308	7454	824	593	430
谢　岗	3	749		830		2282		156	125
常　平	11	2114		3400		8529		585	428
桥　头	5	1462	388	2058	474	5806	1358	593	386
横　沥	4	808		1230		3211		265	197
东　坑	4	875		1271		3301		327	170
企　石	3	884		1238		3417		229	196
石　排	5	996		1212		3304		250	215
茶　山	7	2116	529	2145	398	6642	1713	531	374
松山湖	1			212		524		42	37

14-36 镇街小学情况（2011年）

Basic Statistics on Primary Schools by Town (2011)

镇　街	学校数（所）	毕业生数（人）	招生数（人）	在校学生数（人）	教职工数（人）	#专任教师
全市总计	324	80463	114763	578279	28420	24787
莞　城	9	2363	2142	13036	822	781
石　龙	6	1724	1880	9983	517	459
虎　门	23	5468	6724	36644	1968	1722
东　城	14	4853	6670	33306	1454	1379
万　江	16	3866	4610	25286	1135	1069
南　城	10	2871	4290	21927	1026	991
中　堂	9	2091	2810	14721	751	709
望牛墩	4	1095	1263	6324	389	365
麻　涌	8	1245	1098	6055	476	411
石　碣	8	2583	3922	19155	790	734
高　埗	6	1468	2167	10558	507	471
道　滘	6	1655	1840	10671	460	428
洪　梅	3	370	246	1757	144	121
沙　田	4	1188	1676	8016	390	372
厚　街	15	3544	5029	24295	1294	1169
长　安	22	4175	8365	37072	1819	1463
寮　步	16	3219	5165	26732	1157	1054
大岭山	9	2184	3486	17045	735	670
大　朗	18	3836	6493	30133	1295	1084
黄　江	9	1485	2757	12334	688	519
樟木头	7	1588	2380	12584	562	464
清　溪	9	2008	3605	17178	862	740
塘　厦	13	3605	5508	28044	1361	1118
凤　岗	14	3381	5402	26161	1156	1046
谢　岗	3	975	1198	6214	288	258
常　平	17	4284	5608	29596	1292	1185
桥　头	7	1846	2439	13650	623	576
横　沥	6	1672	2960	13919	635	582
东　坑	7	1600	2666	12606	543	466
企　石	7	1551	1981	9955	504	426
石　排	8	1826	2829	13045	684	607
茶　山	7	2156	3141	15697	759	694
松山湖	2	397	581	3016	184	176

14-37 镇街卫生事业机构、床位及人员数（2011年）

Number of Health care Institutions, Beds and Personnel by Town (2011)

镇街	机构数(个)	#医院	病床床位(张)	卫生工作人员(人)	#卫生技术人员	#执业(助理)医师	注册护士	药剂人员	检验人员
全市总计	2249	72	22814	48142	39582	13644	16217	2352	1427
莞城	55	5	927	1973	1536	512	609	131	59
石龙	27	3	1678	2249	1771	570	707	113	52
虎门	189	7	1836	4257	3614	1146	1522	232	148
东城	161	5	1862	3737	3078	1071	1379	166	145
万江	66	4	2305	4534	3853	1242	1837	216	105
南城	91	4	1052	2967	2460	819	1012	101	98
中堂	55	2	855	899	790	240	331	36	24
望牛墩	31	1	120	336	274	79	81	21	7
麻涌	26	2	422	499	403	134	167	30	18
石碣	40	1	270	943	801	288	336	73	26
高埗	63	2	308	796	607	216	235	33	23
道滘	64	1	120	516	437	149	129	44	20
洪梅	12	1	50	316	256	73	82	24	13
沙田	50	2	165	522	454	153	145	33	15
厚街	125	2	1075	2352	1997	754	891	90	66
长安	109	5	1081	2675	2177	833	940	133	74
寮步	123	2	888	1856	1468	526	580	89	44
大岭山	92	2	380	1126	937	332	365	67	35
大朗	111	3	1082	1670	1371	507	528	67	39
黄江	52	2	650	1244	980	352	369	73	45
樟木头	36	2	510	1107	890	284	359	45	32
清溪	74	1	504	1232	997	375	362	54	49
塘厦	83	2	641	1873	1544	546	588	99	59
凤岗	59	2	999	1567	1274	431	507	77	52
谢岗	20	1	120	302	257	104	87	13	8
常平	144	2	810	1959	1573	616	598	79	51
桥头	51	1	380	772	675	248	260	32	19
横沥	64	1	420	866	690	228	261	39	19
东坑	48	1	250	541	441	154	147	17	18
企石	38	1	448	814	669	188	261	43	19
石排	43	1	306	868	667	242	296	38	21
茶山	45	1	300	686	575	209	222	36	19
松山湖	2			88	66	23	24	8	5

14-38 镇街优抚和社会救济基本情况（2011年）

Basic Statistics on Special Care and Social Relief by Town(2011)

镇　街	敬老院个数（个）	敬老院供养人数（人）	最低生活保障户数（户）	最低生活保障人数（人）	最低生活保障费支出（万元）
全市总计	35	873	12831	31374	6552.48
莞　城	1	32	421	1042	185.93
石　龙	1	35	333	837	227.88
虎　门	1	19	498	1268	331.21
东　城	1	20	45	124	22.73
万　江	1	57	1002	2045	419.72
南　城		6	82	199	41.86
中　堂	1	13	838	2191	437.83
望牛墩	1	86	500	1367	377.22
麻　涌	1	12	1674	3554	728.00
石　碣	1	37	89	261	47.41
高　埗	1	25	271	749	123.03
道　滘	1	43	686	1738	417.61
洪　梅	1	34	663	1334	325.21
沙　田	1	25	1056	1936	320.39
厚　街	2	34	579	1596	253.52
长　安	3	26	8	21	3.63
寮　步	1	28	357	1001	124.80
大岭山	1	26	212	612	117.12
大　朗	1	29	398	1176	285.05
黄　江	1	34	138	350	80.06
樟木头	1	60	130	362	80.20
清　溪	1	32	196	507	120.50
塘　厦	1	16	169	384	82.48
凤　岗	2	8	21	46	13.37
谢　岗	1	13	249	847	129.39
常　平	1	17	256	581	119.47
桥　头	1	35	195	495	76.44
横　沥	1	6	275	704	171.68
东　坑	1	23	311	870	169.80
企　石	1	15	445	1219	269.64
石　排	1	7	527	1386	356.08
茶　山	1	20	207	572	93.20

14-39 镇街专利申请与授权数（2011年）

Basic Statistics on Patents Application Accepted and Granted by Town (2011)

单位：件

镇 街	专 利 申请数	#发明	实用新型	外观设计	专 利 授权数	#发明	实用新型	外观设计
全市总计	24455	4214	10822	9419	19353	758	7977	10618
莞 城	332	90	171	71	225	11	104	110
石 龙	192	37	55	100	174	22	59	93
虎 门	1005	139	534	332	763	26	420	317
东 城	2152	560	928	664	4152	68	555	3529
万 江	805	119	408	278	467	33	262	172
南 城	1568	355	575	638	1391	104	601	686
中 堂	260	61	113	86	127	6	82	39
望 牛 墩	75	15	33	27	71	9	35	27
麻 涌	120	29	73	18	101	21	64	16
石 碣	529	59	251	219	397	13	219	165
高 埗	327	33	115	179	196	26	84	86
道 滘	578	53	199	326	498	12	159	327
洪 梅	212	52	63	97	127	7	61	59
沙 田	367	20	90	257	265	4	99	162
厚 街	1606	64	399	1143	1416	25	347	1044
长 安	1960	475	1062	423	1239	73	746	420
寮 步	1073	188	539	346	652	44	408	200
大 岭 山	1142	79	273	790	726	18	165	543
大 朗	648	121	382	145	359	10	241	108
黄 江	690	64	341	285	550	7	294	249
樟 木 头	435	54	169	212	335	12	110	213
清 溪	994	129	579	286	634	13	404	217
塘 厦	1106	135	555	416	782	19	497	266
凤 岗	500	60	233	207	307	8	129	170
谢 岗	86	17	46	23	53	7	21	25
常 平	1019	206	426	387	532	32	303	197
桥 头	386	28	170	188	239	6	106	127
横 沥	634	42	279	313	560	6	199	355
东 坑	581	33	374	174	440	14	268	158
企 石	393	87	202	104	241	16	162	63
石 排	550	45	232	273	342	3	156	183
茶 山	354	43	207	104	217	9	134	74
松 山 湖	1713	718	729	266	759	73	475	211
其 他	63	4	17	42	16	1	8	7

14-40 镇街总用电量和总供水量（2010-2011年）

Gross Electicity Comsumption and Water Supply by Town(2010-2011)

镇 街	总用电量（万千瓦时）		总供水量（万吨）	
	2010年	2011年	2010年	2011年
莞 城	53903	51232	17699	17707
石 龙	70228	74417	2489	2504
虎 门	390844	396924	11996	11794
东 城	256029	267306	7015	7130
万 江	119324	122094	4831	4849
南 城	95732	102740	1154	1119
中 堂	131490	138213	2937	2867
望 牛 墩	62067	63971	1775	1772
麻 涌	116520	127540	2458	2526
石 碣	155976	157717	3855	4063
高 埗	133411	135669	3066	3053
道 滘	113480	115905	3282	2984
洪 梅	52489	52409	1528	1408
沙 田	105815	104589	3738	3480
厚 街	327126	328340	11043	10796
长 安	540192	547109	13277	13758
寮 步	219715	234053	4634	4980
大 岭 山	169086	171397	3966	4197
大 朗	205043	223665	7584	7857
黄 江	159909	163041	5124	5042
樟 木 头	91847	94807	1883	1751
清 溪	232463	232950	6163	6047
塘 厦	313145	324518	9869	10090
凤 岗	205623	215910	4758	5119
谢 岗	66888	71273	2039	2003
常 平	264291	276345	10351	9522
桥 头	127799	133769	3150	3172
横 沥	119845	124903	3488	3552
东 坑	79618	81416	2260	2292
企 石	71391	77172	1783	1942
石 排	109237	114265	2809	2724
茶 山	128337	131220	4272	4283
松 山 湖	34617	42655	1243	1480

十五、村（居）委会主要指标

Main Indicators of Villagers' (Neighborhood) Committees

15 村(居)委会主要指标（2011年）

Main Indicators of Villagers'(Neighborhood) Committees (2011)

村(居)委会	土地面积(平方公里)	户籍人口(人)	外来暂住人口(人)	户籍从业人数(人)	全部企业及个体户数(个)	#工业企业	当年可支配财政收入(万元)	资产总额(万元)	负债总额(万元)	资产负债率(%)
莞　城										
市桥社区	0.9	31670	1407	10162	2708	2	530	480	23	4.8
东正社区	1.7	21195	3450	12717	685	32	478	450	4	0.9
罗沙社区	1.8	14700	3799	5908	1816	21	446	233	46	19.7
西隅社区	0.6	12014	624	4443	206	3	283	897	207	23.1
北隅社区	1.1	28787	9821	18166	1578	6	560	782	112	14.3
博厦社区	1.0	9059	890	3806	271	11	310	303	44	14.5
兴塘社区	2.6	12876	10807	7185	4093	20	422	315	94	29.8
创业社区	1.5	19436	5266	10830	2566	28	435	221	12	5.4
罗沙联合社							1867	23960	1085	4.5
博厦联合社							561	7482	2260	30.2
细村联合社							2121	16092	1106	6.9
石　龙										
忠 维 村	0.8	990	3623	476	105	13	1493	12588	6667	53.0
林 屋 村	0.7	649	1548	297	105	29	1025	5278	1695	32.1
新 维 村	0.6	548	980	316	484	42	2584	16317	4994	30.6
蒲 溪 村	0.7	617	364	173	10		787	3202	421	13.2
西 湖 村	3.5	2811	4500	1490	585	85	6442	78403	5943	7.6
王屋洲村	3.2	1587	4045	554	275	15	1348	13667	624	4.6
黄家山村	2.5	1919	4200	1188	158	6	956	12902	10909	84.6
中山东社区	0.5	17549	16190	10133	260	11	260	1826	1157	63.4
中山西社区	0.5	20075	4221	9120	547	19	328	5041	3645	72.3
兴龙社区		18396	7509	8759	1520	13	398	1827	1008	55.2
虎　门										
树田社区	4.0	1478	8648	730	411	205	1977	11922	3589	30.1
怀德社区	13.8	6240	27478	3405	909	226	6765	36020	3198	8.9
居岐社区	1.8	1314	13300	798	672	76	2628	13777	1874	13.6
村头社区	1.3	813	9790	433	210	60	2204	13083	5248	40.1
陈村社区	1.3	786	2200	200	45	35	763	5873	1534	26.1
黄村社区	0.9	568	3329	365	86	31	1657	2895	713	24.6
大宁社区	5.4	2738	25822	1219	540	205	8672	61681	4470	7.3
北栅社区	5.9	4621	24800	3008	2073	345	4358	37187	11999	32.3
龙眼社区	3.0	2780	32141	1102	927	302	10380	98451	5528	5.6
赤岗社区	7.5	4346	6000	2665	203	80	2316	26950	9019	33.5
博涌社区	5.9	7009	41496	3575	3010	300	1435	11756	7740	65.8
新联社区	0.6	1169	7680	582	435	65	1601	6314	525	8.3
白沙社区	7.8	7084	17022	3906	1260	221	6396	51368	16986	33.1
镇口社区	1.8	3137	12343	1395	426	123	3507	16550	1667	10.1
金洲社区	4.8	3837	20950	1475	1700	70	6476	20401	14347	70.3

15 续表 1

(2011年)

村(居)委会	土地面积(平方公里)	户籍人口(人)	外来暂住人口(人)	户籍从业人数(人)	全部企业及个体户数(个)	#工业企业	当年可支配财政收入(万元)	资产总额(万元)	负债总额(万元)	资产负债率(%)
小捷滘社区	2.0	897	4380	533	365	102	2191	15368	4972	32.4
南栅社区	8.2	5327	47570	4247	1433	298	9677	96750	28085	29.0
东风社区	2.8	1763	8819	1016	398	63	949	13866	6398	46.1
宴岗社区	1.3	1115	7838	578	176	28	954	7560	1517	20.1
路东社区	5.6	3156	22218	1992	930	217	7233	47704	4717	9.9
沙角社区	11.2	5719	21876	3076	1247	366	5060	39182	16250	41.5
虎门寨社区	2.0	7607	10200	4126	6955	28	3901	22477	2315	10.3
九门寨社区	2.6	1452	7300	675	35	29	1000	11021	3922	35.6
南面社区	7.3	2774	3848	1550	120	25	2197	20273	2892	14.3
北面社区	5.5	2555	4065	1652	75	52	882	11326	5218	46.1
武山沙社区	2.9	2270	5638	792	185	60	936	8791	5111	58.1
东方社区	0.9	9176	3021	5964	725	9	267	557	152	27.3
则徐社区	1.2	14782	10500	8200	2083	55	429	1435	235	16.4
新湾社区	1.0	9895	4341	4000	202	24	1070	3367	2604	77.3
东　城										
温塘社区	11.6	9565	28000	5748	620	65	2639	23955	2401	10.0
桑园社区	4.0	3703	32000	2100	445	125	1660	11268	616	5.5
周屋社区	2.8	2354	8000	1395	365	60	992	6408	616	9.6
余屋社区	2.0	1652	3750	1033	287	65	594	5313	224	4.2
鳌峙塘社区	2.0	1039	2500	518	235	82	571	4154	809	19.5
峡口社区	1.6	1210	2180	510	207	80	721	5582	292	5.2
柏洲边社区	1.0	1077	3850	649	217	58	1107	5827	148	2.5
上桥社区	1.0	1378	3800	768	194	42	3504	3411	170	5.0
下桥社区	2.0	2416	7026	1524	878	47	1358	6949	1403	20.2
樟村社区	3.0	3072	2500	1642	528	43	1880	17354	1559	9.0
梨川社区	1.0	1639	2230	826	584	85	1178	6024	355	5.9
堑头社区	1.5	3098	435	1908	268	30	1757	9303	364	3.9
主山社区	6.6	6011	30020	3676	595	62	2012	14938	610	4.1
石井社区	6.7	2020	2980	1130	145	60	1286	13190	5664	42.9
同沙社区	4.6	2433	4850	1681	412	127	1087	11690	646	5.5
光明社区	1.9	1423	2346	980	143	33	720	9171	132	1.4
牛山社区	11.0	4124	10473	2544	462	104	2032	14987	4631	30.9
立新社区	2.5	3026	5300	1577	523	44	1115	5579	4201	75.3
火炼树社区	1.2	1342	5800	850	485	403	1543	7759	4073	52.5
岗贝社区	1.7	13120	2850	8770	1943	1943	1919	1217	244	20.1
花园新村社区	0.8	1281	1350	855	742		1015	2236	343	15.3
东泰社区	1.4	14163	8500	5628	720		845	4089	229	5.6
星城社区	2.7	7911	22560				495	233	17	7.3
万　江										
万江社区	2.6	4174	3372	2128	82	66	1178	14350	2969	20.7
石美社区	2.5	4067	3660	1820	225	71	1689	15071	3761	25.0
莫屋社区	1.0	1473	1799	913	160	85	664	5432	1479	27.2
拔蛟窝社区	1.3	2033	1963	1012	220	62	4183	20934	3859	18.4

15　续表 2

(2011年)

村(居)委会	土地面积(平方公里)	户籍人口(人)	外来暂住人口(人)	户籍从业人数(人)	全部企业及个体户数(个)	#工业企业	当年可支配财政收入(万元)	资产总额(万元)	负债总额(万元)	资产负债率(%)
黄粘洲社区	0.3	788	983	490	37	22	688	4235	958	22.6
蚬涌社区	2.0	1993	2312	1371	245	102	511	5094	1336	26.2
谷涌社区	2.0	3021	1339	1571	168	25	2904	21415	749	3.5
小享社区	3.8	4991	2741	3411	182	122	2761	16970	454	2.7
滘联社区	2.1	3421	1732	1762	78	37	791	6757	4964	73.5
金泰社区	1.0	2043	2714	1141	132	31	868	5569	1393	25.0
曲海社区	1.2	1565	600	955	31	4	1923	15009	197	1.3
牌楼基社区	1.6	1597	2093	1043	157	41	2129	18032	917	5.1
大莲塘社区	0.8	1020	809	550	70	38	880	8902	285	3.2
水蛇涌社区	1.5	2062	1555	1028	140	41	1407	26676	1297	4.9
共联社区	1.3	1964	6036	1030	178	52	593	5559	611	11.0
新谷涌社区	1.4	2156	1399	1296	87	41	1531	12194	1263	10.4
坝头社区	1.4	1551	1413	985	18	14	1293	13534	3837	28.4
胜利社区	0.9	936	8429	463	30	27	646	2935	215	7.3
官桥滘社区	1.9	1656	1749	662	55	53	1385	9652	768	8.0
简沙洲社区	1.6	1710	2830	1207	134	117	429	4511	3699	82.0
新和社区	3.7	2660	6870	1800	155	119	981	9157	930	10.2
上甲社区	1.4	2441	1600	1431	75	71	964	8008	2138	26.7
严屋社区	0.7	1092	666	632	39	32	594	4766	1129	23.7
大汾社区	2.6	3400	1626	2074	189	69	2107	14089	770	5.5
新村社区	5.8	8017	1860	4917	264	172	1547	15179	3025	19.9
流涌尾社区	2.5	2314	1130	1201	62	51	835	4777	1275	26.7
万江墟社区	1.0	5432	1679	3132	241	24	764	4231	2389	56.5
新城社区		5543	427	4837	467		205	656	40	6.1
南　　城										
胜和社区	4.0	6595	18592	4215	2951	7	4360	45835	29955	65.4
亨美社区	0.5	1826	3335	1050	35	10	2239	28029	10411	37.1
三元里社区	0.4	1102	863	485	31	9	2078	25681	1582	6.2
篁村社区	1.0	3030	6500	2101	760	12	1596	27282	2079	7.6
新基社区	2.0	2759	5576	1716	1518	36	3673	110251	39291	35.6
周溪社区	5.0	3942	6481	2256	172	23	12177	52366	5945	11.4
袁屋边社区	2.0	1919	3500	1071	360	13	18170	43337	504	1.2
白马社区	4.0	3315	7800	2176	1025	43	4510	35906	3958	11.0
石鼓社区	2.0	1768	6852	936	253	24	5365	35135	6218	17.7
蛤地社区	8.0	2765	5600	1447	118	26	2239	30292	13603	44.9
西平社区	3.9	3667	3513	2165	621	12	1329	72755	48463	66.6
水濂社区	6.0	2046	2530	1043	98	27	1432	19663	13306	67.7
雅园社区	1.8	1221	1892	680	129	50	2181	23273	2204	9.5
元美社区	0.4	2623	2296	1162	160	14	849	14160	6656	47.0
鸿福社区		11060	36592							
宏远社区	1.0	8113	21230	4778	954	4				
新城社区	4.5	2328	2019	1378	2256					

15　续表 3

(2011年)

村(居)委会	土地面积(平方公里)	户籍人口(人)	外来暂住人口(人)	户籍从业人数(人)	全部企业及个体户数(个)	#工业企业	当年可支配财政收入(万元)	资产总额(万元)	负债总额(万元)	资产负债率(%)
中　　堂										
潢涌村	9.3	9331	5900	6160	921	106	18794	202606	8909	4.4
三涌村	4.0	3757	2276	2322	343	71	1184	8988	5101	56.8
湛翠村	1.8	2329	1065	1489	123	46	582	4412	1945	44.1
袁家涌村	4.0	5585	2280	3429	421	109	1305	7595	2502	32.9
吴家涌村	3.4	2726	1658	1533	350	74	1519	9471	3268	34.5
凤冲村	1.3	1640	648	1050	85	38	386	1932	1160	60.0
鹤田村	2.2	2233	1823	1435	354	87	583	3338	1678	50.3
东泊社区	2.9	3754	3875	1828	676	171	1821	19871	6334	31.9
中堂村	1.1	1935	935	1125	149	50	442	1518	472	31.1
一村村	0.7	1783	7981	1016	256	30	1204	5835	154	2.6
东向村	2.4	3262	1620	2148	315	87	576	3392	823	24.3
斗朗社区	2.5	2608	946	1694	185	44	1067	9229	4044	43.8
江南社区	2.1	2433	3726	1798	686	157	2161	12950	484	3.7
蕉利村	4.6	4925	3241	3110	526	140	928	6308	2525	40.0
槎滘村	9.4	10097	2346	6395	600	156	2293	27834	2783	10.0
下芦村	1.3	1193	336	737	74	33	559	3023	1336	44.2
马沥村	1.9	1984	496	1076	54	13	759	8912	1643	18.4
四乡村	4.2	3188	290	1927	43	12	239	2584	1380	53.4
红锋社区	0.1	787	77	524	28	4	229	1303	846	64.9
中心社区	0.7	8948	6851	5224	1590	20	228	1925	1356	70.4
望牛墩										
李屋村	0.6	626	1571	340	80	33	358	2079	1120	53.9
望东村	1.4	2044	2100	942	205	21	480	2271	1246	54.9
扶涌村	0.6	885	1200	470	72	11	524	2492	853	34.2
赤滘村	1.9	2901	3100	1832	45	38	1292	11754	5989	51.0
五涌村	1.4	1521	1800	788	69	35	387	2596	1040	40.1
下漕村	3.5	4081	3956	2448	98	42	736	4323	3202	74.1
上合村	1.9	2880	1950	1156	46	34	639	3314	2206	66.6
聚龙江村	0.7	937	2290	460	220	18	968	7320	1229	16.8
望联村	2.8	4998	2665	2998	424	24	926	3526	1086	30.8
洲湾村	1.6	1898	1650	870	45	16	625	3003	1333	44.4
洲涡村	1.9	2439	532	1176	22	15	757	3586	893	24.9
寮厦村	1.4	1428	938	598	23	12	574	4425	1819	41.1
官桥涌村	0.7	941	672	555	22	14	526	3529	334	9.5
芙蓉沙村	0.8	1029	450	626	24	17	433	2928	1337	45.7
杜屋村	1.8	2325	1508	1408	92	30	1290	5437	1049	19.3
横沥村	1.8	2190	350	1392	36	7	540	3367	1405	41.7
福安村	0.6	1052	320	605	16	6	722	3612	665	18.4
官洲村	1.0	1046	456	626	40	13	583	2288	1469	64.2
石排村	0.4	596	420	330	16	7	427	1985	879	44.3
朱平沙村	2.7	3219	2890	2052	40	14	1634	4876	3652	74.9
锦涡村	2.2	1509	730	978	38	7	670	4326	738	17.1
望牛墩社区		4806		2152						

15 续表 4

(2011年)

村(居)委会	土地面积(平方公里)	户籍人口(人)	外来暂住人口(人)	户籍从业人数(人)	全部企业及个体户数(个)	#工业企业	当年可支配财政收入(万元)	资产总额(万元)	负债总额(万元)	资产负债率(%)
麻涌										
麻一村	4.0	4091	1350	2932	255	14	982	4294	2521	58.7
麻二社区	6.8	3615	699	2236	82	4	1501	13061	198	1.5
麻三村	3.7	3790	1321	2243	727	22	1222	9506	884	9.3
麻四村	4.5	4803	830	2820	193	17	1671	13170	1487	11.3
大步村	10.7	7221	3257	4158	349	35	8872	26749	1148	4.3
东太村	4.8	4523	1290	2641	175	11	1326	6748	1264	18.7
新基村	4.4	5691	3958	3383	340	38	2284	8716	300	3.4
川槎村	3.0	3958	2103	2387	228	50	84	589	554	94.1
鸥涌村	2.8	3822	4253	2254	171	16	620	786	308	39.2
黎滘村	1.3	1333	604	695	27	15	396	1747	564	32.3
华阳村	5.5	5303	856	3380	111	10	1827	10065	1064	10.6
南洲村	3.4	2785	1513	1650	181	20	1804	12760	745	5.8
大盛村	6.9	2845	10730	1792	411	12	3152	19672	3048	15.5
漳澎村	29.6	12361	2079	8329	223	9	4381	35363	5484	15.5
麻涌社区		6708		4602						
石碣										
唐洪村	1.0	1814	3395	901	391	40	2185	12251	3196	26.1
水南村	2.8	3539	5517	1555	1284	150	1907	19882	5712	28.7
石碣村	4.6	5272	9588	2998	1528	233	2744	18641	6308	33.8
刘屋村	4.9	4519	5150	2562	509	106	2389	10818	3409	31.5
横滘村	1.6	1963	4694	1117	598	98	2283	10896	4634	42.5
鹤田厦村	2.5	1910	5485	1106	253	25	2061	11586	4389	37.9
四甲村	4.0	4693	7386	2685	833	141	2997	14846	2904	19.6
沙腰村	4.0	3542	3934	2280	279	59	3001	14820	2716	18.3
梁家村	2.0	2449	1740	1365	170	71	2502	13982	7038	50.3
桔洲村	1.2	1450	8630	906	445	76	5629	34677	1053	3.0
单屋村	2.3	1310	2785	795	177	95	1608	13646	2695	19.8
涌口村	1.6	1751	3820	975	522	145	3001	20846	7637	36.6
西南村	2.6	2010	6500	1075	1047	83	7327	43816	5086	11.6
黄泗围村	1.2	703	2185	378	378	78	1963	11061	872	7.9
城中社区		7881	7096	5284	1054	37	926	7426	8863	119.4
高埗										
冼沙村	7.5	7431	25300	4565	440	138	1588	13437	9582	71.3
卢溪村	2.3	1705	6500	820	55	35	796	3915	303	7.7
宝莲村	0.7	1039	1400	512	35	16	354	1441	349	24.2
塘厦村	2.7	1922	2550	1239	102	19	474	2196	418	19.0
草墩村	0.8	805	1500	463	26	22	765	3912	1660	42.4
护安围村	1.9	1115	512	669	93	41	798	4749	685	14.4
保安围村	2.3	2364	1520	1421	72	32	2751	23797	15478	65.0

15　续表 5

(2011年)

村(居)委会	土地面积(平方公里)	户籍人口(人)	外来暂住人口(人)	户籍从业人数(人)	全部企业及个体户数(个)	#工业企业	当年可支配财政收入(万元)	资产总额(万元)	负债总额(万元)	资产负债率(%)
三联村	2.1	1377	550	810	25	5	408	2921	1578	54.0
横滘头村	0.9	1083	830	726	16	8	1128	4746	1502	31.7
低涌村	2.2	2868	11000	1694	400	21	886	5640	2388	42.3
朱磡村	1.0	1477	680	889	25	15	327	1396	744	53.3
欧邓村	0.7	950	760	596	25	9	580	2931	1793	61.2
芦村	1.3	1722	500	850	55	19	491	1921	440	22.9
高埗村	2.1	3281	13250	2012	281	53	1211	7790	4802	61.6
凌屋村	1.2	1256	2100	708	40	8	708	5133	1902	37.1
上江城村	1.9	2327	13000	1492	119	13	811	8344	3304	39.6
下江城村	1.5	1490	2280	973	128	25	1171	5706	2658	46.6
新联村	1.3	1655	1000	996	148	9	311	1716	804	46.9
新创社区		2319								
道滘										
南城村	7.1	4359	3187	2816	602	82	2766	17393	1397	8.0
闸口村	5.2	2810	8175	1722	452	39	2601	12425	1228	9.9
北永村	6.3	3718	3216	2273	246	116	2362	21219	2551	12.0
永庆村	3.1	1660	2515	1196	158	102	2148	9214	342	3.7
厚德村	4.2	2472	4978	1698	182	37	4641	12901	2313	17.9
蔡白村	5.5	4723	4487	2943	302	65	4961	19061	3616	19.0
南丫村	6.8	4143	12370	2775	398	115	5226	27848	5382	19.3
九曲村	4.6	3090	2307	1977	165	53	1036	6239	1612	25.8
大罗沙村	4.5	2872	3473	1727	55	20	1044	7638	1463	19.2
小河村	6.1	5732	3853	3570	215	59	829	6305	1548	24.6
昌平村	3.8	3410	2431	2485	166	36	768	2565	2670	104.1
大岭丫村	4.1	3579	4994	2170	289	76	4196	26281	6761	25.7
大鱼沙村	1.7	1740	1508	1070	213	33	1156	4559	770	16.9
兴隆社区		11775	1467	6084			124	252	201	79.8
洪梅										
洪屋涡村	14.1	6847	2706	3766	148	144	2225	16260	3235	19.9
新庄村	1.0	868	650	498	35	20	523	3325	1672	50.3
梅沙村	3.5	4030	2300	2475	73	27	584	6912	2383	34.5
金鳌沙村	2.3	1355	480	865	30	10	844	4097	2137	52.2
乌沙村	1.5	2189	2610	1400	35	22	685	8978	1000	11.1
尧均村	0.8	599	2023	406	70	11	283	2307	1215	52.7
夏汇村	0.8	710	198	455	6	6	480	2077	1388	66.8
氹涌村	1.6	1910	2510	959	63	9	779	4764	2144	45.0
黎洲角村	1.6	2624	2998	1782	349	10	1504	8942	1938	21.7
洪梅社区	1.0	1055	2351	666			91	28		
沙田										
中围村	0.9	1752	261	965	19	1	1572	14537	3781	26.0
和安村	0.8	3214	185	1860	60	5	1418	12057	3268	27.1

15 续表 6

(2011年)

村(居)委会	土地面积(平方公里)	户籍人口(人)	外来暂住人口(人)	户籍从业人数(人)	全部企业及个体户数(个)	#工业企业	当年可支配财政收入(万元)	资产总额(万元)	负债总额(万元)	资产负债率(%)
大流村	0.5	2054	370	1230	48	1	601	10012	4146	41.4
泥洲村	0.3	3843	331	2500	30	1	1187	22616	15513	68.6
杨公洲村	3.9	1909	12320	1109	496	322	933	8493	2567	30.2
阇西村	5.4	2215	13210	1151	454	71	2470	26770	11712	43.8
民田村	5.2	2569	13446	1600	704	131	1534	12320	3920	31.8
大泥村	4.4	1869	15261	925	844	254	1482	8894	2106	23.7
福禄沙村	3.5	1952	3693	1307	177	65	1454	7946	2765	34.8
西大坦村	0.9	2105	281	1103	6	1	890	9372	2714	29.0
穗丰年村	5.9	2745	4174	1684	250	110	3331	22056	7176	32.5
齐沙村	3.8	2061	15710	1264	851	153	1912	15188	2530	16.7
稔洲村	4.7	2478	22081	1560	1300	246	1708	9455	3142	33.2
义沙村	5.1	1910	11555	1157	343	140	1733	12293	3587	29.2
西太隆村	4.5	2017	12466	1148	468	334	1421	7755	3551	45.8
横流社区	1.0	4606	11230	2253	1267	45	694	6499	1877	28.9
先锋村	0.4	2031	296	960	36	8	512	4999	2351	47.0
厚街										
厚街村	8.0	9064	14577	5848	3190	178	3107	24991	13286	53.2
珊美村	2.1	2467	9200	1480	2308	50	872	9100	2779	30.5
寮厦村	2.5	2381	6855	1480	1632	62	2603	16097	2180	13.5
河田村	9.1	6243	17580	3711	1985	79	4662	19025	8258	43.4
汀山村	4.3	1953	14789	1510	1115	109	4964	38461	4326	11.3
环冈村	4.2	2088	7950	1443	465	45	2680	22269	7035	31.6
三屯村	4.5	2662	15233	1608	1741	152	2865	23864	7819	32.8
宝屯村	3.0	2564	9120	1505	1278	79	3156	21157	10099	47.7
陈屋村	2.0	1529	3560	1052	1369	82	4508	27715	3712	13.4
赤岭村	5.3	3614	15138	2441	1518	133	4838	39404	24702	62.7
桥头村	10.0	7913	10978	4579	1965	129	6152	37235	5167	13.9
南五村	1.6	1501	4589	720	684	62	3392	14654	4031	27.5
溪头村	4.1	3771	13760	1322	884	80	5120	33779	4506	13.3
沙塘村	1.5	2058	3650	1331	255	42	2824	16475	5605	34.0
宝塘村	1.7	1554	6201	940	462	55	5033	23670	5220	22.1
下汴村	2.2	1752	6296	1222	793	95	2983	20252	3175	15.7
白濠村	5.3	5313	14883	2585	1756	226	3722	19777	4447	22.5
新塘村	4.4	5679	9789	3976	1537	116	5013	34723	9662	27.8
双岗村	4.2	6887	5076	4410	1175	98	1758	14295	3801	26.6
涌口村	4.0	5577	15000	3534	1414	132	7316	52511	7598	14.5
大迳村	11.8	3628	2020	2184	251	39	2484	13332	3101	23.3
新围村	15.1	4487	2356	2802	351	45	1202	9459	2150	22.7
竹溪社区		13436	4550	5702	1		361	5207	354	6.8
长安										
涌头社区	4.1	1736	28035	678	1287	178	5606	28396	11041	38.9

15 续表 7

(2011年)

村(居)委会	土地面积(平方公里)	户籍人口(人)	外来暂住人口(人)	户籍从业人数(人)	全部企业及个体户数(个)	#工业企业	当年可支配财政收入(万元)	资产总额(万元)	负债总额(万元)	资产负债率(%)
霄边社区	7.6	3451	57906	1963	2113	119	8093	128244	7835	6.1
咸西社区	3.3	1265	15646	590	1164	85	8715	69276	7958	11.5
锦厦社区	9.7	4295	77450	2185	2320	287	13191	117816	15701	13.3
新安社区	8.5	3429	72471	1758	2359	332	4384	43587	1191	2.7
乌沙社区	10.0	3868	104513	2350	3849	501	11318	48646	6756	13.9
新民社区	2.5	930	27870	386	921	159	3169	33789	16817	49.8
沙头社区	13.4	6245	62360	3380	3865	400	18864	123648	57398	46.4
上沙社区	7.2	2864	50239	1509	2681	365	6925	61375	9435	15.4
厦岗社区	8.7	3212	43784	1545	1926	423	5595	45775	983	2.2
厦边社区	4.4	2490	23003	1302	2416	293	5388	25562	5025	19.7
上角社区	2.9	1318	31157	726	1213	198	8892	54972	20728	37.7
长盛社区	0.8	7203	26532	6601	3497	5	5442	18295	8178	44.7
寮　步										
塘边社区	0.7	1653	3000	855	250	30	664	8748	5003	57.2
西溪村	4.5	4625	8200	2200	371	182	1547	16781	2704	16.1
凫山村	4.0	5945	7100	3780	495	76	1397	12027	4994	41.5
石步村	4.7	4529	3850	1930	245	58	1774	22103	14791	66.9
良边村	2.7	3232	3500	2067	435	265	778	6203	1203	19.4
富竹山村	3.5	1952	2600	1186	75	38	1611	12518	3038	24.3
塘唇村	3.4	2301	2800	1373	118	55	2990	27543	8359	30.4
向西村	2.9	2564	3500	1071	160	85	1241	9837	4124	41.9
下岭贝村	1.8	1518	7421	930	210	15	2781	12204	1415	11.6
岭厦社区	0.9	1030	4500	603	190	60	2540	19574	2599	13.3
新旧围社区	1.4	995	2100	625	215	210	1462	8507	715	8.4
霞边村	1.3	833	1100	525	73	19	1787	6967	840	12.1
横坑社区	5.9	4860	17863	2767	493	467	27806	93877	7335	7.8
竹园村	1.5	891	1300	434	129	32	835	6970	2454	35.2
上屯村	4.5	3345	4000	1758	415	43	1592	13329	1296	9.7
石龙坑村	1.9	3692	5000	2324	402	220	1150	10348	242	2.3
牛杨社区	1.2	1543	5650	1021	110	48	1569	9191	2565	27.9
泉塘社区	2.3	1558	5000	952	52	29	1050	6528	1815	27.8
坑口社区	1.6	1197	3500	660	200	30	1415	14173	1798	12.7
浮竹山村	3.4	1517	3000	928	140	30	1732	15437	5159	33.4
上底村	2.0	1486	1302	804	86	11	515	3493	1706	48.8
刘屋巷村	1.6	567	1680	317	43	30	838	5866	1015	17.3
药勒村	2.4	1138	3300	668	121	40	3881	9704	1424	14.7
陈家埔村	1.6	934	2000	459	63	16	1275	4692	616	13.1
缪边社区	1.6	1205	3000	786	169	36	2859	11153	1425	12.8
寮步社区	1.7	8538	4400	5692	2600	17	1340	4764	2972	62.4
小坑村	1.5	814	1500	400	50	20	1258	5400	332	6.2

15 续表 8

(2011年)

村(居)委会	土地面积(平方公里)	户籍人口(人)	外来暂住人口(人)	户籍从业人数(人)	全部企业及个体户数(个)	#工业企业	当年可支配财政收入(万元)	资产总额(万元)	负债总额(万元)	资产负债率(%)
长坑村	1.5	935	500	485	23	10	902	6220	450	7.2
井巷村	1.1	915	1500	542	35	27	1275	6956	2000	28.8
大岭山										
马蹄岗村	0.8	2226	3988	1471	165	45	741	6402	2397	37.4
大塘朗村	3.0	1615	2189	1095	51	38	472	4686	1437	30.7
新塘村	2.0	2180	6500	1433	270	102	1634	9840	1793	18.2
元岭村	0.3	982	660	478	49	3	1172	15039	533	3.5
金桔村	4.3	3651	8900	2405	540	62	4660	25372	6432	25.4
鸡翅岭村	4.5	1326	3200	705	180	16	1029	6097	1832	30.0
大沙村	3.0	1842	2021	1355	207	151	1520	8420	2898	34.4
旧飞鹅村	3.1	461	1000	300	47	32	1003	3870	87	2.2
连平村	7.2	2907	12000	1090	278	78	1249	5169	1884	36.4
梅林村	1.5	555	7500	306	132	49	846	4113	955	23.2
下高田村	0.5	479	850	312	61	44	749	2181	267	12.2
大环村	2.0	599	841	372	25	15	716	3581	1149	32.1
太公岭村	2.2	1687	5200	1190	180	55	1176	3853	777	20.2
百花洞村	4.8	1300	6300	636	60	45	955	12261	3925	32.0
大片美村	2.6	1020	6000	635	160	18	1059	4120	297	7.2
矮岭冚村	5.5	3640	11880	2450	834	118	1945	15473	6297	40.7
大岭村	7.0	2389	850	1415	77	62	1044	5078	1812	35.7
农场社区	1.0	746	3650	390	445	14	3824	7253	628	8.7
水朗村	4.5	1362	2905	680	25	15	10801	16289	340	2.1
大塘村	8.5	3274	22000	2180	210	200	1779	11291	3122	27.7
杨屋村	12.0	4895	15000	3227	650	146	1512	10812	1633	15.1
颜屋村	3.0	752	6650	367	155	73	879	6004	802	13.4
大岭山社区	10.0	3991	6300	1889	553	13	266	904	461	51.0
大朗										
竹山社区	1.3	1648	2427	820	258	137	1480	11780	777	6.6
高英村	1.7	1839	3598	1054	315	134	1627	16093	5074	31.5
巷头社区	3.5	4400	12456	2493	2519	492	19862	60737	11553	19.0
巷尾社区	1.6	1978	5474	1147	928	267	3178	34230	1203	3.5
求富路社区	1.4	1438	5411	842	591	126	3237	21288	3408	16.0
长塘社区	2.7	4737	9206	2790	1641	250	7262	62042	17597	28.4
大井头社区	4.1	5748	6593	2978	2500	369	8927	62817	3517	5.6
圣堂社区	0.9	1588	2185	960	1308	45	6788	26509	593	2.2
蔡边村	6.1	4226	4355	2043	1228	402	10366	40686	7948	19.5
水口村	3.3	2976	5801	1536	841	313	3251	26953	4916	18.2
洋乌村	2.1	1694	2476	1081	430	249	1231	7087	5078	71.7
洋坑塘村	1.1	1085	4866	687	402	206	1318	11377	964	8.5
松柏朗村	2.5	4162	4133	2335	660	170	1787	16206	8830	54.5

15 续表 9

(2011年)

村(居)委会	土地面积(平方公里)	户籍人口(人)	外来暂住人口(人)	户籍从业人数(人)	全部企业及个体户数(个)	#工业企业	当年可支配财政收入(万元)	资产总额(万元)	负债总额(万元)	资产负债率(%)
黄草朗社区	1.5	2345	4058	1134	827	417	1633	17120	8302	48.5
黎贝岭村	1.9	2264	3016	1438	462	212	1943	14216	805	5.7
佛子凹村	1.1	2430	901	1539	194	79	1484	8351	831	10.0
佛新社区	0.6	876	524	429	218	117	1663	13469	5496	40.8
松木山村	2.7	2632	6339	1605	728	365	2451	20798	3658	17.6
犀牛陂村	8.0	3285	7160	1814	1207	763	2018	16708	2534	15.2
水平村	7.9	1925	3991	1255	448	223	2365	16312	4045	24.8
屏山社区	2.3	510	344	285	64	37	824	3344	575	17.2
宝陂村	0.5	708	102	242	30	8	707	13117	5890	44.9
石厦村	8.0	2990	4416	1745	788	412	2045	18916	1923	10.2
杨涌村	1.5	1380	3271	781	415	155	846	4167	344	8.3
沙步村	3.1	2289	2951	1293	694	394	319	1489	1111	74.6
新马莲村	6.6	1606	3280	1265	310	164	602	2414	1289	53.4
大朗社区	0.3	6526	2070	3949	612	14	548	2329	408	17.5
长富社区	1.5	1995	560	1380						
黄江										
田美社区	11.4	4526	32692	2554	1150	388	4130	33123	4573	13.8
宝山社区	4.9	2703	16031	1544	276	198	4807	28921	3050	10.5
北岸社区	5.9	1581	7831	985	276	58	2053	9219	1021	11.1
三新社区	16.0	2834	12879	1599	697	122	2999	15616	893	5.7
梅塘社区	18.2	4780	26689	3120	887	254	8610	36737	4594	12.5
长龙社区	18.0	2513	13046	1400	260	60	1843	8851	2543	28.7
新市社区	1.6	6554	8322	4520	512		393	892	298	33.4
樟木头										
圩镇社区	4.3	10043	17932	6811	2944	174	2138	18752	13113	69.9
樟罗社区	6.8	3517	19135	2098	2645	72	4347	36657	13171	35.9
百果洞社区	2.4	899	8028	467	1171	26	2364	17566	6803	38.7
樟洋社区	13.5	2436	26471	1396	1695	42	3496	18619	5139	27.6
石新社区	7.3	2319	10843	1086	1730	133	4953	46203	29159	63.1
柏地社区	6.6	1411	7300	708	885	91	1672	21814	7025	32.2
官仓社区	3.0	1109	2225	571	338	36	3056	8264	3114	37.7
裕丰社区	10.0	2021	10436	885	502	57	2825	10877	5637	51.8
金河社区	14.0	1715	12025	959	867	180	3192	10322	3171	30.7
清溪										
罗马村	7.0	1856	7380	1163	339	52	632	3631	1654	45.6
长山头村	4.3	1150	6100	720	75	32	2323	13139	5346	40.7
荔横村	3.4	1525	11100	838	271	59	1287	11197	10563	94.3
浮岗村	3.0	1956	7100	880	628	48	1483	13972	5938	42.5
松岗村	3.9	1264	3824	528	78	45	612	2471	1201	48.6
上元村	4.3	935	3500	630	225	29	737	3590	2096	58.4
重河村	8.4	2672	6800	1325	358	28	1046	8078	1308	16.2

15 续表 10

(2011年)

村(居)委会	土地面积(平方公里)	户籍人口(人)	外来暂住人口(人)	户籍从业人数(人)	全部企业及个体户数(个)	#工业企业	当年可支配财政收入(万元)	资产总额(万元)	负债总额(万元)	资产负债率(%)
清厦村	2.3	1561	4876	917	569	40	1322	7707	5166	67.0
铁松村	5.6	2552	9880	1170	168	85	1595	12393	4998	40.3
铁场村	7.4	794	196	448	23	6	1144	5934	3005	50.6
九乡村	7.5	1719	3100	1071	200	62	828	6785	5624	82.9
大埔村	1.8	725	3000	340	95	30	680	3083	887	28.8
大利村	9.6	2660	12385	1591	952	65	2158	13823	3976	28.8
渔樑围村	2.5	1072	21000	618	310	69	1946	10840	2754	25.4
三星村	2.5	1087	4750	522	112	23	972	3775	3071	81.4
厦坭村	1.7	886	6162	495	339	28	2930	11153	7993	71.7
土桥村	1.2	586	7120	316	328	51	1496	10327	5803	56.2
谢坑村	3.2	790	4500	473	98	59	1254	5127	2094	40.8
三中村	9.0	1781	58430	989	670	135	1862	9926	4976	50.1
青皇村	6.5	1131	3300	695	54	32	908	2626	293	11.2
清溪社区	7.0	7605	13210	3603	1927	18	1419	4995	1961	39.3
塘厦										
林村社区	21.0	5447	44089	3654	1828	243	10661	69466	7570	10.9
莲湖社区	9.0	2184	20963	1220	560	223	3950	20728	6785	32.7
石潭埔社区	6.8	1623	10000	1565	140	65	3529	16722	995	6.0
横塘社区	4.0	1110	7000	698	116	96	3101	9260	1676	18.1
莆心湖社区	6.1	2063	16000	1331	190	69	6086	27505	1734	6.3
诸佛岭社区	2.4	1126	12638	702	296	50	3706	29088	5376	18.5
振兴围社区	2.4	979	11000	621	170	56	1890	15379	538	3.5
四村社区	4.0	1075	11000	503	435	280	3136	15440	4960	32.1
蛟乙塘社区	4.9	1434	9998	710	325	95	10224	21543	928	4.3
沙湖社区	4.0	600	5932	225	98	75	2360	11487	1406	12.2
大坪社区	13.0	1366	11368	760	74	60	5605	25891	4607	17.8
田心社区	4.5	861	8500	470	95	93	1583	16511	2074	12.6
龙背岭社区	8.2	976	10000	533	252	70	3634	14085	1782	12.7
石鼓社区	6.4	2538	16000	1273	305	96	4247	27535	2894	10.5
石马社区	2.7	489	6120	326	172	61	1013	5733	1755	30.6
清湖头社区	4.1	1377	16500	849	185	142	3404	22119	3643	16.5
平山社区	4.8	773	8100	505	117	107	9912	19994	1579	7.9
桥陇社区	2.8	1021	9521	668	150	65	2246	12227	5456	44.6
凤凰岗社区	3.5	1334	9377	710	310	82	3986	14740	4142	28.1
塘厦社区	0.9	15925	48836	13320	2200	353	415	2251	348	15.5
三局社区		2733								
凤岗										
雁田村	21.8	3725	20029	2190	3692	512	20037	225309	25643	11.4
官井头村	10.4	1896	15097	1225	1167	165	6567	96113	4574	4.8
油甘埔村	6.9	2017	21854	955	777	372	4729	38574	12391	32.1
凤德岭村	3.4	1268	5424	605	373	112	2159	13168	3583	27.2

15 续表 11

(2011年)

村(居)委会	土地面积(平方公里)	户籍人口(人)	外来暂住人口(人)	户籍从业人数(人)	全部企业及个体户数(个)	#工业企业	当年可支配财政收入(万元)	资产总额(万元)	负债总额(万元)	资产负债率(%)
塘沥村	6.7	1929	26215	910	278	72	1270	6959	2269	32.5
黄洞村	11.7	2242	17496	1288	241	109	1421	12761	1080	8.5
竹塘村	5.7	1294	11378	500	391	135	1444	6876	2122	30.9
竹尾田村	1.5	744	5305	280	155	15	1362	8178	465	5.7
三联村	3.4	1494	6615	805	833	40	698	3258	1646	50.5
五联村	5.6	1348	9054	559	238	170	1839	19760	12843	65.0
天堂围村	4.2	1105	8133	699	338	120	2067	21061	3739	17.8
凤岗社区	1.1	5956	1777	3253	435	22				
谢岗										
黎村村	11.0	3768	3430	2140	163	31	1964	9828	1708	17.4
南面村	39.6	1497	738	750	42	18	800	2972	519	17.5
窖山村	11.3	527	1695	360	51	23	338	2511	762	30.4
大龙村	5.6	1046	2290	636	54	23	522	2408	1158	48.1
大厚村	5.6	1024	6900	590	110	53	565	4338	467	10.8
谢山村	4.0	589	2290	330	140	50	765	4869	294	6.0
谢岗村	14.0	2961	3086	1880	110	70	1116	8648	963	11.1
赵林村	3.8	1694	4961	695	136	71	1566	5611	1182	21.1
曹乐村	6.6	2164	5720	1318	228	187	1099	4838	704	14.6
五星村	1.6	1298	3838	1047	49	21	487	1574	1362	86.5
稔子园村	2.5	637	1671	411	60	37	468	2401	180	7.5
泰园社区		3456	7581	1860	652	78	194	600	748	124.7
常平										
常平社区	4.0	16672	23465	9647	863	31	594	1044	647	62.0
下墟村	0.4	834	2100	458	130	36	582	2230	855	38.3
岗梓村	2.7	2549	8500	1573	120	70	1974	9815	5446	55.5
桥梓村	2.0	2485	6012	1283	211	88	3280	22714	6117	26.9
塘角村	1.1	962	3200	598	140	118	2311	10615	2117	19.9
苏坑村	4.0	3602	4685	1426	250	210	1142	8564	2016	23.5
袁山贝村	5.0	3574	8810	1337	650	349	2729	20625	4697	22.8
金美村	3.0	2428	9000	1310	308	145	4818	42166	13406	31.8
还珠沥村	5.5	2802	17020	1697	395	153	1702	13855	5479	39.5
朗贝村	4.0	1963	6500	775	270	70	954	6042	210	3.5
板石村	3.4	1956	11200	1138	654	44	610	4891	606	12.4
桥沥村	9.8	3493	35000	1570	762	248	2179	12612	1557	12.3
卢屋村	3.0	843	3650	530	199	109	518	1609	190	11.8
土塘村	8.7	2827	29206	1552	1081	144	3843	25666	1725	6.7
麦元村	2.4	1103	3183	413	153	23	1316	9649	778	8.1
九江水村	9.0	1436	6344	705	305	68	1822	21265	1078	5.1
朗洲村	4.1	622	1322	426	113	29	639	3906	1067	27.3
陈屋贝村	2.2	1115	5860	703	180	41	1436	10322	909	8.8
司马村	8.1	2800	12511	1648	502	84	4502	24925	4059	16.3

15　续表 12

(2011年)

村(居)委会	土地面积(平方公里)	户籍人口(人)	外来暂住人口(人)	户籍从业人数(人)	全部企业及个体户数(个)	#工业企业	当年可支配财政收入(万元)	资产总额(万元)	负债总额(万元)	资产负债率(%)
霞坑村	1.6	742	4539	398	254	23	2527	6735	441	6.5
漱旧村	2.0	1132	4250	699	140	28	801	4534	309	6.8
漱新村	2.4	1266	6100	850	595	140	1122	6529	1895	29.0
黄泥塘村	1.0	896	1900	450	119	55	505	2611	1529	58.6
元江元村	1.9	1482	5300	698	154	56	1045	8464	1866	22.0
横江厦村	5.0	2774	4716	1274	232	90	925	7267	2953	40.6
田尾村	2.1	1557	4400	950	56	36	762	4085	1987	48.6
白花沥村	1.0	701	226	273	10	10	527	2017	1211	60.0
沙湖口村	1.4	1020	3210	690	91	28	612	4496	2520	56.0
白石岗村	5.0	3726	6119	1291	111	101	1446	6996	4210	60.2
松柏塘村	3.8	2347	5698	1081	84	34	922	6739	3619	53.7
上坑村	1.3	923	1700	523	115	45	1511	10675	3796	35.6
木榆村	3.5	2090	6584	1143	497	60	4526	25681	2581	10.1
桥　头										
东江村	4.8	2389	1825	1532	193	42	1137	7749	3860	49.8
山和村	2.5	971	2650	497	56	24	925	6149	1592	25.9
屋厦村	2.0	701	1458	447	102	37	1270	6151	1833	29.8
岗头村	0.6	485	2612	307	50	30	817	3612	1222	33.8
李屋村	2.3	1602	2425	855	58	40	2098	17004	5723	33.7
邓屋村	2.7	1865	10300	1011	55	38	3938	24569	8198	33.4
朗厦村	4.1	1594	5000	830	93	78	2059	16941	3734	22.0
邵岗头村	1.3	852	1120	493	40	34	877	5265	2405	45.7
桥头社区	1.0	1335	2100	540	285	48	2725	21430	1000	4.7
迳联社区	1.5	1753	3168	809	109	47	3683	24898	6770	27.2
田新社区	2.2	2182	3700	1095	402	230	2824	21365	6448	30.2
岭头社区	1.3	1165	3500	728	258	55	1998	14710	1786	12.1
石水口村	7.8	4485	7300	2363	538	130	4214	32667	9549	29.2
大洲社区	4.6	3253	3439	1595	141	73	2793	20281	4446	21.9
禾坑村	1.5	993	1050	612	75	23	1060	6130	1471	24.0
田头角村	1.2	756	1952	432	76	47	1176	6533	1891	28.9
莲城社区	15.6	9978	55345	4902			102			
横　沥										
石涌村	3.7	1782	5878	1023	786	158	2633	14750	3610	24.5
隔坑村	2.2	2696	7300	1732	706	70	2294	11979	6546	54.6
半仙山村	2.2	1605	3275	937	984	16	2253	18740	14008	74.7
横沥村	4.6	2914	3200	1685	738	51	1265	14927	7101	47.6
田头村	4.1	2522	4865	1342	793	57	2458	12385	3801	30.7
田坑村	4.8	2823	4990	1809	1036	76	1082	7346	2024	27.6
村头村	3.5	2301	4550	1295	572	83	1971	9265	2839	30.6
长巷村	2.1	1651	900	1040	71	20	617	4927	1975	40.1
田饶步村	2.8	1840	1725	934	249	56	1432	14072	6792	48.3

15 续表 13

(2011年)

村(居)委会	土地面积(平方公里)	户籍人口(人)	外来暂住人口(人)	户籍从业人数(人)	全部企业及个体户数(个)	#工业企业	当年可支配财政收入(万元)	资产总额(万元)	负债总额(万元)	资产负债率(%)
六甲村	1.4	1093	3215	618	179	43	1537	7229	3255	45.0
村尾村	2.7	1484	3664	943	416	48	1295	11252	4221	37.5
水边村	4.0	2776	5535	1956	290	40	764	8004	3265	40.8
新四村	2.9	2061	6199	1328	403	110	226	2006	1842	91.8
山厦村	2.3	1065	3365	582	241	45	915	11736	765	6.5
月塘村	0.5	1114	1439	621	124	26	719	12996	1504	11.6
张坑村	1.0	624	883	357	79	33	642	7400	1900	25.7
恒泉社区	0.2	6912	2425	3741	1857	28	265	1257	724	57.6
东坑										
东坑村	2.0	3065	13000	1848	236	55	2525	15308	6776	44.3
黄麻岭村	0.8	1080	3008	420	42	42	858	6035	3395	56.3
长安塘村	1.3	1878	950	1170	110	87	1354	7470	5392	72.2
寮边头村	0.8	1589	2988	849	247	28	1194	6363	2928	46.0
塔岗村	2.1	1766	5200	1107	74	60	1318	8677	2085	24.0
坑美村	2.2	1939	2680	1037	133	70	804	6263	1325	21.2
新门楼村	2.1	1699	7183	925	145	11	1549	9403	5646	60.0
井美村	1.9	2514	2997	1558	525	50	2127	9910	4702	47.4
初坑村	2.8	2489	8460	1321	428	55	581	2334	1282	54.9
凤大村	0.3	734	1320	477	312	7	2821	5044	2271	45.0
丁屋村	1.1	1084	1200	590	15	9	754	3766	1624	43.1
彭屋村	2.1	1901	5220	1180	226	8	882	4435	1128	25.4
黄屋村	2.0	1968	4518	1172	518	28	1928	9561	2187	22.9
角社村	2.4	3413	5000	2177	173	71	2698	24398	2455	10.1
草塘社区	0.1	3036	410	1861	92	4				
企石										
铁岗村	5.8	2486	1786	1592	40	30	1452	11208	3613	32.2
深巷村	4.1	2239	2346	1235	124	51	899	6095	2718	44.6
湖美村	1.0	811	441	386	31	15	553	4030	1926	47.8
博夏村	6.7	3540	635	1689	51	17	1133	6831	849	12.4
上洞村	5.3	2659	1512	1945	151	24	735	5372	933	17.4
清湖村	4.6	2028	1830	1218	35	25	736	6275	2436	38.8
江边村	5.0	2977	1486	1700	50	22	753	3975	1028	25.9
旧围村	3.8	1941	1082	700	58	30	373	4103	868	21.2
东平村	1.5	725	2504	472	207	26	710	3807	2749	72.2
上截村	0.8	1158	1008	468	53	10	806	5729	4241	74.0
下截村	1.2	1452	1069	811	45	18	1090	7291	3578	49.1
东山村	6.2	4336	5859	1502	411	95	3474	28629	10264	35.9
铁炉坑村	3.4	3096	2028	1380	112	65	1323	9642	3211	33.3
企石村	1.5	1383	517	775	39	18	685	6638	2136	32.2
杨屋村	0.8	649	423	327	46	11	363	3783	2084	55.1
莫屋村	1.0	1228	615	630	48	26	477	2338	1143	48.9
霞朗村	1.0	891	1817	182	256	32	2054	13176	4960	37.6

15 续表 14

(2011年)

村(居)委会	土地面积(平方公里)	户籍人口(人)	外来暂住人口(人)	户籍从业人数(人)	全部企业及个体户数(个)	#工业企业	当年可支配财政收入(万元)	资产总额(万元)	负债总额(万元)	资产负债率(%)
新南村	2.8	2119	1500	1442	315	41	1396	8648	2838	32.8
南坑村	1.5	1219	1197	811	85	28	974	7362	304	4.1
宝石社区	0.5	5386	7087	3710	438		171	114	24	21.1
石排										
石排村	2.4	3651	4238	1735	615	63	937	2429	910	37.5
下沙村	3.4	2614	3733	1587	488	90	616	3742	1283	34.3
庙边王村	3.7	2410	8055	1518	631	202	932	4706	1152	24.5
福隆村	5.6	5872	9932	3729	1070	313	1629	17435	6681	38.3
沙角村	3.4	2572	4527	1538	131	33	772	3722	1144	30.7
黄家壆村	2.4	1926	2486	1251	150	30	1520	12167	363	3.0
赤坎村	3.2	1406	2275	685	230	50	1538	8608	2166	25.2
向西村	2.0	1206	5843	569	496	61	1174	6874	1437	20.9
水贝村	3.5	3212	4547	1825	215	81	1016	5915	696	11.8
田寮村	3.3	1968	1529	1162	123	48	934	6177	704	11.4
横山村	3.8	2037	4527	1336	166	45	778	3362	1576	46.9
谷吓村	3.1	1864	4228	990	118	58	542	4429	1889	42.7
埔心村	2.2	1588	10085	747	689	388	1387	9679	439	4.5
塘尾村	1.6	1097	4578	641	275	76	778	7874	533	6.8
李家坊村	0.9	929	3174	539	196	92	597	4653	1327	28.5
田边村	4.2	2115	3146	1096	176	70	574	3429	2156	62.9
中坑村	3.2	2308	3585	1582	135	29	936	10673	670	6.3
燕窝村	4.3	1739	5497	1032	480	88	1062	8334	2446	29.3
太和社区		2817		1548			291	1358	987	72.7
茶山										
上元村	4.5	3174	7531	1900	130	125	532	2571	929	36.1
茶山村	1.3	1734	4850	1010	752	54	1512	12378	5401	43.6
下朗村	1.0	1402	1666	913	68	29	2214	14160	1941	13.7
横江村	3.7	3064	5755	2135	136	79	908	14122	3038	21.5
卢边村	3.3	2727	2000	1495	92	88	2635	10333	1791	17.3
寒溪水村	1.3	963	1570	605	71	58	713	3581	866	24.2
增埗村	6.0	7185	12008	4150	617	400	1050	10665	6611	62.0
南社村	6.9	3580	10972	2160	148	98	2057	31240	2724	8.7
塘角村	4.7	2955	8735	1594	325	155	1723	12170	1716	14.1
京山村	3.5	2467	5800	1401	328	41	2320	18394	8962	48.7
博头村	1.2	643	1850	350	39	15	623	4877	471	9.7
冲美村	0.8	760	1080	442	88	39	1287	7207	419	5.8
粟边村	3.2	1974	3175	1034	186	66	803	7150	1234	17.3
刘黄村	0.8	995	3184	615	258	71	1045	7786	2964	38.1
孙屋村	0.6	724	960	468	45	23	350	2463	968	39.3
超朗村	8.2	2947	3071	1780	160	160	1181	18296	696	3.8
茶山圩社区	1.0	6989	3585							

十六、历年国民经济和社会发展主要指标

Main Indicators of National Economy and Social Development over Years

16 历年国民经济和社会发展主要指标

Main Indicators of National Economy and Social Development over Years

年　份	户籍人口(万人)	常住人口(万人)	外来暂住人口(万人)	户籍人口自然增长率(‰)	外来暂住从业人员(万人)	城镇在岗职工人数(万人)	城镇在岗职工平均工资(元)
1949	68.24						
1952	71.68						
1957	77.48					3.90	400
1962	79.64					2.93	552
1965	86.46			29.60		3.17	524
1970	98.56			20.60		3.29	534
1975	107.94			14.51		3.80	577
1978	111.23			13.81		8.20	474
1979	112.04			19.00		9.68	650
1980	112.70			19.31		9.86	750
1981	114.46			16.57		10.66	887
1982	116.19			14.14		11.41	1095
1983	117.59			11.53		11.59	1197
1984	118.95			10.60		11.76	1383
1985	120.85			10.83		12.30	1456
1986	123.01		15.62	11.56	10.41	13.27	2616
1987	124.86		25.29	11.67	18.03	13.67	2067
1988	126.76		36.89	12.09	29.25	12.71	2757
1989	128.76		47.19	12.39	40.53	13.10	3320
1990	131.85	175.62	65.59	12.31	57.20	13.16	3552
1991	133.65	200.01	80.58	13.34	70.20	14.59	3777
1992	136.06	227.78	114.48	14.50	107.10	15.47	4531
1993	138.92	259.41	121.70	13.41	112.68	17.66	6228
1994	141.40	295.43	139.09	13.37	124.18	16.09	8360
1995	143.65	336.45	142.18	12.75	126.54	17.87	9682
1996	145.25	383.17	143.32	11.97	127.66	17.50	10382
1997	147.12	436.38	144.68	12.09	130.73	16.50	10691
1998	148.77	496.97	199.11	10.86	183.19	16.40	11422
1999	150.82	565.98	244.81	10.22	216.15	16.39	12557
2000	152.61	644.84	254.72	7.52	244.84	16.41	14051
2001	153.89	654.43	457.82	7.01	449.68	16.42	16183
2002	156.19	654.84	433.65	5.91	426.01	16.42	17804
2003	158.96	655.25	440.45	5.65	432.73	16.60	22598
2004	161.97	655.66	486.95	5.96	473.39	17.54	25326
2005	165.65	656.07	584.98	6.02	553.42	18.86	28253
2006	168.31	685.66	586.76	5.86	566.98	19.99	31135
2007	171.26	717.02	557.80	5.98	538.95	20.56	35284
2008	174.87	750.60	552.50	6.23	530.30	20.72	39516
2009	178.73	786.08	429.96	6.31	413.46	22.60	42585
2010	181.77	822.48	411.47	6.23	391.23	22.63	46576
2011	184.77	825.48	413.62	6.13	394.71	24.61	50398

注：城镇在岗职工人数与平均工资1952–1975年是全所有制单位资料，1978–1999年为城镇职工资料，2000年起为城镇在岗职工资料。

16 续表 1

年份	地区生产总值（万元）	第一产业	第二产业	工业	建筑业	第三产业	人均地区生产总值（元）
1949							
1952							
1957							
1962							
1965							
1970							
1975							
1978	6.11	2.72	2.68			0.71	553
1979	6.62	2.65	2.92			1.05	593
1980	7.22	2.63	3.33			1.26	643
1981	9.11	3.28	4.30			1.54	802
1982	11.43	3.73	5.81			1.89	991
1983	13.03	3.98	6.90			2.15	1115
1984	15.96	4.57	7.81			3.59	1350
1985	22.60	6.15	11.66			4.80	1885
1986	30.02	8.14	13.57	10.54	3.03	8.30	2462
1987	39.29	9.82	17.72	14.24	3.49	11.74	3170
1988	55.46	11.89	28.28	25.05	3.23	15.29	4408
1989	60.92	12.66	27.97	27.22	0.75	20.29	4768
1990	80.44	13.28	40.53	39.18	1.34	26.63	6173
1991	95.91	13.45	50.32	48.34	1.98	32.13	5095
1992	110.89	14.41	59.27	56.63	2.64	37.21	5038
1993	157.05	14.40	87.31	82.89	4.42	55.34	5850
1994	217.03	17.48	119.49	110.77	8.72	80.06	6357
1995	296.29	21.43	166.97	154.19	12.78	107.89	7421
1996	361.75	24.86	199.48	187.85	11.63	137.40	8444
1997	448.60	25.64	243.28	230.79	12.50	179.68	9747
1998	558.00	25.94	305.68	290.69	14.99	226.37	11265
1999	667.24	25.79	367.05	349.53	17.52	274.40	12494
2000	820.25	25.91	450.71	430.45	20.25	343.64	13679
2001	991.89	26.10	540.51	517.03	23.48	425.28	15268
2002	1186.94	24.88	648.81	621.86	26.96	513.25	18131
2003	1452.52	22.82	798.20	757.18	41.01	631.51	22174
2004	1806.03	22.71	1016.04	968.01	48.03	767.28	27554
2005	2183.20	20.55	1227.86	1173.23	54.63	934.78	33287
2006	2627.98	12.01	1506.60	1441.69	64.91	1109.37	39173
2007	3160.05	11.90	1754.66	1681.83	72.83	1393.49	45057
2008	3703.60	14.83	1901.61	1819.22	82.38	1787.17	50471
2009	3763.91	14.79	1823.08	1741.53	81.55	1926.04	48988
2010	4246.45	16.57	2160.82	2078.45	82.37	2069.07	52798
2011	4735.39	17.88	2366.20	2288.41	77.79	2351.32	57470

注：1. 本表按当年价格计算。
2. 人均生产总值1990年及以前年份按年平均户籍人口计算，1991年起按年平均常住人口计算。

16 续表 2

上年=100

年 份	地区生产总值指数	第一产业	第二产业	工 业	建筑业	第三产业	人均地区生产总值指数
1949							
1952							
1957							
1962							
1965							
1970							
1975							
1978							
1979	99.5	86.5	107.0			146.4	98.6
1980	102.7	90.3	117.3			113.9	102.0
1981	116.6	115.0	122.1			110.8	115.4
1982	116.9	105.3	131.0			117.6	115.1
1983	110.4	104.8	115.7			111.3	108.9
1984	114.2	109.0	107.0			140.9	112.9
1985	132.3	118.9	144.5			132.7	130.5
1986	126.1	111.9	110.3			174.7	124.0
1987	122.5	111.6	127.7	125.8	147.0	126.0	120.5
1988	115.7	90.6	143.7	151.4	77.9	103.0	114.0
1989	107.1	99.8	106.2	106.4	103.7	113.7	105.5
1990	123.2	104.4	127.6	130.6	76.4	128.0	120.8
1991	117.5	103.1	121.5	121.8	113.2	118.6	108.8
1992	108.3	100.0	112.6	113.7	78.0	105.1	92.6
1993	127.9	79.4	139.2	138.5	168.1	129.0	104.8
1994	122.5	107.2	124.7	124.3	138.5	122.3	96.3
1995	127.4	110.5	135.1	135.3	128.3	116.8	108.9
1996	117.5	109.4	115.5	116.2	91.2	123.5	109.5
1997	119.6	104.5	119.8	120.1	106.1	121.8	111.3
1998	121.8	100.9	122.1	122.2	115.1	124.5	113.1
1999	119.7	102.3	120.6	120.7	115.2	120.3	111.0
2000	119.7	99.8	120.7	120.9	110.5	120.0	106.6
2001	119.9	103.0	121.6	122.0	113.0	118.9	110.7
2002	120.5	97.6	122.6	123.0	114.1	119.1	119.6
2003	120.5	90.2	122.3	121.4	143.5	119.7	120.4
2004	121.0	90.0	125.6	126.5	106.8	115.8	120.9
2005	119.5	102.3	120.0	120.2	113.5	119.3	119.4
2006	119.2	58.9	121.9	122.0	118.7	117.1	116.6
2007	118.3	89.9	114.8	115.0	108.7	123.3	113.1
2008	114.0	110.6	106.1	106.4	100.9	124.0	109.0
2009	105.3	102.3	99.7	99.4	104.7	111.4	100.5
2010	110.3	101.6	116.7	117.5	97.1	104.1	105.3
2011	108.0	100.5	107.0	107.7	87.8	109.0	105.4

注：本表按可比价格计算。

16 续表 3

年　份	固定资产投资总额(亿元)	地方财政一般预算收入(亿元)	地方财政一般预算支出(亿元)	居民消费价格指数(上年=100)	商品零售价格指数(上年=100)	农林牧渔业总　产　值(亿元)	农林牧渔业总产值指数(1978=100)
1949						0.54	
1952		0.28	0.02			0.66	
1957		0.32	0.04			0.78	
1962		0.31	0.07			0.76	
1965		0.47	0.07			1.28	
1970		0.48	0.08			1.47	
1975		0.65	0.11			2.53	
1978	0.23	0.66	0.18		100.4	4.24	100.0
1979	0.16	0.66	0.19		102.6	4.15	96.5
1980	0.24	0.67	0.20		110.9	4.19	98.0
1981	0.38	0.68	0.21		109.3	5.04	102.1
1982	1.81	0.81	0.26		101.2	5.59	117.6
1983	1.84	0.86	0.28		99.6	5.64	117.4
1984	3.01	0.85	0.30	99.3	98.6	7.02	126.7
1985	7.06	1.11	0.50	106.5	106.9	9.12	138.9
1986	11.52	1.61	0.99	104.2	104.4	12.30	174.6
1987	14.19	2.02	1.25	112.0	112.2	14.84	186.4
1988	16.55	2.71	1.75	136.0	132.8	20.37	182.1
1989	5.01	3.19	2.16	122.0	122.4	22.11	181.9
1990	7.51	3.57	2.28	96.6	94.9	23.64	195.3
1991	13.75	4.44	2.75	102.4	101.4	24.26	199.5
1992	18.88	5.62	3.82	109.2	107.7	27.13	211.3
1993	32.76	9.38	7.29	121.8	119.5	28.45	175.5
1994	140.76	7.69	8.90	123.5	118.4	34.75	188.4
1995	63.14	11.56	12.42	113.9	109.7	42.69	207.8
1996	67.62	9.65	12.41	106.8	104.7	49.72	216.3
1997	65.89	11.41	14.85	101.5	99.7	51.44	225.0
1998	77.00	15.10	17.91	99.9	98.7	53.60	227.3
1999	88.32	18.26	21.26	97.9	95.9	53.74	242.8
2000	102.89	30.47	33.61	101.5	100.1	54.64	243.3
2001	125.49	45.02	47.86	96.6	97.8	55.93	246.3
2002	191.57	55.29	64.96	98.1	99.1	53.67	263.2
2003	319.39	67.45	76.52	100.7	101.7	49.02	209.7
2004	454.87	82.64	94.16	103.0	103.2	44.19	213.5
2005	597.24	103.97	117.04	102.4	103.0	42.05	222.2
2006	705.45	128.94	147.90	101.2	102.8	21.26	121.0
2007	841.21	186.45	193.10	103.1	104.2	19.98	105.6
2008	944.34	209.22	218.26	105.5	107.9	25.53	118.3
2009	1094.08	231.16	232.62	96.9	95.3	25.31	122.2
2010	1114.98	277.84	289.83	102.8	103.2	28.31	126.2
2011	1079.77	313.06	351.92	104.9	104.7	30.66	126.1

注：农林牧渔总产值1952－1970年按1957年不变价计算，1975年按1970年不变价计算，1978年起按当年价计算。

16　续表 4

年　份	农作物总播种面积(千公顷)	#粮食	粮食产量(万吨)	油料产量(万吨)	水果产量(万吨)	肉类产量(万吨)	水产品产量(万吨)
1949	141.26	127.26	21.07	0.15			0.32
1952	167.61	149.68	26.95	0.35			0.34
1957	188.98	165.53	28.80	0.33			0.42
1962	155.97	138.18	33.12	0.38			0.63
1965	158.97	121.64	43.71	0.72	4.54		0.99
1970	174.60	127.25	45.08	0.96	6.95		1.62
1975	202.00	137.03	50.72	1.11	3.68		2.19
1978	190.63	138.15	53.23	1.42	2.65	2.69	3.09
1979	172.36	129.16	53.53	1.91	2.33	2.92	2.23
1980	162.41	117.12	52.94	2.90	2.37	2.77	2.55
1981	151.17	107.13	44.75	3.55	4.69	2.80	2.49
1982	146.96	106.68	54.33	2.99	5.82	3.30	2.77
1983	146.21	109.02	56.12	1.97	7.72	3.57	3.03
1984	144.35	105.12	55.82	2.31	10.59	3.33	3.25
1985	130.01	93.05	48.87	2.10	18.94	3.33	3.26
1986	119.41	83.81	45.52	2.01	30.77	4.33	4.65
1987	119.73	83.40	46.28	1.70	36.31	4.61	6.57
1988	119.53	82.42	46.09	1.51	26.37	5.61	6.81
1989	122.27	85.61	48.76	1.37	22.14	5.86	6.23
1990	123.25	85.74	49.43	1.34	28.24	6.22	6.85
1991	119.42	81.77	47.37	1.15	34.32	6.88	6.90
1992	104.10	64.26	36.81	0.93	34.48	6.80	7.32
1993	71.20	36.74	20.21	0.56	27.13	7.66	6.50
1994	67.30	35.75	20.24	0.37	26.49	8.54	6.74
1995	71.89	39.90	22.74	0.37	24.32	9.76	7.48
1996	72.23	41.89	24.32	0.31	20.63	11.61	8.11
1997	72.17	41.61	24.69	0.29	16.50	12.90	9.19
1998	73.46	41.63	24.72	0.26	11.41	15.35	9.69
1999	72.59	41.77	24.73	0.22	13.63	15.99	9.40
2000	65.73	35.18	20.41	0.20	12.94	17.90	9.51
2001	56.95	22.56	12.84	0.16	15.01	19.84	8.96
2002	42.28	9.88	5.37	0.09	18.93	18.88	8.24
2003	33.97	5.65	3.05	0.04	14.64	15.46	7.58
2004	30.82	5.41	3.04	0.02	17.54	14.62	7.15
2005	27.38	4.14	2.00	0.01	15.13	17.17	6.74
2006	22.26	2.29	1.00	0.01	13.96	3.49	4.71
2007	21.37	2.15	0.99	0.01	13.16	2.03	4.73
2008	23.48	2.72	1.20	0.01	10.15	2.41	7.23
2009	24.72	2.77	1.19	0.01	9.15	2.55	7.33
2010	24.62	2.79	1.25	0.01	7.55	2.88	7.63
2011	24.46	2.76	1.29	0.01	7.39	2.60	7.82

16 续表 5

年份	工业企业单位数(个)	工业增加值(亿元)	工业增加值指数(上年=100)	规模以上工业增加值(亿元)	总供电量(亿千瓦时)	总售电量(亿千瓦时)	建筑业总产值(亿元)	建筑业增加值(亿元)
1949	1							
1952	23							
1957	262							
1962	280				0.08	0.07		
1965	260				0.36	0.32		
1970	220				0.71	0.60		
1975	324				1.24	1.11		
1978	1290				1.64	1.49		
1979	1250				1.93	1.73		
1980	1293				2.17	1.97		
1981	1479				2.22	1.99		
1982	1862				2.69	2.35		
1983	1964				3.15	2.75		
1984	2329				3.26	2.84		
1985	4187				3.82	3.39		
1986	5949	10.54		6.96	3.93	3.51		3.03
1987	8106	14.24	125.8	8.68	6.43	5.71		3.49
1988	8408	25.05	151.4	15.03	9.48	8.47		3.23
1989	8757	27.22	106.4	15.54	12.09	10.84	1.03	0.75
1990	9892	39.18	130.6	23.76	18.01	16.15	1.27	1.34
1991	10094	48.34	121.8	31.54	24.05	21.67	2.19	1.98
1992	11639	56.63	113.7	38.21	32.00	28.87	3.19	2.64
1993	12449	82.89	138.5	59.08	43.62	39.40	5.39	4.42
1994	14086	110.77	124.3	78.43	58.58	53.02	7.99	8.72
1995	15215	154.19	135.3	111.02	68.00	61.68	9.49	12.78
1996	15326	187.85	116.2	140.89	80.03	72.71	9.66	11.63
1997	16857	230.79	120.1	177.71	94.93	86.65	28.73	12.50
1998	16406	290.69	122.2	240.22	109.48	100.91	35.92	14.99
1999	16877	349.53	120.7	292.58	132.78	123.42	40.73	17.52
2000	16975	430.45	120.9	360.11	178.03	169.06	40.45	20.25
2001	18094	517.03	122.0	410.67	207.72	196.59	50.13	23.48
2002	21313	621.86	123.0	542.03	258.55	246.97	65.84	26.96
2003	21935	757.18	121.4	673.59	321.65	283.54	76.48	41.01
2004	22156	968.01	126.5	826.58	372.84	350.28	77.01	48.03
2005	21868	1173.23	120.2	979.34	415.66	396.59	84.35	58.61
2006	22447	1441.69	122.0	1186.20	464.45	445.52	94.58	64.91
2007	22587	1681.83	115.0	1388.34	507.89	482.56	112.87	72.83
2008	25656	1819.22	106.4	1602.98	507.35	487.32	108.81	82.38
2009	31160	1741.53	99.4	1453.37	488.85	478.19	99.40	81.55
2010	38273	2078.45	117.5	1708.31	556.89	543.66	122.06	82.37
2011	46413	2288.41	107.7	1642.45	579.35	566.69	130.85	77.79

16 续表 6

年　份	公路通车里程(公里)	民用汽车拥有量(万辆)	旅客周转量(万人公里)	货物周转量(万吨公里)	邮电业务收入(万元)	本地电话用户(万户)	移动电话用户(万户)
1949	204	0.002					
1952	219	0.002	1350	139			
1957	373	0.005	2100	195			
1962	598	0.007	4120	293			
1965	882	0.010	4725	457			
1970	1134	0.012	2800	900			
1975	1173	0.025	3890	694			
1978	1259	0.06	9425	15148	686	0.20	
1979	1225	0.11	11162	15290	790	0.21	
1980	1225	0.20	13584	16353	927	0.31	
1981	1225	0.30	13845	15606	962	0.34	
1982	1225	0.34	16026	17185	940	0.35	
1983	1225	0.45	54075	108634	1018	0.39	
1984	1240	0.61	62107	140113	1263	0.48	
1985	1240	0.79	95237	171591	1560	0.77	
1986	1248	0.86	127458	126898	2015	0.88	
1987	1261	1.00	159117	174942	3410	1.63	
1988	1302	1.36	173335	169112	5728	2.52	
1989	1325	1.63	240999	186626	9620	4.30	0.02
1990	1325	1.94	322236	184700	17555	4.90	0.05
1991	1759	2.07	373284	194101	27733	7.50	0.11
1992	2055	3.26	503973	232752	42155	9.70	0.30
1993	2260	4.81	577800	248230	65699	14.98	0.72
1994	2292	6.16	595134	273053	102238	23.19	2.41
1995	2327	8.83	446230	264605	152761	31.57	4.77
1996	2330	9.08	477466	267193	207573	36.91	8.24
1997	2330	10.34	511592	278649	284278	42.65	15.29
1998	2377	11.34	577452	285889	376708	50.13	26.17
1999	2467	12.70	804278	300410	515916	60.87	51.01
2000	2518	15.37	1001906	404678	724593	78.12	123.68
2001	2570	18.36	1031579	406247	1225474	98.96	295.76
2002	2641	22.01	1091821	420684	1816802	127.93	412.39
2003	2688	25.56	1126964	422822	1051220	206.11	660.86
2004	2759	31.97	1166262	423669	1207778	281.35	856.09
2005	2871	40.66	1185290	424829	1328172	384.52	1016.41
2006	3891	48.93	1213809	336783	1466871	461.31	1216.34
2007	3924	60.89	1264982	356677	1619048	469.17	1408.23
2008	4001	70.16	2248521	1747489	1723829	439.41	1454.29
2009	4713	79.56	1053469	1016490	1563077	378.40	1409.29
2010	4751	92.08	1290692	1090340	1553352	332.42	1607.60
2011	4828	106.14	1458811	1874802	1648579	319.55	1677.77

注：1. 公路通车里程2006年起含专用公路和村道。
　　2. 邮电业务收入2003年以前为邮电业务总量，按1990年不变价计算，2003年起为邮电业务收入。

16 续表 7

年 份	社会消费品零售总额(亿元)	进出口总额(亿美元)	出口额	进口额	协议(合同)规定外商投资额(亿美元)	实际利用外资(亿美元)	#外商直接投资
1949							
1952							
1957			0.02				
1962			0.04				
1965			0.08				
1970			0.10				
1975			0.25				
1978	2.13		0.39				
1979	2.50		0.54		0.05	0.02	
1980	3.16		0.77		0.11	0.09	
1981	4.02		0.92		0.08	0.05	0.001
1982	4.81		1.09		0.08	0.07	0.005
1983	5.23		1.19		0.16	0.09	0.003
1984	7.39		1.30		0.32	0.19	0.07
1985	9.36		1.75		0.68	0.35	0.14
1986	12.24		2.33		0.34	0.45	0.15
1987	15.05		2.68		1.85	1.32	0.21
1988	24.65		3.18		6.22	2.99	0.64
1989	27.04		3.49		2.34	2.73	0.84
1990	31.97	10.82	5.68	5.14	3.02	2.56	1.00
1991	36.50	31.75	16.52	15.23	6.45	2.83	1.47
1992	44.35	50.90	26.03	24.87	20.88	4.81	3.29
1993	63.69	67.56	32.11	35.45	35.55	10.49	7.92
1994	85.16	88.30	42.94	45.36	34.97	11.95	7.79
1995	113.01	153.91	77.99	75.92	33.09	11.58	6.72
1996	125.53	178.42	91.87	86.55	20.89	13.10	6.95
1997	146.04	212.99	113.68	99.31	12.14	15.16	8.80
1998	175.16	232.73	130.61	102.13	16.37	15.48	9.30
1999	202.30	284.63	151.54	133.09	14.72	17.89	9.71
2000	235.16	320.45	171.59	148.86	18.36	19.54	10.87
2001	275.71	344.55	189.89	154.65	20.98	20.29	11.47
2002	321.24	442.47	237.36	205.11	24.89	23.48	14.59
2003	369.78	521.06	280.02	241.04	32.56	27.72	17.54
2004	426.47	645.18	351.92	293.25	41.32	33.47	21.39
2005	506.29	743.72	409.29	334.42	47.52	42.48	14.68
2006	599.32	842.21	473.76	368.45	55.28	50.04	18.08
2007	722.45	1068.73	602.32	466.41	62.51	60.07	21.18
2008	881.15	1132.99	655.37	477.62	39.37	47.09	24.47
2009	959.07	941.55	551.69	389.86	20.30	42.12	25.94
2010	1108.06	1213.38	695.98	517.40	30.73	31.63	27.32
2011	1266.31	1352.24	783.29	568.95	37.02	32.18	30.51

注：1. 出口总额1990年起为海关口径，1990年以前为外经贸口径。
　　2. 实际外商直接投资2004年起为新口径，是以验资作为统计标准，与往年数不可比。

16 续表 8

年 份	国际及港澳台旅游者（万人次）	国际旅游外汇收入（万美元）	接待国内游客人次（万人次）	旅 游总收入（亿元）	各项人民币存款余额（亿元）	城乡居民储蓄存款余额	各项人民币贷款余额（亿元）
1949							
1952						0.003	0.004
1957						0.02	0.26
1962					0.08	0.04	0.75
1965					0.16	0.09	0.81
1970					0.39	0.16	0.87
1975					0.96	0.41	1.39
1978					1.05	0.54	1.96
1979					1.49	0.72	2.13
1980					2.61	1.17	3.08
1981					3.80	2.03	4.02
1982					4.51	2.77	4.55
1983					6.05	3.86	5.76
1984					11.03	6.18	12.19
1985					13.49	9.19	14.24
1986	11	554	69		19.59	13.14	20.68
1987	19	453	87		28.48	18.97	31.24
1988	20	710	105		38.05	24.91	41.58
1989	18	504	97		46.82	32.57	49.37
1990	27	1025	98		68.07	45.51	63.04
1991	37	2443	118		94.97	61.47	78.40
1992	47	2473	125		147.34	81.54	105.98
1993	52	2888	117		179.83	107.17	134.31
1994	44	3464	75		249.78	151.54	173.44
1995	27	5679	62		383.68	232.97	254.85
1996	36	6464	139		489.65	318.02	312.81
1997	59	6778	112		671.17	425.82	382.66
1998	75	6601	141		864.01	533.75	442.74
1999	97	7055	156		1040.84	616.34	524.37
2000	106	7617	185		1228.67	672.07	630.84
2001	110	8200	217	39.80	1458.65	799.18	750.18
2002	108	11847	822	72.51	1790.18	1001.69	933.41
2003	80	13825	1006	79.92	2126.78	1231.06	1206.72
2004	149	23437	982	85.70	2462.87	1431.68	1405.25
2005	169	28189	987	90.72	2933.40	1728.28	1500.52
2006	193	33180	1170	96.01	3365.65	2013.40	1730.56
2007	248	42702	1477	118.88	3751.83	2120.74	2154.77
2008	268	45614	1604	128.69	4354.53	2638.04	2380.36
2009	286	51756	1751	151.49	4986.61	2904.57	2903.80
2010	327	67592	1924	191.32	5943.39	3386.85	3329.82
2011	357	90975	2258	249.37	6609.39	3710.99	3716.08

16 续表 9

年 份	在校学生数（万人）			学龄儿童入学率(%)	高考入围人数（人）	#省线入围人数	病床床位数（张）
	普通高等学校	普通中学	小学				
1949		0.20	5.28				219
1952		0.34	7.04				179
1957		0.67	8.80				403
1962		0.97	12.00				1376
1965		1.05	16.09				1308
1970		6.02	11.81				1476
1975		4.96	16.82				1970
1978		7.60	16.11	98.36	846	250	2257
1979		6.23	15.80	98.70	566	166	2271
1980		5.48	15.49	98.85	222	140	2207
1981		4.35	15.09	98.72	239	154	2210
1982		4.17	14.48	99.06	252	115	2292
1983		4.28	13.54	99.75	245	150	2098
1984		4.65	13.46	99.65	619	220	2231
1985		4.66	13.44	99.83	534	285	2323
1986		4.94	14.07	99.90	595	228	3054
1987		5.44	14.43	99.94	644	297	3393
1988		5.93	15.01	99.93	925	315	3640
1989		6.20	15.59	99.92	977	284	3677
1990		6.12	16.27	99.94	759	224	3866
1991		6.01	17.01	99.92	861	268	4085
1992		6.52	17.52	99.94	994	312	4517
1993	0.11	7.53	18.01	99.95	1102	423	4940
1994	0.15	8.58	18.62	99.96	1823	586	5365
1995	0.16	9.25	19.51	99.99	2095	809	5798
1996	0.18	9.52	20.60	99.98	2160	1093	5288
1997	0.20	9.80	22.18	99.99	2212	1215	5505
1998	0.22	10.12	23.58	99.99	2348	1315	5892
1999	0.22	10.55	24.88	99.99	3501	1790	6241
2000	0.32	11.24	27.28	99.99	5017	2646	7081
2001	0.38	12.21	29.54	100.00	5651	3225	7474
2002	0.51	13.53	34.28	100.00	6873	3759	8641
2003	0.69	14.97	38.69	100.00	9167	4509	9820
2004	0.91	17.13	44.83	100.00	10756	5452	10797
2005	1.66	19.10	48.09	100.00	11196	6455	11972
2006	2.20	21.46	49.68	100.00	11359	7652	13293
2007	2.52	23.46	52.07	100.00	13275	9185	15227
2008	2.87	24.84	52.86	100.00	15047	9987	16778
2009	3.40	24.95	51.12	100.00	17487	12569	18080
2010	3.83	25.83	55.24	100.00	18845	13761	19980
2011	4.51	26.31	57.83	100.00	19588	15501	22814

年 份	卫生机构技术人员数(万人)	#执 业(助理)医 师	每万人口拥有		年末参加基本养老保险人数(万人)	年末参加基本医疗保险人数(万人)	城镇居民最低生活保障人数(人)
			床位数(张)	执业(助理)医师(人)			
1949	0.02		3.21				
1952	0.01		2.50				
1957	0.03		5.20				
1962	0.13		17.28				
1965	0.16		15.13				
1970	0.17		14.98				
1975	0.23		18.25				
1978	0.26	0.08	20.29	6.90			
1979	0.29	0.10	20.27	8.67			
1980	0.30	0.12	19.58	10.35			
1981	0.31	0.11	19.31	9.63			
1982	0.33	0.11	19.73	9.44			
1983	0.33	0.11	17.84	9.25			
1984	0.34	0.11	18.76	9.52			
1985	0.33	0.12	19.22	9.94			
1986	0.35	0.12	24.83	9.58			
1987	0.35	0.13	27.17	10.44			
1988	0.38	0.15	28.72	12.13			
1989	0.39	0.16	28.56	12.58			
1990	0.39	0.17	22.01	9.80			
1991	0.39	0.18	20.42	8.77			
1992	0.41	0.18	19.83	8.04			
1993	0.45	0.20	19.04	7.80			
1994	0.49	0.22	18.16	7.52	7.55	7.77	
1995	0.53	0.23	17.23	6.83	8.46	7.60	
1996	0.58	0.24	13.80	6.39	9.16	7.65	
1997	0.63	0.26	12.62	5.97	7.53	8.29	
1998	0.71	0.30	11.86	5.95	7.84	9.05	
1999	0.76	0.31	11.03	5.44	8.35	9.95	
2000	0.81	0.33	10.98	5.13	82.95	88.21	1825
2001	0.81	0.34	11.42	5.24	83.01	84.99	2003
2002	0.90	0.35	13.20	5.38	103.19	105.19	2711
2003	0.98	0.38	14.99	5.74	104.13	105.90	2876
2004	1.31	0.49	16.47	7.43	104.44	105.95	4968
2005	1.88	0.69	18.25	10.52	182.49	189.40	4885
2006	2.29	0.86	22.21	12.58	204.08	212.16	6091
2007	2.88	1.04	21.24	14.57	227.98	236.32	3129
2008	3.31	1.19	22.35	15.81	262.63	513.25	3653
2009	3.58	1.29	23.00	16.39	315.81	536.57	3770
2010	3.75	1.32	24.29	16.07	421.84	592.27	3643
2011	3.96	1.36	27.64	16.53	481.05	602.41	9415

注：每万人口拥有床位数、执业(助理)医师数按常住人口计算。

16 续表 11

年 份	专 利 申请量 (件)	专 利 授权量 (件)	城市居民人均可支配收入 (元)	农 民 人 均 纯收入 (元)	城镇人均住房使用面 积 (平方米)	农村人均生活用房使用面积 (平方米)
1949						
1952						
1957						
1962						
1965						
1970						
1975						
1978				149		
1979				188		
1980				272		
1981				463		
1982				567		
1983				618		
1984				691		
1985			791	803	11	
1986			1033	951	12	
1987			1247	1142	13	
1988			1778	1325	15	
1989			2282	1424	17	
1990	34	30	2508	1542	16	
1991	70	50	3068	1673	16	
1992	102	78	4026	2290	17	
1993	100	90	5970	2903	20	
1994	104	100	8270	3769	23	
1995	325	262	9588	4769	20	
1996	333	312	10824	5554	21	20
1997	725	321	11032	6132	21	41
1998	890	709	11506	6830	26	43
1999	1221	819	12954	7704	29.7	46
2000	1653	1399	14142	8484	31.1	47
2001	2914	1753	16938	9383	39.9	48
2002	3100	2680	16949	10178	41.8	55
2003	3865	2858	18471	11033	41.4	58
2004	4325	3167	20526	11941	41.6	65
2005	6694	3114	22882	13076	42.7	65
2006	9879	4872	25320	14313	45.2	60
2007	13842	6752	27025	15747	43.1	59
2008	14406	8093	30275	16904	40.3	55
2009	19106	12918	33045	18098	40.4	56
2010	21654	20397	35690	20486	44.1	52
2011	24455	19353	39513	22842	49.4	52

十七、东莞与全国、全省、三角洲城市主要指标比较

Comparison of Main Indicators between Dongguan and China, Guangdong Province, the Cities of the Pearl River Delta

17-1 主要年份全国国民经济与社会发展指标

Main Indicators on National Economy and Social Development of China

指标	单位	1980年	1985年	1990年	1995年	2000年	2005年	2010年	2011年
一、人口与劳动力									
年末总人口	万人	98705	105851	114333	121121	126743	130756	134091	134735
年末从业人员人数	万人	42361	49873	64749	68065	72085	74647	76105	76420
#城镇从业人员	万人	10525	12808	17041	19040	23151	28389	34687	35914
二、经济总量									
国内生产总值	亿元	4546	9016	18668	60794	99215	184937	401202	471564
第一产业增加值	亿元	1372	2564	5062	12136	14945	22420	40534	47712
第二产业增加值	亿元	2192	3867	7717	28680	45556	87598	187581	220592
第三产业增加值	亿元	982	2585	5888	19979	38714	74919	173087	203260
人均国内生产总值	元	463	858	1644	5046	7858	14185	29992	35083
三、农业									
主要农产品产量									
粮食	万吨	32056	37911	44624	46662	46218	48402	54678	57121
水果	万吨	679	1164	1874	4215	6225	16120	21401	22768
肉类	万吨		1927	2857	5260	6014	6939	7926	7957
水产品	万吨	450	705	1237	2517	3706	4420	5373	5600
四、工业									
工业增加值	亿元	1997	3449	6858	24951	40034	77231	160867	188572
主要工业产品产量									
机制纸及纸板	万吨	535	911	1372	2812	2487	5404	9833	11034
彩电	万台	3	435	1033	2058	3936	8283	11830	12231
发电量	亿千瓦时	3006	4107	6212	10070	13556	24747	42072	47001
钢材	万吨	2716	3693	5153	8980	13146	39692	80277	88258
五、运输邮电									
货运量	亿吨	54.65	74.58	97.06	123.49	135.87	186.21	324.18	368.50
货物周转量	亿吨公里	12027	18365	26208	35909	44321	80258	141837	159014
客运量	亿人	34.18	62.02	77.27	117.26	147.86	184.70	326.95	351.80
旅客周转量	亿人公里	2281	4436	5628	9002	12261	17467	27894	30936
邮电业务总量	亿元	39	62	156	989	4793	12029	31978	13379
年末程控电话用户	万户	214	312	685	4071	14483	35045	29434	28512
年末移动电话用户	万户			1.8	363	8453	39341	85900	98625

注：城镇从业人员1998年起为城镇在岗职工人数。

17-1 续表

指标	单位	1980年	1985年	1990年	1995年	2000年	2005年	2010年	2011年
六、固定资产投资									
固定资产投资总额	亿元	911	2543	4517	20019	32918	88774	278122	311022
#房地产开发	亿元			253	3149	4984	15909	48259	61740
七、商业									
社会消费品零售总额	亿元	2140	4305	8300	20620	39106	67177	156998	183919
八、物价总指数									
商品零售价格指数	上年=100	106.0	108.8	102.1	114.8	98.5	100.8	103.1	104.9
居民消费价格指数	上年=100	107.5	109.3	103.1	117.1	100.4	101.8	103.3	105.4
九、外贸外经									
海关进出口总额	亿美元	381	696	1154	2809	4743	14219	29740	36421
进口额	亿美元	200	423	533	1321	2251	6599	13962	17435
出口额	亿美元	181	273	621	1488	2492	7620	15778	18986
实际利用外资	亿美元		20	35	375	407	603	1057	1160
十、财政、金融									
财政收入	亿元	1160	2005	2937	6242	13395	31649	83102	103740
财政支出	亿元	1229	2004	3084	6824	15887	33930	87874	108930
各项人民币存款余额	亿元			13943	53882	123804	287170	718238	80.9万
各项人民币贷款余额	亿元			17511	50544	99371	194690	479196	54.8万
十一、人民生活									
在岗职工人均工资	元	762	1148	2140	5500	9371	18364	37147	41799
城市居民人均可支配收入	元	478	739	1510	4283	6280	10493	19109	21810
农民人均纯收入	元	191	398	686	1578	2253	3255	5919	6977
城乡居民人民币储蓄存款余额	亿元	400	1623	7120	29662	64332	141051	303302	351957
十二、教育									
在校学生数									
普通高等学校	万人	114	170	206	291	556	1562	2232	2309
普通中学	万人	5508	4706	4586	5371	7369	8581	7703	7522
小学	万人	14627	13370	12241	13195	13013	10864	9941	9926
十三、卫生									
医院床位数	万张	120	151	187	206	217	245	339	368
卫生技术人员	万人	280	341	390	426	449	456	588	620
#执业（助理）医师	万人	115	141	176	192	208	204	241	251

注：实际利用外资不含对外借款，2005年起为实际使用外商直接投资口径。

17-2 主要年份广东省国民经济与社会发展指标

Main Indicators on National Economy and Social Development of Guangdong Province

指　　标	单　位	1980年	1985年	1990年	1995年	2000年	2005年	2010年	2011年
一、人口与劳动力									
年末常住人口	万人			6347	7387	8650	9194	10441	10505
年末从业人员人数	万人	2368	2731	3118	3551	3989	5023	5752	5961
#城镇从业人员	万人	564	661	785	912	759	904	1119	1238
二、经济总量									
地区生产总值	亿元	250	577	1559	5933	10741	22557	46013	53210
第一产业增加值	亿元	83	172	385	864	986	1428	2287	2665
第二产业增加值	亿元	103	230	616	2900	5000	11357	23015	26447
第三产业增加值	亿元	64	176	559	2168	4755	9773	20712	24098
人均地区生产总值	元	481	1026	2484	8129	12736	24647	44736	50807
三、农业									
主要农产品产量									
粮食	万吨	1682	1604	1896	1803	1822	1395	1317	1361
水果	万吨	29	116	329	415	644	832	1129	1210
肉类	万吨	63	128	202	305	324	384	441	435
水产品	万吨	63	109	208	354	593	695	729	762
四、工业									
工业增加值	亿元	90	186	523	2449	4463	10490	21463	24408
主要工业产品产量									
机制纸及纸板	万吨	31	53	104	288	260	691	1435	1496
彩电	万台	1	79	262	764	1532	4090	4495	4862
发电量	亿千瓦时	109	167	344	821	1293	2163	3101	3607
成品钢材	万吨	45	79	134	247	406	1366	2919	3177
五、运输邮电									
货运量	万吨	14201	58726	85809	111063	119216	133992	205034	234913
货物周转量	亿吨公里	1413	1768	2599	4643	3065	3917	5934	7106
客运量	万人	21444	49848	78046	130998	164791	161357	467049	522002
旅客周转量	亿人公里	114	270	453	936	1219	2043	3342	3853
邮电业务总量	亿元	2	4	26	205	757	2122	4833	1906
年末程控电话用户	万户		24	113	591	1415	3443	3169	3154
年末移动电话用户	万户			1	99	1357	6407	9710	10953

注：2010年年末人口数为第六次全国人口普查数据。

17-2 续表

指 标	单 位	1980年	1985年	1990年	1995年	2000年	2005年	2010年	2011年
六、固定资产投资									
固定资产投资总额	亿元	38	185	381	2327	3234	7164	16113	16933
#房地产开发	亿元			33	564	859	1592	3660	4899
七、商业									
社会消费品零售总额	亿元	118	289	667	2478	4380	7916	17415	20247
八、物价总指数									
商品零售价格指数	上年=100	108.5	113.6	95.6	111.6	99.9	101.8	103.3	105.1
居民消费价格指数	上年=100		114.8	97.5	114.0	101.4	102.3	103.1	105.3
九、外贸外经									
海关进出口总额	亿美元	26	54	419	1040	1701	4280	7849	9135
进口额	亿美元	4	24	197	474	782	1898	3317	3815
出口额	亿美元	22	30	222	566	919	2382	4532	5319
实际利用外资	亿美元	2	9	20	121	146	152	210	223
十、财政、金融									
地方财政一般预算收入	亿元	38	69	131	382	911	1807	4517	5514
地方财政一般预算支出	亿元	27	67	151	526	1070	2289	5422	6716
各项人民币存款余额	亿元			1577	7090	16908	35784	78286	86849
各项人民币贷款余额	亿元			1704	5496	11204	20745	46099	52163
十一、人民生活									
在岗职工人均工资	元	789	1393	2929	8250	13823	23959	40358	45152
城市居民人均可支配收入	元	473	954	2303	7439	9762	14770	23898	26897
农民人均纯收入	元	274	495	1043	2699	3654	4690	7890	9372
城乡居民人民币储蓄存款余额	亿元	30	155	752	3885	8667	19051	36219	40405
十二、教育									
在校学生数									
#普通高等学校	万人	4	7	10	15	30	87	143	153
中等职业教育学校	万人	6	18	45	67	66	71	155	152
普通中学	万人	252	236	234	339	461	612	709	699
小学	万人	749	671	747	883	930	1067	849	822
十三、卫生									
医院及卫生院床位数	万张	8	10	11	14	16	19	28	30
卫生技术人员	万人	14	18	19	23	26	30	45	48
#执业（助理）医师	万人	6	7	8	10	11	12	17	18

17-3 主要经济指标东莞占全国、全省的比重（2011年）

Proportion of Main Indicators of Dongguan to China and Guangdong Province (2011)

指　　标	单 位	绝对值			东莞占全国的比重 (%)	东莞占全省的比重 (%)
		全 国	全 省	东 莞		
一、人口						
年末常住人口	万　人	134735	10505	825.48	0.61	7.86
二、经济总量						
地区生产总值	亿　元	471564	53210	4735.39	1.00	8.90
第一产业增加值	亿　元	47712	2665	17.88	0.04	0.67
第二产业增加值	亿　元	220592	26447	2366.20	1.07	8.95
第三产业增加值	亿　元	203260	24098	2351.32	1.16	9.76
三、工业						
工业增加值	亿　元	188572	24408	2288.41	1.21	9.38
主要工业产品产量						
发电量	亿千瓦时	47001	3607	376.00	0.80	10.42
机制纸及纸板	万　吨	11034	1496	1021.32	9.26	68.27
彩电	万　台	12231	4862	541.00	4.42	11.13
四、农业						
主要农产品产量						
粮食	万　吨	57121	1361	1.29	0.002	0.09
水果	万　吨	22768	1210	7.39	0.03	0.61
肉类	万　吨	7957	435	2.60	0.03	0.60
水产品	万　吨	5600	762	7.82	0.14	1.03
五、固定资产投资额						
固定资产投资总额	亿　元	311022	16933	1079.77	0.35	6.38
六、运输邮电						
货物周转量	亿吨公里	159014	7106	187.48	0.12	2.64
旅客周转量	亿人公里	30936	3853	145.88	0.47	3.79
年末程控电话用户	万　户	28512	3154	305.97	1.07	9.70
年末移动电话用户	万　户	98625	10953	1677.77	1.70	15.32
七、财政、金融						
地方财政收入	亿　元	103740	5514	313.06	0.30	5.68
财政支出	亿　元	108930	6716	351.92	0.32	5.24
各项人民币存款余额	亿　元	80.9万	86849	6609.39	0.82	7.61
各项人民币贷款余额	亿　元	54.8万	52163	3716.08	0.68	7.12
八、外经外贸						
进出口总额	亿美元	36421	9135	1352.23	3.71	14.80
进口总额	亿美元	17435	3815	568.95	3.26	14.91
出口总额	亿美元	18986	5319	783.29	4.13	14.73
实际利用外资	亿美元	1160	223	30.51	2.63	13.68
九、商业、物价						
社会消费品零售总额	亿　元	183919	20247	1266.31	0.69	6.25
商品零售价格指数	上年=100	104.9	105.1	104.7		
居民消费价格指数	上年=100	105.4	105.3	104.9		
十、人民生活						
在岗职工人均工资	元	41799	45152	50398		
城市居民人均可支配收入	元	21810	26897	39513		
农民人均纯收入	元	6977	9372	22842		
城乡居民人民币储蓄存款余额	亿　元	351957	40405	3710.99	1.05	9.18

17-4 主要经济指标东莞占全国、全省的比重（2010年）

Proportion of Main Indicators of Dongguan to China and Guangdong Province (2010)

指标	单位	绝对值			东莞占全国的比重(%)	东莞占全省的比重(%)
		全国	全省	东莞		
一、人口						
年末常住人口	万人	134091	10441	822.48	0.61	7.88
二、经济总量						
地区生产总值	亿元	401202	46013	4246.45	1.06	9.23
第一产业增加值	亿元	40534	2287	16.57	0.04	0.72
第二产业增加值	亿元	187581	23015	2160.82	1.15	9.39
第三产业增加值	亿元	173087	20712	2069.07	1.20	9.99
三、工业						
工业增加值	亿元	160867	21463	2078.45	1.29	9.68
主要工业产品产量						
发电量	亿千瓦时	42072	3101	356.00	0.85	11.48
机制纸及纸板	万吨	9833	1435	933.18	9.49	65.04
彩电	万台	11830	4495	536.00	4.53	11.92
四、农业						
主要农产品产量						
粮食	万吨	54678	1317	1.25	0.002	0.09
水果	万吨	21401	1129	7.55	0.04	0.67
肉类	万吨	7926	441	2.88	0.04	0.65
水产品	万吨	5373	729	7.63	0.14	1.05
五、固定资产投资额						
固定资产投资总额	亿元	278122	16113	1114.98	0.40	6.92
六、运输邮电						
货物周转量	亿吨公里	141837	5934	109.03	0.08	1.84
旅客周转量	亿人公里	27894	3342	129.07	0.46	3.86
年末程控电话用户	万户	29434	3169	298.04	1.01	9.40
年末移动电话用户	万户	85900	9710	1607.60	1.87	16.56
七、财政、金融						
地方财政收入	亿元	83102	4517	277.84	0.33	6.15
财政支出	亿元	87874	5422	289.83	0.33	5.35
各项人民币存款余额	亿元	718238	78286	5943.39	0.83	7.59
各项人民币贷款余额	亿元	479196	46099	3329.82	0.69	7.22
八、外经外贸						
进出口总额	亿美元	29740	7849	1213.38	4.08	15.46
进口总额	亿美元	13962	3317	517.40	3.71	15.60
出口总额	亿美元	15778	4532	695.98	4.41	15.36
实际利用外资	亿美元	1057	210	27.32	2.58	12.99
九、商业、物价						
社会消费品零售总额	亿元	156998	17415	1108.06	0.71	6.36
商品零售价格指数	上年=100	103.1	103.3	103.2		
居民消费价格指数	上年=100	103.3	103.1	102.8		
十、人民生活						
在岗职工人均工资	元	37147	40358	46576		
城市居民人均可支配收入	元	19109	23898	35690		
农民人均纯收入	元	5919	7890	20486		
城乡居民人民币储蓄存款余额	亿元	303302	36219	3386.85	1.12	9.35

17-5 主要经济指标人均水平东莞与全国、全省的比较(2011年)

Comparison of Per Capita Level of Main Economic Indicators between Dongguan and China, Guangdong Province (2011)

指　　标	单 位	人 均 水 平			东莞相当于全国(%)	东莞相当于全省(%)
		全 国	全 省	东 莞		
生产总值	元	35083	50807	57470	163.8	113.1
财政收入	元	7718	5265	3799	49.2	72.2
出口总额	美元	1413	5079	9506	673.0	187.2
各项人民币存款余额	元	60071	82674	80067	133.3	96.8
居民储蓄存款余额	元	26122	38463	44956	172.1	116.9
固定资产投资总额	元	23139	16168	13104	56.6	81.0
社会消费品零售总额	元	13683	19333	15368	112.3	79.5
实际利用外资	美元	86	213	370	429.1	173.9
在岗职工人均工资	元	41799	45152	50398	120.6	111.6
城市居民可支配收入	元	21810	26897	39513	181.2	146.9
农民人均纯收入	元	6977	9372	22842	327.4	243.7
粮食产量	公斤	425	130	2	0.4	1.2
水产品产量	公斤	42	73	9	22.8	13.0
水果产量	公斤	169	116	9	5.3	7.8
工业发电量	千瓦时	3497	3444	4563	130.5	132.5
医院卫生院床位数	张/千人	3	3	3	98.8	94.5
卫生技术人员数	人/千人	5	5	5	104.2	104.9

注：本表人均指标时点数按年末常住人口计算，时期数按年平均常住人口计算。

17-6 主要经济指标人均水平东莞与全国、全省的比较(2010年)

Comparison of Per Capita Level of Main Economic Indicators between Dongguan and China, Guangdong Province (2010)

指　　标	单 位	人 均 水 平			东莞相当于全国(%)	东莞相当于全省(%)
		全 国	全 省	东 莞		
生产总值	元	29762	44736	52798	177.4	118.0
财政收入	元	6213	4390	3455	55.6	78.7
出口总额	美元	1180	4406	8653	733.4	196.4
各项人民币存款余额	元	53593	74979	72262	134.8	96.4
居民储蓄存款余额	元	22639	34689	41179	181.9	118.7
固定资产投资总额	元	20800	15666	13863	66.7	88.5
社会消费品零售总额	元	11741	16931	13777	117.3	81.4
实际利用外资	美元	79	204	340	429.7	166.2
在岗职工人均工资	元		40253	46576		115.7
城市居民可支配收入	元	19109	23898	35690	186.8	149.3
农民人均纯收入	元	5919	7890	25733	434.8	326.1
粮食产量	公斤	409	128	2	0.4	1.2
水产品产量	公斤	40	71	9	23.6	13.4
水果产量	公斤	160	110	9	5.9	8.6
工业发电量	千瓦时	3146	3015	4426	140.7	146.8
医院卫生院床位数	张/千人	3.26	2.65	2.38	72.9	89.7
卫生技术人员数	人/千人	4.36	4.28	4.56	104.6	106.6

注：本表人均指标时点数按常住人口计算，时期数按年平均常住人口计算。

17-7 珠江三角洲国民经济和社会发展主要指标（2011年）

指　　标	单 位	广州市	深圳市	珠海市
一、综合				
行政区域土地面积	平方公里	7287	1953	1654
年末常住人口	万人	1275.14	1046.74	156.76
年末户籍人口	万人	814.58	279.37	106.01
地区生产总值	亿元	12423.44	11505.53	1404.93
第一产业增加值	亿元	204.54	6.55	36.55
第二产业增加值	亿元	4576.98	5343.32	764.41
#工业增加值	亿元	4140.59	4995.10	714.29
第三产业增加值	亿元	7641.92	6155.65	603.98
人均生产总值(按常住人口计算)	元	97588	110421	89794
二、农村经济				
农业产值	亿元	349.78	13.39	67.68
粮食产量	万吨	44.66	0.002	4.34
水果产量	万吨	40.61	0.29	7.77
水产品产量	万吨	44.69	2.68	20.50
三、工业				
规模以上工业企业数	个	4438	5692	893
规模以上工业增加值	亿元	4008.38	4769.43	675.48
规模以上工业企业主营业务收入	亿元	15270.24	20556.94	3464.00
规模以上工业企业利润总额	亿元	958.53	1318.25	165.62
规模以上工业产品销售率	%	97.6	98.1	93.6
四、固定资产投资				
固定资产投资总额	亿元	3412.20	2060.92	637.39
#房地产开发投资额	亿元	1305.36	514.74	255.61
商品房屋销售面积	万平方米	1194.08	496.89	224.03
商品房屋销售额	亿元	1445.25	1060.86	257.53
五、交通、邮电				
民用汽车拥有量	万辆	185.77	193.97	24.10
年末固定电话用户数	万户	587.44	551.11	87.51
年末移动电话用户数	万户	2566.93	2313.20	256.32
全年总用电量	亿千瓦时	663.55	687.90	112.56
#工业用电量	亿千瓦时	361.45	416.95	71.65

Main Indicators of National Economy and Social Development of the Pearl River Delta Economic Zone (2011)

佛山市	惠州市	肇庆市	江门市	东莞市	中山市
3848	11356	14822	9541	2460	1800
723.10	463.36	395.14	446.55	825.48	314.23
374.77	343.03	426.90	393.71	184.77	150.73
6210.23	2093.08	1324.41	1830.64	4735.39	2193.20
118.86	116.51	226.40	138.36	17.88	58.45
3870.95	1223.25	587.30	997.27	2366.20	1223.25
3735.29	1147.79	535.42	953.21	2288.41	1164.62
2220.43	753.32	510.72	695.01	2351.32	911.51
86073	45331	33642	41062	57470	70014
239.60	192.49	344.69	253.97	30.66	100.36
9.74	60.98	113.91	91.78	1.29	7.67
5.01	58.88	111.65		7.39	15.76
57.08	14.67	34.54	69.27	7.82	34.60
6318	1428	1054	2766	4243	3170
2991.38	1013.54	570.95	1069.84	1642.45	1234.73
13957.78	4708.80	2366.82	4442.10	8454.92	5380.34
1006.72	220.16	168.16	311.15	316.54	331.47
97.6	98.8	98.0	95.5	99.6	96.2
1933.96	1024.21	710.03	741.79	1079.31	766.95
596.92	376.54	143.11	146.93	373.76	310.36
873.68	796.30	329.16	321.63	595.61	628.44
702.37	440.87	156.10	171.75	459.61	373.59
104.36	30.64	17.35	31.97	106.14	42.64
283.57	135.20	77.31	112.00	319.55	96.35
1188.70	419.90	230.08	390.23	1677.77	504.53
485.62	209.66	122.09	187.68	566.69	198.55
360.21	145.36	91.54	133.12	445.76	132.51

17-7 续表

(2011年)

指　　标	单 位	广州市	深圳市	珠海市
六、金融、贸易、财政				
年末金融机构人民币存款余额	亿元	25791.70	22782.39	2734.51
#城乡居民储蓄存款余额	亿元	10032.62	7760.84	1085.16
年末金融机构人民币贷款余额	亿元	16333.43	15714.96	1396.04
社会消费品零售总额	亿元	5243.02	3520.87	567.86
预算内地方财政收入	亿元	979.48	1339.57	143.41
预算内地方财政支出	亿元	1181.25	1590.56	190.37
七、对外经济				
海关进口总额	亿美元	596.99	1685.74	276.52
海关出口总额	亿美元	564.73	2455.25	239.87
外商直接投资项目	个	1134	2513	186
合同利用外资金额	亿美元	67.47	76.33	17.76
实际利用外商直接投资	亿美元	42.71	45.99	13.38
八、人民生活、物价				
在岗职工年平均工资	元	57473	55143	40925
城市居民年人均可支配收入	元	34438	36505	28731
城市居民年人均消费支出	元	28210	24080	21162
农民人均纯收入	元	14818		11858
居民消费价格总指数(以上年为100)	%	105.5	105.4	105.0
九、教育、卫生				
学校数				
高等学校	所	79	9	
中等职业技术学校	所	91	13	9
普通中学	所	472	299	59
小学	所	961	334	119
在校学生数				
高等学校	万人	89.61	7.00	11.70
中等职业技术学校	万人	24.92	2.98	2.21
普通中学	万人	56.16	34.69	9.54
小学	万人	81.98	65.13	12.69
医院医疗机构数	个	2363	2481	478
#医院	个	207	116	33
医院床位数	张	55429	22349	5244
执业(助理)医师	人	35289	22683	4520

佛山市	惠州市	肇庆市	江门市	东莞市	中山市
8965.03	2326.05	1197.13	2490.92	6609.39	2916.09
4658.81	1174.34	745.60	1645.28	3710.99	1585.74
5464.49	1295.48	754.35	1133.69	3716.08	1538.54
1931.41	684.72	389.71	759.15	1266.31	756.07
341.73	162.83	92.23	119.17	313.06	183.22
388.68	227.21	157.01	165.30	351.92	192.67
218.04	156.91	24.04	54.39	568.95	96.40
390.94	231.22	33.08	122.53	783.29	245.46
236	425	117		1324	264
32.57	21.68	23.21	13.52	35.08	10.78
21.54	15.69	10.29	7.89	30.51	7.30
40663	35719	34113	31913	50398	48415
30718	26609	19040	23924	39513	27700
23782	20603	14020	17076	27495	20519
13862	10938	9014	9996	22842	17182
105.5	104.9	105.4	104.8	104.9	105.4
3	2	5	3	6	4
38	27	28	23	25	12
185	211	170	184	199	99
416	519	564	322	324	209
4.46	2.20	4.55	4.60	4.51	3.63
7.97	7.13	7.47	5.15	4.82	2.65
32.34	30.77	31.80	25.31	26.31	15.69
44.55	40.40	34.60	29.47	57.83	23.99
1086	809	735	740	1006	473
82	49	43	32	72	47
21255	7793	7691	9569	22276	10593
12376	6824	4875	7142	13644	5337

17-8 长江三角洲国民经济和社会发展主要指标（2011年）

指　　标	单 位	上海市	南京市	苏州市	无锡市	常州市	镇江市
一、综合							
行政区域土地面积	平方公里	6341	6582	8488	4788	4375	3847
年末常住人口	万人	2347.46	810.91	1051.87	643.22	464.97	313.43
年末户籍人口	万人	1419.36	636.36	642.33	467.96	362.86	271.86
地区生产总值	亿元	19195.69	6145.52	10716.99	6880.15	3580.42	2310.40
第一产业增加值	亿元	124.94	163.61	177.45	122.98	111.36	100.41
第二产业增加值	亿元	7959.69	2760.99	5958.04	3728.12	1950.84	1274.23
第三产业增加值	亿元	11111.06	3220.91	4581.50	3029.05	1518.22	935.76
二、农村经济							
农业总产值	亿元	314.11	283.50	308.60		194.70	152.63
三、工业							
规模以上工业增加值	亿元	6798.28	2400.57	6057.30	3346.46	1934.27	1260.01
规模以上工业企业主营业务收入	亿元		10407.93	27570.00	14592.73	8165.30	5016.05
规模以上工业企业利润总额	亿元	2176.13	589.78	1320.00	1113.34	466.40	298.05
四、固定资产投资							
固定资产投资总额	亿元	5067.09	4010.03	4279.98	3169.18	2338.90	1223.45
#房地产开发投资额	亿元	2273.86	896.73	1199.13	877.78	565.91	137.98
五、交通、邮电							
民用汽车拥有量	万辆	329.17	99.71	223.46	128.73	56.00	
年末固定电话用户数	万户	926.40	294.00		212.11	158.70	108.27
年末移动电话用户数	万户	2620.60	1002.10	1440.00	858.83	560.50	330.22
六、金融、贸易、财政							
年末金融机构本外币存款余额	亿元	58186.48	14241.99	16004.17	9722.44	5020.88	2474.45
#城乡居民储蓄存款余额	亿元	17958.22	3968.03	5126.89	3340.09	2171.20	1115.64
年末金融机构本外币贷款余额	亿元	37196.79	11723.52	12776.25	7279.81	3505.80	1835.50
社会消费品零售总额	亿元	6777.11	2670.30	2797.83	2122.72	1236.10	658.07
预算内地方财政收入	亿元	3429.83	635.00	1100.88	615.00	350.88	181.90
预算内地方财政支出	亿元	3914.88	665.99	996.81	592.67	354.22	202.50
七、对外经济							
海关进口总额	亿美元	2276.47	264.79	1336.30	301.35	92.70	44.56
海关出口总额	亿美元	2097.89	308.65	1672.33	423.12	193.60	56.19
实际利用外商直接投资	亿美元	126.01	35.66	90.16	35.05	30.50	18.08
八、人民生活、物价							
城市居民年人均可支配收入	元	36230	32200	34617	31638	29829	26637
城市居民年人均消费支出	元	25102	20763	21046	19780	18893	15513
农民人均纯收入	元	15644	13108	17226	16438	14838	12825
居民消费价格总指数(以上年为100)	%	105.2	105.4	105.1	105.1	105.0	105.0

注：1.湖州、绍兴、舟山固定电话含小灵通。

Main Indicators on National Economy and Social Development of the Yangtze River Delta Economic Zone(2011)

南通市	扬州市	泰州市	杭州市	宁波市	嘉兴市	湖州市	绍兴市	舟山市	台州市
8001	6634	5793	16596	9817	3915	5818	8256	1440	9411
728.90	446.30	462.60	873.80					113.70	
764.88	460.05	507.12	695.71	576.40	343.05	261.05	440.01	96.99	586.79
4080.22	2630.30	2422.61	7011.80	6010.48	2668.06	1518.83	3291.23	765.30	2794.91
287.21	184.54	175.11	236.07	255.76	146.09	116.02	172.16	76.09	188.90
2221.48	1427.87	1308.21	3322.15	3335.37	1536.18	824.55	1843.63	344.82	1443.97
1571.53	1017.89	939.29	3453.58	2419.35	985.79	578.26	1275.44	344.39	1162.04
502.27	330.31		357.63	399.20	247.97	198.36	260.17	149.99	328.90
1981.33	1769.69	1501.57	2337.78	2381.29	1137.22	539.49	1317.86	198.93	709.70
8352.85	6616.22	5770.74	11916.39		5368.25	2902.11			
667.17	486.99	434.23	800.32	614.85	294.72	151.12	461.63	34.45	152.62
2378.36	1476.18	1197.65	3105.16	2392.91	1502.48	809.65	1426.26	500.53	1104.08
379.96	198.46	228.26	1302.27	756.87	384.76	189.66	403.24	119.46	321.68
184.43	80.65	28.24	207.82			27.55		7.37	67.89
279.41		135.50	362.81		121.03	107.73	199.22	53.60	170.99
774.94	441.81	369.13	1225.01		514.23	322.11	484.76	153.39	791.45
5614.56	2860.55	2632.69	18396.57	10659.27	4168.17	2102.05	5510.14	1314.97	3998.90
3068.10	1435.27	1311.60	5547.48	3696.28	1880.45	954.44	2227.67	461.30	2068.79
3408.62	1751.50	1804.45	16573.74	10676.84	3212.74	1712.17	4463.09	1162.66	3470.76
1479.87	846.04	645.27	2548.36	2018.90	948.57	609.89	1006.75	251.71	1132.37
373.69	218.08	218.00	785.15	657.55	226.40	122.12	239.69	76.48	200.12
419.45	248.98	252.48	747.50	750.72	240.61	151.73	253.31	148.10	265.53
78.14	28.30	36.10	224.50	373.60	92.13	13.06	75.20	57.91	34.69
180.30	73.20	74.78	415.21	608.30	192.72	73.56	259.86	74.73	170.35
21.66	21.03	14.17	47.22	28.10	17.21	9.40	8.05	1.08	1.43
25094	22835	23597	32434	34321	31520	29367	33273	30496	30490
16666	16003	15461	22642	21779	19535	19920	20353	19183	22648
11730	11217	11046	15245	16518	16707	15381	15861	16277	13108
105.0	105.1	105.1	104.8	105.3	105.5	104.8	105.4	105.8	106.3

2.苏州、杭州民用汽车拥有量为机动车拥有量,无锡为全社会拥有车辆数。

第三部分　基本单位情况

Part Three　Basic Units

1-1　按行业分的法人单位、产业活动单位数（2011年）

Number of Corporate Units and Industrial Establishments by Sector (2011)

项　　目	法　人 单位数 （个）	单 产 业 法人单位	多 产 业 法人单位	产业活动 单 位 数 （个）	多产业法 人单位的 产业活动 单 位 数
合　　计	81992	80319	1673	91795	11476
采 矿 业	13	13		13	
煤炭开采和洗选业					
石油和天然气开采业	3	3		3	
黑色金属矿采选业					
有色金属矿采选业	3	3		3	
非金属矿采选业	6	6		6	
其他采矿业	1	1		1	
制 造 业	38579	38377	202	38697	320
农副食品加工业	195	190	5	203	13
食品制造业	292	286	6	296	10
饮料制造业	63	58	5	64	6
烟草制品业					
纺织业	1961	1951	10	1970	19
纺织服装、鞋、帽制造业	2114	2095	19	2123	28
皮革、毛皮、羽毛(绒)及其制品业	1538	1531	7	1544	13
木材加工及木、竹、藤、棕、草制品业	348	345	3	350	5
家具制造业	1158	1151	7	1165	14
造纸及纸制品业	1926	1924	2	1930	6
印刷业和记录媒介的复制	1313	1310	3	1312	2
文教体育用品制造业	1136	1131	5	1139	8
石油加工、炼焦及核燃料加工业	38	36	2	38	2
化学原料及化学制品制造业	954	944	10	957	13
医药制造业	47	45	2	46	1
化学纤维制造业	73	73		73	
橡胶制品业	776	775	1	778	3
塑料制品业	4414	4402	12	4419	17
非金属矿物制品业	634	631	3	638	7
黑色金属冶炼及压延加工业	130	130		130	
有色金属冶炼及压延加工业	261	260	1	262	2
金属制品业	4595	4587	8	4604	17
通用设备制造业	1906	1887	19	1906	19
专用设备制造业	2465	2455	10	2472	17

1-1 续表 1

(2011年)

项　　目	法人单位数(个)	单产业法人单位	多产业法人单位	产业活动单位数(个)	多产业法人单位的产业活动单位数
交通运输设备制造业	326	323	3	330	7
电气机械及器材制造业	2680	2658	22	2691	33
通信设备、计算机及其他电子设备制造业	4834	4805	29	4851	46
仪器仪表及文化、办公用机械制造业	546	543	3	550	7
工艺品及其他制造业	1827	1822	5	1825	3
废弃资源和废旧材料回收加工业	29	29		31	2
电力、燃气及水的生产和供应业	147	144	3	174	30
电力、热力的生产和供应业	29	29		31	2
燃气生产和供应业	27	26	1	30	4
水的生产和供应业	91	89	2	113	24
建 筑 业	2684	2653	31	2951	298
房屋和土木工程建筑业	442	436	6	584	148
建筑安装业	742	733	9	804	71
建筑装饰业	1147	1134	13	1180	46
其他建筑业	353	350	3	383	33
交通运输、仓储和邮政业	1380	1341	39	1956	615
铁路运输业	6	6		9	3
道路运输业	431	413	18	561	148
城市公共交通业	72	71	1	74	3
水上运输业	49	48	1	51	3
航空运输业	11	11		16	5
管道运输业	1	1		2	1
装卸搬运及其他运输服务业	602	588	14	710	122
仓储业	106	106		108	2
邮政业	102	97	5	425	328
信息传输、计算机服务和软件业	1416	1394	22	1686	292
电信和其他信息传输服务业	319	309	10	534	225
计算机服务业	835	827	8	874	47
软件业	262	258	4	278	20
批发和零售业	17835	17570	265	20954	3384
批发业	8822	8731	91	9657	926
零售业	9013	8839	174	11297	2458
住宿和餐饮业	1165	1057	108	1723	666
住宿业	581	500	81	615	115
餐饮业	584	557	27	1108	551
金 融 业	239	192	47	1748	1556
银行业	33	21	12	1142	1121
证券业	13	11	2	46	35
保险业	76	46	30	369	323

1-1 续表 2

(2011年)

项　　目	法　人单位数(个)	单产业法人单位	多产业法人单位	产业活动单位数(个)	多产业法人单位的产业活动单位数
其他金融活动	117	114	3	191	77
房地产业	2724	2644	80	3001	357
房地产业	2724	2644	80	3001	357
租赁和商务服务业	8412	8280	132	9495	1215
租赁业	103	103		105	2
商务服务业	8309	8177	132	9390	1213
科学研究、技术服务和地质勘查业	846	837	9	910	73
研究与试验发展	173	172	1	176	4
专业技术服务业	533	525	8	586	61
科技交流和推广服务业	133	133		139	6
地质勘查业	7	7		9	2
水利、环境和公共设施管理业	336	330	6	374	44
水利管理业	61	61		64	3
环境管理业	87	84	3	108	24
公共设施管理业	188	185	3	202	17
居民服务和其他服务业	2073	2051	22	2284	233
居民服务业	654	646	8	777	131
其他服务业	1419	1405	14	1507	102
教　育	1571	1534	37	1913	379
教育	1571	1534	37	1913	379
卫生、社会保障和社会福利业	532	477	55	891	414
卫生	483	429	54	839	410
社会保障业	5	5		5	
社会福利业	44	43	1	47	4
文化、体育和娱乐业	413	409	4	481	72
新闻出版业	13	13		14	1
广播、电视、电影和音像业	61	61		66	5
文化艺术业	114	113	1	117	4
体育	36	36		38	2
娱乐业	189	186	3	246	60
公共管理与社会组织	1626	1015	611	2543	1528
中国共产党机关	54	54		56	2
国家机构	581	529	52	1306	777
人民政协和民主党派	11	11		11	
群众团体、社会团体和宗教组织	362	354	8	472	118
基层群众自治组织	618	67	551	698	631
国际组织	1	1		1	
国际组织	1	1		1	

1-2 按注册类型分的法人单位、产业活动单位数（2011年）

Number of Corporate Units and Industrial Establishments by Registration Status(2010)

项　　目	法　人 单位数 （个）	单产业 法人单位	多产业 法人单位	产业活动 单位数 （个）	多产业法 人单位的 产业活动 单位数
合　　计	81992	80319	1673	91795	11476
内资企业	70125	68593	1532	79230	10637
国有	1449	1336	113	3084	1748
集体	2263	2170	93	2943	773
股份合作	281	277	4	817	540
国有联营	10	10		11	1
集体联营	63	62	1	71	9
国有与集体联营	18	17	1	54	37
其他联营	49	47	2	61	14
国有独资公司	42	42		49	7
其他有限责任公司	18922	18677	245	21011	2334
股份有限公司	949	907	42	2000	1093
私营独资	9643	9596	47	9843	247
私营合伙	2687	2674	13	2730	56
私营有限责任公司	25704	25346	358	27002	1656
私营股份有限公司	1147	1133	14	1197	64
其他内资	6898	6299	599	8357	2058
港澳台投资企业	8504	8427	77	8872	445
与港澳台商合资经营	437	426	11	518	92
与港澳台商合作经营	392	390	2	416	26
港澳台商独资	7430	7367	63	7685	318
港澳台商投资股份有限公司	245	244	1	253	9
外商投资企业	3363	3299	64	3693	394
中外合资经营	258	239	19	346	107
中外合作经营	129	126	3	152	26
外资企业	2844	2804	40	3051	247
外商投资股份有限公司	132	130	2	144	14

1-3 按地域分的法人单位、产业活动单位数（2011年）

Number of Corporate Units and Industrial Establishments by District (2011)

项目	法人单位数（个）	单产业法人单位	多产业法人单位	产业活动单位数（个）	多产业法人单位的产业活动单位数
全市	81992	80319	1673	91795	11476
东城街道	5059	4929	130	5747	818
南城街道	4228	4077	151	4714	637
万江街道	2808	2746	62	3073	327
莞城街道	3821	3663	158	4417	754
石碣镇	2377	2333	44	2668	335
石龙镇	1003	964	39	1286	322
茶山镇	1909	1876	33	2112	236
石排镇	1733	1699	34	1929	230
企石镇	1003	971	32	1153	182
横沥镇	1838	1806	32	2049	243
桥头镇	1999	1969	30	2263	294
谢岗镇	1101	1082	19	1220	138
东坑镇	926	891	35	1106	215
常平镇	3822	3747	75	4369	622
寮步镇	4060	3994	66	4396	402
樟木头镇	2230	2190	40	2557	367
大朗镇	4232	4169	63	4674	505
黄江镇	1856	1829	27	2049	220
清溪镇	2542	2502	40	2787	285
塘厦镇	4496	4438	58	4809	371
凤岗镇	2343	2306	37	2549	243
大岭山镇	2641	2602	39	2883	281
长安镇	6101	6027	74	6777	750
虎门镇	5877	5796	81	6532	736
厚街镇	3278	3243	35	3784	541
沙田镇	1866	1825	41	2047	222
道滘镇	1451	1416	35	1620	204
洪梅镇	564	547	17	663	116
麻涌镇	993	963	30	1151	188
望牛墩镇	687	663	24	790	127
中堂镇	1530	1495	35	1764	269
高埗镇	1243	1204	39	1400	196
松山湖	338	320	18	371	51
虎门港	37	37		40	3
东莞生态园				46	46

1-4 营业收入超5000万元的内资企业（2011年）

Domestic-funded Enterprises with Business Revenue over RMB 50 Million (2011)

单位名称	所属镇街	联系电话	主要产品（或服务）
农副食品加工业			
东莞市双胞胎饲料有限公司	大岭山镇	82760188	饲料
东莞市沙田顺发畜禽实业有限公司	沙田镇	88686610	饲料
东莞市广利饲料有限公司	大岭山镇	83352060	混合饲料
东莞市太粮米业有限公司	樟木头镇	87703313	大米
东莞市领鲜源食品有限公司	寮步镇	22668444	肉制品
东莞市东糖中轻糖业有限公司	中堂镇	88118099	单晶冰糖
东莞市新泰粮食有限公司	樟木头镇	87123620	粮食
东莞市富之源饲料蛋白开发有限公司	洪梅镇	88436030	豆粕
东莞市樟木头食品有限公司	樟木头镇	87718596	牲猪
东莞市穗丰食品有限公司	麻涌镇	88224098	小麦粉
中纺粮油（东莞）有限公司	麻涌镇	88235183	豆油
东莞市东美食品有限公司	高埗镇	88872108	淀粉
东莞市制糖厂有限公司	中堂镇	88812123	制糖
东莞市银华生物科技有限公司	万江街道	22188099	饲料
东莞市海大饲料有限公司	麻涌镇	88237100	畜禽饲料
东莞市康达尔饲料有限公司	麻涌镇	22236928	饲料
东莞市虎门日隆食品厂	虎门镇	85564450	豆制品糕点
东莞市湘大骆驼饲料有限公司	万江街道	23175022	饲料
东莞市煌上煌食品有限公司	洪梅镇	88430678	肉制品
中储粮油脂工业东莞有限公司	麻涌镇	88236688	豆油
东莞市日隆食品有限公司	虎门镇	85564450	麦片
食品制造业			
东莞市真滋味食品有限公司	虎门镇	85151778	预包装食品
内蒙古伊利实业集团股份有限公司东莞分公司	道滘镇	88835173	冰淇淋
东莞市广益食品添加剂实业有限公司	中堂镇	88886882	脱氧保鲜剂
东莞市百味佳食品有限公司	寮步镇	83285888	鸡精
东莞市今麦郎食品有限公司	中堂镇	88118372	方便面
东莞市金富士食品有限公司	东城街道	22621998	饼干
广东丹宝利酵母有限公司	中堂镇	88812123	高活性干酵母
东莞市来一口食品有限公司	谢岗镇	87637375	果冻
东莞市鸿兴食品有限公司	寮步镇	83223122	百利面包粮
东莞市华美食品有限公司	茶山镇	86643036	饼干
广东一品鲜生物科技有限公司	中堂镇	22613911	酵母抽提物
东莞市金娃食品工业有限公司	谢岗镇	87636739	果冻
饮料制造业			
东莞市珠江啤酒有限公司	常平镇	83553033	啤酒
东莞市福地纯水有限公司	南城街道	22404191	饮用水
东莞爱维蒸馏水有限公司	虎门镇	85519666	蒸馏水
纺织业			
东莞市兴业针织有限公司	大朗镇	83311479	针织服装
东莞市大朗民源生毛织制衣有限公司	大朗镇	83186260	针织服装
东莞市逸朗毛织有限公司	大朗镇	82220960	毛织制品
东莞市拓展实业有限公司	茶山镇	86485888	化学纤维
东莞市大朗骏松服饰厂	大朗镇	81119288	针织品
东莞市天伊毛织时装有限公司	大朗镇	83318017	针织衫

1-4 续表 1

(2011年)

单位名称	所属镇街	联系电话	主要产品（或服务）
东莞市惠琪针织有限公司	寮步镇	88909698	毛衣
东莞市成功针织制衣厂	东城街道	22265157	纺织服装
东莞市瑞锋服饰有限公司	大朗镇	86260003	针织毛衣
东莞市胜兴针织有限公司	大朗镇	83189100	针织女毛衣
东莞市富士达针织有限公司	大朗镇	83319826	毛衣
东莞市科纺纺织有限公司	中堂镇	88115588	牛仔布
东莞市信远无纺布有限公司	寮步镇	88951008	无纺布
东莞市众圣针织有限公司	大朗镇	83111739	毛衣
东莞市常平满利针织有限公司	常平镇	83977300	毛衣
东莞市中玲实业有限公司	万江街道	22175828	纺织品
东莞市圣旗路时装有限公司	常平镇	89851115	针织品
东莞市华轩针织制衣有限公司	大朗镇	83181838	针织服装
东莞市建盛针织有限公司	大朗镇	83110188	针织服装
东莞市汇达纺织有限公司	中堂镇	88110468	布料
东莞市众达针织制衣有限公司	大朗镇	83109181	毛衣
东莞市金松针织有限公司	大朗镇	83311811	针织服装
东莞盈豪嘉实制衣实业有限公司	寮步镇	88902688	服装
东莞市汇盛针织时装有限公司	大朗镇	83010618	针织毛衣
东莞市威驰针织有限公司	大朗镇	82811332	针织服装
东莞市金泽服装有限公司	大朗镇	83181322	针织服装
东莞市翔兴针织有限公司	大朗镇	83186788	毛衣
东莞市力豪针织服饰有限公司	大朗镇	83017168	毛织品
东莞市颖祺实业有限公司	大朗镇	83180838	针织服装
东莞市斌斌时装有限公司	虎门镇	88923858	服装
东莞市天元制衣有限公司	大朗镇	83195363	针织服装
东莞长联新材料科技有限公司	寮步镇	81259388	印花染色粘合剂
东莞市德广隆制衣洗水有限公司	麻涌镇	81206362	服装
东莞市大朗翔联服饰厂	大朗镇	82226892	服装
东莞市安盛针织制衣有限公司	大朗镇	83137868	毛织品
东莞市悠派户外用品制造有限公司	茶山镇	84596111	帐篷
东莞市正卉毛织有限公司	大朗镇	83137868	针织毛衣
东莞市明威包装材料有限公司	高埗镇	84996493	绳、索、缆制品
东莞市大朗雅骏服饰厂	大朗镇	83488798	毛衣
东莞市瑞麟毛织有限公司	寮步镇	83280312	毛织
东莞市新阳织造有限公司常平分公司	常平镇	38838288	毛织品
东莞市金广电脑针织有限公司	大朗镇	83182989	针织品
东莞市超翔服饰有限公司	大朗镇	38879801	针织服装
东莞市凫山新兴发针织有限公司	寮步镇	83288868	毛衣
东莞市颖和祺服饰有限公司	大朗镇	81125303	毛衣
东莞市辉骏针织时装有限公司	大朗镇	83183029	针织时装
东莞市欧佳特服饰有限公司	大朗镇	86262988	毛衣
东莞市入世丰针织有限公司	东坑镇	88905668	针织衫
东莞市大朗和利达针织制衣厂	大朗镇	83133988	针织毛衣
东莞市天润服装有限公司	茶山镇	81831883	服装
东莞市长源毛织制衣有限公司	大朗镇	83200838	针织服装

1-4 续表 2

(2011年)

单位名称	所属镇街	联系电话	主要产品（或服务）
东莞市凯纳德针织服饰有限公司	大朗镇	83110775	毛衣
东莞市盛泰针织制衣有限公司	大朗镇	83206828	针织服装
东莞市普莱雅纺织科技有限公司	寮步镇	83288000	针织服装
东莞市广昌隆毛织时装有限公司	大朗镇	83197153	毛织服装
东莞市茶山伟博纺织服装厂	茶山镇	86648311	服装
东莞市伊韵儿服饰实业有限公司	虎门镇	85183089	针、梳织服装、服饰
东莞市雅路家用纺织品有限公司	凤岗镇	87509191	床褥、床单
东莞市盈邦针织有限公司	大朗镇	83482998	针织服装
东莞市清溪康成针织厂	清溪镇	87316438	毛衣半成品
东莞市波路迪针织时装有限公司	大朗镇	83197289	毛衣
东莞市宝丰服装实业有限公司	寮步镇	83216003	毛织品
东莞市汇得佳纺织制衣有限公司	中堂镇	88129398	服装
东莞市业联制衣有限公司	大朗镇	81069908	牛仔服装
东莞市晶晖针织有限公司	大朗镇	83116573	针织服装
东莞市乐祺针织有限公司	大朗镇	83190778	毛织服装
东莞市环宇织造有限公司	大朗镇	83112688	毛织服装
东莞市福轩针织有限公司	寮步镇	83323285	针织品
东莞市国泰华纺织有限公司	大朗镇	86264568	毛衣
东莞市恒帮针织有限公司	大朗镇	83186389	毛织品
东莞市英伟实业有限公司	大朗镇	83102266	针织服装
东莞市琪然电脑刺绣有限公司	虎门镇	85726660	刺绣、服装辅料
东莞市大朗伟航针织制衣厂	大朗镇	83128091	针织品
东莞市高颖针织有限公司	常平镇	83759388	针织服装、毛衣
东莞市中盛针织实业有限公司	横沥镇	83716818	毛衣
东莞市康圣针织制造有限公司	常平镇	83996177	针织品及编织品
东莞市恩基儿服饰有限公司	大朗镇	83129077	针织衫
东莞市金坚制衣有限公司	清溪镇	82997765	服装
东莞市闽盈服饰有限公司	大朗镇	83107020	服装
东莞市盈格织造有限公司	大朗镇	83103588	针织品
东莞市和辉针织有限公司	大朗镇	83133988	针织品
东莞市美姬服饰有限公司	大朗镇	83310268	针织毛衣
东莞市卓越实业有限公司	石排镇	86550111	针织服装
东莞市薏莎实业有限公司	大朗镇	83138999	针织品
东莞市协欣时装有限公司	大朗镇	83193268	毛衣
东莞市凯浚服饰有限公司	大朗镇	83182889	毛织服装
纺织服装、鞋、帽制造业			
东莞市中堂稳发制衣厂	中堂镇	88881891	棉制梳织服装
东莞市鸿锦服饰有限公司	虎门镇	86091828	服装
东莞市原野服装有限公司	虎门镇	85226693	纺织服装
东莞市豪辉服饰有限公司	虎门镇	89030138	服装
东莞市搜于特服装股份有限公司	道滘镇	88320269	设计服装
东莞市慧美实业投资有限公司	茶山镇	86459630	童装
东莞璒录普制衣有限公司	虎门镇	85551363	服装
东莞市新远宏制衣有限公司	虎门镇	82889188	服装
东莞市寮步登辉鞋厂	寮步镇	81199856	鞋材

1-4 续表 3

(2011年)

单位名称	所属镇街	联系电话	主要产品（或服务）
东莞市稳发制衣有限公司	中堂镇	88881891	棉梳织服装
东莞市锦程服装有限公司	望牛墩镇	88559168	皮革压花纺织服装
东莞市都市丽人实业有限公司	凤岗镇	82778888	服装
东莞市盛旺鞋材有限公司	洪梅镇		纺织面料鞋
东莞市由美制衣有限公司	望牛墩镇	88562339	服装
东莞市百思特服饰有限公司	虎门镇	85709002	服装
东莞市东城嘉文制衣厂	东城街道	22267333	梳织服装
东莞市圣隆制衣有限公司	厚街镇	81638100	牛仔服装
东莞市源源制衣有限公司	中堂镇	88126801	服装
东莞市俊颖针织服装有限公司	桥头镇	81027713	服装
东莞市以纯集团有限公司	虎门镇	85520146	纺织服装
东莞市经纬制衣实业有限公司	中堂镇	88411698	牛仔裤
东莞市东辰鞋材有限公司	万江街道	87076238	纺织面料鞋材
东莞市时艺时装制衣有限公司	虎门镇	85260068	针梳织服装
东莞市星达实业有限公司	虎门镇	88620008	服装
东莞市添翔制衣有限公司	万江街道	22277218	服装、针织布
东莞市尚景服装有限公司	石排镇	88590069	纺织服装
东莞市极奇制衣有限公司	企石镇	86664648	衣服
广东金盾服装公司	南城街道	22404168	警察服装
东莞市松鹰实业有限公司	虎门镇	85561999	棉织服装
东莞市盛丰制衣有限公司	万江街道	22658892	服装
东莞市东林制衣有限公司	寮步镇	83238080	毛织品
东莞市永豪制衣实业有限公司	寮步镇	83327589	针织服装
皮革、毛皮、羽毛(绒)及其制品业			
东莞市江顺箱包袋配件有限公司	塘厦镇	87912965	箱包袋配件
东莞市莎米特箱包有限公司	樟木头镇	87712545	旅行包
东莞市新虎威鞋厂	虎门镇	85198313	皮鞋
东莞三元鞋业有限公司	万江街道	22181972	皮鞋
东莞市琪胜鞋业有限公司	厚街镇	88632999	皮鞋
东莞市北谛鞋业有限公司	茶山镇	81833678	皮鞋
东莞市优秀鞋业有限公司	厚街镇	83088530	女鞋
东莞厚街鹏利鞋厂	厚街镇	85906088	皮鞋
东莞市永鸿手袋有限公司	黄江镇	82605681	手袋
东莞市振国皮革制品有限公司	厚街镇	85825356	皮革制品
东莞长安乌沙宝业皮具厂	长安镇	85417333	皮制品
东莞市龙运鞋业有限公司	厚街镇	85933911	鞋类制品
东莞长安霄边兴鹏鞋厂	长安镇	85531541	皮鞋
东莞黄江裕成制鞋厂	黄江镇	83363017	运动鞋
东莞尚科思工艺制品有限公司	寮步镇	81192118	工艺制品、电脑包
木材加工及木、竹、藤、棕、草制品业			
东莞市东上板业有限公司	中堂镇	88128816	硅酸钙板
东莞市易辉纤维板有限公司	桥头镇	81039118	纤维板
东莞市德曼木业有限公司	桥头镇	81037666	木门
东莞市森宝康木业有限公司	洪梅镇	88439626	中密度竹斑板
东莞市中成木业有限公司	道滘镇	88331338	夹板

1-4　续表 4

(2011年)

单位名称	所属镇街	联系电话	主要产品（或服务）
东莞市冠宇木业有限公司	中堂镇	81163188	木制品
家具制造业			
东莞市广纳家具制造有限公司	大朗镇	83136198	家具
东莞市星港家具有限公司	南城街道	22901327	家具
东莞市利普家具有限公司	厚街镇	83082222	家具
东莞市艾伯特家具有限公司	大岭山镇	83356531	家具
东莞市好好家具有限公司	寮步镇	81120825	木制家具
东莞市城市之窗家具有限公司	厚街镇	89982000	家具
东莞市汇雅实业有限公司	道滘镇	85830032	家具
东莞市耀震五金家具有限公司	虎门镇	85550956	家具
东莞市荣圣家具有限公司	凤岗镇	87842272	办公椅
东莞市中意厨房设备有限公司	塘厦镇	82061888	厨柜
东莞市华腾塑钢家具有限公司	洪梅镇	88439399	家具
东莞市中之美家具有限公司	洪梅镇	85927900	木制家具
东莞市楷模家居用品制造有限公司	厚街镇	85961856	家具
东莞市瑞豪家具制造有限公司	高埗镇	88702123	塑胶家具
东莞市桥新家私有限公司	桥头镇	83342337	木制家具
东莞市光润家具制造有限公司	东城街道	86216333	办公家具
东莞市元宗家具有限公司	大岭山镇	85610588	家具
东莞市佳森家具有限公司	大岭山镇	85611222	咖啡桌
东莞市富宝沙发制造有限公司	大岭山镇	85611985	家具
广东大公馆家具制造有限公司	厚街镇	88913333	家具
东莞市嘉梦家具有限公司	常平镇	83826528	床垫、床上用品
东莞市华晟家具制造有限公司	东城街道	22653163	家具
东莞英记来万家私厂有限公司	寮步镇	88908999	沙发
东莞市恒兆实业有限公司	大岭山镇	85627198	家具
东莞市慕思寝室用品有限公司	厚街镇	85058288	沙发
东莞市兆生家具实业有限公司	厚街镇	85921466	家具
东莞市远大家具有限公司	大岭山镇	85617870	木制家具
东莞市森盛家具有限公司	厚街镇	85593555	套房家具
东莞市美迪家具有限公司	洪梅镇	88843128	木制家具
东莞市欣格家具有限公司	石碣镇	86334766	金属家具
东莞润丰金属塑胶有限公司	寮步镇	83320898	五金家具
东莞市时兴家具制造有限公司	高埗镇	88872168	家具
东莞市冠辉五金有限公司	长安镇	85413848	家具
东莞市凯晟家具有限公司	大岭山镇	85785581	家具
东莞佳居乐厨柜有限公司	大岭山镇	85650999	厨柜
东莞市大宇家具有限公司	中堂镇	88180888	办公椅、办公桌
东莞市卓之神家具厂	高埗镇	88704226	木制家具
东莞市德美家具有限公司	大岭山镇	85606228	家具
东莞市东品家具有限公司	凤岗镇	87842343	软体家具
东莞市银通家具有限公司	沙田镇	88686466	玻璃家具
东莞市明晟家具有限公司	东城街道	22653163	木制家具
东莞市华辉家具实业有限公司	厚街镇	85592833	家具
东莞市广丰家具有限公司	厚街镇	85595163	家具

1-4 续表 5

(2011年)

单位名称	所属镇街	联系电话	主要产品（或服务）
造纸及纸制品业			
东莞市同力纸业有限公司	中堂镇		瓦楞芯纸
东莞市同兴纸品有限公司	高埗镇	81303788	瓦楞纸板
东莞市东创纸品制造有限公司	黄江镇	82601888	纸板
东莞市横通纸品有限公司	横沥镇	83378968	纸板
东莞市大步纸业有限公司	麻涌镇	88286883	机制纸及纸制品
东莞市裕杨纸品实业有限公司	茶山镇	86411555	纸箱
东莞市高埗东保纸品厂	高埗镇	88734233	纸板
东莞市龙腾实业有限公司	麻涌镇	88826898	纸制品
东莞市深联造纸有限公司	中堂镇	88818778	瓦楞芯纸
东莞市旗峰纸业有限公司	道滘镇	88328212	纸
东莞市新富发纸业有限公司	万江街道	22711928	灰纸板
东莞市明丰纸品厂	道滘镇	88328688	纸板
东莞市福生造纸有限公司	道滘镇	88320028	瓦楞纸
东莞市鸿业造纸有限公司	中堂镇	88814848	机制纸
东莞清溪现代纸品厂	清溪镇	87295802	纸箱
东莞市厚威包装有限公司	大朗镇	82228320	纸箱
东莞市伟虹纸业有限公司	望牛墩镇	88558198	纸制品
东莞市达成纸品有限公司	麻涌镇	88289898	纸制品
东莞市华兴纸业实业有限公司	万江街道	22279169	纸制品
广东玉兰装饰材料有限公司	东城街道	22652789	墙纸
东莞市金田纸业有限公司	万江街道	22280688	灰板纸
东莞市高安纸品有限公司	高埗镇	88787311	纸板
东莞市伟联纸业有限公司	道滘镇	88382688	纸浆
东莞市晋邦纸业有限公司	大朗镇	81123388	纸箱
东莞市银兴纸品厂	塘厦镇	87816636	纸板
东莞市大田包装有限公司	虎门镇	85269998	纸板
东莞市顺通纸品有限公司	道滘镇	88388266	纸板
东莞市利泰纸业有限公司	望牛墩镇	88554828	纸板及纸制品
东莞市天盛特种纸品有限公司	虎门镇	85169458	无碳复写纸
东莞市智达纸业制品有限公司	沙田镇	88862222	纸制品
东莞市骏业纸业有限公司	道滘镇	88830822	中卡纸
东莞市顺兴造纸有限公司	道滘镇	88328608	瓦楞芯纸
东莞市明天纸业有限公司	望牛墩镇	81310788	纸箱用纸
东莞市上隆纸业有限公司	中堂镇	88187688	高强瓦楞纸
东莞市潢涌银洲纸业有限公司	中堂镇	88899113	挂面箱板纸
东莞市天全纸品有限公司	高埗镇	81338828	纸板
东莞市振诚包装制品有限公司	东城街道	22618027	纸板纸箱
东莞市珠江特种纸业有限公司	中堂镇	88890808	瓦楞纸
东莞市盈泰纸品厂	望牛墩镇	88552289	生活用纸
东莞市道滘东发纸品有限公司	道滘镇	88839018	灰板纸
东莞市上合旺盈印刷有限公司	东城街道	23111888	印刷品
东莞市鸿旭包装印刷有限公司	石排镇	88936668	印刷纸板
广东百顺纸品有限公司	茶山镇	86456233	纸制品
东莞市泓宝印刷有限公司	黄江镇	83669706	包装装潢用品

1-4 续表 6

(2011年)

单位名称	所属镇街	联系电话	主要产品（或服务）
东莞市桐昌纸业有限公司	谢岗镇	82797999	纸箱
东莞市同舟纸品有限公司	企石镇	81928888	纸制品
东莞市宝力造纸厂	洪梅镇	88846388	纸制品
东莞市中堂江南造纸厂	中堂镇	88184305	包装用纸
东莞市中堂镇吴家涌有利造纸厂	中堂镇	88412438	瓦楞纸
东莞市麻涌富林纸品加工厂	麻涌镇	88282629	机制纸及纸板
东莞市凤岗新达纸品有限公司	凤岗镇	87750288	机制纸及纸板
东莞荣辉纸类制品厂	清溪镇	87321128	纸制品
东莞市华利纸品有限公司	高埗镇	88703832	纸板
东莞市致泰纸业有限公司	麻涌镇	88825682	包装用纸
东莞市华通包装有限公司	道滘镇	81332988	纸制品
东莞市强安造纸有限公司	高埗镇	88876118	纸制品
东莞市建航纸业有限公司	中堂镇	88129488	包装纸
东莞市骏利纸制品有限公司	塘厦镇	87922558	纸箱
东莞市泰昌纸业有限公司	望牛墩镇	88852607	卡纸
东莞市银桦纸品有限公司	中堂镇	81163388	包装材料纸箱
东莞市雄东纸业有限公司	洪梅镇	88844928	纸制品
东莞市旭丰纸业有限公司	中堂镇	88121293	瓦楞原纸
东莞市天赐纸品有限公司	高埗镇	88734233	纸板
东莞东兴纸品厂	南城街道	86228785	瓦楞纸板、瓦楞纸箱
东莞市道滘兴隆造纸厂	道滘镇	88381933	制浆
东莞市道窖东发造纸厂	道滘镇	88839018	瓦楞纸
东莞市永安造纸有限公司	望牛墩镇	88818068	瓦楞纸
东莞市顺丰纸品制造有限公司	茶山镇	86176968	纸板
东莞市宝华造纸有限公司	道滘镇	88336328	双灰纸张
东莞市胜源纸品厂	高埗镇	89910165	纸制品
东莞市建桦造纸有限公司	中堂镇	88887988	箱板纸
东莞市易创实业有限公司	寮步镇	81118021	纸制品
东莞市天荣纸品有限公司	大岭山镇	85631665	纸板
东莞市振兴造纸有限公司	高埗镇	88949288	高强芯纸
东莞市常联造纸厂有限公司	常平镇	83337837	机制瓦楞纸
东莞市华深包装材料有限公司	寮步镇	81197702	木质包装箱
东莞市双洲纸业有限公司	中堂镇	88182618	瓦楞纸
东莞市永顺纸品有限公司	望牛墩镇	88551655	纸制品
东莞市贝辉装饰材料有限公司	大朗镇	83199339	装饰材料（浸渍纸）
东莞市东保纸业有限公司	高埗镇	88786298	瓦楞纸、挂面纸
东莞市华柏纸品有限公司	中堂镇	88112269	纸制品
东莞市瑞安纸品实业有限公司	东城街道	22660198	纸箱
东莞市祥兴纸业有限公司	中堂镇	88815238	瓦楞纸
东莞市恒伟纸业有限公司	道滘镇	88323168	纸板
东莞市白天鹅纸业有限公司	万江街道	22172128	纸制品
印刷业和记录媒介的复制			
东莞市金凌印刷有限公司	塘厦镇	87881585	丝印染精
东莞市天华创展印刷有限公司	凤岗镇	87862122	出版物印刷
东莞市东彩印刷包装有限公司	厚街镇	85820822	包装装潢、印刷

1-4 续表 7

(2011年)

单位名称	所属镇街	联系电话	主要产品（或服务）
东莞市二轻包装彩印厂有限公司	东城街道	22699213	包装彩盒
东莞市新广联数码科技有限公司	大朗镇	88289688	只读类光盘复制
东莞市金剑模具制造有限公司	虎门镇	86093538	五金模具
文教体育用品制造业			
东莞市丰泽文具有限公司	虎门镇	85506636	文件夹
东莞市石碣易辉玩具厂	石碣镇	88036081	填充玩具
东莞市生命动力按摩器材有限公司	石排镇	86658583	按摩器材
东莞伟易达电子厂	厚街镇	85581806	电子玩具
东莞市冠艺金属彩印包装有限公司	横沥镇	83371255	文具盒
东莞市天宇玩具制品有限公司	桥头镇	83429729	塑胶玩具
东莞市智乐堡儿童玩具有限公司	石排镇	86550188	玩具
东莞市智高文具有限公司	石碣镇	86634176	彩泥
石油加工、炼焦及核燃料加工业			
东莞市安美润滑科技有限公司	松山湖	83213232	润滑材料
东莞市荣高废油处理有限公司	麻涌镇	88221178	润滑油
东莞市安美化学有限公司	松山湖	83210707	润滑油
东莞市晔联道路改性沥青有限公司	洪梅镇	88439822	储存改性石油沥青
化学原料及化学制品制造业			
东莞市大兴化工有限公司	谢岗镇	87768860	油漆
东莞市盛和化工有限公司	黄江镇	87132012	苯酐
东莞市贝特利新材料有限公司	麻涌镇	88283198	油墨
东莞市保得生物工程有限公司	南城街道	22886693	生物有机肥
东莞市三联科技实业有限公司	寮步镇	83215622	颜料
东莞市雄林新材料科技有限公司	道滘镇	86166013	TPU薄膜
东莞市罗孚化工有限公司	洪梅镇	88328928	万能胶
东莞市汇美淀粉科技有限公司	麻涌镇	88287968	淀粉
东莞市威亮实业有限公司	中堂镇	88886988	洗衣粉
东莞市竣成化工有限公司	厚街镇	85595702	胶水
东莞市高旭新材料有限公司	中堂镇	88110096	重质碳酸钙
东莞市英科水墨有限公司	茶山镇	86481155	水性墨
东莞市瑞德丰生物科技有限公司	大岭山镇	83359225	农药
广东信力特种橡胶制品有限公司	麻涌镇	88220800	橡胶制品
东莞市四辉表面处理科技有限公司	大岭山镇	85628748	抛光蜡
东莞市汇诚塑胶金属制品有限公司	长安镇	87086188	塑胶制品
东莞市合裕粘贴制品有限公司	黄江镇	83369560	胶粘剂
东莞市阳光树脂制品有限公司	石碣镇	86633666	胶粘剂
广东省福利龙复合肥有限公司	高埗镇	88739816	复合肥料
东莞市广华化工有限公司	道滘镇	88328668	酸性蚀刻液
广东中成化工股份有限公司	麻涌镇	88822402	保险粉
东莞市杉杉电池材料有限公司	南城街道	22035233	锂离子电池材料
东莞市成铭胶粘剂有限公司	石碣镇	86319710	胶粘剂
东莞市芙蓉化工有限公司	望牛墩镇	88857923	分散松香胶
东莞市立顿洗涤用品实业有限公司	望牛墩镇	88999999	肥皂及合成洗涤剂
医药制造业			
广东众生药业股份有限公司	石龙镇	86100111	众生丸

1-4 续表 8

(2011年)

单位名称	所属镇街	联系电话	主要产品（或服务）
广东华南药业集团有限公司	石龙镇	86100111	银翘解毒口服液
化学纤维制造业			
东莞市源丰纤维制品有限公司	茶山镇	86645703	涤纶短纤
橡胶制品业			
东莞市石碣东英塑胶制品厂	石碣镇	86631490	塑胶鞋底
东莞市伟捷包装实业有限公司	万江街道	22172183	包装材料
东莞市广海大橡塑科技有限公司	樟木头镇	82022622	橡塑保健用品
东莞市日源盛橡胶绝缘制品有限公司	石碣镇	86289365	绝缘材料
东莞市港源胶粘带制品有限公司	寮步镇	81111360	胶粘带
东莞市迪生塑胶五金工模有限公司	大岭山镇	81600138	五金制品
塑料制品业			
东莞市正新包装制品有限公司	东城街道	22650889	塑料制品
东莞市冠宏包装实业有限公司	望牛墩镇	88518756	BOPP封箱皮
东莞市瑞丰实业有限公司	寮步镇	81192789	聚乙烯环保薄膜
东莞市以诺塑胶制品有限公司	塘厦镇	86957888	塑料制品
深圳市航天远东实业有限公司东莞分公司	凤岗镇	82100375	塑胶制品
东莞市诠盛塑料有限公司	虎门镇	85556378	塑胶制品
东莞市链州日用品有限公司	洪梅镇		日用塑料杂品
东莞联记塑胶原料有限公司	常平镇	83335992	塑胶
东莞市朝阳实业有限公司	企石镇	86722142	塑料制品
东莞市博美包装制品有限公司	塘厦镇	86255725	小型包装制品
东莞市泰至塑料五金有限公司	茶山镇	81821668	pvc管材
东莞市永迪泡绵有限公司	大朗镇	83011091	泡棉、海绵
东莞市永超塑胶科技有限公司	黄江镇	83364226	塑胶制品
东莞新航包装材料有限公司	清溪镇	87312318	发泡胶(泡沫)包材
东莞市铭丰包装品制造有限公司	万江街道	22171188	首饰盒
东莞市丸万塑料包装有限公司	东城街道	22024286	塑料制品
东莞市冠炜塑胶五金制品有限公司	常平镇	83981763	塑胶制品
东莞清溪三钢电器制造厂	清溪镇	87732437	五金、塑胶制品
东莞市兄奕塑胶制品有限公司	樟木头镇	87792188	塑胶制品
东莞市星月实业有限公司	常平镇	86836199	塑料制品
东莞市富利时塑胶制品有限公司	东城街道	22653193	塑胶
东莞市雅居乐日用制品有限公司	石排镇	86598000	PVC台布
东莞市庆盈实业有限公司	茶山镇	86178922	塑料
东莞市日泰鞋材有限公司	万江街道	23036108	鞋材
东莞市合鑫电子厂	石排镇	86537079	塑料电线
东莞市宏磊达电子塑胶有限公司	寮步镇	87070008	LED
东莞市惠德丽实业有限公司	企石镇	86728338	塑料杂品
东莞市天宝五金塑胶制品有限公司	塘厦镇	87914500	五金铁钗
东莞南城添迪制品厂	南城街道	22417969	电脑磁头臂
东莞市荣辉塑料粒有限公司	虎门镇	85154933	塑料粒
东莞市巨祺包装有限公司	常平镇	81093697	塑料瓶盖
东莞市鸿旺包装制品有限公司	清溪镇	87737422	胶袋
东莞市华立实业股份有限公司	常平镇	83333239	塑料板
东莞市华瀚儿童用品有限公司	清溪镇	87867129	婴儿车

1-4 续表 9

(2011年)

单位名称	所属镇街	联系电话	主要产品（或服务）
东莞市华源包装有限公司	茶山镇	86646996	塑料包装袋
东莞市泰和塑胶制品有限公司	桥头镇	83450238	塑料制品
东莞市凤岗油甘埔利联塑胶金属制品厂	凤岗镇	87774139	五金纽扣
东莞凤岗五联威达利塑胶制品厂	凤岗镇	87753728	吸塑罩
东莞市汇泓模具塑胶制品有限公司	长安镇	85353863	模具
东莞清溪三中东扬塑料包装厂	清溪镇	87738456	塑料类包装材料
东莞市汇美实业有限公司	长安镇	85412223	DVD、VCD塑胶面壳
东莞市晟美包装制品有限公司	南城街道	86228778	塑料制品
东莞市海丰塑料包装有限公司	虎门镇	85423300	胶袋制品
非金属矿物制品业			
东莞南玻陶瓷科技有限公司	麻涌镇	88288111	陶瓷磨介
东莞市伍山建材实业有限公司	沙田镇	81560755	混凝土系列外加剂
东莞市双洲水泥制品有限公司	中堂镇	88811668	管桩
东莞市建东水泥制品有限公司	中堂镇	88121288	预制桩
东莞市华佳能电器玻璃有限公司	桥头镇	81029258	钢化玻璃
东莞市银通玻璃有限公司	沙田镇	88868988	玻璃制品
东莞市唯美陶瓷工业园有限公司	高埗镇	81133333	马可波罗瓷砖
东莞市唯美装饰材料有限公司	东城街道	22650006	陶瓷制品
东莞市千色有机玻璃有限公司	虎门镇	81611738	有机玻璃
东莞市金洲羊城管桩厂	中堂镇	88885288	水泥预制管桩
东莞市茶山和兴粉磨站	茶山镇	86404633	粉磨水泥
东莞市隆泰美东镜业有限公司	石龙镇	86310690	玻璃制品
东莞市东成石材有限公司	厚街镇	85596328	大理石花岗的切割
东莞市通州预制件有限公司	高埗镇	88733388	预制件水泥管桩
东莞市拓为塑料五金制品有限公司	寮步镇	84572099	塑料制品
东莞市虎门摩天建材实业公司	虎门镇	85561768	加气混凝土
东莞市华辉玻璃制品有限公司	石排镇	86656791	玻璃镀银、镀铝
广东唯美陶瓷有限公司	高埗镇	81133333	建筑陶瓷制品
黑色金属冶炼及压延加工业			
东莞市锦上钢材有限公司	中堂镇	88186778	PC钢棒
东莞市日月不锈钢有限公司	常平镇	83606259	不锈钢
东莞市东上钢材有限公司	中堂镇	88890107	钢材
东莞市东城东联金属制品厂	东城街道	22291760	铝制品
东莞市亿鑫钢业有限公司	企石镇	86768769	钢结构材料
东莞市恒兴电子五金有限公司	石碣镇	86321888	铝材板
元生有色金属(东莞)有限公司	寮步镇	83281886	铝合金管材
东莞市华雨金属材料有限公司	黄江镇	83131757	铝棒延压
东莞市中一合金科技有限公司	大朗镇	83206618	银铜复合带
东莞市华昌铝合金制品厂	东城街道	22265108	铝材
东莞市永铖铝业有限公司	万江街道	22175338	铝挤型材
东莞市宏顺金属材料有限公司	企石镇	86764001	电镀锌钢板
东莞市铝美铝型材有限公司	厚街镇	83090188	铝制品
东莞市宏发钢铁结构材料有限公司	企石镇	86737153	钢结构材料
东莞市杰夫阻燃材料有限公司	大朗镇	83101593	三氧化二锑

1-4 续表 10

(2011年)

单位名称	所属镇街	联系电话	主要产品（或服务）
金属制品业			
东莞市石排品佳五金加工厂	石排镇	88935678	五金制品
东莞市金达铝业有限公司	道滘镇	88327890	铝型材
东莞市荣杰五金制品有限公司	大朗镇	88609837	皮带扣
东莞市怡丰锁业有限公司	樟木头镇	87795983	五金塑胶
东莞市银朗电梯配件有限公司	中堂镇	88861110	TK5A空心导轨
东莞市泓旭五金制品有限公司	塘厦镇	82064666	五金制品
东莞市硕泰实业有限公司	大岭山镇	81516875	金属压力容器
东莞市林成精密五金有限公司	樟木头镇	87709512	五金配件
东莞市金利怡卫浴有限公司	东坑镇	81013331	水龙头
东莞市饰成实业有限公司	高埗镇		金属片制作
东莞添迪电子五金实业有限公司	南城街道	22417969	磁头臂
东莞竹田金属制品有限公司	塘厦镇	38996398	金属冲压产品
东莞市人本五金有限公司	塘厦镇	86856789	金属制品
东莞市裕隆钢管制品有限公司	塘厦镇	87883188	铁管
东莞市广成五金塑胶实业有限公司	桥头镇	81023992	五金塑胶制品
东莞市奥达铝业有限公司	大岭山镇	81621188	铝材制品
广东华宇钢结构工程有限公司	寮步镇	83218928	金属结构工程网架
东莞市键颖实业有限公司	常平镇	81898898	钮扣
东莞市博丰塑胶五金制品有限公司	企石镇	86739662	吸塑
东莞市华轩幕墙材料有限公司	谢岗镇	82333588	建筑材料
东莞市精丽制罐有限公司	石排镇	81702261	日用不锈钢制品
东莞市坚朗五金制品有限公司	塘厦镇	87943311	点支撑幕墙配件
东莞市宏力实业有限公司金属结构加工厂	沙田镇	88861110	空心导轨
东莞市铁生辉制罐有限公司	企石镇	86710628	金属包装制品
东莞市千岛金属锡品有限公司	塘厦镇	87880129	锡线
东莞市锐嘉精密机械制造有限公司	寮步镇	88908188	机箱
东莞市汇昌金属制品厂	寮步镇	83307988	铝制品
东莞振华特种包装有限公司	麻涌镇	88828115	特种包装铁桶
东莞市协力钢构工程有限公司	厚街镇	85919838	钢构件
东莞市东兴铝材制造有限公司	中堂镇	88813671	铝合金型材
东莞科力钢铁线材有限公司	望牛墩镇	88557276	金属丝绳及其制品
东莞市金瑞五金制品有限公司	道滘镇	88325501	五金制品
通用设备制造业			
东莞市铁志电子有限公司	寮步镇	82311308	碎纸机
东莞市通旺达五金制品有限公司	凤岗镇	87561911	五金配件
东莞市三联机械有限公司	寮步镇	83321381	铸铁件
东莞市寮步兆峰轴承有限公司	寮步镇	83328819	轴承
东莞市勤上金属制品有限公司	常平镇	83395678	铁线
东莞市台冠起重机械设备有限公司	大朗镇	83019666	桥式起重机
东莞市鸿金顺机械制造有限公司	虎门镇	85558848	机械数控设备
东莞市大岭山长虹弹簧厂	大岭山镇	85612812	弹簧
东莞市快意电梯有限公司	清溪镇	87731075	电梯
东莞厚街科技电业厂	厚街镇	85582172	电钻、电锯
东莞市大族粤铭激光科技有限公司	万江街道	22771433	激光雕刻机
东莞市庆新安制冷设备配件有限公司	桥头镇	83341457	制冷空调器

1-4 续表 11

(2011年)

单位名称	所属镇街	联系电话	主要产品（或服务）
东莞市百利电器有限公司	望牛墩镇	88858916	商用冷柜
东莞市达成机械设备制造有限公司	寮步镇	83217777	高度调节板
东莞市隆泰实业有限公司	石龙镇	86611795	煤矿机械
东莞市清辉金属有限公司	望牛墩镇	88560326	金属材料
东莞市快意施耐德电梯有限公司	清溪镇	87736443	电梯
东莞市宝特模具钢加工有限公司	望牛墩镇	88516020	金属制品
东莞市亿杰五金制品有限公司	黄江镇	83623308	金属紧固件
东莞市森中冈金属工业有限公司	大岭山镇	85607016	精密金属棒材
东莞市妙达电动工具制造有限公司	虎门镇	89966022	电动工具
东莞市富士电梯有限公司	东城街道	23062593	电梯
东莞市晟邦机电有限公司	大朗镇	81129292	减速马达
东莞市东城永强弹簧厂	东城街道	22261357	弹簧
东莞市石排同利五金厂	石排镇	86659735	锌合金
东莞市瑞柯电机有限公司	清溪镇	87899858	空压机
东莞市科达机电设备有限公司	万江街道	22188788	蒸发式降温换气机组
东莞市莱钢钢结构有限公司	黄江镇	83666666	钢结构件
东莞市得鑫五金有限公司	大朗镇	81124006	螺丝
东莞市有同电器有限公司	南城街道	22401688	电子变压器用铁心电
东莞市TR轴承有限公司	莞城街道	22461784	滚动轴承
专用设备制造业			
东莞市塘厦赞扬机械厂	塘厦镇	82095156	立式注塑机
东莞市晓铭实业有限公司	长安镇	85390608	塑胶制品
东莞晓达模具科技有限公司	大岭山镇	81881522	模具
东莞市骏朗机械设备制造有限公司	洪梅镇	81336776	设备
东莞瑞升电子有限公司	黄江镇	83633303	印刷电路板
东莞市华之力电子有限公司	虎门镇	85186742	器具开关
东莞市泰康电子科技有限公司	长安镇	85322066	电子连接器
东莞市意隆模具用品有限公司	虎门镇	85236853	模具
东莞市虎门铭锋五金塑胶制品厂	虎门镇	38835099	模具、五金塑胶
东莞市盛星电脑科技有限公司	大朗镇	81065816	电脑横机
东莞市金培电子有限公司	桥头镇	81026999	电子产品
东莞市新泽谷机械有限公司	寮步镇	83286900	电子精密机械
东莞市华茂电子有限公司	长安镇	85319118	五金制品零件
东莞市科光实业有限公司	长安镇	87085877	金属制品
东莞科威医疗器械有限公司	东城街道	21985698	膜式氧合器
东莞市石碣兴铭模具厂	石碣镇		五金模具
东莞市三洋电梯有限公司	厚街镇	85884455	电梯
东莞市南兴木工机械有限公司	厚街镇	89982033	木工机械、木工刀具
东莞市方达实业有限公司	长安镇	85338842	PVC排水器材
东莞市虎门机械厂	虎门镇	85711932	B24小型拉伸机
东莞市三和兴模具钢材有限公司	塘厦镇	82016100	模具钢材
交通运输设备制造业			
东莞市宏运船舶工程有限公司	洪梅镇		船舶修理及拆船
东莞市绿通高尔夫观光车有限公司	洪梅镇	88435388	电瓶车
东莞市大裕摩托车有限公司	中堂镇	88883627	摩托车

1-4　续表 12

(2011年)

单位名称	所属镇街	联系电话	主要产品（或服务）
东莞市佳雅汽车座椅有限公司	中堂镇	88188598	汽车座椅
东莞市永强汽车制造有限公司	寮步镇	83307688	罐式车
东莞市旗丰消声器有限公司	东城街道	22658795	汽车及摩托车消声器
电气机械及器材制造业			
东莞市石碣德昌电子制品厂	石碣镇	88488080	电源线插头
东莞市宾士机电设备有限公司	寮步镇	89161688	发电机组
广东科旺电源设备有限公司	南城街道	22900009	稳压器
东莞市开关厂有限公司	寮步镇	83300801	高低压开关屏
东莞市三友联众电器有限公司	厚街镇	85914551	继电器
东莞市前锋电子有限公司	石碣镇	86633990	电磁炉
东莞市雄丰配电设备有限公司	茶山镇	86647816	高压配电柜
东莞市康达机电工程有限公司	寮步镇	88996233	燃气发电机组
东莞市奥维漆包线有限公司	茶山镇	81810183	漆包绕线组
东莞市科慧电子有限公司	清溪镇	87326186	高频变压器
东莞市精铁机械有限公司	虎门镇	85556166	电线电缆设备
东莞安尚光源有限公司	道滘镇	88311915	节能灯
东莞市日新传导科技股份有限公司	桥头镇	85425888	电子电器配件
东莞市雷洋电子科技有限公司	长安镇	85391369	电子设备
东莞市锐升电线电缆有限公司	虎门镇	86092388	电线
东莞市科菱电线有限公司	虎门镇	85231398	电线
东莞市瑞桥电器有限公司	企石镇	81358668	电器产品及连接线
高达粤电安信电力检修安装有限公司	虎门镇	85561893	机电设备安装
东莞金泰电线电缆有限公司	虎门镇	86093111	电线电缆
东莞市乐科电子有限公司	塘厦镇	87289666	电子产品
东莞格力良源电池科技有限公司	塘厦镇	82991177	锂电池
广东宾士动力科技有限公司	寮步镇	89161688	柴油发电机组
广东特发信息光缆有限公司	寮步镇	86056605	光缆
东莞安尚崇光科技有限公司	道滘镇	88311555	电子节能灯
东莞市金达照明有限公司	万江街道	22284761	水晶灯
东莞市莱尔照明电器有限公司	茶山镇	88930200	照明灯具
东莞勤上光电股份有限公司	常平镇	83395678	LED路灯
东莞市益达实业有限公司	茶山镇	86412628	漆包绕组线
东莞清溪光荣电业制品厂	清溪镇	87300000	吸尘器
东莞市勤上企业有限公司	横沥镇	81107158	烧烤炉
东莞市祺龙电业有限公司	大岭山镇	85152798	电线
东莞市理士奥电源核技术有限公司	塘厦镇	87925180	阀控式蓄电池
东莞市力宇燃气动力有限公司	虎门镇	85015288	发电机
东莞市通宝电线电缆有限公司	大朗镇	83315034	电线
东莞市迈科新能源有限公司	大朗镇	83197555	锂离子电池
广东领亚电子科技有限公司	松山湖	85510688	电线
东莞市亿丰电池有限公司	万江街道	22179288	干电池
东莞市百分百科技有限公司	东城街道	88754800	塑胶塑胶开关
东莞联盈电业有限公司	虎门镇	85152115	电线及电源线
东莞市中亚电缆有限公司	中堂镇	88111000	电线、电缆
东莞市绿雅家用电器有限公司	万江街道	88991088	电扇

1-4 续表 13

(2011年)

单位名称	所属镇街	联系电话	主要产品（或服务）
东莞市力王电池有限公司	塘厦镇	87885755	碱性锌锰电池
东莞市华达电缆厂	大岭山镇	85617836	电缆
东莞市凯晟灯头实业有限公司	企石镇	86787878	铜灯头
东莞塘厦新联电器厂	塘厦镇	87910170	电器制品风筒
东莞市民康电子科技有限公司	茶山镇	88931788	电线
东莞市北航电机有限公司	虎门镇	85157468	电机
东莞市昊恩装饰品有限公司	道滘镇	88328732	台灯
东莞市迈科科技有限公司	大朗镇	83015380	镍氢电池
东莞华旭电线电缆有限公司	虎门镇	85526356	电线电缆、插头
东莞市凌力电池有限公司	万江街道	22271791	干电池
东莞市凌力电池有限公司麻涌电池厂	麻涌镇	88822642	干电池
东莞市昶泰五金制品有限公司	大朗镇	83107188	灯饰制品
东莞市越洋电线电缆有限公司	虎门镇	85167777	电线电缆
东莞莞城协益电子厂	莞城街道	22264550	微型电机及零部件
东莞市汇电电子科技有限公司	长安镇	86240798	电子产品及配件
广东志成冠军集团有限公司	塘厦镇	87722374	不间断电源
东莞市联升电线电缆有限公司	虎门镇	85253317	电线、铜线、电源线
东莞市石碣志业电子有限公司	石碣镇	86318226	电线制品
东莞市欧雷玛电源有限公司	塘厦镇	87865169	铅酸蓄电池
东莞市时唛特电器有限公司	塘厦镇	87987070	电子设备
广东美林电线电缆有限公司	虎门镇	88920098	电线、电缆
东莞市稳畅电子制品有限公司	虎门镇	85521148	电子
广东五星太阳能股份有限公司	万江街道	22176388	太阳能热水器
广东康菱动力科技有限公司	松山湖	22895555	发电机及发电机组
东莞市梅兰电器有限公司	寮步镇	83300022	电器器材
东莞市奥源电子科技有限公司	长安镇	81589595	电子产品及零配件
广东省东莞电机有限公司	南城街道	22810778	交流电动机
东莞市金鸿盛电器有限公司	横沥镇	87060166	空调配件
东莞长安迅诚电业制品厂	长安镇	85413308	漏电保护器插座
东莞市石龙富华电子有限公司	石龙镇	86022222	电源适配器
广东华达电缆有限公司	大岭山镇	83353878	电线
广东中德电缆有限公司	东坑镇	89610888	电缆
东莞市高能电气股份有限公司	东城街道	22291876	绝缘体制品
东莞市民兴电缆有限公司	凤岗镇	87510316	电线电缆
通信设备、计算机及其他电子设备制造业			
东莞市凯运电子有限公司	虎门镇	86232178	USB连接线
东莞桥头技研新阳电器厂	桥头镇	83434514	线圈
东莞市塘厦克琛达塑胶电子厂	塘厦镇	86851777	电子元件
东莞市奕东电子有限公司	东城街道	22200329	电子连接器
东莞市海铭诺信息科技有限公司	清溪镇	86810828	计算机
东莞南城白马荣科电子厂	南城街道	22401145	电子
东莞市东方科技有限公司	厚街镇	85586389	电脑周边设备
威力固设备梅州有限公司	石碣镇		设计电子工业专用设备
东莞市金铭电子有限公司	大岭山镇	85656666	手机
东莞市福地电子材料有限公司	南城街道	22406025	LED芯片

1-4 续表 14

(2011年)

单位名称	所属镇街	联系电话	主要产品（或服务）
广东步步高电子工业有限公司	长安镇	85545555	手机
东莞市长田电子有限公司	塘厦镇	87947610	电子产品
东莞市步步高视听电子有限公司	长安镇	85545555	影碟机
东莞市步步高教育电子产品有限公司	长安镇	85540888	语言复读机
东莞市金业电子科技有限公司	寮步镇	83261111	VCD机
东莞市大朗迅田视讯设备厂	大朗镇	83482898	锌合金分路线
东莞市铭基电子有限公司	塘厦镇	83096688	电脑连接线
广东明家科技股份有限公司	横沥镇	87061828	插座
东莞市金虎电子科技有限公司	清溪镇	87366812	电脑电源
东莞道滘镇协益电子厂	道滘镇	88831848	电气机械
东莞市芊和电子有限公司	石碣镇	81803262	耳机
东莞市凯华电子有限公司	塘厦镇	87915858	电子开关
东莞市金翔电器设备有限公司	万江街道	22704478	电脑机箱
东莞市京硕电子有限公司	塘厦镇	87886667	充电器
东莞市立旺电子塑胶有限公司	大朗镇	83117758	3D眼镜
东莞市众誉电子有限公司	虎门镇	85554168	鼠标键盘
东莞市金河田实业有限公司	厚街镇	85585691	电脑外部设备
东莞市春发电子照明有限公司	谢岗镇	82105188	发光二极管
东莞市奇声电子实业有限公司	麻涌镇	88231648	音响
东莞市金盈电子有限公司	石碣镇	86326328	电源变压器器
东莞市奥莱克电子有限公司	麻涌镇	88226006	组合音响
东莞市美声电器有限公司	东坑镇	83369888	液晶电视
东莞市迅田五金制品有限公司	大朗镇	83181074	锌合金分路线
东莞市德生通用电器制造有限公司	东城街道	23167118	收音机
东莞市华康电脑科技有限公司	横沥镇	83723860	电脑机箱
东莞市铭普实业有限公司	石排镇	81701560	网络变压器
东莞市光普实业发展有限公司	清溪镇	87339849	电脑机箱
东莞市科隆威自动化设备有限公司	寮步镇	83228201	无铅流焊
东莞市欧珀电子工业有限公司	长安镇	85545555	影碟机
东莞市盈聚电子有限公司	石碣镇	86327382	电子配件
东莞市金众电子有限公司	大岭山镇	86077018	线路板
郡懋电子（东莞）有限公司	塘厦镇	87282000	微晶合金
东莞市庭丰电子有限公司	塘厦镇	87926702	电子制品
东莞伟易达电子元器件制造厂	寮步镇	85581806	电子元件
东莞伟易达电子通讯设备厂	寮步镇	85581806	室内无线电话
东莞清溪显讯电子制品厂	清溪镇	87893556	电子
东莞市国登电子有限公司	东城街道	22080805	电子配件
东莞市漫步者科技有限公司	松山湖	23075158	多媒体音箱
东莞市飞尔液晶显示器有限公司	大朗镇	83106619	电子元器件
东莞洪梅电器厂	洪梅镇	88849922	电器开关、安全插头
东莞市澳星视听器材有限公司	塘厦镇	82037888	投影仪
东莞市慧诚电子科技有限公司	厚街镇	85828371	电源
东莞市方达电子工业有限公司	长安镇	85410922	电子产品
东莞市金锐显数码科技有限公司	塘厦镇	86858666	液晶电视主板
东莞市欧谛特光电科技有限公司	塘厦镇	87985588	光电产品

1-4　续表 15

(2011年)

单位名称	所属镇街	联系电话	主要产品（或服务）
东莞市亚马电子有限公司	道滘镇	22024699	电子元件
东莞市耐福电子有限公司	清溪镇	38981500	散热风扇
东莞市新兆电科技有限公司	清溪镇	87330168	电子计算机外部设备
东莞市凯昶德电子科技有限公司	塘厦镇	86851777	电脑连接线
广东欧华电子有限公司	横沥镇	88971888	汽车电子产品
东莞市中之电子科技有限公司	寮步镇	83302928	半导体二极管
东莞市霖玖玖电子科技有限公司	横沥镇	83723861	电脑机箱
东莞市博科电子技术有限公司	大岭山镇	85631002	DVD机
东莞市瑞湖电子有限公司	寮步镇	81256962	电子制品(USB线)
东莞市楚东电子科技有限公司	塘厦镇	82133122	电子元件
东莞市亚力通电子科技有限公司	塘厦镇	82080288	电子元件
东莞市智谦电子有限公司	虎门镇	86235815	手机充电器
东莞华贝电子科技有限公司	松山湖	38960680	GSM手机
东莞市五株电子科技有限公司	石碣镇	81321318	线路板
东莞市隆锐行电子有限公司	望牛墩镇	88512858	电子产品
东莞市东阳光电容器有限公司	长安镇	85315188	电容器
广东易事特电源股份有限公司	松山湖	22897777	不间断电源
东莞市顺茂塑胶电子制品有限公司	虎门镇	85232518	塑胶电子制品
东莞长安日华电子厂	长安镇	85536840	电子
东莞市亿辉电子科技有限公司	塘厦镇	87981885	数码管
东莞市大忠电子有限公司	东城街道	22630563	电子产品
东莞市茵莉电子有限公司	石碣镇	86314889	变压器
东莞海益机械配件有限公司	寮步镇	83220188	传感器零件
东莞厚街下汴电子厂	厚街镇	85591388	CD电唱盘及收音机
东莞市美威电子科技有限公司	虎门镇	85236788	电路板
东莞市石碣东诚电子有限公司	石碣镇	83548862	电子材料
东莞黄江达裕科技电子厂	黄江镇	83531877	液晶显示器
东莞市佳禾电子有限公司	石排镇	86596918	耳机
东莞市奕联实业有限公司	长安镇	86064988	连接线连接器
东莞市森特电子有限公司	石碣镇	86329018	电脑机箱
东莞市亿达音响制造有限公司	大朗镇	22665300	组合音箱
史博森电子-东莞有限公司	桥头镇	83437761	片式元器件
聚信科技有限公司	松山湖	22898612	通信产品
东莞长安上角康扬塑胶五金电子厂	长安镇	85305187	电脑塑胶配件
东莞市粤林电脑科技有限公司	清溪镇	87890888	电脑机箱
东莞市数字印数码科技有限公司	凤岗镇	87510868	数码音乐播放器
东莞市步步高通信设备有限公司	长安镇	85540688	有绳电话机
东莞市嘉田五金塑胶制品有限公司	凤岗镇	87774386	电脑机箱
东莞市佰利电子有限公司	高埗镇	88708002	发光二极管
东莞市冠佳电子设备有限公司	塘厦镇	87914228	电子设备
东莞市旭田电子有限公司	石碣镇	86300036	键盘
东莞市大朗涌韵音膜厂	大朗镇	83138601	振动膜
东莞市龙光电业有限公司	长安镇	85338787	机箱
东莞市华源光电科技有限公司	清溪镇	87336863	太阳能电池板
东莞市维峰五金电子有限公司	长安镇	85358920	电脑连接器

1-4 续表 16

(2011年)

单位名称	所属镇街	联系电话	主要产品（或服务）
东莞市扬明精密塑胶五金电子有限公司	长安镇	85338940	塑胶五金电子制品
东莞市煜弘电子制造有限公司	虎门镇	85014888	音箱、电脑
仪器仪表及文化、办公用机械制造业			
广东万濠精密仪器股份有限公司	长安镇	85316127	投影仪
东莞市远峰科技有限公司	大朗镇	83482500	导航仪
东莞恒宏眼镜有限公司	高埗镇	88873001	眼镜
广东星星光电科技有限公司	石排镇	86921688	视窗防护屏
东莞市南星电子有限公司	沙田镇	88663139	塑胶玩具
东莞寮步铨讯电子厂	寮步镇	83527668	数码相机
东莞市鸿瀚电子材料有限公司	石碣镇	81381535	手机镜片
东莞长安新民冠利精密钟表厂	长安镇	85387288	钟表
东莞市华兰海电子有限公司	麻涌镇	88823105	便携式轴重台
广东正业科技有限公司	松山湖	88985666	电子材料耗材
东莞市邦泽电子有限公司	沙田镇	89191288	碎纸机
工艺品及其他制造业			
深圳市特发信息股份有限公司东莞分公司	寮步镇	86056657	光缆
东莞市钮成服装辅料有限公司	东城街道	22625327	钮扣
东莞市电力燃料有限公司	万江街道	22475222	石油及制品
东莞市金龙珠宝首饰有限公司	厚街镇	81636092	黄金饰品
东莞市昌晖印染器材有限公司	虎门镇	85555020	印刷、印染机械
东莞市金叶珠宝有限公司	厚街镇	85822216	珠宝首饰
东莞太平电镀元件厂	虎门镇	85511047	拉链
电力、热力的生产和供应业			
东莞市城郊供电所	莞城街道	22336600	电力供应管理
东莞市常平供电公司	常平镇	83399778	电力供应管理
东莞市基宁发电有限公司	虎门镇	85136442	火力发电
广深沙角B电力有限公司沙角B火力发电厂	虎门镇	85569688	火力发电
东莞市石碣供电公司	石碣镇	86317627	电力供应管理
东莞市三联热电有限公司	中堂镇	88812123	火力发电
燃气生产和供应业			
东莞市高埗新奥燃气有限公司	高埗镇	83072020	管道燃气供应
东莞市寮步新奥燃气有限公司	寮步镇		管道燃气供应
东莞市九丰能源有限公司	虎门港	88866301	液化石油汽
东莞市东江自来水有限公司	莞城街道	22214443	自来水供应
东莞市大朗镇自来水公司	大朗镇	83318306	自来水供应
东莞市横沥镇自来水公司	横沥镇	83375146	自来水供应
东莞市清溪自来水有限公司	清溪镇	87733362	自来水供应
东莞市东城自来水公司	东城街道	22612699	自来水供应
东莞市长安镇自来水公司	长安镇	85535689	自来水供应
东莞市东江水务有限公司	东城街道	22609238	自来水供应
东莞市沙田自来水厂	沙田镇	88862620	自来水供应
东莞市虎门自来水有限公司	虎门镇	85525510	自来水供应
东莞市塘厦自来水公司	塘厦镇	87724614	自来水供应
东莞市常平镇自来水公司	常平镇	83335588	自来水供应

1-4 续表 17

(2011年)

单位名称	所属镇街	联系电话	主要产品（或服务）
房屋和土木工程建筑业			
东莞市宏泰建筑工程有限公司	南城街道	22813338	建筑施工
东莞市正大建筑工程有限公司	万江街道	22278818	建筑工程
东莞市诚峰建筑工程有限公司	东城街道	22209083	房屋建筑
东莞市虎门建设发展有限公司	虎门镇	85188631	建筑
东莞市企石深巷建筑工程公司	企石镇	86711321	房屋建筑
东莞市鸿高建设工程有限公司	企石镇	86664882	房屋建筑
东莞市东城建筑公司	东城街道	22319001	房屋建筑
东莞市高业建设工程有限公司	高埗镇	88788633	水利工程建筑
东莞市城区市政工程公司	莞城街道	22225634	房屋建筑
东莞市樟木头建筑工程公司	樟木头镇		房屋建筑工程施工承包
东莞市福华建筑工程有限公司	沙田镇	88866688	房屋建筑
东莞市腾飞建筑工程有限公司	南城街道	22425528	房屋建筑
东莞市光大建筑劳务分包有限公司	东城街道	22986086	房屋建筑
东莞市茗鑫路桥建设养护有限公司	莞城街道	81115196	公路路桥建设养护
东莞市裕欣国建筑工程有限公司	高埗镇	88781698	房屋建筑
东莞市百分百建设工程有限公司	东城街道	88754008	房屋建筑
东莞市华固建造工程有限公司	南城街道	23023558	房屋建筑
广东省水利水电第三工程局	塘厦镇	87721441	水利、水电工程施工
东莞市宏达建设工程有限公司	东城街道	22380008	房屋建筑
东莞市华源建筑工程有限公司	厚街镇	85596888	建筑工程
东莞市金斗建造工程有限公司	寮步镇	83300000	工业与民用建筑施工
东莞市南粤建筑工程有限公司	万江街道	22020079	房屋建筑
广东省东莞市石龙建筑工程公司	石龙镇	86116908	房屋建筑
东莞市凤岗建筑工程公司	凤岗镇	87860335	房屋建筑
东莞市中厚建筑工程公司	厚街镇	85582766	房屋建筑
东莞市驰宏建设发展有限公司	虎门镇	85128989	房屋建筑
东莞市健升建筑工程有限公司	南城街道	22302222	房屋建筑
东莞市建工集团有限公司	南城街道	22427888	房屋建筑
东莞市锦新园林绿化有限公司	南城街道	23664092	市政公用工程
广东省东莞市莞城建筑工程公司	莞城街道	22229020	工业与民用建筑施工
东莞市方中建筑工程有限公司	莞城街道	86222001	建筑工程
建筑安装业			
东莞市景安电器安装工程有限公司	长安镇	81762299	电器安装
东莞市输变电工程公司	寮步镇	83237889	电力安装
东莞市高宝电气安装工程有限公司	高埗镇	88786869	安装电力设备
湖南望新建设集团股份有限公司东莞分公司	南城街道	22999910	建筑
广东宏泰照明科技有限公司	南城街道	22880111	房屋工程建筑
东莞市广安电器安装工程有限公司	东城街道	82266666	电器工程安装
东莞市塘厦水电空调设备安装工程有限公司	塘厦镇	87913322	机电设备工程安装
东莞市建安集团有限公司	东城街道	22986086	房屋建筑
广东集明电力工程有限公司	南城街道	22492728	微型电机及零部件
东莞市健升环境科技有限公司	南城街道	22177111	净化空调工程
东莞市顺安电力消防工程有限公司	莞城街道	22481077	消防设施工程
东莞市安利来电气安装有限公司	大朗镇	83010013	电力设施承装
东莞市堃烨装饰工程有限公司	塘厦镇	87933378	装饰工程

1-4 续表 18

(2011年)

单位名称	所属镇街	联系电话	主要产品（或服务）
东莞市良友装饰工程有限公司	高埗镇	88876098	建筑装饰
东莞市誉荣建材有限公司	东城街道	23321108	室内精装
东莞市名雕装饰有限公司	莞城街道	22029268	室内装饰
东莞市附城东城装修设计工程有限公司	东城街道	22618888	装饰装修
东莞市小杨装饰工程有限公司	清溪镇		建筑装饰
东莞市江桦装饰有限公司	寮步镇	83323628	室内装饰
其他建筑业			
东莞市力丰钢结构有限公司	厚街镇	85916822	钢结构安装
东莞市国贸水电安装工程有限公司	东城街道	22760555	水电安装
东莞市广强建筑基础工程有限公司	东城街道	22464088	建筑基础工程
东莞市凤安电力工程有限公司	凤岗镇	82082968	电力设施工程
东莞市东方动力拆迁有限公司	南城街道	22991778	建筑拆迁
东莞市黄江镇建筑工程有限公司	黄江镇	83363938	房屋工程建筑
东莞市金业河建筑基础工程有限公司	南城街道	22985988	基础工程施工
东莞市岭南园林建设有限公司	莞城街道	22450507	园林绿化工程
东莞市东塘电气安装有限公司	塘厦镇	87905273	承装电力设施
道路运输业			
东莞市汽车运输有限公司	莞城街道	22463079	道路旅客运输
东莞市正泰运输服务有限公司	麻涌镇	88222278	货物中转
东莞市玖龙运输有限公司	麻涌镇	88234888	公路货运运输
东莞市交通集团有限公司	万江街道	22701663	交通运输服务
东莞市畅安货物运输服务有限公司	洪梅镇	88561156	道路货物运输
东莞市高步客运站有限公司	高埗镇		客运
东莞市嘉达快运服务有限公司	东城街道	22981833	货物快递
东莞市旺盆运输有限公司	厚街镇	81694271	运输
东莞市三和物流有限公司	寮步镇	83214617	普通货运
东莞市长城客运有限公司	莞城街道	22461975	公路客运
东莞市飞马物流有限公司	黄江镇	86916838	普通货运
城市公共交通业			
东莞市公共汽车有限公司	莞城街道	22211806	交通运输
东莞市城巴运输有限公司	莞城街道	22492259	交通运输
东莞市华悦客运集团有限公司	莞城街道	27231596	交通运输
水上运输业			
东莞市丰海海运有限公司	塘厦镇	87926329	港澳航线运输
广州港集团新沙港务有限公司	麻涌镇	82159033	货物装卸堆存
东莞市海昌船务有限公司	石碣镇	86018810	货物运输
装卸搬运及其他运输服务业			
东莞市一速百优货运代理有限公司	高埗镇	88700684	交通运输、仓储和邮政业
东莞市德邦货运有限公司	南城街道	22907828	货运代理
东莞市南城南方物流有限公司	南城街道	22986935	运输
仓储业			
东莞市百安石化仓储有限公司	虎门港	88666030	化工品仓储
中央储备粮广东新沙港直属库	麻涌镇	88231111	粮食储备
东莞市业荣威通贸易有限公司	洪梅镇	88431919	石化产品仓储

1-4 续表 19

(2011年)

单位名称	所属镇街	联系电话	主要产品（或服务）
邮政业			
东莞市邮政局	莞城街道	22330782	函件
电信和其他信息传输服务业			
中国铁通集团有限公司东莞分公司长安营业厅	长安镇	86249800	电信业务
广东省电信实业集团东莞市有限公司	莞城街道	22482870	电信业务
中国网络通信集团公司东莞市分公司	南城街道	89826085	通讯服务
中国电信股份有限公司东莞分公司	南城街道	22808888	固定电话服务
广东省广播电视网络股份有限公司东莞洪梅分公司	洪梅镇	88430100	有线广播电视传输服务
中国铁通集团有限公司东莞分公司	莞城街道	86272388	电信固定电话服务
软件业			
东莞市智宇计算机科技有限公司	东城街道	23609655	系统集成
广东力优环境系统股份有限公司	松山湖	23076888	开发环境系统应用软件
东莞市泰阳实业有限公司	虎门镇	85136389	计算机网络工程
批发业			
广东省东莞五金矿产进出口有限公司	莞城街道	22227420	进出口代理
广东省东莞国药集团有限公司	莞城街道	22337200	药品
东莞市建晖燃料有限公司	莞城街道	22348877	煤炭
东莞市建森废纸回收有限公司	中堂镇	88121098	废纸回收
东莞市萃华商贸有限公司	桥头镇	83342322	贸易管理
东莞市奇旺商贸有限公司	东坑镇	83887138	服装
东莞主致医药有限公司	南城街道	22036911	医药
东莞市加利石油产品有限公司	沙田镇	88689922	润滑油
东莞市拓顺贸易有限公司	莞城街道	23032773	五金配件
东莞市虎泰能源有限公司	虎门镇	83817777	重油
东莞市银河废纸回收有限公司	中堂镇	88188108	废纸回收
东莞市海天药品有限公司	东城街道	22604555	药品
东莞市恒镒钢铁有限公司	中堂镇	88189477	钢材
东莞市兴盛废纸回收有限公司	中堂镇	88881402	废纸回收
东莞市金汇废纸回收有限公司	中堂镇		废纸回收
东莞市源来废纸回收有限公司	中堂镇	88117972	废纸
东莞市瑞丰石油化工有限公司	松山湖	22893200	成品油
东莞市虎门煤气有限公司	虎门镇	85111140	燃气
东莞市双丰废纸回收有限公司	中堂镇	88182628	废纸回收
东莞市明泰贸易有限公司	南城街道	22824398	国际商业贸易
广东省东莞丝绸进出口有限公司	南城街道	22482892	服装
广东文一朝阳集团有限公司	道滘镇	88327222	书报刊
广东省东莞化工进出口有限公司	莞城街道	22231118	进出口代理
广东洛贝电子科技有限公司	松山湖	22895186	电磁炉
东莞市伟明贸易有限公司	南城街道	23033918	泡棉全棉涂色布
东莞市溢源对外贸易有限公司	东城街道	22201203	代理进出口
东莞市同兴涂料有限公司	高埗镇	88739118	二甲苯
东莞市天牛塑胶原料有限公司	常平镇	86998877	塑胶原料
东莞市银洲燃料有限公司	中堂镇	88181366	煤炭
东莞市万和化工有限公司	万江街道	22273288	洗涤原料用品
东莞市中堂废旧物资回收有限公司中联分公司	中堂镇	88120732	废纸收购
东莞市永信药业有限公司	南城街道	22881314	中成药

1-4 续表 20

(2011年)

单位名称	所属镇街	联系电话	主要产品（或服务）
东莞市东普贸易有限公司	石碣镇	86604338	钢材
广东鸿程油库有限公司	万江街道	88016809	石油及制品
东莞市文成酒业有限公司	东城街道	22110939	酒类
东莞市东建浆纸有限公司	莞城街道	22623930	纸张
东莞市宇阳科技发展有限公司	凤岗镇	87506458	电容
东莞市仲源化工有限公司	谢岗镇	87682277	甲醇
东莞市永祥贸易有限公司	大岭山镇	85787777	燃料油
东莞市中堂废旧物资回收有限公司银洲分公司	中堂镇	88120732	废纸收购
广东省东莞纺织品进出口有限公司	莞城街道	22233804	服装进出口
东莞市津盈实业有限公司	虎门镇	85121693	钢材
东莞市新元素能源有限公司	莞城街道	22763444	重油
东莞市祥兴针车有限公司	石龙镇	86882006	缝纫设备
东莞市中堂废旧物资回收有限公司同力分公司	中堂镇	88120732	废纸收购
东莞市乾洋机电设备有限公司	中堂镇	81139232	五金机电
东莞市天昌塑胶原料有限公司	常平镇	86992933	塑胶原料
东莞市智丰贸易有限公司	大朗镇	83015809	服装
东莞市科裕钢铁贸易有限公司	沙田镇	88867777	钢材
东莞市大洲进出口有限公司	大朗镇	83032998	服装
东莞市华银贸易有限公司	道滘镇	88311866	煤炭
东莞市鸿越实业有限公司	虎门镇	85261330	粉煤灰渣
东莞市恒泰石油制品贸易有限公司	长安镇	85322068	重油
东莞市合联进出口贸易有限公司	大朗镇	83125556	出口毛衣
东莞市文一实业有限公司	道滘镇	88327025	文具
东莞市宝信实业有限公司	高埗镇	88731100	服装
东莞市泰昌石油化工贸易有限公司	樟木头镇	87710980	罐装润滑油
东莞市东伟石油化工有限公司	望牛墩镇	88855108	油
东莞市诚昌纸业有限公司	长安镇	85311598	文具
东莞市中堂废旧物资回收有限公司东江分公司	中堂镇	88120732	废纸收购
东莞市金马经贸有限公司	莞城街道	22307188	进出口代理
东莞市凯盈贸易有限公司	南城街道	23188808	机电产品
东莞市正诚贸易有限公司	东城街道	22680808	进出口业务
东莞市汇鸿纸业有限公司	石碣镇	86010920	纸张
东莞市德利石油化工有限公司	松山湖	85516299	石油及制品
东莞市建筑材料进出口有限公司	莞城街道	22816022	建筑材料
东莞市麒麟机械有限公司	莞城街道	22473938	轴承
东莞市溢安贸易有限公司	麻涌镇	88280993	重油
东莞市年丰饮料有限公司	东城街道	22256391	饮料
东莞市岳化贸易有限公司	谢岗镇	87762745	环已酮
东莞市东辉贸易有限公司	黄江镇	83364788	化工原料
广东省东莞国药集团药材有限公司	莞城街道	22239530	中药材
东莞市中堂废旧物资回收有限公司建桦分公司	中堂镇	88120732	废纸收购
广东省东莞市厚街供销社	厚街镇	85581485	日用百货、建材
东莞市银图贸易有限公司	中堂镇	88412888	塑料
深圳市庆鹏石油化工经销有限公司东莞分公司	沙田镇	88864889	成品油
东莞市富松机械设备有限公司	大朗镇	83200373	机械设备

1-4 续表 21

(2011年)

单位名称	所属镇街	联系电话	主要产品（或服务）
东莞市德凯经贸有限公司	南城街道	23027769	服装出口贸易
东莞市糖酒集团东方配销有限公司	南城街道	22184011	小食
东莞市海通工业煤炭销售有限公司	莞城街道	22239098	煤炭
东莞市新技术进出口有限公司	南城街道	22428678	自营和代理进出口
东莞市中凯进出口有限公司	大朗镇	83101855	出口毛衣
东莞市长安利源石油有限公司	长安镇	85416068	石油
东莞市中堂废旧物资回收有限公司	中堂镇	88811203	收购废品
广东省东莞机械进出口有限公司	莞城街道	22222040	进出口机电产品
东莞市君科进出口贸易有限公司	南城街道	22299128	货物及技术出口
东莞市旗峰对外贸易有限公司	东城街道	22633592	进出口业务
东莞市中堂废旧物资回收有限公司珠江分公司	中堂镇	88120732	废纸收购
东莞市友华机电工程有限公司	莞城街道	23050801	中央空调
东莞市明盛能源有限公司	石碣镇	86313666	煤炭
东莞市港源贸易有限公司	南城街道	22488703	工艺品进出口
东莞市永椿净化设备工程有限公司	寮步镇	81107819	净化设备工程
东莞市惠顺贸易有限公司	东城街道		建材
东莞市华树电脑有限公司	莞城街道	22313954	电子计算机及其配件
东莞市佳森能源有限公司	麻涌镇	88235233	煤炭
东莞市中堂废旧物资回收有限公司建晖分公司	中堂镇	88120732	废纸收购
东莞市隆兴纸业有限公司	石龙镇	86088777	文化用纸
东莞市宏川化工有限公司	松山湖	22893998	化工产品
东莞市利士石油化工有限公司	高埗镇	88731368	石油
东莞市名加石油有限公司	东城街道	81823808	汽油
东莞市雄峰特殊钢有限公司	凤岗镇	87559810	模具钢材
东莞市科虹金属有限公司	石碣镇	86309328	铜材
广东省东莞轻工业品进出口有限公司	莞城街道	22212413	电器
东莞市科大贸易有限公司	沙田镇	88867777	钢材
东莞中茂石油化工贸易有限公司	塘厦镇	81586940	甲醇
东莞市天锐贸易有限公司	长安镇	85545555	电子元件
东莞市东益实业投资有限公司	中堂镇	88815898	钢材
东莞市糖酒集团美宜佳便利店有限公司	南城街道	22465830	小食品
东莞市一君医药有限公司	高埗镇	81306988	中成药
东莞市百业兴经贸有限公司	南城街道	22421328	一般贸易
东莞市汇众进出口有限公司	大朗镇	83209503	针织制品
东莞市高力信塑料有限公司	中堂镇	88411688	塑胶原料
东莞市伟业石油化工有限公司	望牛墩镇	88850666	柴油
东莞市美德石化产品有限公司	谢岗镇	87682025	溶剂油
东莞市永盛燃料有限公司	万江街道	22287225	石油及制品
东莞市创丰科技发展有限公司	南城街道	22855300	自动化设备
广东省东莞快宜外经发展有限公司	南城街道	22421003	商品进出口
东莞市海川进出口有限公司	大朗镇	83113663	服装
东莞市锦茂进出口有限公司	东城街道	22339829	国内商业服务
东莞市南洋计算机软件有限公司	东城街道	22505550	计算机应用软件
东莞市锦多宝能源有限公司	樟木头镇	87780788	汽油、重油、润滑
东莞市昱方钢材有限公司	长安镇	85349788	模具钢材

1-4 续表 22

(2011年)

单位名称	所属镇街	联系电话	主要产品（或服务）
东莞市泽通贸易有限公司	莞城街道	22224050	电器
东莞市恒生进出口有限公司	南城街道	23181991	泡棉机进出口
东莞市振东医药有限公司	东城街道	22323888	药品
东莞市同汇贸易有限公司	东城街道	23360488	代理化工产品
东莞市真映切削工具有限公司	大朗镇	83111711	螺纹切削工具
东莞市莞晟贸易有限公司	中堂镇	88110155	煤炭
东莞市柏百顺石油化工有限公司	樟木头镇	87781216	化工燃料及产品
东莞市众富贸易有限公司	莞城街道	22812638	人造革出口
东莞市瑞展皮革贸易有限公司	厚街镇	85825996	皮革
东莞市寮步根记五金贸易部	寮步镇	83219698	铜制品
东莞市彩虹塑胶颜料有限公司	凤岗镇	87777113	塑胶颜料
东莞市华麟贸易有限公司	莞城街道	22313101	食用香精料
东莞市信佳贸易有限公司	南城街道	23186737	热轧卷板
东莞市巨行实业有限公司	中堂镇	88812373	硅酸钠
东莞市丰和贸易有限公司	万江街道	23179871	商业贸易
东莞市精工轴承有限公司	莞城街道	22451028	轴承
东莞市力宏贸易有限公司	中堂镇	88411005	化工产品
广东省东莞市新华书店有限公司	莞城街道	22115138	教材图书
东莞市蔚欣塑化有限公司	樟木头镇	87703399	塑胶原料
东莞市中堂废旧物资回收有限公司振桦分公司	中堂镇	88120732	废纸收购
东莞市顺盈钢材贸易有限公司	中堂镇	88188790	钢材、五金
东莞市联大特殊金属材料有限公司	樟木头镇	87123992	五金
东莞市万红贸易有限公司	东城街道	22316751	进出口贸易
东莞市对外贸易发展有限公司	东城街道	22265708	代理进出口
东莞市东孚商贸有限公司	万江街道	22772277	化妆品及卫生用品
东莞市巨树食品有限公司	万江街道	22422166	副食
东莞市广弘医药有限公司	万江街道	88899033	中药材及中成药
东莞市达明发展有限公司	东城街道	22363006	出口家具
东莞市嘉宝石油化工有限公司	樟木头镇	87711087	甲基苯
东莞市中泰纸业有限公司	长安镇	85415136	纸张
东莞市荣兴纸业有限公司	石碣镇	86013903	纸类
东莞市先锋特殊钢有限公司	凤岗镇	87777097	钢材
东莞市糖酒集团丰裕贸易有限公司	南城街道	22481231	食品
东莞市中堂废旧物资回收有限公司深联分公司	中堂镇	88120732	废纸收购
东莞市中堂废旧物资回收有限公司汇达分公司	中堂镇	88120732	废纸收购
东莞市景福贸易有限公司	万江街道	22787068	化工产品
东莞市全方圆纸制品有限公司	万江街道	87076226	纸制品
广东省东莞盐业总公司	莞城街道	22380236	盐产品
广东省东莞市谢岗食品公司	谢岗镇	87687328	生猪
东莞市同舟化工有限公司	沙田镇	22365733	甲苯
东莞市汉森金属材料有限公司	中堂镇	88123433	金属材料
广东省东莞医药保健品进出口有限公司	南城街道	22802920	出口服装
东莞市长成纸张有限公司	虎门镇	85269968	纸张
东莞市天泰控股集团有限公司	东城街道	23138888	成品油
东莞市宇兴贸易有限公司	大朗镇	83109968	毛衣

1-4 续表 23

(2011年)

单位名称	所属镇街	联系电话	主要产品（或服务）
东莞市东源投资实业有限公司	南城街道	22855416	煤炭
东莞市庆华能源有限公司	中堂镇	88819933	煤炭
东莞市允新贸易有限公司	寮步镇	83039670	模具钢
东莞市健宇塑胶原料有限公司	常平镇	86991001	塑胶原料
广东烟草东莞市有限公司	东城街道	22210936	烟草
东莞市永联化工贸易有限公司	大朗镇	83112349	过氧化氢
东莞市常平好必来塑胶贸易有限公司	常平镇	86992038	塑胶原料
东莞市澳洁贸易有限公司	常平镇	83750888	日用百货
东莞市广通贸易有限公司	南城街道	22407968	汽车轮胎
东莞市世发贸易有限公司	南城街道	22800368	化工原料
东莞市合润进出口贸易有限公司	南城街道	22827028	镇流器出口
东莞市中堂废旧物资回收有限公司双洲分公司	中堂镇	88120732	废纸收购
东莞市鼎鑫贸易有限公司	东城街道	22314016	贸易
东莞市源源钢铁贸易有限公司	大朗镇	83130830	钢材材料
东莞市金仙峰实业有限公司	南城街道	22416577	白砂糖
东莞市瑞腾贸易有限公司	莞城街道	22223639	农副产品
东莞市万华皮革有限公司	厚街镇	85876266	皮革
东莞市翔顺妇幼用品有限公司	麻涌镇	88281327	奶粉
东莞市富励贸易有限公司	凤岗镇	87508888	化工产品
东莞市华健医药器械有限公司	莞城街道	22687306	医疗器械
中国石油天然气股份有限公司广东东莞销售分公司	南城街道	22022155	成品油
广东省东莞国药集团仁济堂药业有限公司	莞城街道	22484521	中药材
东莞市中堂废旧物资回收有限公司金洲分公司	中堂镇	88120732	废纸收购
东莞市海丽商贸有限公司	松山湖	22508760	架桥剂
东莞市东物剧毒化学物品有限公司	莞城街道	22383672	化工产品
广东钻石世家国际珠宝有限公司	南城街道	22028888	钻石
东莞市中彦进出口有限公司	大朗镇	83315888	服装
广东省东莞市海东石油有限公司	麻涌镇	88232325	油品
东莞市信立实业有限公司	大岭山镇	85633333	农产品贸易
东莞市创力网络科技有限公司	莞城街道	22333968	电脑
东莞市润泰纸业有限公司	长安镇	85499268	纸张
东莞市朝阳药业有限公司	道滘镇	88327952	中成药、中药材
东莞市洋通饮料贸易有限公司	茶山镇	86110722	啤酒
东莞市日之泉食品综合贸易有限公司	中堂镇	88815898	啤酒
广东省东莞包装进出口有限公司	南城街道	22802861	纺织品进出口
东莞市建安贸易有限公司	莞城街道	22321232	轻纺产品服装
东莞市华江石油化工有限公司	樟木头镇	82119266	石油化工
东莞市精骏包装材料有限公司	中堂镇	88180800	电镀锡薄钢板
东莞市彬源塑胶贸易有限公司	厚街镇	85904198	塑胶
东莞市海华五金矿产进出口有限公司	莞城街道	22243170	进出口代理
东莞市成泰化工有限公司	南城街道	22884548	EVA
东莞市日之泉物流有限公司	中堂镇	88815015	钢材
东莞市东江石油化工有限公司	万江街道	87076081	石油及制品
东莞市东糖集团有限公司	东城街道	22613931	成品糖
东莞市中堂废旧物资回收有限公司鸿业分公司	中堂镇	88120732	废纸收购
东莞市环球工艺进出口贸易有限公司	南城街道	22802312	出口家具

1-4 续表 24

(2011年)

单位名称	所属镇街	联系电话	主要产品（或服务）
东莞市乘风实业有限公司	石排镇	86615001	购销包
东莞市中堂物资供销有限公司	中堂镇	88815898	钢材
东莞市龙翔纺织品有限公司	寮步镇	83260051	布料
东莞市汇富进出口贸易有限公司	南城街道	22389322	家具
东莞市虎门粮食有限公司	虎门镇	85511250	粮油
东莞市森和纸业有限公司	厚街镇	85588818	双灰板
东莞市创兴糖业贸易有限公司	万江街道	22784583	糕点、糖果及糖
东莞市东安石油化工有限公司	塘厦镇	88865128	汽油
东莞市豪景商贸有限公司	石龙镇	86118181	机电产品
东莞市利兴糖业贸易有限公司	万江街道	22784583	糕点、糖果及糖
东莞市百业进出口有限公司	南城街道	22421328	一般贸易
东莞市中堂废旧物资回收有限公司有利分公司	中堂镇	88120732	废纸收购
东莞市南腾贸易有限公司	中堂镇	88122189	有机溶剂
广东省东莞市虎门供销社	虎门镇	85513008	家用电子类
广东广浩机电设备有限公司	中堂镇	81312908	五金机电
东莞市中信化工有限公司	黄江镇	86918388	塑胶粒
东莞市泓海贸易有限公司	莞城街道	22340699	纺织品染料
东莞市星辰塑胶有限公司	常平镇	86991286	塑胶原料
东莞市广联通信器材有限公司	石排镇		手机
东莞市华锐塑胶实业投资有限公司	黄江镇	83608800	塑胶原料
中铝洛阳铜业有限公司东莞分公司	虎门镇	85562885	有色金属
东莞市顺安废纸回收有限公司	望牛墩镇	88851243	废纸回收
广东大地通讯连锁服务有限公司	莞城街道	23066666	通讯设备
东莞市亿丰行洗涤产品有限公司	茶山镇	86311487	洗涤用品
东莞市百维食品化工原料实业有限公司	寮步镇	83263989	食品添加剂
东莞市道滘珠洲石油气有限公司	道滘镇	88389233	液化石油气
东莞市鑫泉石油化工有限公司	谢岗镇	85635915	化工产品
东莞市日之泉贸易有限公司	中堂镇	88815015	钢材
东莞市辉明石化产品有限公司	谢岗镇	23183527	石脑油
东莞市欢盈投资有限公司	东城街道		空调
东莞市超捷实业有限公司	麻涌镇	88228979	重油
东莞市华润涂料有限公司	东城街道	22363331	油漆
东莞市瑞峰纸业有限公司	东城街道	22623952	纸张
东莞市东钢金属贸易有限公司	虎门镇	82887122	钢材
东莞市华辉金属材料有限公司	莞城街道	22468979	金属材料
东莞市卓远发展经贸有限公司	黄江镇	87132056	苯酐
东莞市鸿甲五金材料有限公司	凤岗镇	87517744	五金材料
东莞市明旺贸易有限公司	南城街道	22022722	塑胶原料
黑龙江中盟龙新化工有限公司东莞谢岗分公司	谢岗镇	82121261	甲基丙烯酸
东莞市广利食品进出口有限公司	莞城街道	22223344	食品
东莞市华发纸张有限公司	茶山镇	86313868	白纸板
广东省东莞畜产进出口有限公司	东城街道	22206023	五金
东莞市华闽金属材料有限公司	横沥镇	83792951	金属贸易
广东宁兴特钢贸易有限公司	大朗镇	81069989	金属
东莞市华丰盛塑料有限公司	中堂镇	88411688	PC塑料
上海凯群贸易有限公司东莞分公司	厚街镇	85750312	塑胶制品

1-4　续表 25

(2011年)

单位名称	所属镇街	联系电话	主要产品（或服务）
东莞市美星塑胶材料有限公司	南城街道	23120868	塑胶原料
东莞市创辉进出口贸易有限公司	寮步镇	81106328	毛织品
东莞市中油迅兴实业有限公司	中堂镇	88885838	柴油
东莞市恒旭达塑胶贸易有限公司	樟木头镇	87190961	塑胶
东莞市广招贸易有限公司	中堂镇	88893567	锌锭、铝锭
广东新动力能源有限公司	樟木头镇	87188777	石油及制品
东莞市伟力地坪材料有限公司	企石镇	85302795	地坪材料
东莞市岭南进出口有限公司	寮步镇	81197620	电脑配件
东长集团有限公司	望牛墩镇	88566888	重油
东莞市创维电器发展有限公司	东城街道	22292742	家用电器
东莞美的暖通设备销售有限公司	虎门镇	81518680	家用电器
东莞市合泊进出口贸易有限公司	东城街道	23609238	代理进出口
永恩投资(集团)有限公司广东经销部	厚街镇	83085323	服装
东莞市麻涌利南废纸回收有限公司	麻涌镇	88234888	废纸收购
东莞市宜新贸易有限公司	东城街道	22317361	塑料原料
东莞市盈邦贸易有限公司	沙田镇	81631398	重油
东莞市铭骏实业投资有限公司	洪梅镇		建材
东莞市森升化工有限公司	洪梅镇		化工产品
东莞市东长石油化工有限公司	望牛墩镇	88565388	重油
东莞市宝鼎建材有限公司	洪梅镇		建材
鞋柜商贸有限公司东莞经销部	厚街镇		鞋、帽
东莞卓烨能源有限公司	洪梅镇	88436783	重油、罐装润滑油
东莞市宝力金属材料有限公司	洪梅镇		建材
东莞市希贤贸易有限公司	洪梅镇		金属矿
东莞市振乾钢铁贸易有限公司	洪梅镇		金属矿
东莞市展博钢铁有限公司	洪梅镇	21683544	建材
东莞市上钢钢铁有限公司	洪梅镇		金属矿
东莞市宝鑫钢铁有限公司	洪梅镇	82076389	金属矿
东莞市茂晟石化贸易有限公司	中堂镇	81252099	石油及制品
东莞市广济医药器械有限公司	南城街道	22906161	药品
东莞美的制冷设备销售有限公司	虎门镇		家电设备
东莞市东孚石油化工有限公司	寮步镇	82316938	石油产品
零售业			
东莞市盛鑫汽车商贸有限公司	樟木头镇	86268822	汽车
东莞市海雅百货有限公司	东城街道	22031333	百货
东莞市桥头加桥加油站有限公司	桥头镇	22367236	机动车燃料
东莞凯润丰田汽车销售服务有限公司	虎门镇	85133988	汽车
东莞市广物正通达汽车贸易有限公司	寮步镇	83269019	长安品牌汽车
东莞市同庆汽车贸易有限公司	寮步镇	83300188	汽车
东莞市立诚立信贸易有限公司	黄江镇	86919417	塑胶
东莞市时尚电器有限公司	莞城街道	22342220	家用电器
东莞市恒波商业有限公司	大朗镇	83018679	通讯产品
东莞市骐骏汽车销售服务有限公司	樟木头镇	87711038	汽车
东莞东美丰田汽车销售服务有限公司	塘厦镇	82087662	汽车
东莞市华顺汽车贸易有限公司寮步分公司	寮步镇	83230930	东南牌汽车
东莞市新大地汽车贸易有限公司	莞城街道	22266238	汽车

1-4 续表 26

(2011年)

单位名称	所属镇街	联系电话	主要产品（或服务）
东莞市百丰百货商贸有限公司	石碣镇	81816888	用品、食品、生鲜
东莞市恒信汽车销售服务有限公司	东城街道	22767228	汽车
东莞市悦海实业投资有限公司	寮步镇	81254225	服装
东莞市广泰汽车有限公司	虎门镇	85223301	汽车
东莞市永佳丰田汽车销售服务有限公司	厚街镇	81691107	汽车维修
东莞市永虹汽车贸易有限公司	南城街道	22985675	汽车
东莞市合信汽车销售服务有限公司	南城街道	23188228	汔车
东莞东风南方汽车销售服务有限公司	南城街道	22985916	东风日产品牌汽车
东莞市博雅贸易有限公司	常平镇	81090360	长安福特品牌汽车
东莞市华升汽车有限公司	虎门镇	85246601	汽车
东莞市华美汽车销售服务有限公司	虎门镇	85017927	汽车
东莞市嘉祥通讯有限公司	南城街道	88777888	手机
深圳市华德石油化工有限公司东莞分公司	沙田镇	88866342	石油化工产品
东莞东风南方东升汽车销售服务有限公司	厚街镇	85089656	汽车
东莞市沪江五金有限公司	寮步镇	83526022	五金材料
东莞市美的日用家电销售有限公司	莞城街道	22308060	美的电饭煲
东莞润德商业有限公司	厚街镇	89788109	百货
东莞市南城周溪英油加油站	南城街道	22403634	汽油
东莞市东宝能源有限公司	塘厦镇	87905808	重油
东莞市塘厦新奥燃气有限公司	塘厦镇	82019831	燃气供应
东莞市粤美特加油站有限公司	大岭山镇	83351331	汽油、柴油
东莞市嘉誉电子有限公司	清溪镇	82692990	电子产品
东莞龙华英菲尼迪汽车销售服务有限公司	寮步镇	82311999	汽车
东莞市美兴汽车有限公司	寮步镇	82316254	汽车
东莞市顺电商贸有限公司莞城威尼斯分店	莞城街道		家用电器
东莞市兴华燃料贸易有限公司大朗高英供应站	大朗镇	83187988	液化石油气
东莞市广物东捷汽车销售服务有限公司	寮步镇	83269019	商用车（不含乘用车）
东莞市志诚汽车销售服务有限公司	寮步镇	83228331	汽车
东莞市南天大新集团有限公司	桥头镇	83429888	超市百货
东莞市东之捷汽车销售服务有限公司	寮步镇	88952839	汽车
东莞市亚太进出口有限公司	大朗镇		日用品
东莞市世沃汽车销售服务有限公司	寮步镇	81259999	汽车
东莞市南菱博通汽车销售服务有限公司	寮步镇	82392536	汽车
东莞市华熙汽车销售有限公司	寮步镇	81191508	进口汽车
东莞捷运行汽车销售服务有限公司	寮步镇	81118911	汽车
中国石油天然气股份有限公司广东东莞石碣新城加油站	石碣镇	86632870	汽车用汽油
东莞市世奥汽车销售服务有限公司	南城街道	21688006	汽车
东莞市东晖化学工业有限公司	沙田镇	82793166	化工产品
东莞市宝昌汽车销售服务有限公司	虎门镇	88629290	汽车
东莞市东达汽车有限公司	厚街镇	85935999	汽车
东莞市红彤汽车贸易有限公司	寮步镇	82871888	汽车
东莞华多利汽车有限公司	寮步镇	83523000	汽车
东莞市厚街涌口加油站有限公司	厚街镇	85050598	柴油
东莞市会通汽车贸易有限公司	南城街道	22853998	汽车配件
东莞市汇天源汽车销售服务有限公司	寮步镇	83528753	汽车
东莞市骏捷汽车贸易有限公司	厚街镇	83080019	东风本田汽车

1-4 续表 27

(2011年)

单位名称	所属镇街	联系电话	主要产品（或服务）
东莞市羚丰汽车贸易有限公司	南城街道	22981618	汽车
东莞市长久汽车贸易有限公司	东城街道	22663933	汽车
东莞市星高达汽车销售服务有限公司	寮步镇	81105588	斯柯达品牌汽车
东莞东风南方汽车销售服务有限公司樟木头分公司	樟木头镇	83841307	汽车
东莞市石排燕窝加油站	石排镇	86524520	汽油
东莞市励骏实业有限公司	厚街镇	21123920	皮鞋
东莞中汽南方汽车销售服务有限公司	南城街道	86225930	汽车
东莞市永成加油站有限公司	厚街镇	85588949	汽油
东莞市中油西溪加油站有限公司	寮步镇	83328508	汽油
东莞市大朗世达汽车有限公司	大朗镇	81116716	汽车
东莞市广物君豪实业投资有限公司	万江街道	22703999	汽车
东莞市虎门威远加油站有限公司	虎门镇	85040678	机动车燃料
东莞市顺昌贸易有限公司	凤岗镇	87755668	机动车燃料
东莞市兴华燃料贸易有限公司	大朗镇	83132700	液化石油汽
东莞市大参林连锁药店有限公司	南城街道	22884901	药品
广州市好又多（天利）百货商业有限公司世博分公司	东城街道	22763201	百货超市
东莞市常平液化石油气供应有限公司	常平镇	83337820	液化石油气
东莞市君通汽车贸易有限公司	寮步镇	83226599	汽车
东莞市大新汽车贸易有限公司	东城街道	22672268	汽车
东莞市兴隆汽车贸易有限公司	寮步镇	82315618	汽车
东莞市和盈商贸有限公司	万江街道	22422218	日用品
东莞市东众汽车销售服务有限公司	寮步镇	83230999	汽车
东莞市汉阳电器有限公司	东城街道	22670397	电器
东莞市天和商贸有限公司	樟木头镇	22508941	百货
东莞市东悦汽车销售服务有限公司	大朗镇	81069990	汽车
东莞市虎门镇东风加油站	虎门镇	85566666	汽油
东莞市骏丰汽车有限公司	寮步镇	83229371	汽车
东莞市东盛超市有限公司	东城街道	23139067	日用百货
东莞市聚星行汽车销售服务有限公司	厚街镇	82319818	汽车
东莞家乐福商业有限公司	东城街道	22201897	百货
东莞市新天地汽车销售服务有限公司	寮步镇	83523008	汽车
东莞市塘厦林村加油站	塘厦镇	87902608	成品油
东莞市龙成汽车销售服务有限公司	万江街道	22779999	汽车
上海嘉定乐购生活购物有限公司东莞市厚街分公司	厚街镇	88913888	百货
东莞市周通泰汽车贸易有限公司	常平镇	83333390	汽车
东莞市骏宇汽车贸易有限公司	南城街道	22851778	汽车及配件
东莞市东部丰田汽车销售服务有限公司	寮步镇	83285989	丰田品牌车
东莞市中科能源有限公司	黄江镇	83600900	润滑油
东莞市新华利汽车贸易有限公司	寮步镇	81112303	吉利牌汽车
东莞市中昌贸易有限公司	大朗镇	81123383	汽车
东莞市新日水果食品有限公司	莞城街道	22489993	水果、食品
东莞市华顺汽车贸易有限公司	厚街镇	85909050	东南牌汽车
东莞市万江国威加油站	万江街道	22275846	机动车燃料
东莞市东奥汽车服务有限公司	寮步镇	83266998	汽车
上海大众汽车东莞销售服务有限公司	莞城街道	22337006	汽车
东莞市南城丰田汽车销售服务有限公司	南城街道	22987090	汽车

1-4 续表 28

(2011年)

单位名称	所属镇街	联系电话	主要产品（或服务）
广东省东莞国药集团长安医药有限公司	长安镇	85308840	药品
东莞市苏宁电器有限公司	莞城街道	22320266	家用电器
深圳市国美电器有限公司东莞市分公司	莞城街道	22807391	家用电器
东莞市冠骏汽车销售服务有限公司	寮步镇	83230777	汽车
东莞市常平石油供应有限公司陈屋贝加油站	常平镇	83391105	机动车燃料
中国石油化工股份有限公司广东东莞石油分公司	莞城街道	22506200	汽油
东莞市新东联汽车贸易有限公司	寮步镇	83527292	汽车
东莞市中堂镇东泊加油站	中堂镇	88885838	柴油
东莞市大兴汽车贸易有限公司	东城街道	22662646	汽车
东莞市骏标汽车销售有限公司	南城街道	22850962	小轿车
广东省东莞国药集团虎门医药有限公司	虎门镇	85511364	药品
东莞市愉康超市有限公司	长安镇	85536488	百货
东莞市合禾汽车销售服务有限公司	常平镇	82201168	丰田汽车
东莞市常平供销社	常平镇	83331117	百货
东莞市黄江镇江南加油站有限公司	黄江镇	83629433	汽油
东莞市万昌燃气有限公司	凤岗镇	87517320	生活用燃料
东莞市东鑫汽车销售服务有限公司	塘厦镇	82089077	汽车
东莞市鸿鹰汽车销售服务有限公司	南城街道	22981108	汽车
东莞市南方亚飞汽车有限公司	樟木头镇	87193666	汽车
东莞市通利华汽车贸易有限公司	寮步镇	83260006	东风微型汽车
东莞市虎门石油公司虎威加油站	虎门镇	85109138	柴油
东莞市路通汽车贸易有限公司	寮步镇	83232099	商用车
东莞市天虹商场有限公司	莞城街道	23164880	百货
东莞市冠丰汽车有限公司	寮步镇	83525630	汽车
东莞市华康空调电器有限公司	莞城街道	22348888	空调
东莞市东城中油柏洲边加油站	东城街道	22263969	汽油
东莞市志祥汽车销售服务有限公司	寮步镇	83226530	汽车
东莞市永丰行汽车服务有限公司	东城街道	22656866	汽车服务
东莞市银星实业发展有限公司	清溪镇	87737539	汽油、柴油
东莞市昌发汽车贸易有限公司虎门分公司	虎门镇	85131831	汽车
东莞市加仑石油化工有限公司	万江街道	88016889	润滑油
东莞市金美汽车销售服务有限公司	常平镇	83553927	汽车
东莞市天下行丰田汽车销售服务有限公司	常平镇	83558216	汽车
东莞市遂通汽车销售服务有限公司	南城街道	22850555	汽车
东莞市三益汽车有限公司	寮步镇	83526653	汽车
东莞市南城区农机服务站宏伟加油站	南城街道	22404202	汽油
东莞市中油国威油品销售有限公司	虎门镇	85503019	汽油
东莞龙华丰田汽车销售服务有限公司	万江街道	22773388	汽车
东莞市南城海雅百货有限公司	南城街道	23027222	服装
东莞市长安乌沙长盛加油站	长安镇	85548808	石油
深圳市海王星辰健康药房连锁有限公司东莞分公司	莞城街道	22366079	药品
东莞市通力贸易有限公司	南城街道	22987359	饮料
东莞市华安加油站有限公司	东城街道	22298698	成品油
东莞市捷达通贸易有限公司	南城街道	22971218	汽车
中海油销售深圳有限公司大朗分公司	大朗镇	83191686	柴油
东莞市东富实业有限公司	寮步镇	83220559	汽车

1-4 续表 29

(2011年)

单位名称	所属镇街	联系电话	主要产品（或服务）
东莞市同鸿汽车贸易有限公司	寮步镇	83030208	商用车
东莞市丰华汽车销售服务有限公司	樟木头镇	87193088	汽车
东莞市大朗镇松木山加油站	大朗镇	83128021	汽油
东莞市合宝汽车销售服务有限公司	南城街道	22851228	宝马汽车
东莞市塘厦镇诸佛岭加油站	塘厦镇	87926329	成品油
东莞市厚龙燃气有限公司	厚街镇	85817336	液化石油气
东莞东风南方汽车销售服务有限公司寮步分公司	寮步镇	83523042	汽车
东莞市南菱汽车销售服务有限公司	南城街道	22909591	汽车
东莞市江铃汽车销售有限公司	寮步镇	83220527	汽车
东莞市东城丰田汽车销售服务有限公司	东城街道	22019999	汽车
东莞市国贸超级市场有限公司	莞城街道	22117591	副食品
东莞市大通电脑有限公司	东城街道	23071386	计算机软硬件
东莞市华力冷气工程有限公司	莞城街道	23067567	制冷电器
东莞市怡安百货有限公司	长安镇	88612888	服装
东莞市金杯供销有限公司	南城街道	22409128	汽车
东莞市常平石油供应有限公司	常平镇	83022221	汽油、煤油
东莞市顺利汽车贸易有限公司	寮步镇	83305998	商用汽车
中域电讯连锁集团股份有限公司	南城街道	22888888	手机通讯产品
东莞市百力恒丰田汽车销售服务有限公司	长安镇	81603800	汽车
东莞市东城加成加油站有限公司	东城街道	22489229	汽油、柴油
东莞市东瑞汽车有限公司	南城街道	22982189	奇瑞汽车
东莞市桥南加油站有限公司	厚街镇	85882970	汽油
东莞市虎门镇嘉燃加油站（普通合伙）	虎门镇	85110933	汽油
东莞市鸿燕贸易有限公司	南城街道	23303318	汽车
东莞市聚成汽车技术服务有限公司	南城街道	22406200	汽车
东莞市天泰石油化工有限公司	南城街道	22028726	润滑油
东莞市永奥汽车贸易有限公司	寮步镇	83261895	汽车
东莞市英利数控设备有限公司	长安镇	85317431	数控设备
广东省东莞市医药有限公司	莞城街道	22507881	西药
东莞市车友汽车服务有限公司	寮步镇	83220559	奇端汽车
东莞市渝庆汽车销售服务有限公司	寮步镇	83300138	汽车
东莞东风南方东益汽车销售服务有限公司	虎门镇	85133806	汽车
东莞市骏鸣汽车销售服务有限公司	寮步镇	81112813	汽车
东莞市正欣科技有限公司	南城街道	22023588	软件设计
东莞市永升汽车贸易有限公司	寮步镇	81128180	汽车
东莞市南方汽车博览有限公司	樟木头镇	87707666	汽车
东莞市渝州长安汽车销售有限公司	南城街道	23194316	汽车
东莞市华美乐建材超市有限公司	南城街道	22901188	瓷砖
东莞市凯润东成汽车销售服务有限公司	寮步镇	82223988	广州本田汽车
上海嘉定乐购生活购物有限公司东莞市虎门分公司	虎门镇	81613268	百货
东莞市通益汽车销售服务有限公司	寮步镇	81191306	汽车
东莞市永怡汽车贸易有限公司	南城街道	22904057	汽车
上海嘉定乐购生活购物有限公司东莞市常平分公司	常平镇	81896969	百货
东莞市汇福轮胎有限公司	石龙镇	86180598	汽车轮胎
东莞市福丰汽车有限公司	南城街道	22850001	长安福特汽车
东莞市宏宝汽车销售服务有限公司	寮步镇	81106028	汽车

1-4 续表 30

(2011年)

单位名称	所属镇街	联系电话	主要产品（或服务）
东莞市彩怡百货有限公司	莞城街道	22497688	百货
东莞市加南石油供应有限公司	中堂镇		柴油、汽油
东莞市大岭山联英加油站	大岭山镇	83351606	柴油
东莞市金实力油料有限公司	清溪镇		重油
东莞市中维商贸有限公司	东坑镇	83887138	西装
东莞市大朗镇长塘加油站	大朗镇	83319244	柴油、汽油、润滑油
东莞市昊安汽车有限公司	长安镇	85223818	汽车
东莞市永濠汽车销售服务有限公司	南城街道	22904888	汽车
东莞市嘉荣超市有限公司	南城街道	22808810	家用百货
东莞市东仁汽车销售服务有限公司	南城街道	86228588	汽车
东莞市华隆加油站有限公司	松山湖	22367236	汽油、柴油
东莞市寮步横坑加油站有限公司	寮步镇	83301011	汽油
东莞市南城区加油站	南城街道	22417222	汽油
东莞市常平木抡加油站	常平镇	83988331	机动车燃料
住宿业			
东莞市凯景酒店有限公司	中堂镇	88883333	酒店管理服务
东莞市嘉华酒店有限公司	厚街镇	85928888	餐饮、住宿
东莞市石龙名冠金凯悦大酒店有限公司	石龙镇	86188888	餐饮、住宿
东莞宾馆有限公司	莞城街道	22222222	餐饮、住宿
东莞市太子酒店有限公司	黄江镇	83363333	餐饮、住宿
东莞市汇景酒店有限公司	洪梅镇	88848888	餐饮、住宿
东莞市蒂豪花园酒店有限公司	大朗镇	83122222	餐饮、住宿
东莞市华南国际大酒店有限公司	东城街道		餐饮、住宿
东莞市尼罗河酒店有限公司	万江街道	22706666	餐饮、住宿
东莞市景福酒店有限公司	石碣镇	86366666	旅业服务
东莞市松山湖酒店有限公司	松山湖	22891234	酒店管理
东莞市富盈酒店有限公司	厚街镇	85888888	餐饮、住宿
东莞市名冠金凯悦大酒店有限公司	凤岗镇	87759888	餐饮、住宿
东莞市华尔登国际酒店有限公司	桥头镇	81028888	餐饮、住宿
东莞市悦莱花园酒店有限公司	寮步镇	81118888	餐饮、住宿
东莞市樟木头三正半山酒店有限公司	樟木头镇	87799333	餐饮、住宿
东莞市长安国际酒店有限公司	长安镇	85333333	餐饮、住宿
东莞市汇华饭店	常平镇	83938888	餐饮、住宿
东莞市龙泉国际大酒店	虎门镇	85188688	餐饮、住宿
东莞市厚街国际大酒店有限公司	厚街镇	85088888	餐饮、住宿
东莞市丰泰花园酒店有限公司	虎门镇	85708888	餐饮、住宿
东莞市松山湖酒店有限公司凯悦酒店分公司	松山湖	22891234	餐饮、住宿
东莞市塘厦三正半山酒店有限公司	塘厦镇	87299333	餐饮、住宿
东莞市宏远酒店有限公司	南城街道	22418888	餐饮、住宿
东莞市昌明实业有限公司喜来登酒店	厚街镇	85988888	餐饮、住宿
东莞市会展国际大酒店	南城街道	22889999	餐饮、住宿
餐饮业			
真功夫餐饮管理有限公司	松山湖	38792952	快餐饮食服务
东莞市桥头新鸿酒店	桥头镇	83343088	西餐
银行业			
中国建设银行股份有限公司东莞市分行	南城街道	22816118	金融业务

1-4　续表 31

(2011年)

单位名称	所属镇街	联系电话	主要产品（或服务）
东莞市农村商业银行股份有限公司	莞城街道	22103131	金融业务
东莞银行股份有限公司	莞城街道	22118010	金融业务
中国农业银行股份有限公司东莞分行	南城街道	23305742	金融业务
招商银行股份有限公司东莞分行	东城街道	22303888	金融业务
广东发展银行股份有限公司东莞分行	莞城街道	22477888	金融业务
中信银行股份有限公司东莞分行	东城街道	22667876	金融业务
中国银行股份有限公司东莞分行	南城街道	22819888	金融业务
交通银行股份有限公司东莞分行	莞城街道	22505643	金融业务
兴业银行股份有限公司东莞分行	南城街道	22809988	金融业务
中国工商银行股份有限公司东莞分行	南城街道	22481728	金融业务
东莞农村商业银行股份有限公司石碣西南分理处	石碣镇	86631724	金融业务
证券业			
广发证券股份有限公司东莞虎门证券营业部	虎门镇	85521178	证券经纪
东莞证券有限责任公司	莞城街道	22119350	证券经纪业务
保险业			
阳光人寿保险股份有限公司东莞中心支公司	南城街道	88981959	人寿保险业务
中国平安人寿保险股份有限公司东莞中心支公司	南城街道	21683205	人寿保险业务
中国人民财产保险股份有限公司东莞市分公司	东城街道	22313601	财产保险业务
中国太平洋财产保险股份有限公司东莞中心支公司	南城街道	22807699	金融保险业务
中国人寿保险股份有限公司东莞分公司	莞城街道	22488488	人寿保险业务
天平汽车保险股份有限公司东莞中心支公司	南城街道	22992063	车辆保险业务
永安财产保险股份有限公司东莞中心支公司	南城街道	22996100	企业财产损失保险业务
中国大地财产保险股份有限公司东莞中心支公司	东城街道	22361158	财产保险业务
泰康人寿保险股份有限公司东莞中心支公司	南城街道	22994019	人寿保险业务
中国人民健康保险股份有限公司东莞中心支公司	东城街道	22328887	健康保险业务
新华人寿保险股份有限公司东莞中心支公司	莞城街道	22498243	人寿保险业务
太平保险有限公司东莞中心支公司	莞城街道	22476688	财产保险业务
太平人寿保险有限公司东莞中心支公司	南城街道	23188161	人寿保险业务
中国人民人寿保险股份有限公司东莞市中心支公司	东城街道	22306285	人寿保险业务
中国太平洋人寿保险股份有限公司东莞中心支公司	莞城街道	22321518	承保各种人身保险业务
中华联合财产保险股份有限公司东莞中心支公司	莞城街道	22605888	财产保险经营业务
中国平安财产保险股份有限公司东莞分公司	南城街道	22486092	财产保险业务
其他金融活动			
东莞信托有限公司	莞城街道	22366101	信托业务
中国邮政储蓄银行有限责任公司东莞分行	莞城街道	22116366	金融业务
房地产业			
东莞市丰华房地产开发有限公司	莞城街道	22629333	房地产开发
东莞市商业中心发展有限公司	南城街道	22422888	开发建造东莞商业中心
东莞市塘厦镇房地产开发公司	塘厦镇	87722361	房地产开发
东莞市丰泰建设房地产有限公司	虎门镇	85221133	房地产开发
东莞市泰安房地产咨询服务有限公司	东城街道	22470531	房地产开发
东莞市领居房地产开发有限公司	大岭山镇	88988888	房地产项目开发经营
东莞市新世纪丽江豪园商住开发有限公司	茶山镇	86409800	房地产开发经营
东莞市瀚森房地产开发有限公司	横沥镇	81010511	房地产开发
东莞市粤海村（单项)房地产开发有限公司	东城街道	22611621	房地产开发
东莞市翠云轩房地产开发有限公司	寮步镇	22679733	房地产开发

1-4 续表 32

(2011年)

单位名称	所属镇街	联系电话	主要产品（或服务）
东莞市丰源投资发展有限公司	莞城街道	22629333	房地产开发
东莞市金泓地产有限公司	大朗镇	83485807	房地产开发
东莞市东沙港建设发展有限公司	中堂镇	88661823	房地产开发
中惠熙元房地产集团有限公司	东城街道	22360398	房地产开发经营
东莞市三元盈晖投资发展有限公司	万江街道	88778748	房地产项目经营
东莞市沙田镇房地产开发公司	沙田镇	81522888	房地产开发经营
东莞市富怡房地产开发有限公司	厚街镇	85832206	房地产开发经营
东莞市中信康华房地产开发有限公司	南城街道	22482388	房地产开发
东莞市中惠香樟绿洲房地产开发	樟木头镇	22360398	房地产开发
东莞市捷利物业投资有限公司	虎门镇	85124488	房地产开发经营
东莞市广源房地产开发有限公司	寮步镇	22800222	房地产开发经营
中信华南东莞有限公司	东城街道	22482388	房地产开发
东莞市同方房地产开发有限公司	东城街道	22483998	房地产开发
东莞市鼎峰房地产开发有限公司	企石镇	86666016	房地产开发
广东宏远集团房地产开发有限公司	南城街道		城市综合开发
东莞市长佳长安花园开发有限公司	长安镇	85338777	房地产开发
东莞市聚龙物业投资发展有限公司	石龙镇	86116908	物业投资
东莞市东田丽园房地产开发有限公司	常平镇	83989677	开发经营
东莞市黄河集团房地产开发有限公司	虎门镇	85222222	实业投资
东莞市丰泰华园山庄建造有限公司	虎门镇	85188896	房地产开发
东莞市碧水天源物业有限公司	大朗镇	83131976	房地产开发
东莞市致富物业管理有限公司	沙田镇	88868218	物业管理
东莞市麻涌镇房地产开发公司	麻涌镇	88233288	房地产开发经营
东莞市新世纪科教拓展有限公司	凤岗镇	87555552	房地产活动
东莞市星河传说商住区有限公司	东城街道	22031328	房地产开发
东莞市富麟实业有限公司	凤岗镇	87568889	房地产开发
东莞市永江集团有限公司	凤岗镇	87840888	实业投资
东莞市聚豪名轩商住开发有限公司	石龙镇	86088001	房地产投资
东莞市万科物业服务有限公司	莞城街道	88013333	物业管理
东莞市玉泉投资开发有限公司	凤岗镇	87508188	土地开发
东莞市万科阳光房地产开发有限公司	常平镇	83916852	房地产经营
东莞市盈丰房地产开发有限公司	厚街镇	85873818	房地产开发
东莞市松山湖房地产有限公司	松山湖	22892336	房地产开发
东莞市新世纪房地产有限公司	大朗镇	88237666	房地产开发
东莞市龙城房地产开发有限公司	石龙镇	86111268	房地产开发
东莞市新世纪房地产开发有限公司(领居)	大岭山镇	83053693	房地产开发
东莞市樟木头镇物业管理公司	樟木头镇	87713517	物业管理
东莞市幸福花苑开发有限公司	南城街道	23129388	项目开发经营
东莞市世海房地产开发有限公司	东坑镇	22498499	房地产开发
东莞市新世纪润城实业投资有限公司	塘厦镇	88991899	房地产开发
东莞市莞都可苑房地产开发有限公司	中堂镇	22211908	房地产开发
东莞市利丰房地产投资有限公司	石排镇	86555829	房地产开发
东莞市松山居置业有限公司	松山湖	22303989	房地产开发
中信华南(集团)东莞有限公司	东城街道	22482388	房地产开发
东莞市康联房地产开发有限公司	厚街镇	85753088	房地产开发
东莞市佳驹实业有限公司	南城街道	22679733	房地产开发

1-4 续表 33

(2011年)

单位名称	所属镇街	联系电话	主要产品（或服务）
东莞市碧湖花园有限公司	常平镇	83981809	房地产开发经营
东莞市佳兆业房地产开发有限公司	南城街道	22801111	房地产开发
东莞市汇盈豪苑房地产开发有限公司	厚街镇	22388601	房地产开发
东莞市铭可达商住中心开发有限公司	莞城街道	22309112	房地产开发
东莞市大绿地房地产开发有限公司	清溪镇	87388810	房地产开发
东莞市凯东实业投资有限公司	大岭山镇	85609718	实业投资
东莞市阳光海岸实业有限公司	虎门镇	81615333	房地产开发
东莞市新世纪怡岛花园商住开发有限公司	道滘镇	88638888	房地业开发
东莞市山水雅居房地产开发有限公司	常平镇	82206266	房地产开发经营
东莞市合盛房地产开发有限公司	虎门镇	85705222	房地产开发
广东三正集团有限公司	桥头镇	82470333	房地产开发
东莞市清华居建造有限公司	南城街道	23121662	房地产开发
东莞市广盈服务有限公司企石分公司	企石镇	86666698	房屋物业租赁、咨询
东莞市山语湖房地产投资有限公司	常平镇	22032016	房地产开发
东莞市星城国际房地产开发有限公司	寮步镇	26276301	房地产开发
东莞市盈盛房地产开发有限公司	石龙镇	22801111	房地产开发
东莞市新通实业投资有限公司	南城街道	23013547	房地产开发
东莞市华凯帝庭园开发建造有限公司	东城街道	22880098	房地产开发
东莞市凯沣房地产策划有限公司	东城街道	23110366	房地产市场调查
东莞市罗马假日房地产开发有限公司	寮步镇	22319555	房地产开发
东莞市中信广场建造有限公司	东城街道	23282506	房地产开发
东莞市常平房地产开发实业公司	常平镇	83334075	房地产开发
东莞市松湖居置业有限公司	松山湖	23013547	房地产开发
东莞市新万房地产开发有限公司	塘厦镇	25568039	房地产开发
东莞市中润投资实业有限公司	万江街道	28631999	房地产开发
东莞市金贤房地产开发有限公司	厚街镇	85936698	房地产开发
东莞市雍景香江房地产开发有限	洪梅镇	88432228	房地产开发经营
东莞市光大房地产开发有限公司	东城街道	22986086	房地产开发
东莞市中惠沁林山庄房地产开发有限公司	大岭山镇	83716088	实业项目开发投资
东莞市三正房地产开发有限公司	塘厦镇	87299333	房地产开发
东莞市龙泉房地产开发有限公司长安商业广场项目	长安镇	85112323	房地产开发
东莞市高田房地产开发有限公司	东城街道	22386908	房地产开发
东莞市深业房地产有限公司	南城街道	88999686	房地产开发
东莞市石龙镇房地产公司	石龙镇	86116822	镇域房地产监管
东莞市陶然居房地产开发有限公司	长安镇	85533868	房地产开发
东莞市丰泰建设房地产有限公司(丰泰城)	寮步镇	85188701	房地产开发
东莞市德洲房地产开发有限公司	塘厦镇	82093666	房地产开发
东莞市新世纪明上居商住开发有限公司	大朗镇	23013547	房地产开发
东莞市神鹰塑料有限公司	常平镇	86991888	物业管理
东莞市精英世家建造有限公司	南城街道	22413668	房地产开发
东莞市丰盛房地产开发有限公司	南城街道	23183800	房地产开发经营
东莞市瀚森投资集团有限公司	莞城街道	22333488	房地产开发
东莞市阳龙房地产有限公司	长安镇	82289999	房地产开发
东莞市田禾房地产投资有限公司	莞城街道	23030787	房地产开发
东莞市篁城开发有限公司	南城街道	22113388	房地产开发
东莞市新世纪房地产开发有限公司	东城街道	22382251	房地产开发

1-4 续表 34

(2011年)

单位名称	所属镇街	联系电话	主要产品（或服务）
东莞市长银房地产开发有限公司	塘厦镇	87287398	房地产开发经营
东莞市深城投实业投资有限公司	万江街道	23185306	物业投资
东莞市东城区房地产开发公司新	东城街道	22470531	房地产开发
东莞市东城区房地产开发公司	东城街道	22483788	房地产开发
东莞市盈锋房地产开发有限公司	莞城街道	22495555	房地产开发
东莞市桃源商住建造有限公司	松山湖	22986086	房地产开发
东莞市富阳房地产开发有限公司	南城街道	22986888	房地产开发
东莞市塘盛房地产开发有限公司	塘厦镇	87917238	房地产开发
东莞宏远工业区股份有限公司	南城街道	22414228	开发经营工业区
商务服务业			
东莞市虎门城郊供电公司	虎门镇	85527786	电力供应管理
东莞市合鑫膳食管理服务有限公司	东城街道	23111916	膳食管理
东莞市宏图工业开发公司	南城街道	22415322	土地开发
东莞市石龙镇西湖股份经济联合社	石龙镇	86113078	合作社经济管理
东莞市长安镇咸西经济联合社	长安镇	85533868	合作社经济管理
东莞市长安镇综合市场	长安镇	85535310	农贸市场管理
东莞市国际旅行社有限公司	莞城街道	22458168	旅行社
东莞市鸿信实业有限公司	东坑镇	83383786	实业投资
城区资产办	莞城街道	22102722	政府内资产物业管理
东莞市粤龙物业发展有限公司	石龙镇	86181222	企业管理咨询
东莞市桥头供电公司	桥头镇	83341212	电力供应
东莞市沙田对外经济开发总公司	沙田镇	88689966	对外资用地办理立项
东莞市家宝园林绿化有限公司	厚街镇	85088699	商务服务
东莞市盈丰报关服务有限公司	寮步镇	81100932	代理报关服务
东莞市瑞中会计税务服务有限公司石碣分公司	石碣镇	81812200	代理记帐
东莞市山凉劳务派遣有限公司	桥头镇	82366539	劳务派遣服务
东莞市瑞翔旅行社有限公司	东城街道	88996666	旅游服务
广东华强三洋集团有限公司	塘厦镇	87728041	投资、管理属下企业
东莞市凯信知识产权代理有限公司	莞城街道		商标申请代理
东莞市永特利实业投资有限公司	高埗镇	88878778	租赁和商务服务
东莞市信鸿实业投资有限公司	南城街道	22408991	商务服务
东莞市华科防水补漏工程服务有限公司	道滘镇		防水补漏工程服务
富盈集团有限公司	厚街镇	81568888	综合
东莞市南城区资产经营管理有限公司	南城街道	22417250	管理区属资产
东莞市虎门镇路东经济联合社	虎门镇	85567032	合作经济管理
东莞市中堂供电公司	中堂镇	88893288	电力供应
东莞市虎门镇资产经营管理有限公司	虎门镇	85522409	镇属资产产权的管理
东莞市大朗镇长塘股份经济联合社	大朗镇	83318030	合作社经济管理
东莞市南枫佳誉保险代理有限公司	南城街道	22995003	代理保险产品
东莞市桥头镇资产经营管理有限公司	桥头镇	83342135	企业管理服务
东莞市企石振华开发总公司	企石镇	86765688	办理外引内联企业的咨询洽谈
东莞市望牛墩资产经营管理有限公司	望牛墩镇	88853008	镇属资产产权管理
东莞市虎门镇虎门寨股份经济联合社	虎门镇	85509032	合作经济管理
东莞市清溪镇经济联合总社	清溪镇	87733292	咨询服务
上沙股份经济联合社	长安镇	85547208	合作社经济管理
东莞市长安镇沙头经济联合社	长安镇	85544888	经济管理

1-4 续表 35

(2011年)

单位名称	所属镇街	联系电话	主要产品（或服务）
东莞市松山湖工业发展有限公司	松山湖	22891044	房产管理
东莞市凤岗镇资产经营有限公司	凤岗镇	87759398	资产管理
东莞市常平镇资产经营管理有限公司	常平镇	83331431	企业资产管理
东莞市清溪供电公司	清溪镇	87314148	电力供应
东莞市虎门名铺城	虎门镇	85113665	商铺管理
东莞市清溪对外经济发展有限公司	清溪镇	87732058	外引内联企业咨询
东莞市中国旅行社有限公司	南城街道	22218288	旅游服务
东莞市智能市场管理服务有限公司	清溪镇	87738170	市场管理
东莞市丰华集团有限公司	莞城街道	22629333	酒店投资
东莞市华源集团有限公司	厚街镇	85928888	酒店管理
东莞市石碣镇桔洲股份经济联合社	石碣镇	86332030	经联社经济管理
东莞市建华贸易有限公司	清溪镇	87733209	日用品
东莞市塘厦镇资产经营有限公司	塘厦镇	82087792	资产经营管理
东莞市寮步经济发展总公司	寮步镇	83328387	经济贸易咨询
东莞市沙田经济发展总公司	沙田镇	88861003	机构商务代理服务
东莞市大朗供电公司	大朗镇	83316187	电力供应管理
东莞市黄江供电公司	黄江镇	83361290	电力供应管理
东莞市大莹物业管理有限公司	虎门镇	85151566	市场管理
东莞市天纬企业管理咨询服务有限公司	莞城街道	22482678	劳务派遣
东莞市东坑镇经济联合总社	东坑镇	83889698	企业管理机构
东莞市东城供电公司	东城街道	22669826	电力供应管理
东莞市中之进出口有限公司	南城街道	23182111	自营和代理各类商品和技术的进出口
东莞市谢岗供电公司	谢岗镇	87761224	电力供应管理
东莞市横沥镇经济联合总社	横沥镇	83717663	企业管理咨询
东莞市方达集团有限公司	长安镇	85330098	兴办实业
东莞市长安镇霄边经济联合社	长安镇	81882222	合作社经济管理
东莞市常平镇土塘股份经济联合社	常平镇	83553233	合作社经济管理
东莞市樟木头资产经营管理有限公司	樟木头镇	87188978	镇属资产产权管理
广东宏远集团有限公司	南城街道	22414228	经营和代理各类商品的进出口业务
东莞市长安镇锦厦经济联合社	长安镇	85301960	企业管理
东莞市桥头镇田新股份经济联合社	桥头镇	83341032	合作社经济管理
东莞市石碣镇经济发展总公司	石碣镇	86631048	进出口服务
东莞市寮步镇横坑股份经济联合社	寮步镇	83301024	企业管理服务
东莞市桥头镇邓屋股份经济联合社	桥头镇	83341073	合作社经济管理
东莞市南城区工业发展公司	南城街道	22415322	办理开办厂场业务
东莞市塘厦镇林村股份经济联合社	塘厦镇	87721501	企业管理咨询
东莞市桥头镇桥头股份经济联合社	桥头镇	83342308	合作经济管理
东莞市虎门镇北栅经济联合社	虎门镇	85551481	资产管理
东莞市厚街经济发展总公司	厚街镇	85990333	物业租赁
东莞市大岭山供电公司	大岭山镇	83350287	电力供应管理
东莞市万江区资产经营管理有限公司	万江街道	22273273	投资与资产管理
东莞市集源资产经营管理有限公司	黄江镇	83633322	出租房屋服务
东莞康辉国际旅行社有限公司	莞城街道	22001168	国内旅游服务
东莞市长安供电公司	长安镇	85313828	电力供应管理
东莞市东城实业发展总公司	东城街道	22331385	实业投资
东莞市桥光实业集团公司	桥头镇	83341012	咨询业务

1-4　续表 36

(2011年)

单位名称	所属镇街	联系电话	主要产品（或服务）
东莞市景鸿物业管理有限公司	莞城街道	22381011	劳务派遣
东莞市新远高速公路发展有限公司	东城街道	22083200	投资开发高速公路网
东莞市明煜管理咨询有限公司	南城街道	22408845	企业管理服务
东莞市福临门企业咨询服务有限公司	石碣镇	86330555	代办企业登记
东莞市塘厦供电公司	塘厦镇	87727425	电力供应管理
东莞市大岭山镇资产经营管理有限公司	大岭山镇	85788362	经济管理
东莞市凤岗供电公司	凤岗镇	87756877	电力供应
东莞市群策外商投资服务有限公司	南城街道	22813652	企业登记代理咨询服务
东莞市昌明实业有限公司	厚街镇	85598888	实业投资
东莞市石排供电公司	石排镇	86550387	电力供应
东莞市虎门镇南栅股份经济联合社	虎门镇	85561938	合作社经济管理
东莞市石龙粤龙实业公司	石龙镇	86181222	电机、金属机械
东莞市江南市场经营管理有限公司	中堂镇	88183710	市场管理服务
东莞市石碣镇发展实业公司	石碣镇	86631030	企业咨询
东莞市松山湖控股有限公司	松山湖	22898178	第一产业投资
东莞市清溪经济发展公司	清溪镇	87366293	企业管理服务
东莞市南城供电公司	南城街道	22414348	电力供应管理
东莞市高埗供电公司	高埗镇	88781518	电力供应管理
东莞市虎门镇龙眼股份经济联合社	虎门镇	85553988	投资和资产投资
东莞市万江供电公司	万江街道	22788971	电力供应管理
东莞市东城资产经营管理有限公司	东城街道	22331385	资产管理
东莞市麻涌镇经济发展总公司	麻涌镇	88239336	企业管理服务
东莞市厚街供电公司	厚街镇	85585368	电力供应管理
东莞市长安镇长实发展总公司	长安镇	85310368	企业管理
广东智通人才连锁股份有限公司	莞城街道	87078157	人才信息咨询服务
东莞市桥头镇石水口股份经济联合社	桥头镇	83428823	企业管理咨询
东莞市中堂资产经营管理有限公司	中堂镇	88811116	镇属资产经营管理
东莞市凤岗镇雁田经济联合社	凤岗镇	87771631	合作社经济管理
东莞市光华医院有限公司	寮步镇	22668152	医疗卫生
东莞市电化实业集团公司	莞城街道	22461466	实业投资
东莞市中堂镇潢涌股份经济联合社	中堂镇	88881002	合作社经济管理
东莞市寮步供电公司	寮步镇	81113608	电力供应
研究与试验发展			
东莞市万科建筑技术研究有限公司	松山湖	22890188	建筑技术开发
专业技术服务业			
东莞市绿宝石景观建造有限公司洪梅分公司	洪梅镇	22403567	专业技术服务
东莞市清溪工业开发有限公司	清溪镇	87732058	工业开发
东莞市公路桥梁开发建设总公司	东城街道	22083269	规划建设公路桥梁
科技交流和推广服务业			
东莞市方达环宇环保科技有限公司	长安镇	89998656	环保技术的开发转让服务培训
公共设施管理业			
东莞市松山湖公用事业有限公司	松山湖	23306078	园林绿化维护
居民服务业			
东莞市东保押运有限公司	寮步镇	83528016	贵重物品押运

1-4　续表 37

(2011年)

单位名称	所属镇街	联系电话	主要产品（或服务）
东莞市大朗天域康体中心	大朗镇		公共浴室（桑拿）
东莞市大华沐足保健中心	莞城街道	23010766	足浴保健
其他服务业			
东莞市虎门大宁企业发展公司	虎门镇	85553188	办理开办厂场业务
广州志诚科技工程服务有限公司东莞凤岗分公司	凤岗镇		服务
（香港）弘阳国际贸易有限公司东莞代表处	虎门镇		代表处
东莞市桥供废品回收有限公司	桥头镇	83341037	废旧物资回收
东莞市塘厦林村工业发展公司	塘厦镇	87722262	外引内联企业的咨询及洽谈
东莞市酷极动漫设计有限公司	东城街道	23663340	动漫设计
教育			
东莞市东华高级中学	东城街道	22637808	普通高中教育
东莞市黄江镇中心小学	黄江镇	83601630	初等教育
东莞市东华初级中学	东城街道	22659333	初中教育
东莞市北师大翰林实验学校	万江街道	22702988	高中教育
东莞市新民实业投资有限公司	石碣镇	86638529	教育投资
东莞市第一中学	东城街道	22666280	高中教育
东莞市通圣机动车驾驶员培训有限公司	高埗镇		职业技能培训
东莞市东华小学	东城街道	22659823	初等教育
东莞市先进电脑横机技术推广中心	常平镇	89851116	咨询与指导
卫生			
东莞市黄江医院	黄江镇	83636323	综合医院
东莞市南城医院	南城街道	22415129	医疗服务
东莞市长安医院	长安镇	85531104	医疗
东莞广济医院	凤岗镇	87866333	医疗服务
东莞康华医院有限公司	南城街道	22823018	医疗事业服务
东莞市茶山医院	茶山镇	86642066	基本医疗
东莞东华医院有限公司	东城街道	22333333	医疗服务
东莞市樟木头镇石新医院	樟木头镇	87710449	医疗服务
东莞市桥头医院	桥头镇	81037663	医疗护理、保健服务
东莞市寮步医院	寮步镇	83321545	医疗卫生
东莞市东坑医院	东坑镇	83381754	医院服务
东莞市厚街医院	厚街镇	81529815	综合医疗
东莞市东城医院	东城街道	22213790	综合医院
东莞市太平人民医院	虎门镇	85111525	医疗服务
东莞市石龙博爱医院	石龙镇	86118320	综合医院
东莞市石排医院	石排镇	86556333	诊疗
东莞市企石医院	企石镇	86661371	医疗、保健
东莞市石龙人民医院	石龙镇	81368808	医疗、保健
东莞市凤岗医院	凤岗镇	87510815	综合医院
新闻出版业			
东莞日报社	南城街道	23126688	报纸采写编
娱乐业			
东莞市滨河游乐有限公司	樟木头镇		体育、娱乐

1-5 营业收入超5000万元的外资企业（2011年）

Foreign-funded Enterprises with Business Revenue over RMB 50 Million (2011)

单位名称	所属镇街	联系电话	主要产品（或服务）
农副食品加工业			
东莞兴业生物科技有限公司	东城街道	22652130	预混合配合饲料
金钱饲料(东莞)有限公司	麻涌镇	26898096	饲料
东莞益海嘉里粮油食品工业有限公司	麻涌镇	88238760	饲料蛋白
东莞市飞亚达益富可华南油脂有限公司	麻涌镇	88230055	棕榈油
东莞欧陆食品有限公司	长安镇	86246898	西式肉类食品
东莞卡尔吉蛋白饲料有限公司	麻涌镇	88236732	豆油
统一嘉吉(东莞)饲料蛋白科技有限公司	麻涌镇	88225888	豆油
东莞顶志食品有限公司	麻涌镇	88238262	芝麻油
东莞光华饲料有限公司	中堂镇	88817756	猪饲料
中粮新沙粮油工业(东莞)有限公司	麻涌镇	88825601	豆油
食品制造业			
东莞四洲肉类制品有限公司	高埗镇	81339710	禽类罐头
东莞荣华饼家有限公司	石碣镇	86633692	月饼
东莞锦泰食品有限公司	南城街道	22400818	饼干
广东太阳神集团有限公司	黄江镇	83621288	猴头菇胃肠口服液
爱兰特糖果（东莞）有限公司	常平镇	83552285	糖果
华嘉食品有限公司	南城街道	22464101	饼干
东莞徐记食品有限公司	东城街道	22259888	糖果
东莞领驰食品有限公司	樟木头镇	82127116	食品、饮料
百利佳糖果玩具礼品(东莞)有限公司	石排镇	86533119	糖果玩具
东莞万好食品有限公司	横沥镇	81016222	点心、食品
东莞福满多食品有限公司	麻涌镇	88230290	粮食制品
饮料制造业			
东莞捷荣食品有限公司	横沥镇	88971111	咖啡
广东加多宝饮料食品有限公司	长安镇	85331688	罐装王老吉
东莞雀巢有限公司	南城街道	22404088	速溶咖啡
东莞日之泉蒸馏水有限公司	中堂镇	88815015	蒸馏水
金威啤酒(东莞)有限公司	松山湖	22898999	啤酒
华润雪花啤酒广东有限公司	东城街道	88772999	啤酒
东莞石龙津威饮料食品有限公司	石龙镇	86625388	葡锌乳酸菌饮料
可口可乐装瓶商生产(东莞)有限公司	南城街道	22401678	茶饮料及果汁饮料
纺织业			
东莞联丰巨川纤维膊棉有限公司	黄江镇	86914666	人造纤维制品
东莞亿城服装有限公司	长安镇	85311107	纺织品、服装
东莞永丰盛纺织有限公司	寮步镇	83328005	纺织
东莞三江汇聚服装有限公司	横沥镇	83721616	服装
东莞如成服装有限公司	虎门镇	88709991	针织服装
东莞联达毛纺有限公司	横沥镇	83374688	毛纺织品
东莞茶山永联织造厂	茶山镇	88655088	婴儿服装
东莞美商制衣有限公司	南城街道	22902688	服装
东莞奥康德思宏针织品有限公司	常平镇	83828858	针织毛衣
东莞绰荣制衣有限公司	常平镇	83936788	针梳织服装
东莞泉泰服饰有限公司	凤岗镇	86808062	服装
东莞泰富服装有限公司	道滘镇	88830780	服装

1-5　续表 1

(2011年)

单位名称	所属镇街	联系电话	主要产品（或服务）
东莞虎门科艺纺织印花有限公司	虎门镇	85561798	丝绸印花
东莞沙田丽海纺织印染有限公司	沙田镇	88866583	印染布
东莞德永佳纺织制衣有限公司	麻涌镇	88821738	棉针织染整布
东莞嘉鹏纺织有限公司	麻涌镇	88826666	纺织品
东莞南大时装针织有限公司	樟木头镇	87782971	针织毛衣
东莞茶山增埗成衣一厂	茶山镇	86869888	服装
东莞裕源织染有限公司	沙田镇	88863433	针织色布
东莞百和织造有限公司	沙田镇	88862371	粘扣带
东莞联庆纺织有限公司	企石镇	86784606	棉、化纤纺织
东莞艺正制衣洗水有限公司	中堂镇	88120818	针织服装
东莞邦西纺织制衣有限公司	茶山镇	88655083	针织服装
东莞厚宏制衣有限公司	桥头镇	83341382	针织服装
广东联发毛纺织有限公司	东城街道	22262232	纺织
东莞福安纺织印染有限公司	长安镇	85532318	棉针织折用纱线
东莞乐升植绒有限公司	企石镇	86668899	棉、化纤印染
东莞润信弹性织物有限公司	厚街镇	85593366	弹性花边带
东莞光晖针织有限公司	大朗镇	83112278	针织毛衣
东莞东美线业有限公司	道滘镇	88339333	缝纫线、涤纶短纤维线
东莞百宏实业有限公司	沙田镇	88869615	鞋材、运动用品、织带
东莞绰豪制衣有限公司	长安镇	85317168	服装
东莞欣意医疗保健制品厂	黄江镇	83361381	医疗用品
东莞富达染厂有限公司	洪梅镇	88844490	棉针织色布
得福(东莞)制衣有限公司	中堂镇		服装
东莞中玉服装有限公司	常平镇	86997999	纺织
海杰制衣（东莞）有限公司	虎门镇	85237905	针梳织服装
东莞永联弹力织物有限公司	望牛墩镇	88852801	橡根带
东莞勤达针织制衣有限公司	虎门镇	85013599	针织成品
东莞鸿福织造有限公司	虎门镇	85268838	服装
东莞怡力制衣有限公司	横沥镇	81011666	服装
东莞合迅服装设计有限公司	长安镇	86244388	针织化纤内衣
东莞菲力制衣有限公司	高埗镇	88786698	服装
东莞精致针织有限公司	常平镇	86836260	服装
东莞升佳纺织有限公司	沙田镇	88860306	布匹染整
沛恒制衣(东莞)有限公司	石龙镇	86617980	内衣
东莞念辉家饰用品有限公司	常平镇	83392366	桌巾
东莞达生制衣有限公司	常平镇	83919226	泳衣
东莞福泰整染有限公司	道滘镇	88834068	布料整染
东莞世丽纺织有限公司	洪梅镇	88843806	全棉针织色布
东莞富阳针织有限公司	大朗镇	88603688	毛衣
东莞广成线业有限公司	长安镇	85428511	织线产品
东莞宏大制衣有限公司	高埗镇	88468668	针织服装
东莞胜丰针织有限公司	高埗镇	88879742	纺织服装
东莞三骏时装有限公司	长安镇	85326098	针梳织服装
东莞励进制衣有限公司	厚街镇	85822228	全棉男装针织长袖T恤
东莞迅捷环球制衣有限公司	长安镇	85441918	服装

1-5　续表 2

(2011年)

单位名称	所属镇街	联系电话	主要产品（或服务）
东莞泰广玻璃纤维有限公司	道滘镇	88384898	方格布
东莞永达利纺织有限公司	厚街镇	85588751	全棉针织坯布
东莞德福制衣有限公司	常平镇	83335273	毛衣针织
东莞宏宇制衣有限公司	高埗镇	88462208	针织服装
东莞联泰制衣有限公司	凤岗镇	86808117	服装
东莞澳思制衣有限公司	常平镇	83332225	毛衣及针梭织服装
东莞东兴商标织绣有限公司	长安镇	85545888	商标
东莞福怡服装有限公司	沙田镇	88666620	服装
东莞时利制衣有限公司	虎门镇	85709662	服装
东莞励发制衣厂	厚街镇	85822228	全棉男装针织长袖T恤
东莞超盈纺织有限公司	麻涌镇	88231808	双拉布
东莞福井制衣有限公司	长安镇	85440871	服装
东莞福泉制衣有限公司	沙田镇	88666698	棉针织服装
东莞洋得服饰有限公司	寮步镇	83288888	手套
宏达纺织（东莞）有限公司	塘厦镇	87982238	灯芯绒坯布、全棉坯布
东莞聚龙制衣有限公司	长安镇	85538846	服装
东莞市定佳针织服装有限公司	寮步镇	82873688	毛织加工
东莞宝达日用品制造有限公司	大朗镇	83311690	布手套
东莞茂志针织有限公司	大朗镇	83209838	针织服装
东莞润达弹性织造有限公司	厚街镇	85593366	织带
东莞业基工业有限公司	常平镇	83915577	服装
东莞新兴织造厂有限公司	虎门镇	85562795	毛染整精加工
东莞利来远东针织有限公司	南城街道	22851333	服装
东莞明海整染厂有限公司	道滘镇	38831553	染色布
东莞碳盈复合材料有限公司	塘厦镇	82076301	炭纤维布
东莞凯威针织制衣有限公司	常平镇	86830510	布料服装
东莞立春纺织有限公司	沙田镇	88862325	粘扣带
东莞丰泰制衣有限公司	茶山镇	86179848	纺织服装
东莞晶苑毛织制衣有限公司	常平镇	83982212	纺织品
东莞富山纺织漂染有限公司	洪梅镇	88841755	漂染针织布、梳织布
东莞同广纺织品有限公司	厚街镇	85933301	针织胚布
东莞海星服装有限公司	长安镇	85300702	服装
东莞富坊制衣有限公司	虎门镇	85159988	针织服装
东莞市远梦家用纺织品有限公司	厚街镇	85991010	床上用品
纺织服装、鞋、帽制造业			
东莞高埗高胜制衣厂	高埗镇	88876660	内衣
东莞上杰鞋业有限公司	长安镇	81663185	鞋
东莞通盈纺织制衣有限公司	中堂镇	88188015	梳织布
东莞美商新力鞋业有限公司	寮步镇	83261991	运动鞋
东莞盈富制衣有限公司	道滘镇	88838386	男装衬衫
东莞宝升制衣有限公司	长安镇	85549971	服装
东莞通威服装有限公司	凤岗镇	86808613	成衣
联业制衣（东莞）有限公司	清溪镇	87738280	衬衫西裤
东莞冠丽时装有限公司	石碣镇	86016001	服装
东莞永嘉盛针织有限公司	南城街道	22407788	纺织毛衣

1-5 续表 3

(2011年)

单位名称	所属镇街	联系电话	主要产品（或服务）
东莞启松服装有限公司	塘厦镇	87722174	服装
东莞众信制衣有限公司	道滘镇	88318125	服装
东莞达利盛时装有限公司	凤岗镇	87756188	服装
东莞天翔制衣有限公司	万江街道	88751099	梳织针织服装
东莞益豪时装有限公司	石龙镇	86618323	服装
东莞忆凯制衣有限公司	大朗镇	83185898	全棉婴儿毛衣
乐活制衣（东莞）有限公司	横沥镇	83729200	服装
东莞四海时装有限公司	虎门镇	85113514	服装
东莞星华制衣有限公司	万江街道	22179181	梳织服装
东莞中联定型厂有限公司	虎门镇	88921118	针织布定型
东莞海琪运动服装有限公司	虎门镇	85701202	化纤成人运动装
东莞奇兴服装有限公司	东坑镇	83382968	西装
东莞市金巴伦服装有限公司	高埗镇	88738843	制衣
东莞润田服装工艺制品有限公司	石碣镇	86633899	儿童玩具
东莞高芬制衣有限公司	高埗镇	88876660	内衣
东莞市小猪班纳服饰有限公司	樟木头镇	87125086	针织服装
东莞大明制衣有限公司	虎门镇	85192121	服装
东莞福百威制衣有限公司	企石镇	86667111	服装
东莞昱胜鞋业有限公司	沙田镇	88808168	皮鞋
东莞高文内衣制品有限公司	横沥镇	83792939	海棉、脯棉
智诚国际东莞实业有限公司	万江街道	23175238	服装
东莞亮智服装有限公司	寮步镇	83305288	皮革服装
东莞东浩制衣有限公司	东城街道	22265009	服装
东莞胜德织造有限公司	高埗镇	88738293	毛织品
联亚制衣(东莞)有限公司	凤岗镇	82081818	梭织服装
东莞市东方叶杨实业有限公司	东城街道	22634282	羊绒服装
东莞高业制衣有限公司	万江街道	22784602	服装
东莞怡信针织有限公司	常平镇	86836268	服装
东莞成笑服装有限公司	高埗镇	88709991	服装
皮革、毛皮、羽毛(绒)及其制品业			
东莞博励图鞋业有限公司	寮步镇	83266168	女鞋
东莞龙门皮箱有限公司	虎门镇	88625888	箱包
东莞朝冠鞋业有限公司	厚街镇	85588915	皮鞋
东莞瑞邦鞋业有限公司	横沥镇	83712518	女装皮鞋
东莞瑞恩鞋业有限公司	横沥镇	83733253	女装皮鞋
东莞佳泰鞋业有限公司	寮步镇	83213089	皮鞋
东莞精博旅行用品有限公司	东坑镇	83695168	箱包
东莞合雄鞋业有限公司	清溪镇	87734666	人造皮男鞋
东莞金莹鞋业有限公司	厚街镇	85900471	皮鞋
东莞麦斯鞋业有限公司	横沥镇	83375950	皮鞋
东莞福聚皮革有限公司	道滘镇	88326331	皮革鞣制加工
东莞市汉皇鞋业有限公司	横沥镇	83790019	鞋
东莞卫仕皮具有限公司	道滘镇	88386228	皮具
威华(东莞)鞋业有限公司	清溪镇	86816868	鞋
东莞贰发毛绒有限公司	樟木头镇	87718080	静电毛绒

1-5 续表 4

(2011年)

单位名称	所属镇街	联系电话	主要产品（或服务）
东莞奥天奴皮草服装有限公司	企石镇	86786993	皮草服装
东莞纬达皮革有限公司	洪梅镇	88841856	加工牛皮
东莞安阳鞋业有限公司	大朗镇	83318919	牛皮鞋
东莞忠利手袋有限公司	茶山镇	86486422	手袋
东莞昌健鞋业有限公司	厚街镇	85581860	鞋
东莞韦旭鞋业有限公司	长安镇	85321666	皮鞋
东莞欧菲雅有限公司	望牛墩镇	88569688	真皮手袋
东莞德州鞋业有限公司	长安镇	85531584	鞋
东莞力凯鞋业制造有限公司	厚街镇	85583101	运动鞋
东莞南友运动用品有限公司	寮步镇	83268325	运动用品
东莞永信鞋业有限公司	厚街镇	85918310	运动鞋
东莞协和鞋业有限公司	厚街镇	85595058	人造革童鞋
东莞南华户外用品有限公司	洪梅镇	88849281	旅游背袋
东莞大正鞋业有限公司	厚街镇	88633888	鞋
东莞佳展手袋有限公司	高埗镇	88871735	手袋
东莞贯铨鞋业有限公司	寮步镇	83212208	皮鞋
东莞好利包袋制品有限公司	塘厦镇	87906032	钱包、手袋
新百丽鞋业（深圳）有限公司东莞分公司	虎门镇	85261438	皮鞋
东莞东禾鞋业有限公司	东城街道	22662588	鞋
东莞超丰手袋有限公司	东城街道	22627688	手袋
东莞朝代鞋业有限公司	厚街镇	85588915	皮鞋
东莞丽宝鞋业有限公司	道滘镇	86308999	皮鞋
安迈特提箱(东莞)有限公司	大岭山镇	83356051	旅行箱包
东莞大邦鞋业有限公司	石排镇	23066010	鞋
东莞泰亿袋业有限公司	凤岗镇	87862228	皮箱
东莞茂德塑胶制品有限公司	虎门镇	85015628	塑胶制品
东莞星浩手袋有限公司	塘厦镇	87939288	手袋
东莞宏业制鞋有限公司	塘厦镇	86859812	运动鞋、皮鞋
东莞聚美手袋有限公司	长安镇	85374168	手袋
东莞建成鞋业有限公司	清溪镇	87734968	运动鞋
东莞时代皮具制品厂有限公司	厚街镇	85911900	手袋
东莞飞力达鞋业有限公司	寮步镇		女式皮鞋
东莞裕元制造厂	高埗镇	88874202	运动鞋
东莞诚达鞋业有限公司	沙田镇	88806888	休闲鞋
东莞黄江宝亮鞋材厂	黄江镇	83367386	PU人造皮
东莞澳利高太平洋手袋有限公司	常平镇	83824000	手袋
东莞永义鞋业有限公司	厚街镇	85918310	运动鞋
东莞恒辉鞋业有限公司	厚街镇	85594972	人造革运动鞋
东莞钜盛鞋业有限公司	寮步镇	83214345	皮鞋
东莞莱得利皮具有限公司	虎门镇	85554590	皮具
东莞绿洲鞋业有限公司	厚街镇	85880975	鞋
东莞万鑫鞋业有限公司	南城街道	86226699	皮鞋
东莞高埗裕元制造厂第一分厂	高埗镇	88874202	鞋
东莞华南皮革有限公司	茶山镇	86642187	轻革
东莞环艺实业有限公司	东城街道	88755578	手袋

1-5　续表 5

(2011年)

单位名称	所属镇街	联系电话	主要产品（或服务）
东莞永盛鞋业有限公司	厚街镇	85918310	运动鞋
东莞市横沥瑞邦鞋厂	横沥镇	83712518	女装鞋
东莞富程鞋业有限公司	东城街道	22265418	休闲鞋
东莞台威运动用品有限公司	长安镇	85534587	运动鞋、滑板
东莞台昌鞋业有限公司	厚街镇	85980666	鞋
东莞颖龙皮件制品有限公司	高埗镇	88730366	皮箱
东莞汇博鞋业有限公司	厚街镇	85826256	鞋
东莞朗福皮鞋有限公司	谢岗镇	87761380	皮鞋
东莞瑞辉鞋业有限公司	东城街道	22656056	女装牛皮鞋
东莞惠丰鞋业有限公司	厚街镇	85589441	运动鞋
宏盛皮具(东莞)有限公司	东城街道	22665668	皮箱
东莞富华鞋业有限公司	高埗镇	88788166	鞋
东莞伯产合成皮革有限公司	麻涌镇	88820807	PU合成皮革
东莞邦荣鞋业有限公司	厚街镇	85835991	鞋
东莞永益鞋业有限公司	厚街镇	85825298	鞋
东莞雅威鞋业有限公司	塘厦镇	82061966	皮鞋
东莞爱莉莎皮具有限公司	沙田镇	88868969	皮箱、包袋
东莞台育鞋业有限公司	石碣镇	86323168	皮鞋
东莞祥昱鞋业有限公司	寮步镇	88906888	鞋
东莞兴昂鞋业有限公司	大岭山镇	85631888	鞋材和鞋
东莞市怡捷手袋有限公司	望牛墩镇	88569888	手袋
华台鞋业(东莞)有限公司	厚街镇	85917001	皮革鞋靴
东莞高埗彰元鞋材厂	高埗镇	88872837	鞋材
东莞巨辉皮具制品有限公司	厚街镇	89988988	皮具制品
东莞大田鞋业有限公司	清溪镇	87732488	皮鞋
东莞宝基鞋业制造有限公司	厚街镇	85582985	鞋
东莞利威鞋业有限公司	南城街道	22009999	鞋
东莞联运鞋业有限公司	寮步镇	83303350	鞋
东莞泽荣箱包有限公司	寮步镇	83228386	旅行袋
东莞钜旺鞋业有限公司	东城街道	22251840	皮鞋
东莞绿扬鞋业有限公司	厚街镇	85876969	鞋以及鞋材
东莞市圣皇鞋材有限公司	厚街镇	81691206	鞋材
东莞宏国制鞋有限公司	虎门镇	85559400	皮鞋
东莞飞达鞋业有限公司	桥头镇	83344547	运动鞋、皮鞋
金进鞋业(东莞)有限公司	厚街镇	83085185	皮鞋
东莞威霖鞋业有限公司	厚街镇	83093999	运动鞋
东莞捷希皮革制品有限公司	横沥镇	83731678	手袋、鞋
东莞威腾皮革有限公司	厚街镇	85080096	皮革加工
圣马可(东莞)制革皮草有限公司	中堂镇	88124610	皮革
东莞兆成鞋业有限公司	厚街镇	81693311	皮鞋
东莞庆桦皮具有限公司	洪梅镇	88840700	皮具、手袋
东莞鼎力鞋业有限公司	厚街镇	85586102	运动鞋
东莞邦胜鞋业有限公司	厚街镇	85835990	鞋及鞋面
东莞嘉应制鞋有限公司	石碣镇	86631175	皮鞋
东莞华宝鞋业有限公司	南城街道	22908300	鞋

1-5 续表 6

(2011年)

单位名称	所属镇街	联系电话	主要产品（或服务）
东莞昌润皮革制品有限公司	望牛墩镇	88854078	皮革压花
东莞源亨皮具制品有限公司	大朗镇	83312003	手袋
东莞雄师皮具有限公司	长安镇	81663838	皮带
东莞诠立鞋业有限公司	厚街镇	85992586	女装便鞋
东莞旭冠皮具有限公司	东城街道	22251741	手袋
木材加工及木、竹、藤、棕、草制品业			
广东富林木业科技有限公司	常平镇	82202188	造板
亚泰(东莞)木业有限公司	大朗镇	83189105	木制礼品
东莞中城木业有限公司	道滘镇	88331338	装饰板
亿丰（东莞 ）制帘有限公司	常平镇	83988300	木制百叶窗
合和胶板（东莞）有限公司	道滘镇	88381666	装饰防火胶板
家具制造业			
东莞美时家具有限公司	塘厦镇	82031091	办公家具
东莞震兴家私有限公司	虎门镇	85551784	家具
东莞明昌家俱有限公司	沙田镇	88687918	金属家具
东莞志佳木业有限公司	黄江镇	83623301	家具
名隆家具东莞有限公司	大岭山镇	85615322	餐椅
东莞崧崴电子科技有限公司	大岭山镇	86979988	电子产品
东莞新雅美家具有限公司	常平镇	83021686	家具
东莞上丰家具有限公司	寮步镇	83221455	电视架
东莞瑞鸿家用品有限公司	洪梅镇	88385855	家具
世楷家具（东莞）有限公司	常平镇	82826209	文具
东莞柚隆木业有限公司	大岭山镇	83358666	木制家具
东莞承达木材制品有限公司	樟木头镇	87712640	木门
东莞振德家具有限公司	大岭山镇	83359011	木制家具
东莞宜庆家具有限公司	东城街道	22632705	家具
东莞宏展家具有限公司	桥头镇	83433133	家具
东莞大众木业有限公司	大岭山镇	85619320	木制品
东莞雄伟木业有限公司	大岭山镇	83352804	木制家具
宝钜(中国)儿童用品有限公司	清溪镇	87893231	婴儿手推车
东莞创达家具有限公司	桥头镇	83346406	咖啡桌
东莞朝阳家俱有限公司	黄江镇	83621515	家具
瑞丰木业(东莞)有限公司	清溪镇	86810555	家具
东莞威捷家具制品有限公司	塘厦镇	87943088	家具配件
东莞市汇杰木业有限公司	寮步镇	84574557	木桌
普林斯家具(东莞)有限公司	桥头镇	83455777	五金铁艺制品
东莞莱富家具有限公司	桥头镇	83432299	咖啡桌
东莞诺华家具有限公司	道滘镇	88313444	木制家具
东莞益新家私装饰有限公司	大岭山镇	85658912	木制家具
东莞乡源木器业有限公司	大岭山镇	83355145	家具
东莞永鹏家具有限公司	大岭山镇	85617546	家具
东莞超信金属有限公司	寮步镇	83320898	铁制家具
东莞欣鼎五金塑胶制品有限公司	清溪镇	87338888	沙滩桌椅
东莞米德兰五金塑胶制品有限公司	清溪镇	87312071	金属椅
东莞新兴钢具厂有限公司	高埗镇	88872618	办公家具

1-5 续表 7

(2011年)

单位名称	所属镇街	联系电话	主要产品（或服务）
东莞优创家具有限公司	大岭山镇	82780813	家具及配件
东莞琪创家具有限公司	黄江镇	83602123	家具
东莞天山金属家具有限公司	寮步镇	83305743	金属家具
东莞盛家家私制造有限公司	黄江镇	83663291	真皮沙发
东莞拓洋家具有限公司	桥头镇	83420011	木家具
东莞金石家具有限公司	大岭山镇	83355678	家具
东莞鑫固家具有限公司	大朗镇	83100350	五金家具
东莞巨千家具有限公司	石碣镇	86306168	铁制家具
东莞雅克沙发有限公司	厚街镇	85087789	沙发
东莞辰森木制品有限公司	黄江镇	83627078	木制家具
京木木制品（东莞）有限公司	石排镇	86516096	木制家具
东莞欧达家具有限公司	大岭山镇	83353408	沙发
东莞台升家具有限公司	大岭山镇	83352715	木制家具
东莞富运家私有限公司	大岭山镇	83055888	客厅家具
东莞康桥家具有限公司	大岭山镇	83054021	木制家具
东莞达艺家私有限公司	大岭山镇	83351335	木制家具
富鼎木业（东莞）有限公司	大岭山镇	83357899	家具
东莞宝峰金属制品有限公司	谢岗镇	87136078	铁制品
广东鼎盛家具有限公司	大岭山镇	83355351	沙发
东莞华新五金家具有限公司	东坑镇	83385013	五金制品
东莞世昌五金制品厂有限公司	长安镇	85537699	桌椅
东莞劲伟木业有限公司	长安镇	85414770	木器制品
东莞泰冠时钟有限公司	清溪镇	87730352	婴儿床
优先家具（东莞）有限公司	东城街道	22691495	家具
东莞大欣家具有限公司	东城街道	23160288	沙发
东莞益新家俬装饰有限公司	大岭山镇	83351335	家具
东莞汉平家具有限公司	清溪镇	86814555	木制家具
东莞超艺家具有限公司	凤岗镇	87555491	家具
瑞丰木业（东莞）有限公司三中分公司	清溪镇	87310180	家具
东莞爱迪家私有限公司	大岭山镇	83051999	书架
宇谦木器(东莞)有限公司	大岭山镇	85611718	木制家具
灿荣五金(东莞)有限公司	石碣镇	88488118	电视架
东莞铭晋家具有限公司	东城街道	22653362	木制家具
东莞三发钢木家具有限公司	大岭山镇	85622137	餐桌椅
东莞明辉家私有限公司	大岭山镇	83351928	木制家具
东莞汇川金属家具制造有限公司	谢岗镇	87767778	灯饰
东莞宏盛工艺制品有限公司	大岭山镇	83052999	木器工艺品
造纸及纸制品业			
东莞合意印刷有限公司	樟木头镇	87138221	纸制品
斯默菲石东包装(东莞)有限公司	道滘镇	81331300	瓦楞芯纸
伟兴纸业(东莞)有限公司	望牛墩镇	88559318	纸板
东莞进益纸品有限公司	凤岗镇	87758302	纸箱
东莞浩文纸品有限公司	樟木头镇	87198718	坑纸
东莞台聚包装有限公司	长安镇	85353369	纸盒
正隆（广东）纸业有限公司	厚街镇	82273288	纸板

1-5 续表 8

(2011年)

单位名称	所属镇街	联系电话	主要产品（或服务）
泓达纸业（东莞）有限公司	黄江镇	83633276	纸板
台华纸业（东莞）有限公司	塘厦镇	87885611	纸板
安姆科国际容器(广东)有限公司	寮步镇	83303343	纸制品
东莞金源研磨有限公司	大岭山镇	85618339	砂纸
东莞勤和纸品有限公司	长安镇	85544224	纸制品
东莞利通包装有限公司	南城街道	22408186	纸箱纸板
广源兴纸品（东莞）有限公司	大岭山镇	85631665	纸板
东莞中兴造纸厂有限公司	道滘镇	88323518	原色瓦楞芯纸
永发印务（东莞）有限公司	大岭山镇	85650898	包装装潢印刷品
广东理文造纸有限公司	洪梅镇	88432168	造纸
东莞地龙纸业有限公司	麻涌镇	88234888	牛卡纸
泓达包装纸品(东莞)有限公司	黄江镇	83360902	纸箱
东莞高绮印刷有限公司	大岭山镇	83355498	不干胶贴纸
东莞黄氏锦辉纸品有限公司	常平镇	82200732	纸板
东莞天兴纸业有限公司	虎门镇	85700268	纸品
东莞华成纸业有限公司	塘厦镇	87988111	纸制品
东莞群盛纸品有限公司	虎门镇	85558520	纸箱
东莞建晖纸业有限公司	中堂镇	88888363	涂布白板纸
东莞高昇纸品有限公司	塘厦镇	87983362	瓦楞纸品
东莞扬铭纸品有限公司	万江街道	22773061	纸张裁切
怡高纸品印刷（东莞）有限公司	大朗镇	83122188	纸箱
东莞顺诚纸品有限公司	中堂镇	88180388	纸板
光明（东莞）柯式印务纸品厂有限公司	虎门镇	85553368	彩盒
东莞龙成纸业有限公司	大朗镇	81125111	瓦楞纸板
东莞华南印刷有限公司	清溪镇	82098700	纸盒
新华柏纸品(东莞)有限公司	中堂镇	88110888	彩盒、纸类包装用品
东莞大华纸品有限公司	塘厦镇	87885611	瓦楞制品
东莞信盛纸品有限公司	长安镇	85537000	纸板
东莞瑞麒婴儿用品有限公司	石龙镇	88492212	纸尿裤
东莞佳木纸品有限公司	横沥镇	83375868	纸板
东莞大新彩印纸品有限公司	清溪镇	87736060	纸制品
永丰余纸业（东莞）有限公司	凤岗镇	87566668	高档纸
东莞万诚彩印包装有限公司	大岭山镇	83355238	印刷纸张、印刷包装
东莞声力电子制品有限公司	清溪镇	82013917	音乐贺卡
东莞骏佳纸业有限公司	樟木头镇	87712467	纸类制品
东莞明彩纸品有限公司	樟木头镇	87713003	纸制品
东莞正隆纸制品有限公司	黄江镇	83630032	纸箱
东莞顺盈纸业有限公司	中堂镇	88112123	瓦楞原纸
东莞长安昌众造纸有限公司	长安镇	85534024	铜板纸
东莞中世拓纸业有限公司	厚街镇	85033228	数码打印纸
东莞顺裕纸业有限公司	望牛墩镇	88560003	瓦楞纸
东莞大荣纸品有限公司	清溪镇	87734999	纸箱
坚碧包装制品东莞有限公司	大岭山镇	85780088	包装制品
东莞新丰印刷有限公司	凤岗镇	87142581	书、报、刊印刷
东莞谦泰纸业有限公司	长安镇	85537598	纸品

1-5 续表 9

(2011年)

单位名称	所属镇街	联系电话	主要产品（或服务）
东莞金洲纸业有限公司	中堂镇	88181288	瓦楞纸
东莞顺益纸品制造有限公司	茶山镇	86641635	纸箱
东莞寮步中大纸品有限公司	寮步镇	83211760	纸箱
东莞永联工艺包装有限公司	长安镇	86064889	纸制品
永固(东莞)纸业有限公司	塘厦镇	87932383	纸箱
东莞玖龙纸业有限公司	麻涌镇	88234888	牛卡纸
东莞洪通电脑绣花有限公司	塘厦镇	87722437	标签
东莞洛艺文具厂有限公司	桥头镇	83343998	相簿
东莞海龙纸业有限公司	麻涌镇	88234888	灰底白板纸
东莞诚发纸品有限公司	塘厦镇	87886328	纸箱
耐帆包装工程(东莞)有限公司	大岭山镇	83784130	可折叠木包装箱
有余纸品（东莞）有限公司	大岭山镇	85630000	纸箱
东莞理文造纸厂有限公司	中堂镇	88888168	纸及纸制品
东莞骏成纸业有限公司	凤岗镇	87505300	纸制品
东莞旭明纸业有限公司	大岭山镇	85615218	纸箱半成品
东莞映佳纸业有限公司	万江街道	22277747	纸品
东莞理文纸品有限公司	中堂镇	88888168	纸板
东莞市振兴纸品有限公司	高埗镇	88871188	纸板
印刷业和记录媒介的复制			
东莞东平彩印包装有限公司	虎门镇	85555615	彩盒
东莞富阳彩印有限公司	厚街镇	85824620	彩盒
东莞隽思印刷有限公司	樟木头镇	87712112	彩色纸箱
东莞德宝发包装制品有限公司	塘厦镇	87721296	包装制品
东莞大朗中编印刷厂	大朗镇	83314723	书籍印刷
东莞市智源彩印有限公司	望牛墩镇	88556888	包装装潢印刷
东莞派克奇包装有限公司	茶山镇	85585950	纸制品
东莞佳艺包装制品有限公司	万江街道	22285667	包装装潢印刷品印刷
东莞新扬印刷有限公司	东城街道	22259209	印刷成品书
东莞恒业印刷制品有限公司	长安镇	85099366	包装装潢印刷品印刷
东莞明辉商标织造有限公司	樟木头镇	87797688	布商标
东莞永洪印刷有限公司	樟木头镇	87711961	彩色纸盒
敬业（东莞）印刷包装厂有限公司	虎门镇	85551734	纸盒
东莞冠文彩印有限公司	万江街道	22278166	纸板印刷
东莞忠柏彩印工艺制品有限公司	东城街道	22024071	纸浆
极颖印刷制品东莞有限公司	万江街道	22713688	包装装潢印刷品印刷
东莞新洲印刷有限公司	大岭山镇	85625222	包装印刷
东莞当纳利印刷有限公司	寮步镇	81126499	印刷服务
利丰雅高包装印刷东莞有限公司	大岭山镇	85630000	包装印刷
东莞晨光印刷有限公司	石排镇	86551928	纸张塑料工艺商标印刷品
东莞中编印务有限公司	大朗镇	83314723	书籍印刷
东莞澳科实业有限公司	厚街镇	88566222	印刷
东莞虎彩印刷有限公司	虎门镇	85252189	包装印刷品
东莞昌明印刷有限公司	大岭山镇	83356851	包装物
东莞兴年彩印有限公司	长安镇	85543667	纸品印刷
东莞金杯印刷有限公司	常平镇	83394888	印刷书刊

1-5　续表 10

(2011年)

单位名称	所属镇街	联系电话	主要产品（或服务）
东莞广发印刷钉装有限公司	道滘镇	88339316	书籍
东莞大宝杰松印刷有限公司	洪梅镇	88844488	纸板
东莞永达彩印有限公司	道滘镇	88830968	彩盒印刷
东莞明泰彩色包装印刷有限公司	长安镇	85316011	说明书印刷
文教体育用品制造业			
联志玩具礼品（东莞）有限公司	横沥镇	83737875	塑胶玩具
东莞长安锦厦邦劲电子厂	长安镇	85535441	塑胶发声玩具
东莞塘厦童园玩具厂	塘厦镇	87913892	玩具
东莞广达塑胶制品有限公司	大朗镇	83318515	塑胶玩具
东莞银辉玩具有限公司	虎门镇	85551910	玩具
东莞桥头中星电器厂	桥头镇	83344504	电器配件
东莞育童幼儿用品有限公司	塘厦镇	87925551	儿童推车
东莞龙鑫运动用品有限公司	塘厦镇	86851318	运动器材
东莞富美高文具制品有限公司	清溪镇	87898682	文具
东莞华源玩具有限公司	东坑镇	88455176	塑胶五金玩具
东莞普克运动用品有限公司	塘厦镇		运动用品
东莞凤岗竹尾田玩具厂	凤岗镇	87753128	玩具
东莞龙昌数码科技有限公司	常平镇	86836266	玩具
东莞华兴塑胶制品有限公司	清溪镇	87369935	塑胶电子玩具
东莞柏辉玩具有限公司	沙田镇	88861619	玩具
东莞宏溢塑胶玩具有限公司	大岭山镇	81879388	塑胶玩具
东莞键辉五金塑胶玩具有限公司	清溪镇	87739230	塑胶玩具
东莞鑫达玩具礼品有限公司	横沥镇	83375750	合金塑胶玩具
东莞富龙运动用品有限公司	塘厦镇	87813201	高尔夫球杆
东莞大扬运动器材有限公司	厚街镇	85594466	棒球
东莞太联运动器材有限公司	长安镇	85535757	曲棍球中管、曲棍球球杆
东莞联弘玩具有限公司	横沥镇	83376123	玩具
东莞御丰文具有限公司	虎门镇	85154611	文具
安杰玩具（东莞）有限公司	茶山镇	81822333	玩具
东莞康威玩具制造有限公司	大岭山镇	83357533	合金塑胶玩具
东莞宝柏新威玩具有限公司	东坑镇	83384113	玩具
展恒玩具电子（东莞）有限公司	石排镇	86655372	塑胶玩具
东莞峰达电子有限公司	中堂镇	88811559	玩具
东莞仁景五金塑胶制品有限公司	长安镇	86064789	玩具
东莞兴利玩具有限公司	石排镇	86516288	玩具
东莞冠越玩具有限公司	虎门镇	89968888	塑胶玩具
东莞威保运动器材有限公司	寮步镇	88953278	运动手套、护具
东莞东耀玩具有限公司	虎门镇	81619866	塑胶及毛绒玩具
东莞顺联玩具有限公司	万江街道	22279238	电子塑胶玩具
东莞源泰运动器材有限公司	塘厦镇	87722669	网球拍、壁球拍、高尔夫球杆
东莞上泰高尔夫制品有限公司	塘厦镇	87919854	高尔夫球
东莞华登塑胶制品有限公司	清溪镇	87387555	塑胶电子玩具
东莞中岳旅行用品有限公司	塘厦镇	87925791	文具饰品
东莞虎门南栅国际文具制造有限公司	虎门镇	85561686	文具夹
明珠高尔夫制品（东莞）有限公司	清溪镇	87336186	高尔夫球

1-5 续表 11

(2011年)

单位名称	所属镇街	联系电话	主要产品（或服务）
东莞长安美泰玩具二厂	长安镇	85312683	塑胶玩具
富国运动器材（东莞）有限公司	虎门镇	85252033	运动器材
东莞广声五金塑胶制品有限公司	长安镇	86061888	木制玩具
高仕文具(东莞)有限公司	厚街镇	85585588	文具
东莞英德玩具塑胶电子有限公司	东城街道	22295251	塑胶制品
东莞大发玩具厂有限公司	长安镇	85315256	玩具
东莞南辉塑胶电子有限公司	沙田镇	88861619	塑胶玩具
东莞虎门南栅国际文具制造厂	虎门镇	85561686	文具夹
东莞巨佑体育用品有限公司	沙田镇	85582170	运动鞋
锦美运动用品（东莞）有限公司	清溪镇	87333971	高尔夫球具
东莞易达文具有限公司	常平镇	81032000	文件夹类文具
东莞胜辉健身器材有限公司	清溪镇	82098838	训练健身器材
东莞祥兴玩具有限公司	长安镇	85541020	塑胶玩具
山打根实业(东莞)有限公司	万江街道	22272416	塑胶电子玩具
比美高精密模具(东莞)有限公司	凤岗镇	87753128	橡胶模具制品
长荣玩具(东莞)有限公司	清溪镇	87314418	玩具
东莞钜丰运动器材有限公司	凤岗镇	87758887	球拍
东莞稳健高尔夫球用品有限公司	清溪镇	87739826	高尔夫球用品
东莞意志高纸品有限公司	东城街道	22259730	笔记本
东莞建力体育器材有限公司	清溪镇	87739848	高尔夫球具
明安运动器材(东莞)有限公司	虎门镇	85555321	高尔夫球类用品
东莞旭科电子制品有限公司	塘厦镇	87932700	电子玩具
东莞盈利幼童用品有限公司	清溪镇	87736157	儿童三轮车
东莞怡迪电子塑胶制品有限公司	凤岗镇	87777708	塑胶玩具产品
东莞乐迪卡游戏机制造厂有限公司	虎门镇	85159455	游戏机、电子液晶体显示器
东莞大朗玮丰塑胶厂	大朗镇	83319092	塑胶玩具
东莞广德运动用品有限公司	寮步镇	83236641	背包
东莞镇扬玩具有限公司	清溪镇	87736471	玩具
东莞佳畅玩具有限公司	塘厦镇	86856166	塑胶玩具
东莞长安港芝电子塑胶制造厂有限公司	长安镇	85543500	健身器材
东莞康贝童车玩具有限公司	塘厦镇	87720591	童车
东莞永湖复合材料有限公司	塘厦镇	82035151	棒球棒
东莞登富鞋业有限公司	清溪镇	87736010	运动鞋
东莞利达运动用品有限公司	沙田镇	88806900	运动用品
盛昌布艺制品（东莞）有限公司	望牛墩镇	88516028	玩具
东莞联欣运动器材有限公司	虎门镇	85259998	溜冰鞋
东莞司贸文教赠品有限公司	厚街镇	85598898	文具
东莞浩昌实业有限公司	塘厦镇	87297780	电子玩具
东莞仁美玩具制品有限公司	大岭山镇	83051388	玩具
东莞达成金属制品有限公司	虎门镇	85026632	电镀加工文具夹
东莞宝熊渔具有限公司	塘厦镇	87722967	渔具
东莞凯元高尔夫用品有限公司	东城街道	22699619	高尔夫球袋
东莞冠贺运动器材有限公司	虎门镇	85551210	球类产品及用具
东莞南栅利高文具制品厂有限公司	虎门镇	85561878	五金文件夹
东莞兴发玩具厂有限公司	东城街道	22201697	塑胶玩具

1-5 续表 12

(2011年)

单位名称	所属镇街	联系电话	主要产品（或服务）
东莞飞达玩具制造有限公司	桥头镇	83341136	塑胶玩具
东莞兴华玩具有限公司	石排镇	81818839	玩具
东莞威赢高尔夫用品有限公司	长安镇	85389925	高尔夫用品
东莞达宇运动器材有限公司	东坑镇	83882808	运动器材
东莞开达电子有限公司	中堂镇	88811559	玩具
东莞东发玩具厂有限公司	长安镇	85315256	玩具
石油加工、炼焦及核燃料加工业			
东莞太平洋博高润滑油有限公司	麻涌镇	88823886	发动机油
东莞泰和沥青产品有限公司	沙田镇	88687798	普通沥青
东莞东交沥青有限公司	沙田镇	88807929	改进沥青
化学原料及化学制品制造业			
东莞新东方化工有限公司	黄江镇	83639068	硅橡胶
东莞万泰橡胶有限公司	道滘镇	88833021	橡胶靴、鞋
东莞宝丽美化工有限公司	常平镇	83392980	印染助剂
高宝化妆品(中国)有限公司	常平镇	83392980	护肤品
东莞三联热缩材料有限公司	寮步镇	81120158	热缩套管
东莞冠昱实业有限公司	东城街道	22258668	橡胶粒
东莞大宝化工制品有限公司	大岭山镇	83352051	涂料
东莞杜邦华佳高性能涂料有限公司	万江街道	22288858	涂料
东莞大通电线有限公司	大朗镇	83132896	PVC塑料粒(电线接口用)
东莞誉展化工有限公司	凤岗镇	87509919	涂料油漆
东莞铧冠橡塑制品有限公司	厚街镇	85876868	复合橡胶
东莞南新塑胶制品有限公司	常平镇	83996222	塑胶玩具制品
东莞鸥哈希化学涂料有限公司	大朗镇	83317997	塑胶涂料
东莞中瀛涂料有限公司	茶山镇	86636630	丙烯酸清漆
阿克苏诺贝尔涂料(东莞)有限公司	大岭山镇	86520333	工业涂料
罗门哈斯电子材料(东莞)有限公司	东城街道	86225511	铜添加剂
东莞优立化工有限公司	塘厦镇	87727642	电泳涂料
东莞立茂化工有限公司	道滘镇	88330956	化学用品
东莞宏德化学工业有限公司	长安镇	85533620	胶桨树脂化工类
东莞大洋硅胶制品有限公司	樟木头镇	87712088	硅胶制品
东莞毅兴塑胶原料有限公司	厚街镇	85588755	精色粉
东莞康耀录像盒带制品有限公司	樟木头镇	87711691	录像带空盒
东莞普立万氯乙烯聚合体有限公司	厚街镇	85878800	乙稀昱化合物
东莞扬泰电子有限公司	常平镇	83820380	橡胶件
东莞宏石功能材料科技有限公司	沙田镇	88808241	树脂
维布络安舍(广东)日用品有限公司	东城街道	22253908	合成洗涤刘
东莞大日化工厂有限公司	虎门镇	85556675	ABS粒
日立化成工业(东莞)有限公司	茶山镇	86413898	线路板专用光致抗蚀工膜
广东银禧科技股份有限公司	虎门镇	8515828	改性塑料
东莞捷讯橡胶有限公司	企石镇	86724551	硅橡胶制品
东莞瑞安高分子树脂有限公司	长安镇	85533620	聚丙烯树脂
鲁道夫化工(东莞)有限公司	高埗镇	88466888	纺织品助剂
澳瑞凯骆驼粉末涂料东莞有限公司	凤岗镇	86801888	粉末涂料
集美化妆品(东莞)有限公司	樟木头镇	87948041	化妆品

1-5 续表 13

(2011年)

单位名称	所属镇街	联系电话	主要产品（或服务）
东莞维鸿化工有限公司	桥头镇	83342979	聚素胶树脂成型粉
东莞秉顺制漆有限公司	凤岗镇	86801888	油漆
东莞英铭化工有限公司	常平镇	83919189	聚合树脂
东莞富宏塑胶原料有限公司	凤岗镇	87280088	PVC塑吸原料料加工
欧利生东邦涂料(东莞)有限公司	茶山镇	81866000	化工涂料
东莞威威日用品有限公司	石碣镇	86632080	合成洗涤剂
大丰电研科技(东莞)有限公司	石碣镇	88487888	油墨
东莞市爱粤金属粉末有限公司	道滘镇	88385804	环氧聚酯型粉末涂料
东莞三星道达尔工程塑料有限公司	大岭山镇	82781999	尼龙塑胶
亚化科技(东莞)胶粘制品有限公司	长安镇	85312270	胶粘带
益海(东莞)油化工业有限公司	麻涌镇	88238729	皂粒
汉高胶粘剂技术(广东)有限公司	虎门镇	85563700	粘合剂
东莞丽利涂料有限公司	大岭山镇	83353187	钢木家具涂料
东莞井上五金橡塑有限公司	沙田镇	88863344	印刷机部件
东莞宏柏鞋材制造有限公司	万江街道	22176636	橡胶添加剂
东莞高宝化工有限公司	常平镇	83392980	印染助剂
医药制造业			
东莞保斯医疗器材有限公司	凤岗镇	87756433	手腕固定套
化学纤维制造业			
东莞东港化纤有限公司	东城街道	89505888	丙纶制品
东莞方德泡绵制品厂	寮步镇	88908889	海棉
橡胶制品业			
关西毡子电子(东莞)有限公司	石龙镇	86117447	塑胶制品
东莞新和英特达电子材料有限公司	南城街道	22983601	彩管专用特殊胶带
东莞太洋橡塑制品有限公司	樟木头镇	87197979	硅胶制品
东莞兴宝密封件有限公司	东城街道	22666410	橡胶密封件
东莞市安德固塑料包装物有限公司	东城街道	22259888	塑胶制品
东莞英树电子科技有限公司	中堂镇	88642999	塑胶制品
星海丰电子有限公司	虎门镇	85196313	橡胶制品
诠立电子科技（东莞）有限公司	清溪镇	87294721	橡胶制品
东莞井上福坤五金橡塑有限公司	沙田镇	88804002	橡塑制品、汽车内装饰材料
东莞东昌鞋业有限公司	东城街道	23052402	运动休闲鞋
东莞兴泰鞋材有限公司	大岭山镇	85623238	鞋底
东莞长明复合材料有限公司	大岭山镇	85655922	塑胶粒
东莞彰昱实业有限公司	东城街道	22260168	鞋材
东莞国信鞋业有限公司	塘厦镇	87721640	EVA拖(凉)鞋
中星婴儿用品（东莞）有限公司	石排镇	86652872	婴儿用品
东莞益宝鞋材有限公司	长安镇	85536565	合成橡胶片
东莞新亚华电子材料有限公司	石碣镇	86316960	电子绝缘材料
东莞宝建鞋材有限公司	黄江镇	83631221	PU树脂
登迈塑胶(东莞)有限公司	大岭山镇	85613040	PUC吹气产品
东莞亚华胶粘带有限公司	石碣镇	86316960	橡胶带
东莞大森鞋材有限公司	厚街镇	85901546	鞋材
东莞兴鑫电子科技有限公司	虎门镇	85226956	手机按键
东莞仟麒塑胶五金有限公司	石碣镇	86317056	塑胶制品

1-5 续表 14

(2011年)

单位名称	所属镇街	联系电话	主要产品（或服务）
东莞新桥鞋业有限公司	万江街道	22184688	橡胶鞋底
东莞裕祥鞋材有限公司	黄江镇	83364958	橡胶靴、鞋
塑料制品业			
东莞南部塑料有限公司	凤岗镇	87750023	打印机、复印机塑料制品
东莞厚街创机塑胶制品厂	厚街镇	82728888	塑料制品
泰原塑胶制品(东莞)有限公司	石碣镇	86318157	连接器外壳
东莞晨彩塑胶制品有限公司	樟木头镇	38957888	塑胶制品
东莞晋原电子有限公司	大岭山镇	85601899	塑胶制品
东莞圣纪电子科技有限公司	塘厦镇	82616688	办公用品用塑胶壳
东莞稻畑工程塑料有限公司	石龙镇	86188280	工程塑料
东莞胜乔鞋业有限公司	塘厦镇	87887018	鞋
东莞金富包装材料有限公司	虎门镇	85182565	塑料制品
东莞胜百吉鞋业有限公司	长安镇	81608888	鞋
东莞盛泓五金塑胶制品有限公司	凤岗镇	87772450	复印机等的塑胶五金配件
东莞市乐福塑胶电子有限公司	大岭山镇	88968988	塑胶制品
腾翔精密塑胶(东莞)有限公司	黄江镇	83368096	塑胶制品
东莞益卓电子科技有限公司	大朗镇	86263266	塑胶外壳
晋德塑料科技(东莞)有限公司	塘厦镇	87929956	工程塑料
东莞隆捷塑胶制品有限公司	企石镇	86762711	塑胶制品
伟易达（东莞）塑胶制品有限公司	厚街镇	85581806	塑胶制品
东莞天祥塑胶有限公司	东城街道	88990909	电视机外壳
东莞一化精密注塑模具有限公司	石龙镇	86186078	精密塑胶配件
东莞骏威电子制品有限公司	大朗镇	81119390	塑胶门钟
东莞汇景塑胶制品有限公司	长安镇	85546080	塑胶制品
东莞钨珍电子科技有限公司	谢岗镇	82126950	手机配件
东莞大德电子有限公司	长安镇	85544242	玩具
东莞灿达电子有限公司	常平镇	83917568	五金配件
东莞卓越光像薄膜有限公司	常平镇	83395440	光像薄膜
东莞市翔和塑胶电子有限公司	黄江镇	83056968	塑胶制品
东莞日新塑胶制品有限公司	常平镇	83391824	塑胶机械件
健富塑胶五金制品（东莞）有限公司	清溪镇	87338807	电脑机箱
东莞嘉多利塑胶制品有限公司	凤岗镇	87504968	PVC薄膜
东莞百进五金塑料有限公司	石碣镇	81382666	模具
广东紫泉包装有限公司	东城街道	22679188	瓶盖
东莞穗联包装制品有限公司	凤岗镇	87559119	塑胶瓶
东莞祥曜塑胶制品有限公司	凤岗镇	87758622	塑胶制品
东莞联华鑫精密橡胶有限公司	万江街道	22709712	电解电容器橡胶盖
东莞奇妙包装有限公司	大朗镇	83034888	塑料软包装产品（塑料袋）
东莞德源塑胶制品有限公司	虎门镇	85566181	塑胶制品
东莞钜升塑胶电子制品有限公司	长安镇	88611111	手机模型
富裕注塑制模（东莞）有限公司	横沥镇	83378570	塑胶模具
圣诺盟聚氨酯（东莞）有限公司	塘厦镇	87881068	海棉制品
协隆(东莞)塑胶电子有限公司	塘厦镇	87916200	其他金属加工机械
东莞顶钧塑胶模具有限公司	清溪镇	86815666	塑胶零配件
东莞美哲塑胶制品有限公司	中堂镇	88181588	塑胶地砖

1-5 续表 15

(2011年)

单位名称	所属镇街	联系电话	主要产品（或服务）
东莞欣仪五金塑胶制品有限公司	桥头镇	83439116	五金塑胶制品
东莞誉铭电业科技有限公司	长安镇	85373322	塑胶制品
东莞万善美耐皿制品有限公司	桥头镇	86936888	美耐皿制品
东莞恒骏吸塑制品有限公司	长安镇	85350072	塑胶盖
东莞汉星鞋材有限公司	东城街道		鞋材
东莞精熙光机有限公司	长安镇	85312190	照相机、复印机主要零部件
东莞普能塑料科技实业有限公司	高埗镇	88735183	塑料再生胶粒
东莞远展包装制品有限公司	大岭山镇	83354716	发泡胶
东莞斯曼塑胶制品有限公司	桥头镇	86551920	纤维胶粒
东莞三荣通讯科技有限公司	塘厦镇	86851130	手机键
东莞中央化学有限公司	企石镇	86788666	塑料包装容器
东莞玮锋电子包装材料有限公司	长安镇	85381227	塑料型材
东莞鹏远塑胶有限公司	黄江镇	83638000	塑胶粒
舒尔曼塑料(东莞)有限公司	桥头镇	83422777	工程塑料
新崧塑胶(东莞) 有限公司	长安镇	85079188	非金属制品模具
东莞绿树塑胶制品有限公司	东城街道	22765001	塑胶配件
东莞厚街溪头塑料厂	厚街镇	85599076	加工新塑胶粒
东莞华通发泡塑料制品有限公司	企石镇	86789888	泡沫包装和薄膜
东莞辰泰实业有限公司	清溪镇	87737400	塑胶产品
东莞富利达塑胶制品有限公司	凤岗镇	87750770	PVC薄膜
东莞丽骏塑胶制品有限公司	塘厦镇	87811708	衣架
东莞加能鞋材有限公司	南城街道	22400092	鞋材
东莞三荣日化容器有限公司	茶山镇	86415046	塑料容器瓶
东莞嘉盈电子有限公司	厚街镇	85812455	电脑塑胶配件
金旺塑胶制品(东莞)有限公司	凤岗镇	87515170	窗帘配件
东莞广丰兴塑胶有限公司	塘厦镇	87727051	塑胶色母料
雄进塑料制品(东莞)有限公司	寮步镇	83320081	PVC造革
东莞卓荣实业有限公司	东坑镇	83698138	塑胶衣架
中侨路易塑胶制品(东莞)有限公司	东城街道	22655287	塑胶袋
东莞永捷塑胶制品有限公司	石排镇	86920526	塑胶玩具
东莞贯新幼童用品有限公司	清溪镇	86818999	婴幼儿车
东莞家宝生活用品有限公司	企石镇	86666668	塑料披覆
东莞宇光鞋业有限公司	凤岗镇	87753066	塑料制品
东莞东洋塑胶制品有限公司	塘厦镇	87880688	精密塑胶模具
东莞荒井橡胶制品有限公司	塘厦镇	87925725	传真机、复印机、打印机
东莞荣泰塑化材料有限公司	茶山镇	86869211	PVC塑胶粒
东莞康俊胶布有限公司	常平镇	83913222	胶尼龙布
东莞吉田塑料制品有限公司	常平镇	83395533	机芯塑料件加工
东莞第一精工模塑有限公司	长安镇	85358671	各种精密塑胶件
东莞建航精密模具塑胶五金有限公司	寮步镇	81199678	塑料零件
东莞凯钛塑胶制品有限公司	东城街道	22622027	化妆品器具
东莞怡昌塑胶制品有限公司	横沥镇	82320888	PVC硬质胶布
东莞普隆塑胶制品有限公司	石碣镇	88181588	塑胶地砖(软体)
东莞高登鞋材有限公司	道滘镇	88830578	塑料鞋
东莞丰佳塑胶有限公司	厚街镇	85999799	PCC胶粒

1-5 续表 16

(2011年)

单位名称	所属镇街	联系电话	主要产品（或服务）
东莞百代塑胶制品有限公司	企石镇	86767688	塑胶玩具
东莞塘厦永东电子制品厂	塘厦镇	87903685	电子制品
东莞协宇塑胶制品有限公司	长安镇	85495868	塑胶制品
加福塑胶制品(东莞)有限公司	长安镇	85310681	加工塑胶原料
东莞利富高塑料制品有限公司	石龙镇	86106920	汽车零部件
泽冠塑胶电子(东莞)有限公司	厚街镇	83086666	塑胶配件
东莞长安乌沙新永塑胶零件模具厂	长安镇	85548081	塑胶制品
东莞光群雷射科技有限公司	大岭山镇	85601301	塑料软包装新科技新产品
东莞宇光塑胶制品有限公司	凤岗镇	87753066	吸塑罩
昌煜塑胶(东莞)有限公司	凤岗镇	87750453	塑胶产品
东莞东锋达电脑零配件有限公司	塘厦镇	87987390	塑料制品
东莞利士包装有限公司	常平镇	83910878	塑料罐
东莞兴腾鞋材有限公司	大岭山镇	83058898	鞋材、鞋底
东莞市佑忠电子有限公司	塘厦镇	86801899	发泡胶
东莞百瑞立塑胶五金有限公司	长安镇	85414633	塑胶制品外壳
海格五金（东莞）有限公司	石排镇	86922110	五金制品
比安斯（东莞）热固性复合材料有限公司	桥头镇	83433844	热固性复合材料
东莞木村塑胶制品有限公司	沙田镇	88865581	打印机塑胶配件
港龙包装制品(东莞)有限公司	塘厦镇	87903336	塑料薄膜
睦龙塑胶(东莞)有限公司	长安镇	85395001	塑胶制品
东莞鸿华泡绵制品有限公司	清溪镇	87314688	泡棉
杰斯比塑料(东莞)有限公司	松山湖	88011818	发泡聚丙烯粒子EPP
赫比(东莞)电子科技有限公司	长安镇	81886111	模具、塑胶制品
东莞康佳包装材料有限公司	凤岗镇	86202288	泡沫胶袋产品
东莞敬记容器有限公司	虎门镇	85151012	塑料制品
东莞华美人造皮厂有限公司	道滘镇	88839163	PVC、PU人造革
东莞高富达塑料制品有限公司	东城街道	22636148	塑胶材料
东莞伟嘉塑胶电子制品有限公司	麻涌镇	88232838	塑胶制品
东莞洲进电子塑胶五金有限公司	虎门镇	85724011	塑胶配件
东莞好而优塑胶制品有限公司	塘厦镇	87949595	塑胶玩具
东莞珂维斯日用品有限公司	东城街道	22089885	化妆品
东莞合旺塑胶颜料有限公司	凤岗镇	87758710	颜料塑胶鞋、ABS胶鞋、HIPS胶鞋
东莞杰福瑞包装印刷有限公司	虎门镇	86099000	包装、装潢印刷制品
东莞泛昌窗帘制品有限公司	常平镇		塑胶百叶窗帘
东莞同成塑胶五金制品有限公司	茶山镇	86640256	塑胶五金配件
东莞进升塑料制品有限公司	长安镇	85357081	CD袋
东莞三和塑胶制品有限公司	常平镇	83392589	手握箱
信国五金电子(东莞)有限公司	石碣镇	86316760	电脑零配件
东莞百信塑胶制品有限公司	桥头镇	83456081	塑胶制品
品翔电子塑胶制品(东莞)有限公司	石碣镇	86636668	电子塑胶制品
银禧工程塑料(东莞)有限公司	道滘镇	38855188	工程塑料
东莞增立塑料制品有限公司	沙田镇	88680500	PVC人造革
东莞三阳塑胶有限公司	凤岗镇	87515998	塑胶浴帘
东莞南星塑胶有限公司	樟木头镇	87713408	聚乙烯胶袋(筒)
东莞大泰光电科技有限公司	虎门镇	85503858	照相机配件

1-5 续表 17

(2011年)

单位名称	所属镇街	联系电话	主要产品（或服务）
东莞富增泡棉塑胶有限公司	高埗镇	88462258	塑胶泡棉
东莞劲胜精密组件股份有限公司	长安镇	82288188	塑胶制品
东莞竞业塑胶五金制品厂有限公司	中堂镇	88812843	塑料餐具及厨具
东莞宝狮塑胶五金制品有限公司	凤岗镇	87755030	PVC管材
东莞井上高分子材料有限公司	茶山镇	86176861	聚氨酯橡胶
东莞怡发塑胶制品有限公司	常平镇	83392238	电话充电器胶件
东莞高成精密注塑科技有限公司	黄江镇	83632679	工程塑料及塑料合金
永塑（东莞）塑料有限公司	清溪镇	87331245	塑胶粒
鸿特利塑胶制品（东莞）有限公司	清溪镇	87738200	塑胶制品
东莞塘厦三局建钛塑胶制品厂	塘厦镇	87911516	文件夹
东莞丝丽雅电子科技有限公司	东城街道	88772888	塑胶玻璃、包装容器
东莞衍青塑胶五金制品有限公司	清溪镇	87733701	水杯
康扬塑胶(东莞)有限公司	长安镇	85305187	塑胶配件
东莞保利文塑胶制品有限公司	常平镇	83989198	胶花
东莞信柏塑胶有限公司	塘厦镇	82016888	塑料原料加工
东莞联全鞋材有限公司	东城街道	22250887	鞋材塑胶制品
东莞依科聚合物有限公司	厚街镇	82275897	聚氨酯泡沫
优利（东莞）塑胶材料有限公司	桥头镇	83453008	ABS胶粒
东莞天盈塑料管材有限公司	洪梅镇	88438128	PE管材
东莞冠晖塑胶制品有限公司	南城街道	22404249	塑胶充气制品
晋伦塑料科技（东莞）有限公司	塘厦镇	87929958	尼龙复合塑胶粒
东莞华心塑胶制品厂	凤岗镇	87775513	PVC袋
东莞金金碧电子有限公司	横沥镇	87574026	塑胶制品
东莞大银塑胶制品有限公司	长安镇	85412001	塑料制品
东莞建兴塑胶五金制品有限公司	凤岗镇	87753012	五金日用品
东莞市立新塑胶有限公司	石排镇	86658588	塑胶制品、五金制品
东莞黄江福泰塑料厂	黄江镇	83363017	塑料
东莞良佳五金塑胶制品有限公司	塘厦镇	87725096	五金塑胶制品
东莞伟士塑胶制品有限公司	望牛墩镇	88853722	烧烤炉手拖车
东莞凡进工业模具有限公司	常平镇	81895181	塑胶模具
兆丰（东莞）制帘有限公司	企石镇	86716666	门框形百叶窗
东莞常平美泰塑胶电子制品厂	常平镇	83919988	塑胶配件
东莞怡高塑胶五金电子制品有限公司	常平镇	83394988	汽车CD收放机
东莞大岭山永盛玩具有限公司	大岭山镇	83352625	塑胶五金玩具
东莞华庆塑料有限公司	东城街道	22295808	泡沫塑料
东莞冠诚塑胶模具有限公司	清溪镇	87739270	遥控器
东莞坤胜五金制品有限公司	虎门镇	85564158	五金配件
东莞华宇塑胶制品有限公司	凤岗镇	87753066	塑料制品
东莞中建塑胶有限公司	高埗镇	88788261	塑胶配件
非金属矿物制品业			
信义光伏产业（安徽）控股有限公司东莞分公司	虎门镇	85266666	玻璃
东莞华润水泥厂有限公司	沙田镇	88867510	水泥
东莞南玻工程玻璃有限公司	麻涌镇	88288656	中空玻璃
东莞利冠光学电子有限公司	石碣镇	86387600	镜片
信义汽车玻璃（东莞）有限公司	虎门镇	85266666	汽车玻璃

1-5 续表 18

(2011年)

单位名称	所属镇街	联系电话	主要产品（或服务）
信义超白光伏玻璃（东莞）有限公司	虎门镇	85266666	超白光伏玻璃
台玻华南玻璃有限公司	洪梅镇	88841000	浮法玻璃
东莞美艺宝玻璃制品有限公司	常平镇	83390685	玻璃马赛克
宏达光电玻璃东莞有限公司	大岭山镇	81625988	TFT-LCD显示屏材料
东莞秀特电子有限公司	凤岗镇	87773572	磁石
环球石材(东莞)有限公司	长安镇	85392177	石材
东莞金鲤水泥有限公司	麻涌镇	81206633	水泥
东莞华润混凝土有限公司	道滘镇	88326100	水泥
东莞华润丰诚混凝土有限公司	茶山镇	88326100	预拌商品混凝土
信义汽车部件（东莞）有限公司	虎门镇	85266666	汽车玻璃
东莞住秀电子有限公司	凤岗镇	87552682	钕铁硼磁铁
力美有机玻璃东莞有限公司	塘厦镇	87885398	有机玻璃
东莞泰升玻璃有限公司	沙田镇	85557608	玻璃
东莞金晶铸造材料有限公司	洪梅镇	88841888	覆腊砂
广东可耐福新型建筑材料有限公司	麻涌镇	88222708	环保石膏板
信义玻璃工程（东莞）有限公司	虎门镇	85266666	建筑玻璃
东莞艺华弧形钢化玻璃有限公司	桥头镇	83346884	玻璃
东莞可见优玻璃制品有限公司	清溪镇	87315335	玻璃转盘
信义超薄玻璃（东莞）有限公司	虎门镇	85266666	玻璃
东莞南玻太阳能玻璃有限公司	麻涌镇	88281785	光伏发电盖板玻璃
黑色金属冶炼及压延加工业			
东莞宇新钢材制品有限公司	清溪镇	87313331	电镀锌铁(钢)板
东莞谦华五金厂有限公司	长安镇	85537869	焊接钢管
东莞富威钢铁分条有限公司	凤岗镇	87512068	钢铁分条加工
合胜五金制品(东莞)有限公司	清溪镇	87383625	五金制品
爱思开钢铁(东莞)有限公司	寮步镇	81112111	金属材料剪切加工
东莞川电钢板制品有限公司	长安镇	85543073	加工矽钢片
东莞斯穆碧根柏五金制品有限公司	虎门镇	85191603	钢材
东莞珂霓钢制品有限公司	长安镇	85417742	不锈钢棒
东莞三星钢材加工有限公司	大朗镇	81129215	电镀锌板深加工产品
东莞裕升薄板有限公司	沙田镇	88807688	镀锌薄板
东莞住金物产金属制品有限公司	洪梅镇	88439668	铝材
东莞大洲钢铁有限公司	虎门镇	85557451	五金铁片
有色金属冶炼及压延加工业			
三铃制线（东莞）有限公司	常平镇	83395435	铜线
东莞鸿锦应用材料有限公司	厚街镇	85594855	有色金属复合材料
东莞同亚金属制品有限公司	塘厦镇	82081380	铜片
永金金属材料(东莞)有限公司	长安镇	85330095	锡条
阪和钢板加工（东莞）有限公司	茶山镇	81821038	加工电镀锌钢板
东莞铁和金属制品有限公司	南城街道	22903361	镀钢板
东莞升洋焊锡材料有限公司	谢岗镇	82126112	锡材料、助焊剂
东莞宜安电器制品有限公司	清溪镇	87737777	镁铝合金精密铸件
东莞雄福五金有限公司	横沥镇	83723390	数码相机零配件
东莞津工铜合金材料有限公司	洪梅镇	88431580	铜铁合金带
东莞华昌导体有限公司	虎门镇	85507296	红铜线

1-5 续表 19

(2011年)

单位名称	所属镇街	联系电话	主要产品（或服务）
东莞合立五金制品有限公司	虎门镇	85520161	五金制品
东莞泛亚金属制造有限公司	虎门镇	82888138	铝合金接头
东莞翔腾金属制品有限公司	寮步镇	83036688	金属制品
东莞东峰铝型材制品有限公司	塘厦镇	87913344	铝型材
日立金属（东莞）特殊钢有限公司	茶山镇	81869783	模具钢材
东莞汉华金属制品有限公司	大朗镇	83188845	铜线
东莞兆隆五金有限公司	凤岗镇	87751742	铜线、铝线
东莞佳男五金电镀有限公司	虎门镇	85713636	连续端子、电镀五金制品
东莞升贸锡制品有限公司	虎门镇	85508193	锡制品
东莞中瑞吉电工材料有限公司	桥头镇	83425961	铜型材料
东莞新文钦金属有限公司	中堂镇	88810666	铝合金条
展成电机（东莞）有限公司	常平镇	83917317	铝箔加工
东莞东钜有色金属制品有限公司	茶山镇	86402606	铝合金
东莞金昌金属加工有限公司	虎门镇	85562885	有色金属加工
东莞全良铜铝制品有限公司	虎门镇	85700075	铜制品
东莞市石碣华丰五金厂	石碣镇	86313720	铝合金
倍亿得热传科技（东莞）有限公司	横沥镇	83377088	电脑散热器
金属制品业			
东莞尚馥散热系统有限公司	虎门镇	88623999	铝散热片
东莞恒旺五金有限公司	横沥镇	83737616	冷板
东莞鸿辉五金有限公司	塘厦镇	87933801	铁线
东莞精明五金科技有限公司	凤岗镇	87862898	五金配件
东莞佑能工具有限公司	洪梅镇	88848901	钻头
东莞钜弦电子科技有限公司	虎门镇	85248941	五金制品
东莞鼎翰铝制品有限公司	谢岗镇	87769786	铝制品
益龙建材东莞有限公司	东坑镇	83885678	轻型建材及配套产品
东莞陇亿自行车配件有限公司	塘厦镇	87723781	铁车架
东莞东旭金属表面处理有限公司	虎门镇	85565111	电镀加工
东莞茂森金属冲压有限公司	塘厦镇	84342029	金属冲压件及组件
东莞济安塑胶五金制品有限公司	高埗镇	88870555	五金饰品
东莞世泉家电五金制品有限公司	东坑镇	83885906	五金制品
东莞冠德五金制品有限公司	横沥镇	83723626	冷扎铁、马口铁
东莞凤岗浸校塘有成电器制品厂	凤岗镇		电发剪
东莞东记金属制品有限公司	塘厦镇	87725811	高档建筑五金件
东莞旭升五金电子有限公司	高埗镇	81309888	五金配件
东莞肯上精密五金有限公司	长安镇	85335705	五金塑胶件
东莞特迪五金科技有限公司	清溪镇	86814789	五金配件、散热片
东莞众富五金制品有限公司	塘厦镇	87945998	电器散热片
东莞勤德五金制品有限公司	塘厦镇	87919779	五金制品
东莞惠昌电子有限公司	长安镇	85542566	电子制品
大宝(东莞)模具切削工具有限公司	大朗镇	83182598	模具切削工具
东莞顺传五金制品有限公司	清溪镇	87732273	自行车五金零件
东莞智得电子制品有限公司	塘厦镇	87883069	五金配件
东莞力群金属厂有限公司	麻涌镇	88826058	铁管
东莞铿利五金制品有限公司	樟木头镇	87790560	五金配件

1-5 续表 20

(2011年)

单位名称	所属镇街	联系电话	主要产品（或服务）
东莞宏兴金属制品有限公司	桥头镇	83344310	五金制品
东莞盛新五金制品有限公司	企石镇	86769005	五金制品
首屋尔金属（东莞）有限公司	茶山镇	86414346	五金制品
东莞雅康皮塑五金有限公司	塘厦镇	86957222	电子元器件
东莞普瑞得五金塑胶制品有限公司	沙田镇	88685118	电镀五金
东莞以利沙五金塑胶制品有限公司	塘厦镇	87811756	五金塑胶制品
东莞太阳茂森精密金属有限公司	塘厦镇	87929299	五金冲压产品
东莞番尔康金属制品有限公司	凤岗镇	86803388	铁五金制品
东莞才誉五金有限公司	长安镇	81558628	五金配件
东莞马士基集装箱工业有限公司	麻涌镇	88826668	集装箱
东莞浦和冶金有限公司	虎门镇	85150321	轴承
东莞捷润五金塑胶有限公司	凤岗镇	87751898	五金制品
东莞横沥田头百汇五金塑胶制品有限公司	横沥镇	83375520	五金配件
东莞金鑫金属制品有限公司	长安镇	89993999	五金件
东莞韦腾五金塑胶制品有限公司	大岭山镇	85785101	烤肉炉
东莞维信五金塑胶制品有限公司	长安镇	85411861	金属家具
东莞华尔泰装饰材料有限公司	万江街道	22716312	铝塑复合板
东莞信丰五金机械塑胶工业有限公司	长安镇	85411186	相机镜头连接垫
东莞雄罐印铁制罐有限公司	寮步镇	83226869	马口铁制品、铁罐
东莞华联五金厂有限公司	凤岗镇	87777777	钢材分条
东莞日联精钢有限公司	塘厦镇	22203677	不锈钢螺丝
东莞洲亮通讯科技有限公司	道滘镇	88326318	金属餐具
东莞承光五金制品有限公司	厚街镇	85926110	塑胶制品
东莞颖新五金制品有限公司	长安镇	85533709	金属钮扣
东莞原创金属结构有限公司	沙田镇	88688080	金属结构制品
东莞嘉丰机电设备有限公司	寮步镇	83226777	五金机箱、机柜
东莞群晔五金制品有限公司	厚街镇	85589170	五金制品
东莞均益精密五金制品有限公司	石排镇	88937100	表带、表壳
东莞精锐电器五金有限公司	高埗镇	88941998	金属制品
东莞兴铜五金有限公司	清溪镇	87091803	五金制品
东莞住商益安金属制品有限公司	沙田镇	88863093	加工剪切钢卷
东莞华震电器有限公司	寮步镇	83218666	喇叭金属零件
锌辉扬热浸锌(东莞)有限公司	沙田镇	88661928	热浸锌钢铁件加工
东莞宝金山五金制品有限公司	清溪镇	82068588	五金制品
东莞亿量五金制品有限公司	大朗镇	81160085	线材
东莞四方技研五金制品有限公司	塘厦镇	87811636	精密冲模
东莞信凯五金制品有限公司	虎门镇	85260297	铁毛坯
东莞璋泰五金制品有限公司	清溪镇	87734183	铁制品
东莞力雄五金电器塑胶制品有限公司	凤岗镇	82030633	电箱
东莞荣兴五金制品有限公司	大岭山镇	83355911	割草机消音器
东莞荣成塑胶五金制品有限公司	茶山镇	81811503	塑胶五金配件
东莞万顺昌钢铁制品有限公司	虎门镇	85520198	不锈钢片
东莞万成模具五金制品有限公司	高埗镇	88731998	电脑配件
东莞虎门路东昌华五金制造厂	虎门镇	85561811	加工电镀五金文具夹
东莞清溪鸿益五金厂	清溪镇	87732903	加工五金半成品
美达王板和精密金属(东莞)有限公司	松山湖	22893015	电子、电器零件金属材料

1-5 续表 21

(2011年)

单位名称	所属镇街	联系电话	主要产品（或服务）
东莞泓创五金制品有限公司	塘厦镇	86855688	电脑散热器
志联钢线钢缆(东莞)有限公司	长安镇	85312723	钢材加工
东莞长谷川金属制品有限公司	横沥镇	83721269	铝梯
东莞智信五金制品有限公司	塘厦镇	87925656	五金制品
自力钢构(东莞)有限公司	石碣镇	86310711	钢构房屋承建
东莞茂盈五金科技有限公司	清溪镇	82038300	五金制品及配件
大量（东莞）五金制品有限公司	大朗镇	83110970	金属丝
东莞爱可玛金属线有限公司	大朗镇	87686869	加工铜线
东莞金基金属有限公司	虎门镇	85566550	电镀锌铁片
英联卫浴器材（东莞）有限公司	东坑镇	83387970	水槽
东莞台端电子有限公司	长安镇	85419090	各种端子
东莞明晖不锈钢厨具有限公司	清溪镇	87313210	高身雪柜
同朋金属制品（东莞）有限公司	塘厦镇	87903150	铜带片
东莞友智金属制品有限公司	清溪镇	82130848	五金制品
东莞科达模具机器有限公司	望牛墩镇	88857718	模坯
东莞清溪光华制锁厂有限公司	清溪镇	87731333	锁具产品
东莞伟腾五金塑胶有限公司	厚街镇	85599181	不锈钢餐具、厨具
允丰金属（东莞）有限公司	清溪镇	86987599	烤盘
东莞凤岗雁田财迎五金电子厂	凤岗镇	87770958	摄录机机芯
通用设备制造业			
广东欧科空调制冷有限公司	黄江镇	83660888	制冷设备
东莞正荣金属制品有限公司	企石镇	86786771	五金制品
东莞厚街鸿亮机电设备有限公司	厚街镇	83099888	剪草机
东莞恒达电机制造有限公司	谢岗镇	87680606	小型马达
东莞鸿达机械工业有限公司	道滘镇	88313008	机床
东莞龙佑五金机械制造有限公司	虎门镇	85518848	精密精铣机床
东莞鹏驰五金制品有限公司	黄江镇	83668128	螺丝
东莞创机电业制品有限公司	厚街镇	82728888	电动工具
东莞大雅电子科技有限公司	长安镇	85448999	光磁盘驱动器
东莞市高亿电子五金配件有限公司	塘厦镇	87923840	螺丝
东莞永冠铸造厂有限公司	清溪镇	87739480	五金铸件
东莞华懋五金有限公司	常平镇	83399130	螺丝
东泰机械工具（东莞）有限公司	常平镇	83939183	冲床
东莞珉强五金塑胶制品有限公司	清溪镇	89137168	铁管
东莞佳鸿机械制造有限公司	望牛墩镇	88859861	吹瓶机
东莞长安上角广迎五金塑胶制品有限公司	长安镇	85413055	塑胶机壳
东莞百乐仕汽车精密配件有限公司	塘厦镇	87987779	汽车精密配件
东莞信浓马达有限公司	凤岗镇	87772818	微电机
堂盛机械（东莞）有限公司	谢岗镇	87130055	印刷专业设备
东莞虎邦五金塑胶制品有限公司	长安镇	85544660	运动器材塑胚配件
舜全电气器材（东莞）有限公司	虎门镇	85517988	压敏电阻
东莞日技金属加工有限公司	常平镇	83394631	钢材加工
东莞今富五金机械有限公司	谢岗镇	87632358	针织机
东莞侨元金属制品有限公司	大朗镇	87080988	电脑配件
必诺机械(东莞)有限公司	长安镇	85410555	超声波设备
东莞家利来电器有限公司	常平镇	83390188	风筒

1-5 续表 22

(2011年)

单位名称	所属镇街	联系电话	主要产品（或服务）
东莞益新五金有限公司	常平镇	83393762	五金制品
东莞三美空调配件有限公司	东坑镇	83862444	空调配件接管
东莞泰星五金制品厂有限公司	清溪镇	87386666	螺杆
东莞君雄精密五金制造有限公司	企石镇	86710181	钢铁铸件
东莞双叶金属制品有限公司	大岭山镇	85658197	汽车部件
东莞皇冠螺丝有限公司	长安镇	85418758	精密螺丝
锐德热力设备(东莞)有限公司	长安镇	82380238	回流焊炉
东莞强韧机械铸造有限公司	桥头镇	83455397	铸件
东莞益鑫电子科技有限公司	大朗镇	86263266	手提打钉机
成行精密部件(东莞)有限公司	塘厦镇	87282609	精密部件
东莞建越精密轴承有限公司	洪梅镇	88431300	轴承
东莞东运镁业有限公司	常平镇	83500019	镁合金制品
东莞明勖机械五金有限公司	大朗镇	83010960	冲床
东莞富鸿齐电子有限公司	樟木头镇	87187028	主机轴承
东莞艾尔发自动化机械有限公司	大朗镇	83180326	机械手（注塑机）
东莞高德电动工具有限公司	厚街镇	88639858	木材加工机床
春雨(东莞)五金制品有限公司	大朗镇	83310921	钢材
东莞明耀金属制品有限公司	塘厦镇	87942266	五金制品
东莞奄美弹簧有限公司	长安镇	85537655	弹簧
日立粉末冶金（东莞）有限公司	茶山镇	86170115	气门导管
东莞联志五金制品有限公司	大朗镇	83195767	汽车刹车盘零件
东莞耐力五金配件有限公司	长安镇	85338531	铁螺丝
东莞祥艺机械有限公司	常平镇	82202255	机械
东莞宏威数码机械有限公司	南城街道	22901516	旋涂机
东莞保来得粉末冶金有限公司	大朗镇	83133077	轴承零配件
东莞庆安制冷设备配件有限公司	桥头镇	83341457	分离器
东莞群马电子有限公司	东坑镇	83860001	电子零配件
瑞智制冷机器（东莞）有限公司	虎门镇	85528857	制冷空调设备
东莞瑞智压缩机有限公司	虎门镇	85528857	气体压缩机
东莞东成空调设备有限公司	黄江镇	83632222	中央冷水机
东莞百利达健康器材有限公司	南城街道		健康秤、专用秤
专用设备制造业			
东莞极盛电子有限公司	寮步镇	88953118	激光头塑料配件
泓纬塑胶五金模具制造(东莞)有限公司	黄江镇	83511688	塑胶品
科广电子（东莞）有限公司	寮步镇	83302929	微型二极管
台翰模具制品（东莞）有限公司	长安镇	87087888	精冲模模具标准件
东莞乙宏精密模具有限公司	塘厦镇	87919391	精密模具
东莞联茂电子科技有限公司	虎门镇	88623268	覆铜板
东莞友成精密模具有限公司	桥头镇	83457238	筹办五金塑胶制品
东莞东远机械制造有限公司	常平镇	83501527	送料机
东莞道滘万宝至马达有限公司	道滘镇	88831848	电工机械专用设备
东莞富强电子有限公司	东坑镇	83882225	耳机
东莞冠皇精密模具塑胶有限公司	樟木头镇	82128128	模具
东莞胜方电子有限公司	东城街道	86216886	导电薄膜
兴科电子（东莞）有限公司	虎门镇	85106058	手机按键
东莞塘厦顺扬精密五金厂	塘厦镇	87989888	五金模具

1-5　续表 23

(2011年)

单位名称	所属镇街	联系电话	主要产品（或服务）
东莞骆恒塑胶制品有限公司	清溪镇	87312310	精密成型钢模
东莞保康电子科技有限公司	樟木头镇	87780831	血糖检测器
东莞亿东机器有限公司	大岭山镇	85785003	全自动注塑机及零配件
景旺模具（东莞）有限公司	虎门镇	85504415	模具
东莞隆富精密模具有限公司	长安镇	85311526	加工手机按键
东莞毅昌模具制造注塑有限公司	谢岗镇	87761209	五金模具
峰川模具东莞有限公司	凤岗镇	87513998	五金模具
东莞泛邦电子有限公司	长安镇	85310926	电子产品
毅昌金型（东莞）五金制品有限公司	谢岗镇	87761209	塑胶模具
东莞顺兴电子有限公司	寮步镇	83039160	电子塑胶零配件
东莞盈拓科技实业有限公司	横沥镇	83798101	金属切削机床
东莞豪力机械有限公司	茶山镇	88658999	直线封边机
东莞恒晖彩印机械厂有限公司	凤岗镇	87751438	彩印机器设备
东莞运城制版有限公司	常平镇	83395297	凹印版辊
台光五金制品(东莞)有限公司	谢岗镇	87685123	精密五金模具
东莞富强鑫塑胶机械制造有限公司	大朗镇	83313753	注塑机械
巨力精密设备制造(东莞)有限公司	长安镇	88611555	精冲模
长成电子(东莞)有限公司	东城街道	22035023	非金属制品模具
永大精密模具(东莞)有限公司	长安镇	85312541	精密模具
盘起工业(东莞)有限公司	长安镇	85070387	精冲模
东华机械有限公司	东城街道	22806233	注塑机
东莞永胜医疗制品有限公司	塘厦镇	87948084	医疗器械
保德科技（东莞）有限公司	常平镇	81896936	电动化电渡机械设备
东莞明利钢材模具制品有限公司	大朗镇	83316878	精密型腔模
东莞康佳模具塑胶有限公司	凤岗镇	82071360	模具
东莞柏兆电子有限公司	长安镇	85540381	电脑主板机
东莞立诚电子有限公司	石排镇	86532010	电线
忠信制模(东莞)有限公司	横沥镇	83732298	非金属制品模具
东莞兆旺电子有限公司	塘厦镇	87929567	电子专用设备
一胜百模具(东莞)有限公司	松山湖	22897888	精密型模具
东莞丰裕电机有限公司	塘厦镇	87902888	涂装设备
万昌五金模具（东莞）有限公司	茶山镇	86480208	模具
东莞信易电热机械有限公司	大朗镇	83313588	干燥机
先锐模具配件(东莞)有限公司	长安镇	85376810	热流管
东莞鸿图金属压铸电器制造有限公司	长安镇	86062888	汽车零部件
交通运输设备制造业			
格尔翰汽车配件(东莞)有限公司	石排镇	81828988	汽车配件
东莞凯力船舶有限公司	麻涌镇	88280192	船舶配件
东莞井上建上汽车部件有限公司	沙田镇	88682171	汽车零部件
东莞龙达科技有限公司	塘厦镇	87547932	自行车配件
万宝至精工（东莞）有限公司	虎门镇	85564792	电镀轴芯
东莞新荣精密汽车配件有限公司	大岭山镇	83354742	汽车零部件及配件
东莞三峰精密技术有限公司	寮步镇	81197733	磁盘驱动器部件
广东永强奥林宝国际消防汽车有限公司	寮步镇	83269740	消防汽车
东莞井上橡塑加工有限公司	茶山镇	86176862	汽车配件
东莞泰合复合材料有限公司	黄江镇	86913288	自行车零配件

1-5 续表 24

(2011年)

单位名称	所属镇街	联系电话	主要产品（或服务）
东莞鸿图精密压铸有限公司	长安镇	86062888	铝合金压铸件
东莞果升电子有限公司	常平镇	82207988	汽车影音设备
东莞恩斯克转向器有限公司	东城街道	22620960	汽车零部件及配件
小仓离合机(东莞)有限公司	石碣镇	86361603	离合器
东莞瑞城压铸制品有限公司	凤岗镇	87511225	铝合金制品
东莞京滨汽车电喷装置有限公司	东城街道	22658290	汽车零部件及配件
东莞大和化成汽车零配件有限公司	桥头镇	83421718	汽车固件
爱地雅(东莞)自行车有限公司	寮步镇	88951888	自行车
古河汽车配件(东莞)有限公司	清溪镇	87295600	汽车用电线
东莞广泽汽车饰件有限公司	厚街镇	85903898	汽车饰件
东莞山口实业有限公司	樟木头镇	87128480	汽车塑胶制品
美尔顿车业(东莞)有限公司	寮步镇	81118000	电动助力车
东莞方皓汽车配件有限公司	塘厦镇	87725576	捆绑器
东莞鸿益雨刷有限公司	茶山镇	86646707	汽车雨刷
广东中远船务工程有限公司	麻涌镇	88286988	金属船
东莞山多力汽车配件有限公司	企石镇	86722101	汽车雨刷
东莞吉旺汽车零件有限公司	长安镇	86068932	汽车关键零配件
电气机械及器材制造业			
日本电产三协电子（东莞）有限公司	石龙镇	86111234	微电机
东莞硕宇电子有限公司	虎门镇	85710300	电子灯具
东莞虎门龙眼海克力斯电子有限公司	虎门镇	85554604	电子线加工
东莞欧陆电子有限公司	长安镇	87088788	电子元件
东莞市井南电子有限公司	中堂镇	88410266	新型电子材料
东莞桥历电子有限公司	桥头镇	86937682	塑胶五金
东莞道滘建和五金制品厂	道滘镇	88836680	开关电线接插件
东莞新能源电子科技有限公司	南城街道	88989052	电池
东莞吉联电线电缆有限公司	虎门镇	85551155	PVC电线
东莞唯可灯饰有限公司	樟木头镇	38819898	灯饰配件
东莞新隆漆包线有限公司	茶山镇	86415025	漆包线
东莞超霸电池有限公司	塘厦镇	87910215	电池
东莞乐域塑胶电子制品有限公司	石排镇	86550011	光管手提灯
东莞威德电子科技有限公司	东城街道	23061648	背部按摩椅座垫
东莞巨丰铜线有限公司	东城街道	22266314	漆包线
东莞新能源科技有限公司	松山湖	88989162	高技术绿色电池
东莞光旭太阳能灯饰有限公司	大朗镇	86261866	太阳能电池板
东莞力达电机有限公司	塘厦镇	87727891	微电机及其它电机
东莞威霸清洁器材有限公司	寮步镇	83283988	清地机
东莞冠宏电子有限公司	长安镇	88619858	组合音响、电子钢琴
东莞劲捷电子有限公司	厚街镇	85895863	电池充电器
东莞亿得电器制品有限公司	虎门镇	85554635	电热炉
东莞强盛电线电缆有限公司	石碣镇	86633470	电线、电缆
东莞岳丰电子科技有限公司	石碣镇	86634236	电话线连插头
东莞永成电器制品厂有限公司	清溪镇	87738870	吸尘器
东莞亿泰电线电缆有限公司	虎门镇	85500951	电线
东莞理士电源制品有限公司	塘厦镇	87325187	高能阀控密封蓄电池
东莞固邦灯饰电线有限公司	虎门镇	85553167	节日灯饰、红铜线

1-5 续表 25

(2011年)

单位名称	所属镇街	联系电话	主要产品（或服务）
东莞清溪华晖五金电器厂	清溪镇	86817099	油炸锅
东莞志丰电子有限公司	大朗镇	83183457	蜂鸣器
东莞三星电机有限公司	寮步镇	83305000	电源
大宇（东莞）电器有限公司	东坑镇	83020257	榨汁机
东莞卡妮尔灯饰有限公司	塘厦镇	87723088	台灯
亚弘(东莞)电器有限公司	塘厦镇	86851766	家用电器
东莞首资宝电器制造有限公司	谢岗镇	87130808	电暖器
东莞基立线缆有限公司	塘厦镇	82061078	电脑连接线
东莞丰盛电线电缆有限公司	桥头镇	83343591	漆包线
东莞常禾电子有限公司	虎门镇	85551202	音箱、喇叭、扬声器
东莞市银晖电制品有限公司	塘厦镇	87723007	锂离子电池
东莞安联电器元件有限公司	虎门镇	85500410	电器开关
东莞利通电器二厂	长安镇	86070888	电源供应器
东莞诠盛电器有限公司	厚街镇	85825373	电源插座
东莞赫升机电有限公司	塘厦镇	82095588	机电设备
新宝电机（东莞）有限公司	虎门镇	85504417	线路转换板
东莞伊斯丹电子有限公司	清溪镇	87338301	变压器、整流器和电感器
东莞新元电子有限公司	塘厦镇	87815229	锂离子电池
东莞万宝至电机设备制造有限公司	东城街道	22267409	微电机
东莞启东电线电缆有限公司	沙田镇	88867234	电线、电缆
东莞升隆电线塑胶有限公司	黄江镇	83608118	电线
东莞苏扬灯饰有限公司	桥头镇	83342116	圣诞饰品
东莞雅士电子有限公司	长安镇	85545115	收放组合机
东莞日进电线有限公司	寮步镇	83218997	硅胶电线
东莞鸿呈电子有限公司	厚街镇	88636000	电脑连接插头
金淞制冷设备（东莞）有限公司	常平镇	83394468	移动式冷气机
东莞卡斯特照明有限公司	茶山镇	88655066	照明灯具及其配件
东莞润泰电线电缆有限公司	虎门镇	88620999	电线
永新电线电缆(东莞)有限公司	长安镇	85411045	电线、电缆、电脑连接线
呈威电子（东莞）有限公司	横沥镇	83377756	微型变压器
东莞新南利电业有限公司	长安镇	85318758	电源线
东莞元太电业有限公司	塘厦镇	87881778	电线
东莞世福电器有限公司	塘厦镇	87923483	电源控制盒
东莞迅捷线束有限公司	中堂镇	88412829	电源插头线
东莞星志厨具厂有限公司	石碣镇	86634017	厨具
东莞昌亿电器有限公司	洪梅镇	88847319	电器开关制
东莞千石家电有限公司	横沥镇	83732881	冷气机
东莞艾天电池科技有限公司	横沥镇	88973706	锂离子电池
松普科技（东莞）有限公司	塘厦镇	87937608	宽带接入网通信系统设备
东莞高力电池有限公司	清溪镇	87739390	干电池
乔日电业制品(东莞)有限公司	虎门镇	85562003	开关断路器
东莞东进照明有限公司	东城街道	22024968	灯饰
东莞富钢电子有限公司	常平镇	83399000	电路板组件
东莞泰欣照明有限公司	黄江镇	87135999	灯饰
东莞立贸极细电线有限公司	石碣镇	86302066	电线
东莞蒂雅克电子有限公司	长安镇	85548848	音响视听设备

1-5 续表 26

(2011年)

单位名称	所属镇街	联系电话	主要产品（或服务）
实盈电子（东莞）有限公司	清溪镇	87318688	连接器
富士林电子（东莞）有限公司	东坑镇	83882225	连接线
东莞安硕电子有限公司	塘厦镇	87882595	电子式镇流器、微型变压器
东莞邦达五金有限公司	常平镇	83818660	光控开关
东莞九州电器有限公司	大朗镇	83188854	筒灯
亚士吉灯饰（东莞）有限公司	石龙镇	88492087	灯具、照明装置
万泰光电（东莞）有限公司	虎门镇	88620666	单模光纤
东莞明电电气工程有限公司	万江街道	88750012	高压配电柜
东莞金波罗电业科技有限公司	中堂镇	88886808	电线、电缆
东莞铭励电器制品有限公司	洪梅镇	86227426	电器开关
东莞启益电器机械有限公司	塘厦镇	87989065	变压器
东莞进泰电子有限公司	塘厦镇	87725650	音响
东莞大得电线电缆有限公司	企石镇	86787888	电线、电缆
东莞桥梓周氏电业有限公司	常平镇	83332731	电线、电缆PVC胶粒
东莞文邦电线有限公司	清溪镇	87731000	电线、电缆
意拉德电子（东莞）有限公司	横沥镇	82208902	电子控制板
东莞怡盛电业有限公司	大朗镇	83016688	电线、电缆
东莞达晨电业制品有限公司	石碣镇	86631818	电线
东莞超冠照明实业有限公司	长安镇	81627688	镇流器
荣文灯饰(东莞)有限公司	长安镇	81667888	灯饰及配件
长青林电子(东莞)有限公司	桥头镇	83340851	电线
易事特电力系统技术有限公司	松山湖	21643378	不间断电源
东莞昭和机电有限公司	东城街道	23068915	电子连接线
东莞耐迪电子有限公司	茶山镇	86863101	轴承
东莞联立电器实业有限公司	塘厦镇	87721921	小家电
东莞积信电器有限公司	樟木头镇	87799639	电烤炉
东莞星地电子有限公司	长安镇	85545651	带插头电线
东莞嘉盛照明科技有限公司	虎门镇	85700057	灯具
东莞柏杰灯饰有限公司	虎门镇	85551219	灯饰
东莞堤摩讯传动科技有限公司	横沥镇	87062055	控制器
东莞清溪荔横峻凌电子厂	清溪镇	87734725	电子产品
东莞厚街溪头资科电脑线材厂	厚街镇	85599076	电线
东莞永德电业制品有限公司	塘厦镇	87727278	电线
太阳电线东莞有限公司	南城街道	22401739	电线、电缆
东莞华巨特殊线材有限公司	道滘镇	88389008	镀锡线
东莞统元电源连接有限公司	大朗镇	83101598	电源线连插头
东莞佑茂五金塑胶有限公司	谢岗镇	87686300	电脑五金塑胶配件
日立蓄电池（东莞）有限公司	茶山镇	86400790	汽车铅酸蓄电池
东莞立伟电业有限公司	长安镇	86074558	电子接头
东莞市雅科精密线材有限公司	东坑镇	83888869	电线、电缆
东莞港电电器制品有限公司	石排镇	86518228	直发器
东莞中钜资讯光电有限公司	厚街镇	85994660	电子原配件
东莞市柏洋电子有限公司	石排镇	81369899	开关电源、充电器
东莞汇勋电器制品有限公司	塘厦镇	87880968	电风扇、暖风机、增湿机
东莞维盟电子绝缘材料有限公司	清溪镇	87315040	耐高温电容器
东莞海韵电子有限公司	东城街道	22610501	电子设备

1-5 续表 27

(2011年)

单位名称	所属镇街	联系电话	主要产品（或服务）
东莞华兴电器有限公司	清溪镇	82995698	小型变压器
东莞澳利电器制品有限公司	常平镇	83330419	变压器
东莞健达照明有限公司	企石镇	86781774	照明灯具
东莞莹辉灯饰有限公司	虎门镇	85551445	灯饰
四国电线(东莞)有限公司	清溪镇	87735432	同轴电线
东莞三雄电业制造有限公司	桥头镇	83436611	电源线
飞宏(东莞)电子有限公司	清溪镇	87292966	电源供应器及半成品
东莞瀚宇电子有限公司	大朗镇	83193666	KF线
丰岛电子制品(东莞)有限公司	清溪镇	87312590	精密按键
东莞泰德电机有限公司	东坑镇	83020111	吊扇
东莞德宏电线电子有限公司	塘厦镇	87724535	电线
东莞广宇精密电子有限公司	虎门镇	85509706	电线
光宝电子(东莞)有限公司	长安镇	86070888	电源供应器
东莞毓华电子科技有限公司	企石镇	86668107	开关电源
东莞新光电线有限公司	道滘镇	88316705	电线、电缆
东莞库柏电子有限公司	长安镇	81605288	变压器
东莞庆泰电线电缆有限公司	常平镇	83330265	电线、电源
东莞威煌电器制品有限公司	塘厦镇	87727984	电动剪发器
东莞华新电线电缆有限公司	大朗镇	83195252	8.0铜杆
东莞松藤电子有限公司	桥头镇	83457291	电吹风
春迅电子(东莞)有限公司	寮步镇	88955688	感应灯
东莞长联电线电缆有限公司	虎门镇	85703585	电线、电缆
东莞林发电子有限公司	厚街镇	83085888	音响插头线
正规电线电缆(东莞)有限公司	黄江镇	83624357	电源线连插头
东莞维升电子制品有限公司	黄江镇	83622694	电源线连插头
东莞宇隆电工材料有限公司	茶山镇	86642861	漆包线
金霸王(中国)限公司	南城街道	22403615	电池
东莞艾玛电子有限公司	塘厦镇	87725209	红外线感知灯光控制器
东莞永大电子有限公司	常平镇	83339366	插头连接线
东莞宏大电器制品有限公司	东城街道	22269073	家用电器
东莞惠华金属制品有限公司	大朗镇	83188845	铜线
东莞宏桦电器有限公司	塘厦镇	87935001	电风扇
东莞永力电业有限公司	常平镇	83335989	电源线插头
易达威锐电源设备科技（东莞）有限公司	东城街道	22651108	智能化电源设备系统
东莞光距电子有限公司	塘厦镇	87288988	网络线
东莞金星电线有限公司	大朗镇	83195297	电线、电缆
东莞宏翔电器有限公司	凤岗镇	87772581	电风扇
东莞凤岗奥托泰电器制品厂	凤岗镇	87502980	汽车电灯
东莞立邦礼品灯饰有限公司	塘厦镇	82086818	台灯
东莞苏泊尔电器有限公司	石碣镇	86365011	电磁炉
丽宾电子通讯（东莞）有限公司	寮步镇	81112051	耳机线材
东莞川电电机有限公司	东坑镇	83020001	定子、转子
东莞盛时五金塑胶制品有限公司	塘厦镇	87725890	五金塑胶灯具及配件
东莞巨汉灯饰有限公司	莞城街道	22096948	灯饰
东莞建通电子五金有限公司	虎门镇	85565684	端子
港芝(东莞)电子制造厂有限公司	塘厦镇	87720639	健身器材

1-5 续表 28

(2011年)

单位名称	所属镇街	联系电话	主要产品（或服务）
东莞万利信新材料元件有限公司	长安镇	81882000	铝电解电容器
东莞华明灯具有限公司	清溪镇	87311200	灯具
东莞东马电子厂	寮步镇	83308523	微型马达及附件
东莞塘厦伊南电器制品厂	塘厦镇	87880237	连接线
固邦(东莞)电器有限公司	虎门镇	86096666	节目灯饰品灯饰配件
东莞可比世电子有限公司	黄江镇	83623093	变压器
东莞杰扬五金电器有限公司	东坑镇	83020011	吊灯
东莞日线线缆有限公司	桥头镇	83344845	铜材
永胜(东莞)电子有限公司	塘厦镇	87948084	电脑读书磁头
东莞行特电子有限公司	清溪镇	87388642	连接器
东莞钜权电器有限公司	万江街道	22183056	厨房电器及其它零配件
东莞正扬电子机械有限公司	黄江镇	83533290	液位传感器
东莞大东电业有限公司	桥头镇	83340838	电线、电缆
东莞京洲灯饰有限公司	寮步镇	83305827	嵌灯
东莞南玻光伏科技有限公司	麻涌镇	88288808	晶体硅太阳能电池
东莞亚岑照明有限公司	凤岗镇	87774926	灯具及照明装置
东莞裕新灯饰有限公司	虎门镇	82887578	灯饰
东莞优电电线电缆有限公司	石碣镇	86632563	电线、电缆
东莞清溪合力电器制造厂	清溪镇	87731111	搅拌机
东莞厚街溪头太空梭电线厂	厚街镇	85599076	电线
东莞金力电池实业有限公司	企石镇	86661510	电池
东莞福登机电有限公司	东坑镇	81035111	电机和小型电器
东莞蓝创捷特佳电子有限公司	常平镇	83392420	灯具
世雅电子科技(东莞)有限公司	长安镇	85414388	高效率变频器
东莞金山电池有限公司	塘厦镇	87723007	锂离子电子
东莞诚远家电有限公司	大朗镇	83195040	电风扇
东莞小泉照明有限公司	石龙镇	86189569	灯饰
东莞大淼电器有限公司	东坑镇	83884984	变压器
扬宣电子(东莞)有限公司	茶山镇	81833108	电子元器件
东莞成铭电子有限公司	长安镇	85419999	电子零配件
桑野电子(东莞)有限公司	横沥镇	82329818	连接天线
东莞百实特电子科技有限公司	常平镇	82836825	照明灯、发光标志
东莞名星电线电缆有限公司	常平镇	83556398	电线、电缆
东莞忠佑电子有限公司	凤岗镇	86801899	连接线
东莞龙杰电子有限公司	清溪镇	87734425	电源线插头
东莞爱思丽灯饰有限公司	横沥镇	81012302	灯饰
东莞欣德电子有限公司	塘厦镇	87882386	电线
东莞景盛电线材料有限公司	虎门镇	85157538	PVC胶粒
东莞金准电器有限公司	大朗镇	83312620	灯座
东莞合力电器制品有限公司	清溪镇	87731111	搅拌器
东莞虎门万旭电子有限公司	虎门镇	85552215	电脑连接线
东莞艾坤特电子有限公司	寮步镇	82815981	电子元器件
东莞杰光灯饰有限公司	东城街道	22674459	台灯、落地灯
东莞新能德科技有限公司	寮步镇	88956131	可充电池
东莞名帝电子产品有限公司	虎门镇	85551447	连接线
东莞中美五金制品有限公司	塘厦镇	87981800	五金制品

1-5　续表 29

(2011年)

单位名称	所属镇街	联系电话	主要产品（或服务）
东莞市万丰科技有限公司	横沥镇	86920001	网络线
东莞衡隆电业有限公司	寮步镇	81107395	电线
东莞荣星电线有限公司	塘厦镇	87913003	漆包线
东莞美群电器制品有限公司	塘厦镇	87981800	家用电力器具
东莞贵名精密电子有限公司	虎门镇	85152555	电子绝缘配件
东莞泽龙线缆有限公司	石龙镇	81388600	特种漆包线
通信设备、计算机及其他电子设备制造业			
东莞天铖科技有限公司	厚街镇	85889488	电子产品
东莞锦富迪奇电子有限公司	寮步镇	88956666	TFT-LCD平板显示屏材料
毕索龙电子(东莞)有限公司	塘厦镇	82620705	电子产品
广东生益科技股份有限公司	松山湖	22271828	覆铜板
东莞阳天电子科技有限公司	塘厦镇	82062778	电子元件
宜来特光电（东莞）有限公司	寮步镇	81122970	TFFLCD平板显示屏
东莞首利科技五金有限公司	清溪镇	86812888	线路板组件
东莞普光液晶显示有限公司	厚街镇	81520001	手机液晶显示屏
康展电子（东莞）有限公司	塘厦镇	87915950	电子原件
东莞达伸电子有限公司	横沥镇	88975258	电脑散热风扇
东莞金百升塑胶电子有限公司	常平镇	83391096	塑胶制品
东莞辰达电器有限公司	洪梅镇	86227952	电器开关
日发电子科技（东莞）有限公司	长安镇	85348787	电脑磁盘读写笔
东莞富士通电装电子有限公司	洪梅镇	88848801	电子元件
东莞德宝电子有限公司	莞城街道	38875000	液晶显示器
意创力电子科技（东莞）有限公司	长安镇	81553060	导航仪
东莞南城新科磁电制品有限公司	南城街道	22810033	电子产品
成翔电子（东莞）有限公司	清溪镇	86812888	电源供应器
升荣电子(东莞)有限公司	清溪镇	87311036	电脑周边产品
东莞凯鸿光电科技有限公司	虎门镇	85524576	电器保护管
高效电子(东莞)有限公司	寮步镇	88901888	电脑零配件
东莞大新能率电子有限公司	常平镇	83822950	信息传播工具
精成科技电子（东莞）有限公司	黄江镇	83632679	电脑主机板
亚南电子（东莞）有限公司	寮步镇	83265079	音响
东莞联洲电子科技有限公司	凤岗镇	82091688	液晶电视机
东莞电创电子有限公司	道滘镇	88834807	电子接插件
东莞技研新阳电子有限公司	桥头镇	83434514	电器零配件
东莞汉阳电脑有限公司	清溪镇	86819888	内存
东莞奥得时精密电子有限公司	望牛墩镇	88518719	手机配件
东莞凤岗三和盛科技电子厂	凤岗镇	87862222	计算机及周边设备
东莞铭异精密电子有限公司	石碣镇	86387383	电脑支架
东莞南城新科磁电制品厂	南城街道	22810033	电脑磁头
东莞船井电机厂	黄江镇	83665999	液晶电视机
东莞嘉财电业制造厂	大岭山镇	83359040	电子产品
东莞三协精工科技有限公司	高埗镇	88787202	电子产品
东莞时力科技电子厂	长安镇	85415668	电子元件
千代达电子制造(东莞)有限公司	大岭山镇	88961122	精密机电零部件
东莞通华液晶有限公司	东城街道	88774388	液晶显示板
东莞歌乐东方电子有限公司	东坑镇	83387001	音响

1-5 续表 30

(2011年)

单位名称	所属镇街	联系电话	主要产品（或服务）
东莞清溪旺普登电子厂	清溪镇	87291877	液晶用背光板
东莞鹏龙光电有限公司	石碣镇	88787202	平板显示器件
东莞柏能电子厂	厚街镇	85822002	计算机主板和显卡
东莞皓讯电子有限公司	清溪镇	87313056	电脑电子周边线
东莞柏狮赛格精密电子有限公司	麻涌镇	88233068	半导体
东莞东坑先益电子厂	东坑镇	83381857	发光二极管
东莞长安厦岗成铭电子制品厂	长安镇	85419999	电脑机箱
东莞长安日发电子厂	长安镇	85348787	磁头弹性臂
东莞康特尔电子有限公司	高埗镇	88462888	数字电视机
东莞天籁之音电声制品有限公司	厚街镇	85033501	喇叭
东莞顺晟电脑实业有限公司	凤岗镇	86801188	电脑机箱
东莞耳神电声科技有限公司	万江街道	89027886	音箱
东莞海正机电有限公司	石碣镇	86366010	激光机芯
日本电产日新（东莞）工机有限公司	长安镇	87085211	数码相机镜片
东莞彩显有机发光科技有限公司	清溪镇	87738875	新型平板显示器
东莞怡辉五金有限公司	清溪镇	87386488	五金制品、钢材
东莞爱铭数码电子有限公司	寮步镇	83038000	DVD激光头
京瓷爱克(东莞)电子有限公司	石龙镇	88495099	新型机电元件
东莞王氏港建电子有限公司	常平镇	83903333	电子产品
滨川金属（东莞）有限公司	长安镇	85322971	电脑零配件
东莞奕华电子有限公司	东城街道	88759333	电子产品
东莞荃宝电子制品有限公司	清溪镇	87383811	电脑机箱
诺基亚通信有限公司东莞分公司	南城街道	22402844	移动电话
东莞栢能电子科技有限公司	厚街镇	85822002	电脑主机
伟易达（东莞）电子产品有限公司	厚街镇	85581806	电子玩具
伟易达（东莞）通讯设备有限公司	寮步镇	83231806	室内无线电话
东莞尔来德通讯有限公司	黄江镇	87097800	手机按键
东莞冠坤电子有限公司	清溪镇	87318000	片式电容
大东骏通（东莞）电子有限公司	常平镇	83394379	组合音响
东莞万迪电子有限公司	常平镇	82988519	电子设备
伟易达（东莞）电讯有限公司	寮步镇	83231806	电源控制口
亚电电子（东莞）有限公司	塘厦镇	87982616	黑胶唱机、激光唱机
东莞庆帮电子有限公司	大朗镇	83319425	喇叭
东莞微端电子科技有限公司	常平镇	83975888	新型平板显示器
东莞展胜电子科技有限公司	常平镇	83397671	多媒体接收器
东莞航大电子有限公司	常平镇	83392291	电话单机
东莞安美时电子有限公司	常平镇	83394581	网络控制设备
东莞泰凯电子有限公司	塘厦镇	82996789	VCD解码板
京都电工(东莞)有限公司	长安镇	85428288	电子元器
东莞中探探针有限公司	虎门镇	85151668	电子测试探针
东莞令特电子有限公司	虎门镇	81518186	压敏电阻、敏感元器件
东莞新优电子有限公司	横沥镇	82980583	家用电器及其配部件
东莞卓翰光电科技有限公司	横沥镇	81180610	数码相机零配件
东莞明瑞电子有限公司	长安镇	86072000	调解器
东莞艾太科光电有限公司	高埗镇	81305001	背光源
东莞清溪三清半导体厂	清溪镇	87734139	半导体晶体管

1-5 续表 31

(2011年)

单位名称	所属镇街	联系电话	主要产品（或服务）
平易电子（东莞）有限公司	常平镇	83820333	印刷电路板
东莞东英电子工业有限公司	清溪镇	87328201	DVD机蕊
东莞东骏电器有限公司	南城街道	22401688	电子变压器用铁心片
东莞建冠塑胶电子有限公司	虎门镇	85162899	连接器
泓凯电子科技(东莞)有限公司	黄江镇	83365942	电脑机箱
东莞嘉茂电子科技有限公司	大朗镇	88606888	喇叭
东莞石排联鑫电子厂	石排镇	86591818	彩色电视机
业强科技（东莞）有限公司	长安镇	85421928	新型电子元器件(敏感元器件、热导管)
东莞建永数码科技有限公司	塘厦镇	87880818	CD镭射机
东莞黄江瑞升科技电子厂	黄江镇	83633303	电脑及周边产品
东莞石龙粤龙光学制品厂	石龙镇	86181222	收、放音机
美信音响器材(东莞)有限公司	塘厦镇	86856188	音箱(含喇叭)
东莞泰富电子有限公司	高埗镇	88730138	电话
东莞扩乐格电子器材有限公司	塘厦镇	87923096	数字录放机
东莞辉城电子有限公司	望牛墩镇	88520218	电子组件
东莞全特电子科技有限公司	虎门镇	85555526	塑胶电子制品
东莞百一电子有限公司	大朗镇	83188045	数字视频编解码设备
富相电子科技(东莞)有限公司	高埗镇	88737888	液晶显示器件
东莞超悦电子有限公司	寮步镇	83305007	电脑键盘
东莞科德电子有限公司	常平镇	83391340	铭板
东莞石碣源利电子厂	石碣镇	86638923	液晶显示器
东莞凡振工业电子有限公司	谢岗镇	87635181	电子音响
万事通电子(东莞)有限公司	石碣镇	86633491	耳机
棠裕电子(东莞)有限公司	清溪镇	87332588	液晶显示器
东莞创盟电子有限公司	虎门镇	85505799	电脑连接线
奥托仑光电子（东莞）有限公司	茶山镇	86401060	玻璃光学镜片
东莞三星视界有限公司	厚街镇	85582000	液晶显示片
东莞加炜电子有限公司	石碣镇	86310071	电子连接器
东莞鑫联数码科技有限公司	石排镇	86591818	机顶盒
东莞达电电子有限公司	石碣镇	86323500	耳机
达创科技(东莞)有限公司	石碣镇	86637008	集线器
东莞泰山电子有限公司	虎门镇	85564813	印刷线路版
东莞利保迅电子有限公司	茶山镇	86408844	变压器
东莞洲磊电子有限公司	谢岗镇	87631888	磷化镓
泰科电子(东莞)有限公司	厚街镇	85817613	通讯终端设备
东莞长安镇时力电子厂	长安镇	85533151	磁臂组合半成品
东莞黄江精成科技电子一厂	黄江镇	83632679	电脑主板
东莞欣韵电子有限公司	石碣镇	81399168	电源供应器
东莞国瑞电子有限公司	塘厦镇	82063511	电感器
宝罗电子科技（东莞）有限公司	横沥镇	83712772	新型电子元件
东莞华盛音响制品有限公司	石排镇	86528327	汽车收放音机
东莞永保电子有限公司	桥头镇	81176991	锂离子电子
东莞爱美克电子有限公司	凤岗镇	87775085	放大器
东莞顺牛金属制品有限公司	厚街镇	85931595	金属制品
东莞捷盛电子有限公司	东城街道	22026000	印制电路板
东莞立德电子有限公司	塘厦镇	87727748	变压器

1-5 续表 32

(2011年)

单位名称	所属镇街	联系电话	主要产品（或服务）
东莞呈越电脑配件有限公司	大朗镇	86913168	液晶显示器支架
东莞领航电子有限公司	塘厦镇	87937099	变压器、整流器
东莞中兴电子有限公司	桥头镇	83457860	电子元件
思林菲加热器材(东莞)有限公司	虎门镇	88629188	电子元器件
东莞爱美达电子有限公司	横沥镇	83377651	电脑散热器
东莞首富电子有限公司	樟木头镇	87710688	电子产品
东莞高盛电子有限公司	常平镇	83813136	电话机
东莞宏邦光电有限公司	清溪镇	87322250	扩散片
东莞长安上角福摩斯托电子厂	长安镇	85541200	组合音响
东莞宏智电器配件有限公司	谢岗镇	87136136	家用电器配件
东莞技嘉电子有限公司	黄江镇	83367140	电脑主板
益伸电子（东莞）有限公司	横沥镇	83796198	五金电子
东莞宝桥电子科技有限公司	黄江镇	83632679	新型平板显示器件
东莞环宇电子有限公司	凤岗镇	87774838	电子元件
东莞高惠电子有限公司	长安镇	85319188	连接器
东莞昱欣电子有限公司	大朗镇	83126168	电子元件
东莞石龙华南电子五金制品厂	石龙镇	86624941	电子元件
天弘(东莞)科技有限公司	松山湖	22899333	网络游戏机
恩智浦半导体广东有限公司	黄江镇	83668268	半导体
东莞华强三洋电子有限公司	塘厦镇	87910998	彩电
东莞厚街新塘早川电子厂	厚街镇	85901115	电子配件
东莞首邦电子有限公司	石碣镇	86632772	变压器
东莞利源电子有限公司	横沥镇	83723988	灯光控制器
捷荣模具工业(东莞)有限公司	长安镇	82387988	模具
东莞天扬电子有限公司	塘厦镇	82011299	电力电子元器件
东莞优威王电子塑胶五金有限公司	虎门镇	85701800	计算机用PC塑胶配件
东莞迅德电器有限公司	清溪镇	87739411	小型变压器
东莞万年富电子有限公司	塘厦镇	87724667	线路板
东莞狮龙电子有限公司	寮步镇	83283391	DVD
广东南方宏明电子科技股份有限公司	南城街道	22407479	电容器
东莞台庆精密电子有限公司	黄江镇	83365488	电子零件
东莞颖利电子有限公司	谢岗镇	87769809	收录机机芯
智嘉通讯科技(东莞)有限公司	常平镇	83335430	通讯配件
敦朴光电有限公司	厚街镇	85926660	照相机
伟特移动通迅设备（东莞）有限公司	桥头镇	83340841	移动通讯产品
东莞天意电子有限公司	石龙镇	86080328	彩票终端机
东莞万德镜片科技有限公司	东城街道	22676816	镜片
东莞太华半导体有限公司	寮步镇	83263688	手机用液晶显示器部件
东莞矽德半导体有限公司	清溪镇	87313240	集成电路
东莞欧珀移动通信有限公司	长安镇	85545555	手机
东莞宇龙通信科技有限公司	松山湖	23075096	新型智能手机
东莞鑫佑光电科技有限公司	石排镇	86534198	背光板
阿基里斯电子材料(东莞)有限公司	长安镇	85308801	电子材料
东莞同昌电子有限公司	大朗镇	83318960	PCB
东莞德竹电子科技有限公司	虎门镇	85258301	电子零配件
东莞恒扬光电有限公司	横沥镇	83710660	平板显示屏及显示屏材料

1-5 续表 33

(2011年)

单位名称	所属镇街	联系电话	主要产品（或服务）
东莞大岭山光顺电子厂	大岭山镇	83352904	电子产品
东莞为勤电子有限公司	长安镇	85542016	电子元器件
东莞高埗昭和电子厂	高埗镇	88873451	遥控器
东莞川边电子有限公司	东城街道	22209722	扬声器
三井高科技(广东)有限公司	长安镇	86070008	新型电子元器件
东莞德利信电子有限公司	常平镇	83395111	各种机芯产品
东莞广通事务机有限公司	长安镇	85312190	电子元件及组件
东莞华科电子有限公司	大朗镇	83115168	片式电容
智宝电子(东莞)有限公司	塘厦镇	87914676	电解电容器
茂瑞电子(东莞)有限公司	东城街道	87077888	键盘
东莞加玮华电子有限公司	东城街道	22257469	耳机
永胜电脑五金（东莞）有限公司	东坑镇	83387140	电脑机箱
东莞谢岗钨珍电子厂	谢岗镇	82126950	手机外壳
东莞新洋电子有限公司	茶山镇	86171021	手机外壳
东莞能率科技有限公司	寮步镇	83527668	手机摄像头
东莞迅脉电子有限公司	寮步镇	81196000	新型电子元器件
飞比达电子元器件（东莞）有限公司	横沥镇	83725088	新型电子元器件
东莞久尹电子有限公司	南城街道	22401737	热敏电阻和压敏电阻等
东莞裕光数码电子有限公司	道滘镇	88382101	手机LCD电路板
东莞帝光电子科技实业有限公司	清溪镇	87293808	LED背光源
东莞伍联电子科技有限公司	凤岗镇	82097852	电子计算机外部设备
东莞盛和电子有限公司	长安镇	86076988	电子产品
东莞雅图士电子科技有限公司	塘厦镇	82001800	电子器件
国巨电子(东莞)有限公司	塘厦镇	87720275	电阻器
太阳诱电(广东)有限公司	石碣镇	86636888	电容器
东莞亚锋电脑零配件有限公司	塘厦镇	87727888	电脑零配件
东莞全台电子有限公司	东坑镇	83697606	平板显示器
东莞康佳电子有限公司	凤岗镇	87758888	彩色电视
东莞樟木头十和田电子厂	樟木头镇	87713119	收音机
东莞普思电子有限公司	长安镇	85538871	高频滤波器
东莞生益电子有限公司	万江街道	22272074	多层印刷电路板
东莞芝浦电子有限公司	长安镇	85412371	热敏电阻
奥泰斯电子(东莞)有限公司	黄江镇	83365026	防盗热感应器
特新电路材料（东莞）有限公司	茶山镇	86403328	多层线路板
东莞万德电子制品有限公司	东城街道	88775555	硅胶按键
永捷电路版(东莞)有限公司	厚街镇	85812542	印制电路板
东莞陆和电子有限公司	中堂镇	88885117	键盘
东莞市宝盛五金制品有限公司	清溪镇	87315888	电脑外壳
世擎光电（东莞）有限公司	茶山镇	81821666	手机摄像模组
特新微电子（东莞）有限公司	茶山镇	86403328	电路板钻孔加工
东莞宣得电子有限公司	长安镇	85546400	电子元器件
东莞创慈磁性元件有限公司	石碣镇	86327771	变压器
立维腾电子（东莞）有限公司	桥头镇	81038888	电子元件及组件
东莞市捷伟讯电子有限公司	厚街镇	85993708	手机
品基电子(东莞)有限公司	塘厦镇	87910231	电子元件
东莞弘电电子有限公司	虎门镇	85550979	新型电子元器件

1-5 续表 34

(2011年)

单位名称	所属镇街	联系电话	主要产品（或服务）
坚力电子（东莞）有限公司	横沥镇	81890360	电子手表
程品电子科技（东莞）有限公司	石排镇	88935999	高频变压器
东莞大迪音响器材有限公司	寮步镇	83326201	音箱
东莞音音电子绘本有限公司	黄江镇	83668068	电子式音乐卡
富加宜连接器(东莞)有限公司	沙田镇	88682108	电子连接器
大船科技(东莞)有限公司	松山湖	22899666	精密轴承加工
东莞宝顺力电子塑胶制品厂有限公司	大岭山镇	83353827	电子产品音响
东莞红板多层线路板有限公司	长安镇	86060111	电子元器件
茂成电子科技（东莞）有限公司	黄江镇	83632688	元器件专用材料
东莞嘉耀电子有限公司	厚街镇	85930034	电脑功能卡
台达电子(东莞)有限公司	石碣镇	86639008	线圈
东莞达宏电子有限公司	清溪镇	87736405	电源供应器
台达电子零组件(东莞)有限公司	石碣镇	86639008	电脑散热风扇
永泰电子（东莞）有限公司	常平镇	83918040	电脑连接线
东莞国创电子有限公司	塘厦镇	87720275	片式电阻器
东莞华龙电子有限公司	横沥镇	83376575	变压器
康舒电子(东莞)有限公司	塘厦镇	87915950	电源供应器
东莞黄江威成科技电子厂	黄江镇	83632679	液晶显示屏
良特电子科技（东莞）有限公司	常平镇	83914041	通讯器材配件
雅新电子线路板(东莞)有限公司	石碣镇	86331999	印刷线路板
中名(东莞)电子有限公司	虎门镇	85559636	耳机
东莞相川铁龙电子有限公司	常平镇	83395551	电子元件
东莞山技光电科技有限公司	清溪镇	87388658	扩散膜
东莞益衡电子有限公司	凤岗镇	87755689	电源供应器
唯耀电子（东莞）有限公司	石龙镇	86113818	电源板
品佳电子(东莞)有限公司	沙田镇	88800318	液晶显示器
东莞沛波电子有限公司	石碣镇	86310316	小型变压器
东莞旺鸿五金制品有限公司	清溪镇	87302196	电脑机箱
矽谷电子科技（东莞）有限公司	黄江镇	83366696	液晶显示器
东莞动利电子有限公司	常平镇	83550800	电脑散热风扇
旗利得电子(东莞)有限公司	谢岗镇	87766645	印刷线路板
东莞市亚通光电有限公司	塘厦镇	82006088	光电子器件
东莞东聚电子电讯制品有限公司	石碣镇	86631652	鼠标
东莞昆盈电脑制品有限公司	厚街镇	85825810	鼠标
东莞山本电子科技有限公司	麻涌镇	88227094	印刷线路板
东莞万钧电子科技有限公司	洪梅镇	89138000	线路板
新豪(东莞)电子有限公司	寮步镇	83216200	电脑键盘
东莞诚信电子塑胶有限公司	虎门镇	85507263	变压器胶架
金笔电子东莞有限公司	东城街道	22200489	电子零配件件
华玮电子(东莞)有限公司	长安镇	85307001	加工插座
东莞创群石英晶体有限公司	大朗镇	83119395	石英晶体谐振器
东莞东力电子有限公司	塘厦镇	87723276	DVD机
东莞清溪晶达电子制品厂	清溪镇	87320077	液晶器件
广东升威电子制品有限公司	塘厦镇	87287777	电位器、编码器
东莞美捷电业有限公司	常平镇	83903378	镭射收录机
东莞宝山电子有限公司	樟木头镇	87712264	电子产品

1-5 续表 35

(2011年)

单位名称	所属镇街	联系电话	主要产品（或服务）
东莞友华通信配件有限公司	寮步镇	83326172	天线
东莞高埗微太电子科技有限公司	高埗镇	88876239	数码产品
东莞裕佳电子有限公司	清溪镇	87739418	光盘驱动器
东莞友华电子有限公司	寮步镇	83326171	端子连接器
东莞泉声电子有限公司	石碣镇	86325251	新型电子元器件
东莞七盟电子有限公司	黄江镇	83621007	电子专用设备
东莞汇和电子有限公司	谢岗镇	87768410	印刷线路板
东莞恒忻电子有限公司	塘厦镇	87915567	电感线圈
东莞致力电脑有限公司	清溪镇	87312821	电脑配件
东莞联桥电子有限公司	茶山镇	86485066	印刷电路板
盛恒达电子(东莞)有限公司	石碣镇	86633718	ADLS路由器
极讯电子(东莞)有限公司	寮步镇	88953310	电子元件
联德电子(东莞)有限公司	石碣镇	83072288	电子电源供应器
杰群电子科技（东莞）有限公司	黄江镇	83635267	新型电子元器件
东莞大朗辉鸿电子厂	大朗镇	83018938	喇叭半成品
东莞爱电电子有限公司	桥头镇	83434525	线路板
乐依文半导体(东莞)有限公司	长安镇	85647662	集成电路
奇烨电子（东莞）有限公司	石排镇	86925028	变压器
东莞永腾电子制品有限公司	凤岗镇	87755269	铝制散热片及散热器
东莞东原电子有限公司	寮步镇	83228000	手机充电器
东莞永冠电子科技有限公司	万江街道	22033699	DVD播放机
东莞茂林电子有限公司	虎门镇	85562012	空白线路板
东莞华新半导体有限公司	黄江镇	86968673	集成电路
东莞福摩斯托电子有限公司	长安镇	85541200	家用电子元件
东莞奇力新电子有限公司	清溪镇	87730251	线圈
东莞新进电子有限公司	大岭山镇	85613846	电子计算机外部设备
东莞协盈电脑有限公司	厚街镇	85880090	鼠标器
东莞立亚达电子有限公司	石排镇	86511283	电子产品
东莞市旭进光电有限公司	长安镇	85413789	光学镜头
东莞海盛电子科技有限公司	东坑镇	83385859	新型电子元器件
联一小原光学（东莞）有限公司	长安镇	86240666	加工光学玻璃毛胚
东莞旺宏科技有限公司	长安镇	87200379	鼠标
东莞万士达液晶显示器有限公司	东城街道	22668178	光电子器件及其他电子器件
东莞康创电子科技有限公司	厚街镇	85889989	收音机
东莞光阵显示器制品有限公司	清溪镇	87738870	摄像头
东莞高美电子有限公司	寮步镇	83300880	电子配件
东莞成乐电子有限公司	横沥镇	83713213	电子产品
东莞太阳诱电有限公司	石碣镇	86636888	电容器
东莞益新实业有限公司	塘厦镇	87811000	电子零配件
东莞美城电子电器有限公司	莞城街道	22250946	收录音机
东莞福满生电子有限公司	常平镇	82207777	电脑显示器托架
振曜电子(东莞)有限公司	大朗镇	83188470	网络交换机
东莞成谦音响科技有限公司	长安镇	85380808	喇叭
东莞合宝电器制品有限公司	横沥镇	83715169	电器开关
东莞日矿富士电子有限公司	洪梅镇	88431720	液晶背光源用电极
东莞森玛仕格里菲电路有限公司	茶山镇	81822047	多层线路板

1-5 续表 36

(2011年)

单位名称	所属镇街	联系电话	主要产品（或服务）
华磁电子(东莞)有限公司	石碣镇		电感器
东莞凯升电子有限公司	塘厦镇	87883521	电脑机箱
东莞高伟光学电子有限公司	寮步镇	83307113	手机摄像头
吉嘉电子东莞有限公司	樟木头镇	87790197	多媒体音箱
东莞耀升机电有限公司	清溪镇	87338900	电子零件、压铸产品
富港电子(东莞)有限公司	东坑镇	83882225	变压器
东莞美隆电声器材有限公司	塘厦镇	86856288	喇叭
东莞展翊五金电器有限公司	清溪镇	87735052	电脑机箱
东莞长安发利达电子厂	长安镇	85531414	电子元件加工
东莞建玮电子制品有限公司	清溪镇	87734800	电脑连接线
华容电子(广东)有限公司	石碣镇	83075098	电容器
东莞怡科电子有限公司	长安镇	87086668	汽车移动电话充电器
东莞艾利博电子有限公司	松山湖	22899100	电子词典和显示器
东莞长江电脑制品有限公司	清溪镇	87736209	电脑机箱
东莞塘厦建永塑胶电子厂	塘厦镇	87880818	CD镭射机
东莞实英电子有限公司	厚街镇	88630999	电脑接插件
东莞韵邦变压器有限公司	清溪镇	87731121	变压器
东莞泰硕电子有限公司	大岭山镇	85321851	连接器
旭丽电子(东莞)有限公司	石碣镇	86638923	键盘
东莞骅国电子有限公司	厚街镇	85597201	连接器
东莞近江电子有限公司	桥头镇	81036276	线路主板
东莞华强三洋马达有限公司	塘厦镇	87720523	微型马达
东莞群翰电子有限公司	常平镇	83824816	连接器
东莞友俊电子有限公司	清溪镇	87311900	胶粘带
嘉益电子（东莞）有限公司	东城街道	22207821	印制电路板
东莞福哥电子有限公司	茶山镇	86649438	电子产品、电位器
东莞联宝光电科技有限公司	企石镇	86786368	电子产品
东莞广原电子有限公司	石碣镇	86366010	扬声器
东莞台霖电子通讯有限公司	大岭山镇	85655858	电脑线连插头
群光电子（东莞）有限公司	清溪镇	87311688	电脑键盘
东莞康捷电子有限公司	长安镇	85317669	电子、电机连接器
东莞森泰电子有限公司	凤岗镇	87751663	手机
东莞前盛电子有限公司	塘厦镇	87910575	电源供应器
东莞翊凯电器制品有限公司	清溪镇	86812999	电脑机箱外壳
东莞富饶精密五金制品有限公司	虎门镇	85556266	五金制品
东莞添威电子制品有限公司	凤岗镇	87779805	电源供应器
东莞亨域电子有限公司	望牛墩镇	88859838	恒温器
东莞广濑拓展电子有限公司	石龙镇	86187023	复印线路板
东莞东坑富港电子制品厂	东坑镇	83882225	电子制品
东莞英格尔电子有限公司	塘厦镇	87934928	电子元件
东莞创宝达电器制品有限公司	常平镇	83335747	漏电保护器
东莞宇球电子有限公司	寮步镇	83529888	电子插接件
协发(东莞)电子有限公司	塘厦镇	87720745	电源供应器
东莞基杰五金制品有限公司	清溪镇	87735140	电脑机箱
东莞捷讯电子有限公司	樟木头镇	87712009	手提标签机
东莞嘉德电子科技有限公司	桥头镇	83025777	塑胶配件

1-5　续表 37

(2011年)

单位名称	所属镇街	联系电话	主要产品（或服务）
品嘉电子(东莞)有限公司	厚街镇	85903505	电脑显示卡
东莞得泰电子有限公司	石碣镇	86316090	耳机
富声（东莞）电器配件有限公司	虎门镇	85701082	耳机和多媒体喇叭
东莞磁威电子科技有限公司	企石镇	86787388	宽带网络活音分歧器
日本电产<东莞>有限公司	高埗镇	88873011	大容量光磁盘驱动器
东莞长安科得电子有限公司	长安镇	85546130	主板机
东莞明崴电子科技有限公司	东城街道		光电子器件其他电子器件
台达电子电源(东莞)有限公司	石碣镇	86639008	电源供应器
东莞百音电子有限公司	南城街道	22984320	扬声器
东莞正阳电子有限公司	塘厦镇	87916258	音箱
东莞保辉电子有限公司	塘厦镇	87727701	电子玩具
东莞东源光电有限公司	东城街道	22633913	光纤跳接线
东莞艾斯光电科技有限公司	东城街道	22667703	新型电子元器件
东莞宏致电子有限公司	长安镇	85393066	电子零配件
万裕三信电子(东莞)有限公司	长安镇	86069888	电子电容器
东莞鸿爱斯通信科技有限公司	高埗镇	88783009	电子元件
东莞珀韵电子有限公司	横沥镇	83720950	音圈
东莞华鼎电子有限公司	洪梅镇	88847166	液晶显示器
东莞旭福电脑有限公司	清溪镇	87318190	电脑主机板
东莞信泰光学有限公司	长安镇	85535435	数码相机
东莞龙升电子有限公司	黄江镇	83536698	变压器
广濑电机（东莞）有限公司	常平镇	83817840	连接器
米亚精密金属科技(东莞)有限公司	凤岗镇	86802888	高档五金件
先锋信泰(东莞)光学有限公司	长安镇	85535435	精密光电电器件
雷兹达电子(东莞)有限公司	长安镇	85327532	加工电子连接线
东莞保力电子有限公司	石排镇	86511770	充电器
东莞苏扬电器有限公司	常平镇	83391502	圣诞灯串
东莞东骅电子科技有限公司	清溪镇	33336888	电脑机箱
东莞胜美达(太平)电机有限公司	虎门镇	85111118	电子原件
东莞东煦五金电镀厂有限公司	虎门镇	85564222	LED引线架
东莞美维电路有限公司	东城街道	86228000	印制线路板
锦旭电子(东莞)有限公司	清溪镇	87737118	电脑周边产品
飞磁电子材料（东莞）有限公司	清溪镇	87382420	磁芯、磁环
东莞仲屏电子有限公司	石排镇	81868166	扬声器
东莞富鼎塑胶五金有限公司	高埗镇	86279588	电脑托架
东莞力音电子有限公司	石碣镇	86637826	电子线圈
东莞智富五金制品有限公司	塘厦镇	86853888	电器外壳、散热片、音响面板
东莞明鑫电子有限公司	企石镇	86731868	电子元件及组件
东莞加电电子有限公司	常平镇	86836388	钟控CD收音机
东莞盛世科技电子实业有限公司	黄江镇	86914800	电子元器件
东莞科乐波电子有限公司	寮步镇	83281822	变压器
艾利和电子科技(中国)有限公司	松山湖	22899100	MP3和MP4
东莞翔国光电科技有限公司	茶山镇	81833588	印刷电路板
东莞健益五金制品有限公司	茶山镇	86487999	DVD机芯五金件
东莞友华汽车配件有限公司	寮步镇	83326172	塑胶配件
东莞企达电器制品有限公司	横沥镇	83715169	电子元件

1-5 续表 38

(2011年)

单位名称	所属镇街	联系电话	主要产品（或服务）
东莞宏笙电子有限公司	塘厦镇	87919270	鼠标器
东莞美京电子有限公司	寮步镇	83222370	散热片
快捷达通信设备（东莞）有限公司	常平镇	83936688	电子通迅产品
东莞贯达电子有限公司	高埗镇	88786000	电感
圣华电子(东莞)有限公司	塘厦镇	87882707	电脑连接线
东莞佳汇电子厂	大岭山镇	85602828	电脑显示器
欧姆龙精密电子（东莞）有限公司	清溪镇	86816688	液晶背光板
东莞泉睿精密五金有限公司	麻涌镇	85315643	五金轨制设备
东莞市兴奇宏电子有限公司	企石镇	86731868	电脑主机
东莞善募康科技有限公司	谢岗镇	82121900	手机外壳
东莞亿润电子制品有限公司	高埗镇	88730855	光电子元器件
广东佳彩数码科技有限公司	企石镇	86727181	机顶盒
东莞清溪德丽电子厂	清溪镇	87311036	电脑键盘
东莞易迅电子制品有限公司	高埗镇	88788261	开关电源器CAC/DC换能器
雅新电子(东莞)有限公司	石碣镇	86331999	空白印刷电器板
东莞李洲电子科技有限公司	谢岗镇	87762548	数码管
东莞好万年电子制品有限公司	石碣镇	86633278	收音机
瑞讯电子（东莞）有限公司	东城街道	88753288	网络卡路由器
东莞宇宙电路板设备有限公司	凤岗镇	87569928	电路板水平机组
东莞联聿电子有限公司	长安镇	85322996	电脑机箱
祥发电子(东莞)有限公司	石碣镇	86331999	电源供应器
美锐电路(东莞)有限公司	塘厦镇	87724932	印刷电路板
东莞科达五金制品有限公司	石碣镇	86313419	精密驱动器部件
东莞石龙京瓷光学有限公司	石龙镇	86119611	液晶产品
东莞长安华南电子厂	长安镇	85307366	磁性产品
东莞冠诚塑胶模具有限公司清溪分厂	清溪镇	87315088	遥控器
东莞精恒电子有限公司	横沥镇	88977068	公共广播器材
东莞大泉传感器有限公司	寮步镇	88953366	传感器
东莞樟洋电子有限公司	樟木头镇	87197011	数字摄录机
东莞友讯电子有限公司	长安镇	85318000	网络卡
广东楚天龙智能卡有限公司	凤岗镇	87509999	IC卡
东莞隆盛达电子有限公司	万江街道	22706295	影碟机
东莞惠伦顿堡电子有限公司	黄江镇	83362809	电子元器材
东莞宝星电子有限公司	寮步镇	83288770	微型麦克风
希克斯电子（东莞）有限公司	大岭山镇	85601508	充电器
东莞亚联科技电子有限公司	塘厦镇	87727680	电脑及其周边配件充电器
东莞莫仕连接器有限公司	石碣镇	86310328	电脑连接线
锋创电子(东莞)有限公司	长安镇	85398213	音箱
东莞诚翰电子有限公司	黄江镇	83536633	线圈
东莞艾笛森光电有限公司	横沥镇	81011898	电子产品
东莞明泰电讯设备有限公司	大岭山镇	83356898	电话机
先锋高科技(东莞)有限公司	寮步镇	83287704	磁盘驱动器
最上(东莞)电子有限公司	塘厦镇	87883718	喇叭鼓纸
东莞科泰电子有限公司	南城街道	22806790	合路器
东莞东矽电子有限公司	清溪镇	86200050	电源供应器
东莞新劲电子有限公司	塘厦镇	87810780	电脑周边产品

1-5　续表 39

(2011年)

单位名称	所属镇街	联系电话	主要产品（或服务）
东莞冠智电子有限公司	长安镇	85356948	感应触摸胶片、玻璃片
东莞康源电子有限公司	虎门镇	85562002	线路板
雅邦电子(东莞)有限公司	石碣镇	86331999	电子成品组装
东莞双盈电子有限公司	清溪镇	87310135	电脑接线和手机连接线
东莞环亚高科电子有限公司	长安镇	85316946	个人数码助理
东莞庆章光机有限公司	清溪镇	87381610	分光镜
东莞德英电子通讯设备有限公司	莞城街道	22024422	婴儿监督器
立信杰(东莞)精密模具制造有限公司	凤岗镇	86800088	汽车线材
东莞世技电子有限公司	寮步镇	83224133	防盗器
东莞致通电脑有限公司	清溪镇	87312821	数据机网络卡
东莞宏易电子有限公司	塘厦镇	87881584	音响分频器
东莞捷仕美电子有限公司	大朗镇	83125678	电子连接器(电脑周边设备)
大毅科技电子(东莞)有限公司	常平镇	83394790	新型电子元器件
仪器仪表及文化、办公用机械制造业			
东莞铨讯电子有限公司	寮步镇	83527668	数码相机及组件
东莞奥美佳电子有限公司	凤岗镇	87503835	数码相机
丽声实业(东莞)有限公司	虎门镇	86232333	钟
柯尼卡美能达商用科技(东莞)有限公司	石龙镇	86114964	复印机
东莞贝盈激光仪器有限公司	樟木头镇	86907088	激光仪器
东英精密轴承(东莞)有限公司	沙田镇	88666101	打印机配件
优利德科技(东莞)有限公司	虎门镇	85729892	电器仪表
东莞常平土塘大根电子光学制品厂	常平镇	83395446	扫描器镜头
来利眼镜制品(东莞)有限公司	樟木头镇	82339955	眼镜配件
东京光学(东莞)科技有限公司	石龙镇	86185458	镜头组件
东莞清溪优品电子厂	清溪镇	87311417	计数机
东莞新溢眼镜制造有限公司	长安镇	85540945	眼镜
东莞富鼎兴精密电子科技有限公司	谢岗镇	87686518	电脑周边配件
东莞虎门泰达电子有限公司	虎门镇	85558622	电子计算器
陆逊梯卡华宏(东莞)眼镜有限公司	高埗镇	88870241	金属塑胶眼镜
东莞华春电子有限公司	中堂镇	88888850	电脑显示卡
东莞恒通电子制品有限公司	长安镇	85391182	柔性线路板
盈利时表业(东莞)有限公司	大朗镇	83103333	表带
东莞侨运表业有限公司	厚街镇	83086066	手表
东莞福泰电子有限公司	长安镇	85318100	碎纸机
希比希真空电子(东莞)有限公司	长安镇	82389200	数码相机零配件
东莞新利电子有限公司	塘厦镇	86851599	电子钟表
东莞宝元数控科技有限公司	高埗镇	88874202	控制器
东莞富国橡塑工业有限公司	大岭山镇	85656968	防振垫
东莞快灵通卡西尼电子科技有限公司	寮步镇	83039222	计算器
东莞泰联光学有限公司	长安镇	85535435	照相机
万金机械配件东莞有限公司	凤岗镇	82039188	复印机零配件
广东尼康照相机有限公司	长安镇	85535435	相机
金宝电子(中国)有限公司	长安镇	85321555	加工电子计算机
东莞晓视眼镜制造厂有限公司	凤岗镇	87754133	眼镜
高铁检测仪器(东莞)有限公司	南城街道	22400899	试验机
东莞日精电子有限公司	塘厦镇	86857999	遥控器、打印机、复印机控制面板

1-5 续表 40

(2011年)

单位名称	所属镇街	联系电话	主要产品（或服务）
东莞力维时钟有限公司	清溪镇	87732284	时钟
三和盛电子科技(东莞)有限公司	凤岗镇	87862222	数码相机关键件
东莞新旭光学有限公司	长安镇	86240898	光学镜片组
东莞华仪仪表科技有限公司	清溪镇	87309005	仪器仪表
东莞宏松精密组件有限公司	塘厦镇	28129588	打印机及配件
东莞樟木头来利金属制品厂	樟木头镇	87719522	眼镜及配件
镰仓光学(东莞)有限公司	虎门镇	85562870	望远镜及其配件
东莞应华精密金属有限公司	寮步镇	82316661	数码相机外壳
东莞石龙粤龙办公设备制造厂	石龙镇	86181222	影印机加工
京瓷美达办公设备（东莞）有限公司	石龙镇	86112525	打印机
工艺品及其他制造业			
东莞盈彩塑胶电子有限公司	塘厦镇	87849988	塑料、胶制品
东莞宏冠拉链配件有限公司	沙田镇	88866567	拉链
东莞三大电子科技有限公司	常平镇	83997278	电脑零件
东莞台新纤维制品有限公司	清溪镇	87311541	汽车地毯
东莞西文商标织绣有限公司	长安镇	81767999	商标织绣
东莞市浔兴拉链科技有限公司	大朗镇	82220222	拉链
东莞安居家饰有限公司	清溪镇	87306597	窗帘
东莞爱福赛保安制品有限公司	黄江镇	83631663	五金制品
东莞华艺铜业有限公司	常平镇	83918628	铜杆
东莞富美康电器科技有限公司	谢岗镇	87631613	直发器
欣泰家具(东莞)有限公司	清溪镇	87313008	太阳伞、户外伞
东莞晟富电子科技有限公司	寮步镇	81100168	降频器
东莞海金杜门五金制品有限公司	南城街道	22401768	特殊五金冲压件
东莞星系手袋厂有限公司	塘厦镇	87939288	日用杂品
东莞宜成制罐有限公司	塘厦镇	87723456	马口铁制品
东莞宇源精密金属实业有限公司	黄江镇	86968798	金属工艺品
东莞婴宝幼童用品有限公司	清溪镇	86817000	童车
东莞素艺儿童用品有限公司	道滘镇	88382301	婴儿手推车
东莞塘厦保发珠宝首饰厂	塘厦镇	82621838	18K镶钻石首饰
明门（中国）幼童用品有限公司	清溪镇	87733251	婴儿手推车
东莞华生精密制品有限公司	樟木头镇	87187900	组装音响
东莞杜邦电子材料有限公司	南城街道	22852951	电子浆料
东莞精业拉链有限公司	洪梅镇	88849815	拉链
东莞大信装饰礼品有限公司	常平镇	86293999	蜡烛灯
电力、热力的生产和供应业			
广东广合电力有限公司沙角发电厂C厂	虎门镇	85135124	火力发电
东莞天明电力有限公司	道滘镇	22788336	火力发电
深南电（东莞）唯美电力有限公司	高埗镇	88463006	天然气发电
东莞中科环保电力有限公司	南城街道	22667772	垃圾余热发电
东莞深能源樟洋电力有限公司	樟木头镇	87198888	发电
东莞通明电力有限公司	寮步镇	83525188	天然气发电站的建设经营
东莞市科伟环保电力有限公司	横沥镇	83715838	垃圾焚烧发电
广东省粤电集团有限公司沙角C电厂	虎门镇	85165698	发电
广东电力发展股份有限公司沙角A电厂	虎门镇	85136679	火力发电
东莞虎门电厂	虎门镇	85042288	火力发电

1-5 续表 41

(2011年)

单位名称	所属镇街	联系电话	主要产品（或服务）
东莞中电新能源热电有限公司	东城街道	22688088	电力
燃气生产和供应业			
东莞新奥燃气有限公司	莞城街道	88992299	管道燃气输配与零售
东莞长安新奥燃气有限公司	长安镇	89992288	管道燃气的建设
建筑安装业			
东莞安泰电业工程有限公司	莞城街道	22465497	高低压输变电、配电、设备安装
道路运输业			
广东省虎门大桥有限公司	虎门镇	85509333	高速公路管理养护
东莞发展控股股份有限公司	东城街道	22083225	高速收费
水上运输业			
东莞虎门龙威客运有限公司	虎门镇	85511759	沿海旅客运输
仓储业			
东莞三江港口储罐有限公司	虎门港	88862888	液体化工仓储服务
东莞永得利仓储有限公司	麻涌镇	88236909	物流服务
电信和其他信息传输服务业			
中国移动通信集团广东有限公司东莞分公司	东城街道	10086	移动通信服务
中国联通有限公司东莞分公司	南城街道	89826239	通信服务
批发业			
东莞永泓木业贸易有限公司	大岭山镇	83355145	木板材
东莞华港国际贸易有限公司	长安镇	85416451	塑胶原料
莎罗雅(东莞)清洁用品有限公司	长安镇	85358605	清洁用品
锦江麦德龙现购自运有限公司东莞万江商场	万江街道	22178888	商品批发
金光纸业(广州)有限公司东莞分公司	南城街道	22992511	纸品
隆原(东莞)机电贸易有限公司	长安镇	81607192	柴油发电机
东莞市创盛贸易有限公司	长安镇	82289868	钢材制品
大同机械(东莞)销售有限公司	东城街道	22806163	机械设备
东莞金丰物流设备有限公司	道滘镇	88333981	叉车
东莞加德士石油产品有限公司	东城街道	22367236	石油产品储蓄、批发
嘉顿食品贸易(中国)有限公司	南城街道	23024830	蛋糕
东莞柳道贸易有限公司	长安镇	85394466	热流道及配件
零售业			
东莞仁孚华星汽车服务有限公司	寮步镇	82222080	奔驰轿车
青岛润泰事业有限公司东莞大朗分公司	大朗镇	83034798	百货
东莞百安居装饰建材有限公司	南城街道	22719121	室内装修材料
东莞擎达汽车销售服务有限公司	厚街镇	85580180	汽车
东莞喜威液化石油气有限公司	南城街道	22497388	液化气
东莞仁孚溢华汽车服务有限公司	南城街道	22902080	汽车
广东吉之岛天贸百货有限公司东莞花园广场分公司	东城街道	22600236	百货
东莞意美汽车服务有限公司	南城街道	85050911	汽车
东莞美东汽车服务有限公司	寮步镇	82319819	汽车
东莞樟木头大润发商业有限公司	樟木头镇	86902888	百货
东莞市洛加斯润滑油有限公司	大岭山镇	85617000	润滑油
中油碧辟石油有限公司东莞分公司	万江街道	88338556	机动车燃料
东莞新奥莞樟燃气有限公司	樟木头镇	87780331	管道天然气
东莞永佳中通汽车服务有限公司	厚街镇	81633000	汽车零配件
东莞中升雷克萨斯汽车销售服务有限公司	南城街道	23190999	雷克萨斯汽车

1-5 续表 42

(2011年)

单位名称	所属镇街	联系电话	主要产品（或服务）
东莞德现汽车销售服务有限公司	寮步镇	81117637	现代品牌轿车
伟轮叉车(东莞)有限公司	高埗镇	88736868	叉车
东莞沃尔玛百货有限公司	莞城街道	22323055	百货
中油碧辟石油有限公司东莞宏伟加油站	南城街道	22404202	汽油
广东吉之岛天贸百货有限公司东莞第一国际分公司	南城街道	28632988	百货
安利(中国)日用品有限公司东莞分公司	东城街道	22556455	日用品
住宿业			
东莞海悦花园大酒店有限公司	长安镇	85318888	住宿
东莞丽池海悦酒店有限公司	厚街镇	85885888	住宿
东莞长安酒店	长安镇	85532388	住宿
东莞御景湾酒店	东城街道	22625029	住宿
东莞豪门大饭店	虎门镇	85117888	住宿
餐饮业			
东莞肯德基有限公司	莞城街道	83588288	快餐
东莞麦华食品有限公司	莞城街道	22115051	西式快餐
东莞麦长食品有限公司	长安镇	85530791	快餐服务
东莞泛亚饮食有限公司	樟木头镇	87708232	餐饮服务
东莞旗峰山酒店有限公司	东城街道	23368888	餐饮服务
银行业			
汇丰银行（中国）有限公司东莞分行	南城街道	23093088	金融服务
恒生银行（中国）有限公司东莞分行	东城街道	23138838	金融服务
保险业			
中德安联人寿保险有限公司广东分公司东莞营销服务部	南城街道	22827268	人寿保险
美国友邦保险有限公司东莞支公司	南城街道	22418628	人寿保险
信诚人寿保险有限公司东莞营销服务部	东城街道	22763188	人寿保险
房地产业			
东莞水濂山水库商品住宅建造有限公司	南城街道		房地产开发经营
东莞骏豪房地产开发有限公司	塘厦镇	28022593	房地产开发经营
东莞时富花园开发有限公司	寮步镇	83232328	商品住宅
东莞御花苑商品住宅建造有限公司	南城街道	22402268	房地产开发经营
东莞庄士房地产开发有限公司	沙田镇	88660958	房地产开发经营
东莞市富盈房地产开发有限公司	厚街镇	81226161	房地产开发
东莞市金地房地产投资有限公司	南城街道	88991111	房地产开发经营
东莞市庆丰房地产有限公司	东城街道	22619005	房地产中介
东莞市庆丰房地产咨询服务有限公司	东城街道	22619005	房地产开发
东莞东泰花园建造有限公司	东城街道	22482388	房地产开发
东莞市乐富房地产开发有限公司	樟木头镇	87187088	房地产开发
东莞市阳明渡假山庄开发有限公司	塘厦镇	82275828	房地产开发
商务服务业			
(丹麦)森海塞尔通信有限公司东莞代表处	东城街道	22360850	业务联络
东莞派诺蒙鞋业服务有限公司	东城街道	22491889	鞋设计
研究与试验发展			
东莞新科技术研究开发有限公司	南城街道	22810033	研究开发磁电制品
娱乐业			
东莞峰景高尔夫有限公司	东城街道	22253459	高尔夫球娱乐活动
东莞长安今宇高尔夫球场俱乐部有限公司	长安镇	85539288	高尔夫球娱乐活动
东莞观澜湖高尔夫球会有限公司	塘厦镇	28020888	高尔夫球场及配套设施建设经营管理

1-6 星级酒店名单(2011年)

List of Star-ranking Hotels (2011)

酒店名称	星级	电话	地址
银城酒店	五星	22828888	东莞市莞太大道48号
凤岗金凯悦大酒店	五星	87759888	凤岗镇凤深大道158号
龙泉国际大酒店	五星	85188688	虎门镇连升路金洲段
豪门大饭店	五星	85117888	虎门镇虎门大道
嘉华大酒店	五星	85928888	厚街镇家具大道1号
富盈酒店	五星	85888888	厚街镇赤岭路段
索菲特御景湾酒店	五星	22698888	东城区迎宾路8号
莲花山庄	五星	85538388	长安镇莲花山
长安海悦花园大酒店	五星	85318888	长安镇霄边管理区二环路
东莞柏宁酒店	五星	85333333	长安镇德政路222号
石龙金凯悦大酒店	五星	86188888	石龙镇莞龙路西湖路段
喜来登大酒店	五星	85988888	厚街镇S256省道莞太路段
新都会怡景酒店	五星	87883888	塘厦镇环市东路6号
太子酒店	五星	83363333	黄江镇江北路32号
塘厦三正半山酒店	五星	87299333	塘厦镇迎宾大道
汇华国际饭店	五星	83938888	常平镇常平大道2号
帝豪花园酒店	五星	83122222	大朗镇美景中路769号
丰泰花园酒店	五星	85708888	虎门镇S358省道大板地路段
华尔登国际酒店	五星	81028888	桥头镇广场路3号
桥头三正半山酒店	五星	83341868	桥头镇碧莲路
悦莱花园酒店	五星	81118888	寮步镇香市路8号
寮步金凯悦大酒店	四星	83326328	寮步镇教育路1号
文华大酒店	四星	85911111	厚街镇莞太路新塘路段
东莞宾馆	四星	22222222	莞城区东正路11号
江龙大酒店	四星	85838888	厚街镇S256省道莞太路段
新都会酒店	四星	87713333	樟木头镇维多利商业大道38号
君爵酒店	四星	22288888	万江区石美广深路段
宏远酒店	四星	22418888	南城区宏远路1号
汇美酒店	四星	83918888	常平镇中元路9号
花园酒店	四星	87799888	樟木头镇南城广场

1-6 续表 1

(2011年)

酒店名称	星级	电话	地址
长安酒店	四星	85532388	长安镇中心S358省道旁
司马假日酒店	四星	83391888	常平镇司马管理区
新世纪酒店	四星	83338888	常平镇常平大道8号
梵尔赛酒店	四星	83816888	常平镇下墟工业区
厚街海悦花园大酒店	四星	85885888	厚街镇厚街大道东
汇源华美达酒店	四星	85244888	虎门镇虎门大道
业丰大酒店	四星	83113888	大朗镇莞樟路金朗大道23号
万盈酒店	四星	88828888	麻涌镇麻涌大道
中汇文华酒店	四星	88788888	高埗镇振兴路
方中假日酒店	四星	86866666	茶山镇茶山大道西28号
半岛酒店	四星	83988888	常平镇北环路
华禧酒店	四星	85383888	长安镇S358省道上沙路段
嘉辉会酒店	四星	87563388	凤岗镇官井头嘉辉路
美怡登酒店	四星	83028888	常平镇中元路
天悦酒店	四星	81812222	石碣镇崇焕路18号
华庭花园酒店	四星	81633333	厚街镇广东现代国际展览中心南侧
石龙宾馆	三星	86613333	石龙镇绿化中路2号
广彩城酒店	三星	22402088	南城区莞太路
石碣豪华大酒店	三星	86633333	石碣镇新城区
金湖粤海酒店	三星	87869888	塘厦镇塘厦大道南99号
莲城酒店	三星	85536888	长安镇莲峰路接一环路口
黄江假日酒店	三星	83362888	黄江镇黄江大道3号
西湖大酒店	三星	22822888	南城区西平板岭
明苑大酒店	三星	85122918	虎门镇金龙大道南
篁胜酒店	三星	22463888	南城区体育路11号
宝石大酒店	三星	86662188	企石镇振华路1号
恒丰酒店	三星	83343333	桥头镇恒丰新村2号
金岛泰年酒店	三星	82168888	塘厦镇128工业区
绿洲酒店	三星	88832788	道滘镇振兴路156号
沙头酒店	三星	85418888	长安镇沙头管理区

1-6　续表 2

(2011年)

酒店名称	星级	电话	地址
华通城大酒店	三星	86732288	企石镇湖滨南路
丰田酒店	三星	87771199	凤岗镇雁田管理区怡安路
丽江酒店	三星	88872888	高埗镇捷达工业村13座
嘉福海港酒店	三星	88682888	沙田镇中心区港口大道17号
中明酒店	三星	88883368	中堂镇新兴路1号
御烽酒店	三星	22186888	万江区107国道拔蛟窝路段
莱莉雅酒店	三星	87507888	凤岗镇永盛商业大街中银大厦
东逸酒店	三星	85396388	长安镇莲峰路103号
鸿茂酒店	三星	83508888	常平镇常黄路
四季酒店	三星	88566666	望牛墩镇新电城A8座
宏信假日酒店	三星	87363888	清溪镇香芒西路
美景湾酒店	三星	83739888	横沥镇沿江路1号
天鹅湖酒店	三星	83338388	常平镇天鹅湖路8号
富豪酒店	三星	83998888	常平镇金美路256号
中青旅山水	三星	21988888	东城区东纵大道189号
亚都酒店	三星	85343888	长安镇长中路
金沙亚都酒店	三星	85413888	长安镇靖海中路36号
金澳花园酒店	二星	22496966	东城大道金澳花园A座
耀豪酒店	二星	88865333	沙田镇中心区
银星酒店	二星	83987333	常平镇木抡大道9号
雄狮大酒店	二星	83332198	常平镇振兴路1号
盈丰酒店	二星	83333333	常平镇振兴路中段
新港大酒店	二星	83331000	常平镇新市一街6号
悦华大酒店	二星	83336888	常平镇东兴路275号
海霞酒店	二星	82822888	常平镇板石霞村路段
昇平酒店	二星	83812888	常平镇中元街
冠城酒店	二星	83337788	常平镇中元街常平广场
龙源大酒店	二星	85551028	虎门镇S358省道北栅路段
恒安酒店	二星	88868868	沙田镇横流中心区
海月酒店	二星	85926888	厚街镇涌口海月公园侧
悦凯酒店	一星	83398808	常平镇东元东路28号

1-7 高新技术企业名录（2011年）

List of High-tech Enterprises (2011)

企业名称	所在镇街	行业类别
东莞市TR轴承有限公司	莞城街道	纺织专用设备
广东智通人才连锁股份有限公司	莞城街道	公共就业服务
东莞市弘明空调服有限公司	莞城街道	机织服装
东莞市太平洋计算机科技有限公司	莞城街道	信息系统集成服务
东莞市依时利科技有限公司	莞城街道	信息系统集成服务
东莞市政创软件科技有限公司	莞城街道	信息系统集成服务
东莞市华南信息科技有限公司	莞城街道	计算机、软件及辅助设备零售
东莞市捷联科技有限公司	莞城街道	软件开发
广东华盈光达科技有限公司	莞城街道	信息系统集成服务
东莞市光华实业有限公司	石龙镇	电力电子元器件
东莞泽龙线缆有限公司	石龙镇	电线、电缆
泰阳电子（东莞）有限公司	石龙镇	电子元件及组件
东莞市广安电气检测中心有限公司	石龙镇	质检技术服务
东莞市开普互联信息有限公司	石龙镇	软件开发
东莞市石龙富华电子有限公司	石龙镇	仪器、仪表
广东华南药业集团有限公司	石龙镇	化学药品制剂
广东众生药业股份有限公司	石龙镇	中成药
东莞市龙基电子有限公司	石龙镇	电子元件及组件
东莞市石龙万通实业有限公司	石龙镇	轴承
广东巨龙信息科技有限公司	石龙镇	软件开发
东莞利富高塑料制品有限公司	石龙镇	塑料零件
日本电产三协电子（东莞）有限公司	石龙镇	电子元件及组件
亚士吉灯饰(东莞)有限公司	石龙镇	照明灯具
东莞天意电子有限公司	石龙镇	计算机整机
东莞市广大制冷有限公司	虎门镇	制冷、空调设备
信义汽车玻璃（东莞）有限公司	虎门镇	平板玻璃
东莞虎彩印刷有限公司	虎门镇	包装装潢及其他印刷
东莞市威迪膜科技有限公司	虎门镇	膜分离技术及产品的系统设计、研发
广东银禧科技股份有限公司	虎门镇	初级形态塑料及合成树脂
东莞市霸菱实业有限公司	虎门镇	金属家具
东莞市科达计算机系统工程有限公司	虎门镇	计算机
东莞中探探针有限公司	虎门镇	专业探针
东莞市虎门金山电线电缆有限公司	虎门镇	电线、电缆
东莞市联升电线电缆有限公司	虎门镇	电线、电缆
东莞市天盛特种纸制品有限公司	虎门镇	纸制品制
东莞市中实焊锡有限公司	虎门镇	锡冶炼
优利德科技（东莞）有限公司	虎门镇	电工仪器、仪表
东莞康源电子有限公司	虎门镇	印制电路板
广东奥其斯科技有限公司	虎门镇	照明灯具
信义玻璃工程（东莞）有限公司	虎门镇	玻璃
东莞常禾电子有限公司	虎门镇	汽车零部件及配件
东莞市力宇燃气动力有限公司	虎门镇	发电机及发电机组
东莞市适意机械有限公司	虎门镇	模具
东莞联茂电子科技有限公司	虎门镇	电子元件及组件
东莞令特电子有限公司	虎门镇	电子元件及组件

1-7　续表 1

(2011年)

企业名称	所在镇街	行业类别
兴科电子（东莞）有限公司	虎门镇	电子元件及组件
东莞市平波电子有限公司	虎门镇	计算机、软件及辅助设备零售
东莞市妙达电动工具制造有限公司	虎门镇	电动工具及配件
东莞市锐升电线电缆有限公司	虎门镇	电子工业专用设备
东莞市松庆自动化设备有限公司	东城街道	专用设备
东莞市奕东电子有限公司	东城街道	电子元件及组件
东华机械有限公司	东城街道	塑料加工专用设备
东莞科威医疗器械有限公司	东城街道	医疗诊断、监护及治疗设备
东莞生益电子有限公司	东城街道	印制电路板
东莞市百分百科技有限公司	东城街道	照明器具
东莞市德生通用电器制造有限公司	东城街道	音响设备
东莞市高能电气股份有限公司	东城街道	绝缘制品
东莞市晖速天线技术有限公司	东城街道	通信系统设备
东莞美维电路有限公司	东城街道	印制电路板
东莞市神州视觉科技有限公司	东城街道	光学仪器
东莞市安拓普塑胶聚合物科技有限公司	东城街道	初级形态塑料及合成树脂
广东宏远集团药业有限公司	东城街道	化学药品制剂
东莞市邦臣光电有限公司	东城街道	印制电路板
东莞市凯格精密机械有限公司	东城街道	电子工业专用设备
东莞市桦业土木基础工程有限公司	东城街道	土木工程建筑
东莞康视达自动化科技有限公司	东城街道	专用仪器
东莞市大忠电子有限公司	东城街道	电子元件及组件
东莞市建邦计算机软件有限公司	东城街道	软件开发
东莞市慧达环保有限公司	东城街道	环保设备
东莞市嘉腾仪器仪表有限公司	东城街道	光学仪器
东莞市事通达机电科技有限公司	东城街道	金属制品
东莞市新铂铼电子有限公司	东城街道	电子元件及组件
东莞市源兴光学仪器有限公司	东城街道	光学仪器
东莞通华液晶有限公司	东城街道	电子元件及组件
东莞拓扑实业有限公司	东城街道	涂料
东莞万德电子制品有限公司	东城街道	电子元件及组件
东莞鸿宝锂电科技有限公司	东城街道	电子工业专用设备
东莞市芯飞电子科技有限公司	东城街道	软件开发
东莞市良展有机硅科技有限公司	东城街道	硅胶制品
广东大族粤铭激光科技股份有限公司	万江街道	金属切割及焊接设备
东莞市金翔电器设备有限公司	万江街道	计算机外围设备
东莞市科达机电设备有限公司	万江街道	制冷、空调设备
东莞市至诚涂料有限公司	万江街道	涂料
广东五星太阳能有限公司	万江街道	燃气、太阳能及类似能源家用器具
东莞市银华生物科技有限公司	万江街道	水产饲料
东莞市康源节能科技有限公司	万江街道	风动和电动工具
东莞基业电气设备有限公司	万江街道	输配电及控制设备
广东广视通科教设备有限公司	万江街道	木质家具
东莞市利安达环境科技有限公司	万江街道	环境保护专用设备
东莞市铭丰包装品制造有限公司	万江街道	产品包装的设计

1-7　续表 2

(2011年)

企业名称	所在镇街	行业类别
东莞耳神电声科技有限公司	万江街道	音响设备
东莞市安默琳节能环保技术有限公司	万江街道	模具
东莞市硕源电子材料有限公司	万江街道	无尘纸、无尘布系列产品
东莞市爱克斯曼机械有限公司	万江街道	纺织专用设备
东莞市莱硕光电科技有限公司	万江街道	灯用电器附件及其他照明器具
东莞市朗普工程塑料科技有限公司	南城街道	塑料制品
东莞市华业龙图信息技术有限公司	南城街道	互联网信息服务
东莞宏威数码机械有限公司	南城街道	专用设备
东莞市爱玛数控科技有限公司	南城街道	皮革、毛皮及其制品加工专用设备
东莞市福地电子材料有限公司	南城街道	电光源
东莞华宝鞋业有限公司	南城街道	皮鞋
广东科旺电源设备有限公司	南城街道	变压器、整流器和电感器
东莞市高鑫机电科技服务有限公司	南城街道	科技推广和应用服务
广东百思维信息科技有限公司	南城街道	软件开发
东莞市保得生物工程有限公司	南城街道	有机肥料及微生物肥料
东莞市杉杉电池材料有限公司	南城街道	专项化学用品
广东万维博通信息技术有限公司	南城街道	软件开发
东莞市新雷神仿真控制有限公司	南城街道	电子设备
东莞市中大科教网络科技有限公司	南城街道	软件开发
东莞市凯诺德软件科技有限公司	南城街道	软件开发
东莞市领航通通信科技有限公司	南城街道	信息系统集成服务
广东迪奥技术工程有限公司	南城街道	建筑安装
广东南方宏明电子科技股份有限公司	南城街道	电子元件及组件
广东省东莞电机有限公司	南城街道	电动机
广东开心信息技术有限公司	南城街道	软件开发
东莞新科技术研究开发有限公司	南城街道	计算机零部件
东莞市丰远电器有限公司	南城街道	专用设备
广东迪科思信息科技有限公司	南城街道	软件开发
广东凌康科技有限公司	南城街道	信息系统集成服务
广东天新软件科技有限公司	南城街道	软件开发
东莞市数夫家具软件有限公司	南城街道	软件开发
广东新诚智软件科技有限公司	南城街道	软件开发
东莞市创丰科技发展有限公司	南城街道	机械设备及电子产品批发
东莞市钜大电子有限公司	南城街道	锂离子电池
东莞市广益食品添加剂实业有限公司	中堂镇	食品及饲料添加剂
广东一品鲜生物科技有限公司	中堂镇	食品
东莞市东兴铝材制造有限公司	中堂镇	金属制品
东莞市凯迪克高分子材料有限公司	中堂镇	涂料
东莞理文造纸厂有限公司	中堂镇	机制纸及纸板
金元宝弹簧设备（东莞）有限公司	中堂镇	弹簧
永磁电子(东莞)有限公司	中堂镇	电工机械专用设备
东莞佳鸿机械制造有限公司	望牛墩镇	铸造机械
东莞思威特电子有限公司	望牛墩镇	电子元件及组件
东莞市天尚太阳能有限公司	望牛墩镇	燃气、太阳能及类似能源家用器具
东莞市亚美精密机械配件有限公司	望牛墩镇	电子工业专用设备
东莞山本电子科技有限公司	麻涌镇	印制电路板

1-7　续表 3

(2011年)

企业名称	所在镇街	行业类别
东莞南玻太阳能玻璃有限公司	麻涌镇	玻璃
东莞市奥莱克电子有限公司	麻涌镇	音响设备
东莞市华兰海电子有限公司	麻涌镇	电子测量仪器
东莞海龙纸业有限公司	麻涌镇	机制纸及纸板
东莞玖龙纸业有限公司	麻涌镇	机制纸及纸板
东莞市贝特利新材料有限公司	麻涌镇	油墨及类似产品
东莞市英芝堂生物工程有限公司	麻涌镇	生物药品
广东信力材料科技有限公司	麻涌镇	合成橡胶
广东中成化工股份有限公司	麻涌镇	无机盐
东莞太平洋博高润滑油有限公司	麻涌镇	原油加工及石油制品
广东中远船务工程有限公司	麻涌镇	金属船舶
东莞市康达尔饲料有限公司	麻涌镇	饲料
东莞超盈纺织有限公司	麻涌镇	化纤织物面料
东莞南玻工程玻璃有限公司	麻涌镇	平板玻璃
东莞市山力高分子材料科研有限公司	麻涌镇	初级形态塑料及合成树脂
东莞泉声电子有限公司	石碣镇	电子元件及组件
品翔电子塑胶制品(东莞)有限公司	石碣镇	电子元件及组件
达创科技（东莞）有限公司	石碣镇	通信终端设备
东莞市前锋电子有限公司	石碣镇	家用厨房电器具
台达电子电源（东莞）有限公司	石碣镇	电子元件及组件
台达电子（东莞）有限公司	石碣镇	电子元件及组件
东莞广发制药有限公司	石碣镇	中成药生产
东莞市智高文具有限公司	石碣镇	文具
东莞岳丰电子科技有限公司	石碣镇	电线、电缆
旭丽电子（东莞）有限公司	石碣镇	计算机外围设备
东莞市旭田电子有限公司	石碣镇	计算机外围设备
东莞市盈聚电子有限公司	石碣镇	电子元件及组件
东莞达电电子有限公司	石碣镇	塑料零件
东莞东聚电子电讯制品有限公司	石碣镇	仪器仪表
东莞金富亮塑胶颜料有限公司	高埗镇	塑料制品
东莞宝元数控科技有限公司	高埗镇	炼油、化工生产专用设备
广东福利龙复合肥有限公司	高埗镇	复混肥料
东莞市宏达聚氨酯有限公司	高埗镇	初级形态塑料及合成树脂
东莞市东田厨具设备有限公司	高埗镇	五金产品批发
东莞市开泰激光科技有限公司	道滘镇	专用设备
东莞万泰橡胶有限公司	道滘镇	合成橡胶
东莞洲亮通讯科技有限公司	道滘镇	通信终端设备
东莞市中村绝缘材料科技有限公司	道滘镇	电子元器件
东莞安尚崇光科技有限公司	道滘镇	电光源
广东大众农业科技股份有限公司	洪梅镇	复混肥料
东莞市亚洲制药有限公司	洪梅镇	中成药生产
东莞市骏朗自动化科技有限公司	洪梅镇	汽车零部件及配件
广东理文造纸有限公司	洪梅镇	机制纸及纸板
东莞市绿通高尔夫观光车有限公司	洪梅镇	非公路休闲车及零配件
东莞市邦泽电子有限公司	沙田镇	专用仪器
东莞安达电机有限公司	厚街镇	金属切割及焊接设备

1-7　续表 4

(2011年)

企业名称	所在镇街	行业类别
东莞市金河田实业有限公司	厚街镇	计算机外围设备
东莞市南兴家具装备制造股份有限公司	厚街镇	木材加工机械
东莞市东方科技有限公司	厚街镇	计算机外围设备
东莞市金银丰机械实业有限公司	厚街镇	皮革、毛皮及其制品加工专用设备
东莞市力凯科技发展有限公司	厚街镇	软件开发
东莞市三友联众电器有限公司	厚街镇	仪器、仪表
东莞市意利自动化科技有限公司	厚街镇	皮革、毛皮及其制品加工专用设备
东莞市捷伟讯电子有限公司	厚街镇	通信终端设备
东莞朗诚微电子设备有限公司	厚街镇	电子工业专用设备
万裕三信电子（东莞）有限公司	长安镇	电子元件及组件
东莞市维峰五金电子有限公司	长安镇	光电子器件及其他电子器件
东莞市巨冈机械工业有限公司	长安镇	模具
东莞龙光电子集团有限公司	长安镇	电子元件及组件
东莞市东阳光电容器有限公司	长安镇	电子元件及组件
东莞普思电子有限公司	长安镇	电子元件及组件
广东万濠精密仪器股份有限公司	长安镇	电工仪器仪表
东莞钜升塑胶电子制品有限公司	长安镇	模具
先锐模具配件（东莞）有限公司	长安镇	模具
东莞劲胜精密组件股份有限公司	长安镇	电子元件及组件
东莞市奥普特自动化科技有限公司	长安镇	鬃毛加工、制刷及清扫工具
环球石材(东莞)有限公司	长安镇	建筑用石加工
东莞福泰电子有限公司	长安镇	大型碎纸机
东莞广宏电子有限公司	长安镇	电子元件及组件
东莞鸿图精密压铸有限公司	长安镇	汽车零部件及配件
广东冠辉科技有限公司	长安镇	金属家具
东莞市华鹰电子有限公司	长安镇	光纤、光缆
东莞市胜蓝电子有限公司	长安镇	光电子器件及其他电子器件
东莞市泰康电子科技有限公司	长安镇	电子元件及组件
东莞市扬明精密塑胶五金电子有限公司	长安镇	电子元件及组件
东莞信泰光学有限公司	长安镇	光学玻璃
广东荣文照明集团有限公司	长安镇	照明设计、安装规划、售后服务
东莞市祥鑫汽车模具制品有限公司	长安镇	汽车零部件及配件
东莞市长原科技实业有限公司	长安镇	金属加工机械
东莞市星河精密压铸模具有限公司	长安镇	精密压铸模具设计、制造
捷荣模具工业（东莞）有限公司	长安镇	塑料制品
东莞市奥源电子科技有限公司	长安镇	集成电路
东莞市康捷塑胶模具有限公司	长安镇	塑料制品
东莞市西屋电气设备制造有限公司	寮步镇	电气机械及器材
东莞市金业电子科技有限公司	寮步镇	影视录放设备
东莞三联热缩材料有限公司	寮步镇	塑料制品
广东宏磊达光电科技有限公司	寮步镇	电力电子元器件
东莞市蓝冠环保节能科技有限公司	寮步镇	电子真空器件
东莞市友美电源设备有限公司	寮步镇	输配电及控制设备
东莞市开关厂有限公司	寮步镇	配电开关控制设备
东莞市康达机电工程有限公司	寮步镇	发电机及发电机组
东莞市永强汽车制造有限公司	寮步镇	汽车整车

1-7 续表 5

(2011年)

企业名称	所在镇街	行业类别
东莞市科隆威自动化设备有限公司	寮步镇	电子工业专用设备
东莞市佳景印刷材料有限公司	寮步镇	油墨及类似产品
东莞市达成机械设备制造有限公司	寮步镇	起重机
东莞市铁志电子有限公司	寮步镇	文教办公用品
东莞宇球电子有限公司	寮步镇	电子元件及组件
东莞市新泽谷机械有限公司	寮步镇	电子工业专用设备
东莞市飞新达精密机械科技有限公司	寮步镇	非金属加工专用设备
东莞市骏泰精密机械有限公司	寮步镇	机械设备及电子产品批发
东莞市新志密封技术有限公司	寮步镇	塑料制品
东莞市蓝威实业有限公司	寮步镇	金属制厨房用器具
东莞日进电线有限公司	寮步镇	电线、电缆
东莞市双胞胎饲料有限公司	大岭山镇	饲料加工
东莞光群雷射科技有限公司	大岭山镇	烟草制品
东莞大宝化工制品有限公司	大岭山镇	涂料
东莞市瑞德丰生物科技有限公司	大岭山镇	生物化学农药及微生物农药
东莞市新时代新能源科技有限公司	大岭山镇	电气机械及器材
东莞市奥达铝业有限公司	大岭山镇	铝冶炼
东莞市汇成真空科技有限公司	大岭山镇	通用设备
东莞亿东机器有限公司	大岭山镇	塑料加工专用设备
东莞市宇佳电子实业有限公司	大岭山镇	电子设备
东莞锦弘精密机械有限公司	大岭山镇	木材加工机械
东莞市优富利电子有限公司	大岭山镇	计算机外围设备
东莞富强鑫塑胶机械制造有限公司	大朗镇	橡胶加工专用设备
东莞华科电子有限公司	大朗镇	电子元件及组件
东莞市迈科科技有限公司	大朗镇	雷达及配套设备
东莞信易电热机械有限公司	大朗镇	塑料加工专用设备
东莞市迈科新能源有限公司	大朗镇	雷达及配套设备
东莞市飞尔液晶显示器有限公司	大朗镇	电子元件及组件
东莞市中一合金科技有限公司	大朗镇	电子元件及组件
东莞市台冠起重机械设备有限公司	大朗镇	起重机
大宝(东莞）模具切削工具有限公司	大朗镇	切削工具
东莞艾尔发自动化机械有限公司	大朗镇	金属切削机床
东莞呈越电脑配件有限公司	大朗镇	计算机外围设备
东莞市永兴电子科技有限公司	大朗镇	光电子器件及其他电子器件
广东省东莞市亿达音响制造有限公司	大朗镇	音响设备
东莞宝迪环保电镀设备有限公司	黄江镇	环境保护专用设备
东莞星火机电设备工程有限公司	黄江镇	计算机整机
鹏驰五金制品有限公司	黄江镇	紧固件
广东欧科空调制冷有限公司	黄江镇	制冷、空调设备
东莞惠伦顿堡电子有限公司	黄江镇	电子元件及组件
东莞市莱钢钢结构有限公司	黄江镇	环境保护专用设备
东莞新东方化工有限公司	黄江镇	合成橡胶
泓凯电子科技（东莞）有限公司	黄江镇	计算机零部件
东莞市宏德电子设备有限公司	黄江镇	电子工业专用设备
广东太阳神集团有限公司	黄江镇	保健食品
钰翔精密模具（东莞）有限公司	黄江镇	模具

1-7　续表 6

(2011年)

企业名称	所在镇街	行业类别
东莞市亚勖电子科技有限公司	黄江镇	质检技术服务
东莞市兄奕塑胶制品有限公司	樟木头镇	塑料板、管、型材
东莞市广海大橡塑科技有限公司	樟木头镇	橡胶制品
东莞积信电器有限公司	樟木头镇	家用厨房电器具
东莞市启天自动化设备有限公司	樟木头镇	通用设备
东莞市金铮自动冲压设备有限公司	清溪镇	金属切削机床
东莞华仪仪表科技有限公司	清溪镇	电工仪器仪表
东莞宜安电器制品有限公司	清溪镇	合金压铸
实盈电子（东莞）有限公司	清溪镇	电子元件及组件
东莞光阵显示器制品有限公司	清溪镇	光电子器件及其他电子器件
东莞华明灯具有限公司	清溪镇	照明灯具
广东粤林电气科技股份有限公司	清溪镇	计算机外围设备
东莞顺传五金制品有限公司	清溪镇	脚踏自行车及残疾人座车
东莞致通电脑有限公司	清溪镇	计算机
东莞市快意电梯有限公司	清溪镇	电梯、自动扶梯及升降机
东莞建玮电子制品有限公司	清溪镇	计算机零部件
东莞龙杰电子有限公司	清溪镇	电子设备
模德模具（东莞）有限公司	清溪镇	金属表面处理及热处理加工
东莞市奔迪包装有限公司	塘厦镇	塑料制品
东莞市凯华电子有限公司	塘厦镇	电子元件及组件
东莞市凯昶德电子科技有限公司	塘厦镇	电子元件及组件
东莞市星擎电子科技有限公司	塘厦镇	电子元件及组件
东莞市冠佳电子设备有限公司	塘厦镇	老化（烧机）设备
东莞市理士奥电源技术有限公司	塘厦镇	电池
东莞立德电子有限公司	塘厦镇	电子元件及组件
广东升威电子制品有限公司	塘厦镇	电子元件及组件
东莞市光宇实业有限公司	塘厦镇	照明灯具
东莞丰裕电机有限公司	塘厦镇	金属加工机械
东莞市华联环保工程有限公司	塘厦镇	水污染治理
东莞正阳电子有限公司	塘厦镇	电子元件及组件
广东志成冠军集团有限公司	塘厦镇	汽车整车
广东星河生物科技股份有限公司	塘厦镇	食用菌及食用菌深加工产品
东莞市坚朗五金制品有限公司	塘厦镇	金属门窗
东莞市力王电池有限公司	塘厦镇	雷达及配套设备
东莞市乐科电子有限公司	塘厦镇	集成电路
东莞市千岛金属锡品有限公司	塘厦镇	锡冶炼
东莞市亚力通电子科技有限公司	塘厦镇	通信终端设备
东莞市亚通光电有限公司	塘厦镇	光电子器件及其他电子器件
佳辉设备（东莞）有限公司	塘厦镇	电子工业专用设备
东莞市楚东电子科技有限公司	塘厦镇	电子设备
东莞市欧谛特光电科技有限公司	塘厦镇	光电子器件及其他电子器件
东莞建永数码科技有限公司	塘厦镇	音响设备
东莞启益电器机械有限公司	塘厦镇	电子工业专用设备
东莞市锦润电子有限公司	塘厦镇	光电子器件及其他电子器件
东莞领航电子有限公司	塘厦镇	电子元件及组件
东莞市倍嘉电池科技有限公司	塘厦镇	电池

1-7　续表 7

(2011年)

企业名称	所在镇街	行业类别
东莞勤增实业有限公司	塘厦镇	电子元件及组件
东莞市澳星视听器材有限公司	塘厦镇	幻灯及投影设备
东莞锐发智能卡科技有限公司	塘厦镇	智能卡设备
东莞奥美佳电子有限公司	凤岗镇	电子设备
东莞宇宙电路板设备有限公司	凤岗镇	电子工业专用设备
东莞康佳模具塑胶有限公司	凤岗镇	家用电力器具
广东楚天龙智能卡有限公司	凤岗镇	电子元件及组件
东莞康佳电子有限公司	凤岗镇	电视机
嘉力时灯光设备(东莞)有限公司	凤岗镇	照明灯具
东莞永腾电子制品有限公司	凤岗镇	电子元件及组件
东莞市大兴化工有限公司	谢岗镇	涂料
东莞李洲电子科技有限公司	谢岗镇	光电子器件及其他电子器件
东莞洲磊电子有限公司	谢岗镇	电子元件及组件
良特电子科技（东莞）有限公司	常平镇	通信系统设备
东泰机械工具（东莞）有限公司	常平镇	电工机械专用设备
广东富林木业科技有限公司	常平镇	胶合板
东莞勤上光电股份有限公司	常平镇	照明灯具
东莞市环宇激光工程有限公司	常平镇	电子工业专用设备
东莞市特尔佳电子有限公司	常平镇	专用化学产品
智嘉通讯科技(东莞)有限公司	常平镇	电力电子元器件
东莞市华立实业股份有限公司	常平镇	家具
东莞运城制版有限公司	常平镇	包装装潢及其他印刷
东莞东运机械制造有限公司	常平镇	印刷专用设备
东莞市世通国际快件监管中心有限公司	常平镇	装卸搬运
东莞东海龙环保科技有限公司	常平镇	照明灯具
东莞龙昌数码科技有限公司	常平镇	玩具
东莞欧达电子有限公司	常平镇	电子测量仪器
东莞市鼎聚光电有限公司	常平镇	电子元件及组件
东莞市麦蒂科技有限公司	常平镇	软件开发
东莞市维信电脑科技有限公司	常平镇	信息系统集成服务
东莞市金隽机械有限公司	常平镇	塑料加工专用设备
永泰电子（东莞）有限公司	常平镇	电力电子元器件
快捷达通信设备（东莞）有限公司	常平镇	通信系统设备
东莞市天益生物工程有限公司	桥头镇	调味品、发酵制品
东莞市日新传导科技股份有限公司	桥头镇	电线、电缆
广东新一信通信发展有限公司	桥头镇	通信系统设备
东莞市金培电子有限公司	桥头镇	计算机外围设备
东莞巨扬电器有限公司	横沥镇	电光源
东莞市安达自动化设备有限公司	横沥镇	通用设备
广东明家科技股份有限公司	横沥镇	社会公共安全设备及器材
东莞盈拓科技实业股份有限公司	横沥镇	金属切削机床
忠信制模(东莞)有限公司	横沥镇	模具
意拉德电子（东莞）有限公司	横沥镇	电子元件及组件
东莞雷笛克光学有限公司	横沥镇	灯用电器附件及其他照明器具
东莞市艾炜特电子有限公司	东坑镇	电视机
广东中德电缆有限公司	东坑镇	电线、电缆

1-7 续表 8

(2011年)

企业名称	所在镇街	行业类别
东莞市新望包装机械有限公司	企石镇	包装专用设备
广东佳彩数码科技有限公司	企石镇	广播电视接收设备及器材
东莞市兆明光电科技有限公司	企石镇	电光源
东莞明鑫电子有限公司	企石镇	计算机外围设备
东莞市智乐堡儿童玩具有限公司	石排镇	玩具
东莞市富士达电子科技有限公司	石排镇	电子元件及组件
东莞市铭普实业有限公司	石排镇	电子元件及组件
东莞鑫佑光电科技有限公司	石排镇	电子元件及组件
东莞宇隆电工材料有限公司	茶山镇	铜压延加工
东莞市箭冠汽车配件制造有限公司	茶山镇	汽车零部件及配件
东莞荣成塑胶五金制品有限公司	茶山镇	塑料零件
东莞市英科水墨有限公司	茶山镇	油墨及类似产品
东莞市源殿电子科技有限公司	茶山镇	电光源
东莞市益达实业有限公司	茶山镇	电线、电缆
东莞市贻嘉光电科技有限公司	茶山镇	灯用电器附件及其他照明器具
东莞市雄丰配电设备有限公司	茶山镇	配电开关控制设备
东莞森玛仕格里菲电路有限公司	茶山镇	印制电路板
东莞市金昶电线制造有限公司	茶山镇	高级音响线、高级音响插头
艾利和电子科技（中国）有限公司	松山湖	计算机
东莞泛亚太生物科技有限公司	松山湖	食品及饲料添加剂
东莞市安美润滑科技有限公司	松山湖	基础化学原料
东莞市百大新能源股份有限公司	松山湖	锅炉及辅助设备
东莞市贝特电子科技股份有限公司	松山湖	电子元件及组件
东莞市科磊得数码光电科技有限公司	松山湖	印制电路板
东莞市纳明新材料科技有限公司	松山湖	合成材料
东莞市普赛特电子科技有限公司	松山湖	新材料技术推广服务
东莞市瑞柯电机有限公司	松山湖	汽车零部件及配件
东莞市苏普尔电子科技有限公司	松山湖	通信系统设备
东莞市泰斗微电子科技有限公司	松山湖	电子工业专用设备
东莞市腾宇龙机械能源科技股份有限公司	松山湖	皮革、毛皮及其制品加工专用设备
东莞市万科建筑技术研究有限公司	松山湖	水利管理
东莞市星火太阳能科技有限公司	松山湖	太阳能发电
东莞市意普万工程塑料有限公司	松山湖	合成材料
东莞市中之光电科技有限公司	松山湖	照明灯具
东莞新能源科技有限公司	松山湖	雷达及配套设备
广东大普通信技术有限公司	松山湖	电子元件及组件
广东电子工业研究院有限公司	松山湖	电子及新材料的技术开发
广东东阳光药业有限公司	松山湖	化学药品制剂
广东华南工业设计院	松山湖	工业设计
广东力优环境系统股份有限公司	松山湖	制冷、空调设备
广东洛贝电子科技有限公司	松山湖	家用厨房电器具
广东生益科技股份有限公司	松山湖	电子元件及组件
广东易事特电源股份有限公司	松山湖	塑料薄膜
广东雨林木风计算机科技有限公司	松山湖	互联网信息服务
广东正业科技有限公司	松山湖	实验分析仪器
领亚电子科技股份有限公司	松山湖	电线、电缆